Emerging Tools and Applications of Virtual Reality in Education

Dong Hwa Choi
Park University, USA

Amber Dailey-Hebert
Park University, USA

Judi Simmons Estes
Park University, USA

A volume in the Advances in Educational Technologies and Instructional Design (AETID) Book Series

Information Science REFERENCE
An Imprint of IGI Global

Published in the United States of America by
Information Science Reference (an imprint of IGI Global)
701 E. Chocolate Avenue
Hershey PA, USA 17033
Tel: 717-533-8845
Fax: 717-533-8661
E-mail: cust@igi-global.com
Web site: http://www.igi-global.com

Library of Congress Cataloging-in-Publication Data

Names: Choi, Dong Hwa, editor. | Dailey-Hebert, Amber, editor. | Estes, Judi Simmons, 1947- editor.
Title: Emerging tools and applications of virtual reality in education / Dong Hwa Choi, Amber Dailey-Hebert, and Judi Simmons Estes, editors.
Description: Hershey, PA : Information Science Reference, [2016] | Includes bibliographical references and index.
Identifiers: LCCN 2015046870| ISBN 9781466698376 (hardcover) | ISBN 9781466698383 (ebook)
Subjects: LCSH: Virtual reality in education.
Classification: LCC LB1044.87 .E545 2016 | DDC 371.33/468--dc23 LC record available at http://lccn.loc.gov/2015046870

This book is published in the IGI Global book series Advances in Educational Technologies and Instructional Design (AE-TID) (ISSN: 2326-8905; eISSN: 2326-8913)

British Cataloguing in Publication Data
A Cataloguing in Publication record for this book is available from the British Library.

Advances in Educational Technologies and Instructional Design (AETID) Book Series

Lawrence A. Tomei
Robert Morris University, USA

ISSN: 2326-8905
EISSN: 2326-8913

Mission

Education has undergone, and continues to undergo, immense changes in the way it is enacted and distributed to both child and adult learners. From distance education, Massive-Open-Online-Courses (MOOCs), and electronic tablets in the classroom, technology is now an integral part of the educational experience and is also affecting the way educators communicate information to students.

The **Advances in Educational Technologies & Instructional Design (AETID) Book Series** is a resource where researchers, students, administrators, and educators alike can find the most updated research and theories regarding technology's integration within education and its effect on teaching as a practice.

Coverage

- Social Media Effects on Education
- Instructional Design Models
- Digital Divide in Education
- Higher Education Technologies
- Classroom Response Systems
- Game-Based Learning
- Educational Telecommunications
- Bring-Your-Own-Device
- Hybrid Learning
- Adaptive Learning

IGI Global is currently accepting manuscripts for publication within this series. To submit a proposal for a volume in this series, please contact our Acquisition Editors at Acquisitions@igi-global.com or visit: http://www.igi-global.com/publish/.

The Advances in Educational Technologies and Instructional Design (AETID) Book Series (ISSN 2326-8905) is published by IGI Global, 701 E. Chocolate Avenue, Hershey, PA 17033-1240, USA, www.igi-global.com. This series is composed of titles available for purchase individually; each title is edited to be contextually exclusive from any other title within the series. For pricing and ordering information please visit http://www.igi-global.com/book-series/advances-educational-technologies-instructional-design/73678. Postmaster: Send all address changes to above address.

Titles in this Series

For a list of additional titles in this series, please visit: www.igi-global.com

Handbook of Research on Estimation and Control Techniques in E-Learning Systems
Vardan Mkrttchian (HHH University, Australia) Alexander Bershadsky (Penza State University, Russia) Alexander Bozhday (Penza State University, Russia) Mikhail Kataev (Tomsk State University of Control System and Radio Electronics, Russia & Yurga Institute of Technology (Branch) of National Research Tomsk Polytechnic University, Russia) and Sergey Kataev (Tomsk State Pedagogical University, Russia)
Information Science Reference • copyright 2016 • 554pp • H/C (ISBN: 9781466694897) • US $235.00 (our price)

Handbook of Research on Active Learning and the Flipped Classroom Model in the Digital Age
Jared Keengwe (University of North Dakota, USA) and Grace Onchwari (University of North Dakota, USA)
Information Science Reference • copyright 2016 • 450pp • H/C (ISBN: 9781466696808) • US $300.00 (our price)

Handbook of Research on Applied Learning Theory and Design in Modern Education
Elena Railean (European University of Moldova, Moldova) Gabriela Walker (University of South Dakota, USA) Atilla Elçi (Aksaray University, Turkey) and Liz Jackson (University of Hong Kong, Hong Kong)
Information Science Reference • copyright 2016 • 866pp • H/C (ISBN: 9781466696341) • US $400.00 (our price)

Handbook of Research on Strategic Management of Interaction, Presence, and Participation in Online Courses
Lydia Kyei-Blankson (Illinois State University, USA) Joseph Blankson (Ohio Northern University, USA) Esther Ntuli (Idaho State University, USA) and Cynthia Agyeman (Ohio University, USA)
Information Science Reference • copyright 2016 • 611pp • H/C (ISBN: 9781466695825) • US $235.00 (our price)

Intelligent Design of Interactive Multimedia Listening Software
Vehbi Turel (Bingol University, Turkey)
Information Science Reference • copyright 2015 • 448pp • H/C (ISBN: 9781466684997) • US $215.00 (our price)

Utilizing Virtual and Personal Learning Environments for Optimal Learning
Krista Terry (Appalachian State University, USA) and Amy Cheney (Appalachian State University, USA)
Information Science Reference • copyright 2016 • 375pp • H/C (ISBN: 9781466688476) • US $185.00 (our price)

Handbook of Research on Individual Differences in Computer-Assisted Language Learning
Mehrak Rahimi (Shahid Rajaee Teacher Training University, Iran)
Information Science Reference • copyright 2015 • 571pp • H/C (ISBN: 9781466685192) • US $325.00 (our price)

IGI GLOBAL
DISSEMINATOR OF KNOWLEDGE
www.igi-global.com

701 E. Chocolate Ave., Hershey, PA 17033
Order online at www.igi-global.com or call 717-533-8845 x100
To place a standing order for titles released in this series, contact: cust@igi-global.com
Mon-Fri 8:00 am - 5:00 pm (est) or fax 24 hours a day 717-533-8661

This book is dedicated to educational pioneers everywhere who seek to explore opportunities to develop in meaningful and innovative ways as they learn through virtual reality—to all learners and practitioners who are becoming better equipped for the exciting future of the learning landscape that awaits us all.

In memory of my son, Jeremy Blake Estes, who got his first computer in 1983 at the age of 13 and thereafter they were inseparable. -JSE

Table of Contents

Section 2
Virtual Reality Across Disciplines

Section 3
Next Generation of Learning: Catalysts and Considerations in Virtual Reality

Detailed Table of Contents

This chapter is a go-to guide for education professionals (primarily in the undergraduate and graduate college-level degree programs) for understanding and designing Economics classes in World of Warcraft. The premier MMORPG of the Western world, World of Warcraft boasts a number of features that makes it an ideal sandbox for economic education. It was deliberately designed to represent a large number of important real-world institutions like trade, production, cooperation, thus it can become a platform for learning about them. Moreover, since students encounter these institutions in a vibrant virtual world setting, they not only get to verify the learned materials but can practice their applications in their day-to-day dealings with other World of Warcraft denizens. This will lead to more student engagement, better learning outcomes, a more thorough understanding of both the principles of the theory and their applications, and greatly improved knowledge retention.

This book chapter presents, a review of the literature from 2004-2014 regarding the various models of virtual worlds used in foreign language teaching and learning, the impact of virtual world learning environments and the implications of language teaching. The study being reported aims to address the following questions: (1) What are the models of virtual worlds used in language learning instruction in K-12 and higher education; (2) How do VWLEs impact language learning in terms of motivation, communicative competency, intercultural competency, collaborative competency, constructivist learning, and sociocultural competency; and (3) What are the implications of using VWLEs in foreign language teaching and learning? Results indicate that social context and task-based learning enhanced language learners' participation and motivations. Findings also indicate that consistent use of interactional strategies encouraged learners to engage in the tasks and stay motivated. The study suggested that a VWLE offers a motivating, engaging, and multi-dynamic environment for language learners.

Augmented Reality (AR) as an advanced format of Virtual Reality (VR) becomes widely available in numerous appliances, mainly in mobile devices like Smartphones or wearable devices. As the prospective benefits of this technology are said to be immense, tourism marketing education is believed to experience a comprehensive application of AR in coming years. At present, AR technologies are in use in many academic disciplines including medicine, geography, information technology, computer aided entertainment and many more. Out of all of the recently developed technological advancements, those can be termed as 'Innovations', augmented reality can be considered as a key innovation. As coined, due to easier operational capacities, AR is becoming more popular and better fitting in tourism marketing education systems. This chapter outlines the use of AR, termed as an 'Innovation' as per the 'Diffusion of Innovations' theory of Rogers (1962), to meet tourism marketing education demands. The chapter critically examines relevant cross-country cases to support the arguments made above.

Preface

In 1965, Ivan Sutherland posited, "There is no reason why the objects displayed by a computer have to follow the ordinary rules of physical reality with which we are familiar (Sutherland, 1965, para. 13); furthermore, "If the task of the display is to serve as a looking-glass into the mathematical wonderland constructed in computer memory, it should serve as many senses as possible (para. 9)." During the past fifty years, there has been a gradual development of what has come to be known as virtual reality, where ordinary rules of physical reality have been redefined and many senses are being experienced by users, as described in a seminal article by Mazuryk and Gervautz (1996). Today, through various visual and tactile devices, virtual reality (VR) can represent real or imaginary worlds in which the user interacts using multiple senses within a multimedia environment.

VR is being used for a variety of functions: (1) communication spaces, (2) simulation of space (spatial), and (3) experiential space ('acting' on the world), with research primary focused on three topics: participants' affective domain, learning outcomes and social interaction. (Hew & Cheung, 2012). Although the first VR systems were created for the military and aerospace industries, there has been a gradual emergence in the field of education; three-dimensional (3-D) immersive virtual worlds are being used in traditional and distance education classrooms in K-12 and higher education (Dickey, 2005). Applications include use of VR for virtual field trips (Castleberry & Evers, 2010), 3-D models to help students visualize mathematics and science concepts (Bradly & Farland-Smith, 2010; Sun, Lin, & Wan, 2010), and immersive learning environments (Becker & Schuertz, 2003; Orman, 2003).

Integration of virtual reality in educational settings has occurred more slowly than anticipated; "People don't change when you tell them they should, they change when they tell themselves they must" (Friedman, 2005, p. 462). Cuban, Kirkpatrick, and Peck (2001) found that teachers' age, experience, and gender were not significant factors in identifying why technology is not being integrated into instruction; it is a teacher's belief structure about teaching and learning that has been found to inhibit a teacher's development of the technology integration pedagogy. Teacher support was found to be critical in building teachers' confidence levels when first using technology (Redmann & Kotrlik, 2004); administrative support plays a critical role in a teacher's practice of integrating technology into classroom instruction (Shuldman, 2004).

VR holds a possibility for all, regardless of the field of application, "With the virtual reality acting in the education we can discover, explore and build knowledge about places and situations that we could never explore" (Piovesan, Passerino, & Pereira, 2012, p. 295). Perhaps, it is this possibility that has captured the curiosity and interest of the authors who have contributed to this edited collection which promotes research in the use of VR in education, with a focus on higher education. Even though, in higher education, VR has been adopted in areas such as the social sciences and medical fields, faculty need to be more informed and educated about utilizing VR to enhance instruction. The chapters in this collection share possibilities, considerations, and evidence pertaining to the integration of VR and the unique attributes it provides to enrich the student learning process. This collection is sequenced to provide grounding in the existing and emergent research in VR, before moving on to applied models and general principles of practice across multiple disciplines in the field of education from K-12 to higher education. This collection offers a resource to benchmark and examine innovative practices and their linkage to educational settings as VR is connecting students and educators across the globe.

This collection illustrates the connected and globally networked nature of virtual reality in education, through ideas from authors working in five countries, (Australia, Italy, Turkey, United Kingdom, United States), in multiple domains of academia and industry, and across various disciplines. The characteristics and the evolving nature of VR is explored in unique settings from diverse and globalized viewpoints, providing a depth and breadth of understanding on this transformative topic. The collection also looks ahead to explore the next generation of VR in education, and unearths innovative solutions and ethical considerations for future use.

SECTION 1: UNDERSTANDING VIRTUAL REALITY

This collection appropriately begins with four chapters, collectively setting a foundational understanding of VR as a technology that has evolved in the past 26 years, with advances in applications and uses that have included a broadening of definition as well as K-12 and higher education practices unimaginable in 1989 when the term "virtual reality" was coined.

First, in Chapter 1, Nicoletta Melida Sala (Italy) reviews virtual reality-based developments in educational environments. This chapter explores examples of virtual reality in various learning contexts, from primary schools to graduate courses. The author also shares didactical applications in the fields of medical training, foreign language acquisition, chemistry, engineering, architecture and interior design from a global perspective; exploring virtual reality in the United States, Italy, Morocco, Romania, and Switzerland. Conclusively, the author stresses the appreciation for virtual reality in diverse learning environments, and establishes an expectation for potential use of virtual reality as an evolutionary teaching and learning tool.

Building upon this world view, and narrowing the focus more specifically to the context of higher education, Reza Ghanbarzadeh and Amir Hossein Ghapanchi (Australia) provide a robust review of literature on virtual worlds in Chapter 2. This literature review analyzes 164 articles from eight major databases, including both empirical and technical studies on the topic of VR in higher education. These articles were published during the 14 years from 1999-2013. The authors identify five main curricular activities for which three dimensional virtual worlds (3DVW) have been used to date, as well as categorizing 17 virtual environments identified from the literature review. Consequently, the authors provide a framework to discuss various platforms and virtual environments used for educational purposes that emerge.

In Chapter 3, Anita Cassard and Brian W. Sloboda (United States) present information on the methods and approaches used to assess student learning outcomes in virtual environments. The authors explore ADDIE (Analysis, Design, Development, Implementation, and Evaluation) enhanced learning and construct a stance to empower faculty to carefully assess student learning outcomes, which can also be used to support a rationale for the desired integration of virtual reality in learning contexts. The authors suggest that assessment in the virtual environment needs to be enlightened on multiple levels in education, which include diversifying strategies to assess learning outcomes and to assess quality control of three-dimensional (3D) learning platforms. This stance implies that a comprehensive view of assessment issues in virtual environments is essential.

In Chapter 4, James Braman and Yvonne Pigatt (United States) share the implications and lessons learned from their interactive virtual reality project using Second Life as a means to increase student engagement in a community college course. They offer an outline of project requirements, didactical strategies, and pedagogical methodologies from their experiment, and describe the aims of their continued and future work. This chapter concludes with recommendations that are applied to the integration of virtual reality within the higher education coursework.

SECTION 2: VIRTUAL REALITY ACROSS THE DISCIPLINES

Several chapters on virtual reality, in education, across a broad range of course contexts and disciplines, are included in Section II. Each chapter shares a view of virtual reality as a pedagogical tool used to improve student engagement and learning. By providing opportunities to be immersed in natural phenomena, learners can apply knowledge through experience, which contributes to the acquisition of knowledge. These chapters include fields such as teacher preparation, economics, foreign language, mathematics and tourism marketing, each using a variety of tools, platforms, and technologies in the virtual reality landscape.

In Chapter 5, Barbara L. Ludlow and Melissa D. Hartley (United States) describe an application of virtual reality to train graduate level learners in a teacher education program leading to certification in special education (via courses offered online). The authors adopt Constructivism as a pedagogical framework and utilize Second Life to optimize situated and active learning through simulation, as they share ways to bridge the theoretical and practical issues of using virtual reality. The chapter deepens the arguments of the subject and share learners' comments on their training to suggest recommendations for practitioners.

In Chapter 6, the topic shifts from teacher preparation to the field of teaching economics and move from Second Life to the World of Warcraft, one of the most popular Massively Multi-Player On-Line Role-Playing Games (MMORPGs). In this chapter, Andras Margitay-Becht (United States) provides the history of the development of the World of Warcraft and its application in an academic setting. This chapter serves as a guide for professionals who seek to design a more immersive class experience, one which allows learners to build conceptual knowledge while applying principles directly in practice. Real world elements such as trade, production, and cooperation are applied via gamification and can lead to improved retention of student learning as a result.

In Chapter 7, Ellen Yeh and Guofang Wan (United States) provide a systemic review of existing literature on successful models to integrate virtual worlds for foreign language learning. The authors present the pedagogical advantages and technical challenges for using virtual worlds as a collaborative learning tool for foreign language instruction. The impact of integrating the virtual world results in not only improving leaners' communicative skills but the effect can also be observed on individual's competency on social-emotional and cultural levels. Lastly, implications are presented for teaching strategies, assessment tools, administrative support, and professional development programs.

Next, Azizul Hassan and Timothy Jung (United Kingdom) explore the use of augmented reality as a marketing strategy and as a means of marketing education in tourism. The authors present several exemplary cases of applying augmented reality (AR; one of the more advanced and innovative forms of VR) to meet the current trends and demand in the field of business. Interestingly, use of AR as an innovative technology has well established its position in consumers' lifestyle; however, in educational settings, it still remains at the early stage. Conclusively, the chapter proposes that AR should become easily available and accessible to students and practitioners for educational, as well as business, purposes.

Chapter 9 shifts to the discipline of mathematics, as Rebecca Lynne Patterson, D. Cooper Patterson, and Anna-Marie Roberston (United States) explore how virtual reality can revolutionize mathematical thinking. These authors describe how Second Life can be used as a creative space for prototyping, publishing and as a design studio for educational materials, with the power to immerse learners in the shape of numbers through engagement.

SECTION 3: NEXT GENERATION OF LEARNING – CATALYSTS & CONSIDERATIONS IN VIRTUAL REALITY

In this last section of the collection, readers are challenged to explore innovative uses for virtual reality, and also share critical issues to consider in the future.

In Chapter 10, Noah L. Schroeder (United States) introduces the concept of 'pedagogical agents', or virtual characters which facilitate learning in multimedia environments. In this chapter, the author shares research that describes how such agents can be used in learning, explores their effectiveness, and shares potential applications for their use in the future.

In Chapter 11, Celebi Uluyol and Sami Sahin (Turkey) continue with innovative applications for learning in virtual reality in their work on "Connecting Printed Materials with Digital Objects". The use of augmented reality in diverse professional areas are introduced and highlight the benefits of augmented reality (AR) as a means to connect ideas and digital objects through an augmented reality book in education settings. The contribution of augmented reality to learning is discussed on multiple levels.

To continue the exploration of innovative practices using emergent VR tools, in Chapter 12, Amit Goel, William Rivera, Peter J. Kincaid, Michele M. Montgomery, Waldemar Karwowski and Neil M. Finkelstein (United States) provide a critical perspective on ethics in a variety of fields using virtual world environments and present research that exists on the topic. This chapter provides the reader with provocative questions to consider and highlights the responsibility of all researchers and practitioners in this burgeoning field of VR, particularly the need to create awareness for ethical practices.

VR is one of the latest technologies to be integrated into the teaching-learning process. In Chapter 13, Judi Simmons Estes, Amber Dailey-Hebert, and Dong Hwa Choi emphasize that given teachers pivotal role in the process of technology integration, it is imperative to train teachers in computer literacy and the technological skills needed to integrate technology in instruction. The authors propose that training should also include developing a pedagogy and self-efficacy for technology integration.

REFERENCES

Becker, M., & Schuertz, J. (2003). An introduction to ground-water modeling using Virtual Reality Modeling Language (VRML). *Journal of Geoscience Education*, *51*(5), 506–511.

Bradley, J., & Farland-Smith, D. (2010). 3-D teaching models for all. *Science Teacher (Normal, Ill.)*, *77*(3), 33–37.

Castleberry, G., & Evers, R. (2010). Twenty ways to incorporate technology into the modern language classroom. *Intervention in School and Clinic*, *45*(3), 201–205. doi:10.1177/1053451209349535

Cuban, L., Kirkpatrick, H., & Peck, C. (2001). High access and low use of technologies in high school classrooms: Explaining an apparent paradox. *American Educational Research Journal*, *38*(4), 813–834. doi:10.3102/00028312038004813

Dickey, M. D. (2005). Brave new (interactive) worlds: A review of the design affordances and constraints of two 3D virtual worlds as interactive learning environments. *Interactive Learning Environments*, *13*(1–2), 121–137. doi:10.1080/10494820500173714

Friedman, T. L. (2005). The World is Flat: A Brief History of the 21st Century. New York.

Hew, K. F., & Cheung, W. S. (2010). Use of three-dimensional (3-D) immersive virtual worlds in K-12 and higher education settings: A review of the research. *British Journal of Educational Technology*, *4*(1), 33–55. doi:10.1111/j.1467-8535.2008.00900.x

Mazuryk, T., & Gervautz, M. (1996). *Virtual reality: history, application, technology, and future*. Vienna, Austria: Vienna University of Technology.

Orman, E. (2003). Effect of virtual reality graded exposure on heart rate and self-reported anxiety levels of performing saxophonists. *Journal of Research in Music Education*, *51*(4), 302–315. doi:10.2307/3345657

Piovesani, S. D., Passerino, L. M., & Pereira, A. S. (2012). Virtual reality as a tool in the education. *IADIS International Conference on Cognition and Exploratory Learning in Digital Age*, 295-298.

Redmann, D. H., & Kotrlik, J. W. (2004). Technology integration into the teaching-learning process by business education teachers. *Delta Pi Epsilon*, *46*(2), 76–91.

Shuldman, M. (2004). Superintendent conceptions of institutional conditions that impact teacher technology integration. *Journal of Research on Technology in Education*, *36*(4), 319–343. doi:10.1080/15391523.2004.10782418

Sun, K., Lin, C., & Wang, S. (2010). A 3-D virtual reality model of the sun and the moon for e-learning at elementary schools. *International Journal of Science and Mathematics Education*, *8*(4), 689–710. doi:10.1007/s10763-009-9181-z

Sutherland, I. (1965). The Ultimate Display. Proceedings of International Federation of Information Processing (IFIP) (Vol. 2, pp. 506–509). Congress; Retrieved from http://worrydream.com/refs/Sutherland%20-%20The%20Ultimate%20Display.pdf

Acknowledgment

We would like to thank our generous colleagues for their helpful and insightful ideas, reviews, and feedback of the manuscript. They not only critiqued and offered valuable suggestions, but also recommended additional resources to help inform our work and expand our own knowledge base on the topic. Also, we want to acknowledge IGI Global for the many important suggestions along the way and guidance throughout the process. Finally, the editors would like to acknowledge all who contributed their expertise of virtual reality in education to the development of this volume: Ellen Yeh, Guofang Wan, Celebi Uluyol, Sami Sahin, Yvonne Pigatt, James Braman, Andras Hassan, Timothy Jung, Reza Ghanbarzadeh, Amir Mossein, Anita Cassard, Brian Sloboda, Amit Goel, William Rivera, Peter Kincaid, Michele Montgomery, Waldemar Karwowski, Neal Finkelstein, Barbara Ludlow, Melissa Hartley, Rebecca Lynne Patterson, D. Cooper Patterson, Anna-Marie Robertson, Noah Schroeder, and Nicoletta Melida Sala.

Section 1
Understanding Virtual Reality in Education

Sala, 2013a; Stangel & Pantelidis, 1997; Traub, 1991; van Krevelen & Poelman, 2010; Winn, 1993; Youngblut, 1998).

Winn affirmed the reasons for using VR in education. In particular, immersive VR furnishes a non-symbolic experience which helps students in their learning path (Winn, 1993).

Hedberg and Alexander, in 1994, furnished a list of questions that they felt should be asked when contemplating the use of VR in education. They selected 12 questions which are:

1. To what extent is collaboration with peers possible and useful in the VR experience?
2. What use does the learner make of conversations, stories and multiple points of view?
3. What and how does the learner learn in a 'virtual' community of practice?
4. Is there a complex combination of physical and cognitive skills?
5. Are the motivation and the context important?
6. Does the learner need to combine information from different forms of representation (aural, visual, temporal, etc.) and is a context required to limit the cognitive load of the task?
7. Does the learner need to experiment with a scenario which might have dangerous consequences if actually experienced?
8. Does the learned concept require links to objects which behave with a defined set of attributes and relationships?
9. Are the learner's explorations: independent of size of the world being explored (microscopic or macroscopic)?
10. Of physical and improbable phenomena, related to the creation of micro worlds, independent of time explorations with beings real, or historical, within their context)?
11. Is the learned concept a relationship in space independent of physical laws?
12. Does the learner have to work with abstract relationships, manipulate data structures and mathematical functions?

In 1996, Christine Byrne explored VR as an educational tool. She based her doctoral work on testing students' assembling of a virtual molecule of water, using an immersive virtual environment with haptic input. The virtual chemistry world encouraged students to learn by exploring and interacting with the information. The immersive virtual world was created by high school students. Instead of sitting in a classroom and passively viewing images of atomic orbital, students placed electrons into an atom see the atomic orbital appear as the electron buzzes. Her research results were interesting. Byrne claimed that interactivity was found to be significant, but immersion was found to be insignificant. She suggested that issues of training, world design, assessment, hardware resolution, and student population as possible reasons for immersion's lack of significance in her study (Byrne, 1996). She also affirmed that the results of her study have not shown VR to be superior to other methods of instruction; but interactivity, a VR's feature, could be important.

Another interesting survey of research was done by Christine Youngblut during the 1990's. In her 1998 study, she said that VR can be applied in different kind of school (from elementary schools to colleges). This technology introduces important aspects of constructivist learning. The role of the teacher changed to facilitator that helps students in their learning paths, building ideas. Students enjoy using pre-developed applications and developing their own virtual worlds (Youngblut, 1998).

These studies emphasized that VR does not furnish only passive copy of reality, but its reconstruction is a model where users can act. It reacts and behaves as in real environment. This important feature overcomes the inherent limitations of perception, which should be applicable only to objects physically perceptible. As technology continues to improve, VR systems will become pervasive instrumentation for research in education across the disciplines.

VIRTUAL REALITY ACROSS THE DISCIPLINES

In the last twenty years, a set of studies applied VR in different learning paths.

VR became a tool for training undergraduate students in the correct use of instrumentations and for respecting the safety rules in the laboratory activities. VR allows instructors to deliver complex information in a visual way, permitting trainees to simulate, with VR technologies, situations which in real-life could be potentially dangerous.

Bell and Fogler (1995) introduced Vicher (Virtual Chemical Reaction module), an educational application of virtual reality designed to give an aid in the instruction of undergraduate chemical reaction engineering. The goals, in producing Vicher, can be organized in three points, as the authors stated:

- Provide an educational environment in which chemical reactor design students can explore first-hand the concepts which they have studied in class,
- Provide in-depth reactor design and computer programming training to the students who are helping to develop Vicher, and
- Develop a knowledge base concerning the application of virtual reality techniques to educational applications. This knowledge base may be the strongest benefit of the project, as it can then be applied to more complex applications and more advanced hardware in future developments (p.2).

Vicher has been developed at the University of Michigan Chemical Engineering Department and represented the first known application of VR to chemical engineering education, but without difficulties. About the application of VR as an educational tool, Bell and Fogler (1995) observed that in engineering and other technical areas, a lot of simulation difficulties must be identified and solved. For example, the compromise between the speed and the display quality and the price of low-cost PCs.

In 1995, a set of studies described a lot of applications of virtual reality in surgical education and in medicine. For example, Ota, Loftin, Saito, Lea, and Keller (1995) presented VR as an emerging technology that can teach surgeons new procedures and can determine their level of competence before they operate on real patients. They affirmed that VR in medical training could reduce expensive animal training model enhancing the operative field.

Other studies introduced telepresence surgery, 3D visualization of anatomy for medical education, complex medical database visualization, VR surgical simulators, and virtual prototyping of surgical equipment and operating rooms, and rehabilitation (Satava, 1995a, 1995b; Satava, & Jones, 1996). Satava (1995a) wrote:

Today, approximately 90% of the knowledge a physician requires can be obtained through electronic means, such as diagnostic sensors and imaging modalities, directly seeing the patient with a video camera for medical consultation, or using electronic medical records. In addition, with telepresence, a therapy can be effected electronically, regardless of the physical location of the patient. Therefore, it makes sense to send the electronic information or manipulation, rather than sending the patient or blood samples, to obtain tests or to produce a cure. In that these applications are mediated through the computer interface, they are the embodiment of VR as the major force for change in the field of medicine. (p. 12)

Antonietti, Imperio, Rasi, and Sacco (1999, 2000, 2001) propose a prototypal system for machine tools teaching in a virtual reality environment integrated with hypermedia. The goal is to lead undergraduate students involved (54 students divided in studies) not only to understand the structure and function of the lathe, but also to use such a machine. To reach this, the prototype tries to foster conceptual changes in students' mental models and to increase students' control over the learning process. A series of experimental tests have been carried out to assess the educational validity of the instructional tool which has been devised. The aim of the first phase of the project was to assess whether students could easily use the virtual lathe and to verify what they learn about such a machine. The purpose of the second phase was to focus on some critical aspects of the learning process activated by using the virtual lathe in order to realize the instructional procedures which give the best learning outcomes. These studies demonstrated that the VR can help in the comprehension of some core machining concepts. In particular, novice students benefit from free navigation in the virtual environment, training themselves in the use of real lathe. VR allows the training in safety.

All these educational experiences emphasize that one current problem with using VR is the cost to realize immersive VR environments. The price may drop if the market grows, but in terms of products for education, we have to pay much for modest quality hardware and software.

Gerval et al. (2002) have examined VR's potential in the multicultural integration in the primary schools. The project, named EVE (Environment Virtuels pour Enfants), involves nine primary schools from three different countries (France, Morocco and Romania). The EVE application was developed in order to help the primary school children learn French, and especially, reading. The project's goals are:

- To create a new cooperative environment for learning which involves young students from three different countries;
- To realize new kind of pedagogical software tool for primary school children.

From a pedagogical point of view, EVE project intends to promote teamwork, involving children from different countries in cooperative work. They have to achieve a common task together, in hopes that this will encourage the respect in a multicultural framework. This project implements distributed virtual reality technologies. From both perspectives, it is like a NICE-environment, narrative immersive constructionist and collaborative.

Different universities use the Virtual Reality Modeling Language (VRML) to realize VR's low-cost applications. VRML is a language that specifies the parameters to create virtual worlds networked together via the Internet and accessed via Web hyperlinks. VRML was conceived in the spring of 1994, and it was presented to the first annual World Wide Web conference in Geneva, Switzerland (Evans, 1995). Consensus is what enables so many developers with different tools to enrich a single but rapidly expanding universe of VRML objects and worlds, all of which can be experienced by anyone who has a VRML viewer, regardless of who made it (Blackburn, Henderson & Welz, 1996). VRML defines a set of objects and functions for modeling simple 3D graphics. These are known as nodes, which are arranged in hierarchies called scene graphs. There is a top-down arrangement in which nodes that are described earlier in a scene affect later ones, but this can be limited by the use of separator nodes (Bouras & Filopoulos, 1998). The aim of VRML is to bring to the Internet the advantages of 3D spaces, known in VRML as worlds whether they compromise environments or single objects. These are built to be shared between widely distributed users. A VRML file is an ASCII file (with the suffix .wrl), which is interpreted by the browser (for example: Cosmoplayer®, FreeWRL VRML/X3D, Cortona) and converted into a 3D display of the described world. VRML connects virtual reality to the WWW and to cyberspace.

D'Atri, Missikoff, and Pauselli (2002) realized Fairsnet: a virtual environment for supporting business. Fairsnet was developed with the collaboration between IGstudents Foundation (the Italian branch of Young Enterprise Europe, YEE) and the Center for Research on Information Systems (CeRSI) of the Luiss Guido Carli University in Rome. It describes a Web environment for managing real and virtual trade fairs. The aim of the Young Enterprise Europe Programme is to create a connection between the worlds of education and employment (D'Atri, Missikoff, & Pauselli, 2002).

Virtual Reality is a medium for making abstract concepts concrete (Rosemblum & Cross, 1997, Sala, 2013a).

The abstractness of scientific topics creates difficulties in their understanding (Byrne, 1996; Millar, 1991; Sala, 2002, 2013a; Youngblut, 1998; Zoller, 1990) .

In agreement to these considerations, Sala and Sala (2005) analyzed the contribution of multimedia technologies and VR in university courses of mathematics and information technology to a faculty of architecture in Switzerland. In this educational project, the term "virtual reality" has been used to cover both immersive and non-immersive Virtual Reality. The technology was used first to help architecture students to visualize in 3D, since this is arguably the most difficult part of understanding architecture. The topic dedicated to the polyhedra and their interconnections between nature and architecture is an excellent example of an abstract topic that is difficult to learn.

The undergraduate students used the virtual reality technologies in different ways (Sala, 2002a). For example,

- To observe and to rotate the platonic solids and the polyhedra from the different points of view (outside and inside the virtual objects),
- To create some virtual objects using VRML (Virtual Reality Modeling Language),
- To observe and to interact the molecules of carbon (C60 and C70),
- To observe and to manipulate the geodesic domes,
- To study and to observe the symmetry presents in the crystals, and
- To create virtual trees using fractal algorithms.

Figure 6 shows two virtual objects: a molecule of carbon and a geodesic dome, respectively. Students can interact with them, via a low cost VR system. They can go inside the molecule and the dome, observing their symmetries and analogies of the shape. Students have the psychological feeling to interact, in "natural" way, with a molecule; overcoming the dimensional limits imposed in real life.

Figure 6. A molecule of carbon and a geodesic dome created using VRML.

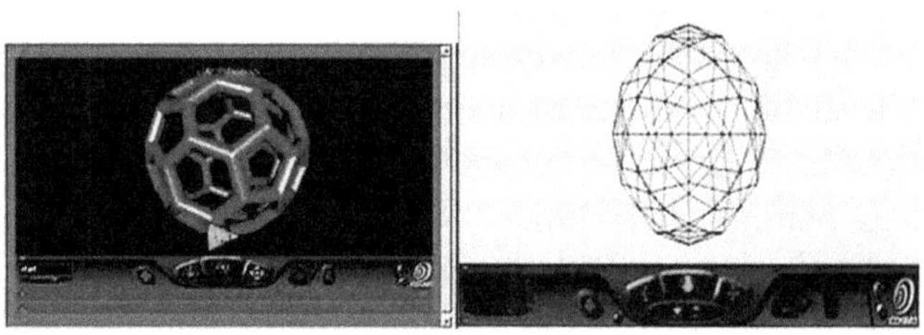

In graduate courses, VR has been analyzed as a medium to create virtual towns and virtual worlds. Students created virtual territories using fractal algorithms and fractal procedures.

During the study, Sala and Sala (2005) emphasized the connections between virtual reality, fractal geometry, and computer graphics to realize some virtual worlds. The students also generated trees, mountains, lakes, and special effects using fractal algorithms (Guérin, Tosan, & Baskurt, 2002; Sala, 2002a, 2009a, 2012; Sala, Metzeltin, & Sala, 2002). Figure 7 shows an example of computer generated virtual terrain using fractal procedures. VR is also connected with the Internet and cyberspace. In particular, it has been interesting to analyze the virtual communities and the virtual cities with their sociology implications (Sala, 2002b).

Virtual reality has been integrated in a training path to visualize the projects connected to the territory or to realize some "virtual buildings" which students can visit (Sala & Sala, 2005).

In order to effectively apply VR as an educational tool in architecture and other technical areas, Sala and Sala (2005) observed a set of problems connected to the technology. For example,

- Low resolution of inexpensive viewing devices which made unrealistic objects,
- Difficulties to maintain high frame rates on personal computers, and
- High costs of hardware and software devices to realize immersive VR.

Sala and Sala (2005) also observed that interaction with virtual objects promotes learning of their features. Knowledge and especially the understanding are better, in quantity and quality, than watching the reality or books' images.

Figure 7. Virtual terrain created using fractal procedures (Fractal landscape, 2015)

VIRTUAL WORLDS

Virtual reality is connected to computer graphics to render virtual worlds (VW) and virtual scenes. Computer graphics, connected to the development of new programming languages and to the advanced computer technologies, have high potentiality, especially in the field of 3D animations for creating online virtual reality environments and virtual worlds.

Virtual worlds are computer-based simulated environments where the users can interact via an alter ego in the computer representation in real time with different devices, for example head mounted displays, and data gloves (Damer, 1997).

This "alter ego" is named avatar. The avatar is: an online manifestation of human's desire to try out alternative identities (Hemp, 2006). The word derives by the Sanskrit "avatāra", an incarnation of the Hindu god Vishnu.

Avatars can move themselves through virtual territories quickly generating with fractal algorithms which can be codified in different computer languages (Java, C++, VRML) (Sala, 2009b).

The technological evolutions of WWW and of computer graphics techniques have generated online virtual worlds, which can be considered virtual communities or scenarios for 3D virtual games. IMVU, Planet Calypso, Planet Arkadia, Woozworld are examples in this field. Other online virtual worlds can offer positive applications in educational fields.

Kamel Boulos, Hetherington, and Wheeler (2007) introduce three-dimensional (3-D) virtual worlds and their educational potential to medical/health librarians and educators. They affirm that the virtual world named Second Life (SL) could be ideal for those studying at a distance from their parent institution, becoming an equitable method of interaction.

Second Life

Second Life is one of the most popular online virtual worlds. It was developed by San Francisco-based Linden Lab and launched on June 23, 2003. This virtual world can be accessed freely via Linden Lab's own client programs, or via alternative Third Party Viewers. The Second Life users are also called "residents". They can create their avatars, which are virtual representations of themselves.

The users can explore this online virtual world. They can meet other residents, they can participate in group activities. They can also create, new buildings and new environments.

Second Life is based on mark-up languages such as HTML (Hypertext Markup Language) and Virtual Reality Modeling (VRML). These languages permit the creation and display of three-dimensional objects on the web, their manipulation and their interaction.

The educational use of SL is the base of a set of research projects and technical papers (Bourke, 2007, 2008; Brown, 2009; Calongne, & Hiles, 2007; Chafer, & Childs, 2008; Childs, 2007, 2010; Duncan, Miller, & Jiang, 2012; Falloon, 2010; Hew, & Cheung, 2010; Inman, Wright, & Hartman, 2010; Jestice & Kahai, 2010; Kamel Boulos, Hetherington, & Wheeler, 2007; Kopp & Burkle, 2010; McKeown, 2007; Mladenovic, Kuvac, & Štula, 2012; Oliver & Carr, 2009; Petrakou, 2010; Salmon, 2009; Trahan, Adams, & Dupre, 2012).

Bourke (2007, 2008) explores the potential of using the online digital world Second Life as a scientific visualization tool, in particular, for remote collaborative exploration of scientific datasets. This virtual world permits to the multiple remote participants to interact with 3D geometry within a virtual environment. He affirms that Second Life offers an interesting and satisfactory for collaborative visualization

Figure 8. Preprocessed spherical projections from inside a crystal including the Hershfield surface computed from Crystal Explorer (Jayatilaka, Wolff, Grimwood, McKinnon, & Spackman, 2006) realized by Bourke (2008)

in the sciences, but there are any limitations which are based on the low geometric complexity. These lacks are strictly connected to the hardware devices and to the algorithmic reconstruction of the virtual environment. He also remarks that Second Life as collaborative experience is perhaps unsurpassed, permitting to multiple participants an interaction with data representations within a 3D virtual environment (Bourke, 2008, p. 7).

Figure 8 shows a preprocessed spherical projections from inside a crystal including the Hershfield surface (Bourke, 2008).

In a 2009 paper titled *Using Virtual Worlds in Education: Second Life As an Educational Tool*, Baker, Wentz, and Woods (2009) claim that Second Life has an high potential for its use in education, but they also suggest:

Do not send the students in to Second Life without some educational objective Teachers have to prepare educational objectives for student learning activities in SL, and share these objectives with the students. Prepare the students for this social experience. SL is similar to a public square, where we can meet people from other cultures or countries. All students have to remember that behind every avatar there is a real person. Consider SL to be one tool in your toolbox. (p. 62)

At National Educational Computing Conference (NECC) 2009 held in Washington D.C., Brown affirms that Second Life provides a sense of presence, and the students, seeing their avatars, have a sense of being in a fixed place (Brown, 2009).

Hew and Cheung (2010) report that virtual worlds can be used for creating special experiential areas.

Childs, in his doctoral thesis, analyzes the experiences of presence in virtual worlds as a specific case of mediated environments, using these technologies in teaching and learning (Childs, 2010). In order to investigate learners' experiences, Childs presents five case studies in Second Life (preceded by a pilot study employing web conferencing).

Grimes and Bartolacci (2012) introduce some of the possibilities for using Second Life as a platform for network and information security training with a focus on the profiling of online behavior. In particular, they refer the initial attempts of its use at one of the Pennsylvania State University's campuses. About SL the authors affirm that SL presents an environment where the cyber eavesdropping, and even would-be criminal acts such as fraud, can be demonstrated with little or no real world harm or consequences. This could create a rift between the virtual world, where anything goes, and the real one, with its rules.

Duncan, Miller, and Jiangin (2012) present a taxonomy for using virtual worlds in education. They classify six categories, according to the content or influence in online education. These categories are the following:

- Population (users aged 18+),
- Educational Activities (for example, visit 3D representation of a cathedral to understand construction techniques),
- Learning Theories (e.g., constructivist or collaborative learning),
- Learning Environment (where the users are working, e.g. inside a simulation of a museum),
- Supporting Technologies (e.g. audio, display or tactile equipment), and
- Research Areas (e.g., case studies on interface).

FUTURE RESEARCH DIRECTIONS

VR was considered to be useful only for the learning of simple manual and operative skills (e.g., hazardous conditions in laboratory activities). Technology evolution is opening new scenarios and applications of VR, now.

For example, Häfner, Häfner, and Ovtcharova (2013) present a teaching methodology for a practical course in virtual reality for undergraduate and graduate students. The course focusses on the learning of virtual reality by simulating interdisciplinary industrial projects, for developing skills such as methodological approach to practical engineering problems, teamwork, and working in interdisciplinary groups. The authors also describe the importance of the course design, task specification and work group composition for a successful realization of the course, referring to some project examples from the past three years.

VR will become a medium to introduce cyber ethics education, too. An example in this field is proposed by Matsuda, Nakayama, and Tamada (2015). They introduce the e-learning material that they developed using three-dimensional Virtual Reality (3D-VR) technology in cyber ethics education. They introduce a new method that teaches students to use three types of knowledge in their analyses of moral judgment problems: knowledge of ethical codes, ICT, and rational judgment. The authors verified that this method is more effective than the conventional method.

A successive and important step in the use of virtual reality could be the introduction of virtual prototyping in courses of engineering and architecture (Sala, 2013a). Virtual prototyping is a construction and testing of virtual prototype which represents a computer simulation of a physical product, which can be analyzed and tested via software (Wang, 2002). This approach can reduce (or even prevent) the construction of physical prototypes, thereby saving time and costs. The use of virtual prototyping, in courses of engineering and architecture, will train the students to new methodologies in design processes. Figure 9 shows an example of virtual prototype.

Figure 9. A virtual prototype (Sala, 2013a, p. 84)

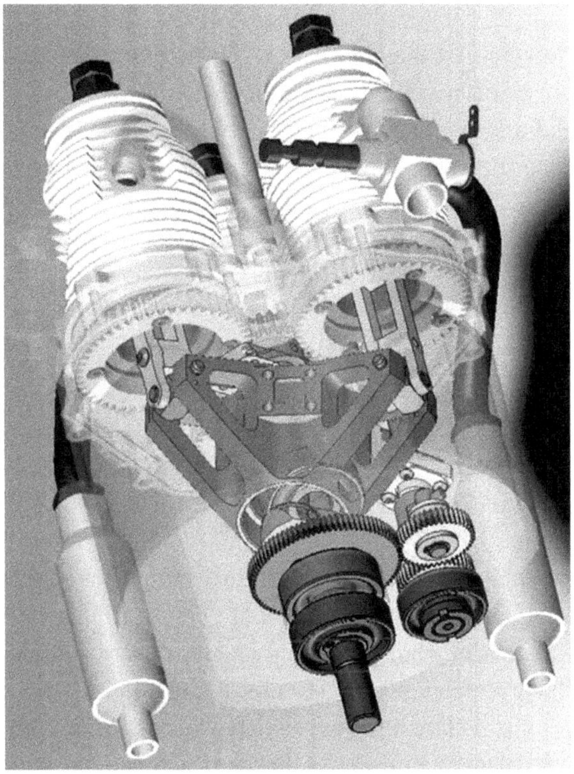

Technological evolution of computer graphics and of WWW will increase online virtual worlds for collaborative learning with social sharing.

For example, Le, Pedro, and Park (2014) propose an online social VR-based system framework which allows students to perform role-playing, dialogic learning, and social interaction for construction safety and health education. They present a system organized in three modules - CDSL, HISC and ASGL- which permits the students to participate in active roleplaying, collaborative and dialogic learning, and social interaction in a 3D virtual world. A prototype system was developed using Second Life environment and its applicability was evaluated with virtual scenarios derived from real accident cases.

Other future research direction will be in the field of interactions between virtual world and architecture. In particular, Second Life could become a virtual world where is possible to build imaginary architectures and shapes based on fractal procedures. Fractal geometry is able to describe the Nature, replacing Euclidean geometry (which dominated our mathematical thinking for hundreds of years). This geometry finds applications for generating virtual landscapes, territories and complex shapes in virtual worlds and in three-dimensional Internet based virtual worlds, using simple geometric rules (Bourke, 2007, 2008; Sala, 2009a, 2009b, 2012, 2013b).

SL is becoming the place to go to do things that you could not normally do in architect-designed buildings (Sala, 2012). SL will be a virtual world with new architecture that will go beyond the real territory, in a new form of space where interactive objects and virtual buildings exist.

CONCLUSION

This chapter presents an overview of the application VR technologies in a variety of teaching and in learning environments, from primary schools to graduate courses.

The application of virtual reality in education can be seen as a set of technologies which influence, support and improve teaching methods, strengthening the educational process and helping to develop new ways of learning.

The wireless networks now blurring the distinction between inside and outside the classroom, and in some sense there are rooms within rooms and spaces within spaces, like Russian dolls, using VR technologies.

Important examples of uses of virtual reality include:

- Medical applications (e.g, training using virtual patients and virtual instruments to acquire a basic level of interpretative and manipulative skills) (Coyle, Traynor, & Solowij, 2015; Gallagher et al., 2005; Ota, Loftin, Saito, Lea & Keller, 1995; Satava & Jones,1996; Satava, 1995a, 1995b; Ziegler, Mueller, Fischer, & Göbel, 1995);
- Foreign language acquisition through immersion in a virtual environment where the language can be heard and its meaning understood (Boudreau & Okada, 1998);
- An educational environment in which chemical reactor design students can explore first-hand the concepts which they have studied in class (Bell & Fogler, 1995, 1997);
- Engineering training in virtual laboratories providing access in remote hazardous environments or in education for manufacturing engineers (Antonietti, Imperio, Rasi, & Sacco, 1999, 2000, 2001, Novak-Marcincin, Janak, Barna, & Novakova-Marcincinova, 2014) ;
- Spaces shared by users in the field of Architecture and Interior Design (Sala & Sala, 2005; Soares Calado, Márcio Soares, Campos, & Correia; 2013); and
- Virtual prototyping in engineering and in architectural education, for creating a new kind of prototypes (Sala, 2013a).

The literature presents the advantages of using virtual reality-based instruction for learning (Merchant, Goetz, Cifuentes, Keeney-Kennicutt, & Davis, 2014).

For example, Chen (2006) affirms that VR is a very important learning tool, but further investigations are necessary. For example, the ways to reach more effective learning when using this technology, and analyzing its impact on learners with different aptitudes.

Pantelidis (2010) is more critical, presenting the guidelines where it is not appropriate to use virtual reality. She affirms that VR is not a positive educational medium if no substitution is possible for teaching/training with the real thing. Virtual environment could be physically or emotionally damaging, and it is a technology too expensive to justify its use, considering the expected learning outcome (p. 65).

Virtual reality, connected to the Internet, to the VRML and to the WWW, is creating virtual spaces and virtual worlds (for example, Second Life) which have high potentiality in education, contributing to help an active learning process, and to improve the teaching impact (Bal, Crittenden, Halvorson, Pitt, & Parent, 2015; Bellotti, Berta, De Gloria, & Primavera, 2010; Kamel Boulos, Hetherington, & Wheeler, 2007; Kopp & Burkle, 2010; Reinsmith-Jones, Kibbe, Crayton, & Campbell, 2015; Zhou, Jin, Vogel, Fang, & Chen, 2011; Waters, 2009).

Second Life is becoming a discrete platform for distance experiences. Using SL in the traditional face-to-face and in hybrid distance education classrooms, this virtual world is promoting a new kind of active didactic where the students can explore Second Life Islands and they can share virtual learning environments (Bal, Crittenden, Halvorson, Pitt, & Parent, 2015; Bourke, 2007, 2008; Jabbari, Sandoval, & Waxman, 2015; Macedo & Morgado, 2009).

Is virtual reality a good educational tool for learning environments? The answer is positive, but it is important to consider that virtual reality and virtual worlds, as Second Life, are not a kind of "panacea" for all educational fields. In fact, they are not appropriate for every instructional objective. There are some teaching scenarios where virtual reality technologies and virtual worlds can be used for improving teaching and learning, and some where they should not be used.

In conclusion, only a deep knowledge of the VR technologies and their effective capabilities, together with a comprehension of psychological and cultural feedback of the students, to such technologies, can help us to create teaching paths where VR will play a central role.

REFERENCES

Adams, E. W. (2004). Postmodernism and the three types of immersion. *Gamasutra*. Retrieved from http://designersnotebook.com/Columns/063_Postmodernism/063_postmodernism.htm

Antonietti, A., Rasi, C., Imperio, E., & Sacco, M. (1999). Virtual reality in engineering instruction: In search of the best learning procedures. *World Conference on Educational Multimedia, Hypermedia and Telecommunications 1999* (Vol. 1, pp. 663-668).

Antonietti, A., Rasi, C., Imperio, E., & Sacco, M. (2000). The representation of virtual reality in education. *Education and Information Technologies*, *5*(4), 317–327. doi:10.1023/A:1012057608694

Antonietti, A., Rasi, C., Imperio, E., & Sacco, M. (2001). Virtual reality and hypermedia in learning to use a turning lathe. *Journal of Computer Assisted Learning*, *17*(2), 142–155. doi:10.1046/j.0266-4909.2001.00167.x

Astheimer, P., Dai, F., Göbel, M., Kruse, R., Müller, S., & Zachmann, G. (1994). Realism in virtual reality. In *N. Magnenat Thalmann & D. Thalmann, Artificial life and virtual reality* (pp. 189–209). New York, NY: John Wiley.

Baker, S. C., Wentz, R. K., & Woods, M. M. (2009). Using virtual worlds in education: Second Life® as an educational tool. *Teaching of Psychology*, *36*(1), 59–64. doi:10.1080/00986280802529079

Bal, A., Crittenden, V., Halvorson, W., Pitt, L., & Parent, M. (2015, January). Second best in Second Life: Teaching marketing cases in a virtual world environment. *Proceedings of the 2010 Academy of Marketing Science (AMS) Annual Conference* (pp. 211-211). Springer International Publishing. doi:10.1007/978-3-319-11797-3_119

Bell, J. T., & Fogler, H. S. (1995). Virtual reality in chemical engineering education. *Proceedings of the American Society for Engineering Education*, Illinois / Indiana Sectional Conference, Purdue University, March 1995. doi:10.1109/VR.2004.1310077

Bell, J. T., & Fogler, H. S. (1997, January 12-15). The application of virtual reality to chemical engineering education. *Proceedings of the 1997 International Conference on Simulation in Engineering Education (ICSEE '97)*, Society for Computer Simulation, San Diego. *Simulation Series*, 29(2). Retrieved from http://citeseerx.ist.psu.edu/viewdoc/download?doi=10.1.1.88.4744&rep=rep1&type=pdf

Bellotti, F., Berta, R., De Gloria, A., & Primavera, L. (2010). Supporting authors in the development of task-based learning in Serious Virtual Worlds. *British Journal of Educational Technology*, *41*(1), 86–107. doi:10.1111/j.1467-8535.2009.01039.x

Benford, S., Greenhalgh, C., Reynard, G., Brown, C., & Koleva, B. (1998). Understanding and constructing shared spaces with mixed-reality boundaries. *ACM Transactions on Computer-Human Interaction*, *5*(3), 185–223. doi:10.1145/292834.292836

Björk, S., & Holopainen, J. (2004). *Patterns in Game Design*. Charles River Media.

Blackburn, D., Henderson, R., & Welz, G. (1996). VRML evolution. *Internet World*, *7*(12), 65–70.

Boudreau, C., & Okada, M. (1998). The foreign language acquisition system of Project Orbis: An example of educational, customizable language exposure in a shared virtual world. In *Future generation computing systems*. Amsterdam: Elsevier.

Bouras, C., & Filopoulos, A. (1998). Distributed virtual reality environments over web for distance education. In *Proceedings of EDEN Conference* (pp. 481-484).

Bourke, P. (2007). *Representing and modeling geometry in Second Life*. Retrieved from http://paulbourke.net/fractals/secondlife/

Bourke, P. (2008). Evaluating Second Life as a tool for collaborative scientific vizualisation. *Proceedings of the Computer Games and Allied Technology in Animation, Multimedia, IPTV & Entertainment (CGAT 08)*. Retrieved from http://paulbourke.net/papers/cgat08/

Brooks, F. P. (1999). What's real about virtual reality? *IEEE Computer Graphics and Applications*, *19*(6), 16–27. doi:10.1109/38.799723

Brown, A. (2009). A second look at Second Life: Virtual worlds and education. *Paper presented at the annual NECC conference*, Washington, D.C.

Burdea, G. C., & Coiffet, P. (2003). *Virtual reality technology* (2nd ed.). New Brunswick, NJ: Wiley-IEEE Press.

Byrne, C. M. (1996). *Water on tap: The use of virtual reality as an educational tool* (Doctoral dissertation, University of Washington).

Calongne, C., & Hiles, J. (2007). Blended Realities: A Virtual Tour of Education in Second Life. In *Proceedings of TCC Worldwide Online Conference 2007* (pp. 70-90). Retrieved from http://etec.hawaii.edu/proceedings/2007/calongne.pdf

Chafer, J., & Childs, M. (2008, November 20-21). The impact of the characteristics of a virtual environment on performance: Concepts, constraints and complications. *Proceedings of the ReLIVE 08 conference*, Open University (pp. 94-105).

Chen, C. J. (2006). The design, development and evaluation of a virtual reality based learning environment. *Australasian Journal of Educational Technology*, *22*(1), 39–63.

Childs, M. (2007). Real Learning in Virtual Worlds. *Warwick International Journal, 30*(2).

Childs, M. (2010). *Learners' experience of presence in Virtual Worlds* [Doctoral dissertation]. Institute of Education. Retrieved from https://files.warwick.ac.uk/mchilds1/files/childs+thesis+final.pdf

Chung, I. C., Huang, C. Y., Yeh, S. C., Chiang, W. C., & Tseng, M. H. (2014). Developing Kinect games integrated with virtual reality on activities of daily living for children with developmental delay. In Advanced technologies, embedded and multimedia for human-centric computing (pp. 1091-1097). Netherlands: Springer. doi:10.1007/978-94-007-7262-5_124

Connolly, P. E. (2008). Virtual reality & immersive technology in education. In C. Van Slyke (Ed.), *Information communication technologies: concepts, methodologies, tools, and applications* (pp. 2168–2172). Hershey, PA: Information Science Reference; doi:10.4018/978-1-59904-949-6.ch158

Coyle, H., Traynor, V., & Solowij, N. (2015). Computerized and virtual reality cognitive training for individuals at high risk of cognitive decline: Systematic review of the literature. *The American Journal of Geriatric Psychiatry*, *23*(4), 335–359. doi:10.1016/j.jagp.2014.04.009 PMID:24998488

Damer, B. (1997). *Avatars! Exploring and building virtual worlds on the Internet*. Retrieved from http://www.digitalspace.com/avatars/book/chtu/chtu1.htm

D'Atri, A., Missikoff, O., & Pauselli, E. (2002). FairsNet: A virtual environment to support business education. *Proceedings IASTED International Symposium on Web-based Education (WBE 2002)*, Cancun, Mexico (pp. 394-398).

Duncan, I., Miller, A., & Jiang, S. (2012). A taxonomy of virtual worlds usage in education. *British Journal of Educational Technology*, *43*(6), 949–964. http://ishbel.host.cs.standrews.ac.uk/Research/SL_Taxonomy.pdf doi:10.1111/j.1467-8535.2011.01263.x

Earnshaw, E., Chilton, N., & Palmer, I. (1997). Visualization and virtual reality on the Internet. In R. Earnshaw & J. Vince (Eds.), *The Internet in 3D information, images and interaction* (pp. 203–222). San Diego, CA: Academic Press.

Encyclopædia Britannica. (2015). *Virtual Reality (VR)*. Encyclopædia Britannica Online.

Evans, C. (1995). *WWW-VRML benefits?* Retrieved from http://www.thinkofit.com/webconf/icde95/0038.htm

Falloon, G. (2010). Using avatars and virtual environments in learning: What do they have to offer? *British Journal of Educational Technology*, *41*(1), 108–122. doi:10.1111/j.1467-8535.2009.00991.x

Fractal landscape. (2015). *Wikipedia, The Free Encyclopedia*. Retrieved from https://en.wikipedia.org/w/index.php?title=Fractal_landscape&oldid=679001052

Gallagher, A. G., Ritter, E. M., Champion, H., Higgins, G., Fried, M. P., Moses, G., & Satava, R. M. et al. (2005). Virtual reality simulation for the operating room: Proficiency-based training as a paradigm shift in surgical skills training. *Annals of Surgery*, *241*(2), 364–372. doi:10.1097/01.sla.0000151982.85062.80 PMID:15650649

Garb, Y. (Winter 1987). Virtual Reality, *Whole Earth Review* (57): 118ff.

Gerval, J. P., Popovici, M., Ramdani, M., El Kalai, O., Boskoff, V., & Tisseau, J. (2002). Virtual environments for children. *Proceedings International Conference on Computers and Advanced Technology Education (CATE)*, Cancun, Mexico (pp. 416-420).

Gerval, J. P., Popovici, M., & Tisseau, J. (2003). Virtual stories authoring tools for pedagogical purposes. *Proceedings of IASTED International Conference on Computer and Advanced in Education*. Rhodes, Greece (pp. 642-646).

Grimes, G., & Bartolacci, M. (2012). Second Life: a virtual world platform for profiling online behavior for network and information security education? An initial investigation. In M. Bartolacci & S. Powell (Eds.), *Research, practice, and educational advancements in telecommunications and networking* (pp. 285–289). Hershey, PA, USA: IGI Global. doi:10.4018/978-1-4666-0050-8.ch017

Guérin, E., Tosan, E., & Baskurt, A. (2002). *Modeling and approximation of fractal surfaces with projected IFS attractors. Emergent Nature: Patterns, Growth and Scaling in the Science* (pp. 93–303). New Jersey: World Scientific.

Häfner, P., Häfner, V., & Ovtcharova, J. (2013). Teaching Methodology for Virtual Reality Practical Course in Engineering Education. *Procedia Computer Science,* 25, 251-260.

Hedberg, J., & Alexander, S. (1994). Virtual reality in education: Defining researchable issues. *Educational Media International*, *31*(4), 214–220. doi:10.1080/0952398940310402

Hemp, P. (2006). Avatar-based marketing. *Harvard Business Review*, *84*(6), 48–57. PMID:16846188

Hew, K. F., & Cheung, W. S. (2010). Use of three-dimensional (3-D) immersive virtual worlds in K-12 and higher education settings: A review of the research. *British Journal of Educational Technology*, *41*(1), 33–55. doi:10.1111/j.1467-8535.2008.00900.x

Immersion (virtual reality). (2015). In Wikipedia, The Free Encyclopedia. Retrieved from https://en.wikipedia.org/w/index.php?title=Immersion_(virtual_reality)&oldid=690405136

Inman, C., Wright, V. H., & Hartman, J. A. (2010). Use of Second Life in K-12 and higher education: A review of research. *Journal of Interactive Online Learning*, *9*(1), 44–63.

Jabbari, N., Sandoval, S., & Waxman, H. (2015, March). A Meta-Synthesis of Research Using Multiuser Virtual Environments (ie, Second Life) in Teacher Education. *Society for Information Technology & Teacher Education International Conference,* 2015(1), 2375-2381.

Jayatilaka, D., Wolff, S. K., Grimwood, D. J., McKinnon, J. J., & Spackman, M. A. (2006). Crystal Explorer: A tool for displaying Hirshfeld surfaces and visualising intermolecular interactions in molecular crystals. *Acta Crystallographica. Section A, Foundations of Crystallography*, *62*(a1), s90. doi:10.1107/S0108767306098199

Jestice, R. J., & Kahai, S. (2010). The effectiveness of virtual worlds for education: an empirical study. *Paper presented at the Sixteenth Americas Conference on Information Systems (AMCIS)*, Lima, Peru.

Kamel Boulos, M. N., Hetherington, L., & Wheeler, S. (2007). Second Life: An overview of the potential of 3-D virtual worlds in medical and health education. *Health Information and Libraries Journal*, *24*(4), 233–245. doi:10.1111/j.1471-1842.2007.00733.x PMID:18005298

Kopp, G., & Burkle, M. (2010). Using Second Life for just-in-time training: Building teaching frameworks in virtual worlds. [iJAC]. *International Journal of Advanced Corporate Learning*, *3*(3), 19–25. Retrieved from http://www.editlib.org/p/45604/article_45604.pdf

Krueger, M. W. (1991). *Artificial reality* (2nd ed.). Reading, MA: Addison-Wesley.

Le, Q. T., Pedro, A., & Park, C. S. (2014). A social virtual reality based construction safety education system for experiential learning. *Journal of Intelligent & Robotic Systems*, 1–20.

Macedo, A., & Morgado, L. (2009). Learning to teach in Second Life. *Proceedings of EDEN seventh open classroom conference* (pp. 120-126).

Magnenat-Thalmann, N., & Thalmann, D. (1999). Virtual reality software and technology. Encyclopedia of Computer Science and Technology, Marcel Dekker, 41.

Matsuda, T., Nakayama, H., & Tamada, K. (2015). Using 3D virtual reality technology in cyber ethics education: How can we really evaluate and change students' attitudes? In Human rights and ethics: concepts, methodologies, tools, and applications (pp. 1621-1636). Hershey, PA: IGI Global. doi:10.4018/978-1-4666-6433-3.ch089

McKeown, L. (2007). Taking action learning online in the 3D virtual worlds of Second Life. *International Review of Research in Open and Distance Learning*, *8*(3).

McLellan, H. (1996). Virtual realities. In D. H. Jonassen (Ed.), Handbook of research for educational communications and technology (pp. 457-487). New York, NY, USA: Macmillan Library Reference.

McLellan, H. (2003). Virtual realities. In D. H. Jonassen & P. Harris (Eds.), *Handbook of research for educational communications and technology* (2nd ed., pp. 461–498). Mahwah, NJ: Lawrence Erlbaum.

Merchant, Z., Goetz, E. T., Cifuentes, L., Keeney-Kennicutt, W., & Davis, T. J. (2014). Effectiveness of virtual reality-based instruction on students' learning outcomes in K-12 and higher education: A meta-analysis. *Computers & Education*, *70*, 29–40. doi:10.1016/j.compedu.2013.07.033

Milgram, P., & Kishino, F. (1994). A taxonomy of mixed reality visual displays. *IEICE Trans. Information and Systems. E (Norwalk, Conn.)*, *77-D*(12), 1321–1329.

Milgram, P., Takemura, H., Utsumi, A., & Kishino, F. (1994). Augmented reality: A class of displays on the reality-virtuality continuum, *SPIE. Telemanipulator and Telepresence Technologies*, *2351*, 282–291. doi:10.1117/12.197321

Millar, R. (1991). Why is science hard to learn? *Journal of Computer Assisted Learning*, *7*(7), 66–74. doi:10.1111/j.1365-2729.1991.tb00229.x

Mladenovic, S., Kuvac, H., & Štula, M. (2012). Virtual learning environment. In *Virtual learning environments: concepts, methodologies, tools and applications* (pp. 1–16). Hershey, PA: Information Science Reference; doi:10.4018/978-1-4666-0011-9.ch101

Novak-Marcincin, J., Janak, M., Barna, J., & Novakova-Marcincinova, L. (2014). Application of Virtual and Augmented Reality Technology in Education of Manufacturing Engineers. *New perspectives in information systems and technologies, 2*, 439-446.

Oliver, M., & Carr, D. (2009). Learning in virtual worlds: Using communities of practice to explain how people learn from play. *British Journal of Educational Technology*, *40*(3), 14. doi:10.1111/j.1467-8535.2009.00948.x

Ota, D., Loftin, B., Saito, T., Lea, R., & Keller, J. (1995). Virtual reality in surgical education. *Computers in Biology and Medicine*, *25*(2), 127–137. doi:10.1016/0010-4825(94)00009-F PMID:7554831

Pantelidis, V. S. (1993). Virtual reality in the classroom. *Educational Technology*, *33*(4), 23–27.

Pantelidis, V. S. (1997). *Virtual Reality (VR) as an instructional aid: a model for determining when to use VR*. Retrieved from http://www.coe.ecu.edu/vr/vredmod.html

Pantelidis, V.S. (2010). Reasons to use virtual reality in education and training courses and a model to determine when to use virtual reality, *Themes in Science and Technology Education (Special Issue)*, 59-70.

Pantelidis, V. S., & Auld, L. (2002). Teaching virtual reality courses online. *CCAI: The Journal for the Integrated Study of Artificial Intelligence, Cognitive Science and Applied Epistemology.*

Bourke, P. (2008). Evaluating Second Life as a tool for collaborative scientific visualization. Retrieved from http://paulbourke.net/papers/cgat08/

Petrakou, A. (2010). Interacting through avatars: Virtual worlds as a context for online education. *Computers & Education*, *54*(4), 1020–1027. doi:10.1016/j.compedu.2009.10.007

Popovici, D. M., Gerval, J. P., Hamza-Lup, F., Querrec, R., Polceanu, M., Popovici, N., & Zăgan, R. (2009). 3D virtual spaces supporting engineering learning activities. *International Journal of Computers, Communications & Control*, *IV*(4), 401–414.

Reinsmith-Jones, K., Kibbe, S., Crayton, T., & Campbell, E. (2015). Use of Second Life in social work education: Virtual world experiences and their effect on students. *Journal of Social Work Education*, *51*(1), 90–108.

Riva, G. (2006). *Virtual reality, Encyclopaedia of Biomedical Engineering*. London: John Wiley & Sons.

Rosemblum, L. J., & Cross, R. A. (1997). The challenge of virtual reality. In W. R. Earnshaw, J. Vince, & H. Jones (Eds.), *Visualization & Modeling* (pp. 325–399). San Diego, CA: Academic Press.

Sala, N. (2002a). Virtual reality in the educational environments. *Proceedings IEEE International Conference on Advanced Learning Technologies ICALT 2002*, Kazan, Russia(pp. 417-419).

Sala, N. (2002b). From Virtual Reality to the Virtual Cities. *Proceedings International Conference on New Educational Environment*, Lugano, Switzerland (pp. 21-24).

Sala, N. (2009a). Fractal Geometry in Artificial Worlds and in Second Life. *Chaos and Complexity Letters*, *4*(1), 23–34.

Sala, N. (2009b). Fractal Geometry and Computer Science. In J. Gutierrez (Ed.), *Selected Readings on Telecommunications and Networking* (pp. 385–404). Hershey, PA: Information Science Reference; doi:10.4018/978-1-60566-094-3.ch028

Sala, N. (2012). Virtual reality in architecture, in engineering and beyond. In E. Abu-Taieh, A. El Sheikh, & M. Jafari (Eds.), *Technology Engineering and Management in Aviation: Advancements and Discoveries* (pp. 336–345). Hershey, PA: Information Science Reference; doi:10.4018/978-1-60960-887-3.ch020

Sala, N. (2013a). Applications of Virtual Reality Technologies in Architecture and in Engineering. *International Journal of Space Technology Management and Innovation*, *3*(2), 78–88. doi:10.4018/ijstmi.2013070104

Sala, N. (2013b). Fractals, computer science and beyond. In F. Orsucci & N. Sala (Eds.), *Complexity science, living systems, and reflexing interfaces: new models and perspectives* (pp. 268–291). Hershey, PA: Information Science Reference; doi:10.4018/978-1-4666-2077-3.ch014

Sala, N., Metzeltin, S., & Sala, M. (2002). Applications of mathematics in the real world: territory and landscape. *Proceedings International Conference: The Humanistic Renaissance in Mathematics Education*, Città del Mare, Sicilia, Italy(pp. 326-333).

Sala, N., & Sala, M. (2005). Virtual reality in education. In D. Carbonara (Ed.), *Technology literacy applications in learning environments* (pp. 358–367). Hershey, PA: Idea Group Inc. doi:10.4018/978-1-59140-479-8.ch025

Salmon, G. (2009). The future for (second) life and learning. *British Journal of Educational Technology*, *40*(3), 13. doi:10.1111/j.1467-8535.2009.00967.x

Satava, R. M. (1995a). Virtual reality, telesurgery, and the new world order of medicine. *Computer Aided Surgery*, *1*(1), 12–16. doi:10.3109/10929089509106821 PMID:9079422

Satava, R. M. (1995b). Medical applications of virtual reality. *Journal of Medical Systems*, *19*(3), 275–280. doi:10.1007/BF02257178 PMID:7643023

Satava, R. M., & Jones, S. B. (1996). Virtual reality and telemedicine: Exploring advanced concepts. *Telemedicine Journal*, *2*(3), 195–200. doi:10.1089/tmj.1.1996.2.195 PMID:10165542

Soares Calado, A. V., Márcio Soares, M., Campos, F., & Correia, W. (2013). Virtual reality applied to the study of the interaction between the user and the built space: A literature review. *Lecture Notes in Computer Science*, *8014*, 345–351. doi:10.1007/978-3-642-39238-2_38

Stangel, C., & Pantelidis, V. S. (1997). South Greenville Elementary School virtual reality project. *VR in the Schools, 2*(4). Retrieved from http://www.coe.ecu.edu/vr/vrits/2-4so-gr.htm

Trahan, M. P., Adams, N. B., & Dupre, S. (2012). Virtual learning environments: Second Life MUVEs to leverage student ownership. In Virtual Learning Environments: Concepts, Methodologies, Tools and Applications (pp. 200-213). Hershey, PA: IGI Global. doi:10.4018/978-1-4666-0011-9.ch113

Traub, D. C. (1991). Simulated world as classroom: The potential for designed learning within virtual environments. In S. K. Helsel & J. P. Roth (Eds.), *Virtual reality: Theory, practice, and promise* (pp. 111–121). Westport, CT: Meckler Publishing.

van Krevelen, D. W. F., & Poelman, R. (2010). A survey of augmented reality technologies, applications and limitations. *The International Journal of Virtual Reality*, *9*(2), 1–20.

Virtual reality (VR). (2015). In *Encyclopædia Britannica*. Retrieved from http://www.britannica.com/technology/virtual-reality

Wang, G. G. (2002). Definition and Review of Virtual Prototyping. *ASME Journal of Computing and Information Science in Engineering*, *2*(3), 232–236. doi:10.1115/1.1526508

Waters, J. K. (2009). A 'Second Life' for educators. *The Journal*, *36*(1), 29–34.

Wikipedia: "Fractal terrain texture" by Stevo-88 - self-made, used Adobe Photoshop for Perlin noise creation and Terragen for rendering. Licensed under Public Domain via Wikimedia Commons. (n. d.). Retrieved from http://commons.wikimedia.org/wiki/File:Fractal_terrain_texture.jpg#mediaviewer/File:Fractal_terrain_texture.jpghttp://thejournal.com/articles/2009/01/01/a-second-life-for-educators.aspx

Winn, W. (1993). A conceptual basis for educational applications of virtual reality (Technical Report TR-93-9). Seattle, Washington: Human Interface Technology Laboratory, University of Washington. Retrieved from http://www.hitl.washington.edu/publications/r-93-9/

Wu, F., Liu, Z., Wang, J., & Zhao, Y. (2015, March). Establishment virtual maintenance environment based on VIRTOOLS to effectively enhance the sense of immersion of teaching equipment. *Proceedings of the 2015 International Conference on Education Technology, Management and Humanities Science (ETMHS 2015)*. Atlantis Press. doi:10.2991/etmhs-15.2015.93

Youngblut, C. (1998). *Educational uses of virtual reality technology* (IDA Document D-2128). Retrieved from http://www.sustainable-design.ie/sustain/VE_Education-D2128.pdf

Ziegler, R., Mueller, W., Fischer, G., & Göbel, M. (1995, January). A virtual reality medical training system. In *Computer vision, virtual reality and robotics in medicine* (pp. 282–286). Springer Berlin Heidelberg. doi:10.1007/978-3-540-49197-2_36

Zoller, U. (1990). Students' misunderstandings and misconceptions in college freshman chemistry (general and organic). *Journal of Research in Science Teaching*, *27*(10), 1053–1065. doi:10.1002/tea.3660271011

Zhou, Z., Jin, X. L., Vogel, D. R., Fang, Y., & Chen, X. (2011). Individual motivations and demographic differences in social virtual world uses: An exploratory investigation in Second Life. *International Journal of Information Management*, *31*(3), 261–271. doi:10.1016/j.ijinfomgt.2010.07.007

KEY TERMS AND DEFINITIONS

Augmented Reality: It is a direct or indirect view of a real-world environment whose elements are augmented (or supplemented) by computer-generated sensory input such as graphics, sound, and video. For example, the user's view of the world is supplemented with virtual objects, usually to provide information about the real environment. Augmentation is in real-time.

Avatar: It is the graphical representation of the user or the user's alter ego in a virtual world. The word derives from Hindu mythology, and it represents the descent of a deity to the earth in an incarnate form or some manifest shape.

Fractal Geometry: It is geometry used to describe the irregular pattern and irregular shapes present in nature. Fractals display the characteristic of self-similarity, an unending series of motifs within motifs repeated at all length scales. The term derives by the Latin from "fractus", which means irregular.

Immersion: In Virtual Reality, immersion is a perception of being physically present in a non-physical world. The perception is created surrounding the user by the virtual reality technologies and by its devices, for example data gloves, head mounted display, sound or other sensorial stimuli, that provide an engrossing total environment.

Interaction: Into virtual reality, interaction is often described as the ability of the user to move within the virtual world and to interact with the objects of the virtual world. If the user can explore the virtual world and move objects within the interactive environment.

Prototype: In engineering is the first units manufactured of a product. It is tested so that the design can be changed if necessary before the product is manufactured commercially.

Second Life: is one of the most popular online virtual worlds. It was developed by San Francisco-based Linden Lab and launched on June 23, 2003. This virtual world can be accessed freely via Linden Lab's own client programs, or via alternative Third Party Viewers. The Second Life users are also called "residents".

Telepresence: It is a set of technologies, such as high definition video, audio, and other interactive elements that permit the users to feel or appear as if they were present in a location which they are not physically in. Users can influence and operate in a world that is real but in a different location. The users can observe the current situation with remote cameras and achieve actions via robotic and electronic arms. This technology is used as collaborative tool.

Virtual Prototyping (VP): The construction and testing of a virtual prototype is called virtual prototyping. It is a computer simulation of a physical product that can be presented, analyzed, and tested from concerned product life-cycle aspects such as design engineering, manufacturing, service, and recycling as if on a real physical model.

Virtual Reality (VR): A form of human-computer interaction in which a real or imaginary environment is simulated, and users interact with and manipulate that world. It is modern technology which gives its users the illusion of being immersed in a computer generated virtual world with the ability to interact with it. The term was coined in 1989, by American writer and computer scientist Jaron Zepel Lanier.

Virtual Reality Systems: Set of hardware and software components which permit to realize virtual reality environments.

Virtual World: It is a computer-based simulated environment where the users can interact via alter ego in the computer representation in real time with different devices, for example head mounted displays.

Virtual Reality Modeling Language, Originally Known as the Virtual Reality Markup Language (VRML): A language that specifies the parameters to create virtual worlds networked together via the Internet and accessed via the World Wide Web hyperlinks. The aim of VRML is to bring to the Internet the advantages of 3D spaces, known in VRML as worlds whether they compromise environments or single objects. It was conceived in the spring of 1994 and it has been presented to the first annual WWW conference in Geneva, Switzerland. Mark Pesce was one of the inventors of this language, and he is recognized as the man who brought virtual reality into the World Wide Web. The term VRML was coined by Dave Raggett in 1994.

Chapter 2
Applied Areas of Three Dimensional Virtual Worlds in Learning and Teaching:
A Review of Higher Education

Reza Ghanbarzadeh
Griffith University, Australia

Amir Hossein Ghapanchi
Griffith University, Australia

ABSTRACT

Three Dimensional Virtual Worlds (3DVW) have been substantially adopted in educational and pedagogical fields worldwide. The current study conducted a systematic literature review of the published research relevant to the application of 3DVWs in higher education. A literature search was performed in eight high-ranking databases, and following scrutiny according to inclusion criteria, 164 papers were selected for review. The systematic literature review process was summarized, reviews undertaken by the authors, and results about the applicability of 3DVWs in higher education were extracted. A wide variety of application areas for the 3DVWs in higher education were found, and were classified into five main categories. Various 3DVW platforms and virtual environments used for educational goals were also identified. The results revealed Second Life as the most popular 3DVW platform in higher education. This study also found that by using 3DVW technology a wide range of virtual environments and virtual tools have been designed and applied in teaching and learning for higher education.

INTRODUCTION

A Three-Dimensional Virtual World (3DVW) is a computer-based, simulated and graphical environment, usually accessible on the World Wide Web, that is intended for users to inhabit and interact using personalized graphical and animated self-representations, known as avatars (Boulos, Hetherington, & Wheeler, 2007). Virtual worlds are online spaces where individuals can interact with three-dimensional

DOI: 10.4018/978-1-4666-9837-6.ch002

representations of physical locations or phenomena. The simulated environment could appear similar to the real world (with real rules, real-time actions, interactions and communications) or depict a fantasy virtual world. Recently, Internet-based 3DVW have thrived and hold promise to significantly impact the way people communicate and interact with each other.

Inside 3DVWs, people can manipulate elements and experience telepresence. Increasingly, researchers, organizations and educational communities are recognizing these environments as legitimate communication media which can be used as an effective media in teaching and learning. Users of these environments not only have the opportunity to interact with each other in a sociocultural and delightful activities but also can follow virtual wealth through activities such as selling and buying lands as well as creating and trading virtual goods using virtual currencies (Ba, Ke, Stallaert, & Zhang, 2010).

Currently, one of the most popular and active 3DVWs is Second Life (SL), which is an eminent platform that was developed by Linden Lab in 2003. It has an in-world marketplace where users can trade virtual goods for Linden Dollars, which are then convertible currency to US Dollars. To illustrate, according to a report provided by Linden Lab in 2013, over the past decade, almost 36 million accounts have been created in SL and 3.6 billion US dollars spent on virtual possessions inside the wide range of virtual lands. In the ten years since Second Life began, the total time people have spent on this platform is equivalent to almost 217,266 years. Based on the mentioned report, Second Life is visited by more than one million individuals monthly, and almost 400,000 new registrations are completed every month. Approximately 1.2 million daily transactions are conducted for virtual possessions in Second Life, 2.1 million virtual possessions made by users are for sale, and Second Life's landmass now is about 700 square miles (Linden Lab, 2013).

The purpose of this chapter is to 1) identify the main activities in the application of 3DVWs in higher education. 2) highlight various 3D virtual world platforms that researchers have used in learning and teaching. 3) categorize various virtual environments designed for educational purposes. Therefore, the current chapter attempts to answer the following three research questions:

1. For what purposes have 3DVWs been used in higher education?
2. What types of 3DVW platforms have been used by researchers in higher education?
3. What kinds of virtual environments have been created for educational activities using 3DVWs?

BACKGROUND

3DVWs have been broadly adopted to favor socialization and education. These worlds offer the possibility of simulating the real world as it is, or designing unique fantasy worlds. By interacting with these platforms, people can actively experience simulated realities, which can aid in understanding various concepts and support independent viewpoints for users as they accomplish specific tasks. Users can easily share the virtual environment for performing highly synchronous collaborative tasks, manipulating the same virtual objects (De Lucia, Francese, Passero, & Tortora, 2009).

Numerous advances in information technology are transfiguring teaching and learning styles, especially in higher education. During the past decade, educators from a variety of backgrounds have started using the online 3DVWs to support their teaching and learning activities. 3DVWs support a higher level of interactivity and richness for interaction, collaboration and communication than traditional media (Ghapanchi & Ghanbarzadeh, 2014). They also have the potential to create engaging and meaningful experiences for students and learners. In recent years, there has been remarkable growth in the application of these environments for distance education and e-learning. These immersive platforms offer various tools to create sophisticated and highly interactive simulations using in-world programming, modeling and scripting tools. 3DVWs support teaching and learning in an educational context and they offer the functionality and capability to manage the various aspects of education such as lecturing, presentation, administration and assessment of coursework.

A wide variety of organizations, educational groups, and government agencies currently provide regular events, seminars, and workshops in virtual worlds. Furthermore, many educational institutions and organizations are creating virtual learning environments to deliver courses (face-to-face and online) and events that include 3DVW presentations, discussions, simulations and role-playing. Not only do 3DVWs amplify learning beyond the capabilities afforded by teleconferencing and online web presentation tools, they also create opportunities for field trips that go far beyond the traditional learning spaces (Linden Research, 2011).

Many studies have been conducted on the application of 3DVWs in learning and teaching. For example, Hew and Cheung (2013) discussed evidence-based educational approaches related to the application of Web 2.0 technologies in both K-12 and higher education settings. In their study, Saleeb and Dafoulas (2010) analytically derived advantageous and disadvantageous categories and sub-categories of applying 3DVWs for conducting e-learning. Hew and Cheung (2010) reviewed past empirical research studies on the application of 3DVWs in educational settings such as K-12 and higher education and found that virtual worlds may be applied for the communication spaces, simulation of space, and experiential spaces.

RESEARCH METHOD

A systematic literature review of the application of 3DVWs in higher education, based on Kitchenham (2004) guidelines was conducted. A systematic literature review is a methodical approach for identifying, evaluating, and interpreting previous studies conducted on a specific research field. Previously, several studies have used Kitchenham's method to carry out a review on the literature (Amrollahi, Ghapanchi, & Talaei-Khoei, 2013; Ghanbarzadeh, Ghapanchi, & Blumenstein, 2015; Ghanbarzadeh, Ghapanchi, Blumenstein, & Talaei-Khoei, 2014; Ghapanchi & Aurum, 2011; Najaftorkaman, Ghapanchi, Talaei-Khoei, & Ray, 2013; Najaftorkaman, Ghapanchi, Talaei-Khoei, & Ray, 2014).

In this section, the steps in the literature review process will be described including the procedure for inclusion and exclusion of pertinent literature, and data extraction and analysis during the search process will be discussed in detail.

Search Criteria, Databases, and Keywords

To begin the literature review process, inclusion and exclusion criteria were established:

- Both empirical and technical studies were included.
- Studies related to education settings other than higher education were excluded.
- Studies published between January 1990 and November 2013 were included.
- Studies in languages other than English were excluded.

Eight relevant scientific databases were used in the search process for the keywords: ScienceDirect, ProQuest Computing, IEEE Xplore, Association for Information Systems Electronic Library (AISel), Web of Science (via Thomson Reuters), Inspec (via Thomson Reuters), ERIC (Via ProQuest) and PsycARTICLES (via Ovid). The databases were selected based on their comprehensiveness in locating pertinent articles, chapters, presentations, papers; these eight databases cover thousands of sources. The initial result of search operations for the mentioned eight scientific digital libraries is shown in Table 1.

The advanced search option provided by each electronic database was used for the search operations. By using the following 48 search terms, title, abstract and keywords of the articles were searched in accordance with the various search patterns offered by each search engine. The key words that were used in the search are shown in Table 2.

According to Kitchenham's guidelines, the process of searching for and selecting relevant literature for the current study was completed in six different stages. Figure 1 shows this process.

In the first stage, the eight scientific databases aforementioned were selected. In Stage 2, a search of the eight databases, by using above-mentioned keywords, was carried out respectively. As of November 15, 2013, the database searches revealed 1402 primary studies. In Stage 3, 865 papers were excluded

Table 1. Summary of the initial results for search in each scientific digital library

Digital Library	Search in	Number of Papers
ScienceDirect	Title/abstract/key	249
	Title	10
	All fields	13,430
ProQuest Computing	Anywhere except full text	224
	Title	14
	All fields	2,713
IEEE Xplore	Abstract	573
	Title	25
	All fields	1,665
(AISeL) Association for Information Systems Electronic Library	Abstract	23
	Title	1
	All fields	325
Web of Science (via Thomson Reuters)	Title	66
	Topic	1,615
Inspec (via Thomson Reuters)	Title	53
	Topic	2,644
ERIC (via ProQuest)	Abstract	194
	Title	17
	All fields	269
PsycARTICLES (via Ovid)	Abstract	20
	Title	2
	All fields	823

Table 2. Key words used in the search

("3D" OR "3 D" OR "3-D" OR "3_D" OR "three-dimensional" OR "three dimensional" OR "3 dimensional" OR "three D" OR "three-D")
AND
("virtual world" OR "virtual life" OR "virtual space" OR "virtual environment" OR "virtual reality" OR "virtual community" OR "virtual inhabited world" OR "inhabited space" OR "second life" OR "active world" OR "avatar" OR "virtual immersive world" OR "Multi user virtual environment" OR "MUVE")
AND
("educate" OR "education" OR "educational" OR "educating" OR "distance education" OR "distance learning" OR "train" OR "training" OR "lecture" OR "lecturing" OR "pedagogy" OR "pedagogical" OR "learn" OR "learning" OR "teach" OR "teaching" OR "instruct" OR "instruction" OR "instructing" OR "edutainment" OR "university" OR "universities" OR "higher education" OR "tertiary sector" OR "tertiary education")

on the basis of their titles. In Stage 4, 255 papers were excluded from the remaining 537 papers based on their abstracts. In Stage 5, 15 papers were excluded on the basis of the full text. One hundred three papers were replicas or there was no access to the full text. Finally, at the end of the procedure, the total number of relevant papers was 164, which seemed reasonable for generating an appropriate conclusion. Therefore, the search process stopped at the end of Stage 6. Table 3 indicates the number of related papers which were selected from each scientific database.

Figure 1. Stages in the procedure of searching for and selecting studies

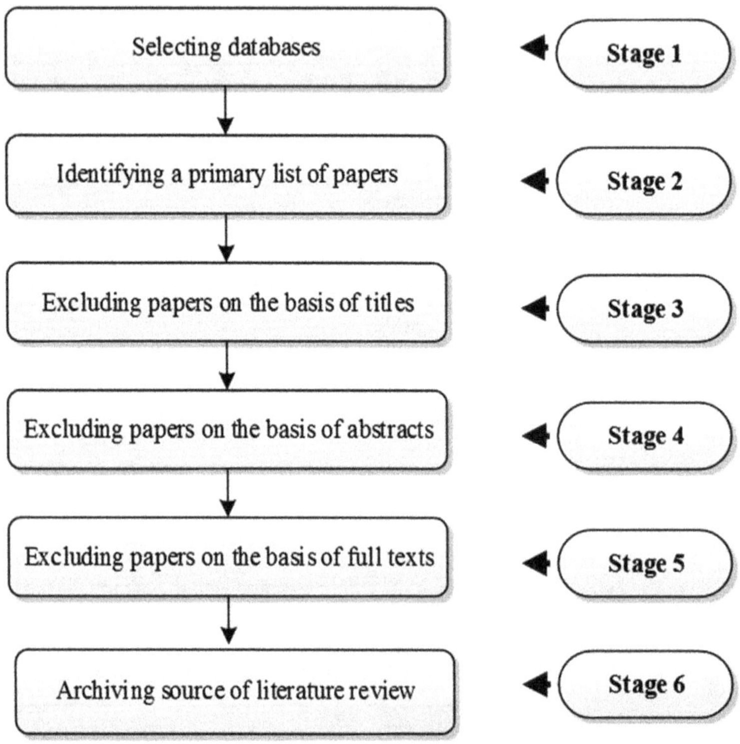

Table 3. Number of related papers selected from each scientific database

Scientific Data Bases	Related Studies
IEEE Xplore	62
ERIC (Via ProQuest)	38
ScienceDirect	27
Inspec (via Thomson Reuters)	19
AISeL	12
ProQuest	5
Web of Science (via Thomson Reuters)	1
PsycARTICLES (via Ovid)	0
Total number of related papers	164

Data Extraction and Analysis

The data extracted from each of the 164 papers identified in the literature search included:

- Performed activities by using 3DVWs for learning and teaching in higher education
- Utilized 3DVW platform
- Created 3D virtual educational environments for the study

To perform a data analysis, the full text of 164 extracted papers were read in their entirety in order to identify all information related to each of the mentioned research questions; then each paper was classified and labeled according to its main area of research and application area of 3DVWs. To make a better classification, the categorizing operation was performed two times. First, each paper was reviewed by one of the authors and an appropriate category code allocated, therefore, all papers were classified in various categories. To clarify the classification, the process was repeated for the second time by the other author. The results were discussed in a meeting with professionals in the similar research field. During the meeting, all categories were discussed and revised, and some of them were merged. Finally, all papers were classified into five major research categories based on the main activity and application areas of 3DWVs: virtual lecturing, discussion, field trip, simulation, and gaming. After this, some demographic information extracted from each paper, then investigated and finalized. Figure 2 shows the procedure undertaken in the data analysis process.

RESULTS

The purpose of this literature review, as stated in the Introduction, was to perform a systematic literature review on the application areas of 3DVWs in learning and teaching in higher education, in order to answer three research questions in relation to the mentioned technology and higher education. In this section a discussion of findings will be presented for each of the research questions.

Figure 2. The procedure of data analysis

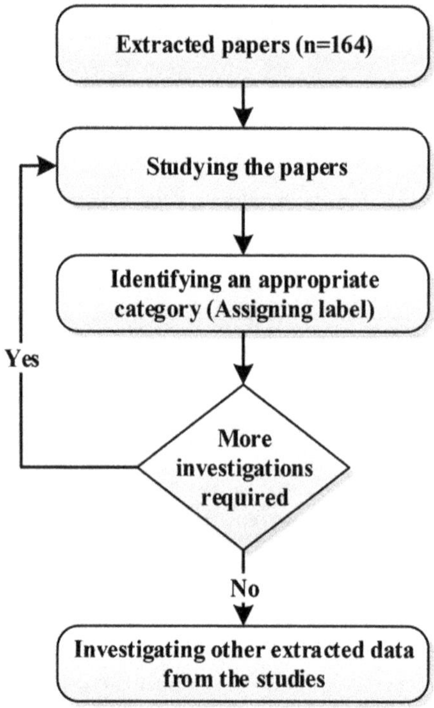

Applications for 3DVWs in Higher Education

The results of this literature review of 164 research articles, revealed that 3DVWs have been adopted and applied in a wide range of areas in higher education for teaching and learning. According to the nature of educational activities performed, articles were sorted into five main categories: virtual lecturing, discussion, field trip, simulation, and gaming. Some of the studies implemented two or more activities simultaneously. Figure 3 depicts the major categories of application areas of 3DVWs in the higher education settings.

Figure 3. The major categories of application areas of 3DVWs in the higher education setting

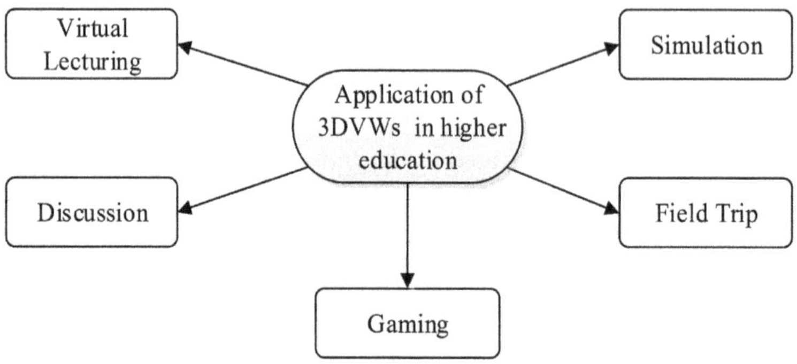

Virtual Lecturing

In this application, by using 3DVWs, a virtual replica of a classroom setting or a laboratory as commonly used for presentations and lectures, is designed. The instructor can use two or more screens for presenting slides, videos, pictures, web resources, and even an online-desktop when a part of the desktop needs to be presented to the students. Students usually attend the virtual classroom using their own avatars and there are possibilities to make contact between the instructor and the students using two mechanisms, text chat and online voice. For voice chat instructor and students need to have microphones and head-sets hooked up to their computers. Around 9% of the investigated studies in the literature have content relevant to virtual lecturing, and they have mainly established a virtual lecturing activity to deliver a course to the students. For example, Barry et al. (2013), Callaghan, McCusker, Losada, Harkin, and Wilson (2009), Dafoulas, Saleeb and Loomes (2012), Dreher, Reiners, Dreher, and Dreher (2009), and Mendonça, Carreira, and Sampaio (2011) carried out studies related to this category.

Discussion

Discussion boards and online meetings are another application in the 3DVW-related virtual learning programs. During the distance discussions or meetings, students engage in several social activities, such as discussions about a subject matter, sharing their perspective(s), presentation of students' projects, consultation, asking questions, etc. For instance, studies of Di Blas and Poggi (2007), Prasolova-Forland (2004), and Zhao, Sun, Wu, and Hu (2010) are classified into this category as they involve virtual meeting or discussion room for various educational purposes.

Field Trip

Field trips are mainly used as an application for self-learning. A virtual representation of a specific place such as a museum, a gallery, a hotel, a hospital, and a scientific site is designed to create visitor awareness about the place and provide information that students need. Students are able to navigate their avatars into the designed environment to visit the virtual site. Students usually perform a virtual trip to a virtual place, visit the site, read the provided information, and observe some activities inside the site. Almost 15% of studies in the literature used 3DVWs for conducting field trip programs. For example, Aydogan, Aras, and Karakas (2010) have built a hydroelectric power plant in Second Life with all its important parts to teach how to produce electricity. Using avatars, students walked around and flew towards the power plant to figure out how it worked. In another study, access to a number of digital 3D models of European theatre designs was provided and participants visited the Theatre of Epidaurus during a virtual field trip; participants also explored Shakespeare's Globe Theatre (Nicholls & Philip, 2012).

Simulation

Other studies in the current systematic review applied 3DVWs for simulation purposes in higher education. Simulation is the act of imitation of a real-world system's or process's operation over time. It is a powerful tool that is commonly used to teach processes that are generally difficult to practice in the real world (Wang & Zhu, 2009). By using virtual worlds' designing and programming tools, as well as simulation techniques, the virtual clones of a specific place or an environment is modelled and designed for training purposes. By working with simulated environments, students get familiar with various concepts which are usually inaccessible in the real world. For example, in a study conducted by Grenfell (2013), students were working to simulate the development of a virtual art exhibition space. In another study, researchers simulated an on-line garment store in Second Life with static objects, such as buildings, sofas, costumes, advertising boards, direction boards, etc. (Dong, Ma, & Wang, 2010).

Gaming

Computer games are effective approaches to teach various educational concepts. Students who play computer games tend to learn the intended concepts, and in most of the cases, they find it a relatively enjoyable experience of learning (Wang & Zhu, 2009). Around 10.5% of the studies in the literature have used games as a provocative tool for teaching and learning. For example, in one of the studies, to determine whether and how a 3DVW enhanced software engineering education, authors designed a Second Life-based game for computer science students (Ye, Liu, & Polack-Wahl, 2007). In another study, authors designed a 3D virtual quest game to enhance English vocabulary acquisition through interaction, negotiation of meaning and observation (Kastoudi, 2011).

3DVWs Platforms Used in Teaching and Learning

Since the advent of the first generation of 3DVWs, various companies have developed their own virtual world platform, and currently, there are a wide variety of 3DVW platforms. Individuals and numerous companies and organizations all around the world are using various samples of these platforms for their own purposes. There are a wide variety of active 3DVW platforms at the moment, however, this literature review sought to identify the platforms most widely used by researchers in their educational programs.

Figure 4 presents percentages of various 3DWV platforms found in the review of 164 studies. Second Life was the most frequently discussed 3DVW platform used for learning and teaching purposes in higher education; Second Life was discussed in 62% of 164 studies. Sixteen percent of the 164 studies used their own, self-developed 3DVW platform mainly using a designed single-purpose virtual world for extending educational activities. Open Simulator was discussed in 8% of 164 studies, as a platform utilised for learning and teaching in higher education. Seven percent of the papers discussed using other platforms such as Vacademia, Zora 3-D, Croquet and AliveX3D. Active World and AET Zone are the other platforms which were discussed respectively in 3% and 2% of studies. In 2% of the studies, authors did not specified the type of 3DVW that they have applied, therefore, the used platforms considered as unknown. Table 4 indicates all 3DWV platforms used in the literature, and the exact number of studies which used each one. According to the findings in the current study, Second Life is the most popular 3DVW platform for higher education, and Open Simulator, Active World and AET Zone were reported the least among the 164 studies.

Gamage, Tretiakov, and Crump (2011) investigated educators' perceptions of Second Life affordances for learning by conducting in-depth semi-structured interviews with 22 educators. Chen, Siau, and Nah (2009) assessed the efficacy of two instruction strategies in Second Life, and their effects on interactivity, social presence, and perceived learning. García-Zubia et al. (2010) described the implementation of a new remote lab that allowed students to control a micro robot from Second Life. Stiubiener, Barbosa, Kamienski, and Schweitzer (2011) in their study presented two tools developed to facilitate the use and automate the process of using Open Simulator for educational purposes. Dickey (2005) presented two

Figure 4. Percentage of applied 3DVWs in higher education

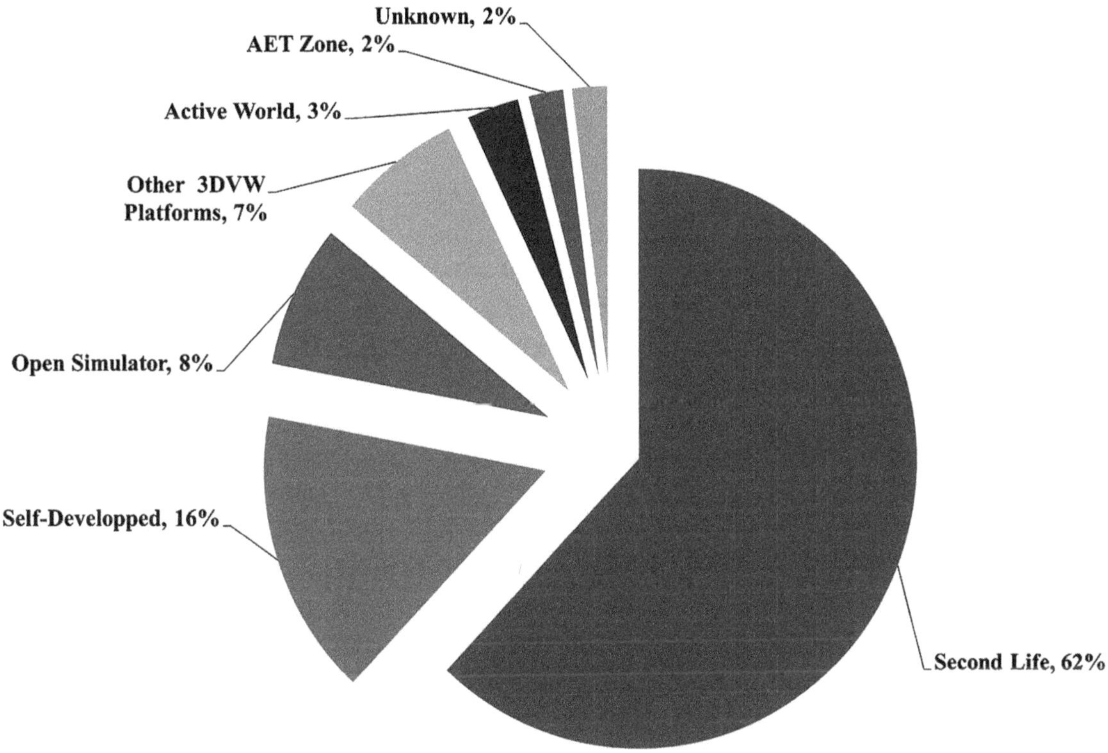

Table 4. Number of studies for each 3DVW platform

3D Virtual World Platform	Number of studies
Second Life	96
Self-Developed	24
Open Simulator	12
Active World	5
AET Zone	3
Unknown	3
Vacademia	2
Barnsborough(AWEDU)	1
Croquet	1
GEARS	1
QA (Quest Atlantis)	1
Virtools Dev	1
Virtual Incubator World (VIW)	1
WonderLands/TEAL	1
Zora 3-D	1
AliveX3D	1

exploratory case studies of different, but exemplary educational activities using Active Worlds for formal and informal education. In another study, Bronack et al. (2008) used the AET Zone platform for their teaching and learning purposes.

Categorization of Learning Environments for Educational Purposes

3DVW technologies provide the ability for users to design and create different kinds of virtual and 3D environments for various purposes. In all of the studies in our systematic literature review, researchers designed and developed specific spaces inside the virtual worlds in relation to their educational activities. The created virtual environments were categorized and 17 categories were identified. The majority of the studies created two or more categories of environments simultaneously. Table 5 shows the list of all virtual environments in higher education as well as the number of papers in each category in the literature.

As it can be noted in Table 5, in 63 studies, researchers designed virtual classroom environments for their programs. These environments resemble actual classrooms or lecture theaters (having a number of seats, a lectern for instructor, a presentation display and video display), where students' and instructors' avatars can attend and communicate with each other using voice or text chat tools. Students can see the presentation slides, educational videos and they can even see the instructor's face in an online and real-time video. For example, Gao, Noh, and Koehler (2009), Loureiro and Bettencourt (2011), Marcelino, Silva, Gruber, and Bilessimo (2012), and Yalcinalp, Sen, Kocer, and Koroglu (2012) designed various virtual classroom environments inside the 3DVW platforms.

Table 5. Virtual environments used in higher education and number of related studies

Virtual Environments	Number of Studies
Virtual classroom	63
Simulated place	31
Meeting area	22
Other environments	21
Virtual campus	15
Virtual laboratory	13
Gaming environment	10
Virtual library	9
Replica of known place	9
Virtual messaging environment	8
Board room	4
Sandbox area	4
Video room	3
Quiz environment	3
Poster room	1
Outdoor environment	1
Staff room	1

In 31 of the 164 studies reviewed, researchers used simulated places for teaching and learning. In most cases, a specific place has been modeled, simulated and created; therefore, students can learn different things by visiting, interacting with and going around these places. For example, Cheng and Wang (2011) designed a 3D virtual supermarket to help business students transform abstract class theory into the concrete application ability in the real world. Brown, Rasmussen, Baldwin, and Wyeth (2012) developed a simulated 3D ICU (Intensive Care Unit) for students to practice key steps in handing over the 24/7 care requirements of intensive care patients during the first hour of a shift. In another study, authors designed a virtual hydroelectric power plant in Second Life to teach students how to produce electricity (Aydogan et al., 2010). Students also can observe the detail of the power plant's structure which cannot be shown even in a technical trip due to the plant being in-service.

Virtual meeting areas have been designed and used by 22 of 164 studies. These areas are mainly furnished by seats and chairs, and they contain presentations and video displays. The avatars can get together in the place and they can use microphones/speakers (voice chat) or text chat tools for sending public or private messages to each other. The main purpose of these places is to hold across-distance meetings with students, instructors or staff. For example, Bronack et al. (2008), Nikolaou and Tsolakidis (2012), and Konstantinidis and Tsiatsos (2008) developed a virtual meeting area to hold educational meetings.

Fifteen of the 164 studies discussed the development of a university campus for their activities. They designed various parts of a real campus and students could enter the campus using their avatars and visit different sections inside. In some cases a replica of a real university campus is designed so the virtual campus exactly resembles the real one. In other cases, researchers designed different buildings and views for the campus and they only inserted the parts, buildings or rooms that students needed to attend or visit. For example, Bers and Chau (2010), Nishide (2011), and Nishide and Ueshima (2004) developed a campus using 3DVWs for their teaching and learning programs in higher education.

Virtual laboratories are the other virtual environments which have been created and developed by researchers for higher education. These laboratories are simulated environments that present the ability to perform most of the activities of the real laboratories in a virtual manner. For instance, Muller, Chilliischi, and Langer (2012) designed a virtual mechatronics lab in Open Simulator, developed for mechatronics training, which combines immersive 3D worlds and real lab equipment. Zhong and Liu (2012) created a virtual chemistry laboratory to discuss the technical difficulties that users face when developing 3D virtual worlds. A physics laboratory was designed by dos Santos, Guetl, Bailey, and Harward (2010) in order to support students understanding of physics concepts.

In nine papers, authors designed a replica of a known and popular place in the world to help students get familiar with the place and atmosphere. These virtual clones are mainly used for field trips and similar activities. For example, Hsu (2012) created a virtual island of France for tourism education. In two other studies, researchers used Second Life to simulate a Saami tent and a Kalasha valley and dwellings for archaeology students (Edirisingha, Nie, Pluciennik, & Young, 2009; Salmon, Nie, & Edirisingha, 2010).

Virtual messaging environments have also been created and used in educational settings for communication purposes. In these environments, users of virtual worlds can have interaction with each other using voice or text chat tools. For example, Traphagan et al. (2010) used a text chat tool for students to complete all course activities collaboratively with group members. Wigham and Chanier (2013) offer a classification of verbal and nonverbal communication acts in Second Life and outline relationships between the different types of acts by using a voice forum.

In addition to the environments mentioned, other virtual spaces have been designed for different educational purposes. Some of the other virtual environments are video rooms, virtual libraries, board rooms, poster rooms, outdoor environments, staff rooms, sandbox areas, and other miscellaneous environments.

FUTURE DIRECTION FOR RESEACH

One of the principle goals of this research was to classify various application areas of 3DVWs in the field of education. Therefore, based on the literature, the authors provide five meaningful categories of applications in higher education (virtual lecturing, discussion, field trip, simulation, and gaming). Hence, future research can explore additional applications of these environments in the education sector. They can identify various criteria to evaluate value-added activities and strategies for effective integration of this technology into a curriculum. Future research also need to be more creative to figure out new effective ways of teaching and learning rather than to replicate the traditional methods of education. In spite of the considerable level of academic research related to the educational application of 3DVWs, research pertaining to the practical applications of such tools are seemingly inadequate, particularly as opportunities continue to arise and continue to evolve in utilizing this technology in the field of education.

The current systematic literature review and the results provide various implications for a wide range of organizations, universities, educational communities, schools, academic staff, educators, instructors and individuals which are able to use this study to consider all the capabilities and derived experiences that are associated with the application of 3DVWs in the professional and pedagogical objectives they want to achieve. This study also identifies any gaps that were apparent in the published research. Despite the fact that researchers paid more attention to educational benefits of 3DVWs, still there are some gaps in the literature and future research should be conducted to explore improvements to previous studies. The mentioned implications as well as existing gaps in conjunction with the topic will be discussed as following:

Collaborative Learning

According to the findings of the current study, the focus of previous studies was mainly on the possibilities of using 3DVWs for delivering distance courses, and the students' learning outcomes in the investigated studies were mostly positive for distance education. Nevertheless, as these technologies provide effective opportunities for students in respect to collaborative learning, team work and self-learning, future studies may best contribute by investigating the impacts of such technologies on individual and group student outcomes and experiences.

Gaming and Machinima

Gaming and machinima aspect of 3DVWs has also received little attention in the higher education field. Machinima, in definition, is the "art of making animated movies in a 3D virtual environment in real time" (Marino, 2004). Entertainment environments and leisure activities as well as using computers and video games have been identified as significant educational resources. Games help impart knowledge, develop course-related skills and reinforce positive habits in students of all ages, in the form of play. Future studies are expected to put more attention to this capability of 3DVWs in teaching and learning programs.

Geographical Context

According to findings of the current study, the majority of studies in the literature in this field, have been done in North America and Europe, and there are only a limited number of studies from other countries of the world. A comparative research within various cultural and social environments is recommended in order to more effectively comprehend the influence of geographical contexts on the use of 3DVWs in higher education.

3DVW-Based vs. Traditional Classroom

One of the significant questions about the applicability of 3DVWs in higher education is whether these technologies can provide comparable learning outcomes for trainees attending real-world classrooms. In the current literature review, the researchers found a wide range of studies that covered this research topic and, according to students' and educators' feedback, they demonstrate that 3DVWs have the ability to enhance teaching and learning outcomes significantly, having a general positive impact on students' achievement and providing more options for delivering education in comparison with real-world and in-person classes.

Distance Learning Opportunities

Due to Internet-based characteristics, 3DVWs, provide effective opportunities to conduct distance learning and e-learning programs for students using this technology. Lectures, seminars, laboratories and workshops can be held easily using this technology, and students and educators can attend courses in the virtual venue using their own avatar from various locations all around the world.

Simulation and Modeling

Modeling is "the act of representing a system or subsystem formally" (Davis II et al., 1999). According to the promising potential of 3DVWs for modeling and simulation purposes, research or practice that may not have been practical or feasible in real life can be created through simulations in 3D virtual environments (Eschenbrenner, Nah, & Siau, 2008), and virtual simulations using these kinds of technologies are an acceptable strategy to deliver scenarios that focus on practical skills. By using the simulation techniques, instructors, educators and trainers are able to collaborate with learners and solve problem-based scenarios in a team. Simulation also allows them to construct technical skills actively through interaction in a 3D virtual environment without having the hazard of risks or danger of making mistakes in a specific activity. Organizations such as universities, manufacturers and educational communities can model and simulate various systems, laboratories, product lines and activities, with virtual instruments and equipment that simulate real-world operations at a very low cost for education. Particularly, utilizing 3DVWs seems to be a proper method to learn design-based and visually-intensive courses like object modeling and computer graphics.

Virtual Field Trips

By using 3DVWs, there is a possibility of holding virtual field trips inside virtual environments for educational purposes. It is a guided and narrated tour of a virtual simulation of a real place or an imaginary location inside a 3DVW that can be selected by educators and arranged so that students can visit, follow the instructions and perform an exploration with just moving around the virtual space. By traveling to virtual locations, students can get familiar with various spectacular, historical and travel points all around the world.

Integration

A 3DVW gives developers the ability to connect and control other hardware and software to add more facilities to virtual learning and teaching environments. For example, developers can control various types of hardware from their virtual land, by adding programs and scripts to their objects within the virtual environment. Developers are also able to connect other educational applications such as Blackboard to some of the virtual worlds like Second Life to take more advantages of those applications inside the virtual learning environment. For example, Second Life supports a specific programming language, Linden Scripting Language (LSL), which is a capable tool allowing control of in-world objects as well as integration and connection with other applications and hardware. On the other hand, as virtual worlds support 3D shape functions, inside these environments students are able to create and sculpt shapes and showcase their individual works to others for peer review; the application of this technology is related to learning as construction or co-construction (Hew & Cheung, 2013). These environments provide facilities for reusing, remixing, and mashing up user-created objects and content; therefore, they can be seen as an effective collaborative tool with which multiple users can experiment with each other.

Virtual Campus

By creating a virtual campus, universities and colleges can provide an attractive virtual environment to extend their educational programs. A virtual campus provides a specific place as a framework for learning activities as well as a set of virtual tools to benefit educational process (Clark & Maher, 2001). Various activities can be done inside the virtual lands of 3DVWs beside the educational programs such as open day programs, orientation programs, public ceremonies or any other extracurricular activities. On the other hand, a virtual campus can be accessed from any Internet-connected personal computer from remote locations providing a more effective learning environment for all its students by giving them the opportunity to access the learning materials and resources from own place.

Barriers and Issues

In the current study, some challenges related to the use of 3DWVs in higher education were identified. As a result, there is also a need for more research into the issues and barriers of using this technology, as current studies tend to deal with only the advantages and positive aspects of the use of 3DVWs in higher education. The problems and barriers of these environments, such as complexity, speed, compatibility, behavior, health, safety, security, cost, user adoption, etc., need to be considered as well as factors associated with adoption and students' intention to use 3DVWs in educational activities. In order to make this technology more accessible and user-friendly, and to reduce the complexity for educators and trainees, especially those who are unfamiliar with designing and programming techniques, further studies and research are required.

CONCLUSION

To provide a big picture of application areas of 3DVWs in the higher education sector, a systematic literature review has been conducted on the available body of knowledge. Consequently, five main category of curricular activities were developed for which 3DVWs have been used to date: virtual lecturing, discussion, field trip, simulation and gaming. The authors also identified the most applied 3DVWs platforms in higher education, and according to their findings, Second Life is the most widely used and well-known platform in the literature in this area. Also the 3D virtual environments created for educational purposes have been identified and classified into seventeen main categories. Virtual classroom, virtual laboratory, virtual meeting area, simulated places and replicas of popular places are the most common 3D virtual environments in the literature that are used for educational pedagogical activities in higher education. The findings offer researchers, educators and educational institutions some informed directions for utilizing these technologies to achieve specific learning outcomes. They are able to use this technology as a creative, powerful and efficient tool to develop new and effective ways of teaching and learning. In order to close the gap between academic research and practical applications some suggestions can be made: First of all, educational applications should be widespread, in accordance with the proposals obtained from the researchers conducting studies in this field. Second, universities and other educational communities and organizations should lead the use of 3DVWs for their educational purposes in the future.

REFERENCES

Amrollahi, A., Ghapanchi, A. H., & Talaei-Khoei, A. (2013). A systematic literature review on strategic information systems planning: Insights from the past decade. *Pacific Asia Journal of the Association for Information Systems*, *5*(2), 4.

Aydogan, H., Aras, F., & Karakas, E. (2010). *An assessment on distance education in a 3D virtual environment: How to produce electricity in a hydroelectric power plant. Paper presented at the Education Technology and Computer (ICETC), 2010 2nd International Conference*. doi:10.1109/ICETC.2010.5529234

Ba, S., Ke, D., Stallaert, J., & Zhang, Z. (2010). Why give away something for nothing? Investigating virtual goods pricing and permission strategies. *ACM Transactions on Management Information Systems*, *1*(1), 4. doi:10.1145/1877725.1877729

Barry, D. M., Kanematsu, H., Fukumura, Y., Kobayashi, T., Ogawa, N., & Nagai, H. (2013). US Students Carry out Nuclear Safety Project in a Virtual Environment. *Procedia Computer Science*, *22*, 1354–1360. doi:10.1016/j.procs.2013.09.224

Bers, M., & Chau, C. (2010). The virtual campus of the future: Stimulating and simulating civic actions in a virtual world. *Journal of Computing in Higher Education*, *22*(1), 1–23. doi:10.1007/s12528-009-9026-3

Boulos, M. N. K., Hetherington, L., & Wheeler, S. (2007). Second Life: An overview of the potential of 3-D virtual worlds in medical and health education. *Health Information and Libraries Journal*, *24*(4), 233–245. doi:10.1111/j.1471-1842.2007.00733.x PMID:18005298

Bronack, S., Sanders, R., Cheney, A., Riedl, R., Tashner, J., & Matzen, N. (2008). Presence Pedagogy: Teaching and Learning in a 3D Virtual Immersive World. *International Journal of Teaching and Learning in Higher Education*, *20*(1), 59–69.

Brown, R., Rasmussen, R., Baldwin, I., & Wyeth, P. (2012). Design and implementation of a virtual world training simulation of ICU first hour handover processes. *Australian Critical Care*, *25*(3), 178–187. doi:10.1016/j.aucc.2012.02.005 PMID:22436543

Callaghan, M., McCusker, K., Losada, J. L., Harkin, J., & Wilson, S. (2009). Integrating virtual worlds & virtual learning environments for online education. *Paper presented at the Games Innovations Conference ICE-GIC International IEEE Consumer Electronics Society.* doi:10.1109/ICEGIC.2009.5293576

Chen, X., Siau, K., & Nah, F. F.-H. (2009). 3-D virtual worlds: Education and learning. *SIGHCI 2009 Proceedings* (p. 13).

Cheng, Y., & Wang, S.-H. (2011). Applying a 3D virtual learning environment to facilitate student's application ability–The case of marketing. *Computers in Human Behavior*, *27*(1), 576–584. doi:10.1016/j.chb.2010.10.008

Clark, S., & Maher, M. L. (2001). *The role of place in designing a learner centred virtual learning environment Computer Aided Architectural Design Futures 2001* (pp. 187–200). Springer. doi:10.1007/978-94-010-0868-6_15

Dafoulas, G., Saleeb, N., & Loomes, M. (2012). The impact of 3D virtual environments on communication patterns. *Paper presented at the Information Technology Based Higher Education and Training (ITHET) 2012 International Conference.* doi:10.1109/ITHET.2012.6246065

Davis, J., II, Goel, M., Hylands, C., Kienhuis, B., Lee, E. A., Liu, J., . . . Reekie, J. (1999). *Overview of the Ptolemy project* (ERL Technical Report). UCB/ERL.

De Lucia, A., Francese, R., Passero, I., & Tortora, G. (2009). Development and evaluation of a virtual campus on Second Life: The case of SecondDMI. *Computers & Education*, *52*(1), 220–233. doi:10.1016/j.compedu.2008.08.001

Di Blas, N., & Poggi, C. (2007). European virtual classrooms: Building effective "virtual" educational experiences. *Virtual Reality (Waltham Cross)*, *11*(2-3), 129–143. doi:10.1007/s10055-006-0060-4

Dickey, M. D. (2005). Three-dimensional virtual worlds and distance learning: Two case studies of Active Worlds as a medium for distance education. *British Journal of Educational Technology*, *36*(3), 439–451. doi:10.1111/j.1467-8535.2005.00477.x

Dong, P., Ma, B., & Wang, F. (2010). Development and Evaluation of an Experiential Learning Service in 3D Virtual World. *Paper presented at the Service Sciences (ICSS) 2010 International Conference*. doi:10.1109/ICSS.2010.37

dos Santos, F. R., Guetl, C., Bailey, P. H., & Harward, V. J. (2010). Dynamic virtual environment for multiple physics experiments in higher education. *Paper presented at the Education Engineering (EDUCON)*. doi:10.1109/EDUCON.2010.5492507

Dreher, C., Reiners, T., Dreher, N., & Dreher, H. (2009). 3D virtual worlds as collaborative communities enriching human endeavours: Innovative applications in e-Learning. *Paper presented at the 3rd IEEE International Conference on Digital Ecosystems and Technologies DEST'09.*

Edirisingha, P., Nie, M., Pluciennik, M., & Young, R. (2009). Socialisation for learning at a distance in a 3-D multi-user virtual environment. *British Journal of Educational Technology*, *40*(3), 458–479. doi:10.1111/j.1467-8535.2009.00962.x

Eschenbrenner, B., Nah, F. F.-H., & Siau, K. (2008). 3-D virtual worlds in education: Applications, benefits, issues, and opportunities. *Journal of Database Management*, *19*(4), 91–110. doi:10.4018/jdm.2008100106

Gamage, V., Tretiakov, A., & Crump, B. (2011). Teacher perceptions of learning affordances of multi-user virtual environments. *Computers & Education*, *57*(4), 2406–2413. doi:10.1016/j.compedu.2011.06.015

Gao, F., Noh, J. J., & Koehler, M. J. (2009). Comparing role-playing activities in Second Life and face-to-face environments. *Journal of Interactive Learning Research*, *20*(4), 423–443.

Garcia-Zubia, J., Irurzun, J., Angulo, I., Hernandez, U., Castro, M., Sancristobal, E., ... Ruiz-de-Garibay, J. (2010). *SecondLab: A remote laboratory under Second Life.* Paper presented at the Education Engineering (EDUCON). doi:10.1109/EDUCON.2010.5492556

Ghanbarzadeh, R., Ghapanchi, A. H., & Blumenstein, M. (2015). Characteristics of Research on the Application of Three-Dimensional Immersive Virtual Worlds in Health [Springer.]. *Information Science*, 213–224.

Ghanbarzadeh, R., Ghapanchi, A. H., Blumenstein, M., & Talaei-Khoei, A. (2014). A Decade of Research on the Use of Three-Dimensional Virtual Worlds in Health Care: A Systematic Literature Review. *Journal of Medical Internet Research*, *16*(2), e47. doi:10.2196/jmir.3097 PMID:24550130

Ghapanchi, A. H., & Aurum, A. (2011). Antecedents to IT personnel's intentions to leave: A systematic literature review. *Journal of Systems and Software*, *84*(2), 238–249. doi:10.1016/j.jss.2010.09.022

Ghapanchi, A. H., & Ghanbarzadeh, R. (2014). 3DVWs: Three-dimensional virtual worlds to support teaching and learning activities. *E-Learning Update*, *47*, 14–18.

Grenfell, J. (2013). Immersive Interfaces for Art Education Teaching and Learning in Virtual and Real World Learning Environments. *Procedia: Social and Behavioral Sciences*, *93*, 1198–1211. doi:10.1016/j.sbspro.2013.10.016

Hew, K. F., & Cheung, W. S. (2010). Use of three-dimensional (3-D) immersive virtual worlds in K-12 and higher education settings: A review of the research. *British Journal of Educational Technology, 41*(1), 33–55. doi:10.1111/j.1467-8535.2008.00900.x

Hew, K. F., & Cheung, W. S. (2013). Use of Web 2.0 technologies in K-12 and higher education: The search for evidence-based practice. *Educational Research Review, 9*, 47–64. doi:10.1016/j.edurev.2012.08.001

Hsu, L. (2012). Web 3D simulation-based application in tourism education: A case study with Second Life. *Journal of Hospitality, Leisure, Sport and Tourism Education, 11*(2), 113–124. doi:10.1016/j.jhlste.2012.02.013

Kastoudi, D. (2011). *Using a Quest in a 3D Virtual Environment for Student Interaction and Vocabulary Acquisition in Foreign Language Learning. European Association for Computer-Assisted Language Learning*. EUROCALL.

Kitchenham, B. (2004). Procedures for performing systematic reviews. Keele University, 33.

Konstantinidis, A., & Tsiatsos, T. (2008). Selecting a networked virtual environment platform and the design of a collaborative e-learning environment. *Paper presented at the 22nd International Conference on Advanced Information Networking and Applications-Workshops AINAW.*

Linden Lab. (2013). SL10B Infographic: Ten Years of Second Life. Retrieved from http://www.lindenlab.com/releases/infographic-10-years-of-second-life

Linden Research. (2011). Second Life education: The virtual learning advantage. Retrieved from http://lecs-static-secondlife-com.s3.amazonaws.com/work/SL-Edu-Brochure-010411.pdf

Loureiro, A., & Bettencourt, T. (2011). The Extended Classroom: Meeting students' needs using a virtual environment. *Procedia: Social and Behavioral Sciences, 15*, 2667–2672. doi:10.1016/j.sbspro.2011.04.167

Marcelino, R., Silva, J., Gruber, V., & Bilessimo, M. (2012). 3D virtual worlds using open source platform and integrated remote experimentation. *Paper presented at the 2012 9th International Conference on Remote Engineering and Virtual Instrumentation (REV).*

Marino, P. (2004). *The art of machinima: 3D game-based filmmaking*. Scottsdale: Paraglyph Press.

Mendonça, R. F., Carreira, S. M., & Sampaio, P. N. (2011). *VirtualLabs@ UMa: A customizable 3D learning platform for experimental activities. Paper presented at the 2011 International Conference on Multimedia Computing and Systems (ICMCS).*

Muller, D., Chilliischi, A., & Langer, S. (2012). *Integrating immersive 3D worlds and real lab equipment for teaching mechatronics. Paper presented at the 2012 9th International Conference on Remote Engineering and Virtual Instrumentation (REV).* doi:10.1109/REV.2012.6293117

Najaftorkaman, M., Ghapanchi, A. H., Talaei-Khoei, A., & Ray, P. (2013). Recent research areas and grand challenges in electronic medical record: A literature survey approach. *The International Technology Management Review, 3*(1), 12–21. doi:10.2991/itmr.2013.3.1.2

Najaftorkaman, M., Ghapanchi, A. H., Talaei-Khoei, A., & Ray, P. (2014). A taxonomy of antecedents to user adoption of health information systems: A synthesis of thirty years of research. *Journal of the Association for Information Science and Technology*.

Nicholls, J., & Philip, R. (2012). Solo life to Second Life: The design of physical and virtual learning spaces inspired by the drama classroom. *Research in Drama Education, 17*(4), 583–602. doi:10.1080/13569783.2012.727628

Nikolaou, A., & Tsolakidis, C. (2012). The role of three dimensional virtual environments in the development of Personal Learning Networks. *Paper presented at the 2012 15th International Conference on Interactive Collaborative Learning (ICL)*. doi:10.1109/ICL.2012.6402114

Nishide, R. (2011). Prospects for digital campus with extensive applications of virtual collaborative space. *Journal of Interactive Learning Research, 22*(3), 421–443.

Nishide, R., & Ueshima, S. (2004). Digital campus project: a" dream university" over the Internet Web. *Paper presented at the Second International Conference on Creating, Connecting and Collaborating through Computing*.

Prasolova-Forland, E. (2004). Supporting social awareness among university students in 3D CVEs: Benefits and limitations. *Paper presented at the 2004 International Conference on Cyberworlds*. doi:10.1109/CW.2004.59

Saleeb, N., & Dafoulas, G. (2010). Pedagogical immigration to 3D virtual worlds: A critical review of underlying themes and their concepts. *Paper presented at the 2010 International Conference on Information Society* (i-Society).

Salmon, G., Nie, M., & Edirisingha, P. (2010). Developing a five-stage model of learning in Second Life. *Educational Research, 52*(2), 169–182. doi:10.1080/00131881.2010.482744

Stiubiener, I., Barbosa, W., Kamienski, C. A., & Schweitzer, C. M. (2011). Using Virtual Worlds in distance learning environments. *Paper presented at the Frontiers in Education Conference (FIE)*. doi:10.1109/FIE.2011.6142822

Traphagan, T. W., Chiang, Y.-V., Chang, H. M., Wattanawaha, B., Lee, H., Mayrath, M. C., & Resta, P. E. et al. (2010). Cognitive, social and teaching presence in a virtual world and a text chat. *Computers & Education, 55*(3), 923–936. doi:10.1016/j.compedu.2010.04.003

Wang, T., & Zhu, Q. (2009). A software engineering education game in a 3-D online virtual environment. *Paper presented at the First International Workshop on Education Technology and Computer Science ETCS'09*.

Wigham, C. R., & Chanier, T. (2013). A study of verbal and nonverbal communication in Second Life–the ARCHI21 experience. *ReCALL, 25*(01), 63–84. doi:10.1017/S0958344012000250

Yalcinalp, S., Sen, N., Kocer, G., & Koroglu, F. (2012). Higher Education Student's Behaviors as Avatars in a Web based Course in Second Life. *Procedia: Social and Behavioral Sciences, 46*, 4534–4538. doi:10.1016/j.sbspro.2012.06.291

Ye, E., Liu, C., & Polack-Wahl, J. A. (2007). *Enhancing software engineering education using teaching aids in 3-D online virtual worlds. Frontiers in Education*. FIE.

Zhao, H., Sun, B., Wu, H., & Hu, X. (2010). Study on building a 3D interactive virtual learning environment based on OpenSim platform. *Paper presented at the 2010 International Conference on Audio, Language and Image Processing*. doi:10.1109/ICALIP.2010.5684986

Zhong, Y., & Liu, C. (2012). User evaluation of a domain-oriented end-user design environment for building 3D virtual chemistry experiments. *Paper presented at the User Evaluation for Software Engineering Researchers (USER)*. doi:10.1109/USER.2012.6226585

ADDITIONAL READING

Fırat, M. (2010). Learning in 3D virtual worlds and current situation in Turkey. *Procedia: Social and Behavioral Sciences*, *9*, 249–254. doi:10.1016/j.sbspro.2010.12.145

Pricer, W. F. (2011). Immersive Education, an Annotated Webliography. *Community College Enterprise*, *17*(1), 41–50.

Saleeb, N., & Dafoulas, G. (2010). Architectural propositions for enhancement of learning spaces within 3D virtual learning environments. *Paper presented at the 2010 International Conference on Information Society* (i-Society).

Wang, F., & Lockee, B. B. (2010). Virtual Worlds in Distance Education: A Content Analysis Study. *Quarterly Review of Distance Education*, *11*(3), 183–186.

Warburton, S. (2009). Second Life in higher education: Assessing the potential for and the barriers to deploying virtual worlds in learning and teaching. *British Journal of Educational Technology*, *40*(3), 414–426. doi:10.1111/j.1467-8535.2009.00952.x

KEY TERMS AND DEFINITIONS

Avatar: A computer user's digital, graphical and animated self-representation which is completely manipulated by its owner.

Blackboard: A virtual learning environment and course management system developed by Blackboard Inc.

E-Learning: A kind of learning which is conducted by using information and communication technologies and electronic media.

Higher Education: Education provided by colleges, universities or similar educational establishments.

Linden Scripting Language: A scripting programming language that gives behavior to Second Life's primitives, objects, and avatars.

Machinima: Use of video game and computer graphics to create animated cinematic production.

Open Simulator: An open source multi-platform and multi-user 3D application server.

Second Life: A 3D virtual world platform developed by Linden Lab Inc. in 2003.

Simulation: The act of imitation of a real-world system's or process's operation over time.

Three-Dimensional Virtual World (3DVW): A computer-based 3D graphical and simulated environment in which users can interact via their own avatars.

Virtual Lecturing: The act of delivering of lectures by utilizing the Internet, Web, and virtual world technologies.

Chapter 3
Faculty Perception of Virtual 3-D Learning Environment to Assess Student Learning

Anita Cassard
University of Phoenix, USA

Brian W. Sloboda
US Department of Labor, USA

ABSTRACT

This chapter presents some of the methods and approaches that are used in the assessment of student outcomes in 3-D virtual learning environments. Distance learning or eLearning that includes the 3-D virtual learning environments have been increasing dramatically because of the rise in demand by students. Because of this advent in eLearning, assessment of the outcomes is crucial when measuring student learning. In addition to the measurement of student learning, the instructional designers will need assessment of student learning as a means to upgrade the 3-D virtual learning environments and maintain the relevancy of the content for students. Much of the research on measurement of outcomes is based on anecdotal evidence provided by students. A comprehensive examination of assessment of the 3-D virtual learning environment becomes paramount, so educators will have a better idea how to carefully assess outcomes of student learning.

INTRODUCTION

As Internet usage soared exponentially since the 1990s, the use of eLearning paralleled this rise as well, which has also revolutionized the delivery of education (Janicki & Steinberg, 2003; Rungtusanatham, Ellram, & Siferd, 2004). Many universities are using the increased availability of online learning tools or electronic learning (eLearning) in both online and traditional classrooms. To provide these online learning tools, many higher education publishing companies are actively integrating Internet technologies into students' course materials. There is a greater level of interest in the impacts of the new tools on the learning outcomes of students in the contemporary classroom. As part of this enhanced learning, virtual worlds or virtual three-dimensional (3-D) environments are available for learning (Kelton, 2008).

DOI: 10.4018/978-1-4666-9837-6.ch003

The delivery of e-learning encompasses multiple schools of thought on learning that include behaviorism, cognitive psychology, and constructivism. Each of these schools of thought can be used with each other in order to develop a productive learning environment and measure positive outcomes for student learning (Salomon & Perkins, 1998).

The use of virtual 3-D environments or virtual worlds provides a robust learning environment for complex text, graphical, and voice-based social interactions and experiences; yet, despite its valuable contributions to student learning, virtual worlds does not have much research (Braman, Jinman, & Trajkovski, 2007). A virtual world is a computer-simulated environment that provides a 3-D graphical representation of a physical environment in which students can interact with each other and manipulate the learning environment to master learning (Dickey, 2005; Minocha & Roberts, 2008). A variety of virtual worlds have been developed in recent years, and the most prevalent platforms that have been created for student learning include Second Life, OpenSim, Active Worlds, and Twinity; Second Life is the most popular platform. (Vickerstaff, 2015). Virtual worlds offer opportunities for more engaging learning experiences and interactions that cannot be easily experienced or replicated through standard eLearning platforms.

Rock and Schwartz (2006) imply that some of the largest leaps in science have emerged from the integration of separate fields. They also suggested that it is imperative to teach people how to learn. Given the demand of talent in education that is not only proficient in academic qualities but also in business life applications, a possible solution is to focus on a person-centered approach. Undeniably, there has been an increase in the demand for eLearning in recent years. With the advent of electronic books, simulations, text messaging, podcasts, wikis, and blogs, the introduction of these new electronic tools have formed a link of pedagogy and technology to meet the needs of students in the two-dimensional (2-D) framework (Rudestam & Schoenholtz-Read, 2010). As understanding increases, regarding how the brain learns, the question arises if neuroscience is an area to be researched and applied in the development of the virtual 3-D environments. The strength of neural connections plays a role in learning and so does the quantity of connections. As more connections are formed, the more effective the learning process becomes (lumosity.com). Do the virtual 3-D environments or virtual worlds better lend themselves to the learning process than traditional education venues or the 2-D learning environments?

There is a concern among educators that the development of 3-D virtual learning platforms is taking precedence in learning, and there is not carefully crafted measurement of outcomes from this learning. There is also little scholarly research that assesses the outcomes of 3-D virtual learning environments. In the sparse literature that does exist, there are some initial reports that the outcomes from these 3-D virtual learning outcomes are positive, and the ease of this technology into various courses has been successful. However, the latter is often based on anecdotal evidence or merely based on reactions (Sletten 2014). A comprehensive examination of assessment of the 3-D virtual learning environment becomes paramount, so educators will have a better idea how to carefully assess outcomes of student learning. This chapter presents some of the methods and approaches that are used in the assessment of student outcomes in 3-D virtual learning environments.

FACULTY PERCEPTIONS OF THE VIRTUAL LEARNING ENVIRONMENT

The exponential use of the 3-D virtual learning environments has prompted a change in role of educators. That is, the dynamics of delivering an education to students may need to be dissected, old models of educational delivery may need to be discarded, new models of educational delivery may need to be constructed and tailored to the subject matter and what can feasibly be taught in 3-D virtual learning environments. More specifically, the virtual classroom is more interactive and students are empowered to take ownership of their learning; consequently, the faculty roles are beginning to shift (Dede, 2005). As a consequence of these shifts in their roles, faculty often has to change roles and delivery of education. When faculty needs to implement new ways to deliver instruction, faculty may have concerns or experience difficulties over the ways they define themselves in the new environment (Giroux, 2002; Oravec, 2003).

Administrators are aware of faculty concerns about new delivery systems in educational content (Rudestam & Schoenholtz-Read, 2010). That leads to the question, how can university administrators ensure that faculty maintains the highest standards of excellence in educational delivery? In the virtual classroom, the high standards of the faculty member translate into leadership, clarity of direction, organization, and vision. Abeles (2007) found that multi-user virtual environments (MUVEs) accommodate the "digital immigrant" who may need to learn at "a pace consistent with their ability" (p. 200). Not all the students in a course will learn at the same pace and the 3-D virtual learning environments provides these students with an atmosphere to learn the material and to be able to apply this new material to new situations.

The early advent of these new technologies prompted the development of the Virginia Tech's Faculty Development Institute (FDI) in 1993 to help faculty acquire teaching strategies that leverage instructional technologies to improve student learning. FDI also represents Virginia Tech's attempt to focus on the knowledge and skills development required for faculty in order to meet today's students' needs for fluency in the use of information technology. A more recent example involved alleviating the concerns of faculty members when introduced to new educational delivery methods, Jarmon and Sanchez (2009) built a virtual Educators Co-op in *Second Life* in conjunction with the University of Texas at Austin Life Sciences Institute. Jarmon and Sanchez also noted that the 3-D virtual learning environments provided an area for faculty to learn about virtual technology, obtain assistance from experts in virtual world building of learning systems, and make these learning systems effective in delivering an instruction to students. Moore, Moore, and Fowler (2005) stated, "Faculty development for existing and future faculty is a pivotal investment for integrating technology in higher education: it can catalyze innovations in learning across generations" (p. 11.1). In addition, the early advent of these new technologies prompted the development of the Virginia Tech's Faculty Development Institute (FDI) in 1993 to help faculty acquire teaching strategies that leverage instructional technologies to improve student learning. FDI also represents Virginia Tech's attempt to focus on the knowledge and skills development required for faculty in order to meet today's students' needs for fluency in the use of information technology.

In dental education, there is a strong presence for the use of haptic technology (sense of touch) along with 3-D-virtual reality graphics, creating lifelike training simulations that led to the development of the dental training simulator system (PerioSim©) (Steinberg, Bashook, Drummond, Ashrafi, & Zefran, 2007). Faculty and practitioners found these images very realistic for teeth and instruments, but not as much for gingiva. In fact, faculty members were enthusiastic about its potential for evaluating students' basic procedural skills in dentistry. The use of virtual reality of training simulation was beneficial for students because PerioSim© may aid students in developing necessary dental tactile skills as required in their dentistry practices.

Janson (2013) conducted a mixed methods approach to assess the faculty perceptions with respect to aspects of the use of educational technology in online education. The results concluded that the faculty wanted a more involved role in strategic planning at their universities. The faculty also perceived a need for more financial, technological, and leadership support from the appropriate university leadership. Having knowledge of faculty perceptions could provide the university leadership with insights into factors to consider in faculty use of virtual worlds and could lead to the development of best practices in the delivery of online learning. Copppola, Hiltz and Rotter (2002) conducted a qualitative study, also for the purpose of assessing faculty perceptions. From their qualitative assessment, the managerial or course management role by the faculty member requires the faculty to pay more attention to the detail, greater structure, and additional student monitoring to ensure student success. Faculty reported that they experienced a change in teaching style and developed greater precision in their teaching and more cognizant in the presentation of course materials and instructions in the completion of course activities. Faculty also experienced a shift to a more Socratic approach, emphasizing enhanced dialogues with the students.

Wasilik and Bolliger (2009) developed a study of faculty satisfaction with online education at a public research university via the Online Faculty Satisfaction Survey (OFSS) with questions related to students, teaching, and institutions. This study included 102 online faculty members. The general theme expressed by the faculty showed moderate satisfaction with teaching online. After collecting the data, the faculty members were divided the faculty members into two groups based on whether they were more or less satisfied with online teaching to conduct further data analysis. Discriminant analysis was applied to the data as a means to evaluate levels of satisfaction between the two groups of faculty based on teaching, student, and institutional-related variables. Those faculty members who were in the satisfied category experienced greater incidences of enhanced faculty-student interactions in an online environment.

In regard to faculty perceptions related to teaching online, themes mainly deal with the achieving learning effectiveness in the virtual learning environments. The most important perception is the need for adoption of technology that emphasizes social community, a while still focusing on pedagogy via a constructivist approach including frequent online feedback of the students' work. Faculty perceptions of needed strategies to enhance online learning include: use of an effective learning management system, an online community built by collaborative activities, and provisions for a quality educational content (Mayes, Ku, Akarasriworn, Luebeck, & Korkmaz, 2011).

Despite the positive experiences by faculty members, some faculty have described technological problems, lack of personal contact with students, and diminished student involvement as drawbacks of virtual learning. A common negative faculty perception is the dissatisfaction with student involvement in the course content. Faculty often expressed satisfaction with flexible schedules, greater access to course materials, and increased access for students who were unable to attend classes in a face-to-face classroom. Some of the literature revealed that a lack of personal contact with students was difficult for the faculty. In fact, faculty only had a moderate interest in teaching online. In one study, thirty eight percent of respondents stated they were satisfied with online teaching as opposed to other delivery methods while ninety three percent of respondents wanted to teach online (Wasilik & Bolliger, 2009).

Jamlan (2004) surveyed faculty about their perceptions toward virtual learning, and found that faculty members viewed virtual learning positively, but the faculty expressed concerns over the economic viability and the reliability in the delivery of virtual reality. Jamlan's findings indicated the following positive attributes in the delivery of virtual learning

- Provides rich resources to students and faculty;
- Makes teaching more efficient;
- Saves faculty members and students time;
- Provides greater access to educational opportunities to students.

An important perception by faculty is their ability to promote positive student outcomes from their online course delivery (Sloan 2006). To achieve these positive student outcomes, there are important intrinsic motivators such as the intellectual challenges and the faculty interest in using the technology to deliver online education (Panda & Mishra, 2007). If the virtual learning environment is positive and a rewarding experience for the faculty, these positive experiences could provide faculty with additional professional development opportunities associated with the virtual learning (Panda & Mishra, 2007; Sloan, 2006). With the goal to achieve positive student outcomes, faculty members need to be recognized for their teaching effectiveness, and this positive recognition increases their satisfaction levels and enhances their perception of virtual learning. Despite their accolades towards use of technology, faculty member cited technology difficulties or lack of access to adequate technology and tools. Consequently, satisfaction by faculty is likely to decrease and their delivery of the virtual learning does not provide the positive outcomes for the students.

CONCEPTS RELATED TO MEASUREMENT AND PERCEPTION OF OUTCOMES FROM VIRTUAL 3-D ENVIRONMENTS

How to Measure Outcomes from Virtual 3-D Environments

The exponential increase in the use of the Internet as a delivery platform in education has allowed colleges and universities to offer courses using a learning management system as well as the use of virtual learning platforms (Sletten, 2014). As in eLearning programs, virtual learning platform developers have an enormous task to continuously improve the delivery of these tools to enhance learning. Thus, the industry must generate a continuous feedback loop to assess these eLearning tools and virtual 3-D environments as well as adhere to the principle "what gets measured gets attention" (Eccles, 1991).

The literature concerning eLearning covers different frameworks that are used in the measurement of the outcomes (Britain & Liber, 2000; Laurillard, 2002). An experimental design is the most common research design when measuring change in student outcome when using eLearning. Typically, students are assigned randomly to two treatment groups: control and experimental. The students are given a pre-test that serves as the baseline for this experiment. Students are then given the intervention (i.e., the eLearning tool), and a post-test follows this intervention. If a significant statistical difference is measured between the pre and post-tests, this change was attributed to the intervention. The later approach to assess student learning in the 2-D learning environment can also be applied to the virtual learning environment (Sletten 2014).

Some course developers/designers have suggested that the traditional models of education and the ADDIE (Analysis, Design, Development, Implementation, and Evaluation) approach is too linear or too structured to be effective in virtual learning. Despite the criticisms of ADDIE, it is the most widely used virtual model in the delivery of education (Atkinson, 2009; Hodge & Collins, 2010). Dawley (2007) argued that traditional instructional design (ID) models have potential shortcomings when applied to the development of virtual 3-D environments. In fact, traditional ID models are often resistant to change and often rigid in their development, and the traditional ID models often fail to incorporate new informational technologies and integrate advances in knowledge (Soto, 2013). Despite some criticisms of the virtual 3-D environments, they have been in use in education for more than a decade, often without the implementation of a need assessment of the effectiveness of demonstrated through an examination of student learning. The development of virtual 3-D environments should be carefully considered by ensuring that there is specificity between what is being learned and the factors that contribute to learning from virtual 3-D environments. That is, good pedagogical methods should be carefully integrated into virtual 3-D environments.

The use of the 3-D virtual learning environment provides constructivist learning because it provides the learners a highly interactive learning environment for active learning (Kim, Park, Lee, Yuk, & Lee, 2001). Constructivist learning is a philosophy of learning that enables learners to acquire knowledge based on their experiences and activities (Jonassen, Peck, & Wilson, 1999; Martens, Bastiaens, & Kirschner, 2007; Reigeluth, 1999). More specifically, constructivist learning is student-centric and focuses on meeting students' needs, and their learning is based on the acquisition of their prior experiences and knowledge (Mergel, 1998; Roblyer, 2003). Consequently, the philosophy of constructivist learning enables students to be more proactive in their learning, control the pace of their learning, and take more ownership of their learning. Chen and Teh (2000) suggested that the various technical capabilities of the 3-D virtual environment adhere to the constructivist learning principles: active learning and learner control over content, sequence, and learning strategy to construct own knowledge. Presente3-D is a virtual learning software tool that is used in various education settings.

Presente3-D changed the engagement level of our students. Students were giving up their lunch and PE periods to have extended learning time with Presente3-D. Our middle school students were sharing their 3-D learning with their parents at home and were helping our teachers convert their PowerPoint presentation. Truly an exciting experience! -Dean of students of a Middle School

Although this example is from a middle school, there is no reason to assume it will not have the same impact on students in higher education. Faculty now has the opportunity to take power points and turn them into stereoscopic presentations with 3-D software, choosing from a variety of companies. Ai-Lim Lee, Wong, and Fung, (2010) examined how 3-D virtual learning environments enhance learning. The statistical analysis revealed that the use of the 3-D virtual learning tools supported the learning outcomes that were mediated by the experience of the interactions and the learning experience. Presence, motivation, cognitive benefits, control and active learning, as well as reflective thinking were learning factors that were used to assess the effectiveness of the learning. Results of this study provided course developers and software developers for the 3-D virtual learning environments, the information necessary to develop effective learning tools to enhance student learning. Delgarno, Hedberg, and Harper (2002) identified eight contributions to 3-D virtual learning environments as summarized in table 1, and these contributions have the objective to enhance the learning of students.

The first five contributions identify a broader range of assessing learning outcomes from the recall of facts to more complex problem-solving. As the goal of learning is to improve conceptual understanding, the remaining contributions focus on the development of conceptual understanding of content. Given these three contributions, the implicit assumption is that by engaging in 3-D virtual learning environments, students will develop a spatial aptitude of the concepts represented, and the development of this spatial aptitude helps develop the conceptual understanding of the material.

These contributions follow the constructivist theory of learning, especially as related to Piaget's theory; students will be actively engage in exploring the content, which ultimately leads to a stronger

Table 1. Contributions of 3-D Environments to Student Learning

Standard Outcomes of Learning
Facilitate familiarization of inaccessible environments
Facilitate task mastery through practice of dangerous or expensive tasks
Improve transfer by situating learning in a realistic context
Improve motivation through immersion
Reduce cognitive load through integration of multiple information representations
Advanced Spatial Development of the Material
Facilitate understanding of complex environments and systems
Facilitate exploration of complex knowledge bases
Facilitate understanding of complex ideas through metaphorical representations

Source: Delgarno, Hedberg, and Harper (2002)

comprehension of the material (Jonassen, 1991). Course developers and faculty need to carefully assess student-computer interactions unique to 3-D environments and the learning objectives need to be measured to the learning process.

What are the Measured (and Measurable) Outcomes from 3-D Virtual Learning Environments?

A typical evaluation of outcomes from eLearning is the comparison of the eLearning and virtual 3-D environment tools with traditional pedagogical tools. Many assessments measure the success of eLearning by evaluating student performance through formal testing of student knowledge of the material and make comparisons with the eLearning tools and traditional learning. The latter approach would be an effective measure of acquisition of learning, but this approach does not indicate how this new knowledge has developed. Hence, the measurement of the outcomes from eLearning and virtual 3-D environments would be no different than measuring outcomes from other modes of education (Kotsilieris & Dimopoulou, 2013).

According to Kirkpatrick (1979), the seminal measurement of educational outcomes evaluates learning using four progressive levels:

Level I: *Reaction* measures the student's reaction to the course (i.e., how did the student like the course?)

Level II: *Learning* measures the learning outcomes of the students (i.e., did the students learn what they were supposed to learn?).

Level III: *Transfer* measures how the learning of this material impacted the students learning (i.e., what were the takeaways of the course's content for the students, and did it contribute to their outcomes of the academic program?).

Level IV: *Results* measure the outcomes on their education because they perceived their education differently.

Level I: Reaction

Level I measures how the students feel about their learning experiences, but it does not measure the outcomes of the program. More specifically, Level I measures the following:

Are students satisfied with what they learned?
Do they regard the material as relevant to their work?
Do they believe the material will be useful to them on the job?

Using these criteria, the results are measured qualitatively, not quantitatively. These experiences by the students will lead to a positive learning experience by the student that can be measured as indicated in level 2.

Level II: Learning

Learning is defined as the principles, facts, and techniques that are mastered and retained by the students. Thus, when educators measure learning, they want to determine how much the students learned by assessing the degree to which the skills, knowledge, or attitudes of the students have changed. To measure the latter is more rigorous because the assessment is not measuring reaction from the learning. To quantitatively measure the results from the learning, educators can use several methods, one of which is a pre-test and post-test to determine how much the students learned through a 3-D virtual learning environments.

When models other than e-learning and virtual 3-D environments are used to deliver education, findings show better results in measuring the outcomes of their learning. Wegner, Holloway, and Garton (1999) revealed that there were no statistically significant differences between the test scores of eLearning and classroom-based students at Southwest Missouri State University. Despite the lack of statistical significant results, this two-semester study yielded qualitative data that indicated that students in the eLearning group experienced more positive feelings about their experiences than did the students receiving their education in a traditional classroom. In another study, Nettles, Dzuuban, Cioffe, Moskal, and Moskal (2000) examined 49 studies that measured outcomes from eLearning environments versus traditional classrooms. While a majority of these studies revealed no statistical significance between eLearning environments and traditional classrooms, approximately 30 percent of the studies reported that eLearning programs provided positive outcomes based on student preference, improved grades, higher cost effectiveness, and a higher percentage of homework completion. In yet another study, Nelson (2001) reported statistically significant differences between the mean grades of 406 university students earned in the traditional classroom and distance education classes, whereby distance learning students outperformed the traditional students.

Level III: Transfer

Well-crafted quantitative or qualitative learning objectives will not typically indicate how the student will use this knowledge in coursework, future coursework, or even on the job. Using these virtual 3-D environments for learning has the objective to change students' learning. Improved student learning is an important outcome in a course, but measuring this change is a more complex task, and eliciting students' feelings or measuring their direct learning through test scores may not be sufficient. There is an assumed connection between measures of behavioral change and the hope for consequence regarding solid academic performance (Level IV). However, in many cases, a well-defined empirical measurement is lacking.

Level IV: Results

This criterion measures the results of the learning as it affects the financial bottom-line of the university or the company that developed the 3-D virtual application. On the surface, this criterion would be difficult to measure because there are many variables and confounding factors that would make it arduous to assess the financial impact of this learning (Kirkpatrick, 1979).

Level V: Return on Investment (ROI)

Phillips (1996) amends the model espoused by Kirkpatrick by adding Level V, which measures the Return on Investment (ROI) or the cost-benefit ratio of the training and the development of these courses. Using the methodology by Phillips to calculate the ROI as an added level to Kirkpatrick's model requires a lengthy and complex evaluation and calculation process. More specifically, the benefits from Level IV are converted to monetary values and compared to the costs of developing these 3-D virtual learning courses.

MEASUREMENT OF CONTENT QUALITY OF 3-D VIRTUAL LEARNING ENVIRONMENTS

The transition from the virtual learning modality from the traditional classroom, the faculty needs to take time to understand their roles and responsibilities in virtual learning (Colaric & Taymans, 2004). In fact, some faculty members may be involved in the curriculum development of these courses, and the faculty needs to remember it is the pedagogical development that is important, not the technology (Appana, 2008; Lewis & Abdul-Humid, 2006; Shieh, Gummer, & Niess, 2008). To transition from the traditional classroom to a virtual learning, the faculty will need to alter their teaching practices as a means to effectively reach out to all learners in the course (Colaric, & Taymans, 2004; Johnson, 2008; Kurzweli & Marcellas, 2008; Panda & Mishra, 2007).

One way to obtain meaningful results is to design more effective assessment methods of the virtual 3-D environments learning tools. In fact, Chen (2010) acknowledged that the traditional instructional development models offer no precise guidance in the development of virtual 3-D environments. In fact, the standard approaches for educational delivery would not meet the expectations for the students in virtual world learning environments. To improve the content quality of the virtual 3-D environments, some course developers would resort to the constructivist approaches to guide the design and development of virtual world activities that allow for a high quality student learning experience. Despite this approach, the existing instructional design to develop effective and high quality instructional tools for the virtual world is virtually nonexistent (Atkinson, 2009).

Yet, the question remains: how do we achieve outcomes in terms of equity and equality? Should balance be created between summative and formative functions of evaluation and assessment? Since virtual 3-D environments are apparently becoming a product in an ever-growing marketplace, content quality may be treated like any other product on the market. Many questions surrounding design and content are concerned with concurrency (i.e., overlapping technical and academic development). It might be possible to develop an expected effects matrix, showing how specific factors combine and produce several different categories for learning.

Moore (1999) noted, "One of the few generalizations that can be made about any distance education program – whatever the communications media used and the content level – is that a good monitoring and evaluation system is likely to lead to a successful program, and a poor system is almost certain to lead to failure (p. 2)." Moore provides the three key elements of a good eLearning platform that can be readily extended to virtual 3-D learning environments. These key elements can be summarized as follows:

1. Clearly providing the learning objectives for the students with the central question: Did the students produce evidence of having met the learning outcomes based on the clearly defined learning objectives? If not, why not?
2. The development of rigorous exercises and handling of the assignments which serves as evidence of the students meeting the learning objectives and provides useful feedback for the course developers.
3. The virtual 3-D learning environment requires an effective data collecting method as well as an efficient reporting system so educators, administrators, and course developers can use the data to make the appropriate assessment.

The development of a high quality virtual 3-D learning environment allows for the students to be fully immersed and engaged in the learning of content. Despite the emphasis on immersion of the students in learning, assessing outcomes of such learning is equally important. Course developers need to be made aware of assessment results so that they will understand what aspects of the content needs to be improved. The implementation of examinations or other assessment tools must be present to assess what students know and can apply to new situations. As an example, for CS 382, a software design class at Colorado Technical University (CTU), the course developers created a 3-D game maze and populated it with traps, sensors, flags, a scoreboard, treasures, and other game features. The purpose of this game was to learn to model a variety of software designs using drawings in a design specification; students played this game on the last night of class, After completing this game, the students were able to design, prototype, and test their designs of the software. In addition, in the execution of this game, the students discovered a minor flaw in the game, and one student fixed the problem while the class tested it during the next run of the game.

After playing a single game, these students were immersed in a learning experience in which the students did not realize was fulfilling the course objectives of several different courses at Colorado Technical University. When the 3-D virtual worlds are crafted carefully, this careful blend of content will remain with the students after the completion of the course (Calongne, 2008).

In today's delivery of education, courses are often designed with content time constraints. That is, the presentation of course material can be a lot of content against some time constraint. To achieve the objectives of the course under such time constraints, eLearning or 3-D virtual learning environments can be used to meet the course objectives and to pique student interest in the material. The 3-D virtual world looks like a game setting, and instructors can guide, observe, and provide feedback and rewards for the students based on their participation in these class activities.

In fact, students often worry that the structure of the course will be poorly defined with opaque course objectives and not managed well. A well-structured course would include a syllabus that defines the course objectives, learning objectives, goals, measurements, a course schedule of activities and assignments, and rubrics for each assessment. In the implementation of virtual world courses, in addition to the standard course materials (e.g., the syllabi), the virtual world courses' syllabi would add information on how projects will be delivered, how class discussions will be evaluated, and how students can benefit from feedback to improve the quality of their work in the remainder of the course or in subsequent courses.

There are other benefits in these 3-D virtual environment courses including: discovering new ways to study, participating in enhanced discussions, engaging in development of creativity, and learning the course subject under the supervision of the instructor. In these types of courses, the faculty becomes the subject matter expert who serves in the role of stimulating and supervising the content of the course for the students while providing structure, guidance, feedback, and assessment for each student (Calongne, 2008).

The development of an effective 3-D virtual environment course would require care, an appropriate mix of course content, and an outline of course competencies to be achieved. The course developers will need to be cognizant of how the course should be developed to meet the course outcomes.

PRACTICAL THEORIES APPLICABLE TO THE VIRTUAL 3-D LEARNING ENVIRONMENT

When introducing a new virtual application for academic learning, it must allow the students to be able to master its use expeditiously, so the students can use it to enhance their learning. Consequently, the difficulties in the use of eLearning tools may create additional stress, and these difficulties will contribute to new barriers between the educators and the virtual reality. The advent of virtual reality tools may provide little evidence of positive outcomes when a newly introduced eLearning platform is introduced. Rogers (2003) alludes to the five attributes that have an effect on a student's decision to use an innovation. These five attributes are as follows: a) what is the advantage of the new innovation over the previous innovation; b) how does this new innovation meet the academic needs to the students; c) how difficult is it to use; d) can the innovation be tested timely; and e) are the outcomes associated with the innovation visible to those around the students.

The costs to develop 3-D virtual learning environments are often borne by foundations and university funds (Bellotti, Kapralos, Lee, Moreno-Ger, & Berta, 2007). For example, the development costs for a Second Life (SL) virtual campus is approximately $25,000 if developed by a commercial entity. A Second Life is a free 3-D virtual world where users can socialize, connect, and create using free voice and text or chat. Although there is an increased demand for gaming, animation, and 3-D visual spaces in higher education, there must be a clear presentation about the benefits associated with the virtual learning (Bellotti, Kapralos, Lee, Moreno-Ger, & Berta, 2007).

For example, how might technical devices such as the Oculus Rift affect and be applied to eLearning? The Oculus Rift is a set of virtual-reality goggles that will work with computers or mobile devices. Tacit knowledge transfer must also be considered. Tacit knowledge is knowledge that is not learned or obtained from sources but personal experiences, e.g., experiences from life's experiences and, the potential for applications to e-learning are almost limitless. If acquiring skills that are physical in nature are needed, the 3-D environment is ideal; if students are able to see and do what faculty and experts in the field do, an opportunity is provided for a safe environment where failing is not a stigma but an opportunity to learn, improve, and emulate. Different groups of students can be aligned with specific topics to use methods relevant to their specific programs. P. Luckey, creator of Oculus Rift, foresees significant changes in the field of education based on the application of 3-D technology (www.gamespot.com).

These potential and monumental changes in higher education will require educators and developers to consider the impact on students' lateral thinking. Lateral thinking is logic related to patterning systems will require methods for "cutting across patterns..." (De Bono, 1985, p. 70). According to De Bono (1985), the latter seems to be especially difficult when change involves moving away from a pattern that has successfully worked in the past. 3-D environment curriculum and evaluation will require developers to map out and understand the logic bubbles of everyone involved in the process. Logic bubbles is a term to describe the set of values, needs, beliefs and experiences that a person sees the world through as described by Edward De Bono. Those suggesting change are usually convinced of the value of the innovation. Yet, the individuals conducting the change reside in their own logic bubbles, and sometimes, they fear the risk associated with the change (De Bono, 1985).

A study about 3-D learning environments conducted by Yilmz, Topu, Goktas, and Coban (2013), showed that "...the motivation and social presence levels of the participants were high," and " factors, which include the particular environment and participant satisfaction, clearly affected motivation while the participants were learning new information" (p. 833). The researchers also found "the participants perceived the environment as warm and sociable"(p. 833). This is important for 3-D designers to understand when developing the new learning platform. Holmberg's (2003) communication and interaction theory plays a significant part in users' motivation levels in the 3-D virtual world. Socialization, the sense of presence, recognition of user differences, satisfaction, and interaction are all related; are important factors to evaluate.

There is much emphasis on the integration of 3-D virtual learning environment in undergraduate and graduate courses in such disciplines as the physical and life sciences, business administration, education and other disciplines (Jarmon, Traphagan, Mayrath, & Trivedi 2009). In recent years, dental educators have been assessing the value of distance education and the steps required to deliver technology-based learning with the objective to provide high quality patient care teaching methods for dentists and dental hygienists. Luciano, Banerjee and DeFanti (2009) focused on the research and development of a prototype dental simulator for training of periodontal procedures. The periodontal simulator allows students to learn performing diagnosis and treatment of periodontal diseases by visualizing a three-dimensional virtual human mouth and feeling real tactile sensations while touching the surface of teeth, gingiva, and calculi with virtual dental instruments. In periodontics, students are required to depend primarily on tactile sensations to perform these periodontal procedures, and the integration of the haptics is crucial for a realistic periodontal simulator to allow students to learn these procedures. In fact, Suebnukarn, Haddawy, Rhienmora, and Gajananan (2010) acknowledged that haptic virtual reality (VR) has revolutionized the acquisition of dentistry skills for dental students. The strength of the haptic VR system is that it can automatically record the outcome and associated kinematic data on how each step of the task is performed. The latter cannot be readily assessed in the traditional learning environments in dental education. They concluded that the novices could learn to perform access opening tasks faster and with more consistency, better bimanual dexterity, and better force utilization. The variables examined showed great promise as objective indicators of proficiency and skill acquisition in haptic VR that can be used to improve the quality of dental care.

Phillips and Berge (2009) demonstrated that the use of SL enhances the current standardized instruction and competency testing and for promoting dental education. In fact, SL is valuable as an adjunct to preclinical teaching methods in virtual problem-solving and communication prior to the students treating patients clinically as well as a resource to provide continuing education for dentists and other dental practitioners. Synchronous distance communication is a reality in the delivery of SL and this can promote resource sharing and collaborations globally among dental practitioners. These enhanced collaborations in dental education globally can improve the quality of dental care. More important, SL offers educational resources that are easy and convenient for dental practitioners to connect globally and collaborate with others.

THE ASSESSMENT OF LEARNING OUTCOMES IN 3-D VIRTUAL LEARNING ENVIRONMENTS

Gee (2003), Steinkuehler (2004), and Delgarno and Lee (2010) have showed that there are relevant outcomes from the virtual learning environment, but there is little conclusive evidence that validates the specific learning benefits of the 3-D virtual learning environment. That is, many of these 3-D virtual learning environments are just "show and tell" and often provide anecdotal or precursory evidence of effective learning outcomes.

Thus, there is a great interest to measure the learning by students in the 3-D virtual learning environments and to discover the contributions to student learning made from these applications. More specifically, Bower (2008) proposes a methodology for matching the affordance requirements of specific learning objectives with the various technological tools, which can assist and inform educators of the specific technological tools that can be used by students to improve student learning. Delgarno and Lee (2010) and Bower (2008) acknowledged that the technologies themselves do not directly cause learning to occur but rather certain learning tasks "themselves *may* result in learning or give rise to certain learning benefits."

In the life and physical sciences, the use of these virtual learning 3-D applications provides informative benefits. For example, a 3-D image of a human skull in an undergraduate human anatomy online laboratory was analyzed. From this implementation, the results revealed statistically significant differences in group means for the main effect of treatment groups 2D and 3-D and for the variables of Identification and Relationship with the 3-D group outperforming the 2D group on both dependent variables (Hilbelink, 2009). The latter begs the following question: does the nature of the courses have greater impact on learning than other courses?

In the virtual 3-D learning environment, instructors would typically use a myriad of evaluation methods: reflections and journaling, peer reviews, presentations with 3-D display panels, interactive quizzes and surveys, 3-D projects, and other methods that demonstrate that learning occurred from the learning activity. However, some faculty still prefer the standard measures of assessing outcomes in learning. As an example, one faculty described how he measured learning outcomes:

So, how do you assess when you are in a traditional space? Well, you give tests and exams. And you do those things because the traditional space is divorced from the actual relevant spaces in which the knowledge and skills and affects that are being learned are to be applied. So tests and quizzes are intermediate for what we really want to be able to measure and those are actual performances. (Chapman & Stone, 2010, p. 674)

As an example, in the 3-D virtual learning environment, the instructors would often allow students to develop their own problems that are meaningful and relevant and to then contextualize that learning around the developed problem. From the latter, the students would be evaluated on a myriad of criteria. Instructors could carefully evaluate the students' work by having the students host a presentation to the class via their avatars. The student would be required to present their work, engage their audience, and be able to answer the questions posed by their classmates. Because the presentation was facilitated via the avatars, the instructor could easily capture digital images of the presentation and other matters pertaining to the presentation for easy reference later for additional evaluation (Chapman & Stone, 2010). Given the latter approach for assessment, the instructor could easily develop grading rubrics that outline the required criteria that are used in the evaluation of the presentation. Using these rubrics, quantitative and qualitative evaluation can be given. Then, the results from these rubrics can be used against the specific outcomes of the course and an evaluation can be made to determine if these outcomes have been met.

Gardner (1964) formulated the idea that "The ultimate goal of the educational system is to shift to the individual the burden of pursuing his own education" (p. 12). On-line learning is at the center of action learning and thus eminently suited to integrate a 3-D environment, which in turn promotes action learning. However, there are potential negatives to the use of 3-D technology. 3-D occurs within a framework of control and instruction, and if not carefully and thoughtfully implemented, it will eventually acquire the formalities and rigidness of other institutional learning devices (Petrina, 2007). Thus, students will return to the previous environment of passively waiting to have learning experiences handed to them.

Research has shown that the more fully a person is engaged in learning, the more he or she will see that there is more to be learned and understood. Continuous new learning requires the psychological achievement of being open-minded. As Rokeach (1960) stated forty-five years ago and remains true today, "it is the extent to which a person can receive, evaluate, and act on relevant information received from outside on its own intrinsic merits unencumbered by irrelevant factors in the situation arising from within the person or outside" (p. 57). Institutional learning models have taught us to think of learning in terms of building blocks (Vaill, 1996). The new 3-D environment of learning enables students to discover how to do something effectively in real-time. 3-D may also address concerns about fostering creativity. As Nobel Prize winner Peter Medawar once said, "The analysis of creativity in all its forms is beyond the competence of any one accepted discipline. It requires a consortium of talents. Psychologists, biologists, philosophers, computer scientists, artists, and poets would all expect to have their say..." (Medawar, 1969).

Foundation of the Assessment of Learning of Student Learning

The Education Commission of the States (1995) has identified the attributes of good practice for higher education to assess student learning from courses. In fact, this Commission posits that that good assessment can lead to the transformation of education when considering that "...when [educators] systematically engage in these good practices, student performance and satisfaction will improve" (p.5). That is, the development of quality assessments becomes crucial. The development of carefully developed assessments provides evidence of successful teaching and outcomes for learning being achieved. In addition, carefully developed assessments provide faculty members the necessary evidence to improve educational delivery (Huba & Freed, 2000). While these recommendations were provided twenty years ago, they still apply today and provide a guide for assessing 3-D learning environments, also. Huba and Freed provide the characteristics for assessments:

- Quality begins with an organization culture that value
  1. High expectations
  2. Respect for diverse talents and learning styles
  3. Emphasis on the early years of study [e.g., general education]
- A quality curriculum requires
  4. Coherence in learning
  5. Synthesizing experiences
  6. Ongoing practice of learned skills
  7. Integrating education and experience
- Quality instruction builds in
  8. Active learning
  9. Assessment and prompt feedback
  10. Collaboration
  11. Adequate time on task
  12. Out-of-class contact with faculty
- Building upon Huba and Freed (2000), Wiggins (1998, p. 106) identifies three types of educational standards:
  1. Content standards: What should students know and be able to do?
  2. Performance standards: How well must students do their work?
  3. Task (work-design) standards: What is worthy and rigorous? What tasks should students be able to do?
- Lissitz and Schafer (2002, pp. 23-26) provide standards for assessing the quality of assessments used by faculty members and other educations:
  1. Quality assessments arise from and accurately reflect clearly specified and appropriate achievement expectations for students.
  2. Sound assessments are specifically designed to serve instructional purposes.
  3. Quality assessments accurately reflect the intended target and serve the intended purpose.
  4. Quality assessments provide a representative sample of student performance that is sufficient in its scope to permit confident conclusions about student achievement.
  5. Sound assessments are designed, developed, and used in such a manner as to eliminate sources of bias or distortion that interfere with the accuracy of results.

Kuhs, Johnson, Agruso, and Monrad (2001) posit that a carefully developed assessment of student learning helps faculty to plan and strategize the instructional needs for the students. More important, faculty can share information with their students concerning their individual progress in their learning. The characteristics of a quality assessment can be answered through the following questions:

1. Does the assessment focus on knowledge and skills that were taught in class and are outlined in district curriculum guides and in state and national content standards?
2. Does the assessment provide information about student learning that represents typical performance?
3. Does the assessment provide opportunities for all types of students to demonstrate what they have learned? (Kuhs et al., 2001, p.4)

Table 2. Kolb Cycle of Learning

Concrete Experience - (Feeling)	Learning from specific experiences and relating to people. Sensitive to other's feelings.
Reflective Observation (Watching)	Observing before making a judgment by viewing the environment from different perspectives. Looks for the meaning of things.
Abstract Conceptualization (Thinking)	Logical analysis of ideas and acting on intellectual understanding of a situation.
Active Experimentation (Doing)	Ability to get things done by influencing people and events through action. Includes risk-taking.

Source: Kolb Learning Cycle (Fry, Ketteridge, & Marshall, 2003, p. 15)

The Kolb (1984) Learning Cycle is also a useful tool based on the work of Kurt Lewin in the early part of the 20th century. Kolb posits that experimental learning is based on the understanding that learning is not fixed; students are constantly refining learning that is formed and re-formed through experiences or learning is a continuous process. The mode of learning promoted by Kolb provides a systematic statement of the theory of experiential learning and how it applies to work, education, and adult development. More important, Kolb developed the theory as a means to explain the connections between the human developmental stages of maturation, learning processes; experience shapes the way students grasp knowledge, which affects their cognitive development. He states there are four stages in learning and each stage of learning follows from each other as shown in table 2.

The Kolb Learning Cycle does not start at the same point for each student. That is, students may enter the learning cycle at any point but will learn the new concept if all four stages of the learning cycle are completed. Here is an example of the application of the Kolb Learning Cycle as applied to learning an application of a 3-D virtual learning environment:

- Active experimentation - Jumping in and using a 3-D virtual learning environment.
- Reflective observation – Students think about what they just did in the application.
- Abstract conceptualization – Students read the manual or other course materials to get a clearer grasp on what was being done in the application.
- Concrete experience – Students using the help features to obtain some additional tips for its use.

Then, the Kolb Learning Style Inventory (KLSI) Version 3.1 is used to categorize students' learning styles. The preferred learning style is dependent on a student's two dominant modes of the four phases of the learning cycle as stated earlier. That is, Kolb espouses that a student will have two dominant modes for learning. However, Chen, Toh and Wan (2005) expanded the assessment of the learning styles as espoused by Kolb and Kolb (2005). The posited that the effects of a 3-D virtual learning environment on students with different learning styles do benefit from this approach to learning the course material despite their learning style. Once the student learning style has been determined, the necessary post-tests can be given to the students to assess their learning as given by the carefully developed learning outcomes and course objectives.

In summary, a 3-D virtual learning environment provides positive benefits irrespective of students' learning style. In a 3-D virtual learning environment students will be assigned a specific assignment to complete, and the students can complete this assignment at their own pace, time and location. Consequently, they can develop their own learning of the course material and be able to apply the material in a different context (Barker & Grossman, 2013).

EFFECTIVE STRATEGIES TO ASSESS OUTCOMES IN 3-D VIRTUAL LEARNING ENVIRONMENTS

Olds and Miller (1998) developed an assessment matrix to evaluate outcomes in eLearning; this matrix will be applied to the 3-D virtual learning environments. The assessment matrix provides faculty members and instructional designers with a formal structure for developing their plan using a series of questions that can lead to a structured approach in the development of a 3-D virtual learning tool that provides a structure to assess outcomes of student learning. Table 3 provides the assessment matrix as outlined by Olds and Miller (1998):

Now the discussion will delve into descriptions of each of the components from the assessment matrix and applications to the development 3-D virtual learning environment.

Objectives and Outcomes

Learning objectives are the first component of the assessment matrix. Course developers and faculty members need to define the broad objectives of the 3-D virtual learning environment. The course developers and faculty need to be able to answer the following questions: "What should students know and be able to do when they complete the course or program?" That is, what are the outcomes from the

Table 3. Assessment Matrix

Objectives
What are the overall objectives of the course or program? How do they complement institutional and accreditation expectations?
Learning Outcomes
What are the program's educational outcomes? What should your students know and be able to do?
Performance Criteria
How will you know the outcomes have been achieved? What level of performance meets each outcome?
Implementation Strategies
How will the outcomes be achieved? What program activities (curricular and co-curricular) help you to meet each outcome?
Evaluation Methods
What assessment methods will you use to collect data? How will you interpret and evaluate the data?
Timeline
When will you measure?
Feedback
Who needs to know the results? How can you convince them the objectives were met? How can you improve your program and your assessment process?

completion of this 3-D virtual learning environment tool, what should the student be able to do? Outcomes need to be clear, precise, and measureable. The outcomes should be written as action verbs using such words as apply, calculate, describe, determine, demonstrate, analyze, evaluate, and avoid such words as learn, appreciate, master and other vague words that are general and not specific (Olds & Miller, 1998).

Performance Criteria

A second component of the assessment matrix is performance criteria. After carefully preparing the objectives and outcomes for the 3-D virtual learning environment tool, the course developers or faculty members should articulate performance criteria for each objective to be evaluated. The type of data that will be collected to provide supportive evidence needs to be specified. The performance criteria shall be able to answer the following questions: How will you know the outcomes have been achieved?" and "What level of performance meets each outcome?" More important, the course developers and the faculty members must carefully agree on the performance levels that they want the students to achieve and what constitutes satisfactory meeting of the outcomes developed earlier (Olds & Miller, 1998).

Implementation Strategies

Implementation Strategies are a third component of the assessment matrix. After the development of the learning outcomes and the performance criteria, how would the 3-D virtual learning environment is implemented? Course developers and faculty members need to be able to answer the following questions as the implementation strategy is carefully crafted: "How will the outcomes be achieved?" and "Which course or program activities help to meet each outcome?" The course developers for the 3-D virtual learning environment tools should avoid broad goals for student achievement, e.g., students will be able to apply these concepts in subsequent courses in their educational program. The latter example would be too broad and not measurable. More important, course developers and faculty members need to allow students to meet the outcomes from the 3-D virtual learning environment and be able to apply in subsequent courses in their academic program. For example, if students are to learn the design process, or how to apply the concepts of supply and demand analysis to business applications, students must have an opportunity within their academic program to apply these concepts. The benefit of the latter is that the course developers and the faculty members will have a better idea how the learning tool(s) can be used in the curriculum and the impact it could have on subsequent outcomes of student learning.

Evaluation Methods

Evaluation methods, a fourth component of the assessment matrix, needs to be incorporated into the process of developing a 3-D learning environment. The purpose of developing effective evaluation methods is to determine if the program or a given course are providing the necessary outcomes for student learning. Valuation methods should attempt to answer the following questions: "What assessment methods will be used to collect data?" and "How will data be interpreted and evaluated?" Consequently, the evaluation methods should provide meaningful quantifiable guidelines that can be used in the evaluation process. Typically, the evaluation process would depend on the time and budgetary resources available. The development of the evaluation process should adhere to the following general guidelines:

- What type of evaluation methods will be used? Quantitative, qualitative, formative, summative? The evaluation approach will depend on the outcomes that are specified earlier in the development of the assessment matrix.
- It is not necessary to rely exclusively on one method but use a combination of methods, (e.g., quantitative and qualitative methods or mixed methods).
- It may be difficult to obtain purely objective assessment results. However, there are advanced methods that can be used to assess these types of outcomes.

Prus and Johnson (1994) delved into the evaluation tools that can be used in a traditional classroom that can be readily extended to the 3-D virtual learning environment formats. These classroom assessments that can be used to compile data for the evaluation process:

- Commercial, norm referenced standardized exams
- Locally developed exams
- Oral examinations
- Performance appraisals
- Simulations
- Written surveys and questionnaires
- Third party reports
- Portfolios
- Archival data
- Behavioral observations
- Exit interviews and other interviews

Timelines

The Timeline component of the assessment matrix asks when the evaluation will be conducted for the 3-D virtual learning environment tool. More specifically, following is the important question to be answered: "When will you measure?" The time to conduct the evaluation will depend on the types of outcomes that were created. For example, some outcomes require formative (midcourse) measurements; others are summative and can be put off until the completion of the course. In some cases it is best a combination of formative and summative assessments will work well. Some skills would take time to assess because the particular academic skill takes time to develop. Because of these skills, these evaluations may just take place at one point during the academic term. For developmental cognitive skills such as oral and written communication skills and critical thinking skills, these skills would be measured by formative assessments and would require assessment periodically as a means to remedy any deficiencies before it is too late. Technical knowledge from specific courses would be best assessed at certain points in the student's academic program. Prus and Johnson (1994) stated there are no clear-cut guidelines to collect data; however, successful assessments often collect longitudinal data on students over the course of the student's academic program. By doing the latter, faculty members can determine if the students are meeting the established learning outcomes. Typically, assessments should be periodic and one summative evaluation does not clearly provide any reasonable conclusions in regard to measuring changes in the learning outcomes of the students.

Feedback

The final part of the assessment matrix is feedback, and feedback is provided to the interested stakeholders, (e.g., faculty, students, other programs, accreditation bodies). The typical feedback questions that are asked include the following: "Who needs to know the results?", "How can you convince stakeholders that the objectives were met?", and "How can you improve your program and your assessment process?" Each of the stakeholders has different needs for the results of the evaluation and these specialized needs should be identified early so the appropriate evaluations can be conducted. To this end, the evaluation reports should be customized to meet the objectives of the appropriate audiences. Finally, if data collected does not provide value-added for any of the stakeholders, then the data should no longer be collected and disseminated.

FUTURE DIRECTIONS

A virtual world earning environment enables students to manipulate time and space, and students are able to learn content without risk and consequence. Despite these obvious advantages of learning in this virtual environment, how are learning outcomes effectively measured? What assessments are needed to ensure that learning actually occurred? Given that course developers must precisely know the learning objectives, course developers must develop the appropriate instructional strategies and learning activities to align with a virtual environment.

This discussion leads to the following two questions posed by Delgarno, Hedberg, and Harper (2002, p. 157).

- What are the important characteristics of learning tasks within a 3-D environment that will facilitate the development of a spatial cognitive model?
- What is the nature of the task support that is required for spatial knowledge development within a 3-D environment, and how should this support be provided within the environment?

This stand as questions to answer with future research. Once these questions are answered, course developers of 3-D virtual learning environments and faculty members will have evidence for best practice to maximize student learning. Finally, knowing precisely what and how to develop a 3-D virtual learning course, the course will do more than simply impress the students with technological "coolness", but actually maximize student learning.

CONCLUSION

The delivery of education has changed dramatically in the past decade as the Internet usage soared exponentially and these changes in delivery has enabled students to purse an education that might have not been possible. In addition to the accessibility to education, 3-D virtual learning environments were introduced to help promote and enhance student learning. However, greater systematic research is needed to confirm that students are actually learning from the 3-D virtual learning environments. As with any form of evaluation, the research must be carefully crafted to assure that meaningful results are obtained. Until a more robust research design is developed for measuring 3-D virtual learning environments, course developers would need to rely mainly on qualitative feedback from students, faculty members, and other academicians that are using 3-D virtual learning environments to deliver an education.

REFERENCES

Abeles, T. P. (2007). Education unbound. *On The Horizon*, *15*(4), 199–203. doi:10.1108/10748120710836219

Ai-Lim Lee, E., Wong, K. W., & Fung, C. C. (2010). How does desktop virtual reality enhance learning outcomes? A structural equation modeling approach. *Computers & Education*, *55*(4), 1424–1442. doi:10.1016/j.compedu.2010.06.006

Appana, S. (2008). A Review of Benefits and Limitations of Online Learning in the Context of the Student, the Instructor and the Tenured Faculty. *International Journal on E-Learning*, *7*(1), 5–22.

Atkinson, T. (2009). Second Life for educators: Teaching and learning. *TechTrends*, *53*(3), 30–32. doi:10.1007/s11528-009-0285-7

Barker, J., & Gossman, P. (2013). The learning impact of a virtual learning environment: Students' views. *Tean Journal, 5*(2). Retrieved from http://bit.ly/AtMwtr

Bellotti, F., Kapralos, B., Lee, K., Moreno-Ger, P., & Berta, R. (2013). Assessment in and of serious games: An overview. *Advances in Human-Computer Interaction*. Retrieved from http://www.hindawi.com/journals/ahci/2013/136864/cta/

Bower, M. (2008). Affordance analysis—matching learning tasks with learning technologies. *Educational Media International*, *45*(1), 3–15. doi:10.1080/09523980701847115

Braman, J., Jinman, A., & Trajkovski, G. (2007). Exploring virtual worlds as an extension to classroom learning. In C. A. Shoniregun & A. Logvynovskiy (Eds.), *Proceedings of the International Conference on Information Society (i-Society 2007)* (pp. 82-86). London, UK: e-Centre for Infonomics. Retrieved from http://air.unimi.it/bitstream/2434/64612/1/i-SocietyProceedings.pdf

Britain, S., & Liber, O. (2000). A framework for the pedagogical evaluation of virtual learning environments. JTAP Report no. 041. Retrieved from http://www.leeds.ac.uk/educol/documents/00001237.htm

Calongne, C. (2008). Educational frontiers: Learning in a virtual world. *EDUCAUSE Review*, *43*(5). Retrieved from http://www.educause.edu/ero/article/educational-frontiers-learning-virtual-world

Chapman, D. D., & Stone, S. (2010). Measurement of outcomes in virtual environments. *Advances in Developing Human Resources*, *12*(6), 665–680. doi:10.1177/1523422310394792

Chen, C. J. (2010). *Virtual reality (VR)-based learning environment: Design, develop, evaluate*. Saarbrücken, Germany: Lambert Academic.

Chen, C. J., & Teh, C. S. (2000). Design issues of desktop virtual reality educational applications. In H. M. Khalid (Ed.), *Virtual reality: select issues and applications* (pp. 63–78). London: Asean Academic.

Chen, C. J., Toh, S. C., & Ismail, W. M. F. W. (2005). Are learning styles relevant to virtual reality? *Journal of Research on Technology in Education*, *38*(2), 123–141. doi:10.1080/15391523.2005.10782453

Colaric, S., & Taymans, J. (2004). Introducing Faculty to Online Learning: An Online Course as Professional Development. In G. Richards (Ed.), *Proceedings of World Conference on E-Learning in Corporate, Government, Healthcare, and Higher Education* 2004 (pp. 549-554). Chesapeake, VA: AACE.

Coppola, N. W., Hiltz, S., & Rotter, N. G. (2002). Becoming a virtual professor: Pedagogical roles and asynchronous learning networks. *Journal of Management Information Systems*, *18*(4), 169–189.

Dawley, L. (2007). *Persistent social learning: An emergent ID model for virtual world design* [Video file]. Retrieved from https://admin.acrobat.com/_a768376479/p17101188/

De Bono, E. (1985). *De Bono's Thinking Course*. New York, NY: Facts On File Publications.

Dede, C. (2005). Planning for neomillennial learning styles. *EDUCAUSE Quarterly*, *28*(1), 1–10.

Delgarno, B., & Lee, M. (2010). What are the learning affordances of 3-D virtual environments? *British Journal of Educational Technology*, *41*(1), 10–32. doi:10.1111/j.1467-8535.2009.01038.x

Dickey, M. D. (2005). Three-dimensional virtual worlds and distance learning: Two case studies of Active Worlds as a medium for distance education. *British Journal of Educational Technology*, *36*(3), 439–451. doi:10.1111/j.1467-8535.2005.00477.x

Eccles, R. G. (1991). The performance measurement manifesto. *Harvard Business Review*, *69*(1), 131–137. PMID:10109469

Education Commission of the States. (1995). *Making quality count in undergraduate education*. Denver, CO: Education Commission of the States.

Fry, H., Ketteridge, S., & Marshall, S. (2003). A handbook for teaching and learning in higher education: Enhancing academic practice (2nd ed.). London; Sterling, VA: Kogan Page.

Gardner, J. W. (1964). *Self-Renewal*. New York: HarperCollins.

Gee, J. P. (2003). *What videogames have to teach us about learning and literacy*. New York: Palgrave Macmillan.

Giroux, H. A. (2002). Neoliberalism, corporate culture, and the promise of higher education: The university as a democratic public sphere. *Harvard Educational Review*, *72*(4), 425–464. doi:10.17763/haer.72.4.0515nr62324n71p1

Hedberg, J., Harper, B., & Dalgarno, B. (2002). The contribution of 3D environments to conceptual understanding. In O. J. McKerrow (Eds.), Winds of Change in the Sea of Learning: Proceedings of *the 19th Annual Conference of the Australasian Society for Computers in Learning in Tertiary Education* (Vol 1, pp. 149-158). Auckland, New Zealand: UNITEC, Institute of Technology.

Hilbelink, A. J. (2009). A measure of the effectiveness of incorporating 3-D human anatomy into an online undergraduate laboratory. *British Journal of Educational Technology*, *40*(4), 664–672. doi:10.1111/j.1467-8535.2008.00886.x

Hodge, E. M., & Collins, S. (2010). Collaborative efforts: Teaching and learning in virtual worlds. [Retrieved fromhttp://www.educause.edu/ero/article/collaborative-efforts-teaching-and-learning-virtual-worlds]. *EDUCAUSE Review*, *45*(3), 62–63.

Holmberg, B. (2003). Distance education in essence: An overview of theory and practice in the early twenty-first century (2nd ed.). Germany: Oldenburg.

Huba, M. E., & Freed, J. E. (2000). *Learner-centered assessment on college campuses: Shifting the focus from teaching to learning*. Boston: Allyn & Bacon.

Jamlan, M. (2004). Faculty opinions towards introducing e-learning at the University of Bahrain. *International Review of Research in Open and Distance Learning*, *5*(2).

Janicki, T., & Steinberg, G. (2003). Evaluation of a computer-supported learning system. *Decision Sciences Journal of Innovative Education*, *1*(2), 203–223. doi:10.1111/j.1540-4609.2003.00018.x

Janson, B. (2013). *Faculty Perceptions of Instruction in Collaborative Virtual Immersive Learning Environments in Higher Education* [Dissertation & Theses Collection]. Paper AAI3558390.

Jarmon, L., & Sanchez, J. (2009). The educator's coop: A model for collaboration and LSI communication research in the virtual world. *The Electronic Journal of Communication*, *19*(1), 1–29.

Jarmon, L., Traphagan, T., Mayrath, M., & Trivedi, A. (2009). Virtual world teaching, experiential learning, and assessment: An interdisciplinary communication course in Second Life. *Computers & Education*, *53*(1), 169–182. doi:10.1016/j.compedu.2009.01.010

Johnson, A. (2008). A nursing faculty's transition to teaching online. *Nursing Education Perspectives*, *29*(1), 17–22. PMID:18330417

Jonassen, D. H. (1991). Objectivism versus Constructivism: Do we need a new philosophical paradigm? *Educational Technology Research and Development*, *39*(3), 5–14. doi:10.1007/BF02296434

Jonassen, D. H., Peck, K. L., & Wilson, B. G. (1999). *Learning with technology: A constructivist perspective*. Upper Saddle River, NJ: Prentice Hall, Inc.

Kelton, A. J. (2008). Virtual worlds? Outlook good. *EDUCAUSE Review*, *43*(5). Retrieved from http://www.educause.edu/EDUCAUSE+Review/EDUCAUSE ReviewMagazineVolume43 /VirtualWorldsOutlookGood/163161

Kim, J. H., Park, S. T., Lee, H., Yuk, K. C., & Lee, H. (2001). Virtual reality simulations in physics education. Retrieved from http://imej.wfu.edu/articles/2001/2/02/index.asp

Kirkpatrick, D. (1979). Techniques for evaluating training programs. *Training and Development Journal*, *33*(6), 78–92.

Kolb, A.Y., & Kolb, D. A. (2005). *The Kolb Learning Style Inventory – Version 3.1: 2005 Technical Specifications*. Haygroup: Experience Based Learning Systems Inc.

Kolb, D. A. (1984). *Experiential learning: Experience as the source of learning and development*. New Jersey: Prentice-Hall Inc.

Kotsilieris, T., & Dimopoulou, N. (2013). The evolution of e-learning in the context of 3-D virtual worlds. *The Electronic Journal of e-Learning. 11*(2), 147-167.

Kuhs, T. M., Johnson, R. L., Agruso, S. A., & Monrad, D. M. (2001). *Put to the test – tools and techniques for classroom assessment*. Portsmouth, NH: Heinemann.

Kurzweil, D., & Marcellas, B. (2008). The faculty - instructional designer dyad. *Proceedings of World Conference on Educational Multimedia, Hypermedia and Telecommunications* (pp. 3445-3446). Chesapeake, VA: AACE.

Laurillard, D. (2002). *Rethinking university teaching: a framework for the effective use of learning technologies* (2nd ed.). London, New York: Routledge/Falmer. doi:10.4324/9780203304846

Lewis, C. C., & Abdul- Hamid, H. (2006). Implementing effective online teaching practices: Voices of exemplary faculty. *Innovative Higher Education, 31(*2), 83-98.

Lissitz, R. W., & Schafer, W. D. (2002). *Assessment in educational reform: Both means and ends*. Boston: Allyn & Bacon.

Luciano, C., Banerjee, P., & DeFanti, T. (2009). Haptics-based virtual reality periodontal training simulator. *Virtual Reality (Waltham Cross), 13*(2), 69–85. doi:10.1007/s10055-009-0112-7

Martens, R., Bastiaens, T., & Kirschner, P. A. (2007). New learning design in distance education: The impact on student perception and motivation. *Distance Education, 28*(1), 81–93. doi:10.1080/01587910701305327

Mayes, R., Ku, H., Akarasriworn, C., Luebeck, J., & Korkmaz, O. (2011). Themes and strategies for transformative online instruction: A review of literature and practice. *Quarterly Review of Distance Education, 12*(3), 151–166.

Medawar, P. (1969). *Induction and Intuition*. Philadelphia: American Philosophical Society.

Mergel, B. (1998). Instructional design & learning theory. Retrieved from http://www.usask.ca/education/coursework/802papers/mergel/brenda.htm

Minocha, S., & Roberts, D. (2008). Laying the groundwork for socialisation and knowledge construction within 3-D virtual worlds. *ALT-J. Research in Learning Technology, 16*(3), 181–196. doi:10.1080/09687760802526699

Moore, A. H., Moore, J. F., & Fowler, S. B. (2005). Faculty development for the net generation. In D. G. Oblinger, & J. L. Oblinger (Eds.), *Educating the Net Generation*: Educause. Retrieved from http://www.educause.edu/educatingthenetgen/

Moore, M. G. (1999). Monitoring and evaluation [Editorial]. *American Journal of Distance Education, 13*(2), 1–5. doi:10.1080/08923649909527019

Nelson, G. (2001). Do no harm: A first measure of effectiveness in small distance education programs. *Proceedings of ED-MEDIA 2001: World Conference on Educational Multimedia, Hypermedia, and Telecommunications*. Tampere, Finland.

Nettles, K., Dziuban, C., Cioffe, D., Moskal, P., & Moskal, P. (2000). Technology and Learning: The 'no significant difference' phenomenon: A structural analysis of research on technology enhanced instruction. In C. D. Dziuban & P. D. Moskal (Eds.), *Distributed Learning Impact Evaluation*. Orlando: University of Central Florida.

Olds, B. M., & Miller, R. L. (1998). An assessment matrix for evaluating engineering programs. *The Journal of Engineering Education*, *87*(2), 173–178. doi:10.1002/j.2168-9830.1998.tb00338.x

Oravec, J. A. (2003). Some influences of online distance learning on US higher education. *Journal of Further and Higher Education*, *27*(1), 89–103. doi:10.1080/03098770305628

Panda, S., & Mishra, S. (2007). E-learning in a mega open university: Faculty attitude, barriers and motivators. *Educational Media International*, *44*(4), 323–338. doi:10.1080/09523980701680854

Petrina, S. (2007). *Advanced teaching methods for the classroom*. Hershey, PA: Information Science Publishing. doi:10.4018/978-1-59904-337-1

Phillips, J., & Berge, Z. (2009). Second Life for dental education. *Journal of Dental Education*, *73*(11), 1260–1264. PMID:19910474

Phillips, J. J. (1996). How much is the training worth? *Training & Development*, *50*(4), 20–24.

Prus, J., & Johnson, R. (1994). A critical review of student assessment options. In T. H. Bers & M. L. Mittler (Eds.), *Assessment & Testing, Myths & Realities. New Directions for Community Colleges, 88* (pp. 69–83). San Francisco: Jossey-Bass Publishers. doi:10.1002/cc.36819948811

Reigeluth, C. M. (1999). What is instructional-design theory and how is it changing? In C. M. Reigeluth (Ed.), *Instructional-design theories and models - a new paradigm of instructional theory* (pp. 5–29). New Jersey: Lawrence Erlbaum.

Roblyer, M. D. (2003). *Integrating educational technology into teaching* (3rd ed.). NJ: Pearson Education.

Rock, D., & Schwartz, J. (2006). *The neuroscience of leadership*. Retrieved from http://www.strategy-business.com/article/06207?gko=6da0a

Rogers, E. M. (2003). *Diffusion of innovations*. New York, NY: Free Press.

Rokeach, M. (1960). *The open and closed mind*. New York: Basic Books.

Rovai, A. P. (2002). A preliminary look at the structural differences of higher education classroom communities in traditional and ALN courses. *Journal of Asynchronous Learning Networks*, *6*(1), 41–56.

Rudestam, K. E., & Schoenholtz-Read, J. (2010). The flourishing of adult online education: An overview. In K. E. Rudestam & J. Schoenholtz-Read (Eds.), *Handbook of online learning* (pp. 1–18). Los Angeles, CA: Sage.

Rungtusanatham, M., Ellram, L. M., Siferd, S. P., & Salik, S. (2004). Toward a typology of business education in the Internet age. *Decision Sciences Journal of Innovative Education*, *2*(2), 101–120. doi:10.1111/j.1540-4609.2004.00040.x

Salomon, G., & Perkins, D. (1998). Individual and social aspects of learning. *Review of Research in Education*, *23*, 1–24.

Shieh, R., Gummer, E., & Niess, M. (2008). The quality of a web-based course: Perspectives of the instructor and the students. *TechTrends: Linking Research & Practice to Improve Learning*, *52*(6), 61–68. doi:10.1007/s11528-008-0220-3

Sletten Sommerseth, K. (2014). *Facilitating collaborative learning in 3-D virtual worlds. A Qualitative meta study* [Unpublished thesis]. Reprosentralen, University of Oslo.

Sloan Consortium. (2006). Faculty satisfaction. Needham, MA: SloanCWiki. Retrieved from http://www.sloan-c-wiki.org/wiki/index.php?title= Faculty_Satisfaction.

Soto, V. (2013). Which instructional design models are educators using to design virtual world instruction? *Merlot Journal of Online Learning and Teaching, 9*(3). Retrieved from http://jolt.merlot.org/vol9no3/soto_0913.htm

Steinberg, A. D., Bashook, P. G., Drummond, J., Ashrafi, S., & Zefran, M. (2007). Assessment of faculty perception of content validity of PerioSim©, a haptic-3-D virtual reality dental training simulator. *Journal of Dental Education*, *71*(12), 1574–1582. PMID:18096883

Steinkuehler, C. A. (2004). Learning in massively multiplayer online games. In Y. B. Kafai, W. A. Sandoval, N. Enyedy, A. S. Nixon, & F. Herrera (Eds)., Embracing diversity in the learning sciences: Proceedings of *the Sixth International Conference of the Learning Sciences (ICLS'04)* (pp. 521–528). Mahwah, NJ: Lawrence Erlbaum.

Suebnukarn, S., Haddawy, P., Rhienmora, P., & Gajananan, K. (2010). Haptic Virtual Reality for Skill Acquisition in Endodontics. *Journal of Endodontics*, *36*(1), 53–55. doi:10.1016/j.joen.2009.09.020 PMID:20003935

Vaill, P. (1996). *Learning as a way of being*. San Francisco: Jossey-Bass Publishers.

Vickerstaff, K. (2015). *Implementation of technology enhanced learning pedagogy and impact on employability and learning within engineering education frameworks* [Unpublished doctoral dissertation]. Plymouth University. Plymouth, UK.

Wasilik, O., & Bolliger, D. U. (2009). Faculty satisfaction in the online environment: An institutional study. *The Internet and Higher Education*, *12*(3-4), 173–178. doi:10.1016/j.iheduc.2009.05.001

Wegner, S. B., Holloway, K. C., & Garton, E. M. (1999). The effects of internet-based instruction on student learning. *Journal of Asynchronous Learning Networks*, *3*(2).

Wiggins, G. (1998). *Educative assessments: Designing assessments to inform and improve student performance*. San Francisco: Jossey-Bass Publishers.

Yılmaz, R. M., Topu, F. B., Goktas, Y., & Coban, M. (2013). Social presence and motivation in a three-dimensional virtual world: An explanatory study. *Australasian Journal of Educational Technology*, *29*(6), 823–839.

KEY TERMS AND DEFINTIONS

E-Learning: Learning conducted via electronic media usually on the Internet.

Logic Bubbles: A term to describe the set of values, needs, beliefs and experiences that a person sees the world through as described by Edward de Bono.

Lateral Thinking: Applying an indirect and creative approach for solving problems and using reasoning that is not immediately obvious by involving ideas that may not be obtainable by using only traditional step-by-step logic as described by Edward de Bono.

Oculus Rift: The Oculus Rift is a set of virtual-reality goggles that will work with computers or mobile devices.

Second Life: A free 3-D virtual world where users can socialize, connect, and create using free voice and text or chat.

Three-Dimensional (3-D) Learning Environment: This type of environment allows interaction with other networked individuals as well as manipulation of objects (Loeffler & Andersen 1994).

Three-Dimensional (3-D) Virtual Learning: Web-based virtual learning provides an opportunity for teaching and learning without the necessity of buying expensive technology and equipment.

Two-Dimensional (2D) Learning Environment: 2D Interactive environments are a form of virtual environment with figurative appearance. Frequently, avatars communicate in bubbles and there can be interactive objects and multimedia imports.

Virtual Worlds: A virtual world is a computer-based online community environment that is designed and shared by individuals so that they can interact in a custom-built, simulated world (techopedia.com).

Chapter 4
Increasing Student Engagement through Virtual Worlds:
A Community College Approach in a Diversity Course

Yvonne Pigatt
The Community College of Baltimore County, USA

James Braman
The Community College of Baltimore County, USA

ABSTRACT

Virtual worlds allow for an immersive 3D experience with rich content and interactive potential for students. Through this richness and interactivity, educators have abundant creative power to design and facilitate meaningful learning experiences and collaboration opportunities. In this chapter, we discuss one such initiative using Second Life as an educational space for a community college course activity as a means to enhance student engagement. A brief literature review on education using virtual worlds will be presented, which underpin our pedagogical methodology for the project framework. Focusing on a community college course titled "Diversity in a Technological Society", the course goals and project requirements will be discussed. The chapter concludes with a detailed description of the proposed methodology for the next phase, recommendations and future work.

INTRODUCTION

Student engagement is one key component that assists in the process of learning and often coincides with attaining learning outcomes (Carini, Kuh, & Klein, 2006). There are many techniques to engage students and to spark additional interest in course topics. Some methods are aimed at classroom activities, while others are more aligned as homework or outside activities for practice and discovery. This can be achieved through the gamification of activities (Domíngues, Saenz-de-Navarrete, de-Marcos, Fernández-Sanz, Pagés, & Martínez-Herráiz, 2013), through flipped classrooms (Roehl, Reddy, & Shan-

DOI: 10.4018/978-1-4666-9837-6.ch004

non, 2013), augmented reality (Dunleavy, Dede, & Mitchell, 2009) and mobile applications (Arnone, Small, Chauncey, & McKenna, 2011), which are just a few methods using technology to engage students through active learning. Selecting the specific technology that best supports student learning depends on the instructional content and core learning outcomes. Certain course topics demand extra focus on specific skill sets and skill levels, while others are designed to sharpen skills in a more general sense. Technology in these courses can greatly enhance an educator's ability to reach students and provide them with unique learning opportunities.

Within the community college environment, teaching a general education course can be challenging due to the diverse set of student skill levels, varied technology literacy, and workload balance. This is compounded by differences in age and enrollment statuses compared to students enrolled in more traditional four-year institutions (Cohen & Brawer, 2003). Adding to this complexity is the many challenges faced when dealing with underprepared (Gabriel & Flake, 2008) or at-risk learners (Zheng, Warschauer, Hwang, & Collins, 2014). Reaching all students and keeping them engaged in the content and context of the class becomes increasingly complex and dynamic.

With the many available technologies and web 2.0 sites available today, educators have a wide array of tools to use in the classroom. Social media for instance now permeates many facets of everyday life and social interaction. Society has grown accustomed to everyday reliance on many forms of digital information (Pew, 2009; Lenhart, Purcell, Smith, & Zickuhr, 2010). However, some technologies do not work or fit well in some contexts, nor are they always appropriate for education. Using technology in the classroom poses its own set of problems and challenges. Instructors may not have knowledge about a particular technology, or even have the resources available. Computing resources, space and internet connectivity all pose potential problems. In some cases, the students may be apprehensive of learning with a new technology, or may have limited use of a particular resource outside of a school setting. While some schools may have open labs or computing resources available through the library, these can be a challenge to maintain or monitor since they are often outside of the instructor's domain of control.

Despite these challenges, for this project the virtual world of Second Life (SL) was selected as the technology of choice. Second Life is a 3-dimensional (3D) virtual world created by Linden Lab that can be accessed through the Internet via a downloadable client application. Users are represented in this world through an *avatar*, where one can interact with other users, content, and explore their surroundings. This online world has seen a large influx of users over the last several years, with an estimated number of "residents" reaching over 36 million accounts worldwide and over 700 square miles of virtual landmass (Linden Lab, 2015).While there are many categories of virtual worlds other than Second Life, each can be defined by their main goal or focus area. Some worlds are designed to be very open-ended and creative, while other worlds are designed to be more game-like or specific for a particular age group. Second Life in particular is not a game in the traditional sense, but an open and collaborative space that lends itself to much potential.

Students are accustomed to working with interactive media for learning and using educational games. While Second Life itself is not a game, it does have several game-like qualities that work well in teaching certain types of content or topics. As students are often attracted by games and other forms of interactive media, Second Life was an intriguing medium to use. Some studies have shown that many users of games also enjoyed being immersed in a simulated environment (Yee, 2006). Following Csikszentmihalyi's research on flow (1990) and applying this into areas of virtual environments to create an engaging and immersive space for learning is a useful goal. Using this approach for assignments can create engaging educational material for students. Additionally virtual environments can provide students with a sense of presence, which some researchers have noted as a key benefit of using the technology (Holmberg & Huvila, 2008; Salmon, 2009).

Other virtual environments, similar to Second Life, are available, such as Twinity, Active Worlds and Minecraft. While these other technologies are competitors, Second Life still has a strong user base and strong attraction for new users, with some attributing its popularity to the large amount of varying in-world activities (Wagner, 2008). There have also been a growing number of available 3D environments that are intended for more targeted users and age groups (Kzero, 2014). Minecraft, in particular, has seen an increase in use for the gamification of material for younger students (Gallagher, 2014).

Virtual worlds and other 3D spaces have been used for an array of educational purposes over the last several years (Kapp & O'Driscoll, 2010; Vincenti & Braman, 2011); including use in the general education curriculum in some schools as a vehicle for research and social exploration (Braman, Meiselwitz & Vincenti, 2013). As virtual worlds continue to grow in popularity, so too will the possibilities of their use. Virtual worlds has also been used in wider areas, such as in theater, art, geography, science and English courses, and many more (Vincenti & Braman, 2010; Vincenti & Braman, 2011). Second Life has been used in more specific domains such as in computer science and in computer ethics (Wang, Dudley, Braman, & Vincenti, 2009). The perception of the use of Second Life in computing courses has generally been positive (Braman, Dudley, Colt, Vincenti, & Wang, 2011).

Second Life was best suited for the pilot study discussed in this chapter due to the authors' experience, the diversity of in-world users, the capabilities of the platform, and the potential for dynamic interactivity through built-in scripting language. . In addition, it is possible to link Second Life to external programs and applications to extend its capabilities. Also, one of the authors had extensive experience conducting workshops and training on Second Life which helped to facilitate the project The purpose of using SL in the diversity course, discussed in this chapter, was twofold: 1) To increase student engagement in the context of the course by increasing participation, student enthusiasm and assignment quality and 2) To teach a new emerging technology. This chapter will begin with background discussion of virtual worlds and creating and using a virtual educational space. Secondly, a pilot study completed at a community college will be described, inclusive of difficulties inside and outside the classroom. A third section will discuss the pilot study and recommendations. Lastly, future research directions and conclusions will be provided.

BACKGROUND

Virtual worlds can be defined as "an electronic environment that visually mimics complex physical spaces, where people can interact with each other and with virtual objects, and where people are represented by animated characters" (Bainbridge, 2007, p. 472). The realism of virtual worlds and the "animated characters" or Avatars, have increased over the years as hardware and video capabilities have improved. The origins of virtual worlds are rooted in online text-based "worlds", referred to as Multi-User Dungeons or Multi-Users Dimension (MUDs) (Bartle, 2003). As technologies have improved, so too have their capabilities, features and representations, which have evolved into the many environments and games seen today. There are other terms that can be used to refer to virtual worlds such as Multi-User Virtual Environments (MUVEs) which can encompass many online worlds, and more specifically, in the context of education, Virtual Learning Environments (VLEs). Typically, VLEs are web-based, are less open-ended compared to MUVEs, and are more focused on learning, communication and include assessment tools (Britain & Liber, 2004). VLEs can be used in a broader sense to include virtual worlds that are focused on education. Common tools are supported in most virtual environments which include capabilities for communication, voice interaction, building tools, polygon mesh, and other 3D support. More recently, a beta version of Second Life has been released which focuses on the use for the Oculus Rift, making for a very immersive experience. The Oculus Rift is a virtual reality head mounted display device that can be used to create realistic immersive experiences for the wearer. With the increase in realism, the potential for new ways of interaction may become more commonplace. There has also been work to enhance the social interaction between users through emotive avatars that capture real expressions, as in the virtual world High Fidelity (High Fidelity, 2015).

While the use of simulations, video and other computerized tools in education are not new, the use of virtual 3D worlds is still experimental. 3D worlds have potential as an educational tool due to the creative nature and capabilities. 3D worlds do present some design challenges in term of creating an educational resource or "space" for the students to work. Unlike the traditional classroom, the virtual classroom has fewer restrictions on time, space and movement. In the next section we examine the creation and use of virtual educational space.

Creating and Using a Virtual Educational Environment

What does it mean to have an education space in a virtual world? What does it look like? In a virtual world, educators are not bound by many of the same physical limitations inherent in the traditional physical classroom. Educators are also not bound by the same limitations of websites or Content Management Systems (CMS) such as Blackboard or Moodle. As John Lester pointed out during his Keynote Talk at the e-LEOT 2014 conference, there is a tendency among educators "to use new tools like old tools" (Lester, 2014). While educators have the power of virtual worlds, which can be used to create new imaginary environments the tendency is to recreate a 3D replica of a traditional classroom. A replica of a classroom in virtual worlds certainly does not guarantee that learning will take place. A virtual world activity for a class needs deliberate planning, testing and integration with specific content to be successful. Unlike some virtual environments where everything is pre-created by the creating company, Second Life relies on the content creation of its residents (users). Content creation in Second Life is more difficult compared to virtual worlds with environments created by software developers, such as World of Warcraft (McArthur, Teather, & Stuerzlinger, 2010). Since many educators may lack the time needed to successfully build all the components needed for their online virtual environment, other options are possible such - as purchasing premade content from other users (via in-world stores or the Second Life Marketplace) or even hiring someone to create the space for a fee. Before designing a space, it is recommended that one spends time in-a virtual world in order to get a sense of the possibilities, and what other educators have designed. Educational spaces can consist of open areas of land which can contain replicas and models of particular systems. These spaces may include interactive kiosks, or somewhat more traditional areas that include meeting spaces like offices with desks.

Students benefit from learning new technological platforms such as Second Life. 3D platforms and games are increasingly commonplace, thus having knowledge of how to operate one can be useful in learning to operate another. Having an avatar can be useful in the operation of various multiuser applications. As noted by Bélisle and Bodur (2010), with the increasing use of consumers today having avatars, it is important to understand how avatars are being used to improve marketing. Many researchers agree that Second Life can provide an engaging learning environment for students compared to current education platforms, including an "around the clock" accessible meeting place (Bradshaw, 2006; Schome Community, 2007; Wang & Braman 2009). Engaging students is also enhanced when instructors maintain additional office hours in-world or include additional training material in a 3D format. A search on video sites, such as www.youtube.com, yield many choices of videos showcasing educational designs. Students may be more willing to interact with an interactive training kiosk in Second Life in addition to lecture notes from class or the required text, rather than reading the textbook alone. As discussed by Antonacci et al. (2008) there are three major educational benefits from using virtual worlds:

1. Virtual worlds give users the ability to carry out tasks that could be difficult for them in the "real world" due to constraints, including cost, scheduling or location;
2. Virtual worlds' persistence allows for continuing and growing social interactions, which can serve as a basis for collaborative education;
3. Virtual worlds can adapt and grow to meet user needs.

These three benefits, particularly for some topics, provide the dynamic flexibility needed to complete projects that would be difficult to complete in the normal time frame of a class.

Duncan, Miller, and Jiang (2012) reviewed virtual world educational literature and summarized six advantages of using virtual worlds in an educational setting; two of the six are from sources other than Duncan et al.

1. The use of SL provides an intuitive modern approach for distance teaching in terms of the use of avatars.
2. Collaboration is greatly facilitated when conducting educational activities in-world.
3. Experimental and constructive learning can be achieved in SL.
4. Higher order thinking, such as analyzing, evaluating and creating can be achieved in virtual words as well as lower order thinking, such as remembering, understanding and applying (Falloon, 2010).
5. As geographical boundaries are broken down in SL, there is a large diverse background among participants.
6. It is possible that the in-world activity is always more interactive than real-world teaching activities (Macías-Díaz, 2008).

As noted previously, the flexibility of the environment to be change and adapted to the dynamics of student needs or to the content of a particular course is quite useful. This is dependent however on the instructor and available resources. Successful lesson plans using a virtual world needs to be carefully planned, often more so than a traditional lecture. These characteristics are indeed important for integration of a virtual environment into any classroom. As engagement though visual and interactive components can promote active learning, attention needs to be placed carefully on this element. Once students are acclimated to the software, teachers can serve as a guide of the lesson plan to facilitate collaboration between students, assist with challenges and problem solving and keep the class on task.

USING SECOND LIFE: A PILOT PROJECT

A computing course titled "Diversity in a Technological Society" was selected for the Second Life Pilot Project. The official course catalogue description reads: "Explores the influences of technology on human diversity. Students are introduced to basic human relationship factors, international cultures, technologies, people with disabilities, human and data communications, artificial intelligence, computer security, and various individuals who have influenced technology". This course was selected due to the nature and flexibility of the course, and due to the instructors schedule to carry out the pilot project. In the course, students were assigned a topic from their normal class textbook which served as a basis for a group project. In semesters, prior to the Pilot Study, students were to work in a small group of three or four people to construct a report on a given course related topic. Once the report was complete, students were to present the topic to the class using Microsoft PowerPoint. The report topics included: Artificial Intelligence, virtual reality, military applications of technology, electronic health records, medical information systems, etc., and several other emerging technology trends. Based on assigned topic, through their own research, and from the textbook information in the chapter, students were to write a summarizing report and presentation (both were graded). This assignment was typical for the course, and was a normal activity assigned at the end of each semester. Students are normally required to attend the presentations of other groups, take notes and ask questions. However, for the pilot study, the "traditional" assignment for the course was altered for the use of Second Life.

Introducing Second Life to Students

In class, students were assigned groups and group topics for the report they would be completing as a course assignment, the same procedure as used pre-pilot study. Students were also asked to create a SL account. Next, the class was introduced to SL in two ways: 1) A homework assignment was administered where students had to watch a documentary on SL and virtual worlds, titled Life 2.0. As part of this homework assignment students were asked to create an avatar; and 2). Students were introduced to SL by means of an in-class lecture and a training session including the in-world navigation controls. When students spend some time learning about virtual worlds and navigation elements before an actual SL graded project, students are better acclimated to the requirements of the assignment and there is less stress related to learning new software.

The initial in-class practice assignment using SL reviewed the main features and controls, such as chatting, basic avatar control, flying and teleportation. In the exercise, all of these features were included and students were asked to explore various aspects of the "grid" while paying extra attention to the layout and design of buildings, stores and general places they visited. Students were asked to make notes of their observations. Students were also introduced to aspects of the economy and how to purchase items if needed. In the last 15 - 20 minutes of class, a brief building tutorial was conducted to give students a very basic understanding on how to build and shape objects. This overview was a beneficial method of showing the class how much time other users put into creating virtual items and buildings.

After students completed these initial practice assignments, the changed aspect of the group project compared to past semesters was revealed. Students were instructed that the presentation for the given topic would not be conducted in the "traditional sense" but instead will be presented to the class through Second Life using their new skills. In addition, each group was asked to upload their final presentations slides into SL, and also to create an interactive kiosk area as an alternative presentation medium for their given topic. For example, if the group's topic was on artificial intelligence, they were asked to create an inviting space to capture their audience's attention, provide a seating area, presentation area and also include decorative items and/or posters or pictures to emphasize their topic. This required some creativity from the students and an understanding of the topic. The group kiosk areas also needed to include several interactive components which could be accessed by the class. The interactive components could include objects that link to external websites and dispense other objects or virtual notecards with additional information. An instructor led discussion on the topics, through the Second Life based learning kiosks, served the class as a content source, while the class was immersed in-world. In order to complete the assignment, students needed prior experience in Second Life to control and manipulate their avatars, understand the interface, and to be able to communicate effectively with other students (as avatars). To facilitate this experience, students were exposed to several deliberate exercises within Second Life to learn the controls. Students needed basic building knowledge and, in some cases, basic scripting knowledge in order to create the interactive kiosks. Thus, an outline was developed for the approach that would be used to teach students how to use SL for completion of a report presentation assignment.

Assignment

Outline for Integrating Second Life into an Assignment

1. Introduce students to Second Life through homework assignments:
   a. Search for basic information online about Second Life and similar virtual worlds
   b. Create a free basic Second Life account by going to http://www.secondlife.com
   c. Watch a video on SL and virtual worlds titled: Life 2.0: http://www.youtube.com/watch?v=aUwD7u7wwcY (example)
2. Class 1 (Lecture / Discussion):
   a. Lecture topic on virtual worlds, SL (in general) and the SL culture. Emphasis on how SL can be used for education, collaboration, business and for entertainment.
   b. Class discussion questions related to virtual worlds
   c. Textbook assignment: "Real Self vs. Virtual Self"
3. Class 2 (Applied Learning):
   a. Using Second Life / Creating an avatar
   b. Learning navigation controls / Flying / Teleporting
   c. Learning Communication / Search /Editing Appearance / Inventory System
   d. In-world Exploration Assignment
   e. Getting started with groups and coordination of Projects
4. Class 3 (Applied Learning):
   a. Groups assigned to in-world spaces
   b. Groups work on designs and upload presentation files in-world
   c. Group Assignment:
      i. Read textbook chapter, complete presentation with interactive kiosk area in SL that discusses an emerging technology topic and group research
5. Class 4 (Applied Learning):
   a. Class exploration and group topic presentations in SL and real life
   b. Class feedback and conclusions

Students were given in-class time to work on their project and to collaborate with their groups to complete the project. Extra time outside of class was also needed as most groups needed extra study time on the topics and also time to complete the presentation files. In Second Life, an area was purchased in the main grid by the instructors, specifically in the Goodnight region. This area was 16,384 square meters and was sufficient for several class sections to work. The virtual space was divided into multiple sections and separated by fences. The space was also sufficient in size to have enough space in between each group area for additional separation. Each group was assigned a specific area to build and to contain their design. It is important to let students know that there is a specific number of virtual objects (or "prims" short for primitive objects) that can housed in an area, so as not to include an excessive amount of unneeded objects in their design. It is also important to remind students not to build in other student areas or disrupt other groups. When students are using the in-world chat feature, other conversations can be "heard" by other groups if they are too close.

By the last in-class building session, student groups had managed to complete most of the assignment. Some groups struggled to build kiosk areas that were related to their topic and some had problems getting their presentation slides uploaded without help (figure 1). On the last day of the project, each of the groups presented the research completed on their assigned topic. The presentations took place in-world and in real life simultaneously. In real life, the presenting group stood in front of the class at the instructor station. One group member was logged into SL at the instructor station with Second Life projected on the overhead screen. The other members of the presenting group were also at the front of the room to assist in their section of the presentation. These students were logged in at their desk computers, but physically located at the front of the classroom. The remainder of the class was able to watch and listen to the presentation though Second Life (by being logged as their self) and in Real Life at the same time. Being in-world and in the real-life class had the advantage of allowing students multiple ways to interact with the content and at the same time provide a real life overlay of the presentation in which they were more accustomed. The class did experience a few technical difficulties during two presentations, which included the platform crashing for one group, and another group had their presentation slides inadvertently reset. Having the real life aspect of the presentation, allowed the group to continue presenting during the challenges. At the conclusion of each presentation, students asked questions to the presenting group via SL through the chat window where each presenting group responded through SL and in person to the class. Several of the presenting groups also posed their own created quiz questions to the class virtually, creating a multi-layered discussion. Figure 2 illustrates a group of students, represented by avatars, in a virtual presentation area.

At the conclusion of the project, the instructors had open discussions with the class to elicit feedback on their experiences with Second Life and the alternate form of presenting. The instructors also wanted to gain key insights into what parts of the project were useful, difficult or lacking in order to make improvements for the future. As mentioned previously, this was a preliminary pilot study in the early testing phase where more in-depth analysis will occur in the future. Feedback was elicited through class discussion and was not explicitly recorded for this pilot study. Student feedback after the project was generally positive on this mixed reality mode of presenting. Many expressed surprise in presenting in this format as it was something very new that they had never before experienced. During the presentations there were very minimal technical problems or complications and by this time in the project, students were much more comfortable being able to navigate and control the avatars for the presentation without help. There were some challenges encouraged in and out of the classroom, beyond those of a technical nature.

Figure 1. Beginning of group kiosk building within fenced in areas

Figure 2. Students in-world listening to a group presentation

Challenges In and Out of the Classroom

This section highlights some issues that were encountered during the Pilot Project, both inside the classroom and for at home assignments.

Inside the Classroom

The real-life classroom was a typical computer lab setting with twenty-four computers. The computers were positioned around the perimeter of the room, so that the instructor could easily assist students that were having problems and keep students on task. This also helped with the collaboration component of the project, as other students could easily maneuver around the class to help other group members. The computers used were 3.2 Ghz with i5 processors with 4GB of RAM, all running the Windows 7 operating system. The instructors were pleasantly surprised regarding the low number of technical difficulties encountered in the classroom.

To make installation and accesses less of a problem, the instructors were able to obtain a large set of 2 gigabyte USB flash drives. These flash drives were generously donated by the college to assist in the Pilot Project. A copy of SL was installed on each flash drive. The intention was to have flash drives readily available with a SL install so that students could use it in class, on another computer on campus, or off-campus. Providing a flash drive, with SL installed was a support system so students could keep working without needing to worry about installing additional software. There were a few issues with defective flash drives, and in those cases the students temporarily installed SL on the lab computer as needed. At the end of the activity, the flash drives were collected back from students who expressed that they would not need the drive or would use Second Life in the future.

Additionally the class did not encounter many problems with the video cards or graphics capabilities during class. Most installations of the SL software defaulted to the highest video settings (which later needed to be adjusted in some instances). During the Project Pilot about 10-15% of the computers experienced periodic crashes, causing SL to need restarting. Lowering the graphic settings one to two levels below maximum seemed to limit the number of crashes. Crashing often occurred when users were moving between regions or teleporting, or when students were located within graphically rich areas. Being close to large bodies of water in SL also seemed to cause problem with some of the graphics cards. The instructors made sure to notify students of these issues as they became known.

Outside the Classroom

A first challenge outside for the classroom pertained to documentary Life 2.0 by Jason Spingarn-Koff that students were asked to watch (http://www.youtube.com/watch?v=aUwD7u7wwcY).While the instructors considered this to be a useful documentary that revealed several motivations of why some people use or are attracted to Second Life, student feedback, was mixed. The class had a discussion about the video, along with several related instructor led questions about how students felt about the video. It is important to that that this discussion was held prior to the students had experience within the virtual world of in Second Life. One perception that was communicated during the discussion was that many students had the impression that users of Second Life were addicted to the environment, led unfulfilled lives and that SL was not a useful space for "normal" people. Other students had opinions that were different, and observed that indeed SL has very useful purposes in many contexts and could be an interesting collaborative and social space. Overall, student's first impressions of SL were more negative than positive. In the future an alternative video that provides more focus on SL content or several shorter introductory videos on virtual worlds will be used.

A second challenge that occurred was related to those students that did not complete the avatar creation assignment prior to class. Students that failed to complete this homework assignment had difficulties creating their accounts while on campus. After a few students created their account, additional students were blocked from registering because the Internet Protocol (IP) address for the campus location was temporarily blocked from creating additional accounts. As of the time of this writing, this is still a problem, and addition accounts cannot be created on campus. The remaining students were able to complete the registration process by using their internet connection on their phone (using their own data plan and connection having a separate IP address). In future semesters, the need to complete the registration process prior to the class, will be stressed in order to alleviate this challenge in the future.

DISCUSSION AND RECOMMENDATIONS

Overall, the Pilot Project using SL in a "Diversity in a Technological Society" course was successful. We gained key insights for increasing student engagement from the project, and additionally identified improvements. The original instructor for the course noted improvement in enthusiasm and detail in submitted projects compared to non-SL usage. Anecdotal evidence from the experience suggests that using a virtual world can have a positive impact on student perception of the project and it can increase enthusiasm for some assignments. Some students did report seeing a positive benefit pertaining to gaining knowledge about virtual worlds for future use. After participating in the assignment, most students that previously had a negative view of SL, had changed their viewpoints. This initial negative opinion may be due to the novelty of the software, but additional research is needed in order to understand preconceived negative perceptions. Understanding these perceptions would be helpful as they could be addressed in the beginning of the assignment.

In future incarnations of this project there are several elements that the instructors wish to change and improve. To assist in streamlining the assignment in the future, the instructors plan on creating additional videos on virtual worlds in addition to video tutorials on how to create objects, upload the presentation files and purchase items in-world. The assignment instructions themselves will also be enhanced to include more detail. Video recorded training sessions will provide additional context for the students of the importance of knowing about virtual world software. It is our wish that other educators can gain insight on how similar projects for their classes may be adapted and used for other diverse content. By placing several of the training videos online, other educators could make use of the information in their classes.

Recommendations

Following is a list of recommendations for integrating the virtual world of SL into a college course using an approach similar to the Pilot Project discussed in this chapter. With each recommendation is a discussed of how the authors plan to implement the changes in future courses.

1. *Include at least two smaller training sessions for students to increase awareness of virtual worlds.* Overall the initial lectures and discussion sessions about Second Life, combined with several

training sessions on the use of SL were helpful for students based on their general comments in class and observations during the project. These training sessions (which included controls, communication, building etc.) were instrumental for student success in using SL to complete the assignment. As students became conformable with the SL technology and understood its application in a wider scope, communication and collaboration expectations were established. Students were able to communicate effectively with their group in-world to complete assigned tasks. Anecdotal evidence, gathered through the author's observations, suggests that training (even at a basic level) greatly improves overall outcomes when using SL for an educational purpose. There are several orientation areas (e.g., Orientation Island) premade and maintained within SL that can be used by students when instructors do not have a readily available class module for orientation.

2. *Require students to complete virtual world activities outside of the classroom.* It is beneficial for both the students and instructors to conduct some preliminary research about virtual worlds outside of the classroom. This allows students to pursue topics related to virtual worlds that may be interesting to them. It would be useful to provide a set of guiding questions, depending on the context of a particular course and how virtual worlds could be useful in that domain. For example, in a business course, an instructor could assign specific readings on the value of virtual goods, or articles on virtual world marketing. In the case of this project students were asked to watch a video related to SL. There are many other such videos available that are more general that may be appropriate. Based on student feedback, an alternate video (yet to be determined) will be selected for future semesters. An additional benefit of having students do a portion of the investigation outside of class time is that more time can be focused on the technology and on the collaboration component. A flipped classroom approach for the individual group project topics is useful.
3. *Evaluate the available resources and technology.* Having backup plans for technical problems will allow for a much smoother class activity. It is important to test the equipment available in the labs especially that of the video card and internet speed. Since SL relies on both components, problems with the video card or internet speeds can easily derail an activity, and frustrate students. Also be sure to check for any scheduled updates for SL as it may pose for some complications if there are any glitches. One major problem that many may face is the lack of ability to install the SL client application on lab computers. Without administrator rights, installation can be difficult or impossible. Also needed updates to the platform that occur periodically can cause problems if instructors lack administrator rights to perform the updates. In this pilot we used flash drives with pre-installed copies of SL which cut down many problems in the classroom. Even though we did have the ability to install software as needed, computers are reset each day which would have required the reinstallation of the program. Be aware however, that the downside of the flash drive approach is the amount of time needed to install the software on each drive. This should be completed well in advance to the actual class activity.
4. *Provide students with sufficient use of context for the use of Second Life.* It is important that students understand the importance of virtual worlds and that it is a technology that is increasingly being used in education, business settings and for social interactions. Having an understanding of the technology and its impacts can be advantageous. To help students become more fluent and comfortable with the technology in a general sense (not just with SL), then sufficient knowledge of virtual worlds is required. If students are able to use a virtual world throughout the semester, and not just for one project, then additional skills may develop. Students can learn more advanced features and skills that can be used in outer areas. If a particular course does not lend itself to us-

ing a virtual world platform all semester, than be sure to provide students with enough context information about how the technology can be used and examples of its current use. For example, show the class how businesses are using the technology to reinforce that it's not just a "game" but a serious place to conduct work. One could also show the class how it could be used in the medical field by describing its usage in medical education for simulation and information display (Meskó, 2008). There are numerous examples of how educators and researchers are using the platforms in many areas.

5. *Aim to reduce costs of conducting an in-class project.* The cost of conducting implementing SL into a course, especially if there are a large number of students or a large land requirement, can be rather expensive. One needs to purchase an area of land, and then in addition to that expense, a monthly land rental fee is assessed. For example, a smaller 2,048 square meter parcel costs $15.00 USD or a 32,768 square meter parcel costs $125.00 USD per month. A full link to the Mainland Pricing and fees can be found at: https://secondlife.com/land/pricing.php. It is important to access the particular needs for implementation prior to purchasing space so as not to incur unneeded costs. There are alternative worlds available, some of which are free that can be hosted locally and customized, such as OpenSim. As an added benefit of using a locally hosted world to that institution, security and control of the space can be better maintained. An additional cost that was incurred as part of this Pilot Project was the purchase cost for each group's PowerPoint presentation boards. In order for the students to present their slides on the topic, they needed a presentation object to do so (discussed more in the next section). For the duration of the Pilot Project each group was given a limited amount of virtual currency (Linden dollars) so that they could purchase a presentation viewer to display their presentation slides. Any additional money that remained could be used by the group to purchase additional decorative items for their space if needed. The students were encouraged to use as many freely available items and content as possible. Students did quickly discover how to obtain and search for free items in the Second Life marketplace: https://marketplace.secondlife.com. Students did learn valuable knowledge on how to make real purchases and how to work with alternate virtual currencies for the project, as well as how to buy from the web, items for their avatar and how to un-package items. There is a large amount of content available in the marketplace and within Second Life for the needs of most projects.
6. *Use a created display board instead of a purchased display board for the activity.* Part of the Pilot Project required that students upload their final version of their presentation files to SL as image files (either in .jpg or .png format) to be integrated into an in-world presenter object. These presenter objects act as an interactive display board, where a presenter can show a slide and then advance to the next one while speaking. It is similar to use the instructor station in a classroom to go through a set of PowerPoint's. Initially, to save time and to allow students a chance to actually purchase goods in SL, the instructors requested that students visit the SL Marketplace to purchase a specific item for the assignment. In order for this to work, each group needed approximately $500L (500 Linden dollars) which was supplied by the instructors. This amount of virtual currency is approximate equivalent to $1.89 USD, but the exchange rate of the virtual current changes daily and is controlled by Linden Lab (Bray & Konsynski, 2008). While this is not a substantial amount of money, it could become problematic if there are a large number of groups across many sections. In the future it is planned to create a specific presentation object for the activity that can be copied and modified by each group for no cost. If time allows, students could be given instructions to

create this presentation object own their own (given adequate time and directions). This would be a more advanced exercise.

7. *Train instructors to be fluent with Second Life and acclimated to the platform.* It is also strongly recommend that educators stay current in topics related to virtual worlds so that they can provide relevance to students about why they are using the technology and how it can be useful for in their future as a technology tool. Providing relevance to using virtual worlds in class can strengthen the relationship of its importance to a learning activity. This can often be accomplished by adding additional readings or discussions that highlight high profile uses of the platform in the business world, by educational institutions, use in government, in medicine, etc. Additionally, due to the technical nature of the software and the many changing features, it is helpful for the students to have an instructor that is able to help if, and when problems occur during use. The students can face an array of challenges and raise many questions during the activity. As some students are hesitant about using the software or quickly overwhelmed by it, having a background in the features often helps to calm student fears if something happens. It is also helpful as an educator to be familiar with many of the advanced features and how to use many of the building tools as one can then create much more inviting and engaging learning spaces. This advanced ability could lend itself to being able to link the learning space to outside resources such as websites or to create very engaging self-directed learning tools for outside class time learning.
8. *Decide on a design for the virtual world space.* As the nature of the virtual learning space is very fluid, the environment can take on many forms. The authors recommended analyzing the needs of a particular project to help determine the form of the virtual space early. The size of the area, the amount of avatars for the class that need to be supported, the need for a sandbox area, and the need for certain tools are all main elements to consider. Visiting public educational areas in SL, to get a sense of what is possible and to see what tools are available in-world (such as display areas, simulations, posters, lecture areas, or video screens, etc.), is recommended. It can be a daunting task to figure out how one's educational space should appear, balancing both functionally and having an interesting and inviting landscape. Often virtual learning environments are designed very differently depending on the subject matter of a course and discipline. Virtual environments can range from being a recreation of a scene from a science fiction novel or a play, which could be used by an English course, or an area that is visually simpler such as a lecture style amphitheater for class presentations. Alternatively the environment could be a replica of a full scale campus. Simulations through Second Life have great potential (Teoh, 2012).

FUTURE RESEARCH DIRECTIONS

In this section, future goals for the Pilot Project are discussed, specifically addressing improvements needed. A first goal is to integrate SL further into the curriculum and also compare retention and learning outcomes in courses integrating SL and those that do not. Although specific measurable feedback from students or grade outcomes from the assignment were not measured at this time, the instructors observed that this Pilot Project, was extremely beneficial in increasing student confidence for using SL in the future and enthusiasm for the assignment. A more detailed and integrated approach using SL earlier in the course, and in multiple assignments would be advantageous. However, further experimentation on selecting specific assignments and best practices are needed.

A second goal is to seek feedback from students using Second Life for class activities. Student feedback is essential for making improvements in the assignment and for understanding strategies that were helpful. Hepplestone et al. (2011) discusses the importance of student feedback regarding technology used within courses and particularly use that encourages engagement (Hepplestone, Holden, Irwin, Parking, & Thorpe, 2011). While the teaching methods and features may be quite different with technology providing a 3D environment compared to more traditional technology, student involvement and feedback is equally essential. Instructors using any virtual world or classroom assignment based on SL should continually seek student comments. These environments change often and content and directions will need to be updated and checked regularly. Using additional student feedback will be useful in implementing changes noted earlier in the chapter.

A third goal, is to use varied quantitative and qualitative methods for collecting detailed feedback from students through discussions, assignments and also through surveys using a more detailed research methodology. Using a more solid project framework that measures student skills and knowledge as well as perceptions about engagement and perceptions would be greatly beneficial. The authors plan to adopt a similar set of survey questions following Wang and Braman (2009) and Braman et al. (2011) with additional questions aimed at engagement and student perception of virtual worlds. A fourth goal is to create and maintain a more permanent space within Second Life that could be used for additional projects, virtual office hours and display of student and faculty projects. Having a fixed space to serve as a location online where students can meet virtually could help improve the project's visibility and encourage more collaboration.

While the future directions pertaining to the Pilot Project provides ideas for those who are interested in the next steps for the authors, there is a need to make specific directions for use of SL in higher education courses in general. To date, use of SL in higher education has been limited. For those readers who have not yet implemented a virtual world tool, following are future directions suggested as an extension of this chapter.

1. Identify colleagues that are interested in identifying tools to engage students in active learning and begin the processing of exploring SL (or other virtual worlds), such as those described in this chapter, for the purpose of increasing instructor knowledge, skills, and self-efficacy with virtual world technology.
2. Meet regularly to share what has been learned individually; use journal articles and book chapters that describe the use of SL in college courses; develop a reference list. The list at the end of this chapter could be an initial resource.
3. Stay current in educational trends related to virtual worlds, and aim to tailor 3D content to be relevant to the course using the technology.
4. Seek continuous student and faculty feedback from those involved in using virtual worlds in a course to enhance content and interaction. Including students in the process is helpful in increasing engagement and for making improvements.

CONCLUSION

In this chapter, the authors have discussed a Pilot Project using Second Life in a diversity course to help foster interest and increase student engagement. As presented in this chapter, there have been many changes in this technology over the years including how it can be used in an educational context. By using tools such as SL to increase student engagement, educators can improve their courses and teach materials in new ways. In this chapter we have provided key background on virtual worlds including how they can be used in higher education. Following, a discussion on a pilot project using SL in a diversity course at a community college where the goal was to increase student engagement and teach a new technology tool. This discussion included the project outline and key activities and student feedback. A discussion about difficulties, both in and out of the classroom was presented as well as a set of recommendations for educators interested in incorporating SL into their own classes. A set of future research goals were also presented as the authors move forward into more detailed research questions and collection of student feedback.

It is a sincere hope that more educators decide to use virtual worlds or similar platforms for educational purposes. SL can be an effective tool to excite and engage students in new ways and extend the capabilities of the traditional classroom setting. With the growing set of features and affordances of virtual worlds, they can become even more commonplace where educators are encouraged to experiment more. While much research is still needed to determine best practices, the literature suggests many positive usages and potential learning outcomes.

REFERENCES

Antonacci, D., DiBartolo, S., Edwards, N., Fritch, K., McMullen, B., & Murch-Shafer, R. (2008). The power of virtual worlds in education: a second primer and resource for exploring the potential of virtual worlds to impact teaching and learning. ANGEL Learning ISLE Steering Committee. Retrieved from http://www.angellearning.com/products/secondlife/downloads/The%20Power%20of%20Virtual%20Worlds%20in%20Education_0708.pdf

Arnone, M., Small, R., Chauncey, S., & McKenna, H. (2011). Curiosity, interest and engagement in technology-pervasive learning environments: A new research agenda. *Educational Technology Research and Development*, *59*(2), 181–198. doi:10.1007/s11423-011-9190-9

Bainbridge, W. (2007). The scientific research potential of virtual worlds. *Science*, *317*(5837), 472–476. doi:10.1126/science.1146930 PMID:17656715

Bartle, R. (2003). *Designing virtual worlds*. United States: New Riders Publishing.

Bélisle, J., & Bodur, H. (2010). Avatars as information: Perception of consumers based on their avatars in virtual worlds. *Psychology and Marketing*, *27*(8), 741–765. doi:10.1002/mar.20354

Bradshaw, D. (2009). New practices in flexible learning: virtual worlds – real learning! Pedagogical Reflections. Retrieved from http://virtualworlds.flexiblelearning.net.au/reports/VWRL_pedagog_reflect.pdf

Braman, J., Dudley, A., Colt, K., Vincenti, V., & Wang, Y. (2011). Gaining insight into the application of second life in a computer course: student's perspectives. *Proceedings of the 14th HCI International Conference on Online Communities and Social Computing*. Orlando, FL.

Braman, J., Meiselwitz, G., & Vincenti, G. (2013). Virtual worlds in the general education curriculum. In R. McBride & M. Searson (Eds.), *Proceedings of Society for Information Technology & Teacher Education International Conference 2013* (pp. 2692-2697).

Bray, D. A., & Konsynski, B. (2008). *Virtual worlds, virtual economies, virtual institutions. Proceedings of the Virtual Worlds and New Realities Conference*. Atlanta, GA: Emory University.

Britain, S., & Liber, O. (2004). A framework for pedagogical evaluation of virtual learning environments. *JISC Technology Applications Program,* (41)

Britain, S., & Liber, O. (2004). A framework for pedagogical evaluation of virtual learning environments. *Research Report.* Retrieved from: https://halshs.archives-ouvertes.fr/hal-00696234/document

Carini, R., Kuh, G., & Klein, S. (2006). Student engagement and student learning: Testing the linkages. *Research in Higher Education*, *47*(1), 1–32. doi:10.1007/s11162-005-8150-9

Cohen, A., & Brawer, F. (2003). *The American community college* (4th ed.). San Francisco: Jossey-Bass Publishing.

Csikszentmihalyi, M. (1990). *Flow: The psychology of optimal experience*. Harper Perennial Modern Classics.

De Freitas, S. (2008). *Serious virtual worlds. A scoping guide: Prepared for the JISC e-Learning Programme, The Joint Information Systems Committee*. UK: JISC.

Domínguez, A., Saenz-de-Navarrete, J., de-Marcos, L., Fernández-Sanz, L., Pagés, C., & Martínez-Herráiz, J.-J. (2013). Pagés, & C. Martínez-Herráiz, J. (2013). Gamifying learning experiences: Practical Implications and Outcomes. *Computers & Education*, *63*, 380–392. doi:10.1016/j.compedu.2012.12.020

Duncan, I., Miller, A., & Jiang, S. (2012). A taxonomy of virtual world usage in education. *British Journal of Educational Technology, 43*(6). DOI: 10:1111/j.1467-8535.2011.01263.x

Dunleavy, M., Dede, C., & Mitchell, R. (2009). Affordances and limitations of immersive participatory augmented reality simulations for teaching and learning. *Journal of Science Education*, *18*, 7–22.

Falloon, G. (2010). Using avatars and virtual and virtual environments in learning: What do they have to offer? *British Journal of Educational Technology*, *41*(1), 108–122. doi:10.1111/j.1467-8535.2009.00991.x

Gabriel, K., & Flake, S. (2008). *Teaching unprepared students: strategies for promoting success and retention in higher education*. Stylus Publishing.

Gallagher, C. (2014). *Minecraft in the classroom: ideas, inspiration, and student projects for teachers*. Peachpit Press.

Hepplestone, S., Holden, G., Irwin, B., Parkin, H., & Thorpe, L. (2011). Using technology to encourage student engagement with feedback: A literature review. *Research in Learning Technology*, *19*(2), 117–127. doi:10.1080/21567069.2011.586677

High Fidelity. (2015). High Fidelity Inc. Retrieved from https://highfidelity.com/

Holmberg, K., & Huvila, I. (2008). Learning together apart: Distance education in a virtual world. *First Monday, 13*(10). Retrieved from http://firstmonday.org/article/view/2178/2033

Kapp, K., & O'Driscoll, T. (2010). *Learning in 3D: adding a new dimension to enterprise learning and collaboration*. Pfeiffer.

KZero. (2014). KZero Reports – Universe Charts. Retrieved from http://kzero.co.uk/

Lenhart, A., Purcell, K., Smith, A., & Zickuhr, K. (2010). Social media & mobile internet use among teens and young adults. Pew Research Center. Retrieved from http://67.192.40.213/~/media/Files/Reports/2010/PIP_Social_Media_and_Young_Adults_Report_Final_with_toplines.pdf

Lester, J. (2014). Augmented mind- The evolution of learning tools from language to immersive reality. *Keynote speech presented at the 1st International Conference on e-Learning e-Education and Online Training*. Bethesda, Maryland, United States.

Linden Lab. (2013). Infographic - 10 Years of Second Life. Retrieved from http://lindenlab.com/releases/infographic-10-years-of-second-life

Linden Lab. (2015). Mainland Pricing and Fees. Retrieved from https://secondlife.com/land/pricing.php

Macías-Díaz, A. (2008). *Survey of e-business module* (MN5553). St. Andrews University: St. Andrews, Scotland.

McArthur, V., Teather, R., & Stuerzlinger, W. (2010). Comparing 3D content creation interfaces in two virtual worlds: World of Warcraft and second life. *Journal of Gaming & Virtual Worlds*, *2*(3), 239–258. doi:10.1386/jgvw.2.3.239_1

Meskó, B. (2008). Unique medical simulation in second life! Science Roll Blog. Retrieved from http://scienceroll.com/2008/08/17/unique-medical-simulation-in-second-life/

Pew Internet. (2009). Internet, broadband, and cell phone statistics. Retrieved from http://www.distributedworkplace.com/DW/Research/Internet%20broadband%20and%20cell%20phone%20statistics%20-%20Pew%20Internet%20Report%20Jan%202010.pdf

Roehl, A., Reddy, S., & Shannon, G. (2013). The flipped classroom: An opportunity to engage millennial students through active learning strategies. *Journal of Family and Consumer Sciences*, *105*(2), 44–49. doi:10.14307/JFCS105.2.12

Salmon, G. (2009). The future for (second) life and learning. *British Journal of Educational Technology*, *40*(3), 526–538. doi:10.1111/j.1467-8535.2009.00967.x

Teoh, J. (2012). Pre-service teachers in second life: Potential of simulations. *Journal of Educational Technology Systems*, *40*(4), 415–441. doi:10.2190/ET.40.4.g

The Schome Community. (2007). The schome-NAGTY teen second life pilot final report: a summary of key findings and lessons learnt. Retrieved from http://kn.open.ac.uk/public/getfile.cfm?documentfileid-11344

Vincenti, G., & Braman, J. (2010). *Teaching through multi-user virtual environments: applying dynamic elements to the modern classroom*. Hershey, PA: Information Science Reference. doi:10.4018/978-1-61692-822-3

Vincenti, G., & Braman, J. (2011). *Multi-User virtual environments for the classroom: practical approaches to teaching in virtual worlds*. Hershey, PA: IGI Global; doi:10.4018/978-1-60960-545-2

Wagner, M. (2008). Second life's popularity rests on breadth of activities. *Information Week*. Retrieved from http://www.informationweek.com/news/personal_tech/virtualworlds/showArticle.jhtml?articleID=210602197

Wang, Y., & Braman, J. (2009). Extending the classroom through second life. *Journal of Information Systems. Special Issue: Impacts of Web 2.0 and Virtual World Technologies on IS Education, 20*(2), 235-247.

Wang, Y., Dudley, A., Braman, J., & Vincenti, G. (2009). Simulating ethical dilemmas: teaching ethics through immersive virtual environments. *Proceedings of the 12th IASTED International Conference on Computers and Advanced Technology in Education*. St. Thomas, US Virgin Islands.

Yee, N. (2006). The demographics, motivations, and derived experiences of users of massively multi-user online graphical environments. *Presence (Cambridge, Mass.)*, *15*(3), 309–329. doi:10.1162/pres.15.3.309

Zheng, B., Warschauer, M., Hwang, J. K., & Collins, P. (2014). Laptop use, interactive science software, and science learning among at-Risk students. *Journal of Science Education and Technology*, *1*(5).

ADDITIONAL READING

Aldrich, C. (2009). *Learning online with games, simulations, and virtual worlds: strategies for online instruction*. John Wiley & Sons.

Balkin, J., & Noveck, S. (2006). *The state of play: law, games, and virtual worlds*. New York University Press.

Castronova, E. (2007). *Exodus to the virtual world: how online fun is changing reality*. Palgrave Macmillan.

Corneliussen, H., & Rettberg, W. (2008). Digital culture, play, and identity: a world of warcraft reader. The MIT Press. Cambridge, Massachusetts. London, England.

Hai-Jew, S. (2010). *Virtual immersive and 3D learning spaces: emerging technologies and trends*. IGI Publishing.

Heaton, J. (2007). *Scripting recipes for second life*. Heaton Research Inc.

Hinrichs, R., & Wankel, C. (2012). *Engaging the avatar: new frontiers in immersive education*. Information Age Publishing.

Hodge, E., Collins, S., & Giordana, T. (2011). *The virtual worlds handbook: how to use second life and other 3D virtual environments*. Jones and Bartlett Publishers.

Nelson, B., & Erlandson, B. (2012). *Design for learning in virtual worlds. Interdisciplinary Approaches to Educational Technology*. Routledge.

Turkle, S. (1995). *Life on the screen: identity in the age of the internet*. New York: Simon & Schuster Paperbacks.

Wankel, C., & Kingsley, J. (2009). *Higher education in virtual worlds: teaching and learning in second life. International Perspectives on Education and Society*. Emerald Group Publishing.

Wankel, C., & Malleck, S. (2009). *Emerging ethical issues of life in virtual worlds*. Information Age Publishing.

KEY TERMS AND DEFINITIONS

Avatar: A 3D representation of a user within a virtual world. Avatars can take many shapes and forms such as a humanoid representation, animal, shape or other figure which allows the use to interact within the world and with other users.

Educational Game: A game in which the main goal is a specific learning outcome. Educational games are often used to increase student engagement.

Educational Space: A web-based, 3D or virtual representation of a classroom or learning area. In relation to virtual worlds, an educational space is often related to the 3D area used for learning which can be represented in a myriad of ways.

Multi-User Virtual Environment: Also known as a MUVE. This term can be used to describe a virtual world that can be used for a collaborative purpose where users can interact in real-time.

Second Life: A popular internet based 3D world created by Linden Labs.

Script: A set of instructions or a small program designed to carry out a specific function or task. In Second Life the Linden Scripting Language is used (LSL) to make objects interactive.

Student Engagement: Increasing student interest, focus and, or motivation for a particular learning activity.

Virtual World: A virtual world often refers to an internet based 3D or 2 ½ D environment where users can interact within the world or with other users through an avatar. Often virtual worlds are persistent environments where a large number of users can participate.

Virtual Reality: A term that can refer to a virtual representation of a scene or reality simulation in 3D. Virtual Reality can be viewed on a traditional display or using immersive VR goggles.

Social Networking Site (SNS): A website that is aimed at social interaction that often includes a public profile, ability to post user generated content and also to connect to other users.

Section 2
Virtual Reality Across Disciplines

Chapter 5
Using Second Life® for Situated and Active Learning in Teacher Education

Barbara L. Ludlow
West Virginia University, USA

Melissa D. Hartley
West Virginia University, USA

ABSTRACT

Preservice and inservice special education teachers used Second Life® as the educational platform in online courses in a graduate level distance education program. Faculty designed the virtual learning experiences to facilitate situated and active learning through the creation of a virtual campus and course-specific learning activities. The purpose of this chapter is to describe how instructors designed environments and activities to optimize learning in a three-dimensional virtual immersive environment, to report students' responses to learning in the virtual world, and to discuss the implications of virtual simulations for teacher education.

INTRODUCTION

Virtual reality applications represent a new technology for use in teacher education programs to assist prospective teachers in acquiring knowledge and skills. Constructivist theories of situated learning and active learning underlie the long-standing and widespread use of educational simulations in teacher education (Richardson, 1997) to help preservice students acquire knowledge and skills in college courses to become effective practicing teachers in their own classrooms in future years. Virtual environments offer new opportunities for creating educational simulations for these teachers-in-training (Calandra & Puvirajah, 2014) to help them acquire and practice skills through project-based activities or roleplaying exercises. The purpose of this chapter is to share how Second Life®(SL), an online virtual world, has been used to support situated and active learning in an online graduate program to prepare special education personnel.

DOI: 10.4018/978-1-4666-9837-6.ch005

BACKGROUND

Constructivist Theories of Learning

Constructivist theories of human learning have emphasized two key principles: learning must be situated and learners must be active. These principles have been widely applied in teacher education for many years and are equally applicable to face-to-face and online program models. Technology-based learning environments such as games and virtual worlds give educators new tools to promote situated and active learning, especially in online courses and programs.

Situated Learning

Situated learning refers to opportunities for the learner to acquire knowledge and skills in meaningful, often natural contexts. Constructivist learning theorists (Brown, Collins, & Duguid, 1989; Lave & Wenger, 1991) have asserted that meaningful learning does not occur through the simple transmission of information from expert to novice but rather results from a learner's co-construction of knowledge through shared experiences and interactions with others in realistic contexts. Situated learning implies that learners need opportunities to learn through being 1) "located" in a real or simulated context through a learning activity such as a project, simulation, laboratory session, or field experience, and 2) provided with opportunities to "be active" as they learn by engaging and collaborating with other learners (Cognition & Technology Group at Vanderbilt, 1993). Teacher education programs have long made extensive use of situated learning through field experiences in schools, problem-based learning activities, and educational simulations that support preservice students in learning concepts and skills related to educational practice (Korthagen, 2010).

Active Learning

Active learning refers to materials and instructions that allow the learner to manipulate objects and interact with others to acquire both physical and social information necessary to develop conceptual understanding and practical skills. Proponents of instructional practices based upon active learning recommended learning activities such as discussion, role playing exercises, case studies, and games (Bonwell & Eison, 1991). Principles of active learning have long been recommended for use at the college level to motivate and engage learners (Meyers & Jones, 1993). More recently, educators have explored how computer- and Web-based applications can be used to design technology-enabled active learning activities (Dorf et al., 2010).

Use of Virtual Environments for Active and Situated Learning

Virtual reality offers new opportunities for instructional design through the creation of learning environments (contextual settings and physical objects) and learning activities (manipulation of objects and interaction with others) that can be accessed on campus or online. Virtual reality applications can be used to design simulations that provide a game-like format that enhances motivation and engagement in learning, a three-dimensional (3D) interface that promotes immersion in the activity, and a personal avatar that enhances the sense of presence in an online environment (Dede, 2009). Virtual simulations avoid the practical constraints and ethical issues sometimes presented by real world activities and settings and allow learners access to a wider range of experiences that might not otherwise be possible (Falconer, 2013).

Virtual environments such as games and online worlds support constructivist learning principles through specially designed contexts that simulate the real world (situated learning) and avatars that enable embodied, immersive, and interactive experiences (active learning) (Dawley & Dede, 2014). They promote situated learning by allowing individuals to explore and interact within authentic and purposeful simulated contexts (Whitton & Hollins, 2008). They also promote active learning by allowing individuals at a variety of remote locations to act upon multiple media as well as collaborate online in real time through movement, text, and speech (Pantelidis, 2009). Several independent literature reviews noted that virtual environments have been used successfully for educational simulations across many fields (Hew & Chung, 2010; Kim, Lee & Thomas, 2012). Ellis, Anderson, and Kibbe (2014) argued that virtual environments may be especially appropriate for educational applications because they integrate the preferences of today's learners for digital technologies, gaming activities, and online social interactions.

Use of Second Life® for Active and Situated Learning

SL is an online virtual world that is available globally, offers free access to a personal avatar and easy-to-use software, and does not require a high degree of technical skill to navigate or design. This virtual world is the one that is most widely used in educational applications, as many colleges and universities have established a presence in-world for online learning activities (Ellis, Anderson, & Kibbe, 2014). SL has been used in higher education for hybrid and online courses, at the undergraduate and graduate levels, and across a variety of disciplines as well as in professional preparation programs in counseling, nursing and education (Wang & Burton, 2013). Cooke-Plagwitz (2009) argued that SL has three primary benefits for instruction: 1) operating in an immersive environment enables contextualized learning; 2) manipulating one's avatar promotes active learning; and 3) interacting with others in-world facilitates collaborative learning.

Jarmon (2008) indicated that SL is effective in supporting both situated and active learning in distance education because learners experience embodiment and social presence through an avatar that can be maneuvered through three-dimensional space as well as engagement and connection through opportunities for interaction and collaboration within shared experiences. Recent research reports have shown that SL has been used to support situated learning in online courses through providing an immersive environment (Falconer, 2012), increasing the sense of social presence through avatar interactions (Annetta, Folta, & Klesath, 2010), and facilitating project completion through participation in learning communities (Messer, Evans, Cownie, & Dawe, 2012). Other reports have indicated that SL also has been used to support active learning through game-like activities that enhance motivation and engagement (Schiller, Goodrich, & Gupta, 2013) as well as interaction and collaboration (Caruso, Morch, Thomassen, Hartley, & Ludlow, 2014).

A CASE STUDY OF VR IMPLEMENTATION IN ONLINE COURSE DELIVERY

Contextual Factors

A major research university, and land-grant institution, in the South has offered an online graduate program leading to initial teaching certification in special education for over a decade. This online program was designed to make training available to individuals living in rural areas near the university and is also available across the U.S. and in approved international locations. Courses are offered through Blackboard Learn 9, an online course management system that provides the platform for asynchronous activities and assessments. Blackboard Collaborate is used as the virtual classroom program for synchronous class sessions in real time. For the past four years, faculty also have incorporated SL for real time activities in courses, creating and using a private virtual island funded by the College and maintained by the department. An island in SL is defined as an island in real life; it's a piece of land surrounded by water on all sides. To date, SL has been used in six different graduate courses totaling 37 course sections, by six individual instructors, and collectively delivered to nearly 700 students.

SL was used as the educational platform for these graduate courses; in many cases, all instructional activities took place within this virtual environment, while in others, instructors also made some use of Blackboard Learn 9 and Blackboard Collaborate. Within each course, students met with the instructor weekly or bi-weekly on the college's virtual campus within SL for activities in real time but some assignments required them to access SL independently at their own convenience. Instructional design efforts focused on two categories: learning environments designed to facilitate situated learning and learning activities designed to promote active learning.

Learning Environments for Situated Learning

Learning environments that represent the critical features of real life contexts are important for situated learning (Herrington & Oliver, 2000). Therefore, one participating faculty member designed learning environments to represent typical learning spaces encountered in college settings as well as in K-12 school settings.

College Campus Environments

To engage students and simulate the experience of being in a college classroom while taking an online course, learning environments within the College's island in SL were carefully crafted, and developed over time. Since the university has two real-life physical campuses, the SL faculty designer built two campuses on the SL island. Students taking campus-based courses use the university's personal rapid transit (PRT) system to get from one campus to another; therefore, a PRT was built and scripted to transport students between the campuses in the SL island. Figure 1 presents a screenshot of a student taking the PRT to commute between campuses.

The SL faculty designer built lecture halls with display boards for interactive lecture, and a common meeting area with stadium style seating for all students to meet at the beginning of class. The SL faculty designer created the lecture halls by linking multiple boxes together, and making the interior of the boxes transparent. After multiple boxes were linked together, the textures of the outsides of the boxes were changed to make the buildings resemble the architectural style of buildings on the actual campus. Figure 2 presents a screenshot of a lecture hall.

Figure 1.

The SL faculty designer also built small group buildings for group work within courses. The small group buildings were positioned so that they were 60 meters apart to minimize conversation interference between groups during group work. Inside the small group buildings, an oval table is available for formal group work, and a comfortable seating area is provided for informal group work. Picture frames were hung around the room for including student photos in each of the group buildings. Students could choose to display photos of themselves, their family, their pets, or any photos they would like to share with their colleagues. Figure 3 is a screenshot showing students working within a small group building.

The SL faculty designer created an SL skill practice tutorial area so that students could become proficient in the skills they would need to use this technology for course activities. The skills included in the practice area were using object view, buying content from a box, retrieving an item from one's

Figure 2.

Figure 3.

inventory, creating a notecard, and sharing a notecard. Using object view involved zooming in on an object to have a better view. For example, when students were viewing the presentation slides on display boards, it helped to zoom in if their avatar was standing behind other students or toward the back of the classroom. Buying content from a box involved right clicking on the box and selecting buy. Once the contents of the box were purchased (for free), the students could locate the content within their inventory in world. Inventory is defined as an archiving of materials one has acquired, much like the download folder in one's computer, and retrieving an item from one's inventory involved opening the inventory and finding the material within a folder. The most common item to retrieve from one's inventory during class was a notecard. Notecards are similar to a Microsoft Word document with only text features, where one can read typed information. In addition to reading content from a notecard, students were also asked to create notecards. One way to create a notecard involved clicking, "Create notecard" in the drop down menu of one's inventory; however, there are many routes to creating a notecard. Lastly, sharing a notecard involved right clicking the notecard, selecting share, and then selecting the individual (avatar name) with whom one would like to share the notecard. However, there are also many different routes to sharing a notecard. Students were asked to practice using these skills in the practice area because these were skills that were typically used in class. Students used object view to see the display boards with the presentation slides when other students' avatars were standing in their line of vision. Students purchased boxes, for $0 Linden dollars (the virtual in-world currency) to obtain the materials for the class session. In order to review the materials purchased from the box, students needed to know how to retrieve the materials from the boxes within their inventory. Finally, students needed to know how to create and send notecards in order to share the information they learned with their instructor.

The college's island was private; therefore, faculty instructors sent students an invitation to join the group accompanied with a landmark for the island. A landmark is defined as a location with coordinates. It could be compared to sending someone else one's location using a "pin" with an iPhone. Once students accepted the group invitation, they could use the landmark to teleport to the virtual College island.

K-12 School Environments

In addition to planning the space on the island for the campuses, the faculty designer also created a primary school on the campus. When students entered the primary school, they were greeted and asked to proceed to the main office. Once they walked over to the main office, their attendance was logged and they received a visitor badge. The primary school was designed for students to practice and engage in instructional activities with K-12 student bots (scripted objects built to resemble students) independent of class time. Within the primary school there was a kindergarten classroom, two resource rooms, a third grade classroom and a fifth grade classroom. Within each classroom, there was a teacher's desk, an area for small group work with a kidney table and chairs, and desks for independent seatwork. Each classroom had a chalkboard and wall decorations that would be appropriate for the age level of the classroom. Within the resource room, there was a file cabinet that included the present level statements for student bots with disabilities. Students could click on the file cabinet drawer they would like to open and obtain a notecard with the present level statement for any students whose name began with the letters reflected on the drawer. The resource room contained a kidney table for small group learning, student desks for independent learning, and a chalkboard. The wall decorations in the room were reflective of the content for the assignments students would be working on in the resource room.

The learning environments on the virtual college campus were designed to facilitate interaction and collaboration as well as skill acquisition, maintenance, and refinement. The primary school was designed for students to practice skills needed by K-12 teachers. The main classrooms were designed for interactive lecture and the small group buildings were designed to facilitate group work without interruption. While these virtual environments were important for facilitating learning and collaboration within a virtual world, the design of activities to promote active learning were critical to addressing the content of each course

Active Learning

Faculty instructors designed the activities within each course to promote active learning. A typical class session included five activity components: begin with an activator, review the activator, deliver an interactive lecture, conduct individual activities, oversee a group activity, and debrief. Figure 4 presents a screenshot of students participating in interactive lecture. During each session, students manipulated objects within SL, interacted with others, and collaborated with others.

Figure 4.

Manipulation of Objects

Within the virtual class sessions, students manipulated objects on a regular basis to acquire information. For example, once on the virtual College island, students teleported to buildings for their specific courses or to K-12 classrooms as required for specific learning activities. In order to teleport to the classrooms, students touched an object and selected *Teleport* from the drop down options. Once inside the classrooms, students navigated the areas by moving their avatars.

Students also manipulated objects through the use of boxes to share information. Depending upon the type of information needed, the instructors shared information through notecards or textures. Notecards were contained within boxes while textures were used to upload and post images, including presentation slides (i.e., PowerPoint or Keynote). Students bought boxes ($0L) to obtain the notecards. To buy the boxes, students touched the boxes and selected buy and then retrieved the notecard(s) from their inventory. After retrieving the notecard(s) from their inventory, students reviewed the information on the notecard(s). After completing the activity on the notecard, students created their own notecard to share their information with the instructor.

In addition to manipulating objects for everyday learning activities, three new activities involving manipulating objects were created. These new activities included: 1) how students accessed the private island, 2) how students were oriented to the learning space, and 3) an activity on classroom configuration.

The first new activity involved how students accessed the virtual private island. In the past, class time was reserved for access and orientation to the College's virtual island; however, faculty wanted to see if students could access the private island independently to maximize class time for learning course content. Since the college's virtual island is private, students previously met the instructor in an area called SPED Retreat on the first SL class session. SPED Retreat was the personal property that accompanied the purchase of a premium avatar and was decorated to look less like a personal residence and more like an office. A handout, with screenshots and detailed directions on how to accept the group's invitation, was given to students through the course management system prior to the first meeting in SL. Once class began, the instructor sent students the invitations during the live class session in case there were any problems with accepting the invitation. Students purchased the landmark for the virtual private island from a box in SPED Retreat for free, and then teleported to the island once they accepted the invitation. This process took approximately 15-30 minutes depending upon the size of the class. Faculty sent the invitations during a live class session because there were concerns that new students may struggle with accepting the invitation and teleporting to the island. However, after nine semesters of sending the invitations during the first class session, faculty decided to send the invitations to students outside of class time. Students were given the same handout, and an additional handout was created to provide directions on how to teleport to the island once students were sent the landmark. Faculty were concerned that students would struggle; however, when talking with a student who was new to SL, the student said, "This has been the easiest part so far."

The second new activity was orienting students to the learning space through experiencing an independent virtual scavenger hunt for the College island orientation. In early semesters of using SL, students were given an orientation to the island during the first class session. After everyone had accepted the group invitation and teleported to the island, the instructor would lead the class through an orientation of the virtual campus. After nine semesters of using class time for the orientation to the campus, faculty decided to create an individual activity where students would acclimate themselves to the virtual campus through a scavenger hunt led by a student bot. When students first arrived at the virtual island, they were greeted by, Marcus, the student bot. Students bought a notecard from Marcus ($0), by clicking on the box on his desk, which contained the directions to the scavenger hunt. The scavenger hunt led students to the tutorial area within the island where they could practice skills regularly used in class, such as object view, buying a box, creating a notecard, retrieving a notecard from one's inventory, and submitting a notecard. After students finished practicing procedural skills in the tutorial area, Marcus prompted them to use the PRT for transportation to the virtual Evansdale campus. To take the PRT, students clicked on the PRT, and selected "teleport" from the drop down menu. When students arrived at the Evansdale campus, Marcus prompted them to enter the Main Classroom and have a seat. The Main Classroom was the area where students would meet for their first class session. To earn credit for participating in the scavenger hunt, students chose to either take screenshots of their avatar practicing the skill, or they created a video of their avatar demonstrating the skills. Faculty were concerned that students may prefer having faculty lead the orientation to the campus. However, one student shared that they preferred completing the orientation independently because they could work at their own pace. The student had taken previous courses in SL where the faculty led the orientation and they felt like they had to rush to keep up with the group; however, during the independent orientation this factor was removed.

Finally, the last newly created activity regarding the manipulation of objects involved planning and implementing classroom configuration. The classroom configuration activity took place within a virtual classroom inside of the virtual Primary School. When students approached the classroom they had the choice between two classroom configuration activities: Assignment A and Assignment B.

For Assignment A, students were given the following scenario, "It is the beginning of the school year, and your task is to arrange your classroom to increase student participation. Your teaching style includes a lot of group work and discussion." Students were also given the following information, "Please arrange the following: 12 student desks, 5 chairs, teacher desk, waste basket, small group table, and computer desk with computer. Please go to the following URL for a video tutorial on how to rearrange the furniture in your room. https://www.youtube.com/watch?v=AolhYGP0xMY" . In addition to the information about the furniture in the room, and a video tutorial on how to move objects in SL, students were also asked to return the furniture to the way they found it when they entered, and were given this task, " Rearrange the classroom & take a screenshot (or multiple if needed) to show how you would arrange the classroom. Please use your text, or additional sources, to support your classroom arrangement to increase participation and facilitate both group work and discussions. Create one word document with the screenshots and your justification."

For Assignment B, students were given the following scenario, "It's the 2nd week of school, and the arrangement of the classroom has been problematic. Your task is to arrange the classroom to optimize independent work & to decide where students should sit." In addition to the scenario, they were given the following names of fictitious students, Jenny, Brian, Sophia, Natalie, Oliver, Olivia, Liam, Carisa, Marcus, Joe, Harper, and Jackson. Students were also given the following additional information to assist them in completing the task, "Olivia and Liam are constantly fighting. Liam picks on Olivia every chance he gets. Carisa is disruptive and is constantly getting out of her seat. She has one non-content related talk out every 9 seconds. Marcus and Joe are friends and like to have side conversations. Harper is easily distracted. Jackson loves to read." They were also given the following task, "Rearrange the classroom & decide where students should sit. Create a Word document with a screenshot showing your classroom arrangement. Then label a screenshot showing where you would have each student sit based upon the additional information. Here is a video tutorial on how to move objects in SL: https://www.youtube.com/watch?v=AolhYGP0xMY"

After selecting Activity A or B, students walked into the classroom where there were 12 desks with chairs, 5 chairs, a teacher desk, a wastebasket, a small group table, and a computer table with a computer all in the middle of the room. After watching a faculty-created video tutorial on how to move objects in SL, students moved the furniture in the room based upon the scenario in the assignment they selected, and then wrote a paper justifying their selection with literature to support their selection.

A Classroom Configuration Activity was offered as a bonus activity to 31 students, of which 12 students completed the activity for bonus points. Graduate student responses to the Classroom Configuration Activity demonstrated their understanding of the importance of classroom configuration in facilitating collaborative learning experiences for K-12 students. One graduate student highlighted evidenced-based practices within his response. Please see Figure 5 for a screenshot of the way this graduate student rearranged his classroom and the classroom reference in his response.

In an effort to increase the participation given my teaching style much of the instruction will take place in the view from picture B. By setting up the 12 desks (the group of 2 would be 4 if there were enough desks in the room.) It allows flexibility of assignments. It allows the use of jigsaw learning, peer tutoring, and the ability to differentiate instruction by group by giving modified assignments to each group that will help accomplish the learning objective. This set up also allows for group debate and instruction. By having this layout it afford me the ability to quickly teach mini lessons to a group that may be struggling. Being close to the chalkboard also allows for information to be shared quickly for guided notes, or "do now" strategies. By using this lay out it would be easy to accomplish, choral response, lecture, class discussions moderated by the teacher, discussion groups, committee report, reading assignments.

Another graduate student also highlighted evidenced-based practices in her decisions for configuring the classroom to promote collaboration.

Figure 5.

I used two Internet sources to influence my classroom layout. On the website http://www.learningandteaching.info/teaching/layout.htm, the author, J.S. Atherton, discussed ideal configurations for varying types of teaching/learning styles. Atherton indicated that for whole group discussion, a U shaped set-up was beneficial and for group work, "tables" were the best option. In the article Seating arrangements that promote positive academic and behavioural outcomes: a review of empirical research, authors Rachel Wannarka And Kathy Ruhl discuss the benefits of rows for behavior management, but acknowledge that grouped seating is useful for collaborative work.

Students are grouped in U shaped "tables" consisting of 4 to 5 seats per group. This will promote conversation during collaborative tasks and for assignments in which students need to share materials, the desks could be pushed together to form a more traditional table shape.

While student responses varied in how they would organize the classroom, each response demonstrated understanding of how to organize a space to facilitate collaboration.

Interaction with Others

Within virtual class sessions, many learning activities were designed to facilitate interaction. Through the design of activities specific to each course, students were expected to interact with both their peers and faculty-created student bots.

Interacting with Peers

During class sessions, students interacted with either their instructor or their peers for approximately 90% of the class session. During the interactive lecture, students completed individual activities related to course content. During these individual activities, students were asked to apply the content that was learned and/or make a personal connection to the content that was learned. An example of an individual activity in the graduate collaboration course included evaluating the professional tone of email exchanges. An example of an individual activity in the mathematics course included determining the types of problems to include on a curriculum-based assessment after reviewing grade level Common Core standards, which are national educational standards for K-12 students.

After students finished their independent work, they were asked to share their work, or ideas, with their peers. Faculty led the debriefing and called on students to share their work; students typically shared their thoughts orally. After students were finished sharing, the class returned to the interactive lecture, participating through the SL chat text feature. While students could respond by speaking during the interactive lecture, a large majority of students chose to type their responses during the lecture.

In addition to interactive lecture, students also interacted with one another during small group activities. Students worked with the same group throughout the semester, and self-selected their group at the beginning of the semester based upon common interests for the specific class they were taking (i.e. disability category, level of mathematics, etc.). To facilitate the group selection process, the course faculty created display boards to show the special education categories (i.e. Vision, Gifted, Autism, Multicategorical K-6, Multicategorical 5-Adult), and asked that students walk over to the display board showing the area where they were working toward certification. Students were asked to join another group if the group already had five people in it. Students could see how many people were in the group by looking at how many avatars were standing in front of the display boards.

Each class session had 45 minutes to one hour dedicated for completion of small group activities. During this time, students role-played to practice skills, worked through case studies, and used their knowledge from their text and other sources to solve common problems in K-12 teacher experience. In order to encourage collaboration, students were asked to solve problems that would be difficult or time consuming to solve independently, or they were asked to practice skills that would require role-playing.

Many students enjoyed interacting with their instructor and peers through SL as demonstrated in the following student reflections:

I appreciate use of the Second Life environment; as a result, I believe this has been my MOST interactive and "inclusive-feeling" online course EVER! It was very powerful to be able to "see" my colleagues and work in small groups with them. I look forward to future classes offered in the Second Life medium.

I love Second Life. I feel like I am really in the classroom.

I learned I a lot during this class and the way we were able to interact with each other and the Second Life program was very interesting.

Second Life is an amazing idea to help in collaboration and also to make me feel like I was actually a part of a group.

I had never used Second Life for any class. However, I have had other instructors require group work without Second Life. The SL program made this class more like a traditional class. Even though I had to get used to the program in the beginning, I felt that SL was a benefit especially to this class.

Out of all the classes I have taken online this was the class that made me feel most like a student in a traditional classroom because of Second

Life. -Interacting with Student Bots

Students not only interacted with one another, but they also interacted with newly faculty-created student bots. There were six student bots with special needs, and 12 general education student bots. Each bot was created to have his/her own personality and had accompanying background information. The bots with special needs had present level statements to let the graduate students know their current levels of academic performance. Each bot was scripted to respond to common academic phrases (i.e. please take out your homework). The bots were scripted using a free scripts available online, and through creation of an accompanying notecard as a "brain" for each bot. The notecard and the script were then added to each bot by dragging each to the content area of the bot. The brain of the bot was created to respond to keywords. Each bot was programmed to respond differently. In addition to the types of responses the bots could give, the bots were also programmed to respond freely a certain percentage of time. This meant that the bots would respond when not called upon directly. Each bot was given a different percentage for his or her free response based upon his/her personality. Due to the ability to respond freely, without being called upon, faculty decided to create learning activities that were graduated in the number of bots with whom the students would work. This decision was made to minimize the anxiety level of graduate students when first working with the bots. Learning activities, incorporating the student bots, were created to transition the graduate students from working with a small number of bots to a larger number of bots. The first activity involved two bots, the second activity involved four bots, and then students could gradually work up to working with the inclusion classroom with all 18 bots. It was hypothesized that beginning with 18 bots could be overwhelming.

To pilot working with the newly created bots, activities were created for 25 graduate students taking a course on how to teach mathematics to students with disabilities. The graduate students began by working in the resource room with two student bots. The resource room activity involved re-teaching mathematics content to the student bots. Before they entered the resource room, graduate students selected the activity, by clicking a box, and reviewed the accompanying notecard.

The students could choose from activities pertaining to topics such as, Factors, Greatest Common Factor, Least Common Multiples, and Algebraic Expressions. The notecards for the activities included the Common Core Standard for the activity, the session objective, and the materials needed to complete it. Students then entered the classroom and walked to the file cabinet to retrieve the students' present levels of academic performance. Following is an example of a present levels statement for Monique, one of the bots in the Resource Room.

Monique is a 13 year old student in 7th grade and is diagnosed with a learning disability. She enjoys reading, watching movies, shopping, and dancing. Monique is very enthusiastic and cares about her school work. She is currently placed in the general education classroom.

When informally assessed with the Math Grade Level Test, Monique scored 16/28 correct, or a 5.0 grade equivalent level (performing at the same level as a student entering the 5th grade).

Monique can multiply two single digit whole numbers (1/1), but struggles with multiplying decimals or single digit numbers by double or triple digit numbers (0/2). She cannot divide double or triple digit numbers by single or double digit numbers (0/2) and incorrectly identified a division sign as a subtraction sign in one problem. Monique struggles with adding, subtracting, multiplying, and dividing fractions or mixed numbers (0/4). She cannot convert between units, although she is able to do so with the assistance of a conversion chart. These difficulties in math inhibit Monique's progress in the general curriculum.

Monique was informally assessed using the Phonological Awareness Inventory and scored 2/3 on rhyme identification, 3/3 on rhyme production, 3/3 on syllable blending, 2/3 on syllable segmentation, 3/3 on syllable deletion, 3/3 on phoneme identification, 3/3 on phoneme isolation (initial), 3/3 on phoneme isolation (final), 3/3 on phoneme blending, and 3/3 on phoneme segmentation. Although mistakes were made on rhyme identification and syllable segmentation, it is not believed that the errors are significant or are inhibiting her reading or comprehension skills.

Monique was informally assessed using the Word ID Fluency Test and scored 30/40 correctly, or a 3.4 grade level equivalent (performing at the same level as a student in the fourth month of the 3rd grade).

Her errors included the omission of letter sounds, especially vowel-consonant-e-syllable words, such as saying "priss" instead of "price" and "futter" instead of "future." She also omitted other letter sounds, such as the "i" in "tailor," saying "taller" instead. Monique made substitutions in letter sounds, such as saying "errand" instead of "around" and "sint" instead of "since." In some cases she reversed sounds by saying "year" instead of "every" and "sever" instead of "served." Monique's disability impacts her involvement in general education by affecting her reading comprehension due to lack of knowledge of word identification skills.

When informally assessed with the Reading Comprehension Grade Level Test, Monique successfully completed the 3rd grade level assessment. She showed text-implicit comprehension by forming opinions and making predictions and showed script-implicit comprehension by relating to the text verbally as she read.

Monique's errors included text-explicit reading comprehension errors, such as incorrectly identifying characters, items, or characters' actions that were directly stated in the text.

Monique's difficulties in recalling information from text through text-explicit comprehension inhibits her progress in the general curriculum.

After reviewing the virtual students' present levels, the graduate students decided which instructional strategies they would use to reteach the information in the activity. When the student bots made errors, the graduate students were asked to determine the type of error that was made (procedural, conceptual, declarative) and what instructional strategies would be most effective for that type of error.

Many students entered the Resource Room and practiced working with the bots before the assignment was due. During the beginning of a class session, students expressed their concerns that no matter how many different strategies they used to reteach the bots that the bots could not get the answers correct. The students were concerned that their grades would be impacted by their inability to get correct responses from the bots. This was a very interesting and unexpected consequence of the activity. Students personalized the bots and attributed human-like characteristics to the bots in that they thought that if they only taught them better the bots would learn, much like real children in real life.

For the assignment, students interacted with the bots through chat text. See Figure 6 for an example of a student working with the bots in the resource room. To use chat text in SL, one types his/her comments in the chat section of the screen. The bots were scripted to respond to keywords that would be common in a math lesson; however, the graduate students were not given the keywords that would assist them in getting a mathematical response from the bots. The bots were scripted to say statements when

Figure 6.

their "brain" did not understand what was being said to them. For example, one bot may say, "I don't understand" while another bot may say, "This is stupid." when he/she did not understand. In order for the graduate students to get a response from the bots, they often had to think of multiple ways to ask the same question because their original question did not include a keyword. Graduate students were not given the keywords for interacting with the bots.

Through interacting with the bots, students were able to apply skills of identifying the types of mathematical errors, and in using evidenced-based teaching strategies as a practice prior to working with children in real life, as is demonstrated in this student's answer to the activity.

When I worked with Vince, I asked him to give me the answer to 2x-3y when x=2 and y=1 he replied "5", when the correct answer is 1. I asked him to give me the answer to question 2, which is "4w+2z when w=-2 and z=5" and he replied "4" when the correct answer is 2. Based on this information, I believe that Vince is making a conceptual error. The reason I believe that it is a conceptual error with Vince is because I don't think Vince understands the concept of substituting a number in for a variable and then multiplying those two numbers together then adding the products together. I believe that Vince is merely guessing at what the correct answer is, which is common with students who do not have conceptual knowledge.

When I worked with Monique, I asked her to give me the answer to 2x-3y when x=2 and y=1 and she replied "260". I asked her to give me the answer to problem 2, which is "4w+2z when w=-2 and z=5" and she replied "152" and the correct answer is 2. Based on this information, I believe that Monique also has a conceptual problem, because I believe that she does not understand the concepts of substituting in the numbers for the variables, multiplying and then adding the two products together. I believe that she is guessing her answers to the problem, which is common when students have a conceptual error. I believe that Monique is guessing really high numbers because she believes that larger numbers would make more sense with these problems given that it is algebra and the problems appear to be long.

The strategy that I have selected to use with Vince and Monique is the graphic advance organizer– modeling "I do" – group guided practice "we do"– independent practice strategy "you do". I chose this strategy because the graphic advanced organizer will give Vince & Monique a better understanding of the concepts of adding, subtracting and multiplying because it will include a pictorial representation of adding, subtracting and multiplying as well as a written form of the problem. With this information readily available for them to use, I feel that the most effective way to reteach this to them would be to first model how to solve these problems, providing both visual demonstration and oral explanation. I would model the first problem for them, giving them an idea of what the problem is asking us to do and what each number and variable in the problem is representing. The next step in the strategy would be to do group guided practice, which means that I will prompt Vince on what the problem means, and how we go about solving it. I will ask him questions on how to start and what to do next, and guide him through the process of solving the problem. We will solve problems 2 and 3 using group guided practice, the first one will be with Vince and the second one will be with Monique. The last part of the strategy is independent practice, which is where Vince and Monique will take the knowledge they (hopefully) gained from the modeling and group guided practice and will use it to solve problems 3-6. I feel that this strategy is the best to use with them so that he can learn to solve these types of algebraic problems.

The graduate student's response demonstrated his ability to determine the type of errors the bots were making and his justification for the determination. The strategy selected demonstrated the student's ability to select a strategy appropriate for remediating conceptual errors, and his response detailed how he would execute the use of the strategy. This level of application demonstrates understanding of how to apply the skills learned from the text.

In addition to demonstrating their ability to apply important skills in teaching mathematics, several themes emerged when reviewing students' reflections on experiences in working in the resource room with the student bots. An interesting, and unintentional consequence of working with bots that were programmed by keywords was that students had to construct their questions in ways that would elicit a response from the bots without knowing the keywords. Since the graduate students did not know the keywords, they often had to rephrase their questions in different ways in order to get a response from the bots. This was evident in the following student reflections.

The experience made me question myself and really made me think about what questions to ask and how to ask them. I realize that I need to apply this more in my classroom and I think that is one of the reasons that you asked us to write this reflection.

I thought this was an interesting experience. It made me think about my own teaching and not just recognizing that my students made a mistake. It is more effective to figure out what kind of mistake your students are making and pick a strategy that will help them more specifically with their errors. Working with the bots was a bit frustrating at times because they wouldn't respond to the question you were asking, but after I thought about it that is also pretty true to real life. There are many times that I ask my own students something and they do not respond in a way that answers my question. In times like that you have to learn to be patient and figure out a different approach to get a desired response. After you have established that they have answered the intended question then you begin working on finding their errors and helping them correct those.

I also believe that you wanted us to work with the bots for our own experience. We had to try different terminologies, ask questions in different ways, feel frustration when things don't go how we expect them to, and resign ourselves to the fact that students (real or virtual) don't always understand what you are trying to explain, no matter how hard you try.

The ability to rephrase questions in multiple ways is an important skill for a special education teacher because students often need questions rephrased in order to understand. If students do not understand the question being asked of them, they will mostly likely be unable to solve the problem; therefore, it is important that future teachers be able to ask questions in a variety of ways to engage all learners.

Another theme that emerged from this experience involved students' comfort level with teaching mathematics involved in the lesson. Many students were not comfortable with teaching mathematics content because they did not plan on nor want to be mathematics teachers, and many students felt completely comfortable with the content. Unlike general education where teachers are certified in one content area, in special education, teachers are typically certified by disability category groups (i.e. mild/moderate, moderate/severe, etc.), and then they complete content area endorsements (i.e. English, math, science, social studies). While certification requirements vary by geographic location, typically once at a school site, special education teachers have some degree of choice in the content area where they would be teaching. Therefore, individuals who do not have a strong background in mathematics could choose to work in other areas once they obtain a position. However, all candidates in this graduate program must complete the course on how to teach mathematics to students with disabilities. The following comments demonstrate the theme of comfort level in teaching mathematics.

The Resource Room activity was very interesting. I do not have a strong math background, so I am a little apprehensive when it comes to teaching math.

For the resource room activity, I chose the greatest common factor assignment. This is a skill that I find myself teaching and re-teaching on a regular basis. I feel very comfortable with my ability to teach this mathematical skill.

For the students who did not feel comfortable teaching mathematics, several shared that working with the bots made them feel more comfortable. The students shared that working with the bots before working with real children made them feel more comfortable in their ability to teach the skills.

Working with the bots allowed me to practice teaching without totally confusing an actual student.

This enabled us to be able to get through feeling uncomfortable and better know how to approach and reteach strategies despite obstacles we may have personally with the subject matter.

It helped in becoming more comfortable in asking questions related to math and how to word and approach the questions. It was also nice to be able to practice before having a larger assignment for those who do not work with students in the math classroom or resource room on regular basis.

There were many learning experiences in piloting the bots, which will be discussed later in the chapter; however, the overall sentiment was that many students enjoyed working with the bots. The following excerpts reflect segments of student reflections on working with the bots in the Resource Room.

Overall, I really enjoyed working with the bots in SL to complete this assignment, because it really did feel like I was working with real students. I think it provides a good opportunity to really think about the types of errors students make, and provides a good opportunity to try to identify the error and find a strategy to try and correct the error. It provides us with good practice in a real life situation. It took words from a textbook and helped us actually apply the ideas, which for me, helps me to really learn what the text is trying to teach.

I was very nervous about starting this activity, which is probably why I waited so long to do it, after I got into the room and started chatting with Vince and Monique I started to relax. Vince and Monique did react like some of the children in my classroom and I was very comfortable with teaching math because I am a math resource teacher.

Overall, I really did enjoy this activity. After hearing most of the other students in our class talk about it, I was very nervous going into the activity. I was pleased that I could actually get the bots to respond with mathematical answers; I had more fun with Monique.

I also like the idea of doing this with bots, instead of real students because I could imagine the insecurities I would feel.

Regardless of enjoyment of the experience, it is pertinent that preservice and inservice special education teachers are able to identify student errors in mathematics and know the evidenced-based strategies that will best remediate the error. While students can read about the types of errors students make in a textbook, it is very different from actually working with a student and determining the types of errors he/she is making during live time. A different level of skill application is involved to be able to determine student errors at a level of automaticity. While the mathematics activities in the resource room were new, it is the intention that graduate students working with the bots will be able to determine the types of errors the bots are making at a level of automaticity by the end of a semester. It is not the expectation that bots will replace working with real children in field experiences; however, it is the hope that practice will the bots in simulations will improve the experiences students have when applying their skills in K-12 schools.

After students completed the activities in the resource room, faculty were ready to pilot the use of a small group of bots at one time. Since students had successfully worked with two bots, faculty were interested in seeing how students would interact with four bots at one time. The activity with the small group of bots was offered as a bonus activity in three graduate courses with the possibility for 56 participants. The bonus activity was offered one week in advance to the due date toward the beginning of the academic semester. One student participated in the bonus activity with the small group of bots.

The small group activity included four bots and language arts curriculum. Graduate students were asked to select an activity by clicking a box, and then were given a notecard. The notecards included the common core standard for the activity, the session objective, and a lesson plan. Students were then asked to teach the lesson to the small group of student bots and assist them with any areas of need. The bots were programmed to respond to keywords, just as they were with the math bots, but they were programmed to respond to keywords for a language arts lesson. For this activity, students were given a specific lesson plan; therefore, the bots were programmed specifically for this lesson. The following is an example of the student's response to the activity.

Before working with the bots, I reviewed each students' present level of performance. All 4 students had a deficiency in reading. Two of the students' reports (Carisa, Marcus) specifically stated that their deficiency was related to decoding. I focused much of the time on conceptual understanding. Before the students could determine the difference between a sentence and a sentence fragment, they needed to understand the format of a sentence, subject and verb. I took it back one step further and reviewed the definitions of a subject and a verb are to ensure they had full understanding before moving forward. After reviewing the basic knowledge of subject/verb, I went through the activity page #1, sentence by sentence, to determine if it was a sentence or a sentence fragment.

I felt more comfortable working with the bots for this assignment than the previous assignment. I felt like I had more realistic expectations of what to expect from the bots this time. I ignored negative behaviors and continued teaching/reviewing the lesson. I also did not become frustrated by the bots' lack of correct answers because my expectations were more realistic toward what they could answer. Although I felt more comfortable with the bots this time, I felt more comfortable teaching the algebraic expression assignment than this assignment.

Figure 7.

The student's response demonstrates the important practice of reviewing students with disabilities present levels of performance from their Individualized Education Plan (IEP) before beginning instruction. Reviewing students' present levels of performance assists the special education teacher in knowing the strengths and areas of need of the student. The student's response also shows that in working with the bots for a second activity, she felt more comfortable in working with them. See Figure 7 for a screenshot of the graduate student working with the four student bots. Further investigation will be needed to determine specific reasons for the increased level of ease in working with the bots.

Once students have completed the activities with the small group of student bots, they would be ready to proceed to the classroom with 18 student bots. For this activity, students would create their own lesson plan, and submit it to faculty. Faculty would then program the bots' responses so that they are customized to the graduate student's lesson. At this point in time, the classroom with 18 bots has only been used by faculty for demonstration purposes.

Collaboration with Others

Learning activities were also designed to facilitate collaboration among graduate students. In addition to small group activities during class sessions with interactive lecture, there were also four collaborative sessions throughout the semester where students work together to solve problems. During these collaborative sessions, students were given the full class session to work collaboratively to solve a problem. The problems assigned were ones that would be difficult for a student to solve independently due to either the size of the project or the need for a variety of skills. To facilitate collaboration, students began the first collaborative session by showing their group members the photo they submitted that is hanging in their small group building, and discussing it. After each student shared their photo(s), they discussed each member's strengths, group norms, and created goals. After this introductory activity, students began their first problem solving activity. Students worked collaboratively, to complete activities, during each class session for the remainder of the semester. Across multiple courses students found that the collaborative activities were helpful to their skill acquisition as related to working with students with disabilities. In the course evaluation of instruction, when responding to the question, "Did collaboratively completing the group activities increase your understanding of the content for that session and ability to demonstrate the skills requested?" students stated that working collaboratively assisted them with the course content, as can be seen in the following comments.

I think that meeting for the group activities was beneficial to increasing understanding of content. The collaborative work helped us to share ideas and learn new methods that we were not previously familiar with.

I believe that collaboratively completing the group activities was very beneficial to the assignment. We had students in our group that had experience in the field and some that were brand new so I believe we worked together in order to succeed.

Yes, because we all learned from each other. Each person also had a role within the group, and that helped keep the groups sessions organized and moving along.

Working in groups helped me to use my own knowledge and my teammates knowledge to correctly complete activities. If I wasn't sure about something, it really helped to have others to rely on.

Yes, I enjoy having group time that is more like a group instead of having to coordinate e-mails for a group project, which I have had to do before and it was not fun. I enjoyed getting to know others in my class and felt we had a great relationship and were able to work well together. This helped us talk about the concepts and each share our ideas to get a better understanding of the concepts.

Using SL as the educational platform for distance education courses promoted collaboration, as students could "see" one another and interacted much like they would do so in a campus-based classroom. Students also responded to questions involving collaboration quantitatively in anonymous course evaluations. The questions had a five-point Likert-type scale with responses including (1) *rarely*, (2) *seldom*, (3) *usually*, (4) *frequently*, and (5) *always*. Of the 700 students who participated in 37 course sections, 122 students anonymously responding to the prompt, "collaborative problem solving and teamwork were encouraged via technologies," 93% (n= 113) of students felt that using SL as the educational platform *always* encouraged collaboration and teamwork. The remaining students (how many) felt that SL *frequently* (n = 7) encouraged collaboration or *usually* (n =2) encouraged collaboration. There were not any students who responded that the use of SL as the educational platform for the course *seldom* or *rarely* encouraged collaborative problem solving or teamwork. The mean score for student responses to this prompt was 4.91, on a five-point scale, demonstrating that a large majority of students indicated that the use of SL as the educational platform for their course encouraged collaboration.

Using the same Likert-type scale, students also responded to the prompt, "Even though we were not physically together in a traditional classroom, I still felt like I was part of a group in the online course." In response to this prompt, 77% (n = 94) of students reported that they *always* felt like they were part of a group using SL as the educational platform for their course, and 13% (n = 16) of students *frequently* felt like part of a group. Therefore, 90% of the students indicated they were *frequently* or *always* part of a group when using the virtual reality for the educational platform in their online course. The remaining students stated that they *usually* (n = 7), *seldom* (n = 3), or *rarely* (n = 1) felt like they were a part of a group when using SL as the educational platform for their online course. The mean score for student responses to this prompt was 4.61, on a five-point scale, demonstrating that a large majority of students responded that they were part of a group even though they were not physically together within a traditional classroom.

SOLUTIONS AND RECOMMENDATIONS

When developing an academic virtual world for the purpose of increasing the skill base of students, it is important to assess/review what worked and what did not work to meet established learning goals. Such a process has been integral to implementing the use of SL in graduate courses for students completing coursework for special education certification. The solutions and recommendations will be discussed within the two categories of instructional design: learning environments for situated learning and learning activities to promote active learning.

Learning Environments

Learning environments should include a skill practice area for students who are new to learning SL, simulate campus-based buildings and classrooms to facilitate instruction, and simulate other environments, such s K-12 classrooms, to provide practice in different contexts. There is a learning curve when learning to use SL, and it is important that the skills needed to access and share information during class are made explicit to students. It is also important to include the skills in a beginning assignment to ensure that students practice the skills. Spaces for educational simulations (i.e., working with K-12 students), should replicate the real life space to the extent possible to provide a life-like context that will promote learning and generalization. While the bots in the pilot study did not always respond like real children, the space looked like a resource room does in a real life school, which resulted in students' feelings of the experience being life-like.

Learning Activities

The recommendations and solutions related to active learning will be discussed within three areas: manipulation of objects, interaction with others, and collaboration with others.

Manipulation of Objects

After 10 semesters of using SL as the educational platform for online courses, it is highly recommended that invitations to the virtual private island and orientation to the learning spaces occur independent of class time. Not only do students prefer it, but it also eliminates the need to address information not directly related to course content during class time. When students completed these activities outside of class time, faculty could devote the first class session in SL to learning course content.

Another area where faculty gained knowledge, involved the classroom configuration activity where students organized the furniture within the room to facilitate different activities based on a case scenario given. Due to everyone having the ability to move the objects within the room and the college being on an island, there were desks in the ocean, and in other rooms of the building because students had lost control of the item and moved it outside of the room. When students need to demonstrate conceptual understanding through the manipulation of physical objects, it is recommended that instructors either script the objects to return to a certain location after a specified amount of time, or make the walls to the room fixed, instead of permeable, to make it impossible for objects to be removed from the room. While instructors were initially concerned that students who were new to SL would lack the skills necessary to move objects for the activity, that was not the case. With a set of instructions and a brief video, which merely included screenshots, students were able to move the objects in the classroom before their second class session in SL was held. Since students had only had one prior class session in SL, this is worth mentioning because if the assignment had been given at the end of the semester, students would have felt much more comfortable completing the assignment. In addition to the learning opportunities surrounding active learning involving the manipulation of objects, instructors also learned from activities involving interactions with others.

Interaction with Others

Students enjoyed using SL as the educational platform for distance education courses. Furthermore, students stated that they enjoyed interacting with their peers in Second Life, and that interacting with their peers within SL made their class experience feel like they were in a traditional campus-based class. It is recommended that studies involving student preference between types of platforms used within distance education, and performance within different types of platforms used within distance education be conducted.

While students interacted with one another, they also interacted with newly created student bots. This initial pilot study with the bots included 25 students in one graduate course at one institution. While the course is an online course with students across the country, there is still a need for more participants; therefore, one recommendation is to include more participants in future studies with the bots. Another recommendation involves the bots' brains and the selection of keywords. Instructors selected keywords for the responses, and need to further tailor the bots' brains to respond to specific keywords for each activity. When tailoring bots' responses, it is recommended that instructors make sure that the errors the bots make are appropriate for the activity. Another recommendation to the initial pilot with the bots is to make the responses of the bots seem more like responses of K-12 students. While several students stated that the bots gave life-like responses, many students stated that the students did not give responses that were similar to real children. When expanding the work with the bots to three courses in the hopes of getting 56 participants, only one student chose to complete the bonus activity with the four bots; therefore, more work with the small group of bots will need to be done before any recommendations can be made.

Collaboration with Others

Qualitative student responses showed that they enjoyed working collaboratively with other students in the courses using SL as the educational platform. Quantitative results also showed students enjoyed the collaborative nature of working together within Second Life. Since many students are new to using SL, it is recommended that instructors consider incorporating collaborative work into learning experiences. The interactive nature of SL promotes collaborative work experiences and students enjoy working together to complete activities.

FUTURE RESEARCH DIRECTIONS

There are many directions for future work in using SL as the educational platform for distance learning. The faculty designer has added a preschool room in the Primary School on the Evansdale Campus in SL and is currently working on building preschool student bots for preschool classroom simulations. The preschool student bots will be used in online graduate courses with preservice and inservice preschool teachers working with children with special needs. The preschool bots will be programmed to facilitate skill acquisition in the use of evidenced-based teaching practices.

The faculty designer is also working on improving the current bots. One improvement includes researching scripting using voice commands instead of text chat so that the student bots could respond to voice and then reply using voice instead of typing. Voice response from the bots would further increase the feeling of the simulation being real while practicing skills. Another improvement to the bots includes working on improving the key words to which the bots respond, and trying to make the interactions as close to a real life experience as possible. The faculty designer would like to more closely tailor the key words to specific activities and align the errors the bots make with common types of errors that students make in K-12 classrooms.

The faculty designer is also researching the use of scripted agents within SL as well as the advantages and limitations to using the scripted agents instead of bots. A scripted agent has been created but has not yet been used in a K-12 classroom. Future developments will include 1) exploring how SL can be used to create machanimations, which could support learning activities in which teacher education students design animated instructional materials for K-12 students; and 2) investigating hardware and software options for creating bots or scripted avatars that use voice rather than text communication to more closely simulate real K-12 classroom experiences.

REFERENCES

Annetta, L. A., Folta, E., & Klesath, M. (2010). *V-learning: Distance education in the 21st century through 3D virtual environments*. New York: Springer. doi:10.1007/978-90-481-3627-8

Bonwell, C., & Eison, J. (1991). *Active learning: Creating excitement in the classroom*. San Francisco: Jossey-Bass.

Brown, J. S., Collins, A., & Duguid, P. (1989). Situated cognition and the culture of learning. *Educational Researcher*, *18*(1), 32–42. doi:10.3102/0013189X018001032

Calandra, B., & Puvirajah, A. (2014). Teacher practice in multi user virtual environments:A fourth space. *TechTrends*, *58*(6), 29–35. doi:10.1007/s11528-014-0800-3

Caruso, V., Morch, A. I., Thomassen, I., Hartley, M., & Ludlow, B. L. (2014). Practicing collaboration skills through role-play activities in a 3D virtual world. In R. Huang, Kinshuk, & N. Chen (Eds.), The new development of technology enhanced learning: Concept, research and best practices (pp. 165-184). Berlin: Springer-Verlag.

Cognition & Technology Group at Vanderbilt. (1993). Anchored instruction and situated cognition revisited. *Educational Technology*, *33*(3), 52–70.

Cooke-Plagwitz, J. (2009). A new language for the Net generation: Why Second Life works for the net generation. In R. Oxford & J. Oxford (Eds.), *Second language teaching and learning in the Net generation* (pp. 173–180). Manoa, HI: National Foreign Language Resource Center, University of Hawaii.

Dawley, L., & Dede, C. (2014). Situated learning in virtual worlds and immersive simulations. In J. M. Spector, M. D. Merrill, J. Elen, & M. J. Bishop (Eds.), *The handbook of research for educational communications and technology* (4th ed., pp. 723–734). New York: Springer. doi:10.1007/978-1-4614-3185-5_58

Dede, C. (2009). Immersive interfaces for engagement and learning. *Science 2*, 323(5910), 66-69. DOI:.10.1126/science.1167311

Dorf, Y. J., Belcher, J., Bessetta, M., Danziger, M., McKinney, A., & Hult, E. (2010). Technology for active learning. *Materials Today*, *6*(12), 44–49.

Ellis, M., Anderson, P. J., & Kibbe, S. (2014). Second Life: Simplifying and enhancing the processes of teaching and learning. In V. C. X. Wang (Ed.), *Handbook of research on education and technology in a changing society* (pp. 483–503). Hershey, PA: IGI Global. doi:10.4018/978-1-4666-6046-5.ch036

Falconer, L. (2013). Situated learning in virtual simulations: Researching the authentic dimension in virtual worlds. *Journal of Interactive Learning Research*, *24*(3), 285–300.

Herrington, J., & Oliver, R. (2000). An instructional design framework for authentic learning environments. *Educational Technology Research and Development*, *48*(3), 23–48. doi:10.1007/BF02319856

Hew, K.F., & Cheung, W. S. (2010). Use of three-dimension (3-D) immersive virtual worlds in K-12 and higher education settings: A review of the research. *British Journal of Educational Technology*, *41*(1), 33–55. doi:10.1111/j.1467-8535.2008.00900.x

Jarmon, L. (2008). Pedagogy and learning in the virtual world of Second Life. In P. Rogers, G. Berg, J. Boettcher, C. Howard, L. Justice, & K. Schenck (Eds.), *Encyclopedia of distance learning* (2nd ed., pp. 1610–1619). Hershey, PA: IGI Global.

Kim, S. H., Lee, J., & Thomas, M. K. (2012). Between purpose and method: A review of educational research on 3D virtual worlds. *Journal of Virtual Worlds Research*, *5*(1), 1–18.

Korthagen, F. A. J. (2010). Situated learning theory and the pedagogy of teacher education: Towards an integrative view of teacher behavior and teacher learning. *Teaching and Teacher Education: An International Journal of Research and Studies*, *26*(1), 98–106. doi:10.1016/j.tate.2009.05.001

Lave, G., & Wenger, E. (1991). *Situated learning: Legitimate peripheral participation*. Cambridge: University of Cambridge Press. doi:10.1017/CBO9780511815355

Messer, S., Evans, S., Cownie, M., & Dawe, C. (2012). Greenbank – A model for situated learning in Second Life. In T. Amiel & B. Wilson (Eds.), *Proceedings of World Conference on Educational Media and Technology 2012* (pp. 844-849). Waynesville, NC: Association for the Advancement of Computing in Education (AACE).

Meyers, C., & Jones, T. B. (1993). *Promoting active learning: Strategies for the college classroom*. San Francisco: Jossey-Bass.

Pantelidis, V. (2009). Reasons to use virtual reality in education and training courses and a model to determine when to use virtual reality. *Themes in Science and Technology Education*, *2*(1), 58–70.

Richardson, V. (1997). Constructivist teaching and teacher education: Theory and practice. In V. Richardson (Ed.), *Constructivist teacher education: Building a world of new understandings* (pp. 3–14). Florence, KY: Psychology Press.

Schiller, S. Z., Goodrich, K., & Gupka, P. B. (2013). Let them play! Active learning in a virtual world. *Information Systems Management*, *30*(1), 50–62. doi:10.1080/10580530.2013.739891

Wang, F., & Burton, J. K. (2013). Second Life in education: A review of publications from its launch to 2011. *British Journal of Educational Technology*, *44*(3), 357–371. doi:10.1111/j.1467-8535.2012.01334.x

Whitton, N., & Hollins, P. (2008). Collaborative virtual gaming worlds in higher education. *ALT-J Research in Learning Technology*, *16*(3), 221–229. doi:10.1080/09687760802526756

KEY TERMS AND DEFINITIONS

Activator: A warm-up activity to activate prior knowledge at the beginning of class.

Bot: An object in SL that is scripted to respond to other users during live time. Bots can be programmed to merely greet users or they can be programmed to interact with users through the use of keywords.

Box: A box is a 3-dimensional shape in SL and users can put contents inside of the box for other users to purchase. Users can determine the cost of the materials within the box, and can make them free.

Individualized Education Plan (IEP): Students who qualify for special education services under the Individuals with Disabilities Education Act (IDEA) have an IEP that states their present levels of academic &/or functional performance, annual goals (with or without short-term objectives), their amount of involvement in general education, their level of participation in state-wide testing, accommodations &/or modifications needed in classes & testing, and transition planning if the student is of age. IEPs serve as the student's road map for instructional decision making.

Island: A piece of virtual land surrounded by water.

Inventory: A virtual place to store materials, much like the document folder in one's computer.

Notecard: A writing feature within SL where users can type information onto a notecard and store the notecard within their inventory in Second Life.

PRT: It stands for Personal Rapid Transportation system, and it carries students between campuses. It travels on tracks above ground.

Object View: A tool in SL where the user can zoom in and out when looking at an object.

Situated Learning: A theory of learning that states that learning occurs as learners construct new understandings through involvement in real or simulated contexts (settings and activities) in which specific knowledge or skills are needed.

Teleport: To physically relocate to another area within Second Life.

Textures: A texture is used to put on an object within SL to change its appearance. For example, if one has a white box, one could put a texture on it of an image and the sides of the box would then display the image.

Chapter 6
Teaching Economics in World of Warcraft

András Margitay-Becht
St. Mary's College of California, USA

ABSTRACT

This chapter is a go-to guide for education professionals (primarily in the undergraduate and graduate college-level degree programs) for understanding and designing Economics classes in World of Warcraft. The premier MMORPG of the Western world, World of Warcraft boasts a number of features that makes it an ideal sandbox for economic education. It was deliberately designed to represent a large number of important real-world institutions like trade, production, cooperation, thus it can become a platform for learning about them. Moreover, since students encounter these institutions in a vibrant virtual world setting, they not only get to verify the learned materials but can practice their applications in their day-to-day dealings with other World of Warcraft denizens. This will lead to more student engagement, better learning outcomes, a more thorough understanding of both the principles of the theory and their applications, and greatly improved knowledge retention.

INTRODUCTION

Virtual worlds, or synthetic worlds (Castronova, 2005) are computer-based simulated environments that can be navigated by a participant (in a gaming context, referred to as a player). While the aim and purpose of these environments vary widely, all share the exploration of a different reality. The multi-user versions of virtual gaming worlds were developed as early as 1973 when Maze War, the forefather of the genre became available through the Advanced Research Project Agency Network (ARPANET – the predecessor of the Internet). The current iteration of the gaming genre is termed Massively Multi-Player On-line Role-Playing Games (MMORPGs).

Modern virtual worlds are nearly exclusively graphical, and most of them represent a three-dimensional (3D) space[1]. Players negotiate this environment via the use of a virtual representation called an avatar. The avatars move like a person; the immersive feedback a player receives is the actual movement of their avatar within the virtual world. To explore the virtual world, players have to guide their avatars as

DOI: 10.4018/978-1-4666-9837-6.ch006

if they themselves were exploring; for example, walking through forests, swimming across lakes, entering houses, mapping caves. Certain virtual worlds implement transportation vehicles like cars, planes, helicopters, horses. Depending on the virtual world used, superhuman navigation options are also available, usually in the form of flight or teleportation.

Virtual worlds are also frequently *themed*. For example, one of the first successful MMORPGs, Ultima Online, was built on the existing mythology of the sword-and-socery themed Ultima games series. EverQuest, a product developed by Sony Corporation, also focused on the sword-and-socery theme. Current popular game titles such as GuildWars and World of Warcraft are also set in sword-and-socery Tolkienesque worlds. Another popular meta-theme is science fiction; Anarchy Online or the cult classic Eve Online are examples. Some virtual worlds combine science fiction with sword and sorcery fantasy themes, such as Star Wars: The Old Republic and Wildstar. There are also theme-less worlds. Second Life, developed by Linden Lab, famously provides only a sand-box environment, and participants are given powerful tools to generate virtual objects. The 3D virtual world of gaming has become so popular that it is being used for educational purposes.

This chapter will provide an in-depth examination of the MMORPG World of Warcraft, discuss the use of virtual environments in education, compare the World of Warcraft with principles of economics, and identify steps to implementing a virtual environment, such as Word of Warcraft, into an introductory economics college course.

EDUCATION IN VIRTUAL WORLDS

Using real-world examples in an undergraduate college program frequently is pointless, as the students are usually inexperienced in the real world. It is not helpful for them to explain that understanding the elasticity of the demand curve will help them formulate the long-term pricing strategy of aluminum, as they have never faced the problem of being responsible for the long-term pricing strategy of aluminum. Social sciences attempt to explain and simplify the complex reality – but these simplifying models themselves are hard to understand without a point of reference. In graduate programs we can assume a working understanding of certain social institutions, and can base our lectures on that; but in the undergraduate setting this is not always realistic. The construction of virtual worlds can bridge this knowledge gap: using the familiar virtual setting, the teacher can introduce both the real-world problem, and the social science model designed to help deal with the problem.

The Knowledge Transmission Mechanism When Using Virtual Worlds for Education

According to Nick Yee (2006), virtual gaming world players can be grouped into three broad categories in relation to their motivation: *achievement*, *social*, and *immersion*. The achievement motivation group encompasses progress, accumulation of power, overcoming challenges both in-game and out-of-game (understanding underlying mechanics, optimization etc.). The social motivation group contains factors like making friends, casual chatting and collaboration. The immersion motivation group contained the joy of discovery, role-playing and escapism, among other factors. It is also important to emphasize that the three motivational groups were not exclusive – they were mostly unrelated.

All three motivations can serve as hooks to which educational applications can be connected. For example, for those who are looking for achievement, power, or technical understanding, the teacher can point out how various in-class concepts can help students progress in the game to higher levels or further understanding of the virtual environment. The social motivation can be connected with exercises in psychology, social sciences, behavioral sciences or management sciences (Margitay-Becht & Herrera, 2013). Immersion, which is characterized by intense engagement can be used for the gamification of tasks and challenges, potentially encompassing both achievement and social motivations.

Most successful MMORPGs incorporate real-world institutions in their core ruleset (frequently the very fabric of the virtual reality itself). As discussed earlier, the three main motivations for players to participate in MMORPGs are of the Achievement, Social and Immersion components. The players have to explore and learn the new setting, navigating an unknown land with unknown rules. They have to understand the physical and social rules to be able to be successful – the immersion leads to the social understanding, which leads to potential achievement. MMORPGs create a community the players can participate in – which leads to them identifying with their in-game roles, avatars; and at the end, greater immersion. This high level of immersion manifests in the players considering participation in MMORPGs an integral part of their life. Some consider this alarming; but this great attachment to the virtual experience can be used for heightened educational experience.

The emotional attachment that develops means that players *care* a lot about the world – and thus are frequently intimately familiar with its workings. Using the connection between the real-world institutions and the virtual world institutions, teachers can build on to and utilize this emotional investment to form a bond between students and the material covered.

As shown in Figure 1, institutions from the physical world are mapped in the virtual world. The institution of trade, for example, appears in World of Warcraft through the institution of the auction house. In the real world, buyers purchase products in stores (themselves physical or on-line). In World of Warcraft, players buy things by going to the auction house. Since both of these institutions are representative of trade, economic models describing trade (like the supply-demand model, or the production possibilities frontier model) describe both the physical and virtual-world institution. Practiced World of Warcraft

Figure 1. Virtual world education transmission mechanism

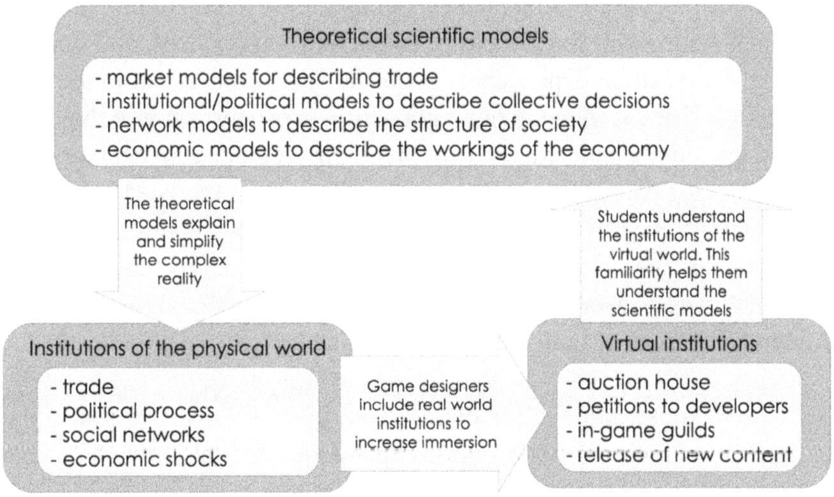

players have an understanding of how the auction house operates – and new players can interact and understand the auction house a lot easier than if they had to understand the physical world counterpart. Using this virtual world understanding makes it easier to explain the underlying theoretical concepts, which then the students can easily try out in their virtual setting. We can then use this advanced understanding of both the virtual world institution and the theory to explain the workings of te real world institution.

Principles of Learning In Virtual Environments

James Paul Gee (2007) organized the major ways of learning into 36 principles. These principles can be grouped into five categories:

1. System-level understanding: the students learn how the environment operates, what are the rules. This learning is active as the players have to explore and probe the environment to learn something about it. Moreover, the very fact of exploration is the conduit of fun, which coincidentally will become the conduit for learning as well. World of Warcraft, the three-dimensional virtual environment is very conducive to experiential learning.
2. Learning process principles: these encompass the trinity of (i) convincing the learner to try difficult tasks, then (ii) getting them to devote lots of time and resources to solving the problem, and finally (iii) providing some kind of reward for the successful solution to complete the feedback loop. An actual implementation of these principles can be observed in World of Warcraft. A few years ago, Blizzard noticed that there is a chronic lack of people who play the “tank” or “healer” roles. To increase participation, they started to provide extra rewards to people playing tank or healer, but that lead to a large influx of inexperienced players. Blizzard then developed an entirely new, self-contained sub-game, called “proving grounds”. These proving grounds are designed to provide a fun, single-player content where the players can practice the common tasks of a given role. By making the experience fun, the players are convinced to try out and spend some time mastering the environment. By requiring the completion of the proving grounds in order to be able to participate in group content, the reward scheme is also in place.
3. Situation-dependent learning: current neuroscientific research seems to (strongly) suggest that learning works by *relating* previous life experiences to solving current problems. Learning is not so much about knowledge generation than about experience generation. Putting the students in an immersive virtual setting will force them to create new experiences, and understand the importance of context and situation-dependence. A hostile enemy player out in the wild might “mean” something else than if she is found in our capital city. In the former case they could be just going about their business, in the latter we can interpret their presence as precursor to aggression.
4. Social principles: being part of the gaming community such as the World of Warcraft community, players will relate to other players, both within the game and without.
5. Educational principles: these principles describe that gradual, step-by-step learning is critical so that the students both learn and keep excited about learning. Successful games, like World of Warcraft, spend considerable amount of design effort to engage players.

Central to Gee’s (2007) description of principles of learning in a virtual world, is the focus on experiential learning: students in a virtual world setting experience their environment, and are able to probe it, experiment with it. This experiential learning process leads to a more thorough understanding of how the environment works, and creates greater immersion as well.

Effectiveness of Using Virtual Worlds in the Classroom

To test the efficacy of using virtual worlds in the classroom, the author, with his co-researcher put together a course as part of a January Term program. During the January Term the professors are invited to offer experimental courses to the students, who take only a single, extra intensive class. The course offered, aimed at discussing introductory level anthropology and economics theories through virtual worlds.

The audience of the course was rather mixed. Students were of mixed majors (sciences, pre-medical, anthropology, economics etc.), though a majority of them majored in business. They also had different gaming backgrounds: some were hardcore gamers, many were casual, and a few did not even have significant experience in virtual worlds.

The course was a combination of lectures and experiential learning. Class sessions started with rigorous discussions of theories and ideas. The students began to experience the virtual environment, where they explored the world, informed by the material covered. To make the experience similar to most students, World of Warcraft was not chosen as the medium. Instead, the class used the theme-less Second Life as one of the virtual worlds, while the other world used was Hellgate: London. Hellgate has just been released (a few weeks prior to the class), and the publishers gave the class access to the servers. Since that environment was brand new, no students had significant experience in that world, so exploration was a critical element for everyone's interaction.

The class was very well received. Pre- and post-tests were conducted to be able to assess student learning, and it found (Margitay-Becht & Herrera, 2008) that student learning was intensive, deep, and knowledge retention great. Students were extremely motivated in the classroom, they were very engaged with the material, and some performed so well that they presented at a conference, despite being only undergraduates themselves.

The experiment was repeated, by that time by the author alone, focusing exclusively on production economics. A companion course on programming was also offered. Both courses had similar positive results.

WORLD OF WARCRAFT OVERVIEW AND FEATURES

World of Warcraft was released in the fall of 2004 by Blizzard Entertainment. To this day, it is one of the most popular MMORPGs that has ever been deployed, and it is the most popular subscription-based MMORPG in the world (MMOs.com, 2015). At the peak of its popularity, World of Warcraft had 12 million subscribers; currently 7 million people participate. This makes World of Warcraft the world's 103rd most populous country, albeit a virtual one (The World Factbook, 2015), placing it between Hong Kong and Bulgaria. The high popularity of World of Warcraft suggests the likelihood that either students are familiar with the game, or can familiarize themselves with its operational procedures relatively easily.

In the developmental stages of World of Warcraft, the developing company Blizzard Entertainment built on the mythology of their existing Warcraft franchise, a series of real-time strategy games focusing on a perpetual conflict between war-like orcs and humans. To lift this spirit of war and conflict into an

MMORPG, players in World of Warcraft were divided into two groups: the ferocious Horde faction, led by the Orcs, and the Alliance faction, led by the Humans.

Most traditional MMORPGs include a strong progression aspect; avatars (called "characters" in World of Warcraft) are continually challenged to move to a higher level of functioning and power. Generally there are two paths to gaining more power: through improving the character itself (generally by gaining "levels" through collecting experience by performing activities), or by gathering more powerful equipment. World of Warcraft incorporates these two routes. At the initial release of the game the maximum attainable level was 60. Once reached, the character could only gain more power by getting better gear[2]. Currently the maximum character level is 100.

The initial focus of the game developers' was on the immersion aspect. The beta version of the game contained few pre-generated tasks, and players were expected to explore the world, and feel as if they were exploring a real place, to feel at home. During beta testing it became obvious that the immersion approach is insufficient. Players were lost and did not know what to do. Blizzard responded by adding quests, pre-generated tasks offered to players by so-called "non-player characters" (avatars operated by the artificial intelligence/world itself, not other players). These quests formed the major source of content in the game for the characters during their leveling progress, sending the player on errand after errand while providing experience and combining the motivations of exploration/immersion with achievement/power. The social aspect of the game was satisfied mostly through chat channels, but some quests and tasks also required cooperation among players.

One of the challenges of content generation for virtual worlds is the proper balance of "things to do" for characters with different levels of power, and for players with different skills and interest. As Figure 2 shows, in World of Warcraft most players play with maximum level characters. This means, that game developers focus most of their efforts in creating content for level 100, as the quests provided for leveling up will not be of interest to players with maximum level characters. To tackle this issue, Blizzard introduced a number of ways to attain more power for level 100 characters. The traditional elite activity is participation in organized, multi-player challenges, either in the form of five-person "dungeons" or 10-30 person "raids". The assembled players face a series of computer controlled enemies, and they use

Figure 2. Activity by character level. Data source: (Toon activity by level, 2015)

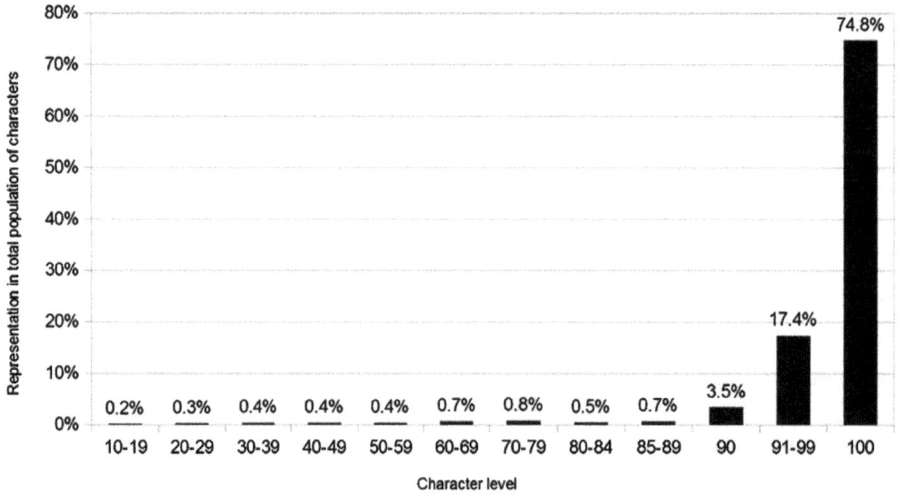

their characters specializing in one of three roles to overcome the opponents. These activities require preparation, a thorough understanding of one's own character and the challenge itself, and serious dedication, as these raids can take many hours to tackle.

For those who want to face other humans and not pre-scripted machine-controlled enemies, Blizzard provided so-called Player Versus Player (PVP) content. Teams of two, three, or five players can face others in same-sized teams in a last-man-standing arena battle. Teams of 10, 15 or 40 can face each other in objective-centric battlegrounds with various goals (capture the flag, zone defense, payload protection). Recently even larger scale Player Versus Player encounters were introduced to create even more epic encounters.

To serve those who are more casual players, Blizzard provided a number of auxiliary activities. Each character can have up to two professions that they can use to gather materials from around the world or use said materials to craft powerful or fun items. These items can be either used by the crafting character, or can be offered up for sale for others through a built-in auction house system. Players can also take part in high level individual or group quests, which either provide powerful rewards or serve as a conduit of storytelling. Key Features of World of Warcraft

There are certain features of World of Warcraft that make it a powerful learning environment. In this section, the following features will be discussed: 3D environment, addons, specializations, group content, Player Versus Player, professions, trade.

3D Environment

The game is implemented as a freely navigable large 3D virtual space. Its total size is approximately 150 square miles (Stoutfoot, 2007), spread among 6 major continents, which themselves are subdivided into smaller areas. One feature that is prominent in World of Warcraft is that each zone has its appropriate "level range" and the content and entities will be scaled to be appropriately challenging only for characters whose level is within that range. This means that a large majority of the 150 square miles is designed for low level characters, thus the overwhelming majority of characters (over 90%) are compressed together in a much smaller area. This feature is by design, and the developers hope to achieve a feeling of liveliness because of the density: people adventuring around in the world do not feel alone. They are not lone wanderers among computer-controlled entities; instead they explore a living, vibrant world.

The fact that the majority of the game world is presented in a 3D setting means that players have to familiarize themselves with the environment, and have to quickly learn the economics of negotiating the setting. What is the optimal way of exploring new areas? How much risk is it worthwhile taking? In World of Warcraft there is little permanent punishment for death (a small amount of in-game resource, gold, has to be sacrificed to repair damaged equipment, but the cost is trivial in most cases). Concurrently, every time a character dies, its soul gets resurrected at a spirit healer, and then the player has to run back to their corpse to revive themselves. These spirit healers are sparsely placed, so it can take minutes to travel the distance and by the time the character arrives at the scene of their death the area might not be safe which leads to further potential deaths and time wasted.

Like most MMORPGs, World of Warcraft also receives regular content updates. This is essential, as the business model of the game (monthly subscriptions) requires the availability of activity for people. As the game itself is over 10 years old, its original content these days would be considered extremely boring, but the content patches and updates give the players newer things to do.

While this primarily serves the interest of continued subscription, the content updates also provide critical educational opportunities, as well. The most obvious opportunity comes from the changing of the environment itself: players have to explore and learn to navigate a new virtual setting. The content patches are frequently also the source of disruptive technologies, changing the trading landscape.

In January 2007, Blizzard released their first major content patch, called the Burning Crusade. This raised the character level limit from 60 to 70, added a whole new continent to the world[3]. The most disruptive technology introduced was the ability for characters to fly. This apparently innocuous change significantly shrunk the perceived size of the world, since characters could not only travel faster between point A and point B with the aid of flying, but it also enabled players to skip content. Before flying was introduced, once players arrived to an area (through the use of the game's built-in mass transportation system), they had to negotiate the environment to complete tasks. This included fighting monsters, avoiding players of the opposite factions, and finding paths to the appropriate area. Both enemies and the environment can be avoided with flying mounts, and players could just swoop in, complete the task and swoop out.

November 2014 saw the release of the most recent content patch, Warlords of Draenor. In this version, Blizzard took the controversial step of removing the ability of players to fly. This was a hotly debated issue, as many felt they are artificially inconvenienced since a capability they used to have was being taken away. Gradually many players realized that this added difficulty and this removal of a powerful option led to a better overall gameplay experience, as players had to actively engage and negotiate the environment, had to spend more time and effort learning.

Addons

When designing World of Warcraft, Blizzard made a progressive decision. They opened to the public, the Application Programming Interface (API) of the World of Warcraft Graphical User Interface. In practice this means that anybody who is familiar with programming can write small programs that run within World of Warcraft, and change the way the game displays information. The entire user experience can be customized this way. This availability provided an immediate educational utilization of World of Warcraft as an entry-level programming experience. The author has taught a very popular and successful Introduction to Programming course using the World of Warcraft API.

The custom user interface elements (called add-ons or addons) can also have special educational value. An addon can be created, for example, that helps communication among group members, improving synchronization and learning about coordination. There are addons available that track individual and group performance (useful for ranking the damage dealers based on how much damage they did, or the healers based on the amount of healing they provided), addons that track trade information, and addons that monitor the chat channels for certain words (easily applicable for educational or research purposes). If the teacher is determined enough, the ability to customize the students' user interface can be an effective addition for the learning experience; not many other virtual worlds provide this opportunity.

Specialization

Like in many MMORPGs, in World of Warcraft players choose a "class" that their character belongs to. This class will then define the abilities and capabilities available to the character. Currently there are 11 classes available, and each class can have three distinct specializations (with the exception of

Druids, who can have four). This leads to overall 34 different playstyles – but they all come down to one of three-four archetypal roles.

The default role is the damage dealer (in World of Warcraft terminology, "dps"); 23 of the available 34 possible playstyles count as dps. Characters with this role deal a lot of damage, but are relatively fragile. They are easily capable of dealing with most content designed for single players, but usually have a hard time surviving the attacks of masses of enemies for an extended period of time. Sometimes the dps role is split into two easily substituting sub-roles: that of the ranged and the melee damage dealer.

The role of tank focuses on survival. These roles (five out of 34 specializations) all have abilities that reduce the damage the character takes, so the role of tank can survive attacks from powerful foes that would decimate members of the other roles – or they live through the onslaught of a horde of weaker foes. To compensate for their increased durability, tank characters usually do lower damage compared to the dps roles.

The final role is that of the healer. Healers have powerful healing abilities such as restoring the lost life of other characters or themselves. Healers further increase the durability of the tank roles, and increase the survival of the dps roles as well. In return for this great utility to others, healers tend to be as fragile as dps characters, and do even less damage than tanks.

The availability of the three different roles (dps, tank, and healer) serve as important lesson in co-operation. Usually single person content is designed with a dps role in mind – and all 11 classes have access to at least one dps role. More challenging content, however, frequently requires groups composed of specialized characters.

Group Content

Building on the concept of specialization, World of Warcraft provides many different kinds of content for groups of players.

Grouped Player Versus Environment (PVE) content is often instanced; instanced means that once a group of players formed a group, they enter a separated virtual space, reserved only for them, where they tackle hard enemies. The so-called dungeons are designed for five players, specifically one tank, one healer and three dps. The enemies are powerful enough that if no tanks are available, all party members die a swift death. Similarly, a healer is required to help keep the tank alive while the dps players kill the enemies. Raids provide a longer, larger challenge, requiring 10-30 people of different roles. These challenges are complex enough that players frequently need direct voice communication with each other to be able to coordinate their actions. An early lesson in this environment is that one misstep can cause the downfall of all. Personal responsibility and societal enforcement mechanisms are the reality of the raiding scene.

In the PVP content players face characters controlled by other players. While in smaller scale encounters (1v1 dueling or the greatly popular 2v2 arenas) the teams frequently are composed of players of the same (dps) role, as more and more players are added, the greater becomes the benefit of variety. The most competitive of these encounters are the 3v3 arenas, fast becoming an e-sport sensation, which in most professional settings require 1 healer and 2 dps roles. It is important to note, that while in the PVE settings most frequently only the role of a character is important, in the PVP content the actual class also becomes a factor. It is the case as in PVE settings the tasks of the players are so specialized, that most players do not (frequently) use their non-damaging utility abilities. In a PVP encounter, however, these secondary abilities (like the small heals of certain DPS roles, or various control capabilities) become the central focus of the gameplay. Because of this, PVP teams are even more varied, with significantly higher level of specialization than PVE teams.

From an educational standpoint the presence of specialization and group content provides valuable lessons. On the surface, specialization and group content enable players to practice their social and co-ordination skills. But perhaps even more importantly they teach the students that following a plan, even a bad plan, can be more beneficial than uncoordinated action.

World PVP

Most MMORPGs constrain PVP combat to instanced, enclosed areas. The developers do this for fear of alienating their player base: it can be rather frustrating to be attacked by other players when one just wants to collect some herbs or ore. World of Warcraft is rare among MMORPGs in that it allows players of the opposite faction to freely attack each other across most of the game world. While EVE Online famously allows any players to attack any other player no matter what, World of Warcraft itself contains both world PVP enabled and world PVP disabled (PVE) servers. Players who play on PVP enabled servers can freely attack each other, while those who play on PVE servers can only be attacked if they explicitly set a flag to allow themselves be attacked (or if they attack someone who can be attacked). Players on both kinds of servers can engage in instanced PVP. Roughly half of the playerbase plays on PVP enabled servers (EURO Quick server stats, 2015).

An interesting element of playing on a world PVP enabled server is that every action a player takes is immediately a high risk action. They cannot only be overcome by computer controlled enemies, but also by enemy players as well. This threat is especially omnipresent if one understands that two of the eleven classes, rogues and druids, are capable of entering "stealth" mode, in which case the opponents cannot see them until they are attacked. This means that in a PVP server players cannot ever feel secure, they can be attacked at any moment. This heightened awareness contributes to the immersion – and will serve as an important lesson in social coordination as well. It is usually challenging for a player to fend off multiple attackers. Because of this, in a PVP environment there is more incentive to form groups, similar to the convoys of the world wars, getting protection and strength in numbers. This behavior parallels the working of unions in the real world: workers of a trade pool their resources to become more powerful in negotiations, and be able to better represent their interests.

Professions

In World of Warcraft, every character can have two primary professions and four secondary professions. These professions are like jobs in the real world: characters of a certain profession are able to produce things other characters, other players might want.

The primary professions can be either gathering (mining, herbalism, skinning) or trade professions (alchemy, blacksmithing, enchanting, engineering, inscription, jewelcrafting, leatherworking, tailoring). The gathering professions simply enable the character to collect resources around the world. Miners and herbalists are able to process mining nodes or herbs in the world; skinners are able to skin furred enemies for leather. These professions simply increase the monetary gain from exploring, by providing additional materials that the player can either sell for someone with a trade profession, or use with their own trade profession as well. Leatherworking, for example, is frequently paired with skinning, as the raw materials from leatherworking are generated from the skinning profession. Herbalism provides similar support to Alchemy and Inscription, Mining supports Blacksmithing, Engineering and Jewelcrafting. Enchanting generates its own raw materials, while the raw materials for Tailoring (pieces of cloth) are gathered from humanoid enemies even without a gathering profession.

The trade professions produce durable and consumable products. Blacksmithing, Leatherworking, Engineering and Tailoring produces clothing and armor, usually expensive durable goods. Jewelcrafting, Inscription and Enchanting can produce a few durable goods, and some semi-consumable items improving the power of the player (in case of inscription) or the player's equipment (in case of Enchanting and Jewelcrafting). Alchemy nearly exclusively focuses on producing magic potions that provide short-time power increases for the players. These alchemical products act as proper consumable goods, as players involved in large-scale Player Versus Environment content (mostly raids) are frequently required to use large quantities of these potions to improve personal performance, and thus group success chance.

Needless to say, it is a critical economic decision to choose which professions should a player choose. Gathering professions are generally easy to use, but they require the player to actively roam the world. Their ease of use means that frequently their profit rate is rather low, as many players choose them. Durable good producing professions usually start with a high profit rate, as opposed to the profit rate of consumable goods, but the profit of durable goods decreases rapidly with the passage of time, while the profit of consumable goods tend to remain constant.

To provide added depth to the already complex system, Blizzard frequently introduces materials to professions that they can produce only in a limited supply (frequently one batch a day). This adds a new time dimension to the cost of production, meaning supply itself is time-limited. This is a critical learning opportunity for students to understand the importance of the distinction between being able to mass-produce something, or being limited by artificial barriers.

The secondary professions are all available for every character, and they produce less powerful products. Fishing allows the character to catch fish from the virtual waters of the virtual world, which are used as raw materials for the many cooking recipes. Cooking, like alchemy, produces temporary performance boosts. While the boost the cooked food provides is less than the boost alchemy produces, since the two are additive, there is usually high demand for the products of cooking as well. First aid can produce weak healing products, while archaeology produces hardly anything of use, and is mostly added to provide additional lore for the interested players.

These professions provide a simple value chain for most products. For example, the sample value chain represented by Figure 3 describes the parts and components of creating the "Shrediron's Shredder Mk. 2" gun. The blue ovals are the professions that generate the linked materials. The green materials are intermediate goods, that can be produced in an unlimited amount, as long as all the raw materials are available. The purple boxes (Gearspring Parts and Alchemical Catalyst) are materials that can only be generated once per day (artificial shortage).

It is easy to see that the production of the "Shrediron's Shredder Mk. 2" gun involves four primary and one secondary professions, which is impossible for a single character to have. This means that producers of this item have to either utilize multiple characters with different professions (a player can have up to 11 characters on one server), in essence creating a vertically integrated value chain, or engage in trading.

Trade

Trade, the willing exchange of goods between two players, has two major conduits in World of Warcraft: the trade channel and the auction house.

Figure 3. Example value chain

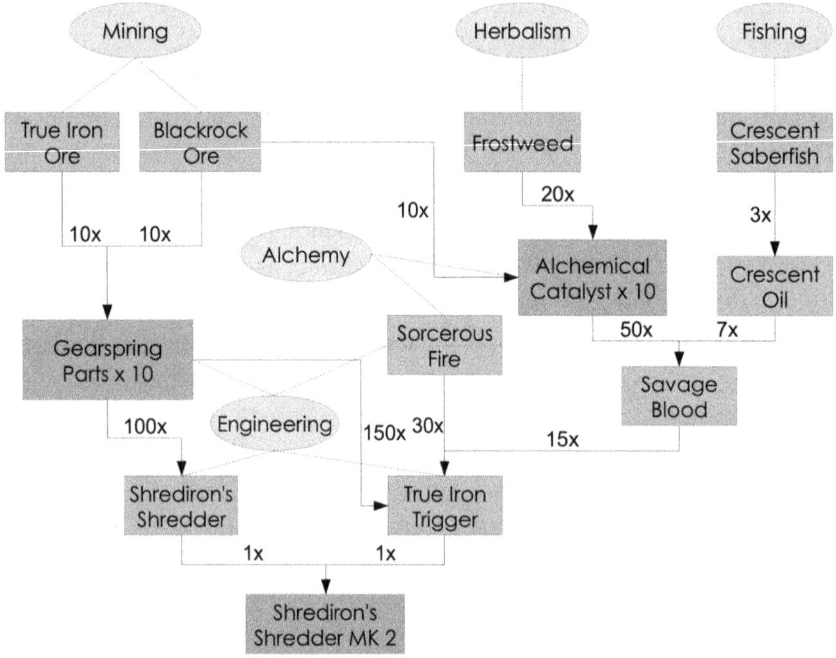

The trade channel is a channel that can be read in all major cities of World of Warcraft, and is designated for buy and sell offers. The buyers or sellers regularly repeat their message on this channel (called *spamming* the channel), in the hopes of someone noticing it and willing to do business. Once two players find each other, they need to get to the same (virtual) location, and then they can exchange their goods with each other.

The other, and by far more popular means of trading is through the auction house. Players can just walk to one of the many auction houses in the world, and list an item (or a stack of an item, in case of commodities) for 12, 24 or 48 hours. The listing contains a bid price and an optional buyout price. When the auction expires, highest bid wins, or if someone paid the buyout price they receive the product immediately. To prevent people from doing high-frequency trading, every time someone posts an item, they have to pay a small fee. If the item sells, they get back this fee, but a fixed % of the sales price will be deducted. If the item does not sell or the seller cancels the auction, they lose the posting fee.

The real lure of using the auction house is that it does not require the buyer and the seller to be at the same place the same time. The seller does not even need to be logged in to World of Warcraft for the sale to go through. Because of this, the trade channel is mostly used to sell high-value products, where the auction cut starts to be a relevant amount.

Observing the behavior of the prices of certain products in the auction house provides a powerful educational experience. The students see whether something sells well (thus low-priced auctions quickly disappear from the listing), or if the demand is insufficient (more and more products appear, undercutting the previous offers).

A further benefit for educational purposes comes from the application of auction house addons. Some of these, like the extensive Auctioneer, provides in-depth statistical data about an item: how its price has been changing over time, what products can it be used for, are there apparent arbitrage opportunities etc.

To make matters even more convenient and useful, Blizzard also implemented an auction house API. Using this it is possible to download all the information from an entire auction house in one easy-to-analyze file. A bit of programming knowledge can lead to a large wealth of economic data. Even for those who lack the programming skills to do so, there are publicly available services which do this in a convenient, easy-to-use way (see: theunderminejournal.com).

ECONOMICS IN WORLD OF WARCRAFT

Multiple MMORPG operators have contracted economists to help run their virtual economy, highlighting the role economics plays in maintaining structural balance in a virtual world.

For example, on June 27, 2007 CCP, the Icelandic company running Eve Online announced that they hired Dr. Eyjólfur Guðmundsson to observe the economy of the game, and help the game operators improve the economy. With his help, CCP was able to curve the rampant inflation plaguing their economy (Roman, 2011). He was in employ until the summer of 2014, when he became the rector of the University of Akureyri.

In March 2012, Valve corporation (running, among other things, the extremely successful Steam platform, which in essence implements a brand new business model for gaming companies) hired Yanis Varoufakis to help run their economy. Today he is the finance minister of Greece, trying to work out deals with the IMF, Germany and the ECB to stabilize his country (Skipper, 2015).

In the following section certain key economic issues, topics, theories and tools will be introduced, and their application in World of Warcraft will be showcased. These theories include: opportunity cost, supply/demand, Economic crises, personal finance/liquidity, inflation, and pathfinding. This section will close with a discussion of using World of Warcraft for research related to economics.

Opportunity Cost

Economics, at its heart, is the science of making decisions in an environment of scarcity. No economic theory showcases this more than that of the theory of opportunity cost. When one makes a choice, by definition they choose something over something else. The potential gain provided by the option *not* chosen becomes the opportunity cost of the choice, and as such becomes the "true cost" of the chosen activity.

A traditional example of opportunity cost would be attending college. Students are asked to describe what it costs for them to attend class. They frequently recognize that *part* of the cost is the tuition they pay, but fail to count the value of time it takes to attend.

The simplest economic model describing opportunity cost is the Production Possibilities Frontier (PPF). The PPF shows the maximum possible production amount among two goods that use the same resources. The more the economy wants to produce of one good, the more resources they need to allocate to the production of that one good, and consequently they have less resources for the production of the other good, whose production then will have to be lowered. The opportunity cost of producing more of the first good is less production of the second good. This model is used to understand the production possibilities of nations, and the rationale behind international trade. The model can also be used to explain individual decisions and resource use as well (the more one works, the less time they have for other things, for example).

There are many occasions the theory of opportunity cost is useful in World of Warcraft. The most obvious is when addressing the optimal use of those crafting materials whose production Blizzard has limited. Limiting production constitutes a real constraint for the crafting characters, as they are available only in a limited supply (and are frequently also not tradable). An example for this could be the introduction of the rare resource "Jard's Peculiar Energy Source" to the game on September 10, 2013. Every character could only create one of resource per day, and it was used in the construction of four products. While the resource itself was not tradable, thus time-limited, the final products were tradable. The most desirable of the final products was a new, rare flying robot the players could use to travel around in the world – yet it required 30 of the new rare resource. Parallel to this, a number of in game toys could also be created by using 15 resources. Clearly, the more of resources used for the creation of the toys, the less could be used to create the flying robots. Each player had to decide for themselves whether it was worth their while to wait until they collected 30 of the resources to make potentially a large amount of money by selling the robot, or if they should use the resources earlier and corner the toy market.

A variant of this problem is the problem of vertical integration – an issue frequently plaguing physical world companies, too. A company is vertically integrated if it does not only produce a single good or service, but also produces either the materials to produce their product (upstream), and/or uses the product to manufacture other products (downstream). Many players choose a crafting profession paired with the gathering profession that produces the raw materials for the crafting profession, thus implementing a vertically integrated value chain: they produce the raw materials as well as the finished products. The vertical integration problem occurs when players with such integrated value chains make the assumption that processing the raw material with the crafting profession will lead to higher profits. If enough players make this assumption without checking the auction house for raw material prices, the assumption will end up being wrong. Players do not realize that they could make more money by selling the raw herbs than processing it to potions – the opportunity cost of the potion is actually greater than the market price, thus the economic profit of potion making becomes negative.

Another use of the opportunity cost concept in World of Warcraft is the discussion of *what to do*? Players have limited time available to play, so choosing any activity inherently means giving up other possible activities. If someone decides to take part in a raid, that is going to take two to three hours that could have been used exploring the world or fighting other players in a PVP setting. This kind of choice is obviously mirrored in the real world by the very choice of whether to invest time in playing World of Warcraft or not. In reality, the two decisions are the same. For a player who really enjoys the challenges of organized PVE (i.e., raiding) content, when their peer group participates in raids, they choose to play World of Warcraft at the expense of physical world activities. If, however, the selfsame player is not interested much in doing other in-game activities, once raid is over they might be inclined to terminate their World of Warcraft presence, and go to the movies or study some more economics instead.

For the casual players it is easy to miss the most direct application of the opportunity cost theory, even though it is extremely central to the gameplay itself. All 34 player class specializations have a combination of resources. Some use a resource that generates by itself over time (called energy or focus) while other classes use resources that generate through the use of other abilities (like warriors, who use rage). Even others use a large pool of magical energy called mana. Many class specializations have more than one resource: they use one resource to generate another resource that they can use with more powerful abilities. When a player plays their class, they continuously make decisions based on these resources. A feral druid, for example, spends most of their time turned into a giant cat fighting enemies. Their base resource is energy, that slowly replenishes over time. They have multiple abilities (shred, rake) that use energy, and both generate a *different* kind of resource, called combo points. They also have multiple abilities that use these combo points to create powerful "finisher" effects. The druid player has to make a decision practically every second about which button to press, what to spend the *scarce* energy or combo point resource on. These questions are complicated enough that answering them is beyond most casual players. There are many websites available where people with advanced knowledge of statistics try to approximate the optimal way of spending resources in different scenarios.

In case of those playing the healer role, the situation becomes even more complicated. All healers use the mana resource, which is initially abundant but regenerates very slowly. Healers thus need to focus on two things: efficiency and throughput. In case of efficiency, they try to maximize the amount of healing they do *per mana spent*. In case of the throughput focus, they are maximizing the amount of healing done *per second*. If a healer chooses to apply spells that do not generate sufficient throughput, they run the risk of not being able to keep the tank alive, and once the tank dies, so does everybody else. If, however, all they focus on is throughput, they will soon run out of mana altogether, leading to no healing and tank death just the same.

In the above gameplay cases the resource scarcity is not just simply a problem players have to tackle, it becomes the *central* source of enjoyment in playing the game. Of course, different players like different play-styles. That is the reason why Blizzard, in essence, provided players with 34 different play-styles, and everyone can find something pleasing for them. At the end of the day, though, the players interact with their chosen characters through the economic principle of opportunity cost.

Supply-Demand

The supply-demand model is generally used in economics to explain the differences in prices of goods. Demand represents people's willingness to pay for the good (technical definition is the "quantity demanded at different price levels"), while supply shows the sellers' willingness to provide the product. The supply-demand model is central to many economics arguments, and included in many introductory economics courses.

The most obvious presence of the supply-demand model is at the auction house. Walking up to the auction house any player can check how much of each good is being offered, and for what price. This, in actuality, is the supply curve of the given good. Checking back frequently one can even get an idea of how this supply is changing – or indeed what the underlying demand might be.

To illustrate, let us use the earlier example about the flying robot. Because of the daily one limitation on its production, 30 days after Jard's Peculiar Energy Source was introduced to the game, was the first time a Sky Golem mount was available for purchase. In World of Warcraft terminology, the day starts at 3 AM (that is when all of the "daily" limits get reset), so the very first Sky Golems appeared at 3AM. For the first few minutes, sellers asked for as much as 200,000 gold for one of the flying robots – an excessive amount of currency. Within 15-20 minutes, the ask price dropped to 150,000, and by the day's end, down to 60,000. In a few days the price stabilized around 30,000 gold, where it stayed for over a year. This drastic change in price can be easily explained by the supply-demand model. Initially there was little supply (not many players were awake at 3AM), so the few people who wanted their flying robot as soon as possible had to pay the exorbitant prices. Later in the day, around 6:30-7:00 AM, as more and more players with engineering professions joined the market, Sky Golems flooded the auction house, driving down prices. Prices increased again around 6:00-7:00 PM where the raiding community joined the servers, and increased the demand for the product.

The above example shows an important but oft neglected aspect of supply-demand: that of timing. Economists traditionally compare two “snapshots” of time – show a supply and demand curve “initially” and another set of supply and/or demand curve “after the fact”. The difference in these two situations is what describes change, an approach called comparative static analysis. This helps economists focus on the *equilibrium* situation, an idealized state where price and quantity traded stabilized. The above example demonstrates that equilibrium might not happen at all; that price and quantity might have a cyclical nature. As students act as members of a dynamically changing society, they understand the transient nature of prices, supply, demand, and thus the importance of timing (being at the right place in the right time).

This daily seasonality can be observed in other products as well. Most notable of course is in the market for consumable goods. To avoid burnout, Blizzard introduced the concept of the “weekly reset”. Large-scale Player Versus Environment encounters like raids and powerful open-world entities can only be defeated for gear once a week. This week resets (on European servers) on Wednesday, at 9 AM. This means, that most hardcore gamers (who tend to be adults with work or school schedule during the day) start their intensive weekly raiding on Wednesdays at 7 or 8pm. It is this periodicity that leads to market demand for consumables vastly rising around 6-6:30pm on weekdays – and especially on a Wednesday. Similarly, the prices for consumables are generally lowest in the wee hours of Monday or Tuesday.

Economic Crises

Another key economic issue is the analysis of economic crises. As mentioned above, Blizzard regularly releases content updates to keep the game fresh. These content updates usually contain more powerful challenges than before, which reward better equipment than that was previously available. To not completely kill off the demand for the products of crafting professions, Blizzard usually also introduces newer craftable equipment. The availability of this improved gear makes the demand for the previously available gear drop drastically. The new gear, however, is usually somehow *gated*: the players have to complete some in-game task to get access to them. This gating can be the need to participate in raids to get access to the recipe, participate in raids to get access to the actual materials for the recipe, perform difficult challenges in the world itself etc. Such gating will lead to a low supply of the products. Paired with the dropped demand for the earlier goods – thus the high demand for these new products, market prices usually start very high. With time, however, more and more producers can overcome the artificial hurdles, thus supply increases. Parallel to that, as time passes more and more weekly lockouts have passed, so more and more equipment became available to players, consequently lowering demand. The net result is that at the launch of a content update the new products are extremely expensive, but with time their prices slowly drops.

The content updates not only impact the demand and supply of durable goods, however. It is understandable that at the launch of a content update there is usually a large influx of players tackling these new challenges. Over time some parts of the player base becomes disinterested in regular activities (most notably raiding), but this lack of interest is swept away at the launch of the content patch. Because of this heightened interest, the demand for consumable goods, such as potions and food, rises dramatically. Also, since a relatively large number of people receive better equipment, the semi-permanent consumable goods produced by jewelcrafters and enchanters also experience increased demand. After a few weeks pass, things slowly return to how they were before. In case of very long patch cycles (at times Blizzard did not release a content update for over a year) millions of players leave the game, reducing the revenue both for in-game artisans and Blizzard itself. But then a new content update re-starts the cycle from the beginning.

Personal Finance, Liquidity

A critical design challenge when creating a virtual world is to make sure the currency has value. Blizzard famously failed at this with their massively successful Diablo II game. Launched in the summer of 2000, Diablo II quickly became critically acclaimed and incredibly successful commercially. At the same time, the game's built-in currency was quickly becoming worthless.

In order for a currency to be successful, it has to be just rare enough. If it is too rare, it cannot fulfill its function as the means of exchange, since nobody has it (money is too valuable). If, on the other hand, like in Diablo II, currency is too abundant, it will lose its value. There were literally no places to spend Diablo II currency. The equipment the in-game vendors were offering for gold were far inferior to the gear found within the game, and the other use for gold, repairing equipment, required only trivial amounts. Because of this, the medium of exchange quickly became a specific type of rare ring, the Stone of Jordan (which had the other kind of problem initially of being too scarce).

To avoid this issue, Blizzard is paying careful attention to the amount of gold entering and exiting the World of Warcraft servers. According to Marco Koegler, Technical Director of World of Warcraft (Marco Koegler, personal communication, November 8, 2014) Blizzard is running an entire economic intelligence unit monitoring the amount of gold flowing in the economy and out. Both the inflows and the outflows have to be carefully designed so as to avoid both extreme poverty for the many – as that would lead to them being dissatisfied with the gaming experience and leave the world, and also to avoid the Diablo II-like devaluation of the currency.

From the student's perspective, this is an excellent opportunity to do some financial planning. First, the student decides on their personal goals. Different goals have different gold requirements. Traditionally, PVP encounters have the lowest gold requirement, as in this context Blizzard wants to emphasize the importance of skill over wealth. Raiding, however, is more expensive. Raiding players have to budget for not only repairing their equipment, which in itself can be somewhat pricey costing a few hundred gold per day, but also for purchasing all of the above mentioned consumable goods to increase performance: flasks, potions, food and augment runes, possibly costing another few hundred. Others might have goals even beyond raiding, like the purchase of a rare and expensive mount (the above mentioned Sky Golem currently costs 11,000 gold, but the extremely rare and desirable Spectral Tiger mount costs over 750,000).

Once the personal goals are set, the player has to select a set of activities to achieve that goal. Some choose to specialize in gathering professions, wander the world and collect resources that they sell. Others try to find niche products that they can reliably sell for high profits. Still others try to optimize the game's built-in money flows (like finding a group of repeatable quests that can be quickly and efficiently completed). The chosen ways of making money, of course, will be a function of individual player preferences, as well: opportunity cost once again becomes the driver of the decision.

Inflation

Another key economic issue is that of inflation. While avoiding excessive inflation is critical, during the launch of larger content patches Blizzard deliberately inflates away the wealth of the players. This is usually somewhat gradual, so the extremely wealthy will remain rich, but the poor will have access to the higher rate of incomes, closing the wealth gap a little.

Detecting the magnitude of inflation, however, is no easy feat. Discussions of inflation are an excellent opportunity for students to understand the complexities of macroeconomic statistics. The basic idea behind inflation is simple: the price of a reference consumption bundle – a selection of goods the "average" consumer purchases – is calculated and then the change of price of this bundle is observed. The problem is that the price of the reference bundle would show a slow and steady decline across the content patch, and when the new expansion launches, the measure would indicate a drastic drop in inflation. The reason for this is that the demand for the goods in the reference basket drops greatly, and a new reference basket needs to be selected. At this point, however, the prices of the two baskets are not comparable. This is an effect that macroeconomic statisticians also have to deal with, but in the case of World of Warcraft, the magnitude of the problem is far greater, as the entire reference bundle has to be replaced, not just a few products substituted in or out.

Research in World of Warcraft

The World of Warcraft is not only ideal for teaching economics, but it is also optimal for performing certain social science inquiries. In this section some ongoing research is showcased, to emphasize how virtual worlds can be places of inquiry for more advanced settings than a simple introductory course.

In a virtual world students and researchers observe the behavior of real individuals; people who follow their own, selfish (and not *primarily* economics-driven) goals. Compared to this, in a business or psychological simulation setting participants can try to figure out what the simulation is all about, how it works. This will change their behavior, so the simulation results might not be lifelike. Even in simulations where they face off other humans, the purpose of the interaction is the simulation itself. Compared to this, observing and engaging the virtual-world players leads to more lifelike results, since their participation in the exchange is not motivated by the simulation, but instead by their own personal goals.

The author of this paper is currently conducting behavioral economic research in World of Warcraft. The question posed was how rational are humans? Economics frequently makes the assumption of the perfectly rational human decision maker, but the author has found frequent and systemic violation of this rule.

Other disciplines have also used World of Warcraft as a research platform. Carnegie Melon's famous Human Computer Interaction Institute, founded by Herbert A. Simon, conducts research projects in World of Warcraft (World of Warcraft Research Assistant, 2015). Due to a bug in the World of Warcraft system, a virtual epidemic started in the world and consequently epidemiologists descended on World of Warcraft to study the spread pattern of infections in human societies (Sydell, 2005). A recent study has been conducted, aimed at figuring out whether World of Warcraft can have therapeutic effects on dealing with the strains of aging (Whitlock, McLaughin & Allaire, 2012). World of Warcraft has even been used to study the formation and impact of diasporas (Herrera, Margitay-Becht & Chagas, 2010).

PRIMER TO INTEGRATING VIRTUAL WORLDS INTO COURSEWORK

In the previous sections the general education transmission mechanism was introduced, then World of Warcraft was introduced, and finally some key critical economics issues were introduced around which coursework can be built. In this section a general primer is being provided on the steps necessary to integrate virtual worlds in a general course.

Before discussing the actual steps to be taken to gamify a course, it is important to call attention to a number of caveats. The most important consideration is the institutional environment. Using virtual worlds or computer games in education might raise negative connotations from both colleagues and students. Despite the fact that a properly structured class integrating virtual worlds creates a more immersive, effective and active learning environment, colleagues could view it as a playful, light-minded class. Students might pick the course expecting an easy course with fewer requirements. However, when a course is well-organized,, students will experience quite the opposite. The first time the author ran a course using World of Warcraft as a teaching tool, students frequently commented that they felt the class was very informative and beneficial, but a lot harder than they expected. Communicating expectations ahead of time, through a detailed syllabus, is critical.

Step 1: Establish the Purpose and Context Of The Course

As the first step in designing a course using virtual worlds, the purpose of the course must be determined, the target audience identified, and it has to be decided whether the course is offered as an alternative to a traditional introductory courses, an elective course, or possibly offered as an upper-division course. The author's personal experience only extends to courses offered as optional classes that students opt in. For these courses, virtual worlds were an effective strategy for expanding on a student's existing interest or knowledge in the field of economics.

Step 2: Select the Virtual World

Depending on the context of the course, a list of potential virtual worlds can be drawn up. It is important to acknowledge that not all virtual worlds and not all genres of digital realities are equally applicable for all discussions. For example, World of Warcraft can be effectively used to discuss economics, Grand Theft Auto can be used to discuss physics, Second Life can be used to discuss economics, business strategy, product design, marketing, etc.

It is of equal importance that the chosen virtual world be a place that the teacher is comfortable with, otherwise they run the risk of losing student confidence and respect. This factor indeed is one of the most dangerous aspects of using virtual realities in education: the appearance of educational capability and authenticity of the teacher might be negatively impacted if they fail to demonstrate competence in the virtual reality itself.

Step 3: Analyze the Virtual World

Once a virtual world is identified, it needs to be critically analyzed to identify aspects and gameplay elements that are conducive in the education of the given material. There are two, complementing necessary conditions to pay attention to. First: is it possible to address all of the critical issues identified in Step 1 using the virtual reality? Second: what do the students gain using this medium over a traditional course? Is it possible to address the critical issues in a clearer manner? Do the students get to practice the theoretical material in the simulated environment? Does the virtual world allow discussion of topics that are hard to address in a traditional setting?

For example, World of Warcraft makes it possible to discuss the supply-demand model, the production possibility frontier, the simple consumer and producer models used in the analysis in microeconomics courses, so it meets the first necessary condition of applicability to teach microeconomics. Is there however any point to doing so? Aside from the greater immersion and student motivation, students tackle the critical assumptions of perfect information and economic rationality, and practice the importance of timing.

Similarly, if the focus is more production oriented, it is possible to use the complex crafting model of World of Warcraft to identify and practice critical economic and value-chain decisions. Which industries should we operate in? Which markets should we sell to? Which production channel should we use to target those markets (trade channel vs. auction house)? What, if any, level of vertical integration should we choose to use? What are the major cycles in the supply and demand of our raw materials? Of our final goods?

Step 4: Review Curriculum and Game Selection

Once the game has been selected and analyzed, a final syllabus can be drawn up. It needs to address not only all the topics discussed during the course, but also pair those topics with the appropriate exercises the students have to conduct in World of Warcraft. Some form of assessment of said exercises also needs to be designed, either through external resources like quizzes, presentations or written reports, or some form of internal tracking mechanisms, possibly through the use of a customized addon.

Once the course is so laid out, it is heavily advisable to compare the results with the initially set constraints. Are all curricular requirements met? Does the course seem to provide sufficient extra value over a traditional course? If the answer is no to any of the questions, a new iteration can be started from Step 2.

CONCLUSION

This chapter discussed the applicability of World of Warcraft to teaching economics in particular, and virtual worlds to college education in general.

The introduction described virtual worlds. Then a generic introduction to how virtual worlds can be used for education was described, building on the mirroring of real-world phenomena within virtual realities. The following section introduced World of Warcraft and its main features, the 3D environment, addons, specialization, group content, world PVP, professions and trade. The economics in World of Warcraft section demonstrated certain key economic features present in the game that can serve as a hook into the educational environment: opportunity cost, supply-demand, economic crises, personal finance and inflation. It also discussed the research potential of World of Warcraft, to highlight its applicability of more advanced coursework as well. The final section generalized the previously introduced ideas to incorporating virtual worlds to any general college course.

Using virtual worlds for education is a challenging endeavor, but is well worth the extra effort. While both the professors and the students have to work significantly harder than in a traditionally conducted course, student outcomes and experience improve dramatically. At the same time, during the current academic social environment, the extra effort might be rewarded with skepticism.

REFERENCES

Castronova, E. (2005). *Synthetic worlds: The business and culture of online games*. University of Chicago Press.

EURO Quick server stats. (2015). Retrieved from http://www.warcraftrealms.com/eu_realmstats.php

Gee, J. P. (2007). *What video games have to teach us about learning and literacy*. Palgrave Macmillan.

Herrera, D. R., Margitay-Becht, A., & Chagas, J. (2010). Cyber-disaporas: The Effects of Migration to Virtual Worlds. In L. DePretto, G. Macri, & C. Wong (Eds.), *Diasporas: Revisiting and Discovering* (pp. 287–298). Oxford: Inter-Disciplinary Press.

Margitay-Becht, A., & Herrera, D. R. (2008). Fun is Learning: A Case Study of Gaming as Education in Virtual Worlds. In C. Nygaard & C. Holtham (Eds.), *Understanding Learning-centred Higher Education*. Copenhagen: Copenhagen Business School Press.

Margitay-Becht, A., & Herrera, D. R. (2013). Teaching Social Skills in Virtual Worlds: A primer for extending existing social science education to business management. In S. D'Agustino (Ed.), *Immersive Environments, Augmented Realities and Virtual Worlds: Assessing Future Trends in Education*. IGI Global. doi:10.4018/978-1-4666-2670-6.ch011

MMOs.com. (2015). Retrieved from http://mmos.com/editorials/most-popular-mmorpgs-world

Roman, D. (2011, February 11). Online Game's Banker Battles Inflation. *The Wall Street Journal*. Retrieved from http://www.wsj.com/articles/SB10001424052748704132204576135931023983542

Skipper, B. (2015, January 27). Greece's new finance minister Yanis Varoufakis is Valve's former Steam Market economist. *International Business Times*. Retrieved from http://www.ibtimes.co.uk/greeces-new-finance-minister-yanis-varoufakis-valves-former-steam-market-economist-1485336

Stoutfoot, T. (2007) *How big is Azeroth?* (Pseudonym) Retrieved from http://tobolds.blogspot.com/2007/01/how-big-is-azeroth.html

Sydell, L. (2005). 'Virtual' Virus Sheds Light on Real-World Behavior. *NPR*, Retrieved from http://www.npr.org/templates/story/story.php?storyId=4946772

Toon activity by level. (2015). Retrieved from http://www.wow-stats.info/pact01.html

Yee, N. (2006). Motivations for play in online games. *Cyberpsychology & Behavior*, *9*(6), 772–775. doi:10.1089/cpb.2006.9.772 PMID:17201605

Whitlock, L. A., McLaughlin, A. C., & Allaire, J. C. (2012). Individual differences in response to cognitive training: Using a multi-modal, attentionally demanding game-based intervention for older adults. *Computers in Human Behavior*, *28*(4), 1091–1096. doi:10.1016/j.chb.2012.01.012

The World Factbook. (2015). Retrieved from https://www.cia.gov/library/publications/the-world-factbook/rankorder/2119rank.html

World of Warcraft Research Assistant. (2015). Retrieved from http://www.hcii.cmu.edu/careers/2011/world-warcraft-research-assistant

ADDITIONAL READING

D'Agustino, S. (Ed.). (2013). *Immersive Environments, Augmented Realities, and Virtual Worlds: Assessing Future Trends in Education*. Hershey, PA, USA: IGI Global.

Alberti, J. (2013). *Rhetoric/Composition/play Through Video Games: Reshaping Theory and Practice of Writing*. Palgrave Macmillan.

Boellstorff, T. (2008). *Coming of age in Second Life: An anthropologist explores the virtually human*. Princeton University Press.

Bowers, C., Smith, P. A., Cannon-Bowers, J., & Nicholson, D. (2008). Using virtual worlds to assist distributed teams. Handbook of research on virtual workplaces and the new nature of business practices (pp. 408-423).

Castronova, E. (2008). *Exodus to the virtual world: How online fun is changing reality*. Palgrave Macmillan.

Castronova, E., Williams, D., Shen, C., Ratan, R., Xiong, L., Huang, Y., & Keegan, B. (2009). As real as real? Macroeconomic behavior in a large-scale virtual world. *New Media & Society*, *11*(5), 685–707. doi:10.1177/1461444809105346

Devlin, K. (2011). *Mathematics education for a new era: Video games as a medium for learning*. CRC Press. doi:10.1201/b10816

Gee, J. P. (2007). *Good video games and good learning: Collected essays on video games, learning and literacy* (New literacies and digital epistemologies).

Gee, J. P. (2014). *What video games have to teach us about learning and literacy*. Macmillan.

Gee, J. P. (2014). *Unified Discourse Analysis: Language, Reality, Virtual Worlds and Video Games*. Routledge.

Kapp, K. M. (2012). *The gamification of learning and instruction: game-based methods and strategies for training and education*. John Wiley & Sons.

Lacasa, P. (2013). *Learning in Real and Virtual Worlds: Commercial Video Games as Educational Tools*. Palgrave Macmillan. doi:10.1057/9781137312051

Mayer, R. E. (2014). *Computer Games for Learning: An Evidence-Based Approach*. MIT Press.

McGonigal, J. (2011). *Reality is broken: Why games make us better and how they can change the world*. Penguin.

Prensky, M. (2005). *Computer games and learning: Digital game-based learning. Handbook of Computer Game Studies, 18*, 97-122.

Shaffer, D. W. (2006). *How computer games help children learn*. Macmillan. doi:10.1057/9780230601994

Sheldon, L. (2011). *The multiplayer classroom: Designing coursework as a game*. Cengage Learning.

Squire, K. (2011). *Video Games and Learning: Teaching and Participatory Culture in the Digital Age. Technology, Education – Connections (the TEC Series)*. Teachers College Press.

Steinkuehler, C., Squire, K., & Barab, S. (Eds.), (2012). *Games, learning, and society: Learning and meaning in the digital age*. Cambridge University Press. doi:10.1017/CBO9781139031127

Whitton, N. (2009). *Learning with digital games: A practical guide to engaging students in higher education*. Routledge.

KEY TERMS AND DEFINITIONS

Avatar: Avatar is the virtual representation of the participant or player in the virtual world.

Blizzard Entertainment: Blizzard Entertainment or Blizzard for short is the name of the gaming company that created and maintains World of Warcraft.

Character: Avatars in World of Warcraft are called character.

Disruptive Technologies: When new technologies arise, if they provide products that are superior to existing products in every way, they disrupt the way business is being done. The better the new product is, the greater the impact of the disruption. Example: the introduction of the iPhone by Apple.

Economics: Economics is the science of making choices in an environment of scarcity.

Experiential Learning: Experiental learning is the collective name for learning techniques that put student engagement and experience at their center.

Gamification: Observing player behavior in virtual worlds and other computer simulated environments, it has been realized that players are greatly motivated to participate. Gamification tries to identify the reason for this motivation, and transplant the motivation mechanisms into other (corporate, educational) settings.

Immersive Experience: Participants of virtual worlds highly identify with their virtual lives lived within the virtual world. It can become similarly important to them as their lives lived outside the virtual setting.

Institutions: In social sciences institutions are everything that describe how things are done in a society. Aside from those obvious institutions like the Central Bank, they also include things like law and trade.

Opportunity Cost: In economics, opportunity cost describes the benefit or gain given up when making a choice, that comes from not choosing another option. It signifies the true cost of everything, as it describes not only the monetary dimension, but all of the other dimensions (time, space, social capital, etc.) as well. For example, if a person can either go to the movies or eat out, the opportunity cost of going to the movies is *not* eating out.

Player Versus Environment (PVE): When participating in PVE activities, the players engage computer controlled enemies or overcome computer-driven challenges.

Player Versus Player (PVP): When participating in PVE activities, the players engage each other, either in dedicated areas (instanced PVP), or in the virtual world at large (world PVP).

Role: In an MMORPG role describes what generic problems certain characters are good at solving. Traditionally there are three roles (frequently called the "trinity" of MMORPGs): tank, healer and dps, but certain virtual worlds include other roles like support as well.

Server/Shard: To balance the load hundreds of thousands or millions of players would cause on a virtual world, virtual world operators usually split the players up across identical copies of the same virtual reality. These copies are referred to as servers or shards. A notable exception is EVE online, where all players are on the same (virtual) shard.

Vertical Integration: A company is vertically integrated if it does not only produce a single good or service, but also produces either the materials to produce their product (upstream), and/or uses the product to manufacture other products (downstream).

ENDNOTES

1. Currently exceptions come mostly in the form of mobile-phone based virtual worlds, like the greatly successful *freemium* games Clash of Clans and Game of War. These have to keep into consideration the fact that smartphones have limited processing and battery power, so they usually use isometric view.
2. At that time there were other avenues to power too. In order to use weapons, characters had to train in weapon skills, so aside from character level and the equipment itself, another leveling process had to be completed. Spellcasters could find rare books of power empowering their spells, providing a combination of item-based and character-based leveling. These additional sources of power were eventually phased out; these days only the two traditional routes to power remain.
3. From the Game Lore's perspective, the new continent, called Draenor, was not a continent at all, instead an entirely new planet. From the players' perspective, however, this distinction hardly matters.

Chapter 7
The Use of Virtual Worlds in Foreign Language Teaching and Learning

Ellen Yeh
Columbia College Chicago, USA

Guofang Wan
Virginia Commonwealth University, USA

ABSTRACT

This book chapter presents, a review of the literature from 2004-2014 regarding the various models of virtual worlds used in foreign language teaching and learning, the impact of virtual world learning environments and the implications of language teaching. The study being reported aims to address the following questions: (1) What are the models of virtual worlds used in language learning instruction in K-12 and higher education; (2) How do VWLEs impact language learning in terms of motivation, communicative competency, intercultural competency, collaborative competency, constructivist learning, and sociocultural competency; and (3) What are the implications of using VWLEs in foreign language teaching and learning? Results indicate that social context and task-based learning enhanced language learners' participation and motivations. Findings also indicate that consistent use of interactional strategies encouraged learners to engage in the tasks and stay motivated. The study suggested that a VWLE offers a motivating, engaging, and multi-dynamic environment for language learners.

INTRODUCTION

Policy-makers, researchers, educators, and learners have paid significant attention to three-dimensional space (3D) virtual world learning environments (VWLEs), which provide learning across curricula and cultures (Deutschmann & Panichi, 2009). 3D virtual worlds learning environments are defined as "persistent virtual environments in which people experience others as being there with them and where they interact with them" (Schroeder, 2008, p.2). Virtual worlds are also described as computer-simulated environments that take place in either realistic settings or imaginary settings (Wickens, 1992). The

DOI: 10.4018/978-1-4666-9837-6.ch007

term "virtual world" has expanded its meaning to a type of online platform. One unique characteristic in virtual worlds is that the systems allow participants to interact simultaneously with other players in a persistent virtual environment.

As learning platforms, VWLEs have four main features that educators may use in various ways: (1) an avatar function that visually represents the participant; (2) various interactive functions for communications including text, audio, and symbolic formats (Dickey, 2005; Dickey, 2011; Wang, Calandra, Hibbard, & McDowell, 2012); (3) a function for a participant to "act" in the virtual world; and (4) a 3D interactive space (Wang et al., 2012). Research studies also reveal that in K-12 and higher education settings, VWLEs provide communication spaces, experiential spaces, and simulation spaces (Hew & Cheung, 2008). The use of virtual worlds in education have been reported in the literature, including Active Worlds, Blaxxun, Community Place, OnLive!, Open Wonderland, Quest Atlantis, Second Life, and Traveler in instruction in academic settings (Berns, Gonzalez-Pardo, & Camacho, 2012; Ibanez et al., 2011).

Among these virtual worlds, Second Life and Active Worlds are the most commonly used in the United States. (Peterson, 2011). These virtual worlds are multi-user virtual environments without fixed storylines or games. The software allows participants to have total freedom to construct their communities, create storylines, and form contexts for communication. Furthermore, Second Life has been popular in higher education settings; at least 300 higher education institutes around the world teach courses or conduct research in Second Life (Deutschmann & Panichi, 2009; Second Life, n.d.). As of 2014, the developer, Linden Labs, reports that Second Life has one million active users daily (Second Life, n.d.).

Educational uses of VWLEs have been studied for the purpose of enhancing the quality of students' learning (Jarmon, Traphagan, Mayrath, & Trivedi, 2008; Wang, Calandra, Hibbard, & McDowell, 2012), expanding learning and life experiences (Jarmon et al., 2008; Wang et al., 2012), and providing collaborative learning opportunities (Erlanson, Nelson & Wilhelmina, 2010; Wang et al., 2012). Research studies show that VWLEs offer opportunities for social interactions, integrating technology in both academic and daily life, and accessing and analyzing information (Wang et al., 2012).

BACKGROUND

In recent years, the rapid advancement of technology has brought easy access to a plethora of open source software, mobile apps, and virtual worlds to the public, which are changing the landscape of foreign language teaching and learning.

Specifically, in the field of computer-assisted language learning (CALL), the features in virtual worlds allow participants to interact with native speakers of their target language in real-time communication and on a high-quality 3D platform with a rich, interesting simulated learning environment (Peterson, 2011). Virtual world software collects written records of participants' linguistic output by recording data in the game so researchers can analyze participants' use of the target language.

The current study aims to review, analyze, and synthesize recent literature on the various models of virtual worlds used in foreign language instruction, the impact of VWLEs on foreign language learning, and the implications of teaching and learning foreign language instruction through virtual worlds.

Research Questions

The study being reported aims to address the following questions: (1) What are the models of virtual worlds used in language learning instruction in K-12 and higher education; (2) How do VWLEs impact language learning in terms of motivation, communicative competency, intercultural competency, collaborative competency, constructivist learning, and sociocultural competency; and (3) What are the implications of using VWLEs in foreign language teaching and learning?

Criteria for Selection of Studies

In order to capture all studies that included use of VWLEs with foreign language learners at the K-12 or higher education levels, the inclusion criteria for studies was intentionally defined broadly. Following are the inclusionary criteria used: discussions of (1) various models of the VWLEs in foreign language learning, (2) the impact of VWLEs on foreign language learning, (3) the implications of using VWLEs in foreign language curricula, and (4) published between the ten year period of 2004 and 2014.

Locating Relevant Studies

The data base of studies include in this literature review was established in two steps: a search of electronic databases and a review of the articles identified in Step 1 to verify that they met the criteria listed. Basic searches were performed using Education Resources Information Center (ERIC), Education Research Complete, and Google Scholar

The following keywords were used: virtual worlds, 3D virtual learning environment, collaborative virtual learning environment, videogame-like applications, Second Life, language learning, teacher education, professional development, intercultural competency, language proficiency, as well as computer-mediated communication (CMC). Through this search, fifty related articles were generated from twenty eight academic journals. These fifty articles focused on using virtual tools in education. However, only eighteen of the fifty articles met the established selection criteria (using virtual tools in language teaching and learning) and were used to answer the research questions (see Table 1). These eighteen related articles were generated from fourteen academic journals.

Coding the Studies

Based on the framework of qualitative evidence synthesis methods, two researchers read through the eighteen articles that met selection criteria and coded them manually and independently, examining the articles for common and major themes related to the research questions; then they discussed and compared their findings and collaboratively identified the common themes to be presented in the results section. The findings were based on pre-established criteria and guidelines for identifying information and keywords related to answering the three research questions. For the first research question (Models of Virtual World Environments Used in Foreign Language), the researchers investigated the methodology section of the literature. More specifically, the researchers examined what types of virtual world model the studies implemented in the language curricula, how the participants interacted with each other, and what types of model language teachers preferred or applied. For the second question (VWLEs Impact on Learning), the researchers focused on the result section of the literature. The researchers investigated

Table 1. Studies Review

Studies	Methods	No. of Subject / Site
Berns, Gonzalez-Pardo, & Camacho (2012)	Qualitative: Observation Quantitative: Survey	85 (college); Spain
Blankenship (2010)	Qualitative: Observation	12 pre-service teachers; southern United States.
Blasing (2010)	Qualitative: In-depth Interview & Observation	5 (college); Russia
Deutschmann & Panichi (2009)	Qualitative: Document analysis Quantitative	9 (college); Russia, Sweden, Italy, Spain, Austria, & Malta.
Deutschmann, Panichi, & Molka-Danielsson (2009)	Qualitative: In-depth Interview & Observation	13 (doctoral); Sweden
Ibanez, Garcia, Galan, Maroto, Morillo, & Kloos (2011)	Qualitative: Observation & Document Analysis	12 (Spanish speakers) and 6 (foreign language teachers); Spain
Jauregi, Graaff, & Canto (2012)	Qualitative: In-depth Interview & Observation. Quantitative: Survey & Oral Tests.	430 (college); Netherlands, Portugal, Russia, & Spain.
Kim & Blankenship (2013)	Qualitative: Observation & Document Analysis	12 (pre-service teachers); Argentina.
Knutzen & Kennedy (2012)	Qualitative: Observation	200 (college); Hong Kong
Ligorio, Cesareni,& Schwartz (2008)	Qualitative: Observation.	10 (13 yrs. old); Italy & Netherlands
Pasfield-Neofitou (2011)	Quantitative: Documents & Interviews	30; Australia & Japan
Peterson (2011)	Literature Review	NA
Shih & Yang (2008)	Qualitative: In-depth Interview & Observation. Quantitative: Survey	20 (20-22 yrs. old); Taiwan
Thorne, Black & Sykes (2009)	Literature Review	NA
Wang, Calandra, Hibbard & McDowell (2012)	Qualitative: Document Analysis	39 (college); China
Wang & Shao (2012)	Qualitative: Document Analysis	39 (college); China
Zhang (2013)	Qualitative: In-depth Interview & Observation	10 (graduate students); China.
Zheng, Young, Wagner, & Brewer (2009)	Qualitative: In-depth Interview, Observation, & Document Analysis	4 (college); China & the U.S.

how the VWLEs influenced language learning and what are some benefits while applying virtual tools in language classrooms. For the third research question (Implications of VWLE Use in Foreign Language Curriculum), the researchers examined both the results and discussion section of the literature. The researchers looked for practical implications, limitations, and future studies.

The researchers applied qualitative evidence synthesis methods, which include elements of applying aggregation approaches (Peterson, 2012). Aggregative synthesis methods involve listing the results of various previous literature and then further organizing and combining them into themes or categories to produce a general description of the certain research issue (Peterson, 2012). The researchers had the three questions listed at the top of a page of paper and as they read each study they wrote down any information that contributed an answer to each of the research questions. Then, they combined all of that data and come up with common themes.

Mainly, aggregative methods are the systematic review method used by the Joanna Briggs Institute, but they also use meta-summary, content-analysis, and thematic analysis, case study, qualitative comparative analysis, and Bayesian meta-analysis (McInnes & Wimpenny, 2008).

RESULTS

Models of Virtual World Environments Used in Foreign Language Instruction

A review of the literature from 2004 to 2014 pertaining to teaching and learning foreign language found nine studies (Blankenship, 2010; Deutschmann & Panichi, 2009; Jauregi, Graaff & Canto, 2012; Kim & Blankenship, 2013; Knutzen & Kennedy, 2012; Peterson, 2011; Wang et al, 2012; Wang & Shao, 2012; Zhang, 2013) which focus on the use of virtual world Second Life, with several studies focusing on other online 3D multiuser virtual environments such as Quest Atlantis (QA), a virtual gaming Active Worlds metaverse (Zheng, Young, Wagner, & Brewer, 2009), OpenSim, a videogame-like application (Berns et al., 2012), Open Wonderland, an open source 3D virtual world development tool (Ibanez et al., 2011), VEC3D, a 3D virtual English classroom (Shih & Yang, 2008), virtual communities via mobile apps, social network sites, video games and online videos (Pasfield-Neofitou, 2011), and the uses of Skye, Google Docs and Active World (Blankenship, 2010; Peterson, 2011; Knutzen & Kennedy, 2012).

The major uses of 3D VWLEs in language instructions include (1) utilizing the resource as the main vehicle for instruction (Blankenship, 2010; Wang et al, 2012; Knutzen & Kennedy, 2012; Deutschmann & Panichi, 2009), and (2) curriculum integration involving both traditional instruction and VWLEs.

3D VWLEs Used In Teacher Training

The professional development program with simulated virtual classrooms in Second Life and Skype allow pre-service teachers to practice competencies of second language (L2) instruction while scaffolded by their instructors and peers (Blankenship, 2010). Cheong (2010, as cited in Kim & Blankenship, 2013) investigated the impact of teaching in Second Life on preservice teachers' efficacy and claimed, "preservice teachers can gain valuable teaching practice in Second Life and that collaborative teaching practice is effective" (p.23). 3D VWLEs programs used to teach L2 and to train L2 teachers: the collaboration and partnership on 3D VWLEs between language instruction programs and pre-service L2 teacher training programs are important features. For example, the L2 in the Global Classroom program (Knutzen & Kennedy, 2012) improved their spoken and listening English while pre-service English language teachers (as partners for the Global Classroom) practiced their skills in teaching English as foreign or second language. The purpose of Deutschmann and Panichi's (2009) study was to identify how supportive moves made by teachers encourage learners to engage with the target language, and what type of linguistic behavior, such as turn length and turn-taking, leads to engagement in others. The researchers analyzed the first and the last sessions from the online oral proficiency course aimed at seven doctoral students and two language teachers in the VWLE Second Life. The study showed that students were able to (1) keep an informal conversation going; (2) be more attentive to the listener's comprehension; (3) be more supportive and interested in a conversation by asking questions, recognizing turn-taking rules, giving constructive feedback, etc.; (4) signal when they didn't understand and when they needed more information; and (5) be aware of cultural differences during the conversation. The findings also suggest that supportive linguistic behavior of teachers is crucial in enhancing learners' engagements. Participants changed their linguistic behavior between the first and the last sessions; they became more active in signaling involvement as the course progressed.

Experimental and Short 3D VWLEs Programs

Exploratory programs created in VWLEs, such as Second Life, showed significant gains in learning among English learners (Wang et al, 2012). The oral proficiency course for doctoral students conducted in the virtual world Second Life, suggests that supportive moves and linguistic behaviors by teachers are important for students' learning and language gains (Deutschmann & Panichi, 2009). 3D virtual English classroom (VEC3D) as a novel language-learning platform, motivated advanced English as a foreign language (EFL) undergraduate students in learning, "acquiring communication strategies, and further extending autonomy in virtual communication through integrating goal-based design, role-play and 3D VR…." (Shih & Yang, 2008, p.66).

Important Trend of 3D VWLE Instruction

Another important trend of using 3D VWLEs in language instruction is integrating VWLEs programs into traditional curriculum as extended programs and activities enrich and innovate foreign language instruction (Berns et al., 2012; Jauregi et al., 2012; Wang & Shao, 2012; Zhang, 2013). In conjunction with classroom instructions, 3D VWLEs are often used as complimentary resources and add-ons to create opportunities for L2 to interact in virtual worlds with native speakers and practice spoken and written forms of target languages (Zhang, 2013). Authentic language learning activities and classroom projects created on 3D VWLEs, such as Second Life, motivated students in language learning. Programs created on other 3D multi-user virtual world, such as Open Wonderland (Ibanez et al., 2011), OpenSim (Berns et al., 2012) and VEC3D immerse learners in real-time communications or interactions in learning (Shih & Yang, 2008; Zheng et al., 2009).

Characteristics of Design

The characteristics of designs of programs created on 3D VWLEs are many; however, authentic situation, immersion, cross-cultural collaboration and goal-based design appear to be prominent in the review studies. The authentic cultural interactions occurring synchronously in virtual worlds allow students to develop their own cultural understanding and language awareness. Jauregi et al. (2012) report L2 experience added values through cross-cultural interactions, besides other benefits. Exchanges and negotiations of meanings both socially and culturally appear while participants collaborate with each other, reflecting on and clarifying concepts, customs, styles, or behaviors on 3D VWLEs. Quest Atlantis (the game-based virtual world) affords language acquisitions (i.e. pragmatics, syntax, semantics, and discourse) via the avatar-embodied intercultural interactions between native English and non-native English speakers (Zheng et al, 2009). Australian learners of Japanese, who participated in language-specific virtual communities (Facebook, Mixi, SNSs, forums), interacted with Japanese native speakers and observed interactions among native Japanese, believe they could model after the language uses by native speakers and that virtual communities provided them with greater access to popular culture and other authentic cultural materials, which were shared by other native speakers and advertisings from website sponsors (Pasfield-Neofitou, 2011).

Authentic Language Communication

Programs in 3D VWLEs put L2 in authentic language/communication situations virtually - where they speak, listen, read and write in the target language with native speakers. This is instrumental for L2 to learn as "the best language learning takes place when the learner is immersed in an environment where the language is natively spoken (Ibanez et al., 2011, p. 2). Pasfield-Neofitou's (2011) natural and social communications on blog, email, SNS, chat room, game profiles and mobile Apps were analyzed and results showed that "gaining access to an authentic audience, was the most important source of motivation for L2 production…." (p.105). Their study reported a four-year long study on virtual communities formed with 12 Australian Japanese learners and 18 Japanese English learners. In the Global Classroom project of Knutzen and Kennedy (2012), 200 participants, half Hong Kong-based English learners and half US-based TESOL students, interacted in a 1950's style American diner created in Second Life. Their instant message (IM) chat and Voice over Internet Protocol (VOIP) voices and behaviors recorded showed that, "Chat proved to be an extremely useful form of interaction for new users…. The immersive virtual environment offers a very good simulation of face-to-face interaction, with its fast-paced small talk and informal language style" (p. 90).

When used appropriately, VWLEs can be beneficial to language learners by developing their socializing and problem-solving skills, providing entertainment, and facilitating learning. Shih and Yang (2008) designed an immersive and interactive virtual English classroom called 3D virtual English classroom (VEC3D). VEC3D is a 3D campus simulated interactive learning environment designed to enhance students' communicative skills and motivation. VEC3D applied task-based and goal-based instructional design (Sadler & Nurmukhamedov, 2008; Thorne, Black, & Sykes, 2009). The results indicate that language learners are inclined to be highly motivated when they are required to search for information to accomplish goals or solve problems in authentic contexts.

Collaboration and Partnerships

Collaboration and partnerships are seen in several reviewed studies. Some collaborate between two countries, involving language learners and native speakers from China and US (Knutzen & Kennedy, 2012; Wang et al., 2012), from Austria and Japan (Pasfield-Neofitou, 2011), Japan and US (Zhang, 2013), and students from three schools in Poland and Spain (Prieto-Arranz, Juan-Garau, & Jacob, 2013). Other 3D VWLEs programs involve foreign language learners interacting with native language teachers-in-training, while both groups benefit from the experience (Kim & Blankenship, 2013). Language learners from multiple countries, Russia, Sweden, Italy, Span, Australia and Maltese are found practicing target languages with native language teachers in Second Life (Deutschmann & Panichi, 2009). The findings of Jauregi et al. (2012) showed that integrating synchronous collaboration projects through video communication and virtual world gaming environments, such as Second Life, have value in linguistic, interpersonal, and motivation issues. They proved that networked sessions offer a positive impact on motivation. Compared to the control group (i.e., the group taking a regular language class), foreign language learners in the experimental group (i.e., the group using Second Life and video communication) were more willing to communicate in their target language, showed significant differences in improvement of the target language, had more positive attitudes towards communication, and had decreased anxiety regarding speaking. Based on the theory of Collaborative Language Teaching (CLT) (Larsen-Freeman, 2007), VWLEs offer an innovative language learning experience with extended immersion in a natural and authentic context with mentoring and support. A virtual world is considered a collaborative and constructivist learning tool. In a qualitative analysis, the study found themes about social boundaries and the anxiety of entering into the virtual world environment.

3D VWLE-Based Programs with Specific Learning Objectives

3D VWLE-based programs with specific learning objectives and goals for language learners are beneficial (Berns et al. 2012; Zheng et al., 2009). Programs that are designed with goal-based and learning outcome-oriented tasks, activities and exercises use technology (3D VWLEs) as a tool rather than an ultimate goal of learning. The supermarket-game created on OpenSim (Berns et al. 2012) introduces students to basic vocabulary related to German food and beverages. Created within Open Wonderland, the natural text chatting with non-player characters, textual tagging of virtual objects, and automatic reading of texts in learning sequences foster students' communication skills (Ibanez et al., 2011). The goal-based instructional design and interactive virtual English classroom, VEC3D, advances student communicative competence and through vivid 3D graphic and real-time voice communication, VEC3D helps enhance learners' English communication skills and promote positive attitude toward learning (Shih & Yang, 2008).

Virtual World Learning Environments Impact on Learning

To answer the second research question, the author create a Virtual World Learning Environment Impact Model to illustrate to what extent VWLEs impact language learning in terms of motivation, communicative competency, intercultural competency, collaborative competency, constructivist learning, and sociocultural competency (See Figure 1).

Motivation

Motivation is one important factor in the learning process, and, as technology has changed the way we learn and interact, it has also affected learner motivation. This section discusses how to benefit from virtual world environments by motivating learners.

Studies claim VWLEs help ELLs learn academic language and culture more effectively and efficiently. As a result, they enhance learners' academic achievement and prepare them for careers (Berns et al., 2012; Blasing, 2010; Jauregi et al., 2012; Knutzen & Kennedy, 2012; Shih & Yang, 2008; Wang et al., 2012). Several studies have found language learners have higher motivation in learning foreign languages through the use of VWLEs. For instance, Blasing (2010) conducted Russian college language learners' interaction and to identify the formation of Russian language in the areas of Second Life. The study investigated participants' second language (L2) identity choices, affective responses (i.e., motivation, anxiety, and confidence) to the virtual world, and learner interaction strategies with target

Figure 1. Virtual World Learning Environment Impact Model

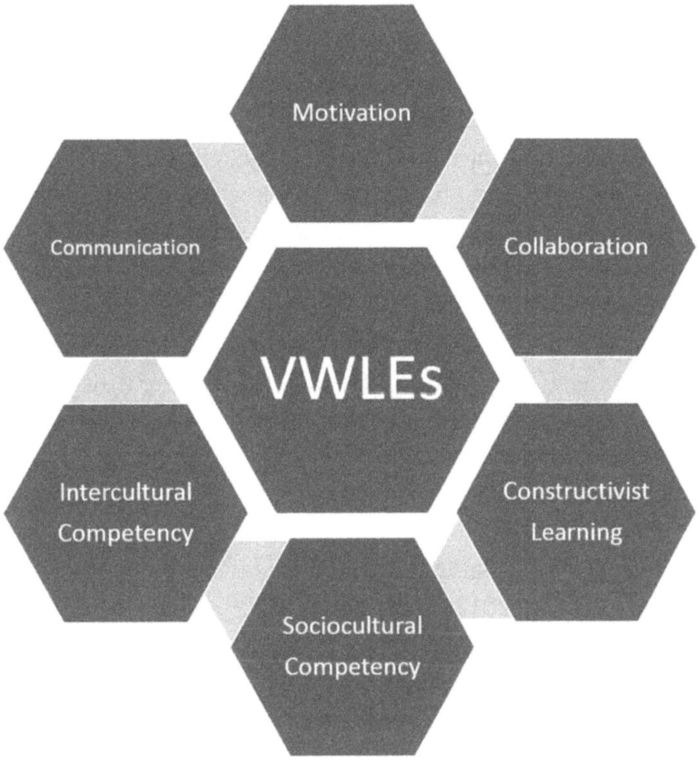

speakers. These communicative strategies could transfer from the VWLE to real-world communication. The results reveal that VWLEs offer learners an authentic setting, which motivates them to participate actively in target language situational practice (for instance, role playing). VWLEs provide captivating social, emotional, and environmental stimuli that traditional EFL/ESL classrooms lack. Two key effects distinguish Second Life from other types of telecommunication tools. First, the virtual element increases anxiety to the level that mimics face-to-face interaction in the target language culture. Second, learners achieve a greater sense of confidence in their interactions with native speakers by selecting avatars in the Second Life gaming world (Blasing, 2010).

Regarding the effects of virtual world use on pedagogical practices, Wang et al. (2012) reported on the effects an experimental EFL program in Second Life had on Chinese EFL learning. The study collected data from 61 Chinese college students; 20 Chinese participants were selected for the Second Life EFL Program as an experimental group, and the rest of the participants were in a control group. The findings revealed that the Second Life EFL Program was significantly effective in EFL learning as measured by pre- and post- language tests. The data analysis from participants' survey, in-depth interviews, and blog reflections showed that the program provides participants with a positive virtual learning platform. Additionally, participants in the experimental group claimed that the Second Life EFL Program is motivating, interactive, and successful.

Communicative Competency

VWLEs provided opportunities for language learners to acquire language in context and to develop communicative competency (Deutschmann & Panichi, 2009; Deutschmann, Panichi, & Molka-Danielsson, 2009; Shih & Yang, 2008; Thorne et al., 2009; Zhang, 2013). Language learners develop various communicative strategies when they encounter difficulties communicating in the target language. Shih and Yang (2008) found that participants' chat transcripts of six synchronous online activities indicated an enhanced acquisition of communicative competence and strategies and the study suggests that VWLEs offer opportunities for participants to repair communication breakdowns by using communicative strategies. Communication breakdowns also allowed the learners to practice discourse skills.

The seven communicative strategies used in order of accuracy and frequency in the conversation were: (1) paraphrasing (i.e., approximation, circumlocution); (2) borrowing (i.e., literal translation, language switch); (3) appeal for assistance; (4) non-linguistic means; (5) avoidance (i.e., topic avoidance, message avoidance); (6) prefabricated patterns; and (7) filler. The application and integration of VWLEs foster learners' communicative competency through role-play and the construction and development of task-based curriculum design.

Preliminary research supports the findings that VWLEs present opportunities for developing communicative skills (e.g., Jauregi et al., 2012; Thorne et al., 2009; Zheng, Li & Zhao, 2008). For instance, Second Life provides opportunities for negotiation for meaning and higher levels of engagement for language learners. Blasing's (2010) study found that there is evidence that language acquisition occurs through interaction and negotiation of meaning within the VWLE. In the virtual world discussion forums, ELLs have opportunities in online interaction and sharing to engage in intense negotiation for meaning (Yeh & Kessler, 2015).

Blasing (2010) also investigated interaction between participants and native speakers in Second Life using the typed chat function as the only means of communication. The findings showed that chatting benefits learners' development of lexicon, improvement in writing skills, and self-correction; it also stimulates focus on form. In addition, the results suggest that participants were able to make connections and learn syntactical structures from native speakers more readily due to the written format of the chat interface. The researchers distinguish the difference from focus on form to focus on formS. According to Long (1991), focus on formS refers to traditional teaching approaches in which the main organizing principle of language learning was the accumulation of grammatical language items, such as plural endings and passives (Long, 1991; Gass & Selinker, 2008). Focus on form, on the other hand, refers to a need for meaning-focused activity in which attention to form is embedded. Long (1991) explained this concept that "overtly draws students' attention to linguistic elements as they arise incidentally in lessons whose overriding focus is on meaning or communication" (pp. 45-46). Virtual worlds can be a valuable tool in providing a learning environment that focuses on form.

Other communicative skills used by language learners include turn lengths and turn-taking patterns. Two studies showed that meaning-focused, task-based design involved authenticity and collaborative components (Deutschmann & Panichi, 2009; Deutschmann et al., 2009). A meaning-focused, task-design refers to students' learning the target language through communication and discussion rather than merely focusing on grammar. Deutschmann et al. (2009) found that meaning-focused activities help students to become supportive and interactive listeners who can ask supportive questions, recognize turn-taking rules, and give constructive feedback. Through these activities, students are able to present their research in a structured and comprehensible way. Students also are more aware of cultural differences through collaboration and communication.

The two research studies were conducted in Kamimo Island, a project funded by the Norwegian University. The studies aimed to "test and evaluate how effective the selected virtual environment was as a learning platform in a life-long learning perspective" and to "test selected learning tools or elements together in the virtual environment to determine if they were suitable to achieve learning through social interaction" (Deutschmann et al., 2009; Molka-Danielsen Richardson, Deutschmann, & Carter, 2007). The findings explore that the voice-chat function is one of the most effective tools in VWLEs.

Intercultural Competency

The intercultural concept is a growing concern for 21st-century citizens and communities pursuing sustainable life satisfaction and global awareness in a digital world (Wan, Yeh & Cheng, in press). Intercultural competency refers to how people from diverse backgrounds and cultures communicate and interact with others and negotiate for meaning in a second language (L2) (Byram, 1997; Kramsch, 1995). Primary studies suggest that language learners spontaneously exchange social and cultural meanings while interacting with native speakers of the target language in the VWLE (Blasing, 2010; Jauregi et al., 2012; Zheng et al., 2009; Wang et al., 2012).

The European NIFLAR project investigated how to integrate intercultural interaction through video communication and virtual worlds into foreign language teaching programs across the Netherlands, Portugal, Russia, and Spain (Jauregi et al., 2012). Researchers collected data from 430 college students. The results indicated that during cross-cultural interactions, participants performed frequent negotiations of meanings in terms of linguistic and cultural perspectives. As participants collaborated with other players, they reflected on and clarified concepts, customs, styles, and behaviors, resorting to their own experiences and cultural values. Participants shared empathy and worked toward creating symmetrical relationships during the interaction exchanges.

Studies also explored how language learners adjusted to the target language culture and how they represented themselves based on their cultural backgrounds in the VWLE (Blasing, 2010; Wang et al., 2012). Blasing (2010) asserts that cultural factors played an important role in the responses of learners in Second Life. For instance, the study found that language learners in Russia (or the "Russian area" of the virtual world) presented others with large, glowing flowers by Russian avatars in honor of International Women's Day because, in Russia, giving flowers to female coworkers is customary on this day. The example shows how such a response from language learners of Second Life extends beyond the level of basic conversation to particular cultural norms and values.

Researchers also applied intercultural perspectives and concepts from ecological psychology to English language learning, as well as content-based learning, in an intercultural avatar-based online environment (Zheng et al., 2009). The study investigated three main areas in terms of negotiation for action (a.k.a. negotiation for meaning), intercultural identity development, and meaning making. The study analyzed the users' chat logs and activities on virtual-world software, Quest Atlantis (QA). The researchers proposed the concepts of negotiation for action to illustrate how interactions and collaborations occurred between native English and non-English native speakers. The findings revealed that participants successfully achieved their desired goals through intercultural collaboration on solving content-based problems, forming intercultural identities, and performing meaning-making tasks. Non-native English speakers also showed enthusiasm for participating in these authentic networking communities, such as chat log, virtual world community, and online multiplayer games. These online learning environments appear to offer significant affordances for language acquisition (Steinkuehler, 2006; Zheng et al., 2009). Contrary to the strict grammar rules students have to practice in the classroom setting, VWLEs enabled language learners to communicate in an authentic environment without worrying about making grammar mistakes.

Collaborative Competency

Collaborative tasks and activities have been suggested as being effective in language learning because they involve "creative and active language use" (Jones & Youngs, 2006; p. 276). In 2006, Hampel claims that collaborative tasks are active, participatory, and meaning-based. Researchers suggest that the benefits of applying collaborative tasks in language classrooms include the delivery of different perspectives and opinions in discussions, resulting in creating controversy, disagreement, resolution, and agreement (Deutschmann et al., 2009; Ligorio, Cesareni, & Schwartz, 2008; Knutzen & Kennedy, 2012; Meskill, 1999; Shih & Yang, 2008). Further, collaborative tasks encourage active participation because there is no single accurate answer for the discussion. Therefore, participants are active agents who are motivated to take active roles and situate themselves in the group.

Knutzen and Kennedy (2012) claim that the integration of intercultural-collaborative virtual learning environments into English courses enhances language learners' collaborative skills. This study explored the integration of Second Life with the curriculum and instruction of EFL courses in Hong Kong. The study collaborated with two TESOL teacher-training classes at Texas A&M University in the United States to examine how collaborative virtual environments affect motivation and engagement in academic settings. Two hundred participants were enrolled in the project, with approximately half from each university. The study also utilized other multimedia tools for collaboration including Moodle, IM-typed chat, and Voice over Internet Protocol (VoIP). The findings indicated that IM typed text chat in Second Life is an extremely useful form of communication for new users. This typing medium allows additional time for language learners to produce their responses. There is also a higher tolerance for learners to make spelling and grammar mistakes compared to a spoken forum in which learners are more anxious, producing incorrect pronunciations or syntax (Beauvois, 1997; Knutzen & Kennedy, 2012). This virtual world learning environment provides an effective simulation of face-to-face communication, with an informal small talk language format. The researchers also trained the language learners on how to use the machine translation built into the chat function to support voice communication. This approach could become extremely important in cross-cultural communication.

A study was conducted in Rome to provoke collaborative and intercultural competencies for language learners (Ligorio et al., 2008). Participants were a group of ten 13-year-old students from junior secondary schools in a Dutch class or an Italian class. The data were collected through observation and seven videotaped sessions in the classroom. The study assigned the participants from one country to build and decorate the cultural houses for the target language country. Therefore, the Italian classes built the Dutch cultural houses, and the Dutch classes built the Italian houses. Participants were required to put their intermediated products online. In this case, the VWLE was a window for the display of products and a platform for the negotiating of meaning, the developing of intercultural understanding, and the building of collaboration skills.

Constructivist Learning

Nine of the eighteen reviewed studies (Deutschmann & Panichi, 2009; Ibanez et al., 2011; Kim & Blankenship, 2013; Shih & Yang, 2008; Wang et al, 2012; Wang & Shao, 2012; Zheng et al, 2009) framed their work around social constructive learning theories. A basis of social constructive learning theory is that learning (cognitive development) takes place socially during scaffolded interactions between the novice and the expert (Vygotsky, 1978). Vygotsky (1978) defines the zone of proximal development (ZPD) as "the distance between the actual developmental level as determined by independent problem solving and the level of potential development as determined through problem solving under adult guidance, or in collaboration with more capable peers" (p. 86). Interactions with peers are effective ways of developing skills and strategies. L2 instructors should design cooperative learning exercises that allow less competent learners to develop with help from more skillful peers within the zone of proximal development.

Within 3D VWLEs, traditional language instruction featuring "silent, solitary acts" become "lively, meaning-making events rich in discussion" (Deutschmann & Panichi, 2009, p. 310), and learners interact with peers and with native speakers in the virtual world. The virtual learning environment features support for knowledge construction, self-direction, immersion, interactivity, and education (Shih & Yang, 2008; Wang et al, 2012). 3D VWLEs also enable the deployment of simulations in realistic-looking environments, where social interactions are possible (Ibanez et al, 2011).

Sociocultural Competency

Several of the reviewed studies (Jauregi et al., 2012; Wang et al, 2012; Zheng et al, 2009) indicate that learning in 3D VWLEs adds value to learners' sociocultural and intercultural competence. Intercultural competence refers to having the knowledge, skills, attitudes, and values to communicate effectively and appropriately with people from other cultures (Byram, 1997).

In short, through learning and social interactions on 3D VWLEs, L2 learners have reportedly had gains on knowledge of target culture and skills on target language uses. As a result, L2 learners are able to communicate in socially and culturally more appropriate ways in target languages and understand the sociocultural aspects of target language better, thus better appreciating target cultures.

Implications of Virtual World Environment Use in Foreign Language Curriculum

To better facilitate and scaffold L2 learning in virtual world environments, the following implications and suggestions are provided for designing, developing, and implementing a curriculum. Four categories of implications are included here: (1) teaching strategies, (2) assessment tools, (3) administrative support, and (4) professional development programs.

Teaching Strategies

Researchers suggest various teaching and learning strategies for L2 learners in VWLEs (Deutschmann et al., 2009; Deutschmann & Panichi, 2009; Peterson, 2011; Wang et al., 2012). First, language teachers should prepare learners for task completion and train learners on how to use virtual tools before projects and tasks are assigned.

Second, teachers can closely monitor and facilitate L2 learners' performance and learning process by reviewing the written texts and audio-recorded conversations that students produce with their language partners (Wang et al., 2012). In this type of student-centered activity, learners have opportunities to interact and communicate without feeling constantly evaluated by the teacher. Virtual world environments offer leeway for learners to make mistakes; however, teachers need to explain explicitly the rubric and assessment rules at the beginning of the activities. It is important for teachers to monitor and scaffold during the activities and to obtain a systematic assessment method and rubric (Berns et al., 2012; Ibanez et al., 2011).

Third, it is crucial for teachers to provide feedback and to encourage learners to conduct post-task reflections (Thorne et al., 2009; Wang et al., 2012) during and after the virtual-world activities. Studies indicated that receiving feedback and writing reflections allow L2 learners to practice higher-level thinking and critical-thinking skills. Feedback provides learners with information about the success (or lack of success) of their spoken and written utterances, as well as gives additional opportunities to focus on production or comprehension (Gass & Selinker, 2008). The activities in VWLEs require a lot of interactions and engagements among students and teachers. Therefore, it is essential for teachers to give appropriate feedback and scaffolding to L2 learners about activities in which they are involved, and that teachers recognize feedback as a crucial part of the learning process (Yeh, 2014).

Fourth, teachers should be aware of the workload and have clear learning objectives for the learners. It's essential to be aware of not increasing learners' workload while using virtual tools (Zhang, 2013) and to set a time limit for any given activity and task (Wang et al., 2012). Teachers need to keep in mind that virtual world tools are supplemental rather than primary means because students need face-to-face interaction and teachers' explicit feedback while completing the assignments on VWLEs. The learning objective need to be communicating clearly, with virtual tools embedded to maintain high learner involvement and participation (Ligorio, et al, 2008).

Fifth, researchers encourage language teachers to provide effective interaction tasks and the opportunities to engage learners in meaningful interaction with higher language-proficiency-level peers or target language speakers (Berns et al., 2012; Ibanez et al., 2011; Jauregi et al., 2012; Peterson, 2011; Wang et al., 2012). Studies show positive relationships between project-based activities and the improvement of L2 skills, such as negotiation of meaning and focus on form (Berns et al., 2012; Peterson, 2011). Furthermore, opportunities to engage in meaningful interaction with target language speakers contributed to improving intercultural competence and communicative skills (Jauregi et al., 2012).

Assessment Tools

Previous studies suggest that applying systematic assessment tools and rubrics are beneficial for learners in project-based learning in VWLEs (Ibanez et al., 2011; Berns et al., 2012). In virtual world learning projects, teachers play facilitator, monitor roles, and the tasks focus on the learning process rather than the product of the learners. Therefore, teachers should conduct not only summative assessments but also formative assessments. Summative assessments refer to assessments that aim to measure, summarize, and evaluate what learners have grasped and typically occur at the end of a project, a course, or a unit of instruction, whereas the purpose of formative assessment is to assist learners during the growth process whiel they are forming skills and competencies. (Brown, 2004).

Administrative Support

Zhang (2013) suggests it is essential to have the support of policymakers and administrators to ensure the pedagogical success of implementing virtual-world learning environments into the language curriculum. Integrating the virtual-world software into the classrooms is a complex process. It is crucial for teachers to recognize that virtual tools are complex programs and require high-speed broadband to run properly (Wang, Song, Xia, & Yan, 2009; Wang & Hsu, 2010; Wang & Shao, 2012). They also usually require updated computers. As a result, administrative support is essential for both technological and financial support.

Professional Development Programs

Development of teachers' computer, media, and virtual world literacy skills are the goals of 21st-century teacher education. Teacher education programs need to offer more global literacy and 21st century skill sets for educators (Yeh & Kessler, 2015); for example, using innovative technological tools for educational purposes (Berns et al., 2012; Zhang, 2013). The goal of using technology is to create projects that are meaningful to the learners, and that help them achieve learning objectives. Teachers can incorporate virtual world tools into the curriculum that are able to engage learners in authentic, meaningful, language-based tasks and allow them to learn at their own pace within a 21st-century learning environment.

DISCUSSION

Limitations

This study reveals that current research on virtual world language learning environments remain largely exploratory in nature and are subject to some limitations. Three main limitations are found: (1) learning difficulties, (2) technical issues, and (3) classroom management.

Learning Difficulties

The scaffolding system in VWLEs was insufficient to satisfy language learners who have lower language proficiency and confidence (Peterson, 2011; Shih & Yang, 2008). Lower language proficiency learner performance and motivation were negatively affected by time pressure; however, synchronous discussions involve both language skills and the ability to react to immediate changes and events during the tasks. Learners with limited typing skills and poor reading and listening comprehension struggled with completing the tasks on time. Also, both studies claim that sociocultural concerns influence language learners' behavior, leading to avoidance and high learning anxiety. Under time pressure, these learners felt less motivated and more frustrated. Teachers need to be aware of meeting the needs of learners at different language proficiency levels, such as making the project more interesting, providing authentic situations, and offering a sense of community. Language teachers should also apply goal-based tasks, a story-centered curriculum, strategic interaction, and appropriate language-level materials to the instructional design of VWLEs.

Technical Issues

While learners enjoyed virtual world learning experiences in general, they also perceived some technical problems that impeded the learning process. Technical issues included poor audio quality during the chats (e.g., echoing and interrupted flow of audio sounds) and frozen screens (Berns et al., 2012; Peterson, 2011; Wang et al., 2012). These problems extremely hindered the flow of communication and task completion in VWLEs.

Classroom Management

L2 learners identified classroom management problems that occurred during the activities (Wang et al., 2012). For instance, in a cross-country or cross-cultural project, due to the time difference, some participants in the United States did not log into the virtual tool system in a timely manner. After waiting several minutes, participants from China would go talk to other participants in the virtual-world locations. Consequently, the American participants were not able to find their partners from China when they logged into the virtual world system. In addition, learners reported distractions, such as an animal regularly jumping from the water and uninvited people suddenly joining the discussion groups or conversations. These issues ought to be addressed when implementing similar curricula in the future.

Future Studies

This study points to the combination of design features and strategies that are distinct to VWLEs. Research studies have showed that these features may create a beneficial environment for language learning (Hislope, 2008); they also indicate directions for future studies (Peterson, 2011). Three areas of future studies that may become beneficial include: (1) models, (2) methods, and (3) learning outcomes.

Models

Research findings indicated that long-term goal-based exercises, task design activities, goal-directed activities, and problem-based collaborative learning with intentional instruction models and interactive models in VWLEs were beneficial for language learning (Berns et al., 2012; Blasing, 2010; Thorne et al., 2009; Zheng et al., 2009). Therefore, future studies should focus on developing and designing goal-based and problem-based tasks while using virtual world learning tools. The concept of collaborating and working together with a target language requires learners to take responsibility for the success and failure to achieve the goal. Learners become active agents while participating in these collaborative problem-solving tasks (Zheng et al., 2009). These types of tasks can enhance learners' skills, including critical thinking, evaluation, problem-solving, collaboration, and communication with team members from different cultural backgrounds. Future research should develop and utilize direct assessments of these 21st-century skills that learners might gain in VWLEs. Studies should also investigate how language learners develop and acquire linguistic competencies in VWLEs that foster learners' intercultural awareness while allowing opportunities for collaboration and interaction.

Methods

Researchers should pay attention to three main methods while conducting research in VWLEs. First, future studies should compare the results of the empirical research with those of the control group (Berns et al., 2012; Zheng, et al., 2009). The majority of the studies in VWLEs are exploratory studies. By comparing an experimental group with a control group, researchers have a better understanding of learning outcomes and how learners make progress.

Second, future studies should involve larger and more diverse learner groups (Ibanez et al., 2011; Zhang, 2013). The sample sizes in previous studies were small and mainly homogenous (Knutzen & Kennedy, 2012; Zhang, 2013). Learners at different universities and countries may vary widely in terms of technology access, media/computer literacy levels, family backgrounds, and school resources. Furthermore, larger and more diverse sample sizes may shed light on the role played by the new types of identity exploration (i.e., avatar characters) made feasible by virtual worlds (Zheng et al., 2009; Zhang, 2013).

Last but not least, future studies should apply discourse analysis methods for data analysis and focus on the analysis of communicative competency components, including phonology, grammar, lexicon, semantics, syntax, nonverbal, and paralinguistic components (Shih & Yang, 2008). Researchers and educators can investigate learners' improvement in communicative competency through transcribing spoken and written discourses and conducting discourse analyses of chat data.

Learning Outcomes

Limited research focuses on identity formation, sociocultural factors, and their effect on learner behavior (Ibanez et al., 2011; Peterson, 2011; Thorne et al., 2009). Thus, future research studies should investigate (1) to what extent sociocultural factors influence identity formation and learner behaviors and (2) to what extent VWLEs offer resources for identity formation and experimentation for language learners. The question of how identity experimentation varies based on the type of virtual tools, learning tasks, virtual representation of avatars, and opportunities for user behavior has not been answered in previous literature (Ibanez et al., 2011; Thorne et al., 2009).

CONCLUSION

A number of studies reveal that virtual worlds can become effective environments for foreign language learning (Deutschmann & Panichi, 2009; Ibanez et al., 2011; Shih & Yang, 2008). These studies indicate three main reasons that virtual worlds may benefit foreign language learning. First, a VWLE provides a 3D, open learning environment and offers opportunities for participants to speak their target languages with native speakers regardless of geographical distance. It is a valuable tool to enhance intercultural competency, motivation, and opportunities for authentic negotiation of meanings and interactions (Deutschmann & Panichi, 2009). For instance, instructors can design a cross-cultural learning community in the virtual world, engaging both native speakers and language learners. Second, a VWLE creates a comfort zone for language learners to work collaboratively with other participants. This enhances language learners' sociocultural competency by scaffolding their team members (Vygotsky, 1978) and reduces anxiety in learning the target language (Krashen, 1987). As many language learners in K-12 and higher education are digital natives (Prensky, 2001), using technology and online platforms to communicate comes naturally to them. Therefore, VWLEs enable language learners to learn a foreign language in a low anxiety setting. Third, a VWLE provides a small virtual community where language learners can develop constructivist learning, communicative competency, and collaborative competency skills. This learning environment is especially valuable for language learners who study languages in non-target language-speaking countries.

In the field of second/foreign language (ESL/EFL) teaching and learning, various linguistic courses have been offered by using virtual worlds, namely English, German, Japanese, Russian, and Spanish (Blasing, 2010; Berns et al., 2012; Erard, 2007; Wang & Shao, 2012). ESL/EFL educators and researchers focus primarily on how to use virtual worlds as learning environments where English language learners (ELLs) have opportunities for authentic interactions with native speakers of their target languages (Deutschmann & Panichi, 2009; Wang et al., 2009). Although literature suggests that VWLEs can assist ESL/EFL teaching and learning, studies also reveal challenges that would influence the instructional use of virtual worlds: Not only is there a steep learning curve for both teachers and students, but also, high-speed broadband is required for running the VWLEs (Wang et al., 2009; Wang & Hsu, 2010; Wang & Shao, 2012). These challenges may prevent ESL/EFL educators from integrating virtual world software into their classrooms. It is important for educators and researchers to recognize that successful language learning and teaching do not rely on technology (Colpaert, 2006); rather, they should focus on how the curricula and instruction are designed. Therefore, this chapter discusses practical implications of using virtual-world learning environments in foreign language curricula.

Previous literature on VWLEs in CALL is limited, especially on how the language learners' use of VWLEs affects learning. It is important to investigate how technology, such as a virtual world, has been integrated into language curricula, and its impact on outcomes of foreign language instruction. This study reveals that VWLEs can provide authentic language environments and rich linguistic, social, and cultural learning experiences for learners. Therefore, this chapter discusses the various ways that virtual worlds have been used for language instruction, the promises and challenges brought by virtual worlds to language learners, and the impact of VWLEs on language teaching and learning in the six areas: (1) motivation, (2) communicative competency, (3) intercultural learning, (4) collaborative competency, (5) constructivist learning, and (6) sociocultural competency.

REFERENCES

Beauvois, M. (1997). High-tech, high-Touch: From discussion to composition in the networked classroom. *Computer Assisted Language Learning*, *10*(1), 57–69. doi:10.1080/0958822970100104

Berns, A., Gonzalez-Pardo, A., & Camacho, D. (2012). Combining Face-to-Face Learning with Online Learning in Virtual Worlds. *Paper presented at the European Association for Computer-Assisted Language Learning (EUROCALL) Annual Conference.*

Blankenship, R. J. (2010). *Using virtual environments as professional development tools for pre-service teachers seeking ESOL endorsement* [Unpublished doctoral dissertation]. University of South Florida, FL.

Blasing, M. T. (2010). Second language in Second Life: Exploring interaction, identify and pedagogical practice in a virtual world. *Slavic and East European Journal*, *54*(1), 96–117.

Brown, H. D. (2004). Language assessment: Principles and classroom practices. White Plains, NY: Addison Wesley Longman.

Byram, M. (1997). *Teaching and assessing intercultural communicative competence*. Multilingual Matters Ltd.

Cheong, D. (2010). The effects of practice teaching sessions in Second Life on the change in pre-service teachers' teaching efficacy. *Computers & Education*, *55*(2), 868–880. doi:10.1016/j.compedu.2010.03.018

Colpaert, J. (2006). Pedagogy-driven design for online language teaching and learning. *CALICO Journal*, *23*(3), 477–497.

Deutschmann, M., & Panichi, L. (2009). Talking into Empty Space? Signaling Involvement in a Virtual Language Classroom in Second Life. *Language Awareness*, *18*(3–4), 310–328. doi:10.1080/09658410903197306

Deutschmann, M., Panichi, L., & Molka-Danielsson, J. (2009). Designing oral participation in Second Life—A comparative study of two language proficiency courses. *ReCALL*, *21*(02), 206–226. doi:10.1017/S0958344009000196

Dickey, M. D. (2005). Engaging by design: How engagement strategies in popular computer and video games can inform instructional design. *Educational Technology Research and Development*, *53*(2), 67–83. doi:10.1007/BF02504866

Dickey, M. D. (2011). The pragmatics of virtual worlds for K-12 educators: Investigating the affordances and constraints of Active Worlds and Second Life with K-12 in-service teachers. *Educational Technology Research and Development*, *59*(1), 1–20. doi:10.1007/s11423-010-9163-4

Erard, M. (2007). A boon to Second Life language schools. Retrieved from http://www.technologyreview.com/communications/18510/page1/?a=f

Erlandson, B. E., Nelson, B. C., & Wilhelmina, C. S. (2010). Collaboration modality, cognitive load, and science inquiry learning in virtual inquiry environments. *Educational Technology Research and Development*, *58*(6), 693–710. doi:10.1007/s11423-010-9152-7

Gass, S., & Selinker, L. (2008). *Second language acquisition: An introductory course* (3rd ed.). New York: Routledge/Taylor Francis.

Hew, K., & Cheung, W. (2008). Use of three-dimensional (3-D) immersive virtual worlds in K-12 and higher education settings: A review of the research. *British Journal of Educational Technology*, *39*(6), 959–1148.

Hislope, K. (2008). Language learning in a virtual world. *The International Journal of Learning*, *15*(11), 51–58.

Ibanez, M., Garcia, J., Galan, S., Maroto, D., Morillo, D., & Kloos, C. (2011). Design and Implementation of a 3D Multi-User Virtual World for Language Learning. *Journal of Educational Technology & Society*, *14*(4), 2–10.

Jarmon, L., Traphagan, T., Mayrath, M., & Trivedi, A. (2008). *Exploration of learning in Second Life in an interdisciplinary communication course. Paper presentation at American Educational Research Association*. New York: AERA.

Jauregi, K., de Graaff, R., & Canto, S. (2012). Integrating Cross-Cultural Interaction through Video-Communication and Virtual Worlds in Foreign Language Teaching Programs: Burden or Added Value? *Paper presented at the European Association for Computer-Assisted Language Learning (EuroCALL) Annual Conference.*

Jones, C. M., & Youngs, B. L. (2006). Teacher Preparation for Online Language Instruction. In P. Hubbard & M. Levy (Eds.), *Teacher Education in CALL* (pp. 267–280). Amsterdam: John Benjamins. doi:10.1075/lllt.14.22jon

Kanuka, H., & Anderson, T. (1999). Using constructivism in technology-mediated learning: Constructing order out of the chaos in the literature. *Radical Pedagogy*, *1*, 1–12. Retrieved from http://www.radicalpedagogy.org/radicalpedagogy/Using_Constructivism_in_Technology-Mediated_Learning__Constructing_Order_out_of_the_Chaos_in_the_Literature.html

Kim, D., & Blankenship, R. J. (2013). Using "Second Life" as a Virtual Collaborative Tool for Preservice Teachers Seeking English for Speakers of Other Languages Endorsement. *Journal of Educational Computing Research*, *48*(1), 19–43. doi:10.2190/EC.48.1.b

Knutzen, B., & Kennedy, D. (2012). The Global Classroom Project: Learning a Second Language in a Virtual Environment. *Electronic Journal of E-Learning*, *10*(1), 90–106.

Kramsch, C. (1995). The cultural component of language teaching. *Language, Culture and Curriculum*, *8*(2), 83–93. doi:10.1080/07908319509525192

Krashen, S. D. (1987). *Principles and practice in second language acquisition*. London: Prentice-Hall International.

Larsen-Freeman, D. (2007). *Techniques and principles in language teaching* (2nd ed.). Oxford: Oxford University Press.

Ligorio, M., Cesareni, D., & Schwartz, N. (2008). Collaborative virtual environments as means to increase the level of intersubjectivity in a distributed cognition system. *Journal of Research on Technology in Education*, *40*(3), 339–357. doi:10.1080/15391523.2008.10782511

Long, M. H. (1991). Focus on form: a design feature in language teaching methodology. In K. de Bot, R. Ginsberg, & C. Kramsch (Eds.), *Foreign Language Research in Cross-cultural Perspective* (pp. 39–52). Amsterdam: John Benjamins. doi:10.1075/sibil.2.07lon

Long, M. H. (1997). The role of the linguistic environment in second language acquisition. In W. Ritchie & T. Bhatia (Eds.), *Handbook of Second Language Acquisition* (pp. 413–468). San Diego, CA: Academic Press.

McInnes, E., & Wimpenny, P. (2008). Using Qualitative Assessment and Review Instrument software to synthesize studies on older people's views and experiences of falls prevention. *International Journal of Evidence-Based Healthcare*, *6*, 337–344. PMID:21631830

Meskill, C. (1999). Computers as Tool for Sociocollaborative Language Learning. In K. Cameron (Ed.), *Computer assisted language learning (CALL): media, design and applications* (pp. 141–162). Lisse: Swets & Zeitlinger.

Molka-Danielsen, J., Richardson, D., Deutschmann, M., & Carter, B. (2007). Teaching and Learning Affectively within a Virtual Campus. *International Journal of Networking and Virtual Organization (Special Issue: Toward Virtual Universities)*, 6(5), 476-498.

Pasfield-Neofitou, S. (2011). Online domains of language use: Second language learners' experiences of virtual community and foreignness. *Language Learning & Technology*, *15*(2), 92–108.

Peterson, B. (2012). It Looks Great but How do I Know If It Fits?: an Introduction to Meta-synthesis Research. In K. Hannes, & C. Lockwood (Ed.), Synthesizing Qualitative Research: Choosing the Right Approach. John Wiley & Sons, LTD: Hoboken, NJ.

Peterson, M. (2011). Towards a Research Agenda for the Use of Three-Dimensional Virtual Worlds in Language Learning. *CALICO Journal*, *29*(1), 67–80. doi:10.11139/cj.29.1.67-80

Prensky, M. (2001). Digital Natives, Digital Immigrants. *On the Horizon*, *9*(5), 1–6. doi:10.1108/10748120110424816

Prieto-Arranz, J. I., Juan-Garau, M., & Jacob, K. L. (2013). Re-imagining cultural identity: Transcultural and translingual communication in virtual third-space environments. *Language, Culture and Curriculum*, *26*(1), 19–35. doi:10.1080/07908318.2012.759585

Sadler, R., & Nurmukhamedov, U. (2008, March). Second Life and task-based learning. *Paper presented at CALICO annual conference*, San Francisco, CA.

Schroeder, R. (2008). Defining virtual worlds and virtual environments. *Journal of Virtual Worlds Research*, *1*(1), 2–3. doi:10.1080/07908318.2012.759585

Second Life. (n. d.). Retrieved from the Second Life Wiki: http://en.wikipedia.org/wiki/Second_Life

Shih, Y., & Yang, M. (2008). A Collaborative Virtual Environment for Situated Language Learning Using VEC3D. *Journal of Educational Technology & Society*, *11*(1), 56–68.

Steinkuehler, C. (2006). Massively multiplayer online videogaming as participation in a Discourse. *Mind, Culture, and Activity*, *12*(1), 38–52. doi:10.1207/s15327884mca1301_4

Thorne, S. L., Black, R. W., & Sykes, J. M. (2009). Second Language Use, Socialization, and Learning in Internet Interest Communities and Online Gaming. *Modern Language Journal*, *93*, 802–821. doi:10.1111/j.1540-4781.2009.00974.x

Vygotsky, L. S. (1978). *Mind in society*. Cambridge, MA: Harvard University Press.

Wan, G., Yeh, E., & Cheng, H. (in press). Digital Media Use by Chinese Youth and Its Impact. In C. K. Cheung (Ed.), *Media Education in China*. Hong Kong, China: Springer.

Wang, C., Calandra, B., Hibbard, S., & McDowell Lefaiver, M. (2012). Learning effects of an experimental EFL program in Second Life. *Educational Technology Research and Development*, *60*(5), 943–961. doi:10.1007/s11423-012-9259-0

Wang, C. X., Song, H., Xia, F., & Yan, Q. (2009). Integrating Second Life into an EFL program: Students' perspectives. *Journal of Educational Technology Development and Exchange*, *2*(1), 1–16.

Wang, F., & Shao, E. (2012). Using Second Life to Assist EFL Teaching: We Do Not Have to Sign in to the Program. *Techtrends: Linking Research and Practice to Improve Learning*, *56*(4), 15–18. doi:10.1007/s11528-012-0582-4

Wang, S.-K., & Hsu, H.-Y. (2010). Using the ADDIE model to design Second Life activities for online learners. *TechTrends*, *53*(6), 76–81.

Wickens, C. D. (1992). Virtual reality and education. *Proceedings of the 1992 IEEE International Conference on Systems, Man and Cybernetics.* doi:10.1109/ICSMC.1992.271688

Yeh, E. (2014). Teaching culture and language through the Multiple Intelligences Film Teaching Model in the ESL/EFL classroom. *Journal of Effective Teaching*, *14*(1), 63–79.

Yeh, E., & Kessler, G. (2015). Enhancing Linguistic and Intercultural Competencies Through the Use of Social Network Sites and Google Earth. In J. Keengwe (Ed.), *Promoting Global Literacy Skills through Technology-Infused Teaching and Learning*. Hershey, PA, USA: IGI Global. doi:10.4018/978-1-4666-6347-3.ch001

Zhang, H. (2013). Pedagogical Challenges of Spoken English Learning in the Second Life Virtual World: A Case Study. *British Journal of Educational Technology*, *44*(2), 243–254. doi:10.1111/j.1467-8535.2012.01312.x

Zheng, D., Li, N., & Zhao, Y. (2008, March). Learning Chinese in Second Life Chinese language school. *Paper presented at CALICO Annual Conference*, San Francisco, CA.

Zheng, D., Young, F. M., Brewer, A. R., & Wagner, M. (2009). Attitude and self-efficacy change: English language learning in virtual worlds. *CALICO Journal*, *27*(1), 205–231. doi:10.11139/cj.27.1.205-231

ADDITIONAL READING

Andreas, K., Tsiatsos, T., Terzidou, T., & Pomportsis, A. (2010). Fostering collaborative learning in Second Life: Metaphors and affordances. *Computers & Education*, *55*(2), 603–615. doi:10.1016/j.compedu.2010.02.021

Girvan, C., & Savage, T. (2010). Identifying an appropriate pedagogy for virtual worlds: A Communal Constructivism case study. *Computers & Education*, *55*(1), 342–349. doi:10.1016/j.compedu.2010.01.020

Herold, D. K. (2010). Mediating media studies—Stimulating critical awareness in a virtual environment. *Computers & Education*, *54*(3), 791–798. doi:10.1016/j.compedu.2009.10.019

Huang, H. M., Rauch, U., & Liaw, S. S. (2010). Investigating learner's attitudes toward virtual reality learning environments: Based on a constructivist approach. *Computers & Education*, *55*(3), 1171–1182. doi:10.1016/j.compedu.2010.05.014

Huang, Y.-C., Backman, S. J., & Backman, K. F. (2010). Student attitude toward virtual learning in Second Life: A flow theory approach. *Journal of Teaching in Travel & Tourism*, *10*(4), 312–334. doi:10.1080/15313220.2010.525425

Inman, C., Wright, V. H., & Hartman, J. A. (2010). Use of Second Life in K-12 and higher education: A review of research. *Journal of Interactive Online Learning*, *9*(1), 44–63.

Larach, D. U., & Cabra, J. F. (2010). Creative problem solving in Second Life: An action research study. *Creativity and Innovation Management*, *19*(2), 167–179. doi:10.1111/j.1467-8691.2010.00550.x

Zhang, H. (2011). Latest developments in the adoption of Second Life in education: A literature review. *China Educational Technology*, *4*, 121–125.

KEY TERMS AND DEFINITIONS

English as a Second Language (ESL): A term originally applied to English language programs at the postsecondary level, but today is used in the K–12 school system to describe students whose native language is not English, regardless of whether they attend language programs or services.

English Language Proficiency: Fluency and competency in the English language in the domains of Basic Interpersonal Communication Skills (BICS) and Cognitive/Academic Language Proficiency (CALP).

First Language (L1): The native language acquired by an individual.

Non-Native English Speakers (NNESs): The term Non-Native English Speakers (NNESs) is defined as those students who speak a language other than English at home. NNESs are inclusive of both competent biliterates and Limited English Proficiency (LEP) students.

Non-Native English Speakers (NNES) Status: NNES status is defined as a linguistic minority status and refers to NNESs' linguistic background in terms of both Basic Interpersonal Communication Skills and Cognitive/Academic Language Proficiency, and language use in home and school settings.

VOIP: Voice over Internet Protocol is a method that turns audio signals into digital data that can be transmitted over the Internet.

Second Language (L2): The second or subsequent language learned by an individual.

Second Language Acquisition (SLA): The learning of another language after the first language has been learned (Gass & Selinker, 2008).

Sociocultural Characteristics: Sociocultural characteristics refer to the notion that knowledge or learning occurs in a social context. Learning is socially mediated, and comes from face-to-face interaction. Learners internalize knowledge and construct it in dyadic interactions through social impact (Gass & Selinker, 2008).

Chapter 8
Augmented Reality as an Emerging Application in Tourism Marketing Education

Azizul Hassan
Cardiff Metropolitan University, UK

Timothy Jung
Manchester Metropolitan University, UK

ABSTRACT

Augmented Reality (AR) as an advanced format of Virtual Reality (VR) becomes widely available in numerous appliances, mainly in mobile devices like Smartphones or wearable devices. As the prospective benefits of this technology are said to be immense, tourism marketing education is believed to experience a comprehensive application of AR in coming years. At present, AR technologies are in use in many academic disciplines including medicine, geography, information technology, computer aided entertainment and many more. Out of all of the recently developed technological advancements, those can be termed as 'Innovations', augmented reality can be considered as a key innovation. As coined, due to easier operational capacities, AR is becoming more popular and better fitting in tourism marketing education systems. This chapter outlines the use of AR, termed as an 'Innovation' as per the 'Diffusion of Innovations' theory of Rogers (1962), to meet tourism marketing education demands. The chapter critically examines relevant cross-country cases to support the arguments made above.

INTRODUCTION

This chapter discusses diverse features and potentials of augmented reality in tourism marketing education and suggests its inclusion in the academic syllabuses to be studied as a key module. Augmented reality (AR), an extension of virtual reality, is an emerging technology that can provide experiences in which real world places and activities are enhanced with computer-generated content, seamlessly mixing and overlapping human perception with two dimensional (2D) and three dimensional (3D) objects (Yuen, Yaoyuneyong, & Johnson, 2011). AR has emerged as an unprecedented use of technology in a number

DOI: 10.4018/978-1-4666-9837-6.ch008

of fields including architecture, construction, military, medical, entertainment, advertising, travel, and marketing. Global brands from different sectors and industries have managed to use AR technology effectively and efficiently, garnering positive responses and support from consumers (Kaufman & Horton, 2015). As a result AR is having an impact on the everyday lives of consumers (Kipper & Rampolla, 2015).

The use of AR in the tourism industry is emerging. As an example, in 2008, Wikitude, a mobile AR software travel guide, was offered as freeware which displays information about the users' surroundings in a mobile camera view, including image recognition and 3D modeling. Tourists traveling in unfamiliar environments naturally require solid sources of data and information; AR applications can meet the demand of personalized, pertinent and rationalized information at a dependable level (Olsson & Väänänen-Vainio-Mattila, 2011). Today, AR applications are being created by tourism organizations all over the world for educational and marketing purposes. Tourism marketing professionals are responsible for advertising and publicizing a variety of goods and services, ranging from tourist sites, lodging establishments, and special events. Positions related to tourism marketing include, but are not limited to, in-house resort marketing representative, tourism specialist for a marketing firm, head of marketing for a resort or cruise line. Students studying to work in the tourism industry must have knowledge and skills in the use of AR in tourism marketing related jobs in order to be competitive in the employment arena.

The purpose of this chapter is to provide an overview of AR applications and platforms, discuss the use of AR applications and platforms within tourism marketing, and to make a case for including AR as a topic of study in institutions of higher education which offer bachelor's and master's degrees in tourism marketing and related programs. Specifically, this chapter is designed to outline augmented reality and its applications in tourism marketing education mainly in three aspects: theoretical, practical, and cross country examples.

BACKGROUND

AR has the potential to incorporate all human senses (sight, sound, taste, smell, touch) into a technological experience (Abernathy & Clark, 2007). AR applications are accelerated mainly by the latest developments in mobile computing, computer graphics, wire-less and sensor technologies. These advances influence and enhance human experiences through providing real time information displays and reviews (Suh, Shin, Woo, Dow, & MacIntyre, 2011). Gartner (2014) expects that, on the basis of continual technological advancements, the general public will be highly accepting the AR technologies. Still, the use of AR application as a tourism marketing tool is developing and may seem futuristic to some individuals (Shen, Ong, & Nee, 2011; Seo, Kim, & Park, 2011). However, AR applications can appear as marketing tools where these are still subject of exploration, where, touristic demand for information source is common (Yovcheva, Buhalis, & Gatzidis, 2012).

AR technology can work on grounds like the Global Positioning System (GPS) and on mobile devices with capacities to add virtual features and to relate them with reality (Azuma, 1997). AR as a medium of displaying requires intensive use of hardware or electronic devices such as camera, display monitors and computing gadgets. The introduction of handheld electronic items like the Smartphone or the smaller version of wearable computers has extended the realms of AR technology (Buchholz, 2014). On the other side, gaming consoles such as the Nintendo DS or similar also are mostly equipped with augmented reality technologies today (Breeze, 2014). The strengths of AR lie in its technological simplicity and capacities to perform as an educational tool.

AR applications used for marketing products may be the most common and popular way that the everyday consumer has been introduced to the concept and practice of augmented reality. AR applications have specifically been used to market brand names in ways that the product becomes memorable to the consumer and subsequently may build brand loyalty. Following are descriptions of three brand name uses of AR for marketing.

Budweiser is one of the world's famous and popular drink brands. As a part of effective marketing, Budweiser brings the Football Association Challenge Cup (FA Cup) directly into the consumers' house by using AR application. The Football Association Challenge Cup is an annual knockout cup competition in English football that is commonly known as the FA Cup in the world (The FA Cup, 2015). The marketing approach of Budweiser is ground breaking and it has managed to immerse AR in conventional marketing strategies. The Budweiser '*Man of the Match*' mobile application enables users to drink from the virtually-generated FA Cup. This application is developed on AR platform of the Aurasma that allows transforming the beer can into a virtual FA Cup trophy as a basic 3D model. Users have to click a selected button of their Smartphone camera for this purpose. Even though this application of AR for marketing can be effective, this entertainment option is limited, and can only be experienced by selected customers (Aurasma, 2015).

High street betting chain Paddy Power® has also made contributions on putting augmented reality into practice. In cooperation with Blippar, Paddy Power developed a special application which turns the Queens face on a £10 bank note into the user's own face. This technology is as simple as to hover on the face of the Queen's and then enjoy. The digital copy of the Queen turns into animation as soon as the Smartphone can recognize the face. The face then moves as interactive and functional that resembles that the Queen is the official sponsor of the Euro 2012 (Preexamples, 2015).

The Muscle Milk® brand has also used AR in marketing. Through the campaign of Shaq the bottle, this company is grabbing the attention of diverse clients and promoters from all over world. The celebration of Shaquille O'Neal was followed by augmented reality application. This initiative took place in the Cleveland market when the muscle milk brand was chosen to market into a new team created with O'Neals joining the team. A special form of AR marker in the shape of a QR code was printed on the back label of each milk bottle. When a webcam was placed on the marker of each bottle, a user could watch the virtual video showing a mini Shaq in Cleveland. Each of the five different flavours of the Muscle Milk® followed five types of videos and these were limited by edition and number (Showcase, 2015).

TOURISM MARKETING

Digital Marketing

Still, no definition of digital tourism marketing has been offered that can be viewed as comprehensive and well accepted. There are still scopes to develop the definition and to turn it into a workable meaning for understanding the central theme and relevancy with existing market structures of tourism (Buhalis & Yovcheva, 2014). In a very general understanding, digital marketing refers to the pattern of marketing that uses technology as the main platform to reach the target bases of consumers. There are numerous techniques of professional practices in tourism marketing and digital marketing that are entirely technology-based. Wider selection of tourism products or services coupled with marketing tactics like branding or promotion is presented before consumers to allow them to reach an agreeable decision of purchase. Internet is the central base of digital tourism while, television, radio or even the mobile telephone devices are used for the purpose. Digital marketing has unparallel dependency on the Internet and thus very often this is termed as Internet marketing (Daim et al., 2012). The use of the Internet is more effective to reach wider consumer segments and, thus, to persuade them to access the available offers, services or products. Unlike conventional patterns of marketing, this Internet-based marketing is more focused; targeted and comprehensive that brings dynamism in marketing and consumer choice enhancements. This also supports consumers to have expanded formats of products or service selection. Technical terms like the search engine marketing (SEM) or search engine optimization (SEO) are quite familiar in digital marketing and have relevancy in numerous platforms of digital media. Other than the SEM or SEO, digital marketing is also relevant in non-mainstream spaces such as the service offers of mobile telephone technologies as the multimedia messaging service (MMS), short messaging service (SMS) or even games (Deighton & Kornfeld, 2007). The central theme of digital marketing is to create a bond between consumers and technology. There is a constant demand that technologies should support human livelihood and thus to create more spaces to understand the demand of tourism product or service consumers. Digital marketing is more engaged in creating and retaining a strong bond between consumers and technology. This pattern of marketing enables business entrepreneurs to become consumer led and also to become more capable to meet the increasing demands of consumers in more manageable ways (Dhir, 2004).

Digital marketing is entirely related to tourism marketing in recent times where, a specific tourism organization uses a digital marketing campaign for branding or marketing (Azim & Hassan, 2013). Other than email, SMS, MMS and social networking, a certain number of advanced options become available for digital marketing. Display supported digital marketing can offer realistic experiences to consumers and thus to select products or services from a more convenient way. The introduction of Smartphones has enabled digital tourism marketers and consumers to reach a mutual standpoint of offerings and accessibilities (Deluna, 2014). Digital marketing is fast, as a message can be shared quickly to numerous consumer bases across the world. However, evidently, digital tourism marketing requires expert knowledge on certain areas and on technical issues to help advancing capacities of both marketers and consumers. The advantages of digital marketing are mostly positive and getting enormous responses from almost all over the world (Wind & Mahajan, 2001). In comparison with direct marketing, digital marketing has specific advantages. These advantages are most similar to digital marketing and come in numerous forms. The main factor of personal attention of consumers is crucial and is related to interaction with customers. Also, digital marketing tends to focus on each of the customers and thus creates more possibilities to generate direct responses. In digital marketing, this is often manageable and possible to create a personalized message to an individual customer (MarketingWeek, 2015). Each customer can be addressed and greeted separately and uniformly. Thus, this promotes personal serviced marketing that is more effective than other conventional forms. Also, digital marketing supports the measurement of responses from customers (i.e. the replies or reactions from messages sent to each of the customers). This is also important to understand the customers and their responses or mindsets. Digital marketing also does not necessarily require specialized forms of knowledge on marketing or technology. This is more customer-tailored and relevant to meet their demands more satisfactorily (Rust, Katherine, & Valarie, 2004). Digital marketing can become an important addition to any existing or potential business evolving in the tourism sector. This helps customers to achieve a target that is more focused to reality and reliability. There is a gap between traditional and digital forms of marketing and this gap is gradually increasing over the years due to the availability of more advanced types of technologies that continuously surpass one another. Digital marketing is a positive and fruitful outcome of the Internet which is supported by diverse forms of technological innovations (Guimaraes, 2012). This is thus convincing that digital marketing continues evolving over the coming years through the adoption of more advanced technological innovations. This is a way to support, promote and expand an existing business or even to reach desired customer bases. Thus, this is important to ensure that the business is getting the maximum exposure from digital forms of marketing, even within a complex pattern of marketing (Hax, 2010). Digital marketing, due to the fact that it does not necessarily require professional expertise and experiences, has very good possibility to gain popularity in tourism.

Digital marketing has become a necessity for today's business world and more supported by technologies than ever before. Also, the tourism sector requires working or practical knowledge in marketing and technology (Mohapatra, 2009). This form of tourism deals with both supply and demand side that involves interests of both marketers and consumers. Digital marketing is beneficial and rewarding in numerous marketing formats and technology applications. Customers normally stay connected with each other on digital platforms. Again, customer response generation relatively becomes more obvious than conventional marketing (Mobile Marketer, 2015). The success and activity of a tourism business enterprise depends on specific marketing factors. These are also related with diverse types of business functionalities including understanding the targeted customer base and becoming able to know their responses in a purposeful manner (Gay, Charlesworth, & Esen, 2007). The success of digital marketing relies on specific strategies or factors. Like conventional marketing approaches, in digital marketing, there are specific goals to reach. In digital marketing, set business goals are wider that target general expansion within the shortest possible time period. The more customers involved with a business enterprise, the more attention from marketers are required to serve their demands more successfully (Rayport & Jaworski, 2004). Digital marketing is particularly important for any business to reach success within the shortest possible timeframe.

AR Uses in Tourism Marketing

As the trend of creating closer interactions between technologies and electronic gadgets, tourism marketing becomes more powerful and it is obvious that AR marketing will gradually contest existing marketing tools. Technologies are dissolving in tourism marketing in faster motions than any other times. This becomes evident from some revolutionary inventions including augmented reality. Technology enhanced marketing strategies are challenging and replacing relatively more rigid theoretical notions. The content, features, and objectives are basically altered by the use of technology in tourism marketing. There are numerous examples, from around the world, of AR being used in an aspect of tourism marketing. Following are examples from six countries, Canada, France, Germany, the Netherlands, Greece, and China.

In Ontario of Canada, the tourism industry witnessed a global event termed as the '2013 Ontario Tourism Summit' that actually gathered academics, scholars, researchers, industry practitioners and AR marketing experts to share their views and ideas. This summit particularly supported general tourism agendas. As an outcome of this summit, experts reached an agreement that mobile devices are becoming reliable for AR marketing and offer enormous potentials to increase the market. The summit concluded that, AR is no longer confined within photo, video, downloads, games or website links. Rather, AR is becoming a powerful marketing tool for tourism (Augmentedmarketing, 2013). In Canada, AR research has already been integrated with academia and Universities like York University and Ryerson University evidently welcomes research programs in AR (augmentedstories, 2015).

In France, AR is being used to promote historic and cultural sites for global audiences. The Louvre -DNP Museum Lab is a specialized research facility designed for AR application development in museums (Louvre -DNP Museum Lab, 2015). The Louvre is now equipped with AR technology enabled displays and devices that offer information about the collections, histories, compilations, and displays with related data and information. Another example from Paris, France involves using Smartphone devices for tourists to download information about historical images. These images are then contrasted with images of the present time in similar places of the city. Users of such applications can travel back as much as one hundred years and view more than two thousands places of interest. These establishments otherwise have to rely on museum attendants or tour operators to convey information to tourists. The AR technology can also help tourists pursue their own areas of interest. Lastly, the Cluny Abbey in Cluny, France has embraced one of the simplest technology displays of AR. In order to promote learning the history, a big size display screen is used to provide tourists with real-life experiences through AR technology. Displays on this screen actually offer tourists historic backgrounds of the city. Therefore, the intervention of AR technology enhances the tourists' experience. On average, millions of tourists make visits and experience this screen to know the past of this city every year. This facility also creates interests among tourists about AR and its application. In general, such interests through AR technology show the huge potentials of AR for tourism marketing. This also demonstrates how AR technology can be diffused for experience generation, sharing, educational and marketing purposes (Digitalmeetsculture, 2015).

In Germany, remarkable advancements in augmented reality application has been jointly offered by the companies Instant Reality and IGD Fraunhofer. These companies have developed a special AR supported photo system that enables tourists to view images of important sites or attractions of Berlin. The exceptional feature that this system offers is to view images of a site or attraction of Berlin in different periods in history. This technological system is supported by wearable or handheld devices such as Smartphones or ultra-mobile personal computer. This technological application allows users to get connected with the central server system and get access to a database of photographs highlighting the city's decade's old growth (Stricker, Pagani, & Zoellner, 2009).

In the Netherlands, the Netherlands Architecture Institute has introduced a free application, Urban Augmented Reality that is available in eight main cities of the country, enabling both the residents and tourists viewing existing urban environment through historic layouts. In order to share views or ideas, tourists can leave their comments on a database linked to it and the public sector policy planners can also then extract themes of such comments and reflect them in public policy frameworks (Caarls, Jonker, Kolstee, Rotteveel, & van Eck, 2009).

In Greece, the process of AR technology application found its way through virtual reconstruction of a prominent ancient temple located in Olympia of Greece. The development of AR technology supported systems is the outcome of many years long research. According to Vlahakis et al. (2002), the development of ArcheoGuide AR system allows tourists to have memorable sensations from tourism marketing education standpoints. Layar is an AR application which uses GPS location to show nearby service facilities on top of the image of a mobile phone's camera. Through the use of Layar, an application that can be downloaded to a Smartphone, a tourist can get the option to point the phone towards the Berlin wall representing a reality based 3D model. In addition, in Seville, Greece the Past View Company has created a program that can offer tourists an entire city tour using AR. The application operates on a type of electronic earphones or video glasses and connects to a Smartphone to present the city's history (Internet-science, 2015).

China, as a global tourism destination with an abundance of tourism resources, is becoming dominant for both present and future tourists. The Yuanmingyuan or the Garden of Perfect Brightness is located in Beijing and was built during the 18th and 19th centuries. During the Anglo-Chinese War, this majestic garden was totally destroyed. However, the attempt to regenerate the garden came into action through the use of both sketches and paintings with little use of photographs or digital formats. However, as soon as AR technology came into practice, a panel of experts of the Beijing Institute of Technology was engaged in creating a reconstruction process of virtual platforms (Wang, Wang, & Fournier, 2000). Facilities for tourists to learn about this garden were supported by numerous initiatives and approaches related to technology use. These included machines that are operated by coins inputted by customers and special facilities like model reconstruction (Lum, 2012).

Most countries in Europe such as Germany, France, Italy, Greece and the United Kingdom with their enriched social, cultural and historic backgrounds are using AR technologies for exhibiting cultural sites for marketing purposes (Hepburn, 2015; Lee, Chung, & Jung, 2015). However, augmented reality can be used in almost all parts of the world, including both technologically developed and under-developed countries by developing technological infrastructures (Neuhofer, Buhalis, & Ladkin, 2013; Jung, Chung, & Leue, 2015).

The use of AR in different marketing areas is immense. In practice, there are numerous examples of brands using augment reality including Topshop Kinect Dressing Rooms, Shisedio Makeup Mirror, American Apparel Colour-Changing App, De Beers 'Forevermark Fitting', IKEA AR Catalogue, Sayduck Furniture Visualizer, IBM App, Converse Shoe Sampler, Burberry Beauty Box, and Moosejaw X-Ray App (Creative Guerrilla Marketing, 2014). This technology becomes a solid platform for creating and maintaining relationship with the public and the general customer base that can be replicated in tourism and can be highlighted in tourism marketing education.

Resistance to AR Marketing

AR can be applied in tourism marketing. Historic establishments can be rebuilt through the use of AR technologies enabling to support experience enhancements and to promote the site. Such regeneration process through images and visuals can be useful for both commercial and prototype educational purposes (Monday, 2015). The demands of tourism learners are diverse and thus relevant learning experience should be offered to satisfy what they seek. If they seek to experience cultural heritage tourism, they should be offered a realistic experience using AR technology (Han, Jung, & Gibson, 2014; Jung & Han, 2014). The rapid advancement of wearable computing, such as Google Glass, adds possibilities of enhancing the learning experience within cultural organizations such as museums and art galleries. A later study by Hassan (2013) in the Whitechapel Gallery of London cited an example of effective technology application in terms of offering learning experience. Another recent study by Leue, Jung, and tom Dieck (2015) reveals specifically that wearable augmented reality application helps visitors see connections between paintings and personalizes their learning experience.

In tourism research, limited theories and models related to technology use have been developed by scholars, researchers or experts. Relevant theories of technology adoption have been mostly applied to understand the pattern of technology adoption by tourism products or service consumers. The Diffusion of Innovation (Rogers, 1962) is an example of those theories or models. However, understanding the relevancy of this theory in AR technology application context is unique. In a simple sense, this theory explains why, how and at what rate a new technology is diffused into a culture. This theory is originally concerned with technologies, artefacts and ideas that normally pass from theory to application stage (Spencer, Buhalis, & Moital, 2012). According to Rogers (2003), sequences that the Diffusion of Innovation Theory follows are: knowledge, persuasion, decision, implementation and confirmation. On the other side, different stages of this theory are: innovators, *early adopters*, early majority, late majority and laggards. The 'Diffusion of Innovations' theory relies on the innovation-decision process that can be seen as valid in diverse cultures. This theory follows that technological innovations are connected through specific channels of the social system and act over a period of time.

Tourism industry is unprecedentedly gaining benefits from technology integration. Arguably, information and communication technologies are required to offer diverse typologies to become beneficial components for tourism marketing in recent times. The involvement of certain features of tourism is also essential in terms of effective use of technologies to make purchase decisions. The world is now better equipped to welcome and apply technological innovations than ever before (McElheran, 2012). Tour guides, travel agents, and tour operators are influenced by the utmost application of technologies; while tourism products or service and consumers are the direct subject of such influences. Results of technology application in tourism can be replicated in similar or emerging market contexts. From the applied viewpoint and most importantly, augmented reality as an innovation is beneficial for the tourism business enterprises, policy planners and business communities for competitive marketing strategy formulations. The basic question stays relevant to delineate consumer and product or service provider to become able to accept augmented reality as innovation. This question also seems as appropriate to explore the position of augmented reality in the Diffusion of Innovation theory. More importantly, concentrations need to be placed to determine the characteristics of augmented reality to incorporate a theory as the Diffusion of Innovation.

Key Practical Challenges to Inclusion of AR

Tourism is the world's leading industry and there are several techniques of professional and practical practices in tourism marketing education where the strategies and patterns are entirely technology-based (World Tourism Organization, 2015). A purposeful selection of tourism products or services coupled with marketing tactics like branding, promotions with augmented reality technology needs to become valid and effective. In fact, this is a real challenge to introduce, support and promote augmented reality in tourism marketing academia. This allows consumers to reach an agreeable decision of purchase that might turn as positive. This chapter suggests two key challenges to apply augmented reality in tourism marketing. In both perspectives of augmented reality and tourism marketing education, the key challenges appear in theory and practice.

In practice, AR is also mostly viewed as a technological innovation and its mass use is mostly restricted. The activities and successes of a tourism business enterprise depend on the selection of specific marketing approaches followed by their effective application (Turban, McLean, & Wetherbe, 2008). In recent times, marketing approaches mostly rely on technologies and to serve the purposes of business enterprises, augmented reality technology can become effective given its proven capacities to attract consumer interests. The greater number of customers that are attracted to a business enterprise, the more opportunities are created for marketing on digital platforms. This requires proper attention of the marketers to each individual customer. Also, setting realistic business targets to ensure that the business is directed towards the desired goal is also important and can be seen as a challenge. The success of digital marketing relies on careful selection of strategies and policies and AR technology application can possibly be a good option. Like unconventional marketing approach, in digital marketing, there have to be specific goals for each individual business enterprise to reach.

TOURISM MARKETING EDUCATION

Tourism marketing education refers to the education that involves tourism marketing in its syllabus. This type of education can support preparing future tourism marketing professionals. Primarily, the use of technologies is crucial. Effective and valid application of technology for professional development including tourism can bring positive outcomes.

Preparing Future Tourism Marketing Professionals

Specific technology like AR is believed to have capacities to create impact among tourism marketing professionals. This impact can lead to influencing consumers. The world is gradually changing and is continuously embracing updated forms of technologies. It is wise to adopt technologies and to apply them effectively for the purpose of marketing (Lewis, Agarwal, & Sambamurthy, 2003). AR marketing, as a type of digital marketing, is relatively more cost effective and can offer better return of investment than traditional forms of marketing (prweb, 2011). AR applications can be useful to develop skills of tourism marketing professionals and can be viewed as a convenient source to create user interests. AR can be an effective means of sales and revenue generation for tourism businesses. This can render possibilities for professionals. AR applications can enhance consumer experiences. In addition, a number of intermediaries and more selectively electronic mediaries (eMediaires) are adopting and using the Internet and AR to reach target customer segments all over the world (Kumar, Venkatesan, & Reinartz, 2006). On the other side, tourists also seek information on their desired services or products on the Internet. Thus, the Internet and in particular AR can be turned into common platforms of marketing. These cost effective and informative platforms are turning as valid and reliable platforms of marketing for tourists. In order to support digital marketing, numerous forms of display patterns are brought to influence a positive form of consumer decision. The Internet is being challenged by the Internet itself in terms of speed, information or accessibility. Visibly, not other platforms can be as reliable and valid for tourism marketing in the most recent tourism marketing contexts. This is termed as unbelievably simple and within the fingertips of customers (Thorpe, Holm, & van den Boer, 2014). Targeted customers are allowed to search for relevant information and thus to get access to it in more convenient ways than ever before with the effective support of AR technology application. This platform is also crucial to promote and make available certain products or services. The conventional types of digital marketing follow e-commerce, website trafficking and e-mail newsletters. All of these types are more conventional and have been in use for a long time. The demand for more advanced forms of digital marketing becomes apparent due to changing choices of consumers and the features of products or services (Song, Liu, & Chen, 2012). The use of AR becomes very effective in terms of getting responses or experiences shared on specific products or services. Blogging is relative less effective than social media but still offers relevant information. Sometimes, information sharing on networking websites becomes critical and thus appears as more capable to offer better service or product qualities with the support of AR technology application. Thus, AR can have a significant role to play to develop skills of marketing professionals in tourism.

In order to prepare more professionals in tourism marketing, marketers need to stress applying technologies for skills development. In tourism, the basic demand to capitalize on technological advancements is to learn operational skills. In many cases, tourism marketers struggle to apply an innovative technology like AR and this can be regarded as a resistance for a relatively new technology such as AR. However, AR, as an innovative technology, is already in use by tourism businesses and marketers. Following the Diffusion of Innovations by Rogers (1962), AR technology can be classified as '*Early Majority*' stage. The basic reason for this categorization is that the tourism marketing and businesses have already advanced significantly to apply AR technology meaning that they are on the '*Early Majority*' stage.

On the other side, government, university and tourism industry should look at the huge potential of AR marketing in tourism and take action to get this included in the academic syllabuses. This can be done by stressing AR technology and include this in both the undergraduate and postgraduate level academic syllabus. Tourism marketing education in almost every country is at the infancy stage with regards to including AR in its academic syllabus. On the other side, skills of the academics also need to reach that desired level to teach AR in tourism marketing education. On the basis of the Diffusion of Innovations theory of Rogers (1962), the present situation of tourism marketing education outlines that AR is an innovative technology at '*Early Adopters*' stage.

Inclusion of AR Applications in Curriculum

Tourism marketing education syllabuses in graduate and postgraduate stage at university level can highlight AR in their academic syllabuses. Numerous evidences and cases from across the world show that the use of AR for marketing purposes is not rare anymore and the number is increasing (Kaufman & Horton, 2015). The effects and influences of augmented reality technology, in particular can hardly be ignored in many areas of tourism marketing. This supports the claim that AR technology needs to be included in tourism marketing education syllabuses. AR as a technology application supports marketing in a unique way that learners need to know. Tourism marketing dynamics outline that the use of AR technologies needs to be widely utilized. This is still a subject matter of consideration both from technology and marketing domains. In the tourism industry, tourists are mostly capable of using AR technologies through their mobile devices like Smartphones. AR is mainly responsible for experience sharing, education and marketing purposes for tourism. This technology can offer experiences of an entire city tour as linked with its basic history, features and related factors. This creates interests in areas of education, marketing and promoting of specific tourist attractions. Unlike conventional tourism marketing education and marketing types, AR marketing is more dependable, target focused and useful. Thus, tourism marketing education evolved as a necessity of today's businesses as solely supported by technological knowledge (Vong, 2015). However, the availability and accessibility of technology are unequal for general learners and consumer segments. There is a strong demand for technological knowledge and use. A comprehensive academic and industry led understanding of tourism digital marketing is yet to be offered. Very often, it is believed that tourism digital marketing has a strong central theme of technology led knowledge and practical application. This possesses capacities to incorporate both existing and future tourism digital marketing. This study cites examples from several countries in the world in terms of AR technology use. Thus, this study advocates AR to be included in tourism marketing education.

Key Theoretical Challenges to Inclusion of AR

The first challenge is theoretical concept on the ground of knowledge exchange and expertise about augmented reality. This challenge is particularly directed for academics, scholars or experts in tourism marketing education. The application of augmented reality in tourism marketing education academia is a challenge. In theory, academic instructors need to possess sufficient knowledge about augmented reality and its application in tourism marketing education. On the other side in particular cases, augmented reality is seen as an element of post modern marketing outlining its relevancies in the marketing academia. Marketing in post modern age is in fact the blend of conventional and modern approaches of marketing. In post modern marketing, consumers typically stay connected and thus the response generation becomes more obvious than conventional marketing (Yang, 2004). Message on services or products pass over within a very short time to numerous consumer bases across the world. Post modern marketing is related with diverse types of business functionalities including identifying the target consumers and becoming able to comprehend their responses in purposeful manners (Petersen & Toop, 1994).

FUTURE DIRECTIONS

The main message of this section is that AR offers features to be included in any tourism marketing education curriculum. The primary reason of such inclusion is its key feature as a technological innovation. Technology is changing the core contents and grounds of tourism marketing education and there is almost no scope left for ignoring the growing importance. Thus, the contribution of technology is gradually increasing in tourism marketing education leaving more impact on both academics and practitioners in these identified grounds. This chapter discusses diverse features and potentials of augmented reality in tourism marketing practice and education and suggests its inclusion in the academic syllabuses to be studied as a key module. Thus, it would be beneficial to include augmented reality in the tourism marketing education syllabus. The very basic benefit that this inclusion can generate is the diversified knowledge of students. On the other side, assigned teachers and researchers in the tourism marketing education discipline would also possibly become aware about the contents and presentations of AR in tourism marketing education. The future of augmented reality as both an academic and research element of tourism marketing education is convincing. Even at present, augmented reality is facing serious challenges but the potentials are enormous to be included in tourism marketing syllabuses across the globe. The key challenge that augmented reality is facing is its complex nature. This technology also requires relevant expertise of concerned academics. The level of knowledge also needs to be well developed to deliver to students. Consequently, this is mostly obvious that augmented reality is expected to manage a strong position in tourism marketing education syllabus in the near future.

The introduction and availability of a technology commonly varies between nations outlining acute differences between nations including the developed and the developing. Technology application cannot be expected to get similar responses in both developed and developing countries across the world. This requires the demand that updated technology needs to be made widely available and particularly for students, academics and researchers. Their involvement and activities would offer positive advancements to view augmented reality as a valid element of tourism marketing education in near future. Thus, this chapter proposes that augmented reality should be offered as an important subject matter of tourism marketing education in the future.

This chapter is a report of thoughts related to AR application in tourism marketing education. This chapter as a report could possibly be converted into comprehensive research supported by empirical data and information. From that perspective, the basic limitation of this chapter is the lack of empirical evidence from respondents through conducting interviews. Primary data and information could possibly enrich contents of this report by highlighting opinions, arguments and justification from user perspectives. This lack is significant in a manner because, a possible interrelationship between academics, students, experts and practitioners related to tourism marketing education could possibly intensify debate and arguments to view augmented reality as an element of an academic syllabus. A balanced interrelatedness between concepts and peoples' ideologies could possibly create a bridge between theories and applications. This is a very generic limitation of this report that needs to be addressed in future research.

CONCLUSION

Conceptually, technology application supports massive consumption across the world where, such consumption patterns are mostly diverse and ever changing. Augmented reality is a computer generated reality but not necessarily fictitious or purely imaginary. Augmented reality supports the reality that is concerned with existing artifacts. Augmented reality as a technology can be termed as innovation on ground of the Diffusion of Innovation Theory (Rogers, 1962). On the basis of the Diffusion of Innovations Theory of Roger's (1962), this study determines position of augmented reality for tourism marketer or business as the '*Early Majority*' and tourism marketing education as the '*Early Adopters*' stage, respectively. Basic logic for this claim is made on the perspective of an emerging trend in tourism marketing education. The very basic reason is that augmented reality as an element of tourism marketing syllabus still remains at the early stage. Academics, students and researchers are still to become fully aware concerning augmented reality in terms of its meaning and application where the technology is not widely available for mass use.

This paper discusses features of augmented reality to be included in the tourism marketing education syllabuses. The features of augmented reality as an advanced form of virtual reality (VR) is interesting and its application values are also relatively high. Recent technological developments of mobile computing, computer graphics, wireless, sensor technologies, Smartphones and wearable devices have created more prospects to view augmented reality as more rewarding. On the other side, global brands are also using this technology for both advertising and marketing purposes. Also, these brands are constantly relying on such technological innovation to create spaces for marketing and connectivity with mass consumers. In addition, global technological appliance manufacturers are constantly aiming to use and develop this technology creating more opportunities for research and employability for students and researchers. These global brands have allowed consumers to view how technological appliances are designed to perform and entertain. Wearable devices like Smartwatches or Smart glasses are also evolving with modifications creating more spaces for general consumers. The development of sensor and visual technologies are also supporting the potentials of augmented reality technology. This thus allows buyers to support and experience what they are going to purchase and how that will look like.

Thus evidently, AR both as a technology and as an innovation has already established the position in consumers' traditional lifestyle. This is visible and evident through the customary use of technological gadgets those are mostly wearable. This chapter cites examples of augmented reality use from several countries of the world including the United Kingdom, Netherlands, Canada, France, Germany, Greece and China to establish the claim of its application.

This chapter outlines the prospects that AR can offer in terms of knowledge, research and practical aspect of employment possibility. Thus, this paper clearly suggests diverse aspects and examples of augmented reality as available and accessible for students, academics and practitioners in tourism marketing. Also, the paper strongly suggests augmented reality to be included in tourism marketing education syllabus to allow students learn about this technology and to become fit for employability. Augmented reality is an excellent and a trendy concept of recent times. This technology is expected to get wider popularity in the near future. Augmented reality shows prospects to turn into a reliable platform in tourism marketing mainly for its increasing capacities.

REFERENCES

Abernathy, W., & Clark, K. B. (2007). Innovation: Mapping the winds of creative distruction. *Research Policy*, *14*(1), 3–22. doi:10.1016/0048-7333(85)90021-6

Augmentedmarketing. (2013). *Ontarion Tourism Summit 2013 features interactive print.* Retrieved from http://bit.ly/1CRuwl6

Augmentedstories. (2015). *Education.* Retrieved from: http://augmentedstories.com/education/

Aurasma. (2015). *The drink of champions.* Retrieved from: http://bit.ly/1Fw66vl

Azim, R., & Hassan, A. (2013). Impact analysis of wireless and mobile technology on business management strategies. *Journal of Information and Knowledge Management*, *2*(2), 141–150.

Azuma, R. (1997). A survey of augmented reality. *Presence (Cambridge, Mass.)*, *6*(4), 355–385.

Breeze, M. (2014). *How augmented reality will change the way we live.* Retrieved from http://tnw.co/1nEDN6O

Buchholz, R. (2014). *Augmented reality: new opportunities for marketing and sales.* Retrieved from http://bit.ly/1nMCLYO

Buhalis, D., & Yovcheva, Z. (2014). *Augmented reality in tourism: 10 best practices.* Retrieved from http://bit.ly/1tphods

Caarls, J., Jonker, P., Kolstee, Y., Rotteveel, J., & van Eck, W. (2009). Augmented reality for art, design and cultural heritage—system design and evaluation. *EURASIP Journal on Image and Video Processing*, *2009*, 1–16. doi:10.1155/2009/716160

Creative Guerrilla Marketing. (2014). 10 examples of augmented reality in retail. Retrieved from http://bit.ly/OxuyHI

Daim, T. U., Letts, M., Krampits, M., Khamis, R., Dash, P., & Monalisa, M. (2012). IT infrastructure refresh planning for enterprises: A business process perspective. *Business Process Management Journal*, *17*(3), 1–16.

Deighton, J. A., & Kornfeld, L. (2007). *Digital interactivity: unanticipated consequences for markets, marketing and consumers*. Boston: Harvard Business School.

Deluna, K. (2014). *10 rockstar examples of augmented reality for 2014*. Retrieved from http://bit.ly/1mIaCib

Dhir, A. (2004). *The digital consumer technology handbook*. Oxford: Elsevier.

Digitalmeetsculture. (2015). Augmented reality: enriching culture. Retrieved from http://bit.ly/1E46st6

Dutra, J.P. (2015). *ARgos – augmented reality in Volos – Greece*. Retrieved from http://bit.ly/1BgTVTw

Edwards, J. (2011). *Digital frontiers media uses augmented reality to market St. Pete/Clearwater tourism with miles media*. Retrieved from http://www.prweb.com/releases/2011/03/prweb5141134.htm

Gartner Incorporated. (2014). *Gartner Technology Research*. Retrieved from: http://Online.gartner.com/technology/home.jsp>

Gay, R., Charlesworth, A., & Esen, R. (2007). *Online marketing: A customer-led approach*. Oxford: Oxford University Press.

Guimaraes, T. (2012). Industry clockspeed's impact on business innovation success factors. *European Journal of Innovation Management*, *14*(3), 322–344. doi:10.1108/14601061111148825

Han, D., Jung, T., & Gibson, A. (2014). Dublin AR: Implementing Augmented Reality (AR) in Tourism. In Z. Xiang & I. Tussyadiah (Eds.), *Information and Communication Technologies in Tourism* (pp. 511–523). Wien, New York: Springer International Publishing.

Hassan, A. (2013). Perspective analysis and implications of visitor management - experiences from the Whitechapel Gallery, London. *Anatolia: An International Journal of Tourism and Hospitality Research*, 24(3), 410-426. doi:.10.1080/13032917.2013.797916

Hax, A. C. (2010). *Reinventing your business strategy*. New York: Springer.

Hepburn, A. (2015). *Top 10 augmented reality examples- digital buzz blog*. Retrieved from http://bit.ly/1nXdp6l

Jung, T., Chung, N., & Leue, M. (2015). The Determinants of Recommendations to Use Augmented Reality Technologies - The Case of a Korean Theme Park. *Tourism Management*, *49*, 75–86. doi:10.1016/j.tourman.2015.02.013

Jung, T., & Han, D. (2014). Augmented reality (AR) in urban heritage tourism. *e-Review of Tourism Research.*

Kaufman, I., & Horton, C. (2015). *Digital marketing: Integrating strategy and tactics with values: A guidebook for executives, managers & students*. New York: Routledge.

Kipper, G., & Rampolla, J. (2014). *Augmented reality: An emerging technologies guide to AR*. London: Elsevier.

Kumar, V., Venkatesan, R., & Reinartz, W. J. (2006). Knowing what to sell when to whom. *Harvard Business Review*, May, 131–145. PMID:16515161

Lee, H., Chung, N., & Jung, T. (2015). Examining the cultural differences in acceptance of mobile augmented reality: comparison of South Korea and Ireland. In I. Tussyadiah & A. Inversini (Eds.), *Information and Communication Technologies in Tourism* (pp. 477–491). Wien: Springer International Publishing New York. doi:10.1007/978-3-319-14343-9_35

Leue, M. C., Jung, T., & tom Dieck, D. (2015). Google Glass Augmented Reality: Generic Learning Outcomes for Art Galleries. In I. Tussyadiah & A. Inversini (Eds.), Information and Communication Technologies in Tourism (pp. 463-476). Wien: Springer International Publishing.

Lewis, W., Agarwal, R., & Sambamurthy, V. (2003). Sources of influence on beliefs about information technology use: An empirical study of knowledge workers. *Management Information Systems Quarterly*, *27*(4), 657–678.

Louvre -DNP Museum Lab. (2015). *Past presentation*. Retrieved from http://www.museumlab.jp/english/tech/04tech.html

Lum, R. (2012). *10 mind-blowing augmented reality campaigns*. Retrieved from http://bit.ly/1kMP8AD

MarketingWeek. (2015). *Online retail will drive innovation in interactive marketing*. Retrieved from http://bit.ly/1nbpjdM

McElheran, K. S. (2012). *Do market leaders lead in business process innovation? The case(s) of e-business adoption*. Boston: Harvard Business School.

Mobile Marketer. (2015). *Mobile augmented reality to drive $1.5B in revenue by 2015*. Retrieved from http://bit.ly/1nbq32r

Mohapatra, S. (2009). *Business process automation*. New Delhi: PHI Private Limited.

Monday, C. (2015). *5 augmented reality examples worth looking at - ignite social media*. Retrieved from http://bit.ly/1mN1qZD

Neuhofer, B., Buhalis, D., & Ladkin, A. (2013). A typology of technology-enhanced tourism experiences. *International Journal of Tourism Research*. doi:10.1002/jtr.1958

Nordin, S. (2003). *Tourism clustering and innovation- paths to economic growth and development. Ostersund*. European Tourism Research Institute.

Olsson, T., & Väänänen-Vainio-Mattila, K. (2013). Expected User Experience of Mobile Augmented Reality Services. *Personal and Ubiquitous Computing*, *17*(2), 287–304. doi:10.1007/s00779-011-0494-x

Petersen, C., & Toop, A. (1994). *Sales Promotion in Postmodern Marketing*. Aldershot: Gower Publishing Ltd.

Preexamples. (2015). *Paddy Power augmented reality campaign brings the Queen's face on £10 note to life*. Retrieved from http://bit.ly/1CRur13

Rayport, J. F., & Jaworski, B. J. (2004). Best face forward. *Harvard Business Review*, *82*(12), 1–12. PMID:15605565

Rogers, M. E. (1962). *Diffusion of innovations*. New York: Free Press.

Rogers, M. E. (2003). *Diffusion of innovations* (5th ed.). New York: Free Press.

Rust, R. T., Katherine, N. L., & Valarie, A. Z. (2004). Return on marketing: Using customer equity to focus marketing strategy. *Journal of Marketing*, *68*(1), 109–127. doi:10.1509/jmkg.68.1.109.24030

Seo, B.-K., Kim, K., & Park, J. (2011). Augmented reality-based on-site tour guide: A study in Gyeongbokgung. *Lecture Notes in Computer Science*, *6469*, 276–285. doi:10.1007/978-3-642-22819-3_28

Shen, Y., Ong, S. K., & Nee, A. Y. C. (2011). Vision-based hand interaction in augmented reality environment. *International Journal of Human-Computer Interaction*, *27*(6), 523–544. doi:10.1080/10447318.2011.555297

Showcase. (2015). *Shaq augmented reality*. Retrieved from http://bit.ly/1BgTZ5F

Song, H., Liu, J., & Chen, G. (2012). Tourism value chain governance- review and prospects. *Journal of Travel Research*, *52*(1), 15–28. doi:10.1177/0047287512457264

Spencer, A. J., Buhalis, D., & Moital, M. (2012). A hierarchical model of technology adoption for small owner-managed travel firms: An organizational decision making and leadership perspective. *Tourism Management*, *33*(5), 1195–1208. doi:10.1016/j.tourman.2011.11.011

Stricker, D., Pagani, A., & Zoellner, M. (2009). *In-situ visualization for cultural heritage sites using novel augmented reality technologies*. Retrieved from http://bit.ly/192Vg5N

Suh, Y., Shin, C., Woo, W., Dow, S., & MacIntyre, B. (2011). Enhancing and evaluating users' social experience with a mobile phone guide applied to cultural heritage. *Personal and Ubiquitous Computing*, *15*(6), 649–665. doi:10.1007/s00779-010-0344-2

The, F. A. Cup. (2015). *About the FA*. Retrieved from http://bit.ly/1GLcZYu

Thorpe, M., Holm, J., & van den Boer, G. (2014). *Discovering the decisions within your business processes using IBM blueworks live*. New York: International Business Machines Corporation.

Turban, E., McLean, E. R., & Wetherbe, J. C. (2008). *Information technology for management*. New Jersey: John Wiley & sons, Inc.

Vlahakis, V., Ioannidis, N., Karigiannis, J., Tsotros, M., Gounaris, M., Stricker, D., Gleue, T., Daehne, P., & Almeida, L. (2002). Archeoguide: An Augmented Reality Guide for Archaeological Sites. *Computer Graphics in Art History and Archaeology, September/October*, 52- 60.

Vong, K. (2015). *How brands are using augmented reality in marketing to engage customers*. Retrieved from http://bit.ly/SrBNTq

Wang, L., Wang, C., & Fournier, C. (2000). Envisioning Yuan Ming Yuan (Garden of Perfect Brightness). *IEEE Computer Graphics and Applications*, *20*(1), 10–14. doi:10.1109/38.814532

Wind, J., & Mahajan, V. (2001). *Digital Marketing: Global Strategies from the World's Leading Experts*. Chichester: John Wiley & Sons.

World Tourism Organization (UNWTO). (2015). *Understanding tourism: basic glossary*. Retrieved from http://bit.ly/1ki2UGS

Yang, C. C. (2004). Exploring factors affecting the adoption of mobile commerce in Singapore. *Telematics and Informatics*, *22*(3), 257–277. doi:10.1016/j.tele.2004.11.003

Yovcheva, Z., Buhalis, D., & Gatzidis, C. (2012). Smartphone Augmented Reality Applications for Tourism. *e-Review of Tourism Research (eRTR)*, *10*(2), 63-66.

Yuen, S., Yaoyuneyong, G., & Johnson, E. (2011). Augmented reality: An overview and five directions for AR in education. *Journal of Educational Technology Development and Exchange*, *4*(1), 119–140.

ADDITIONAL READING

Bridges-to-technology. (2015). *What is Technology Adoption?* Retrieved from http://bit .ly/T5kFnb

Buhalis, D., & Lew, R. (2008). Progress in information technology and tourism management: 20 years on and 10 years after the internet—the state of eTourism research. *Tourism Management*, *29*(4), 609–623. doi:10.1016/j.tourman.2008.01.005

Business Dictionary. (2015). *Consumer buying behaviour*. Retrieved from http://bit.ly/1kICBJX

Candela, G., & Figini, P. (2012). *The economics of tourism destinations*. Berlin, Heidelberg: Springer. doi:10.1007/978-3-642-20874-4

Cantoni, L., & Zheng, X. (2013). *Information and communication technologies in tourism*. Berlin, Heidelberg: Springer.

Change Vision, A. R. M. (2015). *Augmented reality marketing*. Retrieved from http://bit.ly/1gVIqc0

Cooper, C., & Hall, M. C. (2008). *Contemporary tourism: an international approach*. Oxford: Butterworth-Heinemann.

Duffy, J. A. M., & Ketchand, A. A. (1998). Examining the role of service quality in overall service satisfaction. *Journal of Managerial Issues*, *10*, 240–255.

Hassan, A. (2012). Key components for an effective marketing planning: A conceptual analysis. *International Journal of Management & Development Studies*, *2*(1), 68–70.

Hassan, A. (2012). Rationalization of Business Planning Through the Current Dynamics of Tourism. *International Journal of Management & Development Studies*, *2*(1), 61–63.

Hassan, A. (2014). Revising the 'Five - Fold Framework' in Human Resource Management Practices – Insights from a Small Scale Travel Agent. *Tourism Analysis: An Interdisciplinary Journal*, *19*(6), 799–805. doi:10.3727/108354214X14146848084400

Karch, M. (2015). *Apps*. Retrieved from http://abt.cm/1l48Ojv

Li, N., Buhalis, D., & Zhang, L. (2013). Interdisciplinary research on information science and tourism: A systematic review. *Tourism Tribune*, *28*(1), 114–128.

Michopoulou, E., & Buhalis, D. (2013). Information provision for challenging markets: The case of the accessibility requiring market in the context of tourism. *Information & Management*, *50*(5), 229–239. doi:10.1016/j.im.2013.04.001

Mihart, C. (2012). Impact of Integrated Marketing Communication on Consumer Behaviour: Effects on Consumer Decision – Making Process. *International Journal of Marketing Studies*, *4*(2), 121–129. doi:10.5539/ijms.v4n2p121

Morrison, A. M. (2013). *Marketing and managing tourism destinations*. London: Routledge.

SAS Institute Inc. (2015). *Digital marketing-what is it and why it matters*. Retrieved from http://bit.ly/1cRj6SG

The University of Bradford. (2015). *Effective learning service-introduction to research and research methods*. Retrieved from http://bit.ly/1gUwTpo

Tremblay, P. (1998). The economic organization of tourism. *Annals of Tourism Research*, *25*(4), 837–859. doi:10.1016/S0160-7383(98)00028-0

Walters, D. (2002). *Operations strategy*. New York: Palgrave.

Werthner, H., & Klein, S. (1999). *Information technology and tourism - a challenging relationship*. Vienna: Springer-Verlag. doi:10.1007/978-3-7091-6363-4

Wynne, C., Berthon, P., Pitt, L., Ewing, M., & Napoli, J. (2001). The impact of the Internet on the distribution value chain- the case of the South African tourism industry. *International Marketing Review*, *18*(4), 420–431. doi:10.1108/EUM0000000005934

Youngdahl, W., & Loomba, A. (2000). Service-driven global supply chains. *International Journal of Service Industry Management*, *11*(4), 329–347. doi:10.1108/09564230010355368

KEY TERMS AND DEFINITIONS

Augmented Reality: This technology is generally viewed as the later stage of Virtual Reality. In this technology, a computer generated environment is created where, the humans as users act. This blends augmentation with reality.

The Diffusion of Innovation Theory: This theory offered by Rogers in 1962 explains why and how a new technology or idea spreads in a society and at what rate. The theory proposes five stages for such explanation as part of this theory as: innovators, early adopters, early majority, late majority and laggards.

Digital Marketing: Digital marketing represents conducting marketing activities on digital platforms mainly, Internet.

Innovation: Innovation denotes an idea, method or product that is regarded as new.

Tourism Marketing Education: This deals with marketing in tourism education. In more specific understanding, this type education involves marketing aspects in particular grounds of tourism.

Chapter 9
Seeing Numbers Differently:
Mathematics in the Virtual World

Rebecca Lynne Patterson
Dream Realizations, USA

D. Cooper Patterson
CERLabs, USA

Anna-Marie Robertson
Dream Realizations, USA

ABSTRACT

Numbers are the most powerful adjective in the human language, being that they are descriptive and quantifiable. Humans can harness that power with our eyes and our innate ability to see shape patterns. Virtual worlds afford us this opportunity without the physical world hindrances of materials, space, time, or gravity. Explore how language, decimal-centricity, and symbols with their processes have clouded the view of numbers, their shapes, and the discovery of metapatterns: visually recognizable algebraic expressions and equations. The experiences shared in the case study within reveal the need of a working virtual world environment for educational training, prototyping, and studio image capturing. Common Core Standards for Mathematics aspire to bring the student into the understanding of the "why". In the virtual reality of Second Life, the metaphor of seeing the forest before the trees is realized with our example and number patterns: from the earliest subitizing, to multi-digit, multi-base number recognition, to metapatterns, to deriving polynomial equations through differences.

INTRODUCTION

How students learn mathematics hasn't changed for over a century. This includes, but is not limited to numbers, number patterns, symbolic codes for quantity, and number processes. Current teaching practices introduce symbols to children when they are learning their alphabet and their counting words. Students spend some time representing quantities visually and with manipulatives. But with class sizes so large and core curriculum topics so varied, there just isn't time to spend in discovery. Common Core is trying

DOI: 10.4018/978-1-4666-9837-6.ch009

to address these issues with a deeper development of the 'core' lessons in arithmetic. Multiple perspectives are being investigated, and students are asked to find different avenues to explain the why behind the process (CCSS, 2010). Students still find themselves jumping into symbol manipulation: addition, subtraction, fractions, multiplication, division, etc., and spend a lot of time finding roundabout ways to discuss the essence of number. But these ways still leave a lot of students behind, making catching up a difficult journey as they move through the educational process.

Of those capable of taking on the rigor of higher education, 40% of four-year college students will take at least one Math remediation course and 70% of community college students are placed in remedial math (Okimoto & Heck, 2014; CCRC, 2014), only one-third of students taking those remedial math courses pass. Whereas 27% of those students recommended for help, never end up enrolling (Rikoon, Liebtag, Olivera-Aguilar, Robbins, & Jackson, 2014). Students struggle with the abstractness of mathematics (Hiebert, 1984). In a person's early education, the counting numbers are introduced along with the alphabet, impinging a true understanding of quantity. This counting memorization can still be found in teenagers and some adults when asked to do simple addition and fingers are employed in the process. From these realizations and with the help of a virtual world, three foundational problems have been discovered:

1. Conversational Western languages interfere with recognizing number patterns at an early age. The educational emphasis on counting beyond nine further hinders number sense development.
2. Decimal-centricity (focusing mainly on base ten) impedes the very important discovery of place shapes and metapatterns that exist across multiple base number systems. Focusing the learner exclusively on quantity and place value removes broader and more applicable concepts.
3. The push to use number symbols as the primary source for teaching preschool and elementary school mathematics interferes with and sometimes limits the development of a natural understanding of number processes acquired through physical and visual manipulation of *objects*.

The virtual world is the key. Throughout this chapter, instances will be revealed where and how a virtual world such as Second Life (SL) is used in mathematics instruction. SL opened up a plethora of opportunities for advancement, as it is the largest three-dimensional (3D) virtual world created purely by its users. In short, SL is a "3D world where everyone you meet is a real person and every place you visit is built by people just like you" (www.secondlife.com/whatis). Mathematics is still a relatively new topic to teach using this platform, mostly designated as a space to connect for online immersive discussions and tutoring (Burgess & Caverly, 2009), although some are trying to use this space as traditional teaching with negative results (Cheal, 2009). Innovative use of this virtual space affords a different perspective of mathematics. Scripted devices can show quantities in bases two to ten instantaneously and oscillate between two-dimensional (2D) and 3D at the click of a button, an Equation Board tied to those patterns showing the Algebraic representation of those metapatterns, and the base-conversion calculator link them all. In addition we can show the magnitude of number in relation to an avatar for deeper understanding. SL is used, not only as a prototyping, publishing, and design studio for educational materials in world and out, as seen in the attached figures, but also to immerse a student in the shape of number through activity and engagement. Second Life is a viable option for teaching mathematics.

The purpose of this chapter is to describe an innovative system that has been developed to teach mathematics through the use of Second Life, a virtual world application. First, background knowledge is provided on the importance of recognition of patterns in learning mathematical concepts, and the terms Digit Speak and subQuan are introduced. Secondly, Digit Speak and subQuan will be described in-depth as they relate to teaching mathematical concepts using strategies other than the traditional base ten system through the use of Second Life. A third focus of the chapter will be to identify and discuss issues, solutions, and recommendations identified in implementing the program described. A last focus will be on identifying future directions for the use of Second Life in teaching mathematics.

BACKGROUND

Humans are hard-wired to see patterns (Dehaene, 2011): patterns in number, patterns in shape, patterns in sounds, patterns in words, patterns in color, and more. Simple patterns within single digit quantities are overlooked when institutions jump too quickly to symbols. These single digit quantities can be subitized instead of such a heavy reliance on counting. The term, subitize, is derived from the Latin adjective *subitus*, meaning 'sudden'. Humans have an inherent ability to instantly recognize how many items are present in a visual scene when in small quantities, normally between zero and four, the subitizing range. Organized subitizing allows children to see the even- and oddness of number or inherent quantity differences, larger versus smaller. There are no processes to memorize: i.e. dots on the symbols (Cihak & Foust, 2008) nor any singsong rhyming memory verse.

Most languages do not foster an understanding of the patterns in number. The number names ten, eleven, twelve, thirteen etc. break the repetitive pattern and cause English-speaking children to fall behind Chinese-speaking children in their ability to count (Miller, Smith, Zhu, & Zhang, 1995). This is, in part, due to Asian languages using simple ten, ten-one, ten-two, number names. There are only ten counting words in all to reach 99, whereas English-speaking children, along with many other western languages, must learn a total of 27 new vocabulary words to get to 99. The tables in Figure 1 display the words used for number in eight languages. Recent research finds that speaking Mandarin, compared to speaking English, leads to 56% more young children being able to count to 100 (Miller, Kelly, & Zhou, 2005). Though the key difference occurred for the numbers eleven through 20, the fact remains that infants can differentiate syllables and this knowledge should be put to good use (Bijeljac-Babic,

Figure 1. Number names for the digits zero through twenty in various languages.

Single syllable digits have value.

Number	subQuan	English	Spanish	French	German	Sanskrit	Mandarin	Sino-Korean	Japanese
	-ro	zero	cero	zero	null	sunya	ling	yeong	rei
	one	one	uno	un	eins	eka	yi	il	ichi
	two	two	dos	deux	zwei	dvi	er	i	ni
	three	three	tres	trois	drei	tri	san	sam	san
	four	four	cuatro	quatre	vier	catur	si	sa	yon
	five	five	cinco	cinq	fünf	panca	wu	o	go
	six	six	seis	six	sechs	sas	liu	yuk	roku
	-ven	seven	siete	sept	sieben	sapta	qi	chil	nana
	eight	eight	ocho	huit	acht	asta	ba	pal	hachi
	nine	nine	nueve	neuf	neun	nava	jiu	gu	kyū

Yellow tint: words are two or more syllables.
Red arrows: only columns with monosyllables

Indisputable value of reusing number names

Number	subQuan	English	Spanish	French	German	Sanskrit	Mandarin	Sino-Korean	Japanese
	one-ro	ten	diez	dix	zehn	dasa	shi	ship	jū
	one-one	eleven	once	onze	elf	ekadasa	shi yi	shipil	jū ichi
	one-two	twelve	doce	douze	zwölf	dvadasa	shi er	shipi	jū ni
	one-three	thirteen	trece	treize	dreizehn	trayodasa	shi san	shipsam	jū san
	one-four	fourteen	catorce	quatorze	vierzehn	caturdasa	shi si	shipsa	jū yon
	one-five	fifteen	quince	quinze	fünfzehn	pancadasa	shi wu	shipo	jū go
	one-six	sixteen	dieciseis	seize	sechzehn	sodasa	shi liu	simnyuk	jū roku
	one-ven	seventeen	diecisiete	dix-sept	siebzehn	saptadasa	shi qi	shipchil	jū nana
	one-eight	eighteen	dieciocho	dix-huit	achtzehn	astadasa	shi ba	ship-pal	jū hachi
	one-nine	nineteen	diecinueve	dix-neuf	neunzehn	navadasa	shi jiu	shipgu	jū kyū
	two-ro	twenty	veinte	vingt	zwanzig	vimsati	er shi	iship	ni-jū

Yellow tint: words are not two syllables.
Red arrows: columns with logical reuse

Bertoncini, & Mehler, 1993). In addition to a change in number names from ten on, called Digit-speak, it is a hope that the use of -ro (roh) for zero and -ven (ven) for seven will decrease the linguistic burden when dealing with numbers in English. Apparently, every syllable has its cost.

The impact of reusing the words for the single digits has incredible value; 85% of Chinese students can identify 20 objects (stones) between the ages of three and five, when only 45% of U.S. students can do likewise (Miller et al., 1995). This can be attributed to the language differences, especially in regards to the teen number names (Miller & Stigler, 1987). Not only does the reuse of these words allow children to see the patterns in our decimal system, as with far-east languages, making counting easier, but it can also translate into a better number sense when paired with visual numbers as seen in a virtual world.

A suggestion for elementary students is to introduce a specific digit language, called digit-speak, in addition to our conversational speech that would enhance number comprehension. Since humans can quickly recognize number of syllables, each digit should only be one syllable. If you were to hear a number spoken and it had four syllables then it would be a four-digit number. Instead, we currently have a four-syllable word in 27 and yet it is smaller than many two-syllable numbers like 90. Examining a calculator, phone, remote, or keypad of any kind you will notice that there are only ten digits used to represent the numbers, 0 through 9. See Figure 2. This type of numbering is commonly used with a calculator, calling 911 (said 'nine one one' in the U.S. for emergency dialing), reciting decimal numbers, and many other ways.

Ones are the simple number of things. Using instinctual knowledge, number sense, determining even and odds, recognizing and arranging big and small numbers, and performing simple operations of combining becomes trivial. Opposites can also be simply combined by using color. Finally, other research has shown that using single syllables for Ones increases our brain's efficiency when dealing with numbers (Morin & Franks, 2009). Therefore, the recommendation is to use -ro, one, two, three, four,

Figure 2. Various devices using zero to nine interfaces.

Figure 3. Digit-speak allows the patterns of number to be revealed.

Science Technology Engineering Math: STEM

Foundation Problem #1: Number Language (limited to Western Civilization Languages)

Dream Realizations Activity: Language 3

Fill in the blanks with the correct word or write "C" for "clueless".

0	ro*	10	one ro	20	two ro	100	
1	one	11	one one	21			
2	two	12		22			
3	three	13		23			
4	four	14		24		125	
5	five	15		25			
6	six	16		26			
7	ven*	17		27			
8	eight	18		28		789	
9	nine	19		29			

If the above was our numbering language, how many digits would these unclear numbers be?**

wah wah			ik bik bo boo	
wah wah wah wah			oh my my tie tie	

* Extra syllables were removed from zero and seven. Don't worry. We have many numbers that have multiple names. We are adding simpler words for teaching only.

** Conversation was garbled due to poor technical connections (i.e. cell phones, Skype, etc.)

five, six, -ven, eight, nine as the single syllables to build every number, especially numbers that are not in base ten. Ten would be one-ro; eleven, one-one; twelve, one-two; and so on. In this form, students can recognize patterns with more alacrity. This number naming pattern is used in the recognition of visual number patterns: called "digit-speak". See Figure 3.

Children can see large numbers of things when arranged in specific patterns (Patterson, Reiniger, & Robertson, 2012). Support from Dehaene (2011), among other researchers, is readily available in which babies, in addition to birds, fish, and mammals, can recognize the difference between one, two or three objects, one, two or three movements, and one, two or three syllables (Antell & Keating, 1983). In other words, humans instinctually know, subitize, these smaller quantities without having to count (Penner-Wilger et al., 2007; Butterworth, 2005). This natural reality corroborates the findings and foundation of subQuan and place shapes.

With the research backing subitizing and the ability to organize and order numbers quickly in a virtual world, a short name for ordered-organized-groupings-that-can-easily-be-subitized needed to be coined. The word subQuan is derived from the ancient Latin words, subitas quantitas, for 'sudden quantity'. Quantity and subQuan are synonymous in base ten (base A). In all other bases the subQuan is different from the actual quantity. [Example: $12_A \neq 12_8$ ('A' is the single digit representation for base ten)] Mathematicians have long since investigated the same quantities in different bases, but have ignored the same subQuan in different bases. [Example: 23_6, 23_7, 23_8, 23_9 each having different quantities: 15, 17, 19, 21 respectively.]

Linguistically, a difference between the quantity (base ten) words, which is called conversational language, and subQuan language, which is called digit-speak, reveals much. The quantity 23_A is default for twenty-three, whereas 23_5 is said two-three base five. Decimal words like ten, eleven, twelve, and so on do not apply to any other base besides base ten. Any multi-digit numbers learned have been decimal words for quantities, but consider that quantity is only valid for base ten. subQuans are valid for all bases. So as to avoid confusion, digit-speak for subQuans is used and the traditional English number words for quantity, base ten numbers only.

Ordered organized visual patterns of things can be seen as quantities and, in fact, many school systems have base ten blocks for students to manipulate quantities. However, the decimal-centricity of quantity prevents the student's from seeing other base patterns. With the help of a virtual world, a new way of viewing changing quantities of recognizable shape patterns called subQuans can be seen. There is a distinct and repetitive shape to place value in different bases that is visually identifiable. When place value is taught in elementary school, words are introduced for periods: ones, tens, hundreds, thousands, and millions. Students may recognize a repetition of words, but a picture could be more impactful. Place Shape is defined when a large number is shown as a subQuan, organized into shapes that represent their respective periods, such as Cubes, Squares, and so on. Place Shapes (all bases) are the superset of Place Value (base ten only). The astounding part of this discovery is the recognition that containers aren't always packaged in tens. See Figure 4.

A CASE STUDY IN TEACHING MATHEMATICS USING VIRTUAL REALITY

Discovering the Need to Teach Math in a New Way

This is a story of discovery: an epic tale of encountering numbers. What started in the classroom during 2000, enhanced by an online flash program in 2008 (www.itonlytakes1.org), deepened with a virtual

Figure 4. A collection of various sized containers, otherwise known as bases.

world in 2009. Forming Dream Realizations in 2010, we collected classroom research at all levels: preschool through college. In every situation we find ourselves, students thrive in the play and building of number. Our discoveries would be near impossible to portray without the help of a virtual world, whether through pictures, video clips, or virtual world exploration.

Bring up the idea of teaching multiple base systems and teachers will shut down, stop listening, or feel very discouraged. Historical process-oriented ways of teaching has a whole population scared of numbers. With the introduction of Common Core parents are rebelling with the new thinking being introduced that seems to make problem solving so “hard”. Homework is getting longer as the students are asked the why behind what they think the answer is and to write their thoughts. And yet given some simple opportunities, both online and in person, to build with centimeter unit cubes, individuals can become more attune to a deeper understanding of number

Our first collective encounter with number occurred in some informal research and the participation of two fifth grade classes, an eighth grade after-school group, and a class of 11th & 12th grade students at an alternative high school. The students met in the computer lab and ran through all the discoveries at www.itonlytakes1.org, our flash program. They found out that if they let their minds relax (stopped trying to count) and give their eyes the power to see, then they could recognize 2D ordered and organized number patterns. Some of the students became quite quick and were excited with the ease in which it took. We found that the most difficult group to “let go” of counting was the fifth graders. Their times were inconsistent with other’s improvement which was an indicator that they were all still counting. A second visit to the computer lab with the same 5th grade groups and an emphasis on prohibiting counting, “just guess, don’t be afraid to be wrong”, decreased their recognition times noticeably. It seemed as if they were so enmeshed with process that they couldn’t stop counting without impetus.

With these same groups of students, we were afforded some classroom time to play with multicolored centimeter unit cubes and the Base Number Sheets (BNS). A BNS allows an individual to build a number in different bases, each sheet representing a different container size. A set of BNS shows gray and white vertical stripes to make each place easier to see. The bold outlines are containers. (See figures 5, 6, and 7 for examples.) Each group of students was given an equivalent number of cubes to build a number in a different base on a BNS. Once their numbers were built, we practiced walking around the room saying the subQuans. We only allowed digit-speak. Number recognition came quickly, but building took time. In groups as large as the fifth grade classes, it was difficult to perform these tasks without the four adults in the classroom. We realized at this point that we needed to find a quicker way to make numbers accessible and show that these numbers have shape. Our investigation into containers intensified.

Symbolic Representation

We could see the Square-ness and the Cube-ness of the 2D and 3D number shapes, respectively, but what of the one-dimensional (1D) number shape. If we followed the same pattern for the others, geometrically speaking, then a 1D object would be a line. The problem with this label is that it is defined as infinite and we could see with our eyes that the shape definitely stopped (2 unit cubes in base-two, 3 unit cubes in base-three, etc.). Students we presented with this conundrum were able to determine that our term is a line segment for this shape. And yet staying consistent with single syllable shape names, i.e. Cube and Square, all the students were able to derive a single syllable from line-seg-ment that would signify this shape. Seg was unanimous. The other possibilities simply didn’t make sense. So now we had a consensus of shapes: Cube, Square, Seg, Ones. See Figure 5.

Figure 5. Shapes of number: Cube, Square, _____, Ones. Find a one-syllable word to refer to a line segment.

Just what is a Seg?

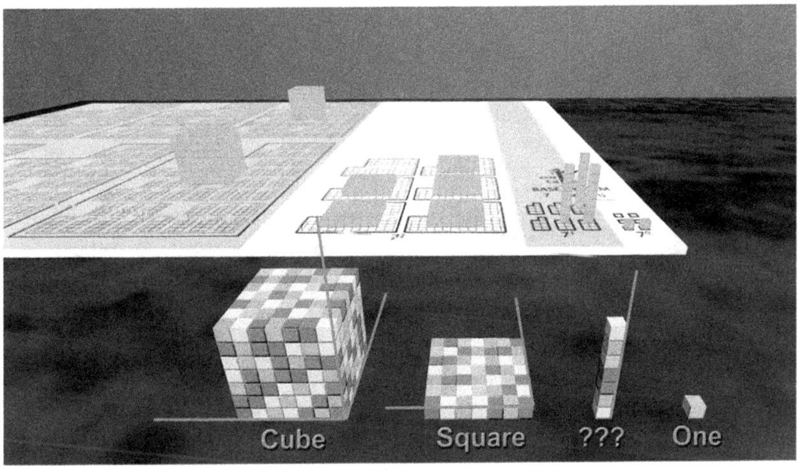

We are looking for a one syllable *word* that follows the sequence of 'cube' for three dimensions, 'square' for two dimensions, and '???' for one dimension. When given this challenge, 5th graders, 8th graders, 11th and 12th graders all came up with same answer. Hint: a line is infinite.

Figure 6. Multiple subQuans on virtual Base Number Sheets (BNS) in 2D help students practice their innate ability.

When learning to subQuan, see the color, then the Segs, then the Ones. There is no need to count. In the 2-dimensional mode of the Seg Sheets below, identify the subQuan. Think green (g) or magenta (m).

The Base 5 Seg Sheet is displaying the subQuan $m41_5$, pronouced 'em four one base five'. Elementary and secondary students can typically identify a Seg subQuan in one to two seconds!

Answers in order from base 3 to base A: $g11_3$, $g23_4$, $m41_5$, $g15_6$, $g53_7$, $m70_8$, $g66_9$, $m78_A$

Figure 7. Physical world base-two BNS above and virtual world binary interactive representation called "The Right Hand" below.

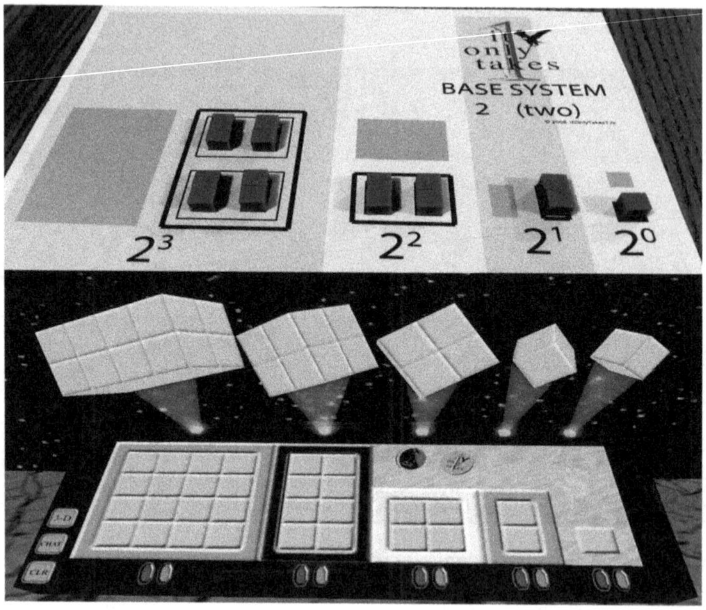

Humans bundle individual items, Ones collected together sometimes in soft containers, sometimes in hard containers, or sometimes in symbols or words in abstract containers using parentheses, braces, and brackets. Regardless of the type of container, we can now see a new type of One, a single container of Ones, called Segs (called Tens in base-ten place value). Segs reveal incredibly rich concepts. Using our instinctual number sense, we can apply the same concepts with Segs as we did with Ones. However, considerable knowledge-power is acquired when Segs are combined with Ones. The changes with evenness, oddness, and order produce useful patterns. A reusable solution to the problem of non-simple combining of Ones becomes apparent and powerful metapatterns can be seen. Research indicates that the numbers ten (10) through nineteen (19), the first Seg, cause problems in the Western World (Miller et al., 2005).

The general name for a system of containers that each holds an identical number of the smaller containers is called a base system. Containers that hold two would be a 'base-two system'. Almost all computers use the base-two system to encode data and programs. The base-two system is also called the binary number system. The base-ten system is called the decimal system. An important fact to remember is that the first place has the first containers so it is where we should look to determine the base of a number. Whenever we write two numbers together, like 24, the four is in the Ones place and the two is in the Tens place as taught in school and pronounced twenty-four. In subQuan, the two is in the 'first place' because it determines the size of container. In a base-ten system, we would have two tens. Whereas, if we were to teach in a multi-base system, for example in base-eight, we would have two containers that held eight items and four items not in a container to make a quantity of 20 items. This is not the quantity 24, but it is the subQuan 24_8 (said "two four base eight"). Our symbolic representations diverge.

When learning to subQuan, first see the color, then the Segs, then the Ones. There is no need to count. In the 2D mode of the Seg Sheets in Figure 6, students can identify the subQuan: green (g) for positive and magenta (m) for negative, although we never express the words fully. For example, the Base 5 Seg

Sheet is displaying the subQuan $m41_5$, pronounces 'em four one base five'. Elementary and secondary students can typically identify a Seg subQuan in one to two seconds. The subscript number represents the base and is only needed in written form with symbols.

[Answers in order from base 3 to A: $g11_3$, $g23_4$, $m41_5$, $g15_6$, $g53_7$, $m70_8$, $g66_9$, $m78_A$ from figure 6.]

Masters Research in 2011 through George Fox University took us into preschool with four- and five-year olds. We investigated the ease of recognizing number in three worlds: physical, virtual, and immersive. Base Number Sheets (BNS) were laid out with three-digit quantities in various bases. We were unconcerned with the base size, but more with order placement (largest to smallest) and correct amount. The children didn't even notice the container size differences and were able to use digit-speak, one digit at a time, to label all subQuans. We were only able to represent four BNS subQuans due to space and time, whereas we proceeded through three Discoveries with ten items each at www.itony-takes1.org. In our Second Life Lab, the children got to see those physical BNS in immersive form and the preloaded subQuans showed quickly. Since the children were tested in pairs, we returned two weeks later to determine retention on an individual basis. All students could recognize and name three-digit subQuans, some counting and some not. Please note that we never once talked about bases, but not one of the subQuans was in base-ten. Our determination here was that we needed a quicker way to get to the 3D-ness of number. It was just too hard to make multiple builds quickly in physical reality. We determined that to show quickly recognizable patterns we must show multiple subQuans in 3D. We rely on the virtual world to make photographs, prototypes, and, in some cases, visit 'in-person', in order to visualize multiple number patterns.

Place Shape on Base Number Sheets

The exponent, mathematically denoted in superscript, assigns a number to each place, highlighted on the BNS as alternate white and gray bars. This relationship between exponent and place is a critical foundational concept that eludes even some math teachers as we discovered in our research. In Figure 7, because it is base two, each container holds two of the containers immediately to the right. The BNS at the top of the figure shows the first four containers, or places, of the base-two system. Notice that the numbering of place shapes start at zero not at one which is consistent with the exponent.

Shapes are defined according to the number of dimensions of the base. Like most ideas, this one is easier to see than explain. All the cubes with each bold outline are arranged in tight groups. In the 2^3 group, the two groups of four Squares stack creating a Cube. The results should look like the bottom picture in Figure 7 of what we call The Right Hand. Five Place Shapes, shown as $g11{,}111_2$, illuminates the power of a virtual world. This interactive virtual device displays base-two in both 2-D and 3-D space. As the 3D shapes spin inworld, students can play with this concept freely. The colors, magenta and green, denote opposites.

Starting with the Cube, notice that it has two smaller unit cubes in its width, depth, and height, or in each of the three dimensions that define a Cube. That means it is a two-Cube. Mathematically we pronounce 2^3 as two-cubed. When we push the four 1 cm cubes together in the 2^2 container, we can see that it is only two cubes wide and deep, the two dimensions of a Square. That means it is a two-Square. Mathematically we pronounce 2^2 as two-squared. The two 1 cm cubes in the 2^1 container only measure

2 in one dimension. We would normally call that a line, but since it is not infinite, we derived a one syllable word from line segment and call it a Seg.

Unit cubes, when contained, create *Segs*, *Segs*, when contained, create *Squares*, and *Squares*, when contained and stacked, create *Cubes*, after which the pattern repeats. This sequence of three shapes aligns nicely with the concept of period. Commas in big numbers surround a period. In the decimal number system each period is named beginning with Ones, then Thousands, then Millions, and so on. Within each period is one, ten, and hundred which coincide with our three shapes (Ones, Segs, Squares), a visual shape pattern recognizable by toddlers. The shapes continue beyond the Cube. We call the next larger shapes: Seg of Cubes, Square of Cubes, and Cube of Cubes, followed by the ever larger Seg of Cube of Cubes, Square of Cube of Cubes, and Cube of Cube of Cubes. Just so the magnitude of these shapes can be understood, a Cube of Cube of Cubes in Base System Ten contains one billion unit cubes, not very easy to play with in a classroom, whereas a Cube of Cube of Cubes in Base System Two (the binary system), comprises of only 512 unit cubes. See Figure 8 (top) for a more inclusive and visual form of Place Shape in addition to and encompassing Place Value.

Using unit cubes in physical reality and programming in a virtual reality allowed us to cement these concepts that lie in viewing multiple bases. All base numbers contain similar shapes: Segs, Squares, and Cubes. These shapes repeat every period. Place Shape instead of Place Value takes precedence and has more meaning. Herein lies the foundation of Algebra and the key to cracking the code behind number symbols. Figure 8 (bottom) shows the consistency of shape patterns in base-two through base-ten.

Figure 8. Numbers have Place Shape in the chart (above), while in virtual world all bases share the same shapes below.

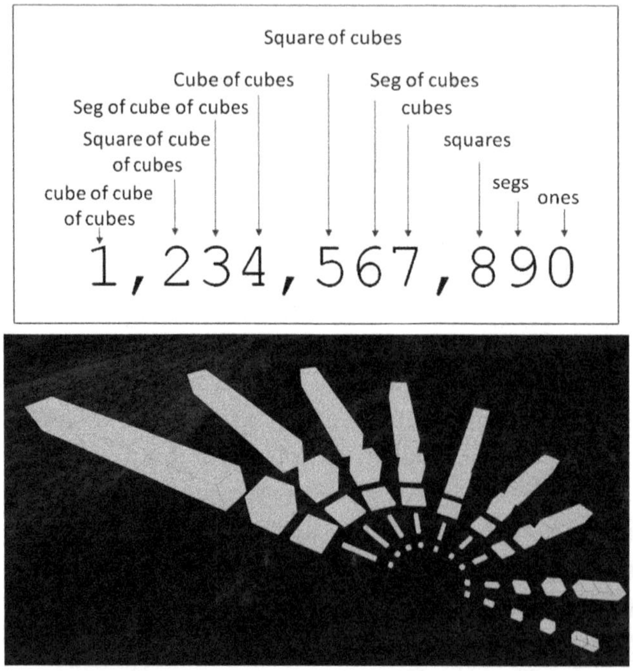

Classroom Experiences

In 2011-12 we worked monthly with 5th and 6th grade homeschool students interspersing many facets of looking at number as a supplement to their rigorous process-driven curriculum. We played with complements, recognizing subQuans, identifying the meaning of bases, and more. Along this same timespan, we presented in multiple educational and technical conferences in a three-series set of workshops: introducing subQuan (how to), metapatterns (recognizing the power of), and differences (deriving equations). In both instances we struggled with the in-person representation of what we were trying to show. We were severely hindered in the physical realm. Large class and conference sizes made building with centimeter cubes difficult to facilitate and a lack of high-speed Internet connection prohibited a functional use of Second Life. We resorted to taking pictures of our inworld creations and put them into PowerPoint presentations. Only on a few occasions were we able to host an inworld work session. We needed a more consistent path.

Our journey brought us into the Community College setting in 2013 where we were asked to teach Basic College Mathematics. The class was to focus on the use of fractions, decimals, percent, integers, and measurements to write, manipulate, interpret, and solve application and formula problems. We were also to introduce concepts of basic statistics. We taught two courses, our student population ranged from 17 to 60 years of age, and we had much coursework to cover. Implementing an interesting class design of pretest, exit exam, and posttest, created a very focused atmosphere. In our first term we taught the material as the text laid it out, while creating supplemental materials of how we'd approach this from a subQuan perspective for the following term.

Once we had worked through the curriculum, we were able to implement some changes and enhancements for the second term. We again had two Basic College Mathematics courses, and we also had one Algebra course. In the Basic courses we spent some time building number, manipulating centimeter cubes and practicing measurement in different bases. Eyes opened with connection as students saw how and why numbers performed the way they did. We didn't have access to the virtual world live, so we brought in virtual world snapshots to share. This second time around, our students received the highest class-grade average, attributable only to the addition of subQuan to the curriculum.

The Introductory Algebra class was to introduce algebraic concepts and processes with a focus on linear equations and inequalities in one and two variables. Applications, graphs, functions, formulas, and proper mathematical notation were emphasized throughout the course. Students used applications, formulas, and reasoning skills to write, manipulate, interpret, solve, and graph linear equations. Concepts were introduced numerically, graphically, and symbolically. Students communicated their results in oral and written form. This was the first of two courses that constituted beginning algebra. This course included, but was not limited to, the arithmetic operations on real numbers, order of operations, properties of real numbers, use of variables, solving basic algebraic equations, beginning problem solving (application problems) using algebraic techniques, and linear equations in two variables (both graphing solutions, lines, and determining linear equations). This course was packed with information to transfer and our time schedule allowed for little extra space.

Every Saturday for five hours, we supplemented the text teaching with manipulatives and building exercises. One Saturday class was left unscheduled for a holiday, so we made class that day optional and reserved a computer lab to take everyone into SL. After getting over the initial hurdles of learning how to walk, the students were able to enter into our teaching locations and practice 'seeing number'. The majority of students truly enjoyed looking at number from a different perspective. These were adults who never understood math as they went through school and for some it was their second or third time trying to pass this course. There were the obstinate few who wanted to be taught only traditional content and seriously balked at what they thought of as a 'waste of time'. We left the Community College with an overall upbeat feeling that we had the opportunity to see remedial curriculum content first hand and open the eyes of a few students who had never understood the math they were taught in their primary and secondary schools.

In the summer of 2013 we taught a six-week, in-person, investigatory math class for Migrant High School students. The student levels ranged from only a basic math understanding to Advanced Algebra. This opportunity enabled us to design and format review curriculum through a subQuan lens. Through the design and implementation, we learned critical components of future subQuan courses and the necessary changes that needed to be made for application in an asynchronous and/or synchronous virtual world space. Little computer access was available, therefore we imported subQuan and SL pictures into PowerPoint, although we took an the opportunity once to have our class tour the Innovation Pavilion at Boise State in Second Life to interact with the sQi3d, a base translator, on a projected screen.

Forms of Number expanded during this time frame as we investigated our "number code" and all that hides behind a number. Figure 9 shows the many different facets of number that show how important an understanding of base becomes. In standard educational settings, only three of the eight Forms are discussed. Due to the flexibility of the virtual world, interactivity with these quantities and subQuans develop visual understanding of the code, the hidden qualities, of numbers. *(In subQuan, base-A is implied when a base is not explicitly stated.)*

Figure 9. Forms of Number break down the informational code hidden within the symbolic representation of number.

Forms	Visual	Symbolic
Standard		1234
Word		One thousand two hundred thirty three
Expanded		1,000 +200 +30 +4
Coefficient		1(1,000) +2(100) +3(10) +4(1)
Exponent		1(10^3) +2(10^2) +3(10^1) +4(10^0)
BaseShape		1 10Cube 2 10Squares 3 10Segs 4Ones
Shape		1 Cube 2 Squares 3 Segs 4 Ones
subQuan		1234
Word		One two three four
subQuan	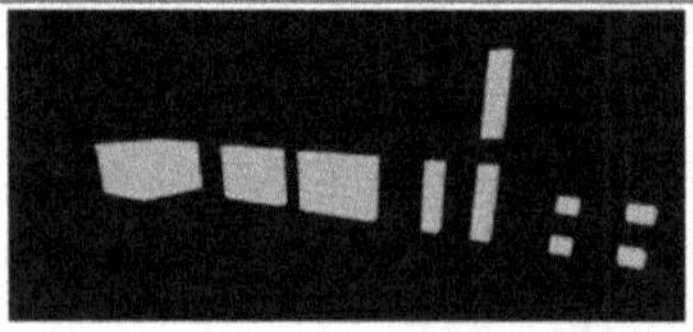	1234b6
Word		One two three four base six
Shape		1 Cube 2 Squares 3 Segs 4 Ones
BaseShape		1 6Cube 2 6Squares 3 6Segs 4Ones
Exponent		1(6^3) +2(6^2) +3(6^1) +4(6^0)
Coeffecient		1(216) +2(36) +3(6) +4(1)
Expanded		216 +72 +18 +4
Standard		310
Word		Three hundred ten

Integrating Second Life into Teaching Mathematics

We began presenting in SL at the Virtual World Best Practices in Education (VWBPE) conference in 2011. Our biggest leap in virtual world development occurred for the 2012 conference; we designed an interactive Sushi Bar. See Figure 10. We developed a virtual calculator (base translator), subQuan interactive 3D device, labeled sQi3d and pronounced Squid, which was programed with viewable shape patterns in multiple bases (6 through A) on placemats and an equation board representing the equations symbolically. We set up tables in the virtual world where avatar educators and conference attendees could sit and we escorted them through a demonstration of subitizing, Place Shape recognition, subQuan, interactive slides, and the metapatterns (algebraic equations).

A difficulty that arose was the inability to make sure that all avatars were looking at the correct space being discussed. Therefore, the following year a virtual world camera control was developed and the Sushi Bar became a permanent setup at Boise State University's EdTech Island. (http://maps.secondlife.com/secondlife/EdTech/87/91/26). We continued to present regularly to educators and post-secondary students about the varied and effective uses of virtual worlds in supporting student engagement, motivation, and learning outcomes, as well as demonstrating an all-encompassing way to look at numbers from subitizing single digit numbers through the foundation of Calculus. It was a 10,000-foot view of mathematics.

An additional space was added on EdTech called the Innovation Pavilion (http://maps.secondlife.com/secondlife/EdTech/105/31/26). At this location individual avatars can practice with the sQi3d and its connection to the equation board and 3D shapes. Color, denoting opposites (positives & negatives), comes alive in this format. Also available are 'The Hands' an interactive base-two device that displays both in 2D and 3D plus chats out the subQuan. This artifact demonstrates ten Place Shapes and supports learners in discovering the reasoning behind container, an effective way of practicing naming and recognition abilities asynchronously.

Continued development in SL supported the drafting of a first in what would become a series of children and parent/teacher discovery books. The first entitled: *The Foundation of Number Sense Series;* Book One: *Seeing Numbers, Introducing subQuan*. This book includes a majority of images pulled from the virtual world to illustrate our discoveries, points, and observations.

Figure 10. A presentation at BSU EdTechIsland familiarizes avatars with their own ability to see number.

Figure 11. Educational Rotunda on OSU's BeaverIsland in SL: Asynchronous learning station in development.

In addition to the SL Presentation location and the Innovation Pavilion, Oregon State University offered a space where we could place an asynchronous teaching rotunda. In its current design, avatars can enter into the learning center, sit down on the stool, and be guided through multiple learning stations with audio, visual, and interactive activities. This application is still in alpha phase, but highlights the power of virtual space. (http://maps.secondlife.com/secondlife/OSU/211/86/24) See Figure 11.

Physically SubQuanning

Winter and spring of 2013-14 found us in an elementary school for 30-minute pull-outs of Kindergarteners, 1st, 4th, 5th, and 6th graders. With these students, the sole design was on the introduction of numbers with a focus on "playing with number." We did not introduce the BNS, but built number as a series of 3D shapes with centimeter unit cubes and showed SL pictures of subQuans as examples. We were unable to use the virtual world to interact. Only the smaller bases were approached: base-two, -three, and –four the majority of the time. We investigated measurement with base-specific rulers as a means of identifying number and we built numbers. Combining, also known as addition and subtraction, was presented visually demonstrating that two different base numbers couldn't be combined. Even the kindergarteners were able to correctly record the number of base shapes in order of size with numbers reaching five and six digits. They were also able to predict the result of combining two four-digit numbers. One male student remarked, "I got number power." The kindergartners and 1st graders were unable to explore numbers beyond base three; the physical manipulation of larger shapes proved difficult for smaller hands though they painstakingly endured the building of a base two Square of Cubes. Whereas the 4th through 6th graders had little difficulty building number with bigger bases, it just took time and a one to five teacher/student ratio. It was becoming clear that to explore larger numbers, young children needed some other form of manipulation.

Time spent building number, especially the subitizable bases (two and three), provides a foundation of understanding for individuals in mathematical operations such as Place Shape, Combining (carrying and borrowing), and Greater than/Less than. It is feasible with less resource consumption of time, matter, and space. Physical reality and human dexterity inhibit the speed of pattern recognition in numbers, so in steps virtual reality where we are not hindered by gravity, materials, space, or time (Patterson, et al, 2012). Building number leads to the discovery of the patterns of number and this assisted discovery benefits learners more than other forms of instruction (Alfieri, Brooks, Aldrich, & Tenenbaum, 2011). This discovery can break the code of symbolic representation of numbers.

Representing the number of place shapes with number symbols is like discovering the number code. An exploration to "uncover" (discover) rather than "cover" (lecture/reveal) takes advantage of multiple intelligences (Gardner, 2011) and assists retention. This discovery could take the place of memorizing processes. Place shapes are very important in creating number codes: the most powerful code mankind has discovered. It enables students to understand how we can assign numbers to really big things, like the stars in the sky and the cells in our bodies. We can use these numbers to predict the future and determine the past, if only everything else in the world was as well behaved as numbers. Discovering number codes is an important step to understanding number, which is one of the most important steps to understanding our world. Scientists, doctors, accountants, mechanics, and all types of occupations could benefit from understanding number and learning the codes.

Practicing building subQuans in physical reality is really quite fun, with just 100 centimeter cubes students can build up to a 10^2 (ten Square), a 4^3 (four Cube), a 3^4 (three Seg of Cubes), or a 2^6 (two Square of Cubes). Getting more than one square using around 100 cubes is impossible for bases eight, nine, and ten. Those bases will have one Square, so a learner can play with that Square, too, not just Segs and Ones. If the larger Place Shapes for bases 8, 9, 10 are premade, it is much easier to manipulate them. But using unit cubes to build anything larger than a Square in these bases would be unwieldy. Base ten becomes awkward and gangly after creating Seg of Cubes and Square of Cubes in base two. In the smaller bases students get excited to be able to write a five-digit number they built themselves. However we live in a base-ten world so we need to address this deficiency that time and space imposes on larger bases. We developed a repository of subQuans at our www.ItOnlyTakes1.org website for extra practice in subitizing ability, but it also fails to address this deficiency. For deeper learning, a virtual world is still the key.

Ordering and organizing place shapes gives the ability to subitize each place and determine the subQuan of numbers in various bases. The major downside of subQuanning physically is that one must be able to reorganize the things to be numbered. Reorganizing is not possible for some things especially if they are big or moving. Fortunately the struggle of ordering and organizing is rewarded with many useful discoveries about numbers in general. Through these exercises students have found that the same quantity doesn't create the same subQuan in different bases. In a virtual world, ordering and organizing happens with the click of the mouse.

Complements, Combining, and Self-Discoveries

As number was further visually investigated, more discoveries awaited including Complements. The research conducted, in teaching numbers, started with a conversation regarding student's use of fingers for the function of adding. Ponder this question, when one represents a number with one's hands, does one start with hands fisted (zero) and then raise fingers one at a time, as if counting "one," "two," "three," etc. Or does one start with all the fingers up (ten) and put down the ones not needed? Or does one do both? The fingers you put down are called complements of the fingers that are up. Putting fingers up only requires enough fingers to represent a number. Putting fingers down requires a base stipulating how many fingers one started with up. For instance, a natural way we represent seven is to point ten fingers

Figure 12. Seg Complements of Ones as shown in base-A (ten) BNS.

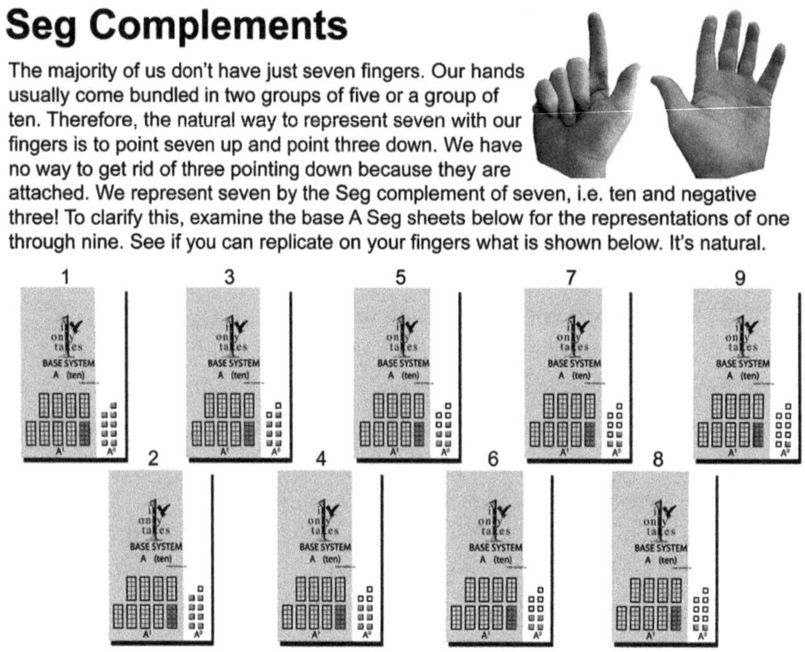

up and then put three down: a representation of seven as a base-A Seg Complement. Negative three is the ten's complement of seven. For example, putting three fingers down out of ten leaves seven up. Examine the base-A (ten) Seg sheets for the complement representations of one through nine in Figure 12.

The green Seg (ten) represents pointing all fingers up and the magenta Ones represent how many individual fingers are put down. Another useful example of different base complements is easy to see and understand with the number four. Using two hands, there are two natural base systems where we can represent four in complement mode. First, one hand with five fingers can be put up, and one finger put down (g1m1b5); or two hands can be used with all fingers up and then six fingers put down (g1m6bA). Every time a student begins counting with all fingers up and then puts some fingers down to reach the desired representative value, the value represented by the fingers put down is the negative complement of the numbers desired.

Combining is the term used for both addition and subtraction, given the two procedures are connected. The theory of 'simple' combining states that when two groups of Ones are combined, the combination is a single-digit. Such is the case in the first four examples of Figure 13. Additionally, color is used to represent opposites. In the first 'simple' example, five subitizable cyan dots are combined with two cyan dots to make a total of seven cyan dots. In the second example, four red dots are combined with four red dots to make a total of eight red dots. In the third example, five cyan dots combine with two red dots. The two red dots cancel out two of the cyan dots and what is left over is three cyan dots. In the fourth example, two cyan dots combine with six red dots to make four red dots after cancelation. All these examples have a single-digit outcome: simple. With Simple Combining no container (base) is needed because the outcome is a single-digit.

Complements make combining easier. The theory of 'not simple' combining states that when two groups of same colored Ones are combined, some results are 'not simple' with an answer containing

Figure 13. Demonstrations of Simple and Not Simple Combining.

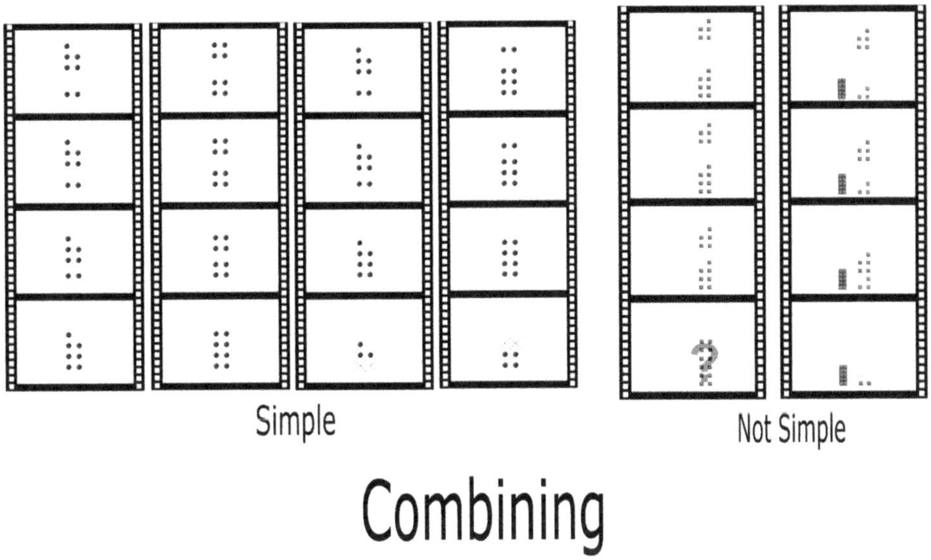

multiple digits. Such is the case for the base-A example in the last two columns in Figure 13. When the result is not simple, the number is greater than or equal to the base; substituting the base Complement for one of the numbers will make it 'simple'. As seen in the last two columns of Figure 13 when two quantities are combined their size is no longer subitizable in the ordered and organized pattern of 'not simple'. Therefore, the Seg Complement, on the right side of the figure, can replace one of the quantities to combine and the new combination becomes 'simple'. In the example pictured, five green cubes are combined with seven green cubes. This combination is 'not simple'. We take the five green cubes and use the Seg Complement for seven, one green Seg and three magenta Ones for base A (ten). Five green cubes combined with three magenta cubes have become 'simple': two green cubes. The outcome is visually 12.

As the concept of subQuans was presented to students in elementary schools, several important discoveries were made. First, students instantly realized why subQuans in different bases couldn't be simply combined. For example, a Cube in base two is not the same as a Cube in base three. While combining these subQuans does make two cubes, students could not state which base because they were clearly different sizes. For the same reason, the Squares in different bases not the same, nor are the Segs. In fact, none of the shapes except Ones are the same in every base because Ones are the only base-independent shape. Second, subitizing place shapes and then combining place shapes leads to the self-discovery of the concept of *carry* in addition. Similarly, *borrow* can be discovered by students. Composing and decomposing shapes, taking a physically built subQuan apart, is a valid alternative to combining using complements, albeit conceptually much more challenging. Decomposing number entails building a number with unit cubes in a certain base and pulling that number apart to show it in uncontained form. Uncontained form leads to more shapes than a base normally allows. For example, in base three; one expresses a number no larger than two in a container. The third figure would move it to the next shape. In uncontained mode, one could have more than two of a shape in base three in any one place: 43 base 3 is uncontained and 120 base 3 is contained, these two quantities are identical. Third, place shapes lead directly to the concept of exponents and exponent operations. The superscript three represents the term cube and, indeed, its shape is a cube. Place value is a subset of place shapes. Fourth, fractions can be represented visually with bases as the denominator. Fifth, when dealing with several different numbers that are represented in different bases sometimes all the subQuans are identical. This observation leads to the discussion of metapatterns.

Metapatterns

So what's the point of representing numbers as subQuans? Seeing one quantity translated into various bases is interesting but not profound. But seeing the same shape pattern in various bases is profound and immediately recognizable. Based on classroom experiences and teaching the concept of subQuan, almost every student can subQuan and therefore see the metapatterns that lead directly to the algebraic concept of polynomials. There are several types of metapatterns: seg metapatterns, square metapatterns, cube metapatterns, and larger metapatterns.

Seg Metapatterns

In Algebra, these are called linear equations and their exploration makes up the bulk of the first year of studying Algebra. Real life applications can be modeled in the virtual world as in the following situation. For example, a little blue-bat dog creature has been discovered. See Figure 14. Its land speed has been measured by time-lapse photography. The seconds are marked in magenta. The forty-foot ruler measures the location of his nose as ordered pairs of seconds and distance: (6, 27), (7, 31), (8, 35), (9, 39) as shown in the chart.

Figure 14. Time-lapse photography caught the data of this Blue-bat Dog running across the field. Data can be put into corresponding BNS to find the visual metapattern.

Seg Metapattern

We've just discovered this little blue bat-dog creature. We decided to measure its land speed by time lapse photography. The seconds are marked in pink. The forty foot ruler yields the location of his nose: (6, 27), (7, 31), (8, 35), (9, 39). In Algebra I, we are taught to determine an equation by process, but if we subQuan the feet (ft) into base sheets selected by seconds (s), then we immediately see the metapattern, g43, for each base. Validating the metapattern yields these set of equations: +4(6)+3 = 27, +4(7)+3 = 31, +4(8)+3 = 35, +4(9)+3 = 39. In general, +4(s)+3 = ft

In Algebra class determining an equation from this data is taught by process, but if the feet (ft) are subQuanned into base sheets selected by seconds (s), then the metapattern can be seen, g43, for each base. Translating the subQuans yields this set of equations:

+4(6)+3=27, +4(7)+3=31, +4(8)+3=35, +4(9)+3=39,

respectively. In general the equation is written, +4(s)+3=ft.

Students of Algebra are learning the first manipulations of letters in mathematics. Research has shown that at this level, students historically disconnect from understanding mathematics in schools (Attewell, Lavin, Domina, & Levey, 2006). So many have had difficulties, that it is now socially acceptable to state that one is "not good at math".

Square Metapatterns

A Square metapattern works in the same fashion as a Seg metapattern. These containers in 3D form beautiful Square containers, a container of containers. The square-ness of objects is how rooms are measured, surface area is calculated, and what makes up the unique characteristic of the diagonal numbers in the multiplication chart. These patterns are parabolic, trinomial, and quadratic equations discussed primarily in the second year of Algebra. From data points alone, individuals can determine many expressions without lengthy and complex processes.

A homogenous (all positive) example on the left of Figure 15, (7, 83), (8, 102), (9, 123), (A, 146), results in the Square metapattern that is instantly seen as g146 (pronounced 'gee one four six') or $+146_x$ (pronounced 'pos one four six') with each of the subQuan digits representing the coefficients of the terms in the equation. Since this pattern is the same in multiple bases we can assume that its algebraic equation is $q_x= +1(x^2) +4(x) +6$ or in subQuan 146_x.

In the example on the right of Figure 15, the Square metapattern is g635 for bases 7, 8, 9. Therefore, the quantities (Q) can be expressed as +6Squares +3Segs +5Ones.

$q_7= +6(7^2) +3(7) +5.\ q_7= 320.$

Figure 15. Two Square Metapatterns examples to determine the algebraic equation of each.

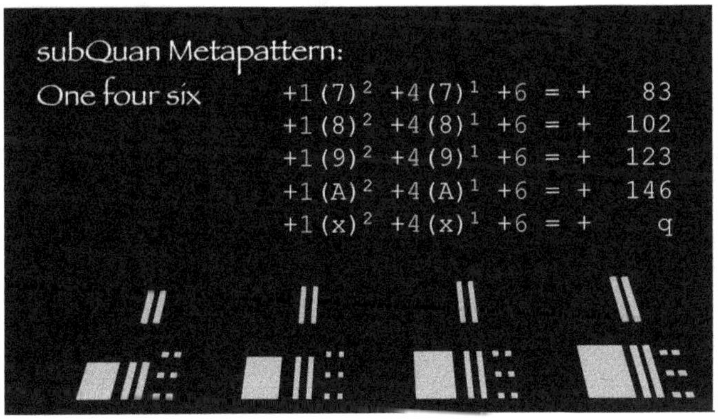

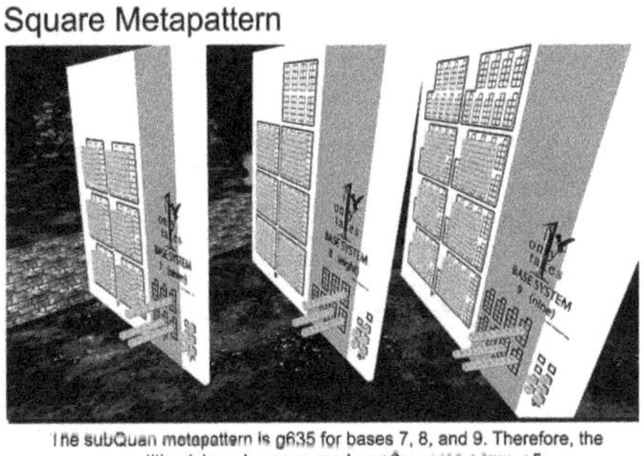

q_8= +6(8^2) +3(8) +5. q_8= 413.

q_9= +6(9^2) +3(9) +5. q_9= 518.

Given the data (7, 320), (8, 413), and (9, 518) we would see the subQuan metapattern g635 or $+635_x$. q_x= +6(x^2) +3(x) +5.

Not all equations derive as homogeneous. Heterogeneous (both positive and negative) patterns can be recognized, too, using color, and complements must be used to determine their equations: patterns within patterns. Our following example shows measurements taken from a bridge. See Figure 16. The equation of the height based on the bridge's span needs to be determined.

Given the ordered pairs for span and height, (6, 8), (7, 16), (8, 26), (9, 38), the Square metapattern is instantly seen as g1m5g2 (pronounced 'gee one em five gee two') or +12 (pronounced 'pos one neg five pos two') with each of the subQuan digits representing the coefficients of the terms in the equation. Since this pattern is the same in multiple bases we can assume the algebraic equation as q_x= +1(x^2) -5(x) +2 or in subQuan 152_x or $+12_x$.

Currently in schools, Advanced Algebra students are manipulating symbolic equations in order to factor quadratic equations, plot points to graph, implement the quadratic formula, and memorize formulas such as point-slope and slope-intercept form, with little understanding. With subQuan, the hope is that quickly seeing the metapatterns will reveal the knowledge hidden in the graphs, equations, and processes of mathematics.

Cube Metapattern

A Cube pattern completes the primary shapes: Cubes, Squares, Segs, and Ones. Large quantities can be represented on Cube base sheets from a petite 8 in base-two to the grandiose 9,999 in base-ten: that's the subQuan $1,000_2$ and $9,999_A$. Cubes are used in measuring volumes such as water tanks, dump truck loads, and gasoline. Moving from 2D pictorial representation to 3D shows that no individual thing is

Figure 16. Homogeneous equations, containing both positives and negatives, are easier to see with color.

absent and that shape is extremely relevant. Accomplishing this task quickly and repetitively can only be facilitated by the virtual world.

Metapatterns on these base sheets are cubic expressions, which are very difficult to derive through symbolic processes. Matrices are what most math classes teach. Instead, through the virtual world, seeing is believing, and the ease of recognizing Cube metapatterns enables students to succeed with cubic expressions when they had previously bogged down in rule-based, memorized steps.

The subQuan metapattern in Figure 17 is m2312 for bases 4, 5, and 6. Therefore, the quantities (q) can be expressed as -2Cubes -3Squares -1Seg -2. Otherwise notated in symbols as:

$q_4 = -2(4^3) -3(4^2) -1(4) -2$. $q_4 = -182$.

$q_5 = -2(5^3) -3(5^2) -1(5) -2$. $q_5 = -332$.

$q_6 = -2(6^3) -3(6^2) -1(6) -2$. $q_6 = -548$.

Given the data (4, -182), (5,-332), and (6, -548) we would see the subQuan metapattern m2312 or $-2{,}312_x$. $q_x = -2(x^3) -3(x^2) -1(x) -2$.

Figure 17. A Cubic subQuan Metapattern.

Larger Metapatterns

In a virtual world quartic and higher degree polynomials can be expressed through pictures and be walked around and explored. The virtual world has no limit to revealing number patterns.

Metapatterns, expressed as polynomials, help to determine past and future happenings in science, technology, engineering, business applications, and more. With such a high percentage of students needing remediation upon entry into college (Bijeljac-Babic et al., 2006), students would benefit greatly from curricular material that explained the why behind the concepts being taught. The use of a virtual world to represent these concepts quickens the pace, interest, and ease of shape configuration. Imagine placing 1,345 individual centimeter cubes in containers of six to represent the pattern. Then build the same subQuan pattern in bases 7, 8, and 9. There simply isn't enough time or patience in the physical world. It is imperative to use technology and a virtual world is at the pinnacle of technological tools.

The astute mathematics instructor will realize sometime during this reading that there has not been any discussion on non-integer based equations. One more topic needs to be introduced to address this limitation. Once a student and/or teacher has the "play time" in Second Life, building and recognizing subQuans, naming metapatterns, and understanding shape value, a step further can be taken in deriving equations from data using *differences*. Finding differences between data points allows the student to remove shapes in order to find the equations of the data: a powerful, pictorial step to connect Calculus to Algebra. Differences are easily explained in the virtual world. See Figure 18.

Common Core Standards and SubQuan

Common Core Standards (2010), developed by state governors and education officers, provide K-12 standards for English language arts/literacy and mathematics, designed to ensure that high school gradu-

Figure 18. Deriving equations from data using differences.

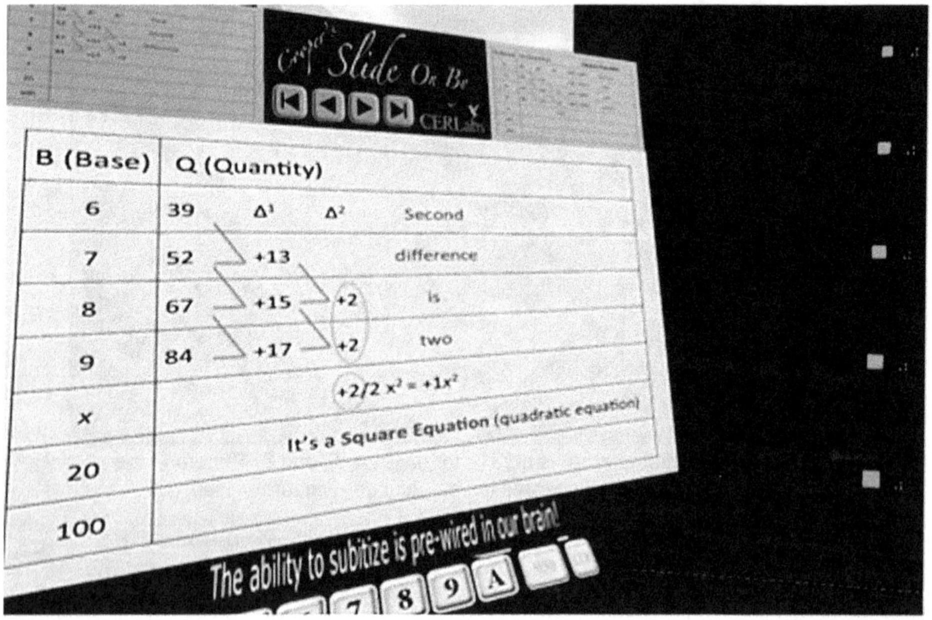

ating students are prepared for college or the workforce. With the implementation of Common Core Standards in 42 states across the United States, as of 2015, there is a greater emphasis on conceptual understanding of mathematical content and procedural knowledge. Students are asked to explain the why, the how of solving problems, and to look at a single problem from multiple perspectives (corestandards.org/mathematics).

According to Common Core Standards (2010), creating solid foundations includes "a solid understanding of concepts, a high degree of procedural skill and fluency, and the ability to apply the math they know to solve problems inside and outside the classroom" (http://www.corestandards.org/other-resources/key-shifts-in-mathematics/). subQuan understanding builds a strong foundation of number and number sense that connects all topics of mathematics, which is the heart of Common Core: cohesion for success in life. Mathematics is "a coherent body of knowledge made up of interconnected concepts" (CCSS, 2010).

Through the process of developing an understanding of number shapes, their patterns, and their symbolic representations, students can conceptualize the "big picture" of mathematics and not be so intimidated by the smaller processes and details. As students develop conceptual knowledge, the initial understanding of number to algebraic pattern recognition and on to polynomial derivation by differences unfolds. To help students meet the standards, educators will need to pursue, with equal intensity, three aspects of rigor in the major work of each grade: conceptual understanding, procedural skills and fluency, and application (CCSS, 2010).

Issues with Teaching SubQuan Using Second Life

There are issues in using the virtual world for mathematics education. First, using a virtual world application in K-12 classrooms was not a common practice within the schools where subQuan was introduced. Most familiarity with virtual worlds is through gaming activities such as playing Worlds of Warcraft or other massively multiplayer online role-playing games (MMORPGs). If teachers have ventured into a virtual world such as Second Life, they may have had become frustrated or found the space to be too open-ended. Virtual worlds are a blank slate where a teacher wishing to use the space must be able to create or have an idea of how their students can create. There is no curriculum guide, no lesson plans, and no worksheets in this virtual space. The "learning curve" is initially very high. Therefore, acceptance of teachers who wish to implement virtual world teaching material in their classroom is also a major stumbling block.

A second issue is the difficulty some students and teachers have in re-conceptualizing mathematical terminology and processes and making the shift to the terminology involved with subQuan. Since our materials span from before school number recognition (subitizing) through number patterns to metapattern recognition and differences, there is a considerable amount of time required to teach these concepts. Students and teachers can have difficulty letting go of previous mathematical learning and adapting to a new way of thinking. The subQuan system emphasizes a new conceptual understanding of mathematics beyond the base ten system.

A third issue involves Internet connectivity. Connectivity is always in question with outdated school district computer equipment and low bandwidth, not to mention firewalls. The consequences of these items result in poor viewing capabilities, increased amount of dropped connections, and glitch interface: rubber-banding, inability to see artifacts, and poor graphics. The effects of these difficulties result in a poor experience and a lack of desire to continue.

Solutions and Recommendations

Next Steps for Teaching SubQuan

As the authors continue to develop subQuan, there are several new directions that are planned which address the issues that arose as the curriculum was implemented with students and teachers.

The advancements with camera control over individual avatars during lessons help ease the transition of learning in a virtual world. Navigation in this learning space is being made as pain-free as possible in order to ease the learning curve. Mitigating most of these barriers and recognizing that some of them are already crumbling from the outside has the authors optimistic as time has moved further into the 21st Century and technology is catching up.

The design of specific teacher training courses is forthcoming, so that with very little hassle, teachers can at least learn at their own pace how to "build number" and find a way around the common phobia revolving base numbers. This training would facilitate their ability to work with their students as they translate their virtual learning into physical reality.

Regarding connectivity issues, an initial thought is to focus on home-school families where parental permissions are easy to obtain and parent involvement is most likely. Teacher-training courses and professional development seminars may be another way to circumvent technological glitches. In these relaxed environments, our innovations could grow to sustain a larger audience.

Even with the drawbacks and our solutions, it is imperative to use the virtual world to implement foundational number sense: a necessary step for education. This platform will continue for prototyping, image creation, mobile development, teacher training, and exploratory classrooms. The authors' goal is to use the virtual world platform as a backdrop for books, mobile interactive resources, and applications as well as developing accessible online resources in the virtual world of Second Life.

FUTURE DIRECTIONS

Teaching mathematics in a virtual world is still a relatively new concept. As mentioned in the introduction, the few who have tried to implement programs have used this space in traditional ways (Burgess & Caverly, 2009; Cheal, 2009; Dickey, 2011; Lim, 2009; O'Connor & Sakshaug, 2009). The authors believe this innovative space requires an innovative approach. Students could learn mathematics with more depth than just "learning by building" (Lim, 2009) or find some "fun" in the traditional learning model because SL looks like a game (Cheal, 2009). Pioneering new mathematics pedagogy requires a paradigm shift and move away from traditional process-oriented symbol manipulations. Common Core desires this shift. Second Life affords teachers the opportunity. Virtual worlds engage students (Wiecha, Heyden, Sternthal, & Merialdi, 2010; Gordon & Koo, 2008). A better use of time, space, material, and financial resources is found through virtual worlds so that children and adults can discover numbers and the patterns hidden behind mathematics with a focus on higher-level thinking and conceptual development. This chapter exemplifies a powerful and game-changing tool and teaching/learning application that showcases virtual worlds' positive impact on education.

CONCLUSION

The purpose of this chapter was to demonstrate how a virtual world, such as Second Life, could be used to teach innovative mathematical concepts and operational processes. A case study approach documented the need to teach math in a new way. A virtual reality was declared the best format through which to illustrate student engagement, visual number acuity, instinctual number sense, and repetitive pattern recognition in an immersive environment.

First, background knowledge was provided on the importance of using visual instinct, single-syllable number words, subitizing, and ordered organized subitizing to increase number sense. Emphasis highlights the recognition of patterns in learning mathematical concepts. The terms Digit-Speak, Place Shape, and subQuan were introduced.

Secondly, Digit Speak, Place Shape, and subQuan were described in-depth as they relate to teaching mathematical concepts using strategies other than the traditional base ten system through the use of Second Life. Classroom experiences were outlined with lessons learned and discoveries made. Difficulties in the physical manipulation of unit cubes when building number limited the ability to see rapidly changing patterns: metapatterns. This deterrent illuminated a need for a better visual platform: virtual reality (Second Life). A virtual reality has all the realities of real life plus some additional qualities: no hindrances of gravity, materials, space, or time. More discoveries were discussed including Complements and Combining.

The third focus of the chapter was to identify and discuss issues, solutions, and recommendations identified in implementing the program described. Common Core Standards align with the depth of understanding that a visual look at numbers employs. Teacher reluctance was discussed not only in learning a new platform, but also a new perspective on a topic they may or may not already understand. The development of camera control and asynchronous/synchronous teacher training is recommended.

A last focus was on identifying future directions for the use of Second Life in teaching mathematics. Virtual reality is not a space in which to teach the same mathematics with a different tool. The mathematics needs to be more engaging, more applicative, and more visual. Innovative and perceptive educators could use this reality to make a great impact on our children.

REFERENCES

Alfieri, L., Brooks, P. J., Aldrich, N. J., & Tenenbaum, H. R. (2011). Does discovery-based instruction enhance learning? *Journal of Educational Psychology*, *103*(1), 1–18. doi:10.1037/a0021017

Antell, S. E., & Keating, D. P. (1983). Perception of numerical invariance in neonates. *Child Development*, *54*(3), 695–701. doi:10.2307/1130057 PMID:6851716

Attewell, P., Lavin, D., Domina, T., & Levey, T. (2006). New evidence on college remediation. *The Journal of Higher Education*, *77*(5), 886–924. doi:10.1353/jhe.2006.0037

Bijeljac-Babic, R., Bertoncini, J., & Mehler, J. (1993). How do 4-day-old infants categorize multisyllabic utterances? *Developmental Psychology*, *29*(4), 711–721. doi:10.1037/0012-1649.29.4.711

Burgess, M. L., & Caverly, D. C. (2009). Techtalk:" Second Life" and Developmental Education. *Journal of Developmental Education*, *32*(3), 42–43.

Butterworth, B. (2005). The development of arithmetical abilities. *Journal of Child Psychology and Psychiatry, and Allied Disciplines*, *46*(1), 3–18. doi:10.1111/j.1469-7610.2004.00374.x PMID:15660640

Cheal, C. (2009). Student perceptions of a course taught in Second Life. *Innovate: Journal of online. Education*, *5*(5), 2.

Cihak, D. F., & Foust, J. L. (2008). Comparing number lines and touch points to teach addition facts to students with autism. *Focus on Autism and Other Developmental Disabilities*, *23*(3), 131–137. doi:10.1177/1088357608318950

Common Core State Standards. (2010). Common Core State Standards for Mathematics. Washington, DC: National Governors Association Center for Best Practices and the Council of Chief State School Officers. Retrieved from http://www.corestandards.org/other-resources/key-shifts-in-mathematics/

Community College Research Center. (2014). What we know about developmental education outcomes. Retrieved from http://ccrc.tc.columbia.edu/media/k2/attachments/what-we- know-about-developmental-education-outcomes.pdf

Dehaene, S. (2011). *The number sense: How the mind creates mathematics*. Oxford University Press.

Gardner, H. (2011). *Frames of mind: The theory of multiple intelligences*. Basic Books.

Gordon, E., & Koo, G. (2008). Placeworlds: Using virtual worlds to foster civic engagement. *Space and Culture*, *11*(3), 204–221. doi:10.1177/1206331208319743

Hiebert, J. (1984). Children's mathematics learning: The struggle to link form and understanding. *The Elementary School Journal*, *84*(5), 496. doi:10.1086/461380

Lim, K. Y. T. (2009). The six learnings of Second Life: A framework for designing curricular interventions in-world.

Miller, K. F., Kelly, M., & Zhou, X. (2005). Learning mathematics in China and the United States. Handbook of mathematical cognition, 163-178.

Miller, K. F., Smith, C. M., Zhu, J., & Zhang, H. (1995). Preschool origins of cross-national differences in mathematical competence: The role of number-naming systems. *Psychological Science*, *6*(1), 56–60. doi:10.1111/j.1467-9280.1995.tb00305.x

Miller, K. F., & Stigler, J. W. (1987). Counting in Chinese: Cultural variation on a basic cognitive skill. *Cognitive Development*, *2*(3), 279–305. doi:10.1016/S0885-2014(87)90091-8

Morin, J. E., & Franks, D. J. (2009). Why do some children have difficulty learning mathematics? Looking at language for answers. *Preventing School Failure: Alternative Education for Children and Youth*, *54*(2), 111–118. doi:10.1080/10459880903217861

O'Connor, E. A., & Sakshaug, L. E. (2009). Preparing for Second Life: Two teacher educators reflect on their initial foray into virtual teaching and learning. *Journal of Educational Technology Systems*, *37*(3), 259–271. doi:10.2190/ET.37.3.c

Okimoto, H., & Heck, R. (2014). Examining the Impact of Redesigned Developmental Math Courses in Community Colleges. *Community College Journal of Research and Practice*, (ahead-of-print), 1-14.

Patterson, D. C., Reiniger, R. L., & Robertson, A. M. (2012). Cross-Reality Math Visualization: The subQuan System Dream Realizations. *Immersive Environments, Augmented Realities, and Virtual Worlds: Assessing Future Trends in Education: Assessing Future Trends in Education*, 57.

Penner-Wilger, M., Fast, L., LeFevre, J., Smith-Chant, B. L., Skwarchuk, S., Kamawar, D., & Bisanz, J. (2007). The foundations of numeracy: Subitizing, finger gnosia, and fine-motor ability. In *Proceedings of the 29th Annual Cognitive Science Society* (pp. 1385-1390). Austin, TX: Cognitive Science Society.

Rikoon, S., Liebtag, T., Olivera-Aguilar, M., Robbins, S., & Jackson, T. (2014). A Pilot Study of Holistic Assessment and Course Placement in Community College: Findings and Recommendations.

Wiecha, J., Heyden, R., Sternthal, E., & Merialdi, M. (2010). Learning in a virtual world: Experience with using second life for medical education. *Journal of Medical Internet Research, 12*(1), e1. doi:10.2196/jmir.1337 PMID:20097652

ADDITIONAL READING

Cathcart, W. G., Pothier, Y. M., Vance, J. H., & Bezuk, N. S. (2000). *Learning mathematics in elementary and middle schools* (p. 106). Prentice Hall Allyn and Bacon.

Cathcart, W. G., Pothier, Y. M., Vance, J. H., & Bezuk, N. S. (2000). Learning and teaching mathematics. *Learning mathematics in elementary and middle schools*, 17-38.

Radin, D. J. (2007). *Coursework on base numeration systems and its influence on pre-service elementary teachers' understanding of place value concepts*. ProQuest.

Slovin, H., & Dougherty, B. (2004). Children's conceptual understanding of counting. *Proceedings of the 28th Conference of the International* (Vol. 4, pp. 209-216).

KEY TERMS AND DEFINITIONS

Assisted Discovery: Assisted discovery involves educators creating scenarios in order to facilitate a student's ability to make discoveries on their own.

Base Systems: Represent varying container sizes for the packaging of objects. Our number codes describe these packages and our school system mainly teaches packaging in ten (the decimal system).

Binary Number System: Base-two system, next larger container holds two of the previous shape.

Combining: A single term for the two processes of addition and subtraction.

Decimal-Centricity: The trend to focus mainly on the base-ten system only. Facilitated by the metric system and excludes greater pattern recognition.

Decimal Number System: Base-ten system, next larger container holds ten of the previous shape.

Differences: Extrapolating the distance from one data point to another in order to remove the largest shape to the smallest shape and determine the metapattern (algebraic equation – otherwise known as deriving polynomial equations) using factorials and subtraction.

Dream Realizations: Dream Realizations is a nonprofit educational support service organization designed to facilitate Colleges, Universities, and other entities in providing effective mathematics instruction.

Metapattern: Pattern of patterns, used in this text for shape patterns (subQuans) of sequential base systems being identical or easily recognizable, like incremental, and signifies an algebraic equation.

Number Codes: Symbolic representations of number (4,352), specifically human shorthand notations by which children learn processes in school to manipulate with little understanding. Different bases may yield the same number code and that has profound meaning.

Place Shape: The optimal shape of each place in a number as each container gets larger: Ones, Segs, Squares, Cubes, Seg of Cubes, Square of Cubes, Cube of Cubes, and so on. These shapes are instantly recognizable in visual form. Ones are identical for all bases. The sizes of all the other shapes are base dependent.

Polynomial Derivation: Finding the pattern of patterns within a set of data: figuring out the equation from a data set.

Subitize: To perceive at a glance the number of items presented, the accuracy limit for humans decays linearly after four unordered and unorganized items derived from the Latin subitus meaning to appear suddenly.

SubQuan: To perceive at a glance the number of items presented, the limit for humans is unknown due to the order and organization of the things but it appears to be approximately 0.5 to 1.0 seconds per place shape. Derived from the Latin subitus quantitus meaning sudden quantity.

Section 3

Next Generation of Learning:
Catalysts and Considerations in Virtual Reality

Chapter 10
Pedagogical Agents for Learning

Noah L. Schroeder
Wright State University, USA

ABSTRACT

Throughout the past two decades, researchers have seen rapid innovations in the field of learning technologies. Virtual reality, video games, and online learning are becoming quite common in educational contexts. Pedagogical agents are often present in a variety of these virtual environments. Pedagogical agents are virtual characters with an on-screen presence that are designed to facilitate learning in multimedia environments. In this chapter the author examines the theoretical rationale for incorporating a pedagogical agent into a learning environment, critically examines their effectiveness for learning, and discusses how they have been implemented in research studies to date. Suggestions for future research in virtual reality environments are highlighted.

INTRODUCTION

Researchers in the field of educational technology have made massive strides in the past few decades. Each year new technologies become available, the cost of many technologies steadily decreases, and new graphic user interfaces make technically challenging programs more user-friendly. As advanced technologies have become more accessible in regard to both the cost and the technical ability needed to utilize them, the research literature has seen a plethora of studies using a variety of digital environments. For instance, virtual reality (e.g., Merchant, Goetz, Cifuentes, Keeney-Kennicutt, & Davis, 2014), mixed reality (e.g., Johnson-Glenberg, Birchfield, Tolentino, & Koziupa, 2014), augmented reality (e.g., Enyedy, Danish, Delacruz, & Kumar, 2012), and other multimedia interfaces such as smartphones (e.g., Huang, Wu, & Chen, 2012) and tablets (e.g., Alegría, Boscardin, Poncelet, Mayfield, & Wamsley, 2014; Alvarez, Brown, & Nussbaum, 2011) are increasingly common in the research literature. In educational contexts, virtual characters often appear within these environments.

There are many types of virtual character. For instance, researchers have investigated the use of avatars (Okita, Turkay, Kim, & Murai, 2013), pedagogical agents (Johnson, Ozogul, Moreno, & Reisslein, 2013;

DOI: 10.4018/978-1-4666-9837-6.ch010

Lane et al., 2013), motivational agents (Baylor, 2011; Baylor & Kim, 2005), and conversational agents (Graesser, 2011). The wide variety of virtual characters has led to their implementation in a number of disciplines. For instance, virtual characters have appeared in content areas such as physics (VanLehn et al., 2007), communications skills (Adcock, Duggan, Nelson, & Nickel, 2006), microbiology (Sabourin & Lester, 2014), and informal science education (Lane et al., 2013).

Virtual characters are not always designed to accomplish the same tasks in the learning environment. For example, conversational agents are equipped with artificial intelligence that allows them to facilitate a conversation by holding a dialogue with the learner (Tegos, Demetriadis, & Tsiatsos, 2014), while motivational agents are designed to facilitate the learner's motivation (Baylor, 2011). In order to accomplish these tasks, virtual characters' features may vary widely depending upon their purpose. For instance, their level of artificial intelligence, their ability to communicate with the learner, how they communicate with the learner, their physical appearance, their ability to move around a virtual space, or even their teaching role in the learning environment (i.e., teacher or peer) can be manipulated in order to achieve different types of human-computer interactions.

Pedagogical agents are virtual characters designed to facilitate learning in multimedia-based environments (Johnson, Ozogul, & Reisslein, 2014). Research surrounding the efficacy of pedagogical agents for learning has yielded mixed results (Heidig & Clarebout, 2011), however a recent meta-analysis found an overall small, positive effect (Schroeder, Adesope, & Barouch Gilbert, 2013). Regardless of their past effectiveness, researchers strive to discover the salient features of agent design and implementation in order to facilitate learning. While the virtual environments used in many studies of pedagogical agents are not likely considered virtual reality environments, it is critical to understand the foundations of pedagogical agent research as instructional designers begin implementing them in novel environments and frameworks, such as virtual reality.

The purpose of this chapter is to review the many uses of pedagogical agents in desktop-based learning environments. The chapter begins with an examination of the theoretical perspectives that have guided pedagogical agent implementation. Second is a brief discussion situating theoretical contributions into practice. Third, the varied findings around pedagogical agents' influence on learning outcomes are discussed. Fourth, a discussion of the different roles a pedagogical agent can play in the learning environment is presented. Finally, the chapter concludes with an examination of the implementation of pedagogical agents in specific knowledge domains and a discussion of the use of pedagogical agents in virtual reality environments. While a wide variety of studies will be reviewed in this chapter, all of those discussed measured learning outcomes when examining the use of a pedagogical agent compared to a non-agent condition

THEORETICAL BACKGROUND

Those in the field of pedagogical agent research have used a number of theories to guide their experimental designs. For the purposes of this chapter, three prominent theories in the literature surrounding how people learn with pedagogical agents are discussed. Specifically, we will examine how pedagogical agent research has been guided by the hypotheses of cognitive load theory (Sweller, 2010), the cognitive theory of multimedia learning (Mayer, 2014a), and social agency theory (Mayer, Sabko, & Mautone, 2003).

Cognitive Load Theory

Cognitive load theory describes how the brain processes information. Broadly, cognitive load refers to the amount of mental effort and mental load required to learn something (Paas, 1992). Paas and Sweller (2014) suggest that the brain is defined by two primary domains, the long-term memory and the working memory.

The long-term memory is the primary information storage structure within the brain. The information one knows, and thus can retrieve when desired, is stored in the long-term memory in organizational structures called schema (Paas & Sweller, 2012). Paas and Sweller (2014) describe two different types of knowledge that can be stored within the long-term memory: rote knowledge and knowledge with understanding. These constructs are analogous to Ausubel's (1963) definitions of rote learning and meaningful learning. Concisely, the long-term memory can hold information that is retained in very similar, if not verbatim ways to which it was learned (i.e., rote learning), or it can hold information that is integrated with pre-existing knowledge structures (i.e., meaningful learning). These types of knowledge are similar to common learning outcome measures in experimental research. For example, retention tasks (i.e., rote learning tasks) often require general recall of information, or use of knowledge in very similar situations to which it was learned. Meanwhile, transfer tasks (i.e., those requiring meaningful learning, or learning with understanding) often require use of the knowledge in a novel situation. These tasks require that the learner must understand the material to a greater extent than it if it were learned through rote processes.

The working memory plays a different role than the long-term memory in human cognitive processes. Paas and Sweller (2014) describe the working memory as the processor of new information. For example, the working memory processes the information brought into the brain from a novel learning task. In addition, the working memory is a limited processor when working with new information, capable of handling only a few pieces of information at a time (Miller, 1956; Paas & Sweller, 2014). However, Paas and Sweller noted that the same limitations do not exist when dealing with information already held within the long-term memory. In these situations the limited capacity of the working memory does not apply, as the information is already stored within the long-term memory's organizational structures (Paas & Sweller, 2014).

Cognitive load theorists have also suggested three different types of cognitive load. The three types of cognitive load have been described as extraneous, intrinsic, and germane (Paas & Sweller, 2014; Sweller, 2010). Extraneous cognitive load is the mental load not directly due to the learning materials, but rather the way they are presented to the learner in the learning environment (Paas & Sweller, 2014; Sweller, 2005, 2010). Accordingly, extraneous cognitive load is dependent upon the instructional design and the presentation of instruction to the learners. For example, presenting students with 15 worksheets when only two are relevant to the instructional task would be introducing extraneous cognitive load. Alternatively, intrinsic cognitive load is caused by the difficulty of the learning material and how many pieces, or elements, of the material must be understood in order for it to be learned (Paas & Sweller, 2014; Sweller, 2010). More interacting elements lead to higher intrinsic cognitive load. For example, a mathematician may find solving a differential equation to be quite simple, and thus, contain low intrinsic load. Yet, a high school student may struggle with the same task because they must first learn many other facts or procedures before solving the problem. Finally, germane cognitive load refers to how the learner utilizes their working memory to deal with the intrinsic cognitive load and process the material (Sweller, 2010). Despite the name, germane cognitive load does not contribute to or influence the working memory's capacity to interpret new information (Sweller, 2010).

To summarize, those designing instruction should strive to minimize extraneous cognitive load, which allows the learner to devote more effort towards processing the necessary intrinsic elements (Paas & Sweller, 2014; Sweller, 2010). It has been argued that pedagogical agents can cause extraneous cognitive load for the learner (Clark & Choi, 2007), however Veletsianos (2007) argued that this could be moderated by the design of the pedagogical agent. Despite the various types of agents prevalent throughout the literature, few studies have shown that pedagogical agents can hinder learning outcomes. Rather, pedagogical agents' impacts on learning are often non-significant (Heidig & Clarebout, 2011).

Cognitive Theory of Multimedia Learning

While cognitive load theory broadly describes how humans process information, the cognitive theory of multimedia learning denotes specifically how we process situations in which we experience multiple medias. Broadly defined, multimedia presentations are composed of information that contains both words and pictures (Mayer, 2014a; Mayer & Moreno, 2003). Relevant examples include a presenter verbally communicating information while referencing on-screen pictures, a traditional textbook that contains both pictures and text, or a virtual reality environment where the learner receives the verbal information through narration.

Mayer (2014a) describes the cognitive theory of multimedia learning as relying upon three primary assumptions. These assumptions are that they eyes and ears each have their own independent working memory processor (dual-processors), that the working memory processors are limited (as described by cognitive load theorists), and that learners actively process information. Mayer suggests that the notion of dual-processors is based on a foundation of cognitive psychology research. More specifically, Mayer suggests that the eyes can bring in information (such as pictures) and process it while the ears can bring in information (such as narration) and process it. This notion of processors dealing with novel information inherently leads to the assumption that each of these processors is limited, as they are essentially working memories (Mayer, 2014a). Thus, the cognitive theory of multimedia learning aligns well with cognitive load theory's model of human cognitive architecture. Finally, within the cognitive theory of multimedia learning framework, Mayer assumes that learners are active processors of information. In other words, in order to meaningfully learn the information the individual must cognitively engage with the content. Mayer denotes that this process involves not only selecting the relevant information, but also organizing it and integrating it into their exiting schemas (i.e., prior knowledge structures).

Given the aforementioned assumptions when learning with multimedia, Mayer (2014a) describes the cognitive processes that take place when students learn. These processes are the selection of appropriate pictures and words, organizing the selected pictures and words, and finally integrating the new information into existing schemas (Mayer, 2014a). Mayer's model denotes that these phases occur within or require the use of the working memory. Recalling the assumptions that words and pictures are processed separately (dual processors) and each working memory is limited, we can see why it is important to present material through both pictures and words in order to maximize the cognitive processing that can occur. After the verbal or pictorial information is organized in its respective processor, the cognitive theory of multimedia learning framework delineates that these two types of information are then integrated together to create a coherent model of the knowledge (Mayer, 2014a). This new knowledge then proceeds through an "*encoding*" (p. 58) phase where it is integrated into the learner's existing schemas.

Finally, Mayer (2014a) describes three types of mental processing that can occur with multimedia learning. All three are analogous to different types of mental load as described in cognitive load theory.

Essential processing takes place when the learner is creating an understandable mental model of the material, a process which requires mental effort identical to that as described by cognitive load theory's intrinsic cognitive load (Mayer, 2014a). Generative processing, which is the same as germane cognitive load, is the mental effort required to learn the information and integrate it into their existing schemas (Mayer, 2014a). Finally, Mayer describes extraneous processing as that which "is caused by poor instructional design" (p. 59). In other words, extraneous processing and extraneous cognitive load describe the same constructs; the mental effort required to learn that is not related to the actual learning task itself, but rather the means of presentation to the learner.

Research surrounding the cognitive theory of multimedia learning has led to a variety of useful instructional design principles and effects. Many of these principles are relevant to the design and implementation of virtual characters. For instance, the modality principle suggests that words should be provided through narration while pictures are presented on screen (Low & Sweller, 2014; Mayer & Pilegard, 2014), implying that instructional designers should create pedagogical agents that speak through narration rather than provide speech bubbles with printed text. In fact, researchers have investigated this effect by conducting experiments where learners in one condition learned with a pedagogical agent that communicated through narration, while the other condition learned with a pedagogical agent that communicated through speech bubbles containing printed text (e.g., Atkinson, 2002; Moreno, Mayer, Spires, & Lester, 2001). Primary studies have shown results supporting the modality principle (Atkinson, 2002; Moreno, Mayer, Spires, & Lester, 2001).

A second principle that can guide the design and implementation of virtual characters is the embodiment principle, which suggests that virtual characters should utilize humanlike gestures (Mayer, 2014b). Researchers have also conducted a variety of studies investigating this effect (e.g., Lusk & Atkinson, 2007; Mayer & DaPra, 2012), with consistent findings suggesting that pedagogical agents should utilize humanlike gestures (Mayer, 2014b).

Finally, a third principle that stemmed from the cognitive theory of multimedia learning that has been applied to pedagogical agent research is the signaling principle. The signaling principle suggests that using visual cues to indicate salient information, such as a pedagogical agent pointing to relevant information on the screen, can increase learning outcomes (Mayer & Fiorella, 2014; van Gog, 2014). Numerous pedagogical agent studies have utilized the agents as cues in the learning environment. In most cases, the pedagogical agent points to relevant pieces of information on the screen such as a section of a diagram or important words in a slide (e.g., Choi & Clark, 2006; Johnson, Ozogul, Moreno, & Reisslein, 2013; van Mulken, André, & Müller, 1998).

Social Agency Theory

Outside of the nuts and bolts of the cognitive processing of new information, Mayer et al. (2003) proposed social agency theory. According to social agency theory, if an individual perceives the computer's interaction as social, it will enact the social conversation schema within the individual, thereby encouraging them to react to the computer as they would a fellow human. Thus, the learner will try to understand what the computer is saying, which helps them engage in learning processes (Dunsworth & Atkinson, 2007). Recently, Domagk's (2010) findings extended social agency theory. Her experiments showed that it is not merely the incorporation of social cues, but also the valence of the social cues that may influence learning outcomes.

Social agency theory has been an important premise in pedagogical agent research. Much of the research surrounding the theory has encouraged researchers to anthropomorphize their virtual characters in an effort to provide relevant social cues. For instance, the use of standard-accented (Mayer et al., 2003), human voices (Atkinson, Mayer, & Merrill, 2005; Mayer et al., 2003), agents likeable in appearance (Domagk, 2010), and embodiment features such as gestures, gaze, and facial expressions (see Mayer & DaPra, 2012) have all been guided by findings of studies investigating different aspects of social agency theory.

Summary

Synthesis of the above theories indicates that pedagogical agent researchers may find themselves in a theoretical quandary. While social agency theory suggests that certain social features of pedagogical agents may help the learners deeply engage in the material, cognitive load theory suggests that pedagogical agents may increase the cognitive load of the learning environment. Through utilizing principles derived from the cognitive theory of multimedia learning (e.g., signaling) researchers have explored ways in which agents can be designed to minimize the impact on cognitive load while facilitating learning.

IMPACT OF THEORY ON RESEARCH AND PRACTICE

While descriptions of theory provide salient background information, it is often challenging to understand how theories guide empirical research and what that means for practice. For example, due to the confluence of the cognitive theory of multimedia learning and cognitive load theory, it can be difficult to grasp the differences without in-depth exploration into the theoretical constructs. As mentioned, pedagogical agent researchers have used the cognitive theory of multimedia learning and cognitive load theory to guide numerous empirical investigations of agent design and effectiveness. These studies are often based on numerous "principles" and "effects" that have been found in prior studies. In this section, select studies will be examined in order to understand how theory has guided research, and how research has expanded theory.

Craig, Gholson, and Driscoll (2002) conducted two different experiments examining the impact of agent design features. Craig et al.'s work was guided by principles that have come out of the cognitive theory of multimedia learning and cognitive load theory. More specifically, in relation to pedagogical agents, they examined the split-attention principle (also referred to as the split-attention effect) and the redundancy effect. The first experiment examined the split-attention principle, or the idea that splitting attention between two sources of information, such as an agent and the picture, could inhibit learning by causing extraneous cognitive load (Clark & Choi, 2007; Craig et al., 2002; Sweller, Ayers, & Kalyuga, 2011; Sweller & Chandler, 1994). The results of their first experiment revealed that the presence of an agent did not facilitate learning, however it did not inhibit learning either. These results were consistent with other research at the time as well as more current reviews of the field (e.g., Heidig & Clarebout, 2011). Their second experiment examined the redundancy effect, which suggests that removing redundant materials can enhance learning outcomes (Craig et al., 2002; Kalyuga & Sweller, 2014; Sweller & Chandler, 1994). Participants interacted with a pedagogical agent that either provided visual, printed text, a pedagogical agent that provided narration, or a pedagogical agent that provided both the printed text and narration. Their results were consistent with the redundancy effect, in that participants who interacted with the agent that provided narration only outperformed students who interacted with an agent that provided narration and visual text. From these studies, we can see that incorporating a pedagogical agent does not always lead to increased or decreased effects on learning, and if an agent is included in the environment, it should communicate with the learner through narration.

Domagk's (2010) work examined implications of social agency theory for pedagogical agent design. She conducted two experiments examining the influence of the agents' appearance and voice on learning and motivational outcomes. In her first experiment, Domagk examined if a likable, dislikable, or neutral pedagogical agent was more or less effective for learning and motivational outcomes than a non-agent condition. The results revealed that the likable agent was rated higher in appeal than the other two agent conditions (Domagk, 2010). In addition, her results showed that while the participants in the agent-based conditions did not perform better on learning outcome tests or motivational measures than those in the non-agent condition, the participants working with the likable agent performed better on transfer tests and reported a higher level of state motivation compared to participants in the dislikable agent condition. In the second experiment, Domagk examined if the agent's appearance (likable and dislikable) and voice (likable and dislikable) impacted motivational or learning outcomes when compared to a control group. No significant differences were found for motivational outcomes or retention outcomes, however the participants who worked with a dislikable agent with a dislikable voice scored significantly lower on the transfer test than the other groups. When taken together, the results from Domagk's experiments reveal that "the valence – not the mere presentation of social cues – needs to be explicitly taken into account" (p. 94) in pedagogical agent design. In other words, the act of including an agent in itself will not increase motivation or learning outcomes. Rather, we must be cognizant of agent design as dislikable agents can impede the learners' ability to learn the material and transfer it to new knowledge domains (Domagk, 2010).

Summary

Researchers in the field of pedagogical agents have conducted thorough empirical investigations into the practical influence of many agent features based on prominent theories of human cognitive processes. As could be expected, a variety of outcomes have been found in regards to learning. As such, researchers have different interpretations of pedagogical agents' effectiveness for helping students learn. In the next section, we examine the influence of pedagogical agents on learning outcomes.

INFLUENCE OF PEDAGOGICAL AGENTS ON LEARNING OUTCOMES

By definition, pedagogical agents are designed to facilitate learning. As such, pedagogical agents often facilitate teaching methods rather than emphasizing purely affective responses. However, researchers' aspirations do not always coincide with empirical results. It is well known that in regards to learning outcomes, mixed results prevail in the field of pedagogical agent research (Dehn & van Mulken, 2000; Domagk, 2010; Heidig & Clarebout, 2011).

The mixed results in the field are exemplified by three recent systematic reviews of the literature. All three reviews examine a similar and often overlapping set of studies. In addition, each review examines the effectiveness of agents to non-agent conditions, and all three reviews examine pedagogical agents' influence on learning outcomes. These similarities notwithstanding, the conclusions drawn by each group of researchers has been different. These differing interpretations epitomize the broad range of views about the efficacy of pedagogical agent implementation. Examination of each review provides important insights into the field.

Heidig and Clarebout (2011) conducted a systematic review of the literature to examine the impact of pedagogical agents on learners' motivation and learning. They searched three databases and located 75 articles, of which, 26 met their inclusion criteria. In order to discuss and examine the findings, Heidig and Clarebout discussed their pedagogical agents-conditions of use model (PACU). The PACU model denotes four related issues in agent implementation: the learner, the learning environment, the agents function, and the agents design. Within agent design, there are three additional levels of design decisions that must be made. Heidig and Clarebout described these levels as follows: the global level determines if the agent is animated, static, human, or cartoon; the medium level has to do with the technical decisions, such as how animated the agent should be; and the detail level has to do with the agent's physical appearance. Collectively, these levels make up the pedagogical agents levels of design (PALD) model (Domagk, 2010). Heidig and Clarebout's analysis of the results indicated that nine of 15 studies showed no difference in learning outcomes between learners who worked with pedagogical agents and those who did not, which led them to the conclusion that "a general motivating or learning facilitating effect of pedagogical agents has be questioned…a more fruitful approach is to ask under what conditions pedagogical agents might be effective for whom" (p. 51).

Schroeder et al.'s (2013) meta-analysis began to approach the question of under what conditions pedagogical agents can be effective. To locate studies, Schroeder et al. searched nine electronic databases, one online paper repository, and the references of three review articles (Gulz, 2004; Kim & Ryu, 2003; Moreno, 2005). Their search revealed 576 research abstracts. Of these 576 abstracts, 28 articles met all of the inclusion criteria. These articles allowed for the extraction of 43 different comparison conditions. In regards to an overall effect size, Schroeder et al. found pedagogical agents provided a small positive effect on learning compared to non-agent conditions, a finding that is consistent with those of other recent reviews (Mayer, 2005, 2014b). Their analysis revealed that significant heterogeneity existed within the sample, and therefore moderator analysis was conducted. Select findings from the study include that the pedagogical agent's appearance as a humanoid or non-humanoid did not make a significant difference on learning, that pedagogical agents were more effective for students in grades 4-7 than college students, and that pedagogical agents were more effective in math and science domains than the humanities. Based on their findings that pedagogical agents can have a positive effect on learning, particularly in certain situations, Schroeder et al. concluded that "researchers should continue to explore the multifaceted features of pedagogical agents" (p. 20) and thus encouraged researchers to continue examining the features of pedagogical agents, such as those delineated by the PALD model (Domagk, 2010; Heidig & Clarebout, 2011).

Mayer (2014b) conducted a review examining the impact of pedagogical agents on learner's scores on transfer tests compared to non-agent conditions. Mayer's review is unique in that it only considers transfer outcomes, or those that should require meaningful learning. According to social agency theorists, pedagogical agents should be able to effectively facilitate meaningful learning. If this were the case, the effect sizes should be positive, indicating that the pedagogical agent was more effective at facilitating learning as interpreted through transfer tests than the non-agent conditions. Mayer's analysis of the 14 experiments included in the review indicated a small positive effect. Based on his findings, Mayer concluded "there is not strong support for adding the speaker's image to the screen...people do not necessarily learn more deeply from a multimedia lesson when a speaker's image is added to the screen" (p. 360).

In summary, the mixed findings in recent reviews reveal a difference in research methodology and interpretation of the findings. However, together the three recent reviews provide interesting insights. For instance, Heidig and Clarebout's (2011) systematic review concluded that the broad question of pedagogical agent effectiveness is not a meaningful way to examine the literature due to the diverse nature of the primary studies. Schroeder et al.'s (2013) meta-analysis provided a quantitative synthesis approach and highlighted a few areas in which agents may be particularly effective. In his review, Mayer (2014b) found an effect size consistent with Schroeder et al.'s meta-analysis, but he interpreted the overall effect size differently. While Mayer concluded that the current evidence does not support the inclusion of an agent, Schroeder et al. concluded that agents may be useful in some situations, and Heidig and Clarebout highlighted a number of areas for future research. Therefore, many may still argue that it is difficult to say what an agent should look like or actually do to be effective in any given implementation. Hence, the author reiterates other researchers' calls for additional research into effective pedagogical agent design (Heidig & Clarebout, 2011; Kim, in press; Schroeder et al., 2013).

Due to the diverse findings in relation to the effectiveness of incorporating a pedagogical agent into a learning environment, it is productive to examine the roles pedagogical agents can play in the learning environment. An understanding of what pedagogical agents actually do in the learning environment will facilitate understanding of the nuances involved with implementing pedagogical agents within different learning domains.

ROLES OF PEDAGOGICAL AGENTS

Pedagogical agents are a type of software agent. Therefore, within the broad boundaries of helping students learn, their ability to perform a task is limited only by software restrictions and the capabilities of the designer. Accordingly, the description of a software agent as a pedagogical agent does not limit its role or capabilities in the environment, as long as the agent is designed to aid the learning process. As such, the pedagogical agent's appearance, features, or role in the environment may change depending on the specific implementation.

Technology has reached a point where it can be quite simple to create basic virtual characters. There are websites that let you create three-dimensional talking characters (e.g., Oddcast Inc., 2015) as well as websites that allow for the creation of a two-dimensional animated scene that contain virtual characters (e.g., GoAnimate, 2015). Alternatively, creating and implementing a fully-animated, custom scripted three-dimensional character in an immersive virtual reality environment still requires specialized software and skills. In other words, while it is currently rather simple to create a talking head that delivers a monologue, it is more difficult to create a three-dimensional agent that demonstrates a task. Due to this reality it is not surprising that most pedagogical agents' actions are scripted (Veletsianos & Russell, 2014). In essence, the limitations of pedagogical agent capabilities are more restricted by software skills, finances, and time than the existence of technologies themselves.

One may still question what a pedagogical agent can actually do in the learning environment. To investigate this question, we consider not only the instructional role of the pedagogical agent as an instructor, but also its role in facilitating the learning process. While these constructs are closely related, the former examines how the agent appears, acts, and speaks, while the latter examines what teaching methods or pedagogies the pedagogical agent utilizes to facilitate learning.

In regards to the instructional role of the agent as an instructor, Baylor and Kim (2005) suggested three distinct types of agents: the expert, the mentor, and the motivator. In their studies, the expert agent was operationalized by speaking authoritatively, professionally, and appearing as a college professor. The mentor agent spoke confidently and less formally then the expert agent, and appeared slightly younger than the expert agent. Finally, the motivator agent appeared similar in age to the learners and it spoke very enthusiastically. These roles highlight a few potential design considerations, as different applications denote the need for different instructional roles. While not all studies acknowledge designing their agent according to these roles, examples can be found in the literature that exemplify all three. For instance, Murray and Tenenbaum (2010) utilized an instructor (i.e., expert) agent. In Murray and Tenenbaum's study, the instructor agent appeared as an adult (the participants were children). Schroeder and Adesope (2013) utilized a mentor agent. In their study, the pedagogical agent appeared around the same age as the students and used informal language. Finally, van der Meij (2013) utilized a motivator agent. In his study, the agent was designed according to the ARCS-model of motivation (see Keller, 2010) and often referred to its own state of mind by using words like "Cool" (p. 850).

Alternatively, Clarebout, Elen, Johnson, and Shaw (2002) described pedagogical agent roles by what they actually do to support the learning process. According to Clarebout et al., there are six different roles the agents can play: testing, demonstrating, scaffolding, supplanting, modeling, and coaching. Clarebout et al. described a testing agent as one that tests the learner's knowledge. In other words, it acts as a test administrator. A demonstrating agent is one that physically shows how a task is performed. Once the task is completed, the agent then watches the learner demonstrate the same task (Clarebout et al., 2002). The scaffolding agent is described as one which assists the learner by completing activities that the learner cannot yet due themselves due to a lack of knowledge. According to Clarebout et al., this is distinct from the role of supplanting, in which the agent performs the tasks for the learners while they watch. The modeling agent is also similar to the demonstrating and supplanting agent, yet the modeling agent explains their process as they model how to complete the task (Clarebout et al., 2002). Finally, the coaching agent is described as one that can provide tips to the learner as they complete the task.

As presented above, there are many different instructor roles and ways that pedagogical agents can facilitate learning process, especially if more than one technique is used in tandem. In the next section, an overview of how pedagogical agents have been used in the different knowledge domains is examined.

USE OF PEDAGOGICAL AGENTS IN DIFFERENT DOMAINS

Teaching in the disciplines, while they may share commonalities, often may call for specialized techniques. Hence, one can find numerous specializations in these fields, such as chemistry education, biology education, and engineering education. In this section, we'll examine pedagogical agent studies in the broader domains of science, mathematics, and the humanities in order to understand how pedagogical agents have been used to help students learn.

Science

An early pedagogical agent study that compared the use of a pedagogical agent to a non-agent condition was conducted by van Mulken et al. (1998). In their study, students learned from either a pedagogical agent that signaled their attention to relevant parts of the screen or a non-agent condition in which an arrow pointed to the relevant parts of the screen. The learning material in the first experiment contained information about pulley systems and how they work. Van Mulken et al. examined the students' recall and comprehension of the learning material. Analysis of the results revealed that there were not significant differences between groups. They concluded that any motivating effect the pedagogical agent may have provided could have been mitigated by the visual distraction caused by the agent, therefore causing no significant increase or decrease in learning outcome scores (van Mulken et al., 1998).

Another early pedagogical agent study in the domain of science is Moreno et al.'s (2001) work with Herman the Bug. Herman is the animated pedagogical agent embedded in the Design-A-Plant micro-world meant to teach students about different features of plants. In their first experiment, Moreno et al. found that college students performed better on transfer tests after working with the pedagogical agent compared to a non-agent condition. However, there were not significant differences found on the retention test. The results of their second experiment indicated that seventh-grade students had similar outcomes after working with a pedagogical agent compared to a non-agent condition. Their results indicated that the students who worked with an agent performed significantly better on transfer tests than those in the non-agent condition, but did not perform significantly better on the retention test. Accordingly, their results demonstrated that while pedagogical agents can help students perform better on transfer tests, the same cannot be said for strictly retention tasks.

Johnson, Ozogul, and Reisslein (2014) examined the effectiveness of a pedagogical agent for teaching students about a single-resistor electric circuit. In their study, students either worked with a pedagogical agent that signaled to relevant parts of the screen, an agent which did not signal, a control condition where an arrow signaled to relevant parts of the screen, or another control condition in which the arrow was absent. Their results revealed that while the presence of a pedagogical agent did not significantly improve learning overall, the inclusion of an agent did significantly impact students depending on their prior knowledge level. More specifically, students with low prior knowledge learned more with an agent while students with high prior knowledge learned more without an agent present. In addition, Johnson et al. did not find a significant difference in learning outcomes between students with high prior knowledge and low prior knowledge when an agent was present. Therefore, one could conclude that the inclusion of an agent helped the low prior knowledge learners attain a higher score, while perhaps slightly inhibiting the abilities of the high prior knowledge students.

A review of the literature indicates that the role of the pedagogical agent in studies investigating topics within the scientific domain tend to use the agent as an information source. In essence, the pedagogical agent generally appears on the screen, provides verbal instructions, and signals the learner's attention to specific parts of the screen. The sciences in particular have numerous opportunities for future pedagogical agent research, as there are many topics in which the agents could model and demonstrate how certain processes, cycles, or functions take place.

Math

When compared to non-agent conditions, pedagogical agents have only occasionally been investigated in mathematics fields. Schroeder, Adesope, and Barouch (2013) meta-analysis found only eight comparison conditions in mathematics domains, yet the studies produced an encouraging effect on learning. However, it should be noted that six of the eight comparison conditions in the analysis came from one research laboratory. Next, three studies that examined the use of pedagogical agents in mathematics fields are reviewed.

Atkinson (2002) conducted two experiments with college students investigating the impacts of combining a pedagogical agent environment with worked examples in mathematics. The agent in his study was Peedy, an animated parrot that would signal the learner's attention to certain parts of the screen through movement, gaze, and gesture. The first experiment compared a control condition, text-only condition, a narration-only condition, an agent that communicated through text condition, and an agent that communicated through narration condition. His analysis revealed that the participants who worked with the agent that provided narration performed significantly better on near and far transfer tests. In the second experiment, participants worked with either a text-only condition, a narration-only condition, or an agent with narration condition. Analysis of the results indicated that the learners in the pedagogical agent condition performed significantly better on a near transfer test than the students in the text-only condition, and they also performed significantly better on the far transfer test than the students in either the text-only and narration-only conditions (Atkinson, 2002). From the results of the experiments, one could conclude that pedagogical agents that provide instructions through narration can be effective for learning when coupled with worked examples.

Lusk and Atkinson (2007) examined the extent to which a fully embodied pedagogical agent that could talk, gaze, walk, and gesture influence learning compared to a static agent or a voice only condition. The agent in this experiment was Peedy the Parrot (as in Atkinson, 2002). Similar to Atkinson's work, students once again learned about solving worked examples. Lusk and Atkinson's results revealed that students working with the fully embodied pedagogical agent significantly outperformed students who worked with the voice only condition on both the near transfer and far transfer tests. Thus, their results indicated that having an animated agent present in the learning environment can facilitate learning compared to a non-agent condition.

A study by Plant, Baylor, Doerr, and Rosenberg-Kima (2009) examined if a male or female pedagogical agent would be more effective at changing student attitudes about engineering and math performance than a non-agent condition. The participants were middle school students, and the agent conditions consisted of either a male or female pedagogical agent that was designed to appear attractive, young, and cool. The agents delivered a 20 minute monologue about female engineers. In addition, the agents discussed a few benefits of a career in engineering. Plant et al. found that learning with the male agent did not lead to significantly better scores on the mathematics test. However, the students who learned with the female agent scored significantly higher than both the students in the male agent condition and the students in the no agent condition. The results of Plant et al.'s study adds to the literature base suggesting that the characteristics of the agent are salient in the design process.

Due to the limited amount of studies investigating the use of agents compared to non-agent conditions in the mathematics domain, there are many opportunities for novel agents to be developed. For instance, to date, the vast majority of studies use agents to facilitate the teaching with worked examples of word problems. However, there are many other fields of mathematics, and agents could presumably model and explain how to solve nearly any mathematics problem. Examples include topics such as basic mathematics (addition and subtraction) or even more advanced mathematics such as calculus.

Humanities

The meta-analysis conducted by Schroeder et al. (2013) indicated that while there were 16 comparison conditions in the fields of the humanities, pedagogical agents were not significantly effective for learning compared to non-agent conditions. In this section, three pedagogical agent studies in the humanities fields are reviewed.

Choi and Clark (2006) investigated the effectiveness of an animated pedagogical agent, Genie, for college students learning English relative clauses. The specific question was whether or not Genie was more effective for learning than a condition that contained narration and arrows (i.e., no on-screen character). Results indicated that there were no significant differences in learning outcomes between the group that learned without an agent and the group that learned with an agent. Furthermore, their additional analyses provided preliminary evidence that student characteristics (in this case, prior knowledge) can influence cognitive outcomes when students learn with animated pedagogical agents. As a side note, the experimental design used was particularly important in minimizing confounding variables, a persistent experimental design issue which has consistently influenced the understanding of pedagogical agent studies (Clark & Choi, 2005).

Theodoridou (2009) conducted an experiment to examine the effects of a pedagogical agent to help students learn Spanish vocabulary. The agent used in the study was Laura, a female agent that appeared in her mid-to-late twenties. Laura was a relatively static agent in that she did not gesture, but she had lip synchronization, head movements, and the ability to gaze different directions. Laura was also artificially intelligent, having a Spanish knowledge base that Theodoridou created using Artificial Intelligence Markup Language. Students either worked with Laura or they worked with a web-based program that did not contain the agent. Theodoridou examined students' knowledge through the use of immediate and delayed post-tests. Analysis of the results revealed that there were not statistically significant differences in learning outcomes between groups. As such, this particular pedagogical agent was not more effective at facilitating students' learning than a control condition. However, it is noteworthy that the students' in the agent group did not perform significantly worse than the non-agent group. Therefore, the next step would be to examine what features of the pedagogical agent could make it more effective for specifically teaching language learning, yet very little research exists in the area that compares a pedagogical agent to a non-agent condition.

Murray and Tenenbaum (2010) investigated the impacts of pedagogical agents on middle school students' health and fitness knowledge. In their study, students in one condition interacted with a teacher agent and a peer agent, in another condition the students only interacted with the teacher agent, and in the control condition the students were provided with written materials. Analysis of their results indicated that while students in both agent conditions significantly outperformed the control condition on the knowledge test, the students who worked with only the instructor agent outperformed those who also worked with a peer agent as well as the control group. Murray and Tenenbaum's study is notable as it is one of the few longitudinal studies in the field, having consisted of five instructional sessions over the course of five weeks.

The humanities fields have seen numerous instances of pedagogical agents being implemented, yet the results tend to produce insignificant effects on learning outcomes compared to other knowledge domains (Schroeder et al., 2013). It is difficult to hypothesize why the findings of studies of pedagogical agents in the humanities have not found similar results to those in the mathematic or scientific domains.

Summary

As shown above, pedagogical agents have been incorporated in a wide variety of subject domains in efforts to help students learn. However, they have been explored in relation to non-agent conditions from relatively limited perspectives. Agents are often providing the instruction to learners rather than helping their learning through scaffolding, demonstrating, or modeling. In the future, researchers should begin examining more roles of pedagogical agents in learning environments, particularly with agents that can model or demonstrate tasks (Moreno, 2005). When creating these agents, researchers in the field may consider collaborative projects with those in the field of intelligent tutoring systems, as they continue to be found effective for learning (e.g., Ma, Adesope, Nesbit, & Liu, 2014; Steenbergen-Hu & Cooper, 2014; VanLehn, 2011). Artificially intelligent agents that can help scaffold student learning throughout the learning process may hold great promise.

THE FUTURE: PEDAGOGICAL AGENTS IN VIRTUAL REALITY ENVIRONMENTS

Many of the studies described in this chapter have often occurred in more "traditional" multimedia learning environments in which the learner could not explore a virtual space. To generalize, in the majority of studies cited above, the learners were presented with a designated, very controlled learning environment that contained a pedagogical agent and the agent would provide instruction. The background of the environment was generally a solid color, and generally, the learner couldn't move around or explore the virtual space. In a sense, the learners often watched a pedagogical agent talk, similar to watching a video, and then they solved the learning problems. Interaction with the software or pedagogical agent was often limited. To summarize, there has been limited work that examines the influence of pedagogical agents compared to non-agent conditions in virtual reality environments.

As mentioned previously, integrating virtual characters of any variety into a virtual reality situation can be expensive, time consuming, and require specific technical skill sets. This is true regardless of whether the virtual human takes the role of a pedagogical, motivational, or conversational agent. Fortunately, technologies are emerging that are making the process of creating simulations, educational games, and other virtual reality environments more practical and accessible. One example is the Virtual Human Toolkit (Hartholt et al., 2013). The Toolkit assists in the integration of lifelike characters into virtual reality environments. The Toolkit works in conjunction with Unity3D (Unity Technologies, 2015), a popular game development software. By assisting with the creation of virtual humans, the Toolkit could facilitate the creation of conversational agents, pedagogical agents, and other types of virtual characters.

The Toolkit contains a number of modules that facilitate virtual human integration. Due to the broad scope of all the modules within the virtual human toolkit, a full description is outside the realm of this chapter. For detailed information, please refer to Hartholt et al. (2013). However, a few brief examples will highlight some of the many features within the modules provided in the virtual human toolkit. For instance, the *MultiSense* module allows for the tracking and analysis of the user's physical response to the environment, such as body posture and facial expressions (Hartholt et al., 2013). In addition, the Toolkit includes modules that assist in creating basic artificial intelligence. For example, the *NPCEditor* module allows the instructional designer to write questions learners may ask the agent and then write in a number of appropriate responses for the agent to reply with (Hartholt et al., 2013).

As tools such as the Virtual Human Toolkit (Hartholt et al., 2013) become more commonly available and usable by non-specialists, it is plausible that the use of pedagogical agents will increase. This is especially true as game development platforms become more widespread and continue to fall in price. As mentioned previously, Unity3D (Unity Technologies, 2015) is a common game development software. Another option for game development software is Unreal Engine 4 (Epic Games Inc., 2015). Either platform can be used to develop immersive virtual environments that contain virtual characters.

Research with Virtual Characters in Virtual Reality Environments

The use of virtual reality environments for creating simulations and games holds much potential for researchers in the field who want to explore new types of research with pedagogical agents. Within the larger context of pedagogical agent research, researchers could explore the influence of pedagogical agents on learning when playing different roles in the virtual environment. As previously mentioned, the influence of pedagogical agents on learning when modeling or demonstrating a task has not yet been examined compared to a non-agent condition. Virtual reality environments present an exceptional opportunity for exploring these questions. For instance, in a chemistry context, in one condition a pedagogical agent could demonstrate how to perform titrations and properly mix chemicals. In the control condition, the pedagogical agent's character could be removed. In the domain of nursing, a pedagogical agent could demonstrate how to interact with a patient. In a control condition, the pedagogical agent's image could be removed. Studies of this sort can help explore if the inclusion of a virtual character facilitates learning when the agent is demonstrating or modeling a task.

Meanwhile, there are many more aspects of pedagogical agent design that could be considered in virtual reality environments. More specifically, Domagk's (2010) PALD model presents an excellent foundation for research in virtual reality environments. This is because virtual reality environments allow for the creation of contextually relevant agents (for a description of contextually relevant agents, see Veletsianos, 2007; Veletsianos, 2010) that are not only relevant to the content being taught, but also to the environment in which they appear. For example, in a nursing simulation a virtual patient can be dressed in civilian clothing and the virtual nurse could be dressed as they would in the local area hospitals. In a control condition, the clothing could be changed to not be relevant. For instance, the virtual nurses in the simulation could be dressed in street clothes rather than traditional hospital nursing attire. Studies such as this would allow for insights into different levels of the PALD model.

Virtual Reality Environments Benefit From Iterative Design

One drawback of the use of virtual reality environments is the amount of work that must be done prior to implementing the intervention. A non-exhaustive list of tasks includes designing a narrative, creating the virtual space, creating assets for the virtual space, programming the environment for different levels of interaction, and the creation of animation loops. Due to the confluence of many techniques that must all work in tandem, virtual reality environments can benefit from iterative design. For instance, educational games can benefit from iterative design informed by play or usability testing (Moreno-Ger, Torrente, Hsieh, & Lester, 2012; Olsen, Procci, & Bowers, 2011; Warren, Jones, & Lin, 2011). This process can be time consuming and resource intensive, requiring numerous iterations of game development and testing. In addition, data should be collected at each point and the results of the analysis should guide revisions to the environment. While educational games may appear to be a specialized environment, other virtual reality environments benefit from play testing and usability testing as well. For instance, when developing a nursing pain assessment and management simulation, Romero-Hall, Watson, Papelis, and Garcia (2014) used a form of usability testing. In their study, the instructional designer went through the virtual environment through both the correct and incorrect order in an attempt to find bugs in the system.

While the benefits of iterative design are increased functionality and optimization, researchers in the field have suggested numerous methodologies that all constitute different forms of play or usability testing. The specifics of the method may not be generalizable to all virtual reality environments. Optimizing player experience can highly depend on the purpose of the intervention. Accordingly, the questions that should be examined at each stage of design and play testing are likely different depending upon the application. However, the author notes that collecting both qualitative and quantitative data may be beneficial. Quantitative data can help collect ratings to quantify the learner's perceptions, but qualitative data may be informative for guiding revisions. Through the triangulation of numerous data sources the researcher can likely find more meaningful insights than through one data source alone. As such, those creating virtual environments that contain virtual characters may find it fruitful to utilize both qualitative and quantitative data sources collected over numerous points in the iterative design process. Furthermore, these results can be systematically reported to help the field create a framework for usability and play testing for specific applications.

Summary

A benefit of the movement towards virtual reality environments is that researchers can take what we've learned about pedagogical agent design and test them in new ways. However, a drawback is that while we are just getting access to technologies that make pedagogical agents easier to implement in traditional multimedia environments, implementing an agent in a virtual reality situation still requires specialized skills and software. Presumably the next decade will see drastic improvements in the accessibility of these environments. Researchers should take advantage of this to further explore the influence of pedagogical agents on learning outcomes.

CONCLUSION

As shown, pedagogical agent researchers have explored numerous salient research questions encompassing a wide variety of content domains. Pedagogical agents have played a number of different roles in the virtual environment, but there is a dearth of research that explores the influence of a pedagogical agent when it is demonstrating or modeling a task compared to a control group (i.e., a non-agent condition). The continuing rise of virtual reality and immersive game-based environments offer much promise to pedagogical agent researchers. Allowing the virtual character to appear within a more immersive environment can foster its "*deictic believability*" (Lester, Voerman, Towns, & Callaway, 1999, p. 384), or its ability to move around and reference its environment in an appropriate, meaningful way. As new technology tools become increasingly accessible, it is plausible to expect the number of pedagogical agent studies to continue to increase.

While the discussion within this chapter was limited to studies examining the influence of a pedagogical agent compared to a non-agent control condition, whether or not pedagogical agents generally impact student learning remains a major question in the field. Recent quantitative reviews of the field have found that pedagogical agents can have small, positive effects on learning outcomes (Mayer, 2014b; Schroeder et al., 2013). Still, the question remains as to how we can most effectively design pedagogical agents to best facilitate increased learning outcomes. While it may seem natural to omit the control (non-agent) condition in experimental designs, doing so would retain the issue of the broader question of pedagogical agents' overall influence on learning. Heidig and Clarebout (2011) suggested that the question is simply too broad to answer. However, meta-analytic procedures can not only examine the question of overall agent effectiveness, but also examine the conditions in which the pedagogical agents are most effective (or ineffective) compared to a non-agent condition. These insights are important as if there are content areas or specific situations where pedagogical agents are not particularly effective, it may not be worth devoting the resources needed to implement one. As such, the author concurs with Heidig and Clarebout (2011) that experimental designs such as those used in Domagk (2010), which contain experimental groups with different features as well as a non-agent control group, may be the most fruitful as the field continues to expand.

REFERENCES

Adcock, A. B., Duggan, M. H., Nelson, E. K., & Nickel, C. (2006). Teaching effective helping skills at a distance: The development of project CATHIE. *The Quarterly Review of Distance Education*, *7*(4), 349–360.

Alegría, D. A. H., Boscardin, C., Poncelet, A., Mayfield, C., & Wamsley, M. (2014). Using tablets to support self-regulated learning in a longitudinal integrated clerkship. *Medical Education Online*, *12*. PMID:24646438

Alvarez, C., Brown, C., & Nussbaum, M. (2011). Comparative study of netbooks and tablet PCs for fostering face-to-face collaborative learning. *Computers in Human Behavior*, *27*(2), 834–844. doi:10.1016/j.chb.2010.11.008

Atkinson, R. K. (2002). Optimizing learning from examples using animated pedagogical agents. *Journal of Educational Psychology*, *94*(2), 416–427. doi:10.1037/0022-0663.94.2.416

Atkinson, R. K., Mayer, R. E., & Merrill, M. M. (2005). Fostering social agency in multimedia learning: Examining the impact of an animated agent's voice. *Contemporary Educational Psychology*, *30*(1), 117–139. doi:10.1016/j.cedpsych.2004.07.001

Ausubel, D. G. (1963). Cognitive structure and the facilitation of meaningful verbal learning. *Journal of Teacher Education*, *14*(2), 217–222. doi:10.1177/002248716301400220

Baylor, A. L. (2011). The design of motivational agents and avatars. *Educational Technology Research and Development*, *59*(2), 291–300. doi:10.1007/s11423-011-9196-3

Baylor, A. L., & Kim, Y. (2005). Simulating instructional roles through pedagogical agents. *International Journal of Artificial Intelligence in Education*, *15*(2), 95–115.

Choi, S., & Clark, R. E. (2006). Cognitive and affective benefits of an animated pedagogical agent for learning English as a second language. *Journal of Educational Computing Research*, *34*(4), 441–466. doi:10.2190/A064-U776-4208-N145

Clarebout, G., Elen, J., Johnson, W. L., & Shaw, E. (2002). Animated pedagogical agents: An opportunity to be grasped? *Journal of Educational Multimedia and Hypermedia*, *11*(3), 267–286.

Clark, R. E., & Choi, S. (2005). Five design principles for experiments on the effects of animated pedagogical agents. *Journal of Educational Computing Research*, *32*(3), 209–225. doi:10.2190/7LRM-3BR2-44GW-9QQY

Clark, R. E., & Choi, S. (2007). The questionable benefits of pedagogical agents: Response to Veletsianos. *Journal of Educational Computing Research*, *36*(4), 379–381. doi:10.2190/2781-3471-67MG-5033

Craig, S. D., Gholson, B., & Driscoll, D. M. (2002). Animated pedagogical agents in multimedia educational environments: Effects of agent properties, picture features, and redundancy. *Journal of Educational Psychology*, *94*(2), 428–434. doi:10.1037/0022-0663.94.2.428

D'Mello, S. K., & Graesser, A. (2010). Multimodal semi-automated affect detection from conversational cues, gross body language, and facial features. *User Modeling and User-Adapted Interaction*, *20*(2), 147–187. doi:10.1007/s11257-010-9074-4

Dehn, D. M., & van Mulken, S. (2000). The impact of animated interface agents: A review of empirical literature. *International Journal of Human-Computer Studies*, *52*(1), 1–22. doi:10.1006/ijhc.1999.0325

Domagk, S. (2010). Do pedagogical agents facilitate learner motivation and learning outcomes? The role of the appeal of agent's appearance and voice. *Journal of Media Psychology*, *22*(2), 84–97. doi:10.1027/1864-1105/a000011

Dunsworth, Q., & Atkinson, R. K. (2007). Fostering multimedia learning of science: Exploring the role of an animated agent's image. *Computers & Education*, *49*(3), 677–690. doi:10.1016/j.compedu.2005.11.010

Enyedy, N., Danish, J. A., Delacruz, G., & Kumar, M. (2012). Learning physics through play in an augmented reality environment. *International Journal of Computer-Supported Collaborative Learning*, *7*(3), 347–378. doi:10.1007/s11412-012-9150-3

Epic Games Inc. (2015). *Unreal engine 4* [computer software]. Retrieved from https://www.unrealengine.com/

GoAnimate. (2015). *Make professional animated videos*. Retrieved from http://goanimate.com/

Graesser, A. C. (2011). Learning, thinking, and emoting with discourse technologies. *The American Psychologist*, *66*(8), 746–757. doi:10.1037/a0024974 PMID:22082403

Gulz, A. (2004). Benefits of virtual characters in computer based learning environments: Claims and evidence. *Educational Research Review*, *6*, 27–54.

Hartholt, A., Traum, D., Marsella, S., Shapiro, A., Stratou, G., Leuski, A., . . . Gratch, J. (2013). All together now: Introducing the virtual human toolkit. *Proceedings of the International Conference on Intelligent Virtual Humans.* Retrieved from http://ict.usc.edu/pubs/All%20Together%20Now.pdf

Heidig, S., & Clarebout, G. (2011). Do pedagogical agents make a difference to student motivation and learning? *Educational Research Review*, *6*(1), 27–54. doi:10.1016/j.edurev.2010.07.004

Huang, H. W., Wu, C. W., & Chen, N. S. (2012). The effectiveness of using procedural scaffoldings in a paper-plus-smartphone collaborative learning context. *Computers & Education*, *59*(2), 250–259. doi:10.1016/j.compedu.2012.01.015

Johnson, A. M., Ozogul, G., Moreno, R., & Reisslein, M. (2013). Pedagogical agent signaling of multiple visual engineering representations: The case of the young female agent. *The Journal of Engineering Education, 102*(2), 319–337. doi:10.1002/jee.20009

Johnson, A. M., Ozogul, G., & Reisslein, M. (2014). Supporting multimedia learning with visual signaling and animated pedagogical agent: Moderating effects of prior knowledge. *Journal of Computer Assisted Learning*. doi:10.111/jcal.12078

Johnson-Glenberg, M. C., Birchfield, D. A., Tolentino, L., & Koziupa, T. (2014). Collaborative embodied learning in mixed reality motion-capture environments: Two science studies. *Journal of Educational Psychology, 106*(1), 86–104. doi:10.1037/a0034008

Kalyuga, S., & Sweller, J. (2014). The redundancy principle in multimedia learning. In R. E. Mayer (Ed.), *The Cambridge handbook of multimedia learning* (2nd ed., pp. 247–262).

Keller, J. M. (2010). *Motivational design for learning and performance. The ARCS model approach.* New York, NY: Springer. doi:10.1007/978-1-4419-1250-3

Kim, M., & Ryu, J. (2003). Meta-analysis of the effectiveness of pedagogical agent. In D. Lassner, & C. McNaught (Eds.), *Proceedings of World Conference on Educational Multimedia, Hypermedia and Telecommunications 2003* (pp. 479-486). Chesapeake, VA: AACE.

Kim, Y. (in press). Pedagogical agents. In M. Spector, et al. (Eds.), *Encyclopedia of Educational Technology.* Thousand Oaks, CA: Sage Publications. Retrieved from http://works.bepress.com/cgi/viewcontent.cgi?article=1056&context=yanghee_kim

Lane, H. C., Cahill, C., Foutz, S., Auerbach, D., Noren, D., Lussenhop, C., & Swartout, W. (2013). The effects of a pedagogical agent for informal science education on learner behaviors and self-efficacy. In *Artificial Intelligence in Education* (pp. 309–318). Springer Berlin Heidelberg. doi:10.1007/978-3-642-39112-5_32

Lester, J. C., Voerman, J. L., Towns, S. G., & Callaway, C. B. (1999). Deictic believability: Coordinated gesture, locomotion, and speech in lifelike pedagogical agents. *Applied Artificial Intelligence, 13*(4-5), 383–414. doi:10.1080/088395199117324

Low, R., & Sweller, J. (2014). The modality principle in multimedia learning. In R. Mayer (Ed.), *The Cambridge handbook of multimedia learning* (2nd ed., pp. 227–246). New York, NY: Cambridge University Press.

Lusk, M. M., & Atkinson, R. K. (2007). Animated pedagogical agents: Does their degree of embodiment impact learning from static or animated worked examples? *Applied Cognitive Psychology, 21*(6), 747–764. doi:10.1002/acp.1347

Ma, W., Adesope, O. O., Nesbit, J. C., & Liu, Q. (2014). Intelligent tutoring systems and learning outcomes: A meta-analysis. *Journal of Educational Psychology, 106*(4), 901–918. doi:10.1037/a0037123

Mayer, R. E. (2005). Principles of multimedia learning based on social cues: personalization, voice, and image principles. In R. Mayer (Ed.), *The Cambridge handbook of multimedia learning* (pp. 201–212). New York, NY: Cambridge University Press. doi:10.1017/CBO9780511816819.014

Mayer, R. E. (2014a). Cognitive theory of multimedia learning. In R. Mayer (Ed.), *The Cambridge handbook of multimedia learning* (2nd ed., pp. 43–71). New York, NY: Cambridge University Press.

Mayer, R. E. (2014b). Principles based on social cues in multimedia learning: Personalization, voice, image, and embodiment principles. In R. Mayer (Ed.), *The Cambridge handbook of multimedia learning* (2nd ed., pp. 345–370). New York, NY: Cambridge University Press. doi:10.1017/CBO9781139547369.017

Mayer, R. E., & DaPra, C. S. (2012). An embodiment effect in computer-based learning with animated pedagogical agents. *Journal of Experimental Psychology. Applied*, *18*(3), 239–252. doi:10.1037/a0028616 PMID:22642688

Mayer, R. E., & Moreno, R. (2003). Nine ways to reduce cognitive load in multimedia learning. *Educational Psychologist*, *38*(1), 43–52. doi:10.1207/S15326985EP3801_6

Mayer, R. E., & Pilegard, C. (2014). Principles for managing essential processing in multimedia learning: Segmenting, pre-training, and modality principles. In R. Mayer (Ed.), *The Cambridge handbook of multimedia learning* (2nd ed., pp. 316–344). New York, NY: Cambridge University Press. doi:10.1017/CBO9781139547369.016

Mayer, R. E., & Pilegard, C., (2014). Principles for managing essential processing in multimedia learning: Segmenting, pre-training, and modality principles. In R. Mayer (Ed.), *The Cambridge handbook of multimedia learning* (2nd ed., pp. 316–344). New York, NY: Cambridge University Press. doi:10.1017/CBO9781139547369.016

Mayer, R. E., Sobko, K., & Mautone, P. D. (2003). Social cues in multimedia learning: Role of speaker's voice. *Journal of Educational Psychology*, *95*(2), 419–425. doi:10.1037/0022-0663.95.2.419

Merchant, Z., Goetz, E. T., Cifuentes, L., Keeney-Kennicutt, W., & Davis, T. J. (2014). Effectiveness of virtual reality-based instruction on students' learning outcomes in K-12 and higher education: A meta-analysis. *Computers & Education*, *70*, 29–40. doi:10.1016/j.compedu.2013.07.033

Miller, G. A. (1956). The magic number seven, plus or minus two: Some limits on our capacity for processing information. *Psychological Review*, *63*(2), 81–97. doi:10.1037/h0043158 PMID:13310704

Moreno, R. (2005). Multimedia learning with animated pedagogical agents. In R. Mayer (Ed.), *The Cambridge handbook of multimedia learning* (pp. 507–524). New York, NY: Cambridge University Press. doi:10.1017/CBO9780511816819.032

Moreno, R., Mayer, R. E., Spires, H. A., & Lester, J. C. (2001). The case for social agency in computer-based teaching: Do students learn more deeply when they interact with animated pedagogical agents? *Cognition and Instruction*, *19*(2), 177–213. doi:10.1207/S1532690XCI1902_02

Moreno-Ger, P., Torrente, J., Hsieh, Y. G., & Lester, W. T. (2012). Usability testing for serious games: Making informed design decisions with user data. *Advances in Human-Computer Interaction*, *2012*, 1–13. doi:10.1155/2012/369637

Murray, M., & Tenenbaum, G. (2010). Computerized pedagogical agents as an educational means for developing physical self-efficacy and encouraging activity in youth. *Journal of Educational Computing Research*, *42*(3), 267–283. doi:10.2190/EC.42.3.b

Oddcast Inc. (2015). *SitePal*. Retrieved from http://www.sitepal.com/

Okita, S. Y., Turkay, S., Mihwa, K., & Murai, Y. (2013). Learning by teaching with virtual peers and the effects of technological design choices on learning. *Computers & Education*, *63*, 176–196. doi:10.1016/j.compedu.2012.12.005

Olson, T., Procci, K., & Bowers, C. (2011). Serious games usability testing: How to ensure proper usability, playability, and effectiveness. In *Design, user experience, and usability: Theory, methods, tools, and practice* (pp. 625–634). Berlin, Heidelberg: Springer. doi:10.1007/978-3-642-21708-1_70

Paas, F., & Sweller, J. (2012). An evolutionary upgrade of cognitive load theory: Using the human motor system and collaboration to support the learning of complex cognitive tasks. *Educational Psychology Review*, *24*(1), 27–45. doi:10.1007/s10648-011-9179-2

Paas, F., & Sweller, J. (2014). Implications of cognitive load theory for multimedia learning. In R. Mayer (Ed.), Cambridge handbook of multimedia learning (2nd ed., pp. 27-42).

Paas, F. G. W. C. (1992). Training strategies for attaining transfer of problem-solving skill in statistics: A cognitive-load approach. *Journal of Educational Psychology*, *84*(4), 429–434. doi:10.1037/0022-0663.84.4.429

Plant, E. A., Baylor, A. L., Doeer, C. E., & Rosenberg-Kima, R. (2009). Changing middle-school students' attitudes and performance regarding engineering with computer-based social models. *Computers & Education*, *53*(2), 209–215. doi:10.1016/j.compedu.2009.01.013

Romero-Hall, E., Watson, G. S., Papelis, Y., & Garcia, H. (2014). Nursing pain assessment and management: A 3D interactive simulation. *International Journal of Designs for Learning*, *5*(1), 43–56.

Sabourin, J. L., & Lester, J. C. (2014). Affect and engagement in game-based learning environments. *IEEE Transactions on Affective Computing*, *5*(1), 45–56. doi:10.1109/T-AFFC.2013.27

Schroeder, N. L., & Adesope, O. O. (2013). How does a contextually-relevant peer pedagogical agent in a learner-attenuated system-paced learning environment affect cognitive and affective outcomes? *Journal of Teaching and Learning with Technology*, *2*(2), 114–133.

Schroeder, N. L., Adesope, O. O., & Gilbert, R.B. (2013). How effective are pedagogical agents for learning? A meta-analytic review. *Journal of Educational Computing Research*, *49*(1), 1–39. doi:10.2190/EC.49.1.a

Steenbergen-Hu, S., & Cooper, H. (2014). A meta-analysis of the effectiveness of intelligent tutoring systems on college students' academic learning. *Journal of Educational Psychology*, *106*(2), 331–347. doi:10.1037/a0034752

Suter, W. N. (2012). *Introduction to educational research: A critical thinking approach* (2nd ed.). Thousand Oaks, CA: Sage Publications.

Sweller, J. (2005). Implications of cognitive load theory for multimedia learning. In R. Mayer (Ed.), The Cambridge handbook of multimedia learning (pp. 19-30). New York, NY: Cambridge University Press.

Sweller, J. (2010). Element interactivity and intrinsic, extraneous, and germane cognitive load. *Educational Psychology Review*, *22*(2), 123–138. doi:10.1007/s10648-010-9128-5

Sweller, J., Ayres, P., & Kalyuga, S. (2011). The split-attention effect. In *Cognitive Load Theory* (pp. 111–128). Springer New York. doi:10.1007/978-1-4419-8126-4_9

Sweller, J., & Chandler, P. (1994). Why some material is difficult to learn. *Cognition and Instruction*, *12*(3), 185–233. doi:10.1207/s1532690xci1203_1

Tegos, S., Demetriadis, S., & Tsiatsos, T. (2014). A configurable conversational agent to trigger students' productive dialogue: A pilot study in the CALL domain. *International Journal of Artificial Intelligence in Education*, *24*(1), 62–91. doi:10.1007/s40593-013-0007-3

Theodoridou, K. D. (2009). *Learning with Laura: Investigating the effects of a pedagogical agent on Spanish lexical acquisition* (Doctoral dissertation). University of Texas at Austin, Austin, TX.

Unity Technologies. (2015). *Unity3D* [computer software]. Retrieved from http://unity3d.com/unity/download

van der Meij, H. (2013). Motivating agents in software tutorials. *Computers in Human Behavior*, *29*(3), 845–857. doi:10.1016/j.chb.2012.10.018

van Gog, T. (2014). The signaling (or cueing) principle in multimedia learning. In R. Mayer (Ed.), *The Cambridge handbook of multimedia learning* (2nd ed., pp. 263–278). New York, NY: Cambridge University Press. doi:10.1017/CBO9781139547369.014

van Mulken, S., André, E., & Müller, J. (1998). The persona effect: How substantial is it? In *People and computers XIII* (pp. 53–66). Springer London. doi:10.1007/978-1-4471-3605-7_4

VanLehn, K. (2011). The relative effectiveness of human tutoring, intelligent tutoring systems, and other tutoring systems. *Educational Psychologist*, *46*(4), 197–221. doi:10.1080/00461520.2011.611369

VanLehn, K., Graesser, A. C., Jackson, G. T., Jordan, P., Olney, A., & Rose, C. P. (2007). When are tutorial dialogues more effective than reading? *Cognitive Science*, *31*(1), 3–62. doi:10.1080/03640210709336984 PMID:21635287

Veletsianos, G. (2007). Cognitive and affective benefits of an animated pedagogical agent: Considering contextual relevance and aesthetics. *Journal of Educational Computing Research*, *36*(4), 373–377. doi:10.2190/T543-742X-033L-9877

Veletsianos, G. (2010). Contextually relevant pedagogical agents: Visual appearance, stereotypes, and first impressions and their impact on learning. *Computers & Education*, *55*(2), 576–585. doi:10.1016/j.compedu.2010.02.019

Veletsianos, G., & Russell, G. (2014). Pedagogical agents. In M. Spector, D. Merrill, J. Elen, & M.J. Bishop (Eds.), *Handbook of Research on Educational Communications and Technology* (4th ed., pp. 759-769). Springer Academic. Retrieved from http://www.veletsianos.com/wp-content/uploads/2013/08/pedagogical_agents_synthesis_veletsianos_handbook.pdf

Warren, S., Jones, G., & Lin, L. (2011). Usability and play testing: The often missed assessment. In L. Annetta & S. Bronack (Eds.), *Serious educational game assessment: Practical methods and models for educational games, simulations and virtual worlds* (pp. 131–147). Netherlands: Sense Publishers. doi:10.1007/978-94-6091-329-7_8

KEY TERMS AND DEFINITIONS

Cognitive Outcome: The outcome of a learning task, such as a retention test or a transfer test.

Cognitive Load Theory: A theory describing how the brain processes information through the working and long-term memories.

Cognitive Theory of Multimedia Learning: A theory describing how individuals learn with multimedia. The theory is built upon the notion that the human brain can utilize two processors when presented with information, an auditory processor and a visual processor, and each has their own working memory limitations.

Conversational Agent: A type of software agent meant to facilitate a conversation with the user.

Domain: A domain is a broad field of study, such as science, mathematics, or the humanities.

Meta-Analysis: A statistical technique that allows researchers to analyze the results of different studies collectively.

PACU: Pedagogical agents-conditions of use model (see Heidig & Clarebout, 2011).

PALD: Pedagogical agents levels of design model (see Heidig & Clarebout, 2011).

Pedagogical Agent: A type of visually represented software agent, often in the form of a character, meant to aid in the learning process.

Social Agency Theory: A theory that describes how humans can interpret interactions from a computer in a similar way to how they would interpret interactions from another human.

Virtual Human Toolkit: Computer software that assists in the creation of virtual humans (see Hartholt et al., 2013).

Chapter 11
Augmented Reality: A New Direction in Education

Çelebi Uluyol
Gazi University, Turkey

Sami Şahin
Gazi University, Turkey

ABSTRACT

Augmented Reality (AR) is an emerging technology that bridges the gap between the computer-generated digital information and the reality in real time. Despite the use of AR in numerous disciplines such as architecture, e-learning system, entertainment, medicine, engineering, and e-commerce, it has also potential implications in education. Therefore, in this study, augmented reality use in education is considered in all aspects. After the advantages and disadvantages of AR use in education is explained detailed, the phases of augmented reality book development are discussed. As a result, researchers should work on experimental studies to investigate how AR applications can be applied in educational settings in the future.

INTRODUCTION

In the last decade there has been a significant increase in the use of mobile technologies such as handheld devices, tablet computers and personal digital assistants (Dieterle & Dede, 2006; Lenhart & Madden, 2007). A learner's choice of technology is dependent on the educational environment and on his or her access to different technologies. Providing access to effective information technology at any time and place in a rapidly changing society is a vital factor in classroom and school settings. Augmented reality (AR) is one technology that shifts the location and timing of training.

Researchers have explored using Augmented Reality (AR) applications within various disciplines such as medicine (Liu, Jenkins, Sanderson, Fabian, & Russell, 2010; Sielhorst, Feuerstein, & Navab, 2004), e-commerce (Zhu, Owen, Li, & Lee, 2004), architecture (Billinghurst & Henrysson, 2009), and interior design (Phan & Choo, 2010). The field of education has also demonstrated an interest in integrating AR, including distance learning environments (Cho, Lee, Soh, Lee, & Yang, 2007; Liarokapis, Petridis,

DOI: 10.4018/978-1-4666-9837-6.ch011

Lister, & White, 2002), science education (Kerawalla, Luckin, Seljeflot, & Woolard, 2006; Shelton & Hedley, 2002), engineering education (Liarokapis et al., 2004), and mathematics and geometry education (Kaufmann & Dünser, 2007). Educational technologists and researchers have stressed the need for more research that investigates whether and how these technologies can be used in an effective and useful way for learning (Means & Haertel, 2004).

The 2010 and 2011 Horizon reports (New Media Consortium, 2011), which predict the impact of emerging technologies on different sectors, emphasized that AR will be used widely on US college campuses in the coming years. The reports also indicated that AR can positively impact learning and lead to a creative education. In this chapter, the topic of augmented reality will be explored, as well as the use of augmented reality in education. A case is made for AR being a viable an effective technology tool for teaching and learning in higher education.

DEFINING AND DESCRIBING AUGMENTED REALITY

AR is a technology in which the real environment or object is enhanced by digital content that is tied to certain activities, places or objects. AR allows digital content to be mixed into the perception of reality. 2D or 3D digital objects such as texts, audio materials, animations, graphics and pictures can be combined with individuals' perceptions of the real environment. These digital objects aim to aid and improve users' knowledge and understanding of what is going on around them.

AR was first described by researchers in terms of specific tools, such as head mounted displays (HMDs). Zhou, Duh, and Billinghurst (2008) define the three main characteristics of AR as (1) the combination of real-world and digital objects, (2) which are interactive in real-time, and (3) in which the display of digital information is tied to real-world orientation. Höllerer and Feiner (2004) similarly describe AR environments as those which integrate "real and computer generated information in a real environment, interactively and in real time, and virtual objects with physical ones" (p. 150). Ludwig and Reimann (2005) describe AR as "human-computer-interaction, which adds virtual objects to real senses that are provided by a video camera in real time" (p. 387). Zhou, Duh, & Billinghurst (2008) describes it as a technology "which allows computer generated virtual imagery to exactly overlay physical objects in real time" (p. 387).

According to Milgram, Tekamura, Utsumi, and Kishino (1994), augmented reality is closely linked to virtual reality (VR). They also emphasize that AR is an extension or variation of VR, very similar to VR. Both AR and VR of them are challenging, interactive and contain information sensitivity. As Azuma (1997) states, the user's frame of reference is fully tied to the virtual environment in VR, whereas in AR the user's perception is still centered within reality. The Second Life environment is an example of VR. On the other hand, sport games in game consoles such as the Xbox, Playstation and Nintendo Wii and smart phone applications that utilize GPS data or tie digitally-generated objects to real world places are the best-known examples of AR applications.

As Johnson, Levine, Smith, and Stone (2010) observe, AR applications can occur in two forms: marker-based or markerless-based. Marker-based applications contain three features, which include a booklet for introducing marker information, a gripper for taking information through the booklet and a cube for rendering information on the screen (Johnson et al., 2010). On the other hand, markerless-based applications contain a tracking system, a compass and an image recognition device instead of the three components of marker-based environments. Markerless-based applications have widespread use because they can be operated anywhere, without the need for supplemental points and special labeling.

Augmented Reality Applications

There are two methods of providing access to computer-generated content in augmented reality applications. One of these methods is Quick Response (QR) technology. It is possible to access the AR application through this special two-dimensional barcode technology from the camera of a mobile device. Barcodes that provide access to digital content can be placed on any surface, such as in the booklet, in the image, or on a separate sheet of paper. When this environment-carrying barcode object is placed in front of the web cam, the AR application works on the system and the display shows the results that are connected to the system. If the material is moved in front of the web cam, the direction of the AR application on the screen also changes. The augmented reality object changes depending on the direction of the user's movement.

A second method that provides access to AR applications is the use of a special set of glasses, which is called a Head-Mounted Display (HMD). These glasses are larger and more functional than the glasses we use in everyday life and the lenses of the glasses function as small computer screens. Users can access digital content by looking at various objects in the real world while wearing the HMD glasses. The digital content to be connected can be displayed both on the screens of the lenses or on another big screen that is connected with the glasses. However, such an environment may only be implemented in a laboratory prepared for this purpose.

AR application consists of four components, real object; display screen; data and connection; and software. Nowadays, anyone who uses technological devices can develop simple AR applications. Therefore, it is important for developers and people to know the system components (figure 1).

Figure 1. The four components of augmented reality applications

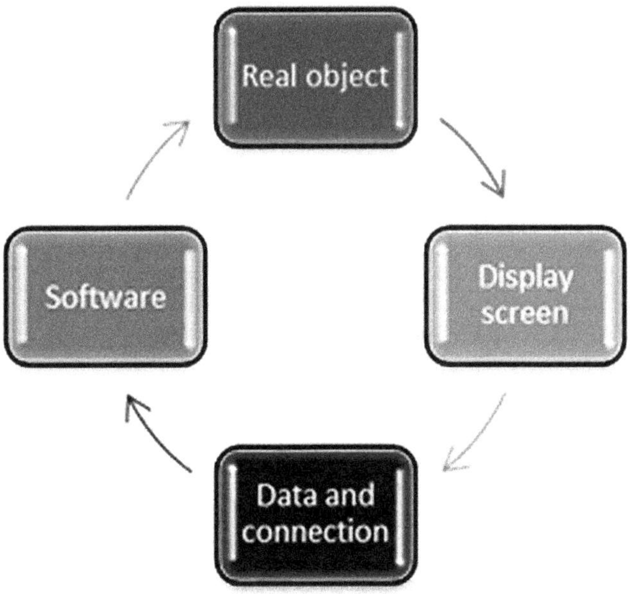

- **Real Object:** The first element is reality or a real object. This can be a car, a house, a tree, a place, or anything in the real world. If there is not a reliance on reality in the environment, we cannot call the application an augmented reality application.
- **Display Screen:** The results, which combine both computer-generated objects and reality in an augmented reality application, should be displayed on a display screen. These screens can be an HMD, a television, a computer screen or any other display screen, such as a mobile or tablet PC screen.
- **Data and Connection:** The digital content that will be displayed on the screen is perhaps the most important matter. The design of the content to be displayed is an entirely different topic. Content may be accessed in two different ways: either digital content can be placed on a local database, or the Internet may be used to provide access to digital content.
- **Software:** Software that recognizes real objects and allows access to digital content should be used. The task of the augmented software is to detect objects in the external world, connect them to digital content, and show the results on the screen successfully. Many companies have their own augmented reality software and browsers.

Augmented Reality Browsers

The important point of augmented reality is the software. AR programs are written in some software development kit programs and are runned and tested throughout AR browsers. It is possible to reach many AR browsers working on both mobile devices and tablet computers. Some of these browsers are shown in Figure 2 below.

It is not the intent of this chapter to review all available AR broswers, but there are three whose utilization rates are high, so each of these will be discussed: Wikitude, Layar and Junaio.

Wikitude: Operations using the Wikitude AR browser can be summarized as follows:

- Exploring a place or showing it in a map with using augmented reality
- Browsing more than 100 million places and interactive content
- Quickly searching many restaurants and accessing information
- Adding bookmarks to content preferences

Figure 2. Examples of augmented reality browsers

- A structure that is constantly updated
- Ability to search through many different categories
- Opportunity to find tweets, events, Wikipedia articles and ATMs
- Opportunity to find many more locations in your environment with recommendations from Yelp, Qype, TripAdvisor, and hotels.com
- Ability to find deals, discounts and mobile coupons that can be used at stores and shops near you

Layar: Layar is one of the well-known AR browsers in the world. Operations using Layar can be summarized as follows:

- Opportunity to develop augmented reality environments without any programming language knowledge
- Easy to use
- Support for graphics
- Adding any videos to content quickly and easily
- Providing the opportunity to interact with the content (e.g., adding a button to the application)
- Giving a chance to design and customize the applications
- Has the support of various applications
- Support through the Web page, advanced blog site, Facebook and Twitter
- Giving the opportunity to share layers with others

Junaio: The Junaio browser is one of the best-known AR browsers and is often used on mobile devices. It is developed by Mctaio, which is one of the leading augmented reality research institutions. Operations using Junaio can be summarized as follows:

- Giving an opportunity to developers without no programming language knowledge
- Having a special programming language called AREL within, and PHP, HTML 5, and Javascript support for programmers who want to develop advanced AR network applications
- An easy way to develop augmented reality applications for iPhone, iPad, Android and tablet computers
- Advanced statistical analysis
- Opportunity for applications developer to develop layers

Augmented Reality vs. Virtual Reality

In spite of the fact that AR is an extension of Virtual Reality (VR), there are some differences between them. In a VR environment, real world objects are simulated and created, and users interact completely with the simulated objects. In an AR environment, computer-generated objects such as images, animation, graphics or sounds are used to strengthen the user's visual feelings by adding these virtual objects to reality. As Hsieh and Lin (2011) posit that virtual reality is designed to take the place of the real environment and augmented reality is designed to augment reality with virtual objects generated by a computer. Some of different areas that use AR and VR is seen in Figure 3.

Figure 3. Various disciplines that use AR and VR

AUGMENTED REALITY IN EDUCATION

Despite a wide range of studies during the past decades, the use of AR in educational settings is still ripe for engagement and research, particularly because there are some issues with its integration due to traditional teaching methods, the costs for the design, implementation and maintenance of the AR system, and resistance to new technologies. However, considering developments in smart phones and the increased usage of tablet PCs with higher Internet connection, AR use in educational settings must have a more streamlined approach (with wider adoption) than ever before. In addition to that, some technological developments that make AR possible are increasingly efficient and effective and compact enough to deliver AR applications to academic environments through faster personal computers and smart devices. AR technology in education is more feasible because of the rapid increase in camera-equipped mobile technologies, such as handheld devices, tablet PCs and other electronic devices. Kerawalla, Luckin, Seljeflot, and Woolard (2006) state that AR's potential and pragmatic tasks have only just begun to be investigated and utilized. AR has the potential to make students more engaged and motivated in discovery, learning and applying their studies to the real environment in new and innovative ways that have never been developed before.

There is also a wide range of ongoing studies that aim to enhance the applicability of AR into real life. However, there are still some questions about AR use in education, including cost effectiveness issues and efficiency between AR applications and methods.

Although there has been intensive study on AR, Wu, Lee, Chang, and Liang (2013), and Cheng and Tsai (2012) emphasize that AR is still in its infancy. In these studies, researchers indicate that research on AR should continue in depth and should focus on the differences between this technology and others. Chen and Tsai (2012) state that the research on AR in educational applications has just began a new era. Dunleavy, Dede, and Mitchell (2009) specify that "we are only beginning to understand effective instructional designs for this emerging technology" (p. 20).

In this section, AR use in education will be reviewed in the five sub-headings as follows: Types of AR in education, advantages of AR in education, limitations of AR in education, AR resources for higher education and a focused look at AR Book use in education.

Table 1. Types of AR use in education

Category	f	%
Marker-based	19	59.38
Marker-less	4	12.50
Location-based	7	21.88

Types of AR in Education

The results regarding the types of AR use in education in presented in Table 1 (Bacca, Baldiris, Fabregat, Graf, & Kinshuk, 2014).

According to the results shown in Table 1, three types of AR use are considered, as also emphasized by Wojciechowski and Cellary (2013). For the augmented reality applications, it is seen that mostly marker-based applications are used (59.38%). Other types of AR use in education are marker-less (12.50%) and location-based (21.88%).

Advantages of AR in Education

The results regarding the advantages of AR use in education in presented in Table 2 (Bacca et al., 2014).

According to Table 2, it is seen that AR presents various advantages. The major advantages of AR use in education are learning gains (43.75%) and motivation (31.25%). This means that AR can contribute to

Table 2. Advantages of AR use in education

Advantage	f	%
Learning gains	14	43.75
Motivation	10	31.25
Interaction Support	5	15.63
Collaboration	6	18.75
Low cost	4	12.50
Increasing the experience	4	12.50
Just-in-time learning	4	12.50
Exploration of the world	4	12.50
Student-centred	3	9.38
Gaining student attention	3	9.38
Enjoyment	3	9.38
Situated learning	3	9.38
Increasing innovation	2	6.25
Creating positive attitudes	2	6.25
Awareness	1	3.13
Anticipation	1	3.13
Authenticity	1	3.13

improving students' learning performance and motivation. This result is very important when we consider that one of the problems faced in an educational environment is motivation. AR technology can be used in some applications to increase student motivation in educational settings. Some other reported advantages of AR use are interaction support (15.63%), collaboration (18.75%), low cost (12.50%), increasing the experience (12.50%), just-in-time learning (12.50%) and exploration of the real world (12.50%).

AR use has been most frequently studied in higher education (Bacca et al. 2014). This is followed by primary education, lower secondary education, upper secondary education, informal learning and short-cycle tertiary education. In these studies, AR was used to motivate learners, explain course topics and add information. As an example, İbili and Sahin (2013) studied augmented reality to find evidence that AR supports elementary-level geometry learning. They developed an augmented reality environment called ARGED3D using Visual Studio 2012 and Microsoft Silverlight. They implemented the environment as an AR book in an experimental setting. As a result, they found that the AR book improved students' ability to learn abstract and complex geometry concepts. In addition, they observed that external use of an AR marking system increased interaction and ease of use. According to Bacca et al. (2014), there was no evidence of augmented reality use in the field of early childhood education, post-secondary non-tertiary education, master's or equivalent level and doctoral degree.

One of the benefits of AR is that the system combines face to face collaboration with access to a computer generated object, permitting students have their own experiences and control over the virtuality, while preserving visual contact with others. Furthermore, augmented reality leverages situated cognition, by allowing the learner to access the digital world by simply displaying a camera in the real world, inside or outside the school. This behavior is beneficial to learners because appropriate information may be procured to satisfy the learner's interest. Learner motivation can also be augmented through augmented reality applications because it changes learner perceptions of real world and provides experiences with individually suitable content. Augmented reality applications should also allow learners to control the course content, as well as have individualized views of the content. However, researchers need to further explore in order to specify these advantages in experimental studies. According to these results, there is a need to validate the advantages of augmented reality use in education and experimental studies in real educational settings.

Limitations of AR in Education

In contrast, Bacca et al. (2014) summarize the limitations or disadvantages of AR use in education. The results of limitations identified from the studies are shown in Table 3.

Table 3. Limitations of AR use in education

Category	f	%
Implementation for a specific domain	1	3.13
Teachers cannot create any content	1	3.13
Difficulties in maintaining information	3	9.38
Too much attention to virtuality	2	6.25
Short periods of validation	1	3.13
Intrusive technology	2	6.25

According to the results in Table 3, the most frequently reported limitations are difficulties maintaining information (9.38%), students' attention to virtuality (6.25%) and intrusive technology (6.25%). Students can feel frustrated if the AR application does not work properly or if it is difficult for learners to use the markers to see the augmented information. To overcome these issues within the applications, there is a need to improve new algorithms, in engineering disciplines in particular. Usability studies are offered for future research on AR applications in educational settings. Paying too much attention to virtuality is related to the novelty of that technology when it is used for the first time in the classroom. Learners may be distracted by the virtual information itself. Using an HMD (Head mounted display) is also a limitation because the device can interrupt interaction between learners. One of the final limitations of AR use is related to teachers. Teachers often do not have the technical skills to create augmented reality environments. So, in the future, studies should be undertaken to assist teachers with using authoring tools to create these environments easily.

There are some limitations or challenges emphasized in other researches in the use of augmented reality in education. Dunleavy, Dede, and Mitchell (2009) found that GPS error is a limitation in augmented reality systems. Resarchers stated that GPS error is prohibitively high for large-scale implementations. GPS failure rates of 15–30% were observed in their study. When the learners were asked what they did not like about learning using an augmented reality system, GPS error was the highest reply. They also emphasized two major errors: "(1) software instability, and (2) the research team incorrectly setting up the mobile device configurations" (p. 13).

The second challenge in an AR environment as specified by Dunleavy et al. (2009) is logistical support and lesson management. There is a high management overhead that accompanies an augmented reality simulation design and implementation. The investigation and interview data from the study show the reality that some instructors could not design and develop the augmented reality unit. In addition to providing the GPS signal during development, the support team in the study also emphasized some points. These points are: "(1) distributed and collected all hardware, (2) tried to keep groups together, (3) answered content and handheld interface questions, (4) provided alternative handhelds to students whose machines had crashed (average 2 out of 15 per class), and (5) corralled the students out of the Street" (p. 16). Briefly, as a result, maintaining sufficient support to the instructors during the development was crucial. The researchers stated that a minimum of two people on web site duties were needed to support teachers with implementing and collecting data.

The last limitation in an AR environment reported by Dunleavy et al. (2009) is student cognitive overload. According to the study findings, students reported feeling frequently overwhelmed and confused by the material and the complexity of tasks they could handle throughout the simulation. Learners were exposed to and requested to rapidly apply various mixed skills: "geo-spatial navigation, collaborative problem solving, handheld manipulation, as well as the mathematics and literacy problems presented within the narrative" (p. 14). While it could be advocated that in isolation any of those skills would be smootly successful, the synthesis of all those skills was doubtful.

Augmented Reality Resources for Higher Education

Science Center to Go (www.sctg.eu) The LifeLong Learning project was supported by the European Union. In this project, an augmented reality technology was implemented in science education. This project converted an augmented reality system for educational use. Some educational scenarios were designed to be used by hundred of instructors, learners, and science teachers within the project. Teachers and students actively manipulated the experiments and played active roles in the environment. Thus, augmented reality experiences were experimented with in education by all stakeholders in the school. The results of the project can be summarized as follows: "(1) It is possible to combine reality with computer generated objects and to place suitable information into real surroundings, (2) AR technology has a potential to be used in education, (3) Augmented reality tools can visualize the invisible onto a real environment object, (4) AR applications allow learners to interact physically with educational learning scenarios materials, (5) Teachers and students can control their learning and teaching themselves, (6) the usability, availability and the prices of AR technology are making it soon available for everyday education" (p. 6).

Construct3D (www.ims.tuwien.ac.at/research/construct3d/) is a development kit for investigating geometry. It takes aspects of computer-aided design (CAD) and combines them with augmented reality to design and implement an educational tool aimed at increasing interaction with other students. The Construct3D tool was mostly used in an experimental study. Research results showed that the AR application was useful as a learning tool, allowing the learner to focus on the actual task rather than the application itself. It is suitable for learners to have the opportunity to investigate on their own initiative, in collaboration with each others. Learners work more effectively with each other if they can share a common workspace. By using an augmented reality system based on a tangible interface metaphor, real objects can have computer generated digital objects tied to them, allowing learners to engage with them in an intuitive way and collaborate and communicate in a more natural way within the real environment.

The LearnAR Project in the United Kingdom (http://www.learnar.org) designed an augmented reality curriculum resource that instructors and learners can investigate in different environments. AR systems have been used in a flexible way, allowing instructors to make demonstrations to a classroom. The same technology can be used by learners in a classroom through tablet computers, mobile devices, netbooks and desktop computers, and by learners independently outside of the school. There is no need for any extra tools, just access to the Web and a device.

The ARiSE Project was also developed to use augmented reality in a school setting. The project combines real and digital objects and lets learners communicate either in close vicinity to each other or from a remote location to administrate virtual objects related to their own culture. Various aspects of augmented reality were observed in the project, and results indicated that the recommended solution has been well received by learners and instructors and is well matched for collaborative learning. In another augmented reality project, called AR Volcano Kiosk (www.hitlabnz.org/wiki/AR_Volcano), the eruption of a volcano was displayed in interactive animated 3D. It demonstrated how augmented reality provides spatial and temporal assistance to the student.

The EXPLOAR Project (www.ea.gr/ep/exploar) is an augmented reality project that involved visitors to science locations such as museums in playful learning. This project looks upon informal training as an opportunity to transcend traditional museum visits and foster an emotional and interactive user experience. A set of scenarios, interactive visualisation technologies and learning paradigms were used in the Project. The EXPLOAR proposes a service that demonstrates the potential of AR to cover the emerging need for continuous updates, innovative exhibits, new exhibitions, new creative materials, new programmes and approaches to visitors.

AR systems can be applied both in higher education and K-12 settings. In relation to the use of augmented reality in K-12, Freitas and Campos (2008) created SMART (System of augmented reality for teaching), which is an educational application using augmented reality technology. This system superimposes 3D models such as cars, airplanes and trucks at 2nd grade-level concepts. Several experimental studies by Freitas and Campos (2008) were performed with 54 students in various schools in Portugal. They concluded that SMART helps increase student motivation and has a positive impact on student learning, especially among less academically successful students. On the other hand, as Lee (2012) states, augmented reality is also a very productive technology for higher education. Students who are studying at university and colleges can develop their abilities, especially when it comes to complicated theories or systems. Regarding this idea, Liarokapis, Petridis, Lister, and White (2002) demonstrated that augmented reality technology can make difficult mechanisms and theories in higher education clearer for learners using contextually enriched interaction.

Additionally, El Sayed, Zayed, and Sharawy (2011) presented courses differently using AR environments so students could handle a wide range of computer-generated objects in an interactive way. Klopfer (2008) also emphasized that AR systems can facilitate skill acquisition. He concluded that AR mobile games can be used in educational setting to arrange, investigate and evaluate data and information.

Some essential knowledge in todays's society can also be organized through AR learning systems (Rosenbaum, Klopfer, & Perry, 2007). For example, in Rosenbaum et al.'s (2007) study, AR learning systems increase students' understanding of complex concepts. Moreover, AR systems could increase learners' interest and motivation and help them improve their abilities and gain more accurate knowledge (Sotiriou & Bogner, 2008). Learners' skills can be enhanced after utilizing cooperative augmented reality applications (Kaufmann, Steinbugl, Dunser, & Gluck, 2005; Martin-Gutierrez et al., 2010). Other skills that can be improved in augmented reality systems are psychomotor-cognitive skills, because augmented reality can make use of visual markers to improve learners' knowledge (Feng, Duh, & Billinghurst, 2008). Kotranza, Lind, Pugh, and Lok (2009) stated that users could receive real time, in-situ responses that may enhance their performance and improve psychomotor skills in cognitive tasks by using an augmented reality system. Liu (2009) concluded that an AR learning environment may help learners overcome learning issues and develop their English speaking and listening skills.

Augmented Reality Book Use in Education

One example of AR use in education is the AR-Book. One of the most well known AR-Books is called the "Magic Book" (Billinghurst, Kato, & Poupyrev, 2001). A booklet can become interactive – or "magic" – using AR technology. This makes users' imaginations a part of the story by using both a printed book and a camera-equipped device. In the Magic Book, while the user can turn the pages of the book, look at the images and read the text without any interactive assistance, he or she can also view 3D models appearing out of the pages through a handheld AR display. Billinghurst, Kato, and Poupyrev (2001) emphasized that younger people especially can read pages in more interactive and effective ways by using AR technology along with printed books. They also concluded that users are able to view three-dimensional scenes from different perspectives simply by moving the augmented reality device along the Magic Book. Moreover, Johnson et al. (2010) stated that AR-Books such as the Magic Book can be converted into an augmented reality version after publication by installing special software called AR Toolkits on users' personal computers. After installing the software on a personal computer or a smart phone, the user can view computer-generated digital objects on the device screen through an embedded camera. Figure 4 shows an example of what a typical AR-book might look like. The scene on the screen shows real booklet with digital supports, such as text, graphics and pictures.

Figure 4. An example of what a typical AR-Book might look like. It shows the reality with such digital supports, such as text, graphics and pictures

The Application Tool

There are many different tools for both programmers and non-programmers to create augmented reality applications. The Metaio Creator is one augmented reality tool for non-programmers in which the user can prepare augmented reality scenarios ranging from simple to complex environments through simply "dragging and dropping." The program has also some highlights such as the ability to rapidly import content, multi-platform support and a complete tracking solution. Due to the various features of the mentioned tool, in this study, the Metaio Creator augmented reality software was used to prepare the AR-Book.

The Augmented Reality Browser

AR browsers have now become one of the major commercial AR applications. There are many AR browsers running smoothly on iOS or Android platforms; examples include Wikitude, Layar, Argon, AR Browser, Aurasma, Google Goggles, and Daqri. All these browsers can be downloaded easily and run on mobile platforms in a few steps. Junaio is an AR platform that allows the user to unlock digital information from places, products and sights around him or her. It is powered by Metaio and available for some glasses such as Epson, Vuzix and Google. Due to the many advantages of the browser, in this study, the Junaio augmented reality browser was used to test and run the designed and developed AR-Book.

Application Development Phases

All applications were developed in Creator demo mode, which has some limitations: (a) only 2 trackables (tracking references) can be loaded, (b) only 2 AR resources can be loaded, and (c) limited access to your channel & contents via QR code only. When the program runs, the user will see the screen shown in Figure 5.

Figure 5. The new project window in the Metaio Creator

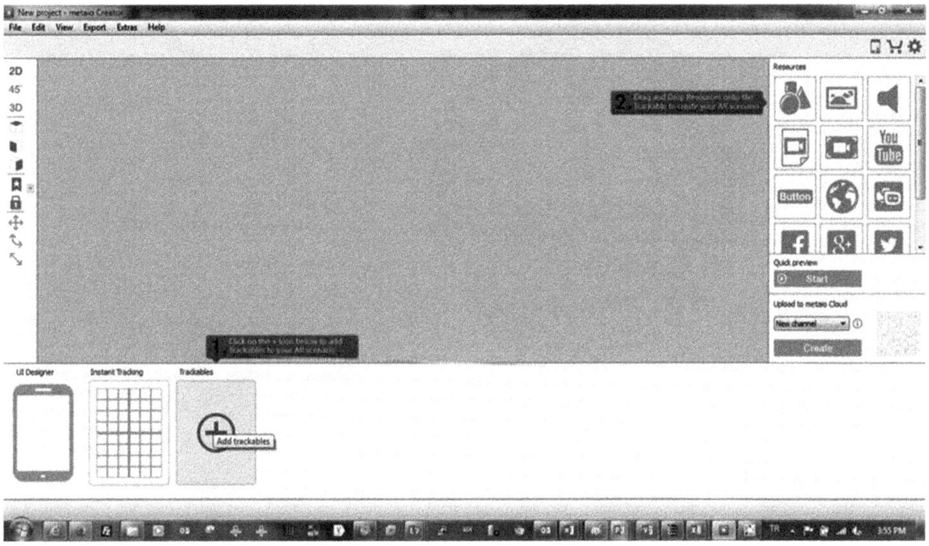

In the new project window, after clicking the "Trackables" button at the bottom left, Figure 6 will appear. In this window, the user should choose tracking technology. We chose "image tracking" for preparing our AR material.

When "image tracking" has been chosen, the user will be prompted to select a picture from the hard drive. We chose the Faculty of Education logo, as seen in Figure 7.

The application cycle will be completed after matching the camera with the pointer. The user must choose an action, which can be a video, music, picture, or other. We chose a hyperlink as an action and wrote the faculty official web site address in the opening window, as seen in Figure 8.

The last step in the application is to create a new channel to upload the material to Metaio Cloud. After clicking the "create" button, the user will be asked the name of this new channel. In this study, we named it "education_faculty," as seen in Figure 9.

The channel with a barcode will be created a few minutes later, as seen in Figure 10.

Figure 6. Different tracking technologies which can be chosen to prepare AR material

Figure 7. An image placed on the application layer

Figure 8. Adding a hyperlink to the picture

Figure 9. Creating and naming a new channel

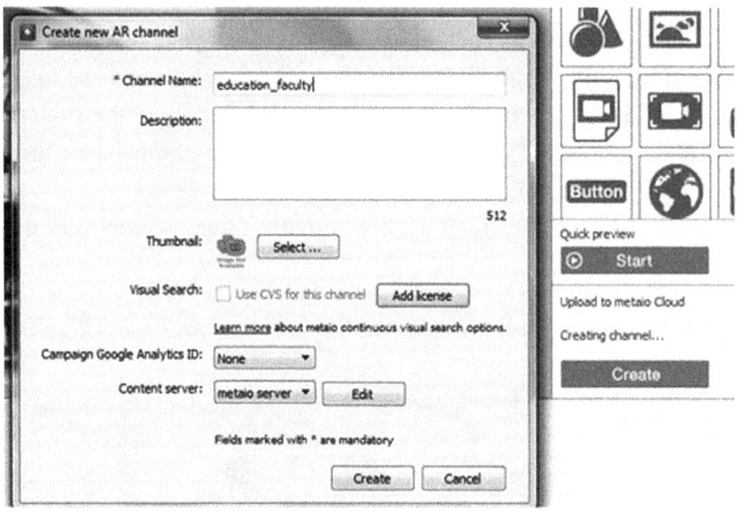

When the user opens Junaio browser on his or her tablet computer, smart phone or handheld device, after scanning the barcode in the browser screen, the device will recognize the application and will open the faculty web site any time it sees the faculty logo. The faculty logo and the created barcode can be printed closely on a booklet and the augmented reality application can be easily tested. A user working with a mobile operating systems such as iOS or Android can drive the application while reading the book.

Figure 10. The created channel with a barcode

When the user scans the QR-Code, the Junaio augmented browser will connect to the Metaio server and download the application to the mobile platform.

CONCLUSION

Given the rapid changes and properties of AR as a growing technology, researchers emphasize that augmented reality has potential implications and various advantages and benefits for educational settings (Billinghurst, 2002; Cooperstock, 2001; Shelton & Hedley, 2002). In today's society, learners can begin to use AR applications quickly. They can download AR browsers/software to their technological devices such as laptops, tablet computers or smartphones. They can also create their own applications and run and test the applications themselves easily.

Although AR applications are not new, the AR-Book is still in its infancy in education. There are still many problems to explore and overcome regarding the use of AR in education. Augmented reality content is still quite difficult for an instructor to design, develop and create. This study illustrates the simplicity of designing the AR-Book for educators who have no programming and coding skills or technical knowledge. In the future researches, experimental studies should be done about the use of AR-Book in education. Educators and researchers should monitor the impact of AR on learning, evaluate the implications of AR use for training and investigation and seek to determine how AR systems can be best applied to learning environments. Researchers should work with educators to explore how AR applications and systems can best be applied in the school environment.

REFERENCES

Azuma, R. T. (1997). A survey of augmented Reality. *Presence (Cambridge, Mass.)*, *6*(4), 355–385.

Bacca, J., Baldiris, S., Fabregat, R., & Graf, S., & Kinshuk. (2014). Augmented Reality Trends in Education: A Systematic Review of Research and Applications. *Journal of Educational Technology & Society*, *17*(4), 133–149.

Billinghurst, M. (2002). *Augmented Reality in Education. New Horizons for Learning*. Retrieved from http://www.newhorizons.org/ strategies/technology/billinghurst.htm

Billinghurst, M., & Henrysson, A. (2009). Mobile architectural augmented reality. In X. Wang, & M. Schnabel (Eds.), *Mixed Reality In Architecture, Design And Construction* (pp. 93–104). The Netherlands: Springer. doi:10.1007/978-1-4020-9088-2_6

Billinghurst, M., Kato, H., & Poupyrev, I. (2001). The Magic Book — Moving seamlessly between reality and virtuality. *IEEE Computer Graphics and Applications*, *21*(3), 2–4.

Chen, C.-M., & Tsai, Y.-N. (2012). Interactive augmented reality system for enhancing library instruction in elementary schools. *Computers & Education*, *59*(2), 638–652. doi:10.1016/j.compedu.2012.03.001

Cheng, K.-H., & Tsai, C.-C. (2013). Affordances of augmented reality in science learning: Suggestions for future research. *Journal of Science Education and Technology*, *22*(4), 449–462. doi:10.1007/s10956-012-9405-9

Cho, K., Lee, J., Soh, J., Lee, J., & Yang, H. S. (2007). A realisitc e-learning system based on mixed reality. *Proc 13th Intl Conference on Virtual System and Multimedia* (pp. 57- 64). VSMM.

Cooperstock, J. R. (2001). The classroom of the future: Enhancing education through augmented reality. *Proceedings of HCI International* (pp. 688-692). New Orleans: Lawrence Erlbaum Associates, Inc.

Dieterle, E., & Dede, C. (2006). Building university faculty and student capacity to use wireless handheld devices for learning. In M. van't Hooft (Ed.), *Ubiquitous computing: invisible technology, visible impact* (pp. 303–328). Mahweh, NJ: Erlbaum.

Dunleavy, M., Dede, C., & Mitchell, R. (2009). Affordances and limitations of immersive participatory augmented reality simulations for teaching and learning. *Journal of Science Education and Technology*, *18*(1), 7–22. doi:10.1007/s10956-008-9119-1

El Sayed, N. A. M., Zayed, H. H., & Sharawy, M. I. (2011). ARSC: Augmented reality student card – an augmented reality solution for the education field. *Computers & Education*, *56*(4), 1045–1061. doi:10.1016/j.compedu.2010.10.019

Feng, Z., Duh, H. B.-L., & Billinghurst, M. (2008). Trends in augmented reality tracking, interaction and display: A review of ten years of ISMAR. *Paper presented at the 7th IEEE/ACM international symposium on mixed and augmented reality (ISMAR)*, Cambridge, UK. doi:10.1109/ISMAR.2008.4637362

Freitas, R., & Campos, R. (2008). SMART: A system of augmented reality for teaching 2nd grade students. *Proceedings of the 22nd British computer society conference on human-computer interaction (HCI 2008)* (pp. 27-30). Liverpool John Moores University, UK.

Hsieh, M. C., & Lin, H. C. K. (2011). A Conceptual Study for Augmented Reality E-learning System Based on Usability Evaluation. *CISME*, *1*(8), 5–7. doi:10.5963/CISME0108002

İbili, E., & Şahin, S. (2013). Software design and development of an interactive 3D geomety book using augmented reality: ARGE3D. *Afyon Kocatepe University Journal of Science and Engineering*, *13*(1), 1–8. doi:10.5578/fmbd.6213

Johnson, L., Levine, A., Smith, R., & Stone, S. (2010). *The 2010 Horizon Report*. Austin, Texas: The New Media Consortium.

Kaufmann, H., & Dünser, A. (2007). Summary of usability evaluations of an educational augmented reality application. Virtual Reality, *LNCS* (Vol. *4563*, pp. 660–669). doi:10.1007/978-3-540-73335-5_71

Kaufmann, H., Steinbugl, K., Dunser, A., & Gluck, J. (2005). General training of spatial abilities by geometry education in augmented reality. *Cyberpsychology & Behavior*, *8*(4), 330.

Kerawalla, L., Luckin, R., Seljeflot, S., & Woolard, A. (2006). Making it real: Exploring the potential of augmented reality for teaching primary school science. *Virtual Reality (Waltham Cross)*, *10*(3-4), 163–174. doi:10.1007/s10055-006-0036-4

Klopfer, E. (2008). *Augmented learning: Research and design of mobile educational games*. Cambridge, MA: MIT Press. doi:10.7551/mitpress/9780262113151.001.0001

Kotranza, A., Lind, D. S., Pugh, C. M., & Lok, B. (2009, October). Real-time in-situ visual feedback of task performance in mixed environments for learning joint psychomotorcognitive tasks. *Paper presented at the 8th IEEE international symposium on mixed and augmented reality (ISMAR)*, Orlando, FL.

Lee, K. (2012). Augmented reality in education and training. *TechTrends*, *56*(2), 13–22. doi:10.1007/s11528-012-0559-3

Lenhart, A., & Madden, M. (2007). *Social networking websites and teens: an overview*. Washington, DC: Pew Internet & American Life Project.

Liarokapis, F., Mourkoussis, N., White, M., Darcy, J., Sifniotis, M., & Petridis, P. (2004). Web 3D and augmented reality to support engineering education. *World Transactions on Engineering and Technology Education*, *3*(1), 11–14.

Liarokapis, F., Petridis, P., Lister, P., & White, M. (2002). Multimedia Augmented Reality Interface for E-learning (MARIE). *World Transactions on Engineering and Technology Education*, *1*(2), 173–176.

Liu, D., Jenkins, S. A., Sanderson, P. M., Fabian, P., & Russell, W. J. (2010). Monitoring with head-mounted displays in general anesthesia: A clinical evaluation in the operating room. *Society for Technology in Anesthesia*, *110*(4), 1032–1038. PMID:20357147

Liu, T.-Y. (2009). A context-aware ubiquitous learning environment for language listening and speaking. *Journal of Computer Assisted Learning*, *25*(6), 515–527. doi:10.1111/j.1365-2729.2009.00329.x

Ludwig, C., & Reimann, C. (2005). Augmented reality: Information at focus. *Cooperative Computing & Communication Laboratory*, 4(1). Universitat Paderborn.

Martin-Gutierrez, J., Saorin, J. L., Contero, M., Alcaniz, M., Perez-Lopez, D. C., & Ortega, M. (2010). Design and validation of an augmented book for spatial abilities development in engineering students. *Computers & Graphics*, *34*(1), 77–91. doi:10.1016/j.cag.2009.11.003

Means, B., & Haertel, G. D. (2004). *Using technology evaluation to enhance student learning*. New York: Teachers College Press.

Milgram, P., Tekamura, H., Utsumi, A., & Kishino, F. (1994). Augmented reality: A class of displays on the reality-virtuality continuum. *Telemanipulator and Telepresence Technologies*, *2351*, 282–292. doi:10.1117/12.197321

New Media Consortium. (2011). The Horizon Report 2011 Edition. Retrieved from http://www.nmc.org/pdf/2011-Horizon-Report.pdf

Phan, V. T., & Choo, S. (2010). Interior design in augmented reality in environment. *International Journal of Computers and Applications*, *5*(5), 16–21. doi:10.5120/912-1290

Rosenbaum, E., Klopfer, E., & Perry, J. (2007). On location learning: Authentic applied science with networked augmented realities. *Journal of Science Education and Technology*, *16*(1), 31–45. doi:10.1007/s10956-006-9036-0

Shelton, B. E., & Hedley, N. R. (2002). Using augmented reality for teaching earth-sun relationship to undergraduate geography students. *Proceedings of the First IEEE International Augmented Reality Toolkit Workshop* (pp. 1-8). Darmstadt, Germany: IEEE. doi:10.1109/ART.2002.1106948

Sielhorst, T., Feuerstein, M., & Navab, N. (2008). Advanced medical displays: A literature review of augment reality. *Journal of Display Display Technology*, *4*(4), 451–467. doi:10.1109/JDT.2008.2001575

Sotiriou, S., & Bogner, F. X. (2008). Visualizing the invisible: Augmented reality as an innovative science education scheme. *Advanced Science Letters*, *1*(1), 114–122. doi:10.1166/asl.2008.012

Wojciechowski, R., & Cellary, W. (2013). Evaluation of learners' attitude toward learning in ARIES augmented reality environments. *Computers & Education*, *68*, 570–585. doi:10.1016/j.compedu.2013.02.014

Wu, H.-K., Lee, S. W.-Y., Chang, H.-Y., & Liang, J.-C. (2013). Current status, opportunities and challenges of augmented reality in education. *Computers & Education*, *62*, 41–49. doi:10.1016/j.compedu.2012.10.024

Zhou, F., Duh, H. L., & Billinghurst, M. (2008). Trends in augmented reality traching, iteraction nd display: A review of ten years in ISMAR. *Proceedings of the Mixed and Augmented Reality, ISMAR 7th IEE/ACM International Symposium* (pp. 193-202). Cambridge: IEEE.

Zhu, W., Owen, C., Li, H., & Lee, J.-H. (2004). Personalized in-store e-commerce with PromoPad: An augmented reality shopping assistant. *Electronic Journal for E-commerce Tools and Applications*, *1*(3), 1–19.

KEY TERMS AND DEFINITIONS

AR-Book: A book which becomes interactive or "magic" using AR technology.

Augmented Reality: Augmented Reality (AR) is a technology that combines computer-generated digital objects and reality in real time.

Augmented Reality Browsers: Augmented reality browsers run AR applications which are operated on mobile devices.

Digital Objects: Computer-generated objects such as text, pictures, graphics, sound and animation are called digital objects.

HMD: Head mounted device is a display device which has a small optic in front of each eye and allows to see virtual objects with reality in real environments.

Junaio: Junaio is a AR browser which allows to create and run AR applications.

Metaio Creator: Metaio Creator is one of the AR kits to design and develop AR applications.

Virtual Reality: Real world objects are simulated and created in virtual reality environments, and users interact with the simulated objects completely.

Wikitude: Wikitude is an AR browser that lets the user to explore a place or show it in a map using augmented reality.

Chapter 12
Ethics in Virtual World Environments Research

Amit Goel
University of Central Florida, USA

William A. Rivera
University of Central Florida, USA

Peter Kincaid
University of Central Florida, USA

Michele Montgomery
University of Central Florida, USA

Waldemar Karwowski
University of Central Florida, USA

Neal M. Finkelstein
US Army Research Laboratory, USA

ABSTRACT

With increased use of virtual worlds in education, training, military, arts, engineering, architecture, astronomy, medical, physical sciences, and many other fields, research in the field of distributed virtual world simulation environments has increased manifold in the last decade. This astounding growth has motivated us to think seriously about issues related to ethics in such research. Awareness of ethical issues is not only a responsibility of the researcher conducting research in virtual worlds, but also for ethics committees and institutional review board members. In this chapter we provide an overview of the past and current research attempting to identify ethics issues related to distributed virtual world simulation environments research. We raise questions related to virtual world research ethics that researcher and ethics committee members should ponder, and we provide several references for the reader to engage in thought provoking further study and discussion.

INTRODUCTION

Virtual worlds have grown beyond merely being a tool for gaming and enjoyment, and have become prolific in many areas of human life, being used for modeling, simulation, analysis, social interactions, and conducting business transactions. In addition, virtual world simulation environments are being used for conducting research in diverse areas such as education (Balula & Moreira, 2014), training (Gomes, Abade, Campos, Harriso, & Silva, 2014), military (Scacchi, Brown, & Nies, 2012), medical (Diener, Windsor, & Bodily, 2009; Gomes et al., 2014), physics, astronomy (Henckel & Lopes, 2010; Lopes,

DOI: 10.4018/978-1-4666-9837-6.ch012

2009), arts (Duran & Villagrasa, 2013), engineering (Duran & Villagrasa, 2013), architecture (Duran & Villagrasa, 2013), and many other fields. Overall, millions of users worldwide are involved with some kind of virtual world.

Events related to ethical issues in virtual worlds have been studied, including cyber rape (Dibbell, 1993, 1994) in LambdaMOO and Facebook's emotional contagion experiment (Kramer, Guillory, & Hancock, 2014). The Facebook experiment manipulated user feeds without users being aware of it, resulting in an outcry from the public that included a call for a review of ethical questions such as issues of informed consent before conducting human subject research. In response, some researchers voiced the opinion that in online contexts it is difficult to determine when research requires informed consent (Rosenberg, 2010). These examples demonstrate us it there are situations that make us think about issues of ethics in virtual worlds.

The purpose of this chapter is to raise awareness regarding issues related to ethics in the use of virtual reality in research. First, background information is provided on virtual worlds, ethics, and a brief literature review of published articles related to the topic of ethics and the use of virtual reality. Second is a discussion of ethical issues, including moral and ethical context, human subjects, public and private space. Third is a discussion of ethics in research including military research, ethics in mobile learning for K-12 and ethics in SecondLife. Fourth is a discussion of future research directions, followed by concluding remarks.

BACKGROUND

In this section we provide a brief overview of virtual worlds and ethics followed by related work in ethical issues in virtual worlds, their usage in general, and their usage n particular in research.

Virtual Worlds

A virtual world is computer-based interactive simulation environment where users take the form of an avatar, own virtual assets, perform virtual actions, and interact with other users and computer-controlled actors known as bots or non-player characters (NPC) (Bell, 2008; Schroeder, 2008).

Virtual worlds include three-dimensional (3D) interactive environments such as Second Life and OpenSimulator. Furthermore, the term virtual world represents Multi User Virtual Environment (MUVE), Massively Multiplayer Online Game (MMOG), Massively Multiplayer Online Role-Playing Games (MMORPG), and Massively Multiplayer Online Social Games (MMOSG). Note that there are subtle differences in each of the above-mentioned terms, but those subtleties make no difference while discussing the issue of ethics. For example, MMORPG focuses on structured objective-based game play, whereas MMOSG focuses on social interaction and communication without a pre-defined structure.

Metaverse is the collective sum of all virtual worlds, virtual reality and augmented reality. The term metaverse was coined in a futuristic science fiction novel titled Snow Crash authored by Neal Stephenson in 1992 (Stephenson, 1992). In the Snow Crash novel human-controlled avatars interact with each other and with computer controlled agents known as bots, in a 3D space that uses the metaphor of the real world. In virtual worlds, users immerse themselves in a 3D environment using avatars to socialize, move around, buy objects, construct objects that they can sell or share, and communicate with other avatars and bots. Thus the immersive and global nature of virtual worlds with large number of users and complex interactions with elements of role-playing are attracting researchers from all fields to experiment using virtual worlds (McKee & Porter, 2009).

Ethics

Ethics is a branch of philosophy that conceptualizes right and wrong conduct in a moral context; ethics deals with morality, good vs. bad, right vs. wrong, virtue vs. vice, justice, legality, and crime (Robinson & Garratt, 2000). Ethics, for virtual world research, has evolved from ethics for the Internet, computer science, software engineering, and information technology. However, the virtual world research has a different context for application of concepts, theory and practice of ethics (McKee & Porter, 2009). The difference in context stems from the nature of virtual worlds. Virtual worlds contain spaces and avatars. Should these spaces be considered public or private? Should the avatars be treated the same as if they were human beings or should they just be treated as an object? How does informed consent take shape in such worlds? Does informed consent apply to some action of the avatar or the human controlling the avatar? In context of Virtual Worlds research, the researcher has to be immersed in the Virtual World itself by using an Avatar. Thus the context of Virtual Worlds Research has some additional and different aspects.

It is beyond the scope of this chapter to provide details of computer and the Internet ethics, but ample resources are available. (See Bynum & Rogerson, 2003; Bynum, 2000, 2001; Coleman, 2007, 2010; Floridi & Sanders, 2001; Floridi, 1999, 2004, 2005, 2010; Harshman, Gilsinan, Fisher, & Yeager, 2005; Himma & Tavani, 2008; Himma, 2007; Johnson, 2005, 2009; Noorman, 2014; Patrignani & Whitehouse, 2014)

Most institutions engaged in research have ethics related rules, regulations and responsibilities for their researchers. These rules and regulations are usually administered through an institute-wide body such as Institutional Review Board (IRB), Independent Ethics Committee (IEC), or Ethical Review Board (ERB).

For example, at the University of Central Florida (UCF), the Office of Research and Commercialization (ORC) administers ethics and compliance, and ensures that the research at UCF complies with regulatory guidelines and meets the highest standards of responsible conduct. The Institutional Review Board (IRB) is an independent body at ORC and is a committee established to protect rights and welfare of human participants in research[1]. The Office of Animal Welfare at ORC protects animals from abuse in research.

Ethical Issues

In a search, using popular and academic search engines and scholarly databases, a comprehensive critique of ethical issues in virtual worlds and metaverse research was not located. Papers, book chapters and books on topics related to ethical issues in design, use and applications of virtual worlds were identified.

Robert W. Kerbs (2005) identified several activities that could lead to ethical issues in the virtual world such as gaming addiction, chatting in chat rooms, cyber stalking, child neglect and abuse. Gaming addiction may lead to destructive behavior towards self and others such as manipulation of situation to ones' own advantage. An example of destructive behavior due to games is a young player who was found dead in a cyber café after playing virtual world game for several hours at a stretch. Public chartrooms often lead to privacy and security of information issues. Cyber stalking has become a prevalent crime and can take many forms such as stalking a female or male virtual world participant, to the extent of harassing them with information obtained from stalking. Access of virtual worlds by children raises concerns that are almost identical to concerns in real life. Thus, the activities identified by Kerbs lead to ethical issues in the virtual world that may also impact the work of researchers in the virtual world. His work also provides suggestions for preventive measures. Some of the preventive measures that he suggests include regulation of virtual world games, using public email identities, creating restricted online profiles for youngsters and kids, and browsing the web anonymously.

Warren and Lin (2012) discuss ethical consideration for virtual worlds design and development in learning published in the handbook of research on practices and outcomes in virtual worlds and environments (Yang & Yuen, 2012). Warren and Lin provided a discussion from the point of view of the designer for learning games and simulations in virtual worlds, and concluded with some interesting questions in the area of educational virtual worlds design. For example the authors discuss the questions of appropriateness of a virtual world game or simulation to their target audience. They also raise questions on measuring the effectiveness in learning and of the measuring the risks associated with the virtual world game or simulation.

Work by Wankel and Malleck (2009) related to ethical issues in the use of virtual worlds such as copyrights, violence, sex, difference, disability, and medical education, etc. Although the authors emphasize that the virtual worlds have to play a very important role in the context of developing twenty first century, the novel ethical problem arising from proliferation of virtual worlds cannot be ignored. The issue of copyright is discussed from ethical and legal dimensions in the virtual worlds and online gaming and the concept of gaming capital is discussed from an ethical viewpoint. The authors also discuss the abuse of the virtual worlds by adult players who use child avatars for engaging in sexual activities in virtual worlds. Second Life had a section called Wonderland for such child-avatar-sex activities that was allowed to continue in the name of free speech. Later this area was shut down due to overwhelming negative reaction and feedback from community. The authors discuss the ethical and moral implications of such activities in the virtual worlds in depth. The authors also discussed ethical issues for usage of virtual worlds in medical education. The ethical dilemmas discussed included whether or not virtual worlds sufficiently prepare students for real life. Overall this work provides a modern outlook and overview towards emerging ethical issues in virtual world and its recent usage in diverse areas.

Grimes, Fleischmann, and Jaeger (2010) discuss research pertaining to ethics from stakeholders' point of view. They provide a detailed discussion on different internal and external stakeholders related to virtual worlds research, and give some generic suggestions for researchers. Understanding how each stakeholder might be affected by research actions or data collection helps researchers alleviate some of ethical issues. See Table 1 for a summary of stakeholders and research ethics considerations.

However, there are additional considerations with respect to ethics for researchers engaged in researching about Virtual Worlds, which were not identified by earlier researchers, hence not listed in above table. This chapter attempts to raise awareness of some of those considerations in following sections.

Ethics in Virtual World Research

Virtual worlds are such a fertile ground for data that they have attracted various disciplines for social, behavioral, and educational modeling, simulation and research. This has led to increased focus on ethics in such research. Grimes et al. (2009, 2010) argue that as a result of the lack of information on ethics in virtual worlds research, a researcher may get approval for research that might be harmful or unethical. However, just because an Institutional Review Board approved the research, does not absolve the researcher, and probably the institution, from legal and ethical responsibilities.

Table 1. Our identification of Research Ethics Considerations for Stakeholders adapted from Grimes et al. (Grimes, Fleischmann, & Jaeger, 2009, 2010)

	Stakeholder	Research Ethics Considerations
Internal	Administrators	• Extra load on administrators including maintenance and scaling of servers because of research activities should be considered. • Impact on infrastructure due to research actions should be considered.
	Managers	Managers should be informed and their interest in retention of user community should be considered.
	Designers	• Creative rights of virtual world designers should be protected. • Impact of research activity on artistic integrity of work should be considered.
	Users	Vulnerable users such as minors, elders, disabled should be considered in research design.
External	Governments	Government interests should be considered such as: • Taxing the virtual property and citizens • Preventing virtual worlds being safe havens for terrorist activities • Providing legal infrastructure for virtual world contracts and disputes
	Investors	Potential financial damages to investors internal and external to virtual worlds should be considered because such financial damages can have ramifications percolated to other stakeholders.
	Researchers	Conflict of role and impact on other researchers in similar field should be considered.

Moral and Ethical Context

In this section, research questions guide the discussion on the context of ethics in virtual worlds research. Moral and ethical context identification is important, since without the contextual awareness, the discussion of ethical issues tends to be lost in technicalities. Examining the context sets the backdrop against which the researchers have to evaluate the general and particular cases of ethics in virtual world research.

Research Question(s)

- Is there a moral and ethical context and content in interactions and actions that happen in virtual worlds?
- Where does the "virtual" end and "real" begin?
- Do we have the same responsibilities in virtual worlds as we do in the real world?

Discussion

With regards to above questions, some researchers agree and provide their reasoning and analysis supported by theories from social science and philosophy. Thomas M. Powers (2003) argues in favor of the presence of morality and the ethical context. In order to provide reasoning for the existence of context, he extends Austin's speech act theory (Austin, 1975) and Rawl's conception of social practice (Rawls, 1955), with his own arguments. The various forms of communications in online communities are equated to examples of speech acts on the lines of Austin's speech theory. According to Thomas, the connection between speech acts and realism about intentions suggests an inclusive realism in virtual worlds. Thus real people act in virtual worlds in a way that establishes moral context and brings strong identification between themselves and their online identities. Further, Thomas establishes the relationship between rules, expectations, and practices in virtual worlds, based on Rawl's (Rawls, 1955) conception of social practice. The rules of virtual world are akin to real laws, sense of ownership of identities and objects is "stage-setting", and the social irreplaceability of characters draws parallels to morality of real people. However, Thomas denies the presence of a moral context in game-based virtual worlds because the difference in respective expectations between online game-based virtual worlds and non-game based virtual worlds. The game-based virtual worlds have minimal rules and participants are punished for violating the rules. Whereas non-game based virtual worlds have either no rules or community-based guidelines and policies. Thus participants are under more harm in non-game based virtual worlds thus establishing a moral and ethical context.

Ren Reynolds (2012) further argues that criteria applied by Thomas M. Powers was too restrictive, and under a different set of criteria, even the game virtual worlds also have moral context Reynolds' paper is centered around the following acts in game-based virtual worlds: *Griefing*, *Cheating*, *Harassment*, *Power Imposition*, *Greed Play*, *Scamming*, *Kill-Stealing*, *Trains*, *Camping*, *Begging*, *Twinkling*, *Power Leveling*, *Ganking*, and *Ninja Looting*. The acts are looked at in context of three major objections to ethical context in game based virtual world: Virtuality, Fantasy, and Gameness. *Virtuality* refers to the concept that game-based virtual worlds are virtual, not real. *Fantasy* refers to the concept that acts in game-based virtual worlds are based on a storyline or narrative and thus unreal. *Gameness* refers to the concept that interactions, events and transactions in game-based virtual worlds are just part of game, or an entertainment play. Reynolds thus modify the Powers' criteria (Powers, 2003) to justify the moral context by refuting above three objections. The modified criteria is based on the fact that acts trade on trust; thus there is identification and attachment with aspects of virtual world; hence there are moral and ethical expectations of behavior in the circumstances under consideration.

According to Grimes et al. (2009, 2010), the assumption that virtual worlds are just sandboxes for research, without any lasting harmful impact, is naive and dangerous. Authors emphasize that avatars are psychological extensions and that avatars project the identities of the virtual world users.

Researchers that disagree with the existence of ethical and moral context in the game-based virtual worlds, base their reasoning on some of the following misconceptions:

- Virtual worlds are "virtual", they do not exist in reality, and hence they are outside the consideration of ethics (Johnson, 1997).
- Virtual worlds have elements of fantasy and role-play; such as flying actions by an avatar in Open Simulator and Second Life, thus they are not within context of ethics (Consalvo, 2003; Southern, 2001).
- Virtual worlds are just games and hence not a serious activity. Games are set with nontraditional norms such as acts of lying, violence, and no fear of law or society (Consalvo, 2003; Southern, 2001).

Human Subjects

In this section, the issues around use of human subjects in virtual worlds research is discussed. Important and critical questions provide the basis for discussion.

Research Question(s)

- What are the ethical issues for using human subjects?
- Are they actually human subjects or just their virtual avatars?
- Are they still considered human subjects if we are not seeing, knowing or interacting with them physically?

Discussion

Use of human subjects in virtual worlds research is as common as any other research. Therefore the role of ethics is very important in order to avoid any kind of harm to such human subjects. Grimes et al. (2009, 2010, p. 79) provide a list of ethical issues and factors when conducting human subject based virtual world research:

- Psychological importance and emotional attachment to virtual objects

Human subjects may develop emotional attachment to virtual objects and identities. A human subject may start loving his virtual pet or virtual girlfriend to the extent of disturbing his real life. Human subjects may start giving more importance to their virtual assets such as virtual house, virtual money, virtual friends, and virtual family.

- Importance of privacy, confidentiality, anonymity, and reputation of users and their avatars

The virtual identity of human subject needs to be protected just like his/her real identity. The concepts of privacy, confidentially, and anonymity apply to virtual identities as well. In virtual world reputation has to be built and maintained, whether it is the reputation with respect to moral character, friendliness, technical skill or social behavior.

- Respect for the virtual world and the preservation of the social ecology

The social ecosystem in virtual world drives the interactions and growth. As in real life, users do not wish to venture into virtual worlds where the social ecosystem is missing. In real life we respect the social contracts and behaviors, such as not littering on streets or not playing loud music in public. Similarly in virtual worlds, researchers have to observe the respectfulness for virtual society such as taking consent before conducting research or before releasing information.

- Financial importance of virtual objects and virtual economy

Virtual economy is sustained by actions of users through their avatars. Thus researchers have to make sure that their actions do not bring virtual economy to a halt, just like mortgage crisis and other financial crisis in real life bring the real economy down.

- Inconsistencies of contractual documents in terms of legal restrictions

Human subject based research should ensure that there are no inconsistencies in contracts and other legal documents. Further, the restrictions posed by such documents on human documents should not take away their real life rights earned from so many centuries of human development and struggle.

- Issues of legal and social requirements of multiple jurisdictions and national boundaries

When using human subjects in virtual world research, it may be possible that human subjects from different geographical areas and different nations are participating. Researchers should be careful of legal requirements involving multiple jurisdictions imposed by different nations. Further, the area of jurisdiction should be clearly stated, in case a dispute or conflict arises. Similarly cross-cultural aspects should also be considered while using human subjects from across the national boundaries in virtual world research.

- Ethical considerations of artificial life and software agents

While using human subjects, researchers should be careful about the impact of a mixed use of human subjects with artificial software agents. How would human subjects respond to the artificial life of theirs and of other software agents, also popularly known as bots? It may be the case that bots are threatening to human subjects. If bots are not well designed, human subjects may develop anxiety and frustration while dealing with such bots in artificial life.

This list is not exhaustive; there is a need to consider other factors that are related to specific issues and concerns in other diverse domains where virtual worlds are being used as a research tool. For example, we provide additional factors to consider for using virtual worlds research in military context and K-12 Mobile Education.

Public and Private Space

A public space is considered accessible to anyone, and in context of virtual worlds public space includes a place, conversation or piece of information. On the other hand a private space is supposed to be only accessible by its intended audience, owner or originator. In this section a discussion pertaining to public and private spaces in virtual worlds is provided.

Research Question(s)

- Should the virtual worlds be considered public spaces?
- What areas, if any, are private?
- Does the data collected by virtual world hosting company belong to public domain?
- Can avatar communications, interactions, and activities be studied, recorded, analyzed, and reported without informed consent?
- What would be an appropriate way of getting informed consent from hundreds or thousands or millions of users?

Discussion

In virtual worlds research, private spaces are difficult to lockdown as they are in real world, because of the current nature of virtual worlds being open spaces accessible to everyone. Hence, it is critical for virtual world researchers to understand their responsibilities about respecting private spaces.

McKee and Porter (2009) report that concerns about public and private spaces on the Internet and online communities have been discussed in online and Internet research, and these concerns are similar to the concerns in the virtual worlds research. However, virtual worlds have different context for such earlier discussions to apply. For example, in virtual worlds, researchers collect data not only as a passive observer, but also most of the time researchers have to participate in the virtual world in order to study and analyze the elements of interactions. This is different from Internet and Online Communities context where the researchers usually collect data in form of logs and transcripts without actively participating in the community.

Rosenberg's work provides a detailed commentary with respect to public vs. private spaces in virtual worlds (Rosenberg, 2010). Authors propose the idea of private places, conversations, and information. They also recognize the public spaces with varying degrees of privacy. The authors suggest that researchers should determine the kind of relations that predominate the particular online context. Identifying the relationship types facilitates researchers in deciding the best approach to handle the issues of public and private space in presence of such relationships.

Military Related Virtual World Research

Military forces have been a leader in the use of virtual reality. In this section, questions are raised related to military use of virtual worlds research. The importance of raising these questions can be judged from the fact that military use can cause more harm than anything else since military is designed to use force for defensive actions.

Research Questions

- What are possible concerns from military's use of virtual world for research?
- Should it be bound by any ethical restrictions because military is using it for national interest?
- What are the issues military researchers need to be aware of while performing virtual world research?

Discussion

The military as a government entity provides a core function of protecting the states and country from external enemies, at times by using lethal force and weapons. Even though the core task of any military force is to defend, sometimes the military is also used to wage war against other countries. During peace times, the military engages in training exercises and may be called on to provide support for internal functions of state such as emergency services, social ceremonies and guarding important installations such as nuclear power plants or important infrastructure sources.

Military forces worldwide use Virtual Worlds for variety of purposes such as education and training, simulation of wartime or peacetime scenarios, "strategic, tactical and operational" analysis and planning, battlefield rehearsals, research and situational awareness (Aguiar & Monte, 2011; Allen & Demchak, 2011; Maxwell, Griffith, & Finkelstein, 2014; Thompson, 2011).

Ethics in military research of virtual worlds include traditional military ethics related questions such as:

- What are the overarching laws of engaging in war?
- What is the justification of using military force?
- What to target and how does the military select and justify targets for attack or defense?
- What kinds of weapons to use and how to decide whether weapons chosen are excessive or not?
- What are the laws protecting rights of countries who lose the war?
- What are the laws governing the handling of military force of losing side and handling of civilian and military personnel of opposing side imprisoned during war?
- What are the laws, standards, and processes governing violations of war ethics?

From an analysis of above listed questions, we see that use of virtual worlds for military research brings additional ethics related issues into the fold. Critically examining and answering these issues will make sure that military research in virtual worlds conforms and addresses ethical concerns. From examining the issues raised in military ethics, it's evident that military force is designed to use force, however, the ethical discussions revolve around the use of force, or around amount of force and, or around the time of use. Military use mandates examination of such questions in virtual world research context.

No literature was located pertaining to virtual world research ethics in military use setting. The second research question, pertains to whether military should be allowed to break ethics guidelines, policies or principles set by virtual world. If military is given unrestricted access to virtual worlds, they may be able to pursue their research, but it may be harmful to other virtual world users. For example, military offices might want to use virtual worlds for doing data mining research, surveillance, and trouble detection. Another possible use might be to track down suspected users who are identified as potential threats. However, these threats might be unreal due to users assuming fake identities and avatars. Also, users might engage in meaningless fake conversations and unserious jokes assuming that virtual worlds is just a game play and fantasy, that might lead them to being suspects by virtual world research using virtual worlds for research. Having said that, we lay emphasis that military use of virtual worlds research needs to be investigated in detail further and readers are encouraged to read the literature from military ethics and other areas of virtual worlds research to apply to military context.

K-12 Related Virtual Worlds Research

Mobile learning communities and virtual worlds for K-12 has seen an increase in recent years. A large number of educators and institutions are discovering the potential of virtual worlds as a useful tool for classroom education. For some, virtual worlds are a supplemental tool, and for others it is replacement of real-world classroom. In this section we raise questions for ethical issues in mobile learning virtual worlds. Mobile learning virtual communities and virtual worlds, if not analyzed from ethics context, may cause potential harm among young users such as children, hence our motivation to study this context in the light of virtual world research.

Research Questions

- What considerations must be taken for parents and for their children?
- Does the content belong to the platform, the children or the parents?
- What should and shouldn't be shared with parents?

Discussion

The availability of mobile devices has become more widespread because of their affordability and popularity. Mobile devices offer the advantages of portability, shared interaction, individual customization, interconnectivity and real time context sensitivity which allows the user to be connected anywhere at any time. The ubiquitous nature of these devices offers new learning experiences that are both flexible and pervasive.

An emerging area of research is the ability to connect virtual worlds to mobile learning platforms. During our search of popular and academic search engines we were not able to locate any literature that highlighted the ethical challenges of mobile learning virtual communities research. The literature that we found was limited to only technological and pedagogical concerns of mobile learning platforms (Dionisio, Iii, & Gilbert, 2013; Franklin, 2011; Pegrum, Oakley, & Faulkner, 2013; Pereira & Rodrigues, 2013; Rachel, Cobcroft, Towers, Smith, & Bruns, 2006; Sharples, Taylor, & Vavoula, 2005; Suslov, 2012). Since the current chapters is about ethics in virtual worlds research, hence we are not covering the above found literature in detail, however, reader is encouraged to read and bring some of those concepts in virtual worlds research ethics discussion.

An issue with the use of mobile devices is digital distraction which may have health considerations. Recent study suggests adverse health issues and sleep disturbances caused from the inappropriate use of mobile devices after hours (Munezawa et al., 2011). Aside from health concerns other ethical considerations for researchers include content and privacy rights for material collected from different context. This includes knowing what can be collected, from whom and how often. Special considerations for diverse age groups, religion and cultural backgrounds are also paramount considerations.

Mobile learning provides pervasive formal, informal and social learning but this access can also expose user content to external unauthorized users. Student records, images and institutional information must also be safe guarded at all times and proper training must consider how to handle data and how to report incidents. This is not limited to hackers but also to sharing content with friends or family which may be in violation of privacy rights.

Astronomy and Astrophysics Related Virtual World Research

Meta Institute of Computational Astrophysics (MICA) pioneered the use of Astrophysics Virtual World Research (Djorgovski et al., 2010). MICA is a professional scientific and educational, non-profit organization based in virtual worlds that researched problems in astrophysics using virtual world platforms such as SecondLife, OpenSim and ScienceSim. StellarSim (Henckel & Lopes, 2010; Lopes, 2009) is a plugin architecture framework for automated creation and population of stellar object in cosmological environments in virtual worlds. Thus the field of Astronomy and Astrophysics is embracing the virtual worlds for research purposes. From explorations of academic journals and search engines, literature discussing ethical concerns in virtual world research in the field of Astronomy and Astrophysics was found lacking, thus motivating to raise the questions listed below:

Research Questions

- What are ethical considerations for the astronomers and the astrophysicists in virtual worlds research?
- What are the ethical considerations in outreach research activities on virtual worlds?
- Do virtual worlds provide an accurate and stable platform for sharing and conducting astronomical simulations and research?

Discussion

Astronomy is a science mostly based on observations, theories, models and simulations. In astronomy, large-scale experiments are not feasible to conduct, as an example, researchers cannot go out in space and make two galaxies to collide to see the results, or they cannot explode a star to experiment if theory of star explosion is correct. Thus virtual worlds provide a natural stage for running these simulations and for conducting research.

The ethical issues and concerns in astronomical and astrophysical research in virtual worlds are not as grave as other fields discussed above. Such research is mostly simulations and does not affect the individuals or the avatars, as there is almost no interaction with the avatars or the individuals outside the research group. However, outreach research in virtual words does involve interacting with large community of virtual world users and thus the ethical context issues we discussed so far in this chapter apply to such research in virtual worlds.

Accuracy and stability of virtual world platform is a matter of concern in astronomical research. Since astronomical research relies on observations, models and simulations, thus accuracy and stability provided by research platform greatly affects the research results. The ethical context here relates to the fact that accuracy in research builds the trust and confidence in science and in researcher doing the research. It would be unethical to convey or report results from an unstable research.

Ethics in Second Life

In this section the adequacy of ethics in virtual world research is described for publicly available virtual worlds such as Second Life. Second Life has become a popular platform for usage among diverse users, hence, many different kinds of virtual worlds research is pursued in Second Life platform. This raises the questions of ethics and protecting the users from harm.

Research Questions

- Are the standards, guidelines and policies provided by Second Life adequate for researchers?
- Do they cover all aspects of researchers' use of Second Life?

Asking and discussing such questions are important because the standards, guidelines and policies provided by Second Life seem to be designed only for users, and not for researchers.

Discussion

Second Life is a 3D Interactive Virtual World developed and promoted by Linden Research Inc., also known as Linden Labs. The Second Life Environment is known as Second Life Grid, where virtual residents create and own objects. A user may register a free basic account or a paid premium account that comes with extra features and capabilities. The Second Life Grid may be accessed by Second Life Viewer or many of the freely available open source viewers. A viewer is almost like a 3D browser for virtual worlds.

Second Life Community Standards are provided with the goal of respectful treatment of each other without harassment. These standards list six behaviors that are considered unethical, hence result in punishment by suspension or in case of repeat offenses, expulsion from Second Life: Intolerance, Harassment, Assault, Disclosure, Adult Regions, Groups and Listing, and Disturbing the Peace.

Second Life's official wiki provides guidelines of ethical behavior to be observed at all times while using the virtual worlds. Also, Second Life's etiquette available at their wiki describes the manners and customs for living in Second Life. Reader is encouraged to read the latest guidelines from SecondLife's website for more details.

These etiquettes and community standards (mentioned above) are applicable to researchers participating in SecondLife to research about Virtual Worlds, just like any other SecondLife Resident. However, there is not enough evidence or research that these standards cover the special context of virtual world research itself. Perhaps Second Life hosting company itself is conducting virtual world research and does not want to impose any restrictions on themselves.

FUTURE RESEARCH DIRECTIONS

As the virtual worlds continues to be used by researchers of various diverse fields for research, the need to address the concerns and issues related to ethics in such research has become a fertile ground of ethics research. In this regards, various professional societies have their own code of ethics. These codes of ethics cover both the practice of profession. Since the area of virtual worlds research ethics is in its nascent stage and a paucity literature is available, it is important to extend this research by evaluating code of ethics from various professional societies related to virtual world researchers, such as:

- Association of Computing Machinery
- IEEE (Institute of Electrical and Electronics Engineers) Computer Society
- Association of Information Systems
- American Psychological Association
- Association of Virtual Worlds
- Association of Internet Researchers
- American Association for Advancement of Science

The playgrounds for virtual worlds research are diverse and broad. Hence gaining insight into the awareness of code of ethics among these researchers, and how they are encountering and solving ethical issues in virtual world research, is an important research direction that has not been addressed.

Continued research on ethics in virtual worlds environments needs to be explored in the diverse fields such as Military, Education, Medicine, Astronomy, Engineering, and Architecture etc. Additional synergies in such multi-disciplinary research can be accomplished by sharing experience of researchers from diverse fields and skill areas.

CONCLUSION

Virtual worlds have penetrated many different fields for modeling, simulation, and analysis while conducting research. This increased usage has led to the questions and concerns related to ethical issues in such research. As discussed in this chapter, virtual worlds pose different and newer challenges for the field of ethics.

Studying ethics is very important for researchers and users of virtual worlds. Awareness of issues related to ethics in virtual worlds research enables the researcher to better design his or her experiments such that harmful effects can be avoided. This awareness is not only important for researchers, but also for ethics committees examining and evaluating requests related to ethical clearance for virtual world research.

In this work, we have discussed some critical issues in virtual world research ethics related to moral and ethical context, human subjects, public and private spaces, military research and Second Life. The big questions to explore are the existence of moral and ethical context for objects, subjects, and interactions in virtual world. We raised some interesting issues with respect to the usage of human subjects in virtual worlds. Although everything in virtual worlds can be in a public space by virtue of being online, but researchers should respect the private spaces within the context. We also commented on use of virtual worlds and ethical issues for domains of military research and astronomical research. Finally we presented issues related to effectiveness of guidelines issued by Second Life for virtual world researchers.

ACKNOWLEDGMENT

The authors acknowledge Mr. Doug Maxwell of the Simulation and Training Technology Center (STTC) of United States Army Research Laboratory for generously providing computational resources and support. The authors would also like to acknowledge Dr. Brian Goldiez, Dr. Paul Wiegand and Dr. Glenn Martin from Advanced Research Computing Center at University of Central Florida for sharing their thoughts and ideas.

REFERENCES

Aguiar, S., & Monte, P. (2011). Virtual Worlds for C2 Design, Analysis and Experimentation. *Proceedings of the 16th International Command and Control Research and Technology Symposium (ICCRTS 2011), Quebec City, Quebec, Canada, June 21-23, 2011.*

Allen, P. D., & Demchak, C. D. (2011). Applied Virtual Environments: Applications of Virtual Environments to Government, Military and Business Organizations. *Journal of Virtual Worlds Research, 4*(1).

Austin, J. L. (1975). *How to do things with words.* Oxford University Press. doi:10.1093/acprof:oso/9780198245537.001.0001

Balula, A., & Moreira, A. (2014). e-Teaching evaluation in higher education. In Evaluation of Online Higher Education: Learning, Interaction and Technology (pp. 1–11). Springer. doi:10.1007/978-3-319-05425-4

Bell, M. W. (2008). Toward a Definition of "Virtual Worlds". *Journal of Virtual Worlds Research, 1*(1).

Bynum, T. W. (2000). The foundation of computer ethics. *ACM SIGCAS Computers and Society, 30*(2), 6–13. doi:10.1145/572230.572231

Bynum, T. W. (2001). Computer ethics: Its birth and its future. *Ethics and Information Technology, 3*(2), 109–112. doi:10.1023/A:1011893925319

Bynum, T. W., & Rogerson, S. (2003). *Computer Ethics and Professional Responsibility: Introductory Text and Readings.* Cambridge, MA, USA: Blackwell Publishing.

Coleman, K. G. (2007). Casuistry and Computer Ethics. *Metaphilosophy, 38*(4), 471–488. doi:10.1111/j.1467-9973.2007.00494.x

Coleman, K. G. (2010). Computing and Moral Responsibility. Retrieved from http://plato.stanford.edu/archives/win2010/entries/computing-responsibility/

Consalvo, M. (2003). It's No Videogame: News Commentary and the Second Gulf War. *Proceedings Level Up Conference.* Retrieved from http://citeseerx.ist.psu.edu/viewdoc/summary?doi=10.1.1.77.44

Dibbell, J. (1993). A Rape in Cyberspace. *The Village Voice.*

Dibbell, J. (1994). A Rape in Cyberspace: How an Evil Clown, a Haitian Trickster Spirit, Two Wizards, and a Cast of Dozens Turned a Database into a Society. *Annual Survey of American Law*, 1994, 471–481.

Diener, S., Windsor, J., & Bodily, D. (2009). Design and development of clinical simulations in SecondLife. *Proceedings of the EDUCAUSE Australasia Conference* (pp. 1–13).

Dionisio, J. D. N., Iii, W. G. B., & Gilbert, R. (2013). 3D Virtual worlds and the metaverse. *ACM Computing Surveys, 45*(3), 1–38. doi:10.1145/2480741.2480751

Djorgovski, S. G., Hut, P., McMillan, S., Vesperini, E., Knop, R., Farr, W., & Graham, M. J. (2010). Exploring the use of virtual worlds as a scientific research platform: The meta-institute for computational astrophysics (MICA). In *Facets of virtual worlds* (pp. 29–43). Retrieved from http://link.springer.com/chapter/10.1007/978-3-642-11743-5_3

Duran, J., & Villagrasa, S. (2013). Teaching 3D arts using game engines for engineering and architecture. *Proceedings of the 5th International Conference on Virtual, Augmented and Mixed Reality (VAMR 2013) held as part of HCI International (HCII 2013)* (pp. 113–121). Springer. doi:10.1007/978-3-642-39420-1_13

Floridi, L. (1999). Information ethics: On the philosophical foundation of computer ethics. *Ethics and Information Technology*, *1*(1), 33–52. doi:10.1023/A:1010018611096

Floridi, L. (2004). Open Problems in the Philosophy of Information. *Metaphilosophy*, *35*(4), 554–582. doi:10.1111/j.1467-9973.2004.00336.x

Floridi, L. (2005). Information ethics, its nature and scope. *ACM SIGCAS Computers and Society*, *35*(2), 3. doi:10.1145/1111646.1111649

Floridi, L. (Ed.). (2010). *The Cambridge Handbook of Information and Computer Ethics*. Cambridge University Press. doi:10.1017/CBO9780511845239

Floridi, L., & Sanders, J. W. (2001). Artificial evil and the foundation of computer ethics. *Ethics and Information Technology*, *3*(1), 55–66. doi:10.1023/A:1011440125207

Franklin, T. (2011). Mobile learning: At the tipping point. *Turkish Online Journal of Educational Technology*, *10*(4), 261–275.

Gomes, T., Abade, T., Campos, J. C., Harriso, M. D., & Silva, J. L. (2014). A Virtual Environment based Serious Game to Support Health Education. *ICST Transactions on Ambient Systems*, *1*(3), e5. doi:10.4108/amsys.1.3.e5

Grimes, J. M., Fleischmann, K. R., & Jaeger, P. T. (2009). Virtual guinea pigs: Ethical implications of human subjects research in virtual worlds. *International Journal of Internet Research Ethics*, *2*(1).

Grimes, J. M., Fleischmann, K. R., & Jaeger, P. T. (2010). Research ethics and virtual worlds. In C. Wankel & S. Malleck (Eds.), *Emerging Ethical Issues of Life in Virtual Worlds* (pp. 73–99). Information Age Publishing.

Harshman, E. M., Gilsinan, J. F., Fisher, J. E., & Yeager, F. C. (2005). Professional Ethics in a Virtual World: The Impact of the Internet on Traditional Notions of Professionalism. *Journal of Business Ethics*, *58*(1-3), 227–236. doi:10.1007/s10551-005-1417-4

Henckel, A., & Lopes, C. V. (2010). Stellarsim: A plug-in architecture for scientific visualizations in virtual worlds. In *Facets of Virtual environments* (pp. 106–120). Springer-Verlag Berlin Heidelberg. Retrieved from http://link.springer.com/chapter/10.1007/978-3-642-11743-5_9

Himma, K. E. (2007). Foundational issues in information ethics. *Library Hi Tech*, *25*(1), 79–94. doi:10.1108/07378830710735876

Himma, K. E., & Tavani, H. T. (Eds.). (2008). *The Handbook of Information and Computer Ethics*. John Wiley & Sons. doi:10.1002/9780470281819

Johnson, D. G. (1997). Ethics online. *Communications of the ACM*, *40*(1), 60–65. http://dl.acm.org/citation.cfm?id=242857.242875 doi:10.1145/242857.242875

Johnson, D. G. (2005). Computer Ethics. In R. G. Frey & C. Heath Wellman (Eds.), *A Companion to Applied Ethics*. Oxford, UK: Blackwell Publishing; doi:10.1002/9780470996621.ch45

Johnson, D. G. (2009). *Computer Ethics* (4th ed.). Pearson.

Kerbs, R. W. (2005). Social and ethical considerations in virtual worlds. *The Electronic Library*, *23*(5), 539–546. doi:10.1108/02640470510631254

Kramer, A. D. I., Guillory, J. E., & Hancock, J. T. (2014). Experimental evidence of massive-scale emotional contagion through social networks. *Proceedings of the National Academy of Sciences of the United States of America*, *111*(24), 8788–8790. doi:10.1073/pnas.1320040111 PMID:24889601

Lopes, C. V. (2009). The massification and webification of systems' modeling and simulation with virtual worlds. Proceedings of the 7th joint meeting of the European software engineering conference and the ACM SIGSOFT symposium on The foundations of software engineering (pp. 63–70). ACM; Retrieved from http://dl.acm.org/citation.cfm?id=1595708

Maxwell, D., Griffith, T., & Finkelstein, N. M. (2014). Use of Virtual Worlds in the Military Services as Part of a Blended Learning Strategy. In K. S. Hale & K. M. Stanney (Eds.), *Handbook of Virtual Environments: Design, Implementation and Applications* (2nd ed., pp. 959–1000). CRC Press. doi:10.1201/b17360-45

McKee, H. A., & Porter, J. E. (2009). Playing a Good Game : Ethical Issues in Researching MMOGs and Virtual Worlds. *International Journal of Internet Research Ethics*, *2*(1).

Munezawa, T., Kaneita, Y., Osaki, Y., Kanda, H., Minowa, M., Suzuki, K., & Ohida, T. et al. (2011). The association between use of mobile phones after lights out and sleep disturbances among Japanese adolescents: A nationwide cross-sectional survey. *Sleep*, *34*(8), 1013–1020. doi:10.5665/sleep.1152 PMID:21804663

Noorman, M. (2014). Computing and Moral Responsibility. Retrieved from http://plato.stanford.edu/archives/sum2014/entries/computing-responsibility/

Patrignani, N., & Whitehouse, D. (2014, July 30 – August 1). Slow Tech: The Bridge between Computer Ethics and Business Ethics. In K. Kimppa, D. Whitehouse, T. Kuusela, & J. Phahlamohlaka (Eds.), *Proceedings of 11th IFIP TC 9 International Conference on Human Choice and Computers (HCC11 2014), Turku, Finland* (Vol. 431, pp. 92–106). Berlin, Heidelberg: Springer. doi:10.1007/978-3-662-44208-1

Pegrum, M., Oakley, G., & Faulkner, R. (2013). Schools going mobile: A study of the adoption of mobile handheld technologies in western Australian independent schools. *Australasian Journal of Educational Technology*, *29*(1), 66–81. doi:10.1234/ajet.v29i1.64

Pereira, O. R. E., & Rodrigues, J. J. P. C. (2013). Survey and Analysis of Current Mobile Learning Applications and Technologies. *ACM Computing Surveys*, *46*(2), 27:1–27:35. doi:10.1145/2543581.2543594

Powers, T. M. (2003). Real Wrongs in Virtual Communities. *Ethics and Information Technology*, *5*(4), 191–198. doi:10.1023/B:ETIN.0000017737.56971.20

Rachel, S., Cobcroft, R., Towers, S., Smith, J., & Bruns, A. (2006). Mobile Learning in Review: Opportunities and Challenges for Learners, Teachers, and Institutions. *Proceedings of the Online Learning and Teaching (OLT) Conference 2006*. doi:10.1016/S0190-9622(06)01179-0

Rawls, J. (1955). Two concepts of rules. *The Philosophical Review*, *64*(1), 3–32. doi:10.2307/2182230

Reynolds, R. (2012). Ethics and practice in virtual worlds. In J. R. Sageng, H. Fossheim, & T. M. Larsen (Eds.), *The Philosophy of Computer Games* (Vol. 7, pp. 143–158). Springer; doi:10.1007/978-94-007-4249-9_10

Robinson, D., & Garratt, C. (2000). *Introducing Ethics*. Totem Books.

Rosenberg, A. (2010). Virtual world research ethics and the private/public distinction. *International Journal of Internet Research Ethics*, *3*, 23–36.

Scacchi, W., Brown, C., & Nies, K. (2012). Exploring the Potential of Virtual Worlds for Decentralized Command and Control Point of Contact. *Proceedings of the 17th International Command and Control Research and Technology Symposium (ICCRTS 2012)*. DTIC Document.

Schroeder, R. (2008). Defining virtual worlds and virtual environments. *Journal of Virtual Worlds Research*, *1*(1).

Sharples, M., Taylor, J., & Vavoula, G. (2005). Towards a Theory of Mobile Learning. *Proceedings of mLearn*, *1*, 1–9.

Southern, M. (2001). The cultural study of games: More than just games. Retrieved from http://www-bcf.usc.edu/~anthonyb/itp101/articles/cultural.doc

Stephenson, N. (1992). *Snow Crash*. Random House Publishing Group.

Suslov, N. (2012). Krestianstvo SDK towards end-user mobile 3D virtual learning environment. *Proceedings of the 10th International Conference on Creating, Connecting and Collaborating through Computing, C5 2012* (pp. 9–14). doi:10.1109/C5.2012.8

Thompson, C. W. (2011). Next-Generation Virtual Worlds. *IEEE Internet Computing*, *15*(1), 60–65. doi:10.1109/MIC.2011.15

Wankel, C., & Malleck, S. (Eds.), (2009). *Emerging Ethical Issues of Life in Virtual Worlds*. Charlotte, NC, USA: Information Age Publishing.

Warren, S., & Lin, L. (2012). Ethical considerations for learning game, simulation, and virtual world design and development. In H. H. Yang & S. C.-Y. Yuen (Eds.), *Handbook of Research on Practices and Outcomes in Virtual Worlds and Environments* (Vol. 1). Hershey, PA, USA: IGI Global. doi:10.4018/978-1-60960-762-3.ch001

Yang, H. H., & Yuen, C.-Y. S. (Eds.). (2012). Handbook of Research on Practices and Outcomes in Virtual Worlds and Environments (Vol. 2). Hershey, PA, USA: IGI Global.

KEY TERMS AND DEFINITIONS

Ethics: Ethics is a branch of philosophy that conceptualizes right and wrong conduct in moral context. Ethics deals with morality, good vs. bad, right vs. wrong, virtue vs. vice, justice, legality, and crime.

Metaverse: Metaverse is the collective sum of all virtual worlds, virtual reality and augmented reality on the Internet.

MMOG: Massively Multiplayer Online Game refers to Internet or online based games that allow hundreds or thousands of players to play the game at the same time, mostly in competitive or collaborative pursuit of some goals.

MMORPG: Massively Multiplayer Online Role-Playing Games refers to Internet or online based games that encourage role-play among players such that players can choose and play different roles from ones available.

MMOSG: Massively Multiplayer Online Social Games refers to Internet or online based games that allow players to interact with social goals and practices such as community building and trading.

MUVE: Multi User Virtual Environment refers to virtual environments that can be accessed by multiple users at the same time and allow users to be aware of each other's' presence and interact with each other.

NPC: Non-player character is a persona or character in virtual games that is not controlled by any human player. Non-players characters are automated programs that usually employ artificial intelligence techniques.

Opensimulator: Opensimulator is an open-source software program for simulation of the virtual worlds and the metaverse. The Opensimulator program mainly refers to the server component that is hosted on the Internet. The users connect to this server using Openserver or compatible client program in order to participate and play in the virtual world hosted by Opensimulator.

Private Space: A private space is supposed to be only accessed by its intended audience, owner or originator.

Public Space: A public space is accessible to anyone whether it is a place, conversation or piece of information.

ScienceSim: ScienceSim is a virtual world grid hosted using the OpenSimulator platform. ScienceSim is created for scientists to showcase science-based visualizations to the users.

SecondLife: SecondLife is a 3D Interactive Virtual World developed and promoted by Linden Research Inc., also known as Linden Labs. Users can use SecondLife or compatible client program for accessing the virtual world. Although anyone can register for free, and there are lots of virtual world areas and objects available for free, but users can also buy, sell and trade stuff using virtual money called Linden dollars.

SecondLife Grid: The SecondLife Environment is known as Second Life Grid, where virtual residents create and own objects.

Virtual World: A virtual world is computer-based interactive simulation environment where users take the form of an avatar, own virtual assets, perform virtual actions and interact with other users and computer-controlled actors known as bots or non-player characters (NPC).

Chapter 13
Integrating Technological Innovations to Enhance the Teaching-Learning Process

Judi Simmons Estes
Park University, USA

Dong Hwa Choi
Park University, USA

Amber Dailey-Hebert
Park University, USA

ABSTRACT

Virtual reality is one of the latest technologies to be integrated into the teaching-learning process and it holds significant potential to enhance instructional processes and impact student learning. Historically, technology integration for instruction has been initiated primarily within institutions of higher education, while K-12 integration has been gradual to become part of mainstream education. Likewise, as teachers play a pivotal role in the process of technology integration, it is imperative to train teachers not only in computer literacy, but also in the requisite technological knowledge and skills needed to use technology in instruction. Furthermore, such training should be accompanied by support for teachers in developing a pedagogy and self-efficacy for technology integration. Self-efficacy can also serve as a foundation of motivation for teachers to keep abreast of new technologies and to determine how and when to use such emergent tools to enhance instruction.

AN INTRODUCTION TO VIRTUAL REALITY

Virtual Reality (VR) is a computer-generated environment designed to simulate three-dimensional (3D) physical environments that provide user interaction. Three-dimensional immersive virtual worlds are one of the most exciting technologies being used today and have been successfully implemented to promote learning in K-12 and higher education (Dickey, 2005a). Immersive VR, such as Oculus Rift and Magic Lead, have transformed education due to the ability to transport conventional learning environment to any virtual learning environment imaginable (Afshar, 2014). While these emergent technologies offer a unique venue to enact learning and practice skills, they also require teacher training, support, and opportunities for experimentation. Therefore, it is important to understand the broad scope through defining VR, identifying characteristics of VR, and describing VR in practice.

DOI: 10.4018/978-1-4666-9837-6.ch013

Defining Virtual Reality

While there are countless uses for VR in education and industry, there are equally as many definitions; definitions of VR have shifted as the related hardware and software applications have evolved, moving from a single user interface to massively multiplayer online worlds (MMOW). For example, in 1996 Schroeder first posited that computer-generated display allows or compels users to have a sense of being present in an environment, other than the one they are actually in, and to interact with that environment (Schroeder, 2008). By 2003, Sherman and Craig expanded the definition of VR when they defined it as "a medium composed of interactive computer simulation that senses the participant's position and actions and replaces or augments the feedback to one or more senses, giving the feeling of being mentally immersed or present in the simulation (a virtual world)" (p. 13). More recently, Kapp and O'Driscoll (2010) defined a virtual world as an "immersed 3D virtual environment in which a learner acts through an avatar to engage with the other avatars for the explicit purpose of learning" (p. 55). Hence, as the capabilities and applications of the VR functions have expanded, definitions and instructional uses for VR have changed. Often, visual, auditory, and other perceptual stimuli are incorporated within software and hardware applications of technology in a sequence of programmed events to which a person is expected to react.

The environment created through virtual reality is referred to as a virtual world (VW), virtual world environment (VWE), and/or a virtual world learning environment (VWLE). Simply, a VWE is an artificial physical environment created using digital technology viewed two-dimensionally (2D); a complex 3D environment contains digital objects and human avatars in real-time. VWLE's can accommodate a wider range of learning styles and goals, encourage collaborative and resource-based learning and allow greater sharing and re-use of resources (Britain, 1999). These VR environments are used to support multiple learning styles and encourage such collaborative exchange through social learning as well. This focus evolved when innovators of VR noticed that users were responsive to the collaborative community and in 2003, the immersive virtual world of Second Life was launched (Linden Lab, 2013), allowing users opportunities for interaction, exploration, and collaboration. In Second Life, the user typically has some digital representation of self, known as an avatar. Users create their own identity and embody themselves through their avatars and by representing self as avatars, users report feeling socially and psychologically connected (Biocca, Harms, & Burgoon, 2003). Additionally, users can interact and communicate with each other in real time by using voice and text chat and/or gestures. It is notable that Tokel and Karrats (2014) found Second Life was the most commonly used platform given that it was used in 85% of virtual world studies. As VWE's have evolved so have the characteristics of VR.

Characteristics of Virtual Reality

Designs of virtual worlds are quite diverse, ranging from the replication of real classrooms to imaginary worlds (Prasolova-Førland, 2008). Dickey (2005a) posited that 3-D virtual worlds typically share three features: 1) the illusion of 3-D space, 2) avatars that serve as visual representations of users and 3) an interactive chat tool for users to communicate with one another. Five years later, Hew and Cheung (2010) added a fourth feature; 4) the ability for a user to 'act' on the virtual world; this added feature provides the user with more opportunity for active engagement within the virtual world environment. For example, objects have properties that allow them to be taken or dropped, which makes it possible for students to learn by doing rather than simply learning by listening to the instructor or reading assigned content in a text. Bojonova (2011) suggested that through avatars, users can navigate, explore, create, and communicate in a virtual space as if it were an extension of the real world, but without the physical limitations and risk of the real world. One of the most attractive features of virtual worlds, and their use in learning environments, is the ability to extend beyond mere text and lecture to promote active learning, the application of knowledge and skills, and the ability to put learning into practice. Hence, VWs serve as optimal learning environments to promote the application of both content knowledge and procedural knowledge in a safe space (Noteborn, Dailey-Hebert, Bohle-Carbonell, & Gijselars, 2013).

Furthermore, VR promotes 'knowledge creating cultures' (Scardamalia & Bereiter, 2006), which allow learners to not only collaborate virtually, but to create and produce new knowledge and experiences together. Regardless of specific hardware, software, or uses for VR, Smart, Cascio and Paffendof (2007) found that while VWs may appear in different forms, they possess a number of recurrent features:

- Persistence of an in-world environment.
- Shared space allowing multiple users to participate simultaneously.
- Virtual embodiment in the form of an avatar (a 3-D representation of the self).
- Interactions that occur between users and objects in a 3-D environment.
- Immediacy of action such that interactions occur in real time.
- Similarities to the real world (topography, movement, physics); a sense of being in the environment.

Collectively, these features influence and have been influenced by the practices that evolved in using VR.

Virtual Reality in Practice

In 2007, the Horizon Report predicted a two to three year time frame for the adoption of virtual worlds in education (The New Media Consortium, 2007). Similarly, the subsequent Australia- New Zealand Horizon Report enthusiastically identified virtual worlds as "spaces for truly immersive forms of learning and for a level of collaboration that is erasing traditional boundaries and borders rapidly" (Johnson, Levine, & Smith, 2008, p. 6). In 2008 and again in 2009, virtual worlds in higher education were at the peak of their hype cycle (Lowendahl et al., 2008) and there was a prediction that 80% of Internet users would have an avatar in a virtual world by the end of 2011 (Stamford, 2007). However, despite the persistence of interest, and with the development of many teaching facilities in VWs, teaching in these environments has not become mainstream, and the numbers of educators using such environments for teaching is in fact decreasing. This is evidenced by the number of underutilized and disused builds that are seen in virtual worlds (Gregory et al., 2015). According to Tokel and Karratas (2014), in analyzing studies from 2008 through 2013, the results showed that participants in VW studies were higher education students (53%), adult learners (20%), primary students (7%), and secondary students (4%). While innovative uses of VR technologies is reportedly lagging in education, the potential and promise for innovative uses of such technologies is evident in fields other than education.

Today, outside of education, VR is being used to help rehabilitate stroke victims (Saposnik & Levin, 2011), to enhance the design and manufacturing process in industry (Ong & Nee, 2013), to train medical staff in a virtual clinical learning lab (Pulse Simulation Technology, 2008), to take a jury through a crime scene (Hullinger, 2015), and to customize a virtual shopping experience and explore merchandise from the comfort of one's own home (Chang, 2015). The possibilities, applications, and uses for virtual reality continue to be explored and continue to enhance these domains as a result. While VR and related technological knowledge has grown exponentially in the past two decades, the depth and breadth of knowledge on this subject remains relatively shallow and requires further development and research, particularly as it relates to *educational* applications. These applications are important to note because applications of VR in fields other than education may have educational applications.

EDUCATORS USE OF VIRTUAL REALITY

The world of education has changed from an orderly world of disciplines and courses to a world in which communication technologies are increasingly important. It is clear that we see a major restructuring of our social, industrial and educational institutions, and an increased reliance on telecommunications for work and education (Friedman, 2005;Molnar, 1990; Pink, 2006). When properly applied, technology can provide an effective means for learning; technologies are now available to significantly augment the skills that are necessary for the dynamic and globally connected workforce that exists today. For instance, within teacher preparation programs, the flexible and low impact affordance of a multi user virtual environment (MUVE) can allow teacher candidates to concentrate on certain discrete aspects of being a teacher, such as classroom management, conducting parent-teacher conferences, and application of instructional strategies without the need to attend to the myriad of other activities and responsibilities teachers take on during a normal teaching session or workday (Yilmaz, Topu, Goktas, & Coban, 2013).

The Importance of Pedagogy, Content, and Technology

Even though multiple benefits of using technology have been recognized, it needs to be noted that teachers' roles are easily misconceptualized or minimized when education technology is used. With every new technology tool or application, it is still teachers who figure out how to use technology for student learning According to Umbach and Wawrzynski (2005), "faculty behaviors and attitudes affect students profoundly, which suggests that faculty members may play the single-most important role in student learning" (p. 176). In order to use technology effectively in the classroom, teachers should be able to plan out a whole teaching process with relevant knowledge and skills in technology. These knowledge and skills have been discussed in a variety of ways including (1) technological pedagogical content knowledge as well as relevant knowledge of information and communication (AACTE, 2008) and (2) pedagogical technology integration of content knowledge (Brantley-Dias, Kinuthia, Shoffner, DeCastro, & Rigole, 2007).

The development of innovative technology-integrated pedagogy lies in a teacher's interpretation of the newly learned technology and the value of that technology to the instructional and learning process. Teachers are constantly making decisions about what learning experiences are going to most efficiently and effectively deliver content to students and which technology will augment the student experience. Huang, Rauch, and Liaw (2010) argued that, "educators or instructional designers, as they apply a new VR technology to educational settings, need to consider carefully how pedagogy or a learning theory may influence the learning process" (p. 1172). Studies on the integration of technology into classrooms have shown the importance of the presence of technology as well as the pedagogy-supported use of technology (Bozkurt, 2011). Indeed, the power to develop innovative technology supported pedagogy lies in the teacher's interpretation of the technology's value for instruction and leaning in the classroom.

This interpretation is mediated by past experience and accumulated knowledge (Bransford & Schwartz, 1999). Zhao, Pugh, and Sheldon (2002) noted that technological innovations perceived to be far from teacher's own practice are less likely to be established which means that effective technology integration depends on a consideration of the interactions among technology, content, and pedagogy. Teachers' pedagogical knowledge on how to utilize technology for particular content in a certain context plays a critical role in learning outcomes. For example, contrary to common assumptions that assert beginning teachers more easily integrate technology, experienced teachers who often have less technology experience are more poised to integrate technology simply because they possess more knowledge and experience with making connections between learning and the contexts of teaching (Zech, Gause-Vega, Bray, Secules, & Goldman, 2000).

If teachers are going to be able to prepare their students to be technologically capable, they need to have, at the very least, basic technology skills. This expectation is reflected in International Society for Technology in Education (ISTE, 2008) National Educational Technology Standards for Teachers (NETS-T), which were first published in 1998. As seen below, the NETS-T define a set of pedagogical knowledge and skills that teacher are expected to demonstrate in the digital age.

- Facilitate and inspire student learning and creativity: Teachers use their knowledge of subject matter, teaching and learning, and technology to facilitate experiences that advance student learning, creativity, and innovation in both face-to-face and virtual environments.
- Design and develop digital age learning experiences and assessments: Teachers design, develop, and evaluate authentic learning experiences and assessments incorporating contemporary tools and resources to maximize content learning in context and to develop the knowledge, skills, and attitudes identified in the Standards.
- Model digital age work and learning: Teachers exhibit knowledge, skills, and work processes representative of an innovative professional in a global and digital society.
- Promote and model digital citizenship and responsibility: Teachers understand local and global societal issues and responsibilities in an evolving digital culture and exhibit legal and ethical behavior in their professional practices.
- Engage in professional growth and leadership: Teachers continuously improve their professional practice, model lifelong learning, and exhibit leadership in their school and professional community by promoting and demonstrating the effective use of digital tools and resources. (ISTE, 2015)

The importance of teacher competency in applying technology with sound pedagogical knowledge for particular content is well recognized by Cerniamo et al. (2010, p. 10). According to Cerniamo et al. in order for "optimal" technology integration to occur, teachers need to know how to:

- Identify which technologies are needed to support specific curricular goals.
- Specify how the tools will be used to help students meet and demonstrate those goals.
- Enable students to use appropriate technologies in all phases of the learning process including exploration, analysis, and production.
- Select and use appropriate technologies to address needs, solve problems, and resolve issues related to their own professional practice and growth.

To successfully teach in VWs, educators must not only learn the skills to use the space but also to understand ways in which pedagogy is involved (Smith-Robbins, 2011). For example, upon initial use of a VR tool, educators often use virtual worlds primarily as a replacement to an instructional strategy typically used, in order to first explore the feasibility of using the virtual tool, before using VWs technology as a new and innovative experience (Hughes, 2005). However, it is important for educators to move beyond using technology simply to support lecture-based instruction; using VWs as a replacement technology is not recommended best practice (Lawless & Pellegrino, 2007; Partnership for 21st Century Skills, 2007).

Further expanding upon these pedagogical understandings, "heutagogy" is a learner-centered approach that builds on the theory of constructivism and self-determined learning (Hase, 2013). In more recent years, heutagogy has seen innovation through the application of VR and other e-learning to apply competencies to situations through learner generated content, personal empowerment, and learner centric training programs suggesting the importance of the learner and educator simultaneously in such co-created, co-experienced learning environments (Blaschke & Hase, 2015).

Virtual Reality to Support Student Learning

Today's learners are 'digital natives' (Prensky, 2001) who have grown accustomed to the integration of technology in all aspects of life: for entertainment, communication, consumerism, and education. What makes digital natives unique is their ability to create and produce new knowledge in globally networked collaborative groups, rather than simply absorbing existing knowledge. As such, the experiential elements of learning in the VW are particularly appealing. Falloon (2009) stated, "The multimedia capabilities of virtual learning environments cater for a range of learning preferences and styles, enhancing engagement and enabling learners to set their own pace and blend the range of audio, video, graphic and text-based resources to match their own informational needs" (p. 112). This type of individualized learning pathway offers a more customized educational experience that is more specific to the learner's needs. For educational purposes, 3-D virtual worlds make accessing information easier, and can increase the motivation of users by engaging them actively in a learning process (Mishra, 2009).

While VR can provide customized learning for the individual, it also offers opportunities for collaborative knowledge sharing and exchange, each of which is valued by today's learners. Therefore, features of 3-D environments, such as interactions between users and between individual users and the environment, increase the users' learning capacities through participation in the provided activities, and the feeling of truly being in the environment (Mishra, 2009). Student engagement is influenced by the feeling students get when they are present in the classroom and connected with peers and teacher. The concept of presence has been defined by Slater and Wilbur (1997) as the subjective feeling and psychological sense of "being present" in the VR environment. Slater and Steed (2000) suggested that a feeling of presence determines the level of immersion felt by each individual; level of immersion relates to a sense of feeling and behaving as if in a real world environment and the consequent learning that occurs from the VR experience. The sense of being present can vary person-to-person while in the same digital environment (Bowman & McMahan, 2007), however, the concept of presence is a key element in research related to VR effectiveness (Schuemie, Van Der Straaten, Krijn, &Van der Mast, 2001). In VW 3D environments, users enjoy exploring the simulated environment simultaneously with other users. In a sense, participation in the virtual environment is a social activity, while separated in real-life, a connectivity occurs through the interactions that the avatars have with one another and/or through exploring the VLE with others (Biocca, Harms, & Burgoon, 2003). Users who have fun, are interactive, and cooperate within 3-D virtual worlds tend to be more motivated (Arya, Hartwick, Graham, & Nowlan, 2011) and pay attention for longer durations of time (Bouta, Retalis, & Paraskeva, 2012). Through the use of collaborative communities, which are found in VR, the value of peers as lifelong teachers is often demonstrated.

Promoting Critical Thinking and Problem-Solving Skills

Technology can support the development of problem-solving and critical thinking, as well as working within a collaborative community. There has been a major paradigm shift in education from theories of "learning" to theories of "cognition." Cognitive science approaches teaching and learning in a different way. It addresses how the human, as an information processor, functions and uses information. Rather than focusing on teaching facts through expository lectures or demonstrations, the emphasis is, instead, on developing higher-order, thinking and problem-solving skills. The cognitive approach is important because it recognizes human information processing strengths and weaknesses, and the limits of human perception and memory in coping with the information explosion. It focuses, instead, on organizing information to fit human capacity, and has changed the emphasis in education from learning to thinking (Gagne, 1980; Reinick, 1983). In information processing, VR contributes to make information concrete, highly visual, and/or spatial, especially for those who experience difficulties in processing merely abstract, verbal, or lineal information or those who prefer graphs, images, or more interactive ways of data collection. VR provides highly interactive and direct operations by the action of the learner (Barilli, 2012).

Educators in higher education positively influence student cognitive growth, development, and persistence of college; and model intellectual work, promote mastery of knowledge and skills, and help students make connections between their studies and post-graduate plans (NSSE, 2014).

Living in an unscripted future, in which it is difficult to predict, anticipate, or prepare for the uncertain workplace that waits, it becomes more imperative to strengthen such technological competencies (Dailey-Hebert, Donnelli-Sallee, & DiPadova-Stocks, 2008). For example, Thomas Frey (a senior Futurist at the DaVinci institute and Google's top rated futurist speaker) identified 55 jobs of the future jobs that do not even exist today but which will most likely be created by 2020. Some jobs include: augmented reality architects, global systems architects, business colony managers, avatar designers, etc. (Frey, n.d.). The majority of these 55 jobs would benefit from experience learning and working in VR. More recently, researchers have found that learning in the VR environment may even translate to greater success in the workplace (Heili & Michel, 2011). Furthermore, as knowledge workers today have more flexibility and mobility in the spaces in which they work (Moravec, 2008), becoming proficient in such tools will be a marketable and important skillset to possess. While technology can increase productivity of students and teachers, it can be related to more than productivity when integrated with instruction. These are skills that are also beneficial in the workplace, particularly one that requires a more highly skilled work force with a broader education and a greater familiarity with the tools and theories of science. Competitiveness depends not only on the discovery of new innovations, but the speed at which that knowledge is transmitted through our educational systems, to create highly skilled workers who can apply knowledge, critical thinking, and problem-solving skills. To achieve the kinds of technology uses required for 21st century teaching and learning, educators need to understand how to use technology to facilitate meaningful learning (Lai, 2008), and may need professional development to gain the requisite skills.

The Benefits of Professional Development

Technology is not consistently being used to support student-centered active learning and other kinds of instruction believed to be most powerful (ISTE, 2008; Partnership for 21st Century Learning, 2007). Rogers (2003) theorized that individual adoption rates of technological innovations can be visually represented with a bell-shaped curve with representing five categories of users: (a) innovators (2.5%), (b) early adopters (13.5%), (c) early majority (34%), (d) late majority (34%), and (e) laggards (2.5%). Professional development and training opportunities can support all educators but especially those who are classified as 'late majority' 'laggards' in adopting new technologies.

Working with colleagues in a professional learning community can provide a support system that can be invaluable to a teacher learning a new set of technology skills (Ertmer, Ottenbreit-Leftwich, & York, 2006). Participating in a professional learning community can be a supportive experience for teachers and contribute to their confidence and sense of self-efficacy (Putnam & Borko, 2000). ISTE placed an emphasis on collegial *community* in a white paper, *Technology, Coaching, and Community,* which emphasizes the value of having a technology coach within a school setting (Beglau et al., 2011). The technology coach essentially establishes and nurtures a professional learning community of teachers. These learning communities enable their members to share ideas and resources among each other, to create a shared knowledge base of best practices, and to provide "a sense of collective accountability" (Wong, 2010, p. 633).

ISTE (2011, p. 16) offers ten strategies in creating a transformational professional development model inclusive of technology, coaching and community.

- Learning with Technology Is More Important Than Learning about Technology: Technology should be used to increase skills and expand or enhance learning across all skills and subject areas.
- Relevance Wins: Adult learners learn best when knowledge is relevant. Position your program as an opportunity for teachers to improve their craft based upon their own needs and interests.
- Keep Millennial in Mind: Develop a millennial point of view. Give younger teachers learning opportunities that meet their learning styles: collaborative, on-line, and technology-driven.
- Relationships Matter: Allow coaches to build trust one teacher at a time. Your collaborative, technology-rich coaching presence should be perceived as a personal trainer, not an unwelcomed monitor.
- Be Inclusive: Don't work on your own. Tap into your school or district's professional development agenda when developing your technology coaching plan.
- Trust the Process: Implementation dips are likely to occur, yet sticking with a long-term plan that allows for iterative improvement over time yields stronger results than one-off skill-building events.
- Share Your Progress: One of the key indicators an administrator uses to determine the success of a professional development program is seeing that teachers are actually implementing what they are learning. Having an active communication plan to report progress and successes is crucial.
- Make the Most of Your Time: Coaching programs are having success regardless of whether they allow for full time coaches or peer-embedded support with other practicing teachers. Put your best thinking forward in determining a process that will work within budget and time variables.

- Take Technology Mainstream: Every professional development initiative can benefit from the integration of technology. Together, you're better.
- Leverage the World: Resist the temptation to reinvent the wheel. Use technology, coaching methods, and learning communities as "power partners" to tap into existing resources, experts, and support structures.

Having a readily available support system for building professional knowledge and integrating new knowledge with practice can be beneficial to all teachers and particularly those new to the profession and/or with limited experience. It is important to note that one time workshops are not as effective as a system of on-going professional development, in regard to being most effective in supporting teachers' ability to develop the knowledge, skills, new teaching strategies, and technology integration change in classrooms (Cifuentes, Maxwell, & Bulu, 2011). Ideally, effective professional development provides teachers a "new set of experiences, skills, resources, and knowledge that will support them as they implement the ideas they have studied in the field" (Holmes, Signer, & MacLeod, 2010, p. 76). The practice and application of professional development is particularly important, as applying technology to content specific learning goals helps a teacher integrate new technology knowledge and skills more easily. Ideally, participating in professional development that is collaborative and subject specific, within technology inquiry groups, supports a teacher's ability to integrate technology into their subject areas. (Hughes, 2005).

eMINTS: Professional Development for Integrating Technology Into Instruction

Currently, institutions of higher education faculty have not universally accepted and employed the practice of a learner-centered approach to teaching (Weimer, 2010), nor have they integrated technology into their own teacher practice. A model has been developed to support teachers in the acquisition of skills so that they will, in turn, provide students with assignments that integrate the use of technology; Enhancing Missouri's Instructional Networked Teaching Strategies (e-MINTS) is a model of learner-centered instruction powered by technology, for P-20 classrooms (see Estes, 2015). The eMINTS National Center at the University of Missouri, is a non-profit organization that has provided comprehensive research-based professional development services to educators since 1999. eMINTS professional development uses interactive group sessions and in-classroom coaching/mentoring to help teachers integrate technology into their teaching using an instructional model that a) authentic learning, b) high-quality lesson design, c) community of learners, and d) powered by technology.

- **Authentic Learning:** Through the use of real-world projects, students become problem-solvers, collaborators, critical thinkers, inventors, and creators. Through the use of global content, students begin to ask and think about their world in new and innovative ways.
- **High-Quality Lesson Design:** The best teaching and learning take place inclassrooms where teachers value self-directed learning. Through the use of varied instructional and assessment strategies teachers have the opportunity to create the kinds of lessons that meet the needs of learners.
- **Community of Learners:** Fundamental to eMINTS practice is the community of learners, not only within the classroom, but also among teachers and among trainers, as well as showing students how continuous life-long learning takes place in a community. eMINTS helps teachers and other participants learn the importance of building a community of learners where learners share,

take risks, respect and push each other as they find their own best ways to learn and engage in deep content with one another.

- **Powered by Technology:** Seamless integration of technology with authentic learning and differentiated instruction bring about true learning. Technology adds excitement and motivation for students and teachers as they use digital tools to enhance and expand learning beyond the classroom walls. (eMINTS National Center, 2014).

Teachers trained in e-MINTS self-report improvement in their inquiry-based teaching activities, their computer use, and their perception of their own computer skills (Office of Social and Economic Data Analysis, 2001). Integrating the e-MINTS model into teacher preparation curriculum is inclusive of professional development that has been found to be most effective: training occurs over a two year period, using a cohort model, and with mentoring to meet needs of the individual attendees, as well as an annual national conference to keep abreast of emerging technology and applications. Through the process of developing a skill base in using technology to enhance instruction, seeds of self-efficacy become rooted for many educators.

Educators, Technology, and Self-Efficacy

A teacher's belief structure about teaching and learning is one of the most important factors in determining whether or not a teacher will take steps to integrate technology into instruction (Becker, 2001; Hernández -Ramos, 2005; Windschitl & Sahl, 2002). Although teachers might believe that technology helps them to be more efficient in completing personal and professional tasks, teachers tend to be hesitant to incorporate technology tools into instruction for a variety of reasons including the lack of relevant knowledge (Lawless & Pellegrino, 2007), low self-efficacy (Mueller et al., 2008), and existing belief systems (Subramaniam, 2007). In addition, time to learn how to use new technology, the lack of training in the use of new technology, and the unreliability of technology were significant inhibitors to the adoption of technology integration strategies (Cuban, Kirkpatrick, & Peck, 2001). Rogers (2003) posited that adapting to innovative practices is a social process and that "an important factor regarding the adoption rate of an innovation is its compatibility with the values, beliefs, and past experiences of individuals in the social system" (p. 4).

Bandura (1997) discussed the idea of self-efficacy as having confidence in one's abilities to organize and execute an action; self-efficacy is a kind of self-confidence. Although knowledge of technology is necessary, it won't be enough if teachers don't also feel confident using that knowledge to facilitate student learning. In a survey of 764 teachers, Wozney, Venkatesh, and Abrami (2006), found that one of the two greatest predictors of teachers' technology use was their confidence that they could achieve instructional goals using technology. This suggests that time and effort should be devoted to increasing teachers' confidence for using technology, not just to accomplish administrative and communicative tasks, but to facilitate student learning.

Teacher's competency for technology plays a critical role in using technology in instruction has been addressed. "Although computer related variables, in general, continue to impact a teachers' ability to integrate technology, it is through positive experiences with computers in the classroom context, that build a teacher's belief in computer technology and confidence in its potential as an instructional tool" (Mueller, Wood, Willoughby, Ross, & Specht, 2008, p.1533). There are many variables that contribute to a teacher's sense of self-efficacy in regard to using technology integrated instruction. One of these variables is allowing enough time for teachers to familiarize with technology by manipulating it (Somekh, 2008). Being introduced to a new technology and gaining skills is not enough; there must be time to gain confidence through experimenting and learning the nuances of the technology. When teachers are taught technological knowledge and skills, but do not have an opportunity to relate the knowledge and skills to the instruction they provide for students, the meaning of the experience can be lost. When given opportunities to apply knowledge and skills learned in small steps and applied in small successful experiences, teacher confidence increases. Additionally, providing successful experience in technology, support systems through peer interaction or leaning community, or customized professional training contribute to developing teachers' self-competency in technology (Ertmer & Ottenbreit-Leftwich, 2010).

Institutional Support

As early as 1991, Fullan and Stiegelbauer discussed the process of change that teachers often experience as they began to explore technology integration with instruction; the dimensions of

change involved (a) beliefs, attitudes, or pedagogical ideologies; (b) content knowledge; (c) pedagogical knowledge of instructional practices, strategies, methods, or approaches; and (d) novel or altered instructional resources, technology, or materials. When institutional systems are put into place to support teachers in these four dimensions of change, teachers will be more likely to be interested in learning the requisite knowledge and skills and have the motivation to invest needed time, energy, and effort in the process of integrating technology with the teaching-learning process. Given that it can take five years for a teacher to evolve from a direct instruction teacher to a constructivist teacher (Ertmer, 1999), providing institutional support and guidance is needed when teachers are first employed.

Implementing a VR environment affects several different stakeholders in the educational environment including students, faculty, and instructional technology personnel (Miller, 2014). In addition, institutional leadership also become stakeholders due to the expense of technology involved (particularly when providing a VR environment) and also require any VR implementation to be consistent with the mission and vision of the institution. A significant opportunity for school leadership is to create, with teachers, a shared vision for technology integration with the teaching-learning process. This shared vision should place emphasis on including technology as part of the definition of effective teaching. This can be achieved by creating standardized expectations that are articulated through professional development plans that include a technology component.

Giving teachers an opportunity to engage in professional goal setting, specifically related to technology is important (Somekh, 2008). Undoubtedly, a lack of resources and support can be a barrier to teacher technology use (Hew & Brush, 2007) and contribute to lack of faculty interest, use, and innovative endeavors. One suggested reason for the disinterest is the lack of support educators are afforded, in terms of technical and pedagogical support or provision of additional time to develop virtual world lessons (Smith-Robbins, 2011). As has been described earlier, technology is ever changing and the need for faculty growth and development is on-going. Not only do teachers need to continually keep themselves abreast of technology advances, teachers must be supported to decide how the learned knowledge and skills can be used within the instructional process to most efficiently and effectively engage students and teach content.

VIRTUALY REALITY: PAST, PRESENT, & FUTURE

Within schools, effectively integrating technology into instruction has been ever evolving. There have always been 'early adopters' of innovation (initiated by a few), and gradual adaptations of innovation by many. Technology integration into instruction is actually a developmental process with more than a 70-year history, receiving policy and fiduciary support from governmental agencies in some instances. In this section, a brief history of emergent technology use in education will be presented, followed by some of today's most innovative projects, and developments that we can anticipate in the future.

Emergent Technology Adoption in Education: A Brief History (1944-2015)

Today, Silicon Valley is viewed as the U.S. birthplace of technological innovations. However, institutions of higher education have been the historical venues of new technological knowledge. In fact, the first operational computer was introduced in 1944 at Harvard with early educational uses primarily occurring within departments of mathematics, science and engineering for the purposes of critical thinking and problem-solving (Levien, 1972). As early as 1954, B. F. Skinner combined his theories related to direct instruction and programmed learning to provide students with individualized instruction; the skill base of each student was targeted and sequentially higher level skills were provided based on successful responses. Skinner referred to the technology that he developed as *teaching machines* (https://www.youtube.com/watch?v=jTH3ob1IRFo).

Shortly thereafter, the U.S. National Defense Education Act legislation made money available for new technology in schools, primarily in vocational education (http://web.csulb.edu/~murdock/histofcs.html). In 1959, at the University of Illinois, Donald Bitier began the first, large-scale project for the use of computers in education, serving elementary school reading programs, a community college, and undergraduate programs (Office of Technology Assessment, 1982). In 1963, only 1% of U.S. secondary schools used computers for instructional purposes, by 1974, 55% of the schools had access to computers, over two million students used computers in their classes and 23% of these classrooms were using computers primarily for instruction (Molnar, 1975).

The Office of Technology Assessment, established in 1972, was intended to provide Congress with objective and authoritative analysis of the complex scientific and technical issues of the late 20th century. A report, *Teachers and Technology: Making the Connection* (Office of Technology Assessment, 1995), included one chapter focused specifically on *Helping Teachers Learn About and Use Technology Resources* (https://www.princeton.edu/~ota/ns20/year_f.html), recognizing the importance of training teachers (as the person responsible) for integrating technology into instruction.

In 1981, IBM became the first mainframe manufacturer to develop a personal computer (PC) used primarily for drill & practice, and by 1986, 25% of high schools used PCs for college and career guidance, while K-8 schools were primarily buying Apple II and Macintosh computers (http://web.csulb.edu/~murdock/histofcs.html). In 1992, the Office of Science and Technology Policy (OSTP), a department of the Executive Office of the President, initiated a government-wide effort to dramatically expand the U.S. portion of the Internet; the purpose was interconnecting the nation's educational infrastructure to its knowledge and information centers so that all may could share access to digital libraries, databases and diverse scientific instruments (OSTP, 1992).

As early as 1994, digital video, VR, and 3-D systems captured the attention of many business professionals. Digital video systems were the forerunners of VR emerging as a new paradigm in computer technology. Object-oriented authoring systems such as HyperCard, Hyperstudio, and Authorware were growing in popularity and use, particularly as a resource for instructional delivery by teachers, however in many K-12 schools there was a lack of availability to students (http://web.csulb.edu/~murdock/histofcs.html). The original educational intent of VR was for the learner to interact with electronically generated artificial environments as if they were real and to develop procedural knowledge in the process. In early 1990, Howard Rheingold expanded the concept and use of VR to the gaming industry (Rheingold, 1991; Mazuryk & Gervautz, 1996) but the cost and clunky nature of VR goggles and data gloves inhibited mass adoption during the 90's (Virtual Reality, n.d.).

The Internet did not became commercialized and decommissioned until 1995 (Harris & Gerich, 1996) and as the internet grew in access, capability, and use, so did the VR movement. Such developments and applications highlighted the need to consider the future of VR from both the technical and social aspects (Mazuryk & Gervautz, 1996). By 2000 innovators of VR noticed that users were responsive to the collaborative community and in 2003, the less immersive virtual world of Second Life was launched (Linden Lab, 2013), where they could create their own avatars and socialize in a virtual space together. It is evident that between 1997 and today, the growth of the internet has expanded far faster than most predicted, becoming the world's largest database of information, graphics, and streaming video, making it an invaluable resource for educators.

Virtual Reality in Education Today: Challenges and Opportunities

Hew and Cheung (2010) conducted a literature review of the uses of VR in K-12 and higher education and found that the majority of studies were conducted in polytechnics and university settings (69%), followed by secondary schools (19%) and primary schools (12%). Within polytechnic and university settings, Hew and Cheung identified VR research in the following content areas: media arts (18.8%), health and environment (18.8%), education (12.5%), commerce (12.5%), computing (12.5%), others (12.5%), teaching of foreign language (6.3%), and librarianship (6.3%). In this study and others, not only do we see a low adoption rate for VR technology in education and across the disciplines, we also see the need to identify overarching challenges and opportunities that exist to implement VR.

Challenges

There remains a paucity of literature documenting the challenges in adapting VR technologies to the teaching and learning curriculum (Woods, 2009). The learning curve is steep for building knowledge, skills, and application for integration of VR with instruction. Having a research base to draw from would be an asset. For example, a scoping study undertaken in Australia and New Zealand reviewed and analyzed the use of 3D virtual worlds in teaching and learning in higher education and various categories of challenges were formulated from the feedback collected from educators using virtual worlds, including "[lack of] technology, support, funding and time, usability and familiarity, equity and ethics, inherent limitations of virtual worlds, acceptance of virtual worlds, and management and planning" (Dalgarno, Gregory, Carlson, Lee, & Tyson, 2013, p. 10).

A second challenge, and another related to research is that unfortunately, the literature that should help to inform our education and training tends to be dated and limiting in study design and global scope. In a comprehensive review of the literature, Hew and Cheung (2010) located 470 papers, but 455 were discarded because they were opinion papers, conceptual papers, non-empirical descriptions of program implementations, or non-K-12 and higher education related; finally fifteen papers were located, with fourteen of the fifteen using descriptive research methodology. A variety of data collection methods were used in the descriptive research, including questionnaire (most frequently used), interviews, observations, online log files (e.g., chat transcripts) and one study used exam scores. Only one study used an experimental design (Holmes, 2007).

A third challenge is that the diversity and global scale of VR related studies are scant. Hew and Cheung (2010) in their review of the literature found a majority of the studies located (87%) involved participants from countries in North America and Europe, compared with other countries. There is a continual need to study participants in other countries in order to better understand how different geographical contexts might influence the use of virtual worlds differently, and this continues to be a significant limiting factor in the study of VR.

Fourth, despite early projections for innovative applications, VR, avatar-centric environments have not yet resulted in a mainstream adoption among educators (Waters, 2014). Likewise, students also face a steep learning curve and difficulty in adoption of VR. Student dislikes related to virtual world technology include: (a) inability to access the virtual world environment through older computers, (b) technical requirements involving the need for robust computing and Internet connectivity, (c) general prohibition of the use of such virtual world software in public computers, (d) having to instantaneously formulate answers and responses and needing fast typing skills in order to communicate textually through the chat tool, (e) no provision of turn taking or threaded discussion because of the chat function and (f) unfamiliarity with the virtual world software (Dickey, 2005b; Miller, 2014).

A final challenge is keeping pace with the constant state of flux and advancements within the field of emergent technologies. As VR technologies continue to morph, advance, and evolve, it is likely that the definitions and their applications will also continue to evolve – hence, the more challenging it becomes to remain current and properly trained on such developments as they occur. Therefore, a significant need exists which focuses on more support, training, and access for students and educators.

Opportunities

While there is no question that challenges exist for the adoption of educational innovations for VR use, the opportunities that exist in the realm of VR and learning are exponential with many examples within the chapters of this book. There is significant growth in the use of VR within academic organizations for offering virtual campus tours, the expansion of digital libraries, institutional museums and much more. Some leaders in innovation who seek to provide a more rich understanding of VR include Stanford's *Virtual Human Interaction Lab*. With numerous projects and dozens of publications, they investigate topics related to social issues, interactions, and applications for VR. (https://vhil.stanford.edu/pubs/) (Ahn, Bostick, Ogle, & Bailenson, 2015; Cummings & Bailenson, 2015). Standford is not alone in dedicated work to better understand and explore the VR space for learning. The University of Minnesota's *Virtual Realty Design Lab* represents an interdisciplinary partnership between the College of Design and Computer Science & Engineering for a six-year project focused on a more immersive experience using perception headsets to investigate the learning effects of "Social VR". (http://vr.design.umn.edu).

Other academic institutions are also leading the way to explore this unknown frontier, such as the University of Southern California's *Institute for Creative Technologies* Medical Virtual Reality Group, that specializes in mental health therapy, motor and cognitive skills rehabilitation, assessment, and clinical skills training (http://medvr.ict.usc.edu). Today, these immersive learning-scapes have become quite popular particularly in medical and engineering programs that require the practical application of skills or the building and modeling of a design. The medical profession has typically served as an early adopter of emergent technologies and has been proactive in their uses for VR as well. One example includes the work of PULSE (developed in part by Texas A&M University Corpus Christi), a simulation game for health care professionals that "allows them to train and practice on avatars without the risk of harming patients. Players work in virtual hospitals where they respond to emergency situations to diagnose and treat patients at they would in the real world" (http://www.healthgamesresearch.org/games/pulse-the-virtual-clinical-learning-lab). Many universities and learning institutions are not only using VR in practice, but are dedicating research centers and funding collaborative efforts to support the expansion of such work on their campuses.

In regard to strategies that support educators, the concept of a virtual technology coach and its potential to support NETS*C (National Educational Technology Standards for Coaches) still needs to be considered in future studies (Sugar & Slagter van Tryon, 2014). Virtual communities of practices for teachers (e.g., Lewis, Koston, Quartley, & Adsit, 2011) have been offered in an online setting. A key facet of school technology integration needs point to the alignment between the NETS*C, International Society for Technology in Education's (2012) education coach standards for skills necessary in promoting teachers' classroom integration of technology, and the apparent value teachers place on their ability to learn more deeply about technology integration within a collaborative community. To better support and offer additional training and guidance, we also see potential for avatar-based, avatar-led instruction and training on demand through e-coaching (Warner, 2012). Such options could utilize VR to train educators on VR, which could be attractive for busy professionals (like teachers) and could offer hands-on experience using the virtual world from the learner perspective.

Research suggests that students like using the virtual worlds because of the following reasons: the ability to fly and move around freely in a 3-D space, to socialize and meet new people and to experience virtual field trips and simulated experiences (e.g., learners, in a sense, were embodied in the learning content and context (Dickey, 2005b), as opposed to the traditional flat, one-dimensional, text-driven digital displays. In addition to the content and procedural knowledge students can develop using VR, it helps to better prepare learners for the unscripted future they face, a future that is dynamic and constantly changing as a result of emergent technologies that shape it (Dailey-Hebert, Donnelli-Sallee, & DiPadova-Stocks, 2008). Providing a state-of-the- art learning experience for students will not only benefit the colleges and universities in their competitive environment, but also aid in preparing students for their entry into the workforce (Miller, 2014). This opportunity provides one key to moving forward with a vision for the future of virtual reality in education.

Moving Forward: A Vision for the Future of Virtual Reality in Education

A vision for the future of virtual reality in education can be highlighted by a few examples of curricular innovations that are and will continue to, shape the future of VR as we currently know it and beyond.

Innovative Education

Innovative Education is an initiative developed in Icelandic Schools with the InnoEd Project, a virtual learning environment with European schools; the purpose is to provide a pedagogical model, based on the use of a virtual reality learning environments, with supporting internet and database technologies to facilitate virtual classrooms on the web (Thorsteinsson & Page, 2008). "Of particular interest are the emphases within Innovative Education on: ethical issues, the motivational potential of close relationships with the students' home environment, ideation, use of Information and Communications Technology to support and develop ideation, communication through use of posters, presentations and internet presentations" (p. 33).

GemInGame

VR expansion into the gaming world grew significantly and continues to be the most popular application of VR reality today (Chouhan & Sharma, 2015). For example, KZero's radar charts indicate that the number of virtual worlds and Massively Multiplayer On-line Role Playing Games (MMORPGs) totaled 900 as of 2013; KZero's universe chart revealed 1,899 million registered users in virtual worlds and massively multiplayer online games (MMOs) as of 2013 (KZero, 2013). Given the popularity and engagement of such VR games, serious games as a learning tool have emerged and been effective at shaking up the slow to adapt world of academia and having positive affects in the workplace (Heili & Michel, 2011; Michel, 2013). In Grenoble France, professors developed a new curriculum they call *GemInGame*, in which students create, develop, and co-brand serious games as part of their curriculum. They are able to partner with external organizations in the area to create and co-brand serious games for employee training – giving students the opportunity to not only engage in a gaming system for the sake of learning, but to create and produce new serious games for market in the VR environment.

Oculus Rift

Oculus Rift is an evolving technology that was created in 2012, as a head-mounted display device that is worn like goggles to experience an immersive virtual world experiences. Already a leader in virtual reality technology, the Oculus company was purchased by the social media leader Facebook in 2014; CEO Mark Zuckerberg blogged, "We're going to make Oculus a platform for many other experiences. Imagine enjoying a courtside seat at a game, studying in a classroom of students and teachers all over the world, or consulting with a doctor face-to-face (The Associated Press, 2014, para.1). The technology is being explored by several universities as a tool for taking a virtual tour of campus. An example can be viewed of a Yale University tour using the YouVisit virtual tour site (http://www.youvisit.com/tour/yale). While some technical problems remain and scalability for the general market continues to be a problem, there is promise for using such tools to enhance the educational teaching-learning process in the future.

CAVE Automatic Virtual Environment

Although it was originally presented in1992, the CAVE system holds promise for more mainstream uses of virtual reality and scientific visualization. Individual immersion in a VR environment is actualized through using immersive display devices, such as a head-mounted display. The device has a small optic display/screen in front of each eye in which the user sees a pre-programmed 3-D environment. Another example is the Cave Automatic Virtual Environment (CAVE). A CAVE system, when programmed well, can closely represent an environment by highly resembling the real world in full-scale. One advantage of using a CAVE system is that it allows the user to move naturally in the space surrounded by digitally created environmental cues. When users are immersed in a VR environment, they can interact in real time with digital objects and avatars. CAVE assures superior quality and resolution of viewed images, and a wider field of view in comparison to HMD based systems (Mazuryk & Gervautz, 1996).

Scalable Game Design

Alexander Repenning, Director of Scalable Game Design (SGD), housed at the University of Colorado in Boulder leads a 15 year effort to reinvent computer science education in public schools through game design starting at the middle school level (http://sgd.cs.colorado.edu/wiki/Scalable_Game_Design_wiki). SGD teachers computational thinking and critical thinking as well as problem-solving during the process of teaching students and teachers how to program virtual reality games. With over 10,000 students hundreds of teacher K-16, taking the SGD training, SGD is conducting the largest US study of computer science education which included middle schools in urban core areas, remote rural areas, and Native American communities (http://scalablegamedesign.cs.colorado.edu). Computational thinking tools that have evolved as game and simulation authoring systems include AgentSheets™ for two-dimensional games and AgentCubes™ for three-dimensional games (see Repenning, Webb, & Ioannidou, 2012). Results indicate that students, across genders and ethnicities, are not only highly motivated to learn computer science through game design but they also learn essential computational thinking skills. (Webb, Repenning, & Kuh, 2012).

Mobility of Virtual Reality

One final opportunity to consider involves the mobility of VR. While former VR accessories, such as clunky headgear or gloves, made accessibility cost prohibitive and intimidating, breakthroughs just this year plan to make VR accessible as never before. Advances in VR now plan to offer an accessory such as goggles, compatible with a cell phone, that allow for the VR experience (Pierce, 2015) which provides an untethered mobile experiences, immersing users with 360 panoramic views, and applications available from the Oculus VR app stores.

The cell phones and mobile device revolution, being merged with the VR revolution, is the next marriage of innovation that will also offer affordability and accessibility.

CONCLUSION

The premise of this chapter is that integrating VR into the teaching-learning cycle is a next step in a historical and on-going process of determining ways in which technology innovations can enhance instructional processes and student learning outcomes. The purpose of education is not simply for students to acquire knowledge and skills, but to be interested and engaged in the learning process, to successfully collaborate with peers, to develop critical thinking and problem-solving skills to tackle unforeseen challenges, and to view self as a life-long learner who is capable of applying knowledge and skills to real-life situations. The utilization of VR to promote such development has been evident in the past and holds great promise for the future, as the evolution of technology tools, features, and functionalities continues to evolve.

Educators play a pivotal role in the process of technology integration. In spite of the fiduciary impact on institutions when educators are not motivated and able to stay current in their knowledge of technological advances and strategies for integration into instruction, there is a paucity of institutional support, training, and professional development opportunities provided for K-12 and higher education educators.

Needed educator support includes not only requisite technology skill development, but as importantly providing guidance in the process of developing pedagogy and self-efficacy for technology integration. What is desperately needed is for educators to be motivated to keep abreast of new technologies and to have the self-efficacy to determine how and when to use such emergent tools to enhance instruction. Today's technology innovation is VR; tomorrow's technology innovation has not yet been imagined, much less brought to fruition. Regardless of the technology tools available, ways to support educators toward the meaningful integration of such tools for the benefit of lifespan learning, remains imperative.

REFERENCES

AACTE Committee on Innovation and Technology. (2008). *Handbook of technological pedagogical content knowledge (TPCK) for educators*. New York: Routledge.

Afshar, V. (2014). 10 Hottest Technologies in Higher Education. Retrieved from http://www.huffingtonpost.com/vala-afshar/10-hottest-technologies-i_b_6089740.html

Ahn, S. J., Bostick, J., Ogle, E., & Bailenson, J. N. (2015, August 6-9). Embodying nature's experiences: Taking the perspective of nature with immersive virtual environments to promote connectedness with nature. *Paper to be presented at the Annual Association for Education in Journalism and Mass Communication (AEJMC) Conference*, San Francisco, CA.

Arya, A., Hartwick, P., Graham, S., & Nowlan, N. (2011, May). Virtual space as a learning environment: Two case studies. *Paper presented at the meeting of the International Education Technology Conference*, Istanbul, Turkey.

Bandura, A. (1997). *Self-efficacy: The exercise of control*. New York: Freeman.

Barilli, E. (2012). Virtual Reality Technology as a Didactical and Pedagogical Resource in Distance Education for Professional Training. In P. B. Muyinda (Ed.), *Distance education*. Retrieved from http://cdn.intechopen.com/pdfs-wm/39200.pdf

Becker, H. (2001). How are teachers using computers in instruction? Paper presented at the 2001 Meeting of the American Educational Research Association, Seattle, WA. Retrieved

Beglau, M., Hare, J. C., Foltos, L., Gann, K., James, J., Jobe, H., . . . Smith, B. (2011). *Technology, Coaching and Community*. International Society for Technology in Education (ISTE). Retrieved from http://www.iste.org/learn/coaching-white-paper.aspx

Biocca, F., Harms, C., & Burgoon, J. K. (2003). Toward a more robust theory and measure of social presence: Review and suggested criteria. *Presence (Cambridge, Mass.)*, *12*(5), 456–480. doi:10.1162/105474603322761270

Blaschke, B., & Hase, S. (2015). Heutagogy, technology and lifelong learning for professional part-time learners. In A. Dailey-Hebert & K. Dennis (Eds.), *Transformative perspectives & processes in higher education*. London: Springer. doi:10.1007/978-3-319-09247-8_5

Bojanova, I. (2011). Physical presence through virtual worlds. *IT Professional*, *13*(4), 4–5. doi:10.1109/MITP.2011.66

Bouta, H., Retalis, S., & Paraskeva, F. (2012). Utilizing a collaborative macro-script to enhance student engagement: A mixed method study in a 3D virtual environment. *Computers & Education*, *58*(1), 501–517. doi:10.1016/j.compedu.2011.08.031

Bowman, D. A., & McMahan, R. P. (2007). Virtual reality: How much immersion is enough? *Computer*, *40*(7), 36–42. doi:10.1109/MC.2007.257

Bozkurt, A. (2011). A classroom observation-based evaluation of elementary teachers' use of technology in the classrooms in Turkey. *Educational Research Review*, 2011, 367–373.

Bransford, J. D., & Schwartz, D. L. (1999). Rethinking transfer: A simple proposal with multiple implications. In A. Iran-Nejad & P. D. Pearson (Eds.), Review of research in education (pp. 61-100). Washington, DC: American Educational Research Association.

Brantley-Dias, L., Kinuthia, W., Shoffner, M. B., DeCastro, C., & Rigole, N. (2007). Developing pedagogical technology integration content knowledge in preservice teachers: A case study approach. *Journal of Research on Computing in Teacher Education*, *23*, 143–149.

Britain, S. (1999). A framework for pedagogical evaluation of virtual world learning environments. JISC Technology Applications Programme, Report 41: Joint Information Systems Committee of the Higher Educational Funding Council. Manchester, UK.

Cerniamo, K. S., Ross, J. D., & Ertmer, P. A. (2010). *Technology integration for meaningful classroom use: A standards-based approach*. Belmont, CA: Wadsworth, Cengage Learning.

Chang, L. (2015, June 29). Go shopping from the comfort of your own home with your virtual reality headset. *Digital Trends*. Retrieved from http://www.digitaltrends.com/cool/retail/

Chouhan, R., & Sharma, G. K. (2015). Virtual Reality: In gaming. *International Journal of Multidisciplinary Consortium*, *2*(2), 36.

Cifuentes, L., Maxwell, G., & Bulu, S. (2011). Technology integration through professional learning community. *Journal of Educational Computing Research*, *44*(1), 59–82. doi:10.2190/EC.44.1.d

Cuban, L., Kirkpatrick, H., & Peck, C. (2001). High access and low use of technologies in high school classrooms: Explaining an apparent paradox. *American Educational Research Journal*, *38*(4), 813834. doi:10.3102/00028312038004813

Cummings, J. J., & Bailenson, J. N. (2015). How immersive is enough? A meta-analysis of the effect of immersive technology on user presence. *Media Psychology*, 1–38. doi:10.1080/15213269.2015.1015740

Dailey-Hebert, A., Donnelli-Sallee, E., & DiPadova-Stocks, L. (2008). Service-eLearning as integrated pedagogy: An introduction. In A. Dailey-Hebert, E. Donnelli-Sallee, L. & DiPadova-Stocks (Eds.), Service-eLearning: Educating for citizenship (pp.1-5). Charlotte, NC: Information Age Publishing.

Dalgarno, B., Gregory, S., Carlson, L., Lee, M. J. W., & Tynan, B. (2013). *A systematic review and environmental analysis of the use of 3D immersive virtual worlds in Australian and New Zealand higher education institutions* (Final Report) (pp. 1–226). Armidale, Australia: DEHub: Innovation in Distance Education, University of New England. Retrieved from http://www.dehub.edu.au/downloads/VWSSP_Report_V2_TD_200613_dehub.pdf

Dickey, M. D. (2005a). Brave new (interactive) worlds: A review of the design affordances and constraints of two 3D virtual worlds as interactive learning environments. *Interactive Learning Environments*, *13*(1–2), 121–137. doi:10.1080/10494820500173714

Dickey, M. D. (2005b). Three-dimensional virtual worlds and distance learning: Two case studies of Active Worlds as a medium for distance learning. *British Journal of Educational Technology*, *36*(3), 439–451. doi:10.1111/j.1467-8535.2005.00477.x

eMINTS National Center. (2014). Instructional model. Retrieved from http://www.emints.org/professional-development/instructional-model/

Ertmer, P. A. (1999). Addressing first and second order barriers to change: Strategies for technology integration. *Educational Technology Research and Development*, *47*(4), 4761. doi:10.1007/BF02299597

Ertmer, P. A., & Ottenbreit-Leftwich, A. (2010). Teacher Technology Change: How Knowledge, Confidence, Beliefs, and Culture Intersect. *Journal of Research on Technology in Education*, *42*(3), 255–284. doi:10.1080/15391523.2010.10782551

Ertmer, P. A., Ottenbreit-Leftwich, A., & York, C. (2006). Exemplary technology-using teachers: Perceptions of factors influencing success. *Journal of Computing in Teacher Education*, *23*(2), 55–61.

Estes, J. S. (2015). A call for teacher preparation programs to model integrating technology into the instructional process. In J. Keengwe (Ed.), *Handbook of research on educational technology integration and active learning* (pp. 62–77). Hershey, PA: IGI. doi:10.4018/978-1-4666-8363-1.ch004

Falloon, G. (2010). Using avatars and virtual environments in learning: What do they have to offer? *British Journal of Educational Technology*, *41*(1), 108–122. doi:10.1111/j.1467-8535.2009.00991.x

Frey, T. (n. d.). 55 Jobs of the Future. Retrieved from http://www.futuristspeaker.com/2011/11/55-jobs-of-the-future /

Friedman, T. (2005). *The world is flat. Farrar, Straus and Giroux*. New York: MacMillan Publishers.

Fullan, M., & Stiegelbauer, S. (1991). *The new meaning of educational change*. New York: Teachers College Press.

Gagne, R. M. (1980). Is Educational Technology in Phase? *Educational Technology*, 1980, 7–14.

Gregory, S., Scutter, S., Jacka, L., McDonald, M., Farley, H., & Newman, C. (2015). Barriers and Enablers to the Use of Virtual Worlds in Higher Education: An Exploration of Educator Perceptions, Attitudes and Experiences. *Journal of Educational Technology & Society*, *18*(1), 3–12.

Harris, S. R., & Gerich, E. (1996). Retiring the NSFNET backbone service: Chronicling the end of an era. *ConneXiona, 10*(4).

Hase, S. (2013). Learning defined learning. In S. Hase & C. Kenyon (Eds.), *Self-determined learning: Heutagogy in action*. London: Bloomsbury.

Heili, J., & Michel, H. (2011, October). Do students Trained using serious games become better sales representatives? An experiment to study the performance of academic serious games. *Proceedings of the European Conference on Games-Based Learning*.

Hernández-Ramos, P. (2005). If not here, where? Understanding teachers' use of technology in Silicon Valley schools. *Journal of Research on Technology in Education*, *38*(1), 39–64. doi:10.1080/15391523.2005.10782449

Hew, K. F., & Brush, T. (2007). Integrating technology into K-12 teaching and learning: Current knowledge gaps and recommendations for future research. *Educational Technology Research and Development*, *55*(3), 223–252. doi:10.1007/s11423-006-9022-5

Hew, K. F., & Cheung, W. S. (2010). Use of three-dimensional (3-D) immersive virtual worlds in K-12 and higher education settings: A review of the research. *British Journal of Educational Technology*, *4*(1), 33–55. doi:10.1111/j.1467-8535.2008.00900.x

Holmes, A., Signer, B., & MacLeod, A. (2011). Professional development at a distance: A mixed-method study exploring inservice teachers' views on presence online. *Journal of Digital Learning in Teacher Education*, *27*(2), 76–85. doi:10.1080/21532974.2010.10784660

Holmes, J. (2007). Designing agents to support learning by explaining. *Computers & Education*, *48*(4), 523–525. doi:10.1016/j.compedu.2005.02.007

Huang, H. M., Rauch, U., & Liaw, S. S. (2010). Investigating learners' attitudes toward virtual reality learning environments: Based on a constructivist approach. *Computers & Education*, *55*(3), 1171–1182. doi:10.1016/j.compedu.2010.05.014

Hughes, J. (2005). The role of teacher knowledge and learning experiences in forming technology-integrated pedagogy. *Journal of Technology and Teacher Education*, *13*(2), 277–302.

Hullinger, J. (2015, June 28). *Six innovative uses for virtual reality. The Idea Factory.* Retrieved from http://theweek.com/articles/562851/6

International Society for Technology in Education. (2008). *National educational technology standards for teachers* (2nd ed.). Eugene, OR: Author.

International Society for Technology in Education. (2011). Technology, Coaching, and Community: Power partners for improved professional development in elementary and secondary schools. Retrieved from http://www.instructionalcoach.org/images/downloads/ISTE_Whitepaper_June_Final_Edits.pdf

International Society for Technology in Education. (2012). Digital age coaching. Retrieved from http://www.iste.org/standards/nets-for-coaches

International Society for Technology in Education. (2015). Standards for teachers. Retrieved from http://www.iste.org/standards/ISTE-standards/standards-for-teachers

Johnson, L., Levine, A., & Smith, R. (2008). 2008 Horizon report Australia-New Zealand edition. In *2008 Horizon Report Australia-New Zealand Edition*. Austin, Texas: The New Media Consortium. Retrieved from http://wp.nmc.org/horizon-anz-2008/

Kapp, K., & O'Driscoll, T. (2010). *Learning in 3D*. San Francisco, CA: Pfeiffer.Lai, K-W. (2008). ICT supporting the learning process: The premise, reality, and promise. In J. Voogt & G. Knezek (Eds.), *International Handbook of Information Technology in Primary and Secondary Education* (pp. 215–230). New York: Springer.

KZero. (2013). Kzero Worldswide. Retrieved from http://www.kzero.co.uk/blog/category/education-and-academia

Lai, K.-W. (2008). ICT supporting the learning process: The premise, reality, and promise. In J. Voogt & G. Knezek (Eds.), *International Handbook of Information Technology in Primary and Secondary Education* (pp. 215–230). New York: Springer. doi:10.1007/978-0-387-73315-9_13

Lawless, K. A., & Pellegrino, J. W. (2007). Professional development in integrating technology into teaching and learning: Knowns, unknowns, and ways to pursue better questions and answers. *Review of Educational Research*, *77*(4), 575–614. doi:10.3102/0034654307309921

Levien, R. E. (1972). *The Emerging Technology: Instructional Uses of the Computer in Higher Education*. New York, NY: McGraw-Hill Book Company.

Lewis, L. A., Koston, Z., Quartley, M., & Adsit, J. (2011). Virtual communities of practice: Bridging research and practice using Web 2.0. *Journal of Educational Technology Systems*, *39*(2), 155–161. doi:10.2190/ET.39.2.e

Linden Lab. (2013). Infographic: 10 years of Second Life. Retrieved from http://www.lindenlab.com/releases/infographic

Lowendahl, J. M. (2013, July 25). Hype Cycle for Education, 2013. *Gartner*. Retrieved from http://www.gartner.com/DisplayDocument?doc_cd=251104

Mazuryk, T., & Gervautz, M. (1996). Virtual reality, history, applications, technology and future, 1-72. Institute of Computer Graphics, Vienna University of Technology, Austria. Retrieved August 29, 2015 from https://www.cg.tuwien.ac.at/research/publications/1996/mazuryk-1996-VRH/TR-186-2-96-06Paper.pdf

Michel, H. (2013, January). From Haute-Couture to Ready-to-Wear: Typology of Serious Games Implementation Strategies in Higher Education. *Proceedings of the European Conference on Games Based Learning* (p. 386). Academic Conferences International Limited.

Miller, R. (2014). The application of virtual reality in higher education distance learning. *Journal of Applied Learning Technology*, *4*(4), 15–18.

Mishra, S. (2009). Virtual worlds. In S. Mishra (Ed.), *E-Learning* (pp. 110-113). New Delhi: IndiraGandhi National Open University. Retrieve from http://webserver.ignou.ac.in/institute/STRIDE_Hb8_webCD/STRIDE_Hb8_Full.pdf

Molnar, A. R. (1975). Viable Goals for New Educational Technology Efforts: Science Education and the New Technological Revolution. *Educational Technology*, *15*(9).

Molnar, A. R. (1990). Computers in education: A historical perspective of the unfinished task. *T.H.E. Journal*, *18*(4), 80–83.

Moravec, J. W. (2008). *Knowmads in society 3.0*. Education Futures.

Mueller, J., Wood, E., Willoughby, T., Ross, C., & Specht, J. (2008). Identifying discriminating variables between teachers who fully integrate computers and teachers with limited integration. *Computers & Education*, *51*(4), 1523–1537. doi:10.1016/j.compedu.2008.02.003

National Survey of Student Engagement. (NSSE) (2014). Center for Postsecondary Research, Indiana University School of Education, Bloomington, IND. Retrieved from http://nsse.iub.edu/NSSE_2014_Results/pdf/NSSE_2014_Annual_Results.pdf#page=8

Noteborn, G., Dailey-Hebert, A., Bohle-Carbonell, K., & Gijselears, W. (2013), Essential knowledge for academic performance: Educating in the virtual world to promote active learning. *Teacher and Teacher Education,* 37(January), 217-234. http://authors.elsevier.com/sd/article/S0742051X1300156X

Office of Science and Technology Policy (OSTP). (1992). *Grand Challenges: High Performance Computing and Communications.* Washington, DC. Retrieved from http://www.hpcc.gov

Office of Social and Economic Data Analysis (OSEDA). (2001). *Final results from the e-MINTS teacher survey*. Columbia, MO: Author.

Office of Technology Assessment. (1982). Informational technology and its impact on American education, 128-133. U.S. Congress, Washington, DC.

Office of Technology Assessment (OTA). (1995). *Teachers and technology: Making the connection.* Washington, D.C.: U.S. Government Printing Office.

Ong, S. K., & Nee, A. Y. C. (2013). *Virtual and augmented reality applications in manufacturing.* Springer Science & Business Media.

Partnership for 21st Century Learning. (2007). *Framework for 21st century learning*. Retrieved from http://www.21stcenturyskills.org

Pierce, D. (2015, March 6). The Future of Virtual Reality is inside your smartphone, Wired, Retrieved from http://www.wired.com/2015/03/future-virtual-reality-inside-smartphone/

Pink, D. H. (2006). *A whole new mind: Why right-brainers will rule the future.* Penguin.

Prasolova-Førland, E. (2008). Analyzing place metaphors in 3D educational collaborative virtual environments. *Computers in Human Behavior*, *24*(2), 185–204. doi:10.1016/j.chb.2007.01.009

Prensky, M. (2001). Digital natives, digital immigrants part 1. *On the horizon*, *9*(5), 1–6. doi:10.1108/10748120110424816

Pulse Simulation Technology. (2008). Retrieved from https://www.youtube.com/watch?v=Q11aWO6dg2Q

Putnam, R. T., & Borko, H. (2000). What do new views of knowledge and thinking have to say about research on teacher learning? *Educational Researcher*, *29*(1), 4–15. doi:10.3102/0013189X029001004

Reinick, L. B. (1983). Mathematics and Science and Learning: A New Conception. *Science*, *220*(4596), 477–478. doi:10.1126/science.220.4596.477 PMID:17816206

Repenning, A., Webb, D., & Ioannidou, A. (2012). Scalable game design and the development of a checklist for getting computational thinking into public schools. Association for Computer Machinery (ACM). Retrieved from http://www.cs.colorado.edu/~ralex/papers/PDF/SIGCSE10-repenning.pdf

Rheingold, H. (1991). *Virtual reality: The revolutionary technology of computer generated artificial worlds*. New York: Simon & Schuster Publishing.

Rogers, E. M. (2003). *Diffusion of innovations* (5th ed.). New York, NY: The Free Press.

Saposnik, G., & Levin, M. (2011). Virtual reality in stroke rehabilitation a meta-analysis and implications for clinicians. *Stroke*, *42*(5), 1380–1386. doi:10.1161/STROKEAHA.110.605451 PMID:21474804

Scardamalia, M., & Bereiter, C. (2006). Knowledge building: Theory, pedagogy, and technology. In K. Sawyer (Ed.), *Cambridge Handbook of the Learning Sciences* (pp. 97–118). New York: Cambridge University Press.

Schroeder, R. (2008). Defining Virtual Worlds and Virtual Environments. *Journal of Virtual Worlds Research*, *1*(1). Retrieved from http://journals.tdl.org/jvwr/article/view/294

Schuemie, M. J., Van Der Straaten, P., Krijn, M., & Van Der Mast, C. A. P. G. (2001). Research on presence in virtual reality: A survey. *Cyberpsychology & Behavior*, *4*(2), 183–201. doi:10.1089/109493101300117884 PMID:11710246

September 21, 2015 from http://www.crito.uci.edu/tlc/FINDINGS/special3/

Sherman, W. R., & Craig, A. B. (2003). *Understanding virtual reality. Interface, application and design*. Boston, MA: Morgan-Kaufmann Publishers.

Slater, M., & Steed, A. (2000). A virtual presence counter. *Presence (Cambridge, Mass.)*, *9*(5), 413–434. doi:10.1162/105474600566925

Slater, M., & Wilbur, S. (1997). A framework for immersive virtual environments (FIVE): Speculations on the role of presence in virtual environments. *Presence (Cambridge, Mass.)*, *6*, 603–616.

Smart, J., Cascio, J., & Paffendof, J. (2007). *Metaverse roadmap: pathways to the 3D web*. Retrieved from http://www.metaverseroadmap.org/overview

Smith-Robbins, J. (2011, December). Are virtual worlds (still) relevant in education? *elearn Magazine: Education and Technology Perspective*. Retrieved from http://elearnmag.acm.org/archive.cfm?aid=207847

Somekh, B. (2008). Factors affecting teachers' pedagogical adoption of ICT. In J. Voogt & G. Knezek (Eds.), *International Handbook of Information Technology in Primary and Secondary Education* (pp. 449–460). New York: Springer. doi:10.1007/978-0-387-73315-9_27

Stamford, C. (2007, April 24). Gartner says 80 percent of active Internet users will have a "Second Life" in the virtual world by the end of 2011. *Gartner Newsroom*. Retrieved from http://www.gartner.com/it/page.jsp?id=503861

Subramaniam, K. (2007). Teachers' mindsets and the integration of computer technology. *British Journal of Educational Technology*, *38*(6), 1056–1071. doi:10.1111/j.1467-8535.2006.00693.x

Sugar, W., & Slagter van Tryon, P. J. (2014). Development of a virtual technology coach to support technology integration for K-12 educators. *TechTrends*, *58*(3), 54–62. doi:10.1007/s11528-014-0752-7

The Associated Press. (2014, March 25). Facebook to buy Oculus virtual reality firm for $2B. Retrieved from http://www.cbc.ca/news/technology/facebook-to-buy-oculus-virtual-reality-firm-for-zb-1,2586318

The New Media Consortium. (2007). *The Horizon Report*. Austin, Texas: New Media Consortium.

Thorsteinsson, G., & Page, T. (2008). Innovative technology education using a virtual reality learning environment, 90, 26-35. Pedagogy Studies/Pedigogika: Vilnius Pedagogical University.

Tokel, S. T., & Karitas, E. C. (2014). *Mersin University Journal of the Faculty of Education*, *10*(1), 1–12.

Umbach, P. D., & Wawrzynsli, M. R. (2005). Faculty do matter: The role of college faculty in student learning and engagement. *Research in Higher Education*, *46*(2), 153–185. doi:10.1007/s11162-004-1598-1

Virtual reality. (n. d.). Retrieved from https://en.wikipedia.org/wiki/Virtual_reality

Virtual reality. (n. d.). Retrieved from http://www.merriamwebster.com/dictionary/virtualreality

Warner, T. (2012). E-coaching systems: Convenient, anytime, anywhere, and nonhuman. *Performance Improvement*, *51*(9), 22–28. doi:10.1002/pfi.21305

Waters, J. (2014, October 9). Could the Oculus Rift redeem virtual reality in higher ed? *Campus Technology*. Retrieved from http://campustechnology.com/articles/2014/10/09/could-the-oculus-rift-redeem-virtual-reality-in-higher-ed.aspx

Webb, D., Repenninga, A., & Koh, K. (2012, February 29-March 3). Toward an emergent theory of broadening participation in computer science education. *Proceeding of the Association for Computer Machinery (ACM) Special Interest Group on Computer Science Conference (SIGCSE)* (pp. 173-178). Raleigh, NC. ACM. doi:10.1145/2157136.2157191

Weimer, M. (2010). *Inspired college teaching: A career-long resource for professional growth*. Hoboken, NJ: John Wiley & Sons.

Windschitl, M., & Sahl, K. (2002, Spring). Tracing teachers' use of technology in a laptop computer school: The interplay of teacher beliefs, social dynamics, and institutional culture. *American Educational Research Journal*, *39*(1), 165–205. doi:10.3102/00028312039001165

Wong, J. N. (2010). Searching for good practice in teaching: A comparison of two subject-based professional learning communities in a secondary school in Shanghai. *Compare: A Journal of Comparative and International Education*, *40*(5), 623-639.

Woods, D. (2009). Experiential learning through real space placements undertaken in 'virtual world' spaces. *Proceedings from Ascilite Auckland 2009*.

Wozney, L., Venkatesh, V., & Abrami, P. C. (2006). Implementing computer technologies: Teachers' perceptions and practices. *Journal of Technology and Teacher Education*, *14*(1), 173–207.

Yilmaz, R., Topu, F., Goktas, Y., & Coban, M. (2013). Social presence and motivation in a three dimensional virtual world An explanatory study. *Australasian Journal of Educational Technology*, *29*(6), 823–839.

Zech, L. K., Gause-Vega, C. L., Bray, M. H., Secules, T., & Goldman, S. R. (2000). Content-based collaborative inquiry: A professional development model for sustaining educational reform. *Educational Psychologist*, *35*(3), 207–217. doi:10.1207/S15326985EP3503_6

Zhao, Y., Pugh, K., Sheldon, S., & Byers, J. L. (2002). Conditions for classroom technology innovations. *Teachers College Record*, *104*(3), 482–515. doi:10.1111/1467-9620.00170

ADDITIONAL READING

Angeli, C., & Valanides, N. (2009). Epistemological and methodological issues for the conceptualization, development, and assessment of ICT-TPCK: Advances in technology and pedagogical content knowledge (TPCK). *Computers & Education*, *52*(1), 154–168. doi:10.1016/j.compedu.2008.07.006

Barbour, M. (2011). The promise and the reality: Exploring virtual schooling in rural jurisdictions. *Education in Rural Australia*, *21*, 1–19.

Blascovich, J., & Bailenson, J. (2011). *Infinite Reality: Avatars, eternal life, new worlds and the dawn of the virtual revolution*. New York: Harper Collins Publishing.

Blascovich, J., & Bailenson, J. (2012). *Infinite Reality: The hidden blueprint of our virtual lives*. New York: Harper Collins Publishing.

Cheong, D. (2010). The effects of practice teaching sessions in second like on the change in pre-service teachers' teaching efficacy. *Computers & Education*, *55*(2), 868–880. doi:10.1016/j.compedu.2010.03.018

Cline, M. (2005). *Power, madness & immortality: The future of virtual reality*. University Village Press eBooks. Retrieved from https://books.google.com/books?id=7OxbJWzIaVEC&pg=PP1&lpg=PP1&dq=Cline,+Mychilo+Stephenson+(2005).+Power,+madness+%26+immortality:+The+future+of+virtual+reality.&source=bl&ots=OrCOjJD787&sig=1CdY3AjD3qj6SdGxGUgQqXkylms&hl=en&sa=X&ved=0CCEQ6AEwAGoVChMIsOSo5LvWxwIV1hSSCh0f_AWl#v=onepage&q=Cline%2C%20Mychilo%20Stephenson%20(2005).%20Power%2C%20madness%20%26%20immortality%3A%20The%20future%20of%20virtual%20reality.&f=false

Dede, C., Nelson, B., Ketelhut, D. J., Clarke, J., & Bowman, C. (2004, June). Design-based research strategies for studying situated learning in a multi-user virtual environment. *Proceedings of the 6th international conference on Learning Sciences* (pp. 158-165). International Society of the Learning Sciences.

Diaz, D. P., & Botenbal, K. F. (2001). Learner preferences: Developing a learner-centered environment in the online or mediated classroom. *Ed at a Distance, 15*(8). Retrieved from http://www.usdla.org/html/hournal/AUGO1_Issue/article03.html

Digenti, D. (1998). Toward an understanding of the learning community. *Organization Development Journal*, *16*(2), 91–96.

Gill, L., & Dalgarno, B. (2010). How does pre-service teacher preparedness to use ICTs for learning and teaching develop during the first two years of teacher training? In C. Steel, M. J. Keppell, P. Gerbic, & S. Housego (Eds.), Proceedings of Ascilite2010 Sydney (pp. 371–381). Retrieved from http://www.ascilite.org.au/conferences/sydney10/Ascilite%20conference%20proceedings%202010/Gillfull.pdf

Hermans, R., Tondeur, J., van Braak, J., & Valcke, M. (2008). The impact of primary school teachers' educational beliefs on the classroom use of computers. *Computers & Education*, *51*(4), 1499–1509. doi:10.1016/j.compedu.2008.02.001

Kay, J., & FitzGerald, S. (2008). *Educational uses of Second Life*. Retrieved from http://sleducation.wikispaces.com/educationaluses

Kock, N. (2008). E-collaboration and e-commerce in virtual worlds: The potential of Second Life and World of Warcraft. *International Journal of e-Collaboration*, *4*(3), 1–13. doi:10.4018/jec.2008070101

Mayo, M. J. (2009). Video games: A route to large scale STEM education? *Science*, *323*(5910), 79–82. doi:10.1126/science.1166900 PMID:19119223

Monahan, T., McArdle, G., & Bertolotto, M. (2008). Virtual reality for collaborative e-learning. *Computers & Education*, *50*(4), 1339–1353. doi:10.1016/j.compedu.2006.12.008

Peterson, M. (2006). Learner interaction management in an avatar and chat-based virtual world. *Computer Assisted Language Learning*, *19*(1), 79–103. doi:10.1080/09588220600804087

Rienties, B. C., Reeb-Gruber, S., Daly, P., & Van den Bossche, P. (2011). *Proceedings of the 18th EDINEB Conference: From Innovation to Crème de la Crème Education.*

Snoeyink, R., & Ertmer, P. A. (2001/2002). Thrust into technology: How veteran teachers respond. *Journal of Educational Technology Systems*, *30*(1), 85–111. doi:10.2190/YDL7-XH09-RLJ6-MTP1

Tapscott, D. (2009). *Grown Up Digital. How The Net Generation Is Changing Your World.* New York: McGraw Hill.

Verloop, N., VanDriel, J., & Meijer, P. (2001). Teacher knowledge and the knowledge base of teaching. *International Journal of Educational Research*, *35*(5), 441–461. doi:10.1016/S0883-0355(02)00003-4

Warburton, S. (2009). Second Life in higher education: Assessing the potential for and the barriers to deploying virtual worlds in learning and teaching. *British Journal of Educational Technology*, *40*(3), 414–426. doi:10.1111/j.1467-8535.2009.00952.x

KEY TERMS AND DEFINITIONS

e-MINTS: Enhancing Missouri's Instructional Network Teaching Strategies; a professional development model that that supports high quality lesson design, promotes inquiry-based learning, creates a technology-rich learning environment and builds community among students and teachers.

Engagement: Student engagement involves active participation, critical thinking, synthesis, and application of content to real-life experiences. Highly engaged students tend to feel a connection to the process of learning, to their peers, and to the institutions of higher education in which they are enrolled.

Information and Communications Technology (ICT): ICT is a commonly used acronym for information and communication technology including the tools and resources used to communicate, create, disseminate, store, and manage information.

ISTE: The International Society for Technology in Education is a not-for –profit organization that provides standards and criteria for what teachers need to teach and what students need to learn, as well as what content needs to be provided by a professional development program in relation to educational technology.

Motivation: Motivation pertains to the general desire or willingness of a student to engage with peers, teacher, and content while enrolled in a course of study.

NETS-T (National Educational Technology Standards for Teachers): Developed by ISTE, the NETS-T standards guide teachers in use and application of technology within the instructional process.

Office of Technology Assessment (OTA): OTA opened as an office of the U.S. Congress from 1972 to 1995 and responsible for providing Congress with authoritative and bipartisan reports on a wide range of issues in science and technology, including issues related to education. Princeton University now hosts the OTA legacy website (https://www.princeton.edu/~ota/).

Pedagogy: Beliefs and theory that guide the practice of teaching; what teachers do, based upon what they believe, when implementing their craft and assist student learning.

Pedagogical Content Knowledge: Pedagogical content knowledge is a synthesis of how teachers related what they know and belief about teaching (pedagogy) with the subject matter, or content that they are teaching.

Scalable Game Design: Scalable Game Design provides professional development for teachers and training for middle school students through use of a computer programming curriculum that begins with the use of simple game design and progressively advancing to the design and use of STEM related real-life simulations, enabling students to explore and create virtual realities.

Self-Efficacy: A person's belief about their ability and competency; a teacher's believe in their technology knowledge, skills, and ability to integrate technology into instruction.

Technology Integration: Technology integration refers to a process of intentionally choosing technology tools that enhance specific instructional strategies during the teaching and learning process.

Compilation of References

AACTE Committee on Innovation and Technology. (2008). *Handbook of technological pedagogical content knowledge (TPCK) for educators*. New York: Routledge.

Abeles, T. P. (2007). Education unbound. *On The Horizon*, *15*(4), 199–203. doi:10.1108/10748120710836219

Abernathy, W., & Clark, K. B. (2007). Innovation: Mapping the winds of creative distruction. *Research Policy*, *14*(1), 3–22. doi:10.1016/0048-7333(85)90021-6

Adams, E. W. (2004). Postmodernism and the three types of immersion. *Gamasutra*. Retrieved from http://designers-notebook.com/Columns/063_Postmodernism/063_postmodernism.htm

Adcock, A. B., Duggan, M. H., Nelson, E. K., & Nickel, C. (2006). Teaching effective helping skills at a distance: The development of project CATHIE. *The Quarterly Review of Distance Education*, *7*(4), 349–360.

Afshar, V. (2014). 10 Hottest Technologies in Higher Education. Retrieved from http://www.huffingtonpost.com/vala-afshar/10-hottest-technologies-i_b_6089740.html

Aguiar, S., & Monte, P. (2011). Virtual Worlds for C2 Design, Analysis and Experimentation. *Proceedings of the16th International Command and Control Research and Technology Symposium (ICCRTS 2011), Quebec City, Quebec, Canada, June 21-23, 2011.*

Ahn, S. J., Bostick, J., Ogle, E., & Bailenson, J. N. (2015, August 6-9). Embodying nature's experiences: Taking the perspective of nature with immersive virtual environments to promote connectedness with nature. *Paper to be presented at the Annual Association for Education in Journalism and Mass Communication (AEJMC) Conference*, San Francisco, CA.

Ai-Lim Lee, E., Wong, K. W., & Fung, C. C. (2010). How does desktop virtual reality enhance learning outcomes? A structural equation modeling approach. *Computers & Education*, *55*(4), 1424–1442. doi:10.1016/j.compedu.2010.06.006

Alegría, D. A. H., Boscardin, C., Poncelet, A., Mayfield, C., & Wamsley, M. (2014). Using tablets to support self-regulated learning in a longitudinal integrated clerkship. *Medical Education Online*, *12*. PMID:24646438

Alfieri, L., Brooks, P. J., Aldrich, N. J., & Tenenbaum, H. R. (2011). Does discovery-based instruction enhance learning? *Journal of Educational Psychology*, *103*(1), 1–18. doi:10.1037/a0021017

Allen, P. D., & Demchak, C. D. (2011). Applied Virtual Environments: Applications of Virtual Environments to Government, Military and Business Organizations. *Journal of Virtual Worlds Research*, *4*(1).

Alvarez, C., Brown, C., & Nussbaum, M. (2011). Comparative study of netbooks and tablet PCs for fostering face-to-face collaborative learning. *Computers in Human Behavior*, *27*(2), 834–844. doi:10.1016/j.chb.2010.11.008

Amrollahi, A., Ghapanchi, A. H., & Talaei-Khoei, A. (2013). A systematic literature review on strategic information systems planning: Insights from the past decade. *Pacific Asia Journal of the Association for Information Systems*, *5*(2), 4.

Annetta, L. A., Folta, E., & Klesath, M. (2010). *V-learning: Distance education in the 21st century through 3D virtual environments*. New York: Springer. doi:10.1007/978-90-481-3627-8

Antell, S. E., & Keating, D. P. (1983). Perception of numerical invariance in neonates. *Child Development*, *54*(3), 695–701. doi:10.2307/1130057 PMID:6851716

Antonacci, D., DiBartolo, S., Edwards, N., Fritch, K., McMullen, B., & Murch-Shafer, R. (2008). The power of virtual worlds in education: a second primer and resource for exploring the potential of virtual worlds to impact teaching and learning. ANGEL Learning ISLE Steering Committee. Retrieved from http://www.angellearning.com/products/secondlife/downloads/The%20Power%20of%20Virtual%20Worlds%20in%20Education_0708.pdf

Antonietti, A., Rasi, C., Imperio, E., & Sacco, M. (1999). Virtual reality in engineering instruction: In search of the best learning procedures. *World Conference on Educational Multimedia, Hypermedia and Telecommunications 1999* (Vol. 1, pp. 663-668).

Antonietti, A., Rasi, C., Imperio, E., & Sacco, M. (2000). The representation of virtual reality in education. *Education and Information Technologies*, *5*(4), 317–327. doi:10.1023/A:1012057608694

Antonietti, A., Rasi, C., Imperio, E., & Sacco, M. (2001). Virtual reality and hypermedia in learning to use a turning lathe. *Journal of Computer Assisted Learning*, *17*(2), 142–155. doi:10.1046/j.0266-4909.2001.00167.x

Appana, S. (2008). A Review of Benefits and Limitations of Online Learning in the Context of the Student, the Instructor and the Tenured Faculty. *International Journal on E-Learning*, *7*(1), 5–22.

Arnone, M., Small, R., Chauncey, S., & McKenna, H. (2011). Curiosity, interest and engagement in technology-pervasive learning environments: A new research agenda. *Educational Technology Research and Development*, *59*(2), 181–198. doi:10.1007/s11423-011-9190-9

Arya, A., Hartwick, P., Graham, S., & Nowlan, N. (2011, May). Virtual space as a learning environment: Two case studies. *Paper presented at themeeting of the International Education Technology Conference*, Istanbul, Turkey.

Astheimer, P., Dai, F., Göbel, M., Kruse, R., Müller, S., & Zachmann, G. (1994). Realism in virtual reality. In *N. Magnenat Thalmann & D. Thalmann, Artificial life and virtual reality* (pp. 189–209). New York, NY: John Wiley.

Atkinson, R. K. (2002). Optimizing learning from examples using animated pedagogical agents. *Journal of Educational Psychology*, *94*(2), 416–427. doi:10.1037/0022-0663.94.2.416

Atkinson, R. K., Mayer, R. E., & Merrill, M. M. (2005). Fostering social agency in multimedia learning: Examining the impact of an animated agent's voice. *Contemporary Educational Psychology*, *30*(1), 117–139. doi:10.1016/j.cedpsych.2004.07.001

Atkinson, T. (2009). Second Life for educators: Teaching and learning. *TechTrends*, *53*(3), 30–32. doi:10.1007/s11528-009-0285-7

Attewell, P., Lavin, D., Domina, T., & Levey, T. (2006). New evidence on college remediation. *The Journal of Higher Education*, *77*(5), 886–924. doi:10.1353/jhe.2006.0037

Augmentedmarketing. (2013). *Ontarion Tourism Summit 2013 features interactive print.* Retrieved from http://bit.ly/1CRuwl6

Augmentedstories. (2015). *Education*. Retrieved from: http://augmentedstories.com/education/

Aurasma. (2015). *The drink of champions*. Retrieved from: http://bit.ly/1Fw66vl

Austin, J. L. (1975). *How to do things with words*. Oxford University Press. doi:10.1093/acprof:oso/9780198245537.001.0001

Ausubel, D. G. (1963). Cognitive structure and the facilitation of meaningful verbal learning. *Journal of Teacher Education, 14*(2), 217–222. doi:10.1177/002248716301400220

Aydogan, H., Aras, F., & Karakas, E. (2010). *An assessment on distance education in a 3D virtual environment: How to produce electricity in a hydroelectric power plant.Paper presented at the Education Technology and Computer (ICETC), 2010 2nd International Conference.* doi:10.1109/ICETC.2010.5529234

Azim, R., & Hassan, A. (2013). Impact analysis of wireless and mobile technology on business management strategies. *Journal of Information and Knowledge Management, 2*(2), 141–150.

Azuma, R. (1997). A survey of augmented reality. *Presence (Cambridge, Mass.), 6*(4), 355–385.

Azuma, R. T. (1997). A survey of augmented Reality. *Presence (Cambridge, Mass.), 6*(4), 355–385.

Bacca, J., Baldiris, S., Fabregat, R., & Graf, S., & Kinshuk. (2014). Augmented Reality Trends in Education: A Systematic Review of Research and Applications. *Journal of Educational Technology & Society, 17*(4), 133–149.

Bainbridge, W. (2007). The scientific research potential of virtual worlds. *Science, 317*(5837), 472–476. doi:10.1126/science.1146930 PMID:17656715

Baker, S. C., Wentz, R. K., & Woods, M. M. (2009). Using virtual worlds in education: Second Life® as an educational tool. *Teaching of Psychology, 36*(1), 59–64. doi:10.1080/00986280802529079

Bal, A., Crittenden, V., Halvorson, W., Pitt, L., & Parent, M. (2015, January). Second best in Second Life: Teaching marketing cases in a virtual world environment.*Proceedings of the 2010 Academy of Marketing Science (AMS) Annual Conference* (pp. 211-211). Springer International Publishing. doi:10.1007/978-3-319-11797-3_119

Balula, A., & Moreira, A. (2014). e-Teaching evaluation in higher education. In Evaluation of Online Higher Education: Learning, Interaction and Technology (pp. 1–11). Springer. doi:10.1007/978-3-319-05425-4

Bandura, A. (1997). *Self-efficacy: The exercise of control.* New York: Freeman.

Barilli, E. (2012). Virtual Reality Technology as a Didactical and Pedagogical Resource in Distance Education for Professional Training. In P. B. Muyinda (Ed.), *Distance education.* Retrieved from http://cdn.intechopen.com/pdfs-wm/39200.pdf

Barker, J., & Gossman, P. (2013). The learning impact of a virtual learning environment: Students' views. *Tean Journal, 5*(2). Retrieved from http://bit.ly/AtMwtr

Barry, D. M., Kanematsu, H., Fukumura, Y., Kobayashi, T., Ogawa, N., & Nagai, H. (2013). US Students Carry out Nuclear Safety Project in a Virtual Environment. *Procedia Computer Science, 22*, 1354–1360. doi:10.1016/j.procs.2013.09.224

Bartle, R. (2003). *Designing virtual worlds.* United States: New Riders Publishing.

Ba, S., Ke, D., Stallaert, J., & Zhang, Z. (2010). Why give away something for nothing? Investigating virtual goods pricing and permission strategies. *ACM Transactions on Management Information Systems, 1*(1), 4. doi:10.1145/1877725.1877729

Baylor, A. L. (2011). The design of motivational agents and avatars. *Educational Technology Research and Development, 59*(2), 291–300. doi:10.1007/s11423-011-9196-3

Baylor, A. L., & Kim, Y. (2005). Simulating instructional roles through pedagogical agents. *International Journal of Artificial Intelligence in Education, 15*(2), 95–115.

Beauvois, M. (1997). High-tech, high-Touch: From discussion to composition in the networked classroom. *Computer Assisted Language Learning, 10*(1), 57–69. doi:10.1080/0958822970100104

Becker, H. (2001). How are teachers using computers in instruction? Paper presented at the 2001 Meeting of the American Educational Research Association, Seattle, WA. Retrieved

Beglau, M., Hare, J. C., Foltos, L., Gann, K., James, J., Jobe, H., . . . Smith, B. (2011). *Technology, Coaching and Community*. International Society for Technology in Education (ISTE). Retrieved from http://www.iste.org/learn/coaching-white-paper.aspx

Bélisle, J., & Bodur, H. (2010). Avatars as information: Perception of consumers based on their avatars in virtual worlds. *Psychology and Marketing*, *27*(8), 741–765. doi:10.1002/mar.20354

Bell, J. T., & Fogler, H. S. (1995). Virtual reality in chemical engineering education. *Proceedings of the American Society for Engineering Education*, Illinois / Indiana Sectional Conference, Purdue University, March 1995. doi:10.1109/VR.2004.1310077

Bell, J. T., & Fogler, H. S. (1997, January 12-15). The application of virtual reality to chemical engineering education. *Proceedings of the 1997 International Conference on Simulation in Engineering Education (ICSEE '97)*, Society for Computer Simulation, San Diego. *Simulation Series*, 29(2). Retrieved from http://citeseerx.ist.psu.edu/viewdoc/download?doi=10.1.1.88.4744&rep=rep1&type=pdf

Bell, M. W. (2008). Toward a Definition of "Virtual Worlds". *Journal of Virtual Worlds Research*, *1*(1).

Bellotti, F., Kapralos, B., Lee, K., Moreno-Ger, P., & Berta, R. (2013). Assessment in and of serious games: An overview. *Advances in Human-Computer Interaction*. Retrieved from http://www.hindawi.com/journals/ahci/2013/136864/cta/

Bellotti, F., Berta, R., De Gloria, A., & Primavera, L. (2010). Supporting authors in the development of task-based learning in Serious Virtual Worlds. *British Journal of Educational Technology*, *41*(1), 86–107. doi:10.1111/j.1467-8535.2009.01039.x

Benford, S., Greenhalgh, C., Reynard, G., Brown, C., & Koleva, B. (1998). Understanding and constructing shared spaces with mixed-reality boundaries. *ACM Transactions on Computer-Human Interaction*, *5*(3), 185–223. doi:10.1145/292834.292836

Berns, A., Gonzalez-Pardo, A., & Camacho, D. (2012). Combining Face-to-Face Learning with Online Learning in Virtual Worlds. *Paper presented at theEuropean Association for Computer-Assisted Language Learning (EUROCALL) Annual Conference*.

Bers, M., & Chau, C. (2010). The virtual campus of the future: Stimulating and simulating civic actions in a virtual world. *Journal of Computing in Higher Education*, *22*(1), 1–23. doi:10.1007/s12528-009-9026-3

Bijeljac-Babic, R., Bertoncini, J., & Mehler, J. (1993). How do 4-day-old infants categorize multisyllabic utterances? *Developmental Psychology*, *29*(4), 711–721. doi:10.1037/0012-1649.29.4.711

Billinghurst, M. (2002). *Augmented Reality in Education. New Horizons for Learning*. Retrieved from http://www.newhorizons.org/ strategies/technology/billinghurst.htm

Billinghurst, M., & Henrysson, A. (2009). Mobile architectural augmented reality. In X. Wang, & M. Schnabel (Eds.), *Mixed Reality In Architecture, Design And Construction* (pp. 93–104). The Netherlands: Springer. doi:10.1007/978-1-4020-9088-2_6

Billinghurst, M., Kato, H., & Poupyrev, I. (2001). The Magic Book — Moving seamlessly between reality and virtuality. *IEEE Computer Graphics and Applications*, *21*(3), 2–4.

Biocca, F., Harms, C., & Burgoon, J. K. (2003). Toward a more robust theory and measure of social presence: Review and suggested criteria. *Presence (Cambridge, Mass.)*, *12*(5), 456–480. doi:10.1162/105474603322761270

Björk, S., & Holopainen, J. (2004). *Patterns in Game Design*. Charles River Media.

Blackburn, D., Henderson, R., & Welz, G. (1996). VRML evolution. *Internet World*, *7*(12), 65–70.

Blankenship, R. J. (2010). *Using virtual environments as professional development tools for pre-service teachers seeking ESOL endorsement* [Unpublished doctoral dissertation]. University of South Florida, FL.

Blaschke, B., & Hase, S. (2015). Heutagogy, technology and lifelong learning for professional part-time learners. In A. Dailey-Hebert & K. Dennis (Eds.), *Transformative perspectives & processes in higher education*. London: Springer. doi:10.1007/978-3-319-09247-8_5

Blasing, M. T. (2010). Second language in Second Life: Exploring interaction, identify and pedagogical practice in a virtual world. *Slavic and East European Journal*, *54*(1), 96–117.

Bojanova, I. (2011). Physical presence through virtual worlds. *IT Professional*, *13*(4), 4–5. doi:10.1109/MITP.2011.66

Bonwell, C., & Eison, J. (1991). *Active learning: Creating excitement in the classroom*. San Francisco: Jossey-Bass.

Boudreau, C., & Okada, M. (1998). The foreign language acquisition system of Project Orbis: An example of educational, customizable language exposure in a shared virtual world. In *Future generation computing systems*. Amsterdam: Elsevier.

Bouras, C., & Filopoulos, A. (1998). Distributed virtual reality environments over web for distance education. In *Proceedings of EDEN Conference* (pp. 481-484).

Bourke, P. (2007). *Representing and modeling geometry in Second Life*. Retrieved from http://paulbourke.net/fractals/secondlife/

Bourke, P. (2008). Evaluating Second Life as a tool for collaborative scientific visualization. Retrieved from http://paulbourke.net/papers/cgat08/

Bourke, P. (2008). Evaluating Second Life as a tool for collaborative scientific vizualisation. *Proceedings of the Computer Games and Allied Technology in Animation, Multimedia, IPTV & Entertainment (CGAT 08)*. Retrieved from http://paulbourke.net/papers/cgat08/

Bouta, H., Retalis, S., & Paraskeva, F. (2012). Utilizing a collaborative macro-script to enhance student engagement: A mixed method study in a 3D virtual environment. *Computers & Education*, *58*(1), 501–517. doi:10.1016/j.compedu.2011.08.031

Bower, M. (2008). Affordance analysis—matching learning tasks with learning technologies. *Educational Media International*, *45*(1), 3–15. doi:10.1080/09523980701847115

Bowman, D. A., & McMahan, R. P. (2007). Virtual reality: How much immersion is enough? *Computer*, *40*(7), 36–42. doi:10.1109/MC.2007.257

Bozkurt, A. (2011). A classroom observation-based evaluation of elementary teachers' use of technology in the classrooms in Turkey. *Educational Research Review*, 2011, 367–373.

Bradshaw, D. (2009). New practices in flexible learning: virtual worlds – real learning! Pedagogical Reflections. Retrieved from http://virtualworlds.flexiblelearning.net.au/reports/VWRL_pedagog_reflect.pdf

Braman, J., Dudley, A., Colt, K., Vincenti, V., & Wang, Y. (2011). Gaining insight into the application of second life in a computer course: student's perspectives. *Proceedings of the 14th HCI International Conference on Online Communities and Social Computing*. Orlando, FL.

Braman, J., Jinman, A., & Trajkovski, G. (2007). Exploring virtual worlds as an extension to classroom learning. In C. A. Shoniregun & A. Logvynovskiy (Eds.), *Proceedings of the International Conference on Information Society (i-Society 2007)* (pp. 82-86). London, UK: e-Centre for Infonomics. Retrieved from http://air.unimi.it/bitstream/2434/64612/1/i-SocietyProceedings.pdf

Braman, J., Meiselwitz, G., & Vincenti, G. (2013). Virtual worlds in the general education curriculum. In R. McBride & M. Searson (Eds.), *Proceedings of Society for Information Technology & Teacher Education International Conference 2013* (pp. 2692-2697).

Bransford, J. D., & Schwartz, D. L. (1999). Rethinking transfer: A simple proposal with multiple implications. In A. Iran-Nejad & P. D. Pearson (Eds.), Review of research in education (pp. 61-100). Washington, DC: American Educational Research Association.

Brantley-Dias, L., Kinuthia, W., Shoffner, M. B., DeCastro, C., & Rigole, N. (2007). Developing pedagogical technology integration content knowledge in preservice teachers: A case study approach. *Journal of Research on Computing in Teacher Education, 23*, 143–149.

Bray, D. A., & Konsynski, B. (2008). *Virtual worlds, virtual economies, virtual institutions. Proceedings of the Virtual Worlds and New Realities Conference*. Atlanta, GA: Emory University.

Breeze, M. (2014). *How augmented reality will change the way we live.* Retrieved from http://tnw.co/1nEDN6O

Britain, S. (1999). A framework for pedagogical evaluation of virtual world learning environments. JISC Technology Applications Programme, Report 41: Joint Information Systems Committee of the Higher Educational Funding Council. Manchester, UK.

Britain, S., & Liber, O. (2000). A framework for the pedagogical evaluation of virtual learning environments. JTAP Report no. 041. Retrieved from http://www.leeds.ac.uk/educol/documents/00001237.htm

Britain, S., & Liber, O. (2004). A framework for pedagogical evaluation of virtual learning environments. *JISC Technology Applications Program,* (41)

Britain, S., & Liber, O. (2004). A framework for pedagogical evaluation of virtual learning environments. *Research Report.* Retrieved from: https://halshs.archives-ouvertes.fr/hal-00696234/document

Bronack, S., Sanders, R., Cheney, A., Riedl, R., Tashner, J., & Matzen, N. (2008). Presence Pedagogy: Teaching and Learning in a 3D Virtual Immersive World. *International Journal of Teaching and Learning in Higher Education, 20*(1), 59–69.

Brooks, F. P. (1999). What's real about virtual reality? *IEEE Computer Graphics and Applications, 19*(6), 16–27. doi:10.1109/38.799723

Brown, A. (2009). A second look at Second Life: Virtual worlds and education. *Paper presented at theannual NECC conference*, Washington, D.C.

Brown, H. D. (2004). Language assessment: Principles and classroom practices. White Plains, NY: Addison Wesley Longman.

Brown, J. S., Collins, A., & Duguid, P. (1989). Situated cognition and the culture of learning. *Educational Researcher, 18*(1), 32–42. doi:10.3102/0013189X018001032

Brown, R., Rasmussen, R., Baldwin, I., & Wyeth, P. (2012). Design and implementation of a virtual world training simulation of ICU first hour handover processes. *Australian Critical Care, 25*(3), 178–187. doi:10.1016/j.aucc.2012.02.005 PMID:22436543

Buchholz, R. (2014). *Augmented reality: new opportunities for marketing and sales*. Retrieved from http://bit.ly/1nMCLYO

Buhalis, D., & Yovcheva, Z. (2014). *Augmented reality in tourism: 10 best practices*. Retrieved from http://bit.ly/1tphods

Burdea, G. C., & Coiffet, P. (2003). *Virtual reality technology* (2nd ed.). New Brunswick, NJ: Wiley-IEEE Press.

Burgess, M. L., & Caverly, D. C. (2009). Techtalk:" Second Life" and Developmental Education. *Journal of Developmental Education*, *32*(3), 42–43.

Butterworth, B. (2005). The development of arithmetical abilities. *Journal of Child Psychology and Psychiatry, and Allied Disciplines*, *46*(1), 3–18. doi:10.1111/j.1469-7610.2004.00374.x PMID:15660640

Bynum, T. W. (2000). The foundation of computer ethics. *ACM SIGCAS Computers and Society*, *30*(2), 6–13. doi:10.1145/572230.572231

Bynum, T. W. (2001). Computer ethics: Its birth and its future. *Ethics and Information Technology*, *3*(2), 109–112. doi:10.1023/A:1011893925319

Bynum, T. W., & Rogerson, S. (2003). *Computer Ethics and Professional Responsibility: Introductory Text and Readings*. Cambridge, MA, USA: Blackwell Publishing.

Byram, M. (1997). *Teaching and assessing intercultural communicative competence*. Multilingual Matters Ltd.

Byrne, C. M. (1996). *Water on tap: The use of virtual reality as an educational tool* (Doctoral dissertation, University of Washington).

Caarls, J., Jonker, P., Kolstee, Y., Rotteveel, J., & van Eck, W. (2009). Augmented reality for art, design and cultural heritage—system design and evaluation. *EURASIP Journal on Image and Video Processing*, *2009*, 1–16. doi:10.1155/2009/716160

Calandra, B., & Puvirajah, A. (2014). Teacher practice in multi user virtual environments:A fourth space. *TechTrends*, *58*(6), 29–35. doi:10.1007/s11528-014-0800-3

Callaghan, M., McCusker, K., Losada, J. L., Harkin, J., & Wilson, S. (2009). Integrating virtual worlds & virtual learning environments for online education. *Paper presented at the Games Innovations Conference ICE-GIC International IEEE Consumer Electronics Society.* doi:10.1109/ICEGIC.2009.5293576

Calongne, C., & Hiles, J. (2007). Blended Realities: A Virtual Tour of Education in Second Life. In *Proceedings of TCC Worldwide Online Conference 2007* (pp. 70-90). Retrieved from http://etec.hawaii.edu/proceedings/2007/calongne.pdf

Calongne, C. (2008). Educational frontiers: Learning in a virtual world. *EDUCAUSE Review*, *43*(5). Retrieved from http://www.educause.edu/ero/article/educational-frontiers-learning-virtual-world

Carini, R., Kuh, G., & Klein, S. (2006). Student engagement and student learning: Testing the linkages. *Research in Higher Education*, *47*(1), 1–32. doi:10.1007/s11162-005-8150-9

Caruso, V., Morch, A. I., Thomassen, I., Hartley, M., & Ludlow, B. L. (2014). Practicing collaboration skills through role-play activities in a 3D virtual world. In R. Huang, Kinshuk, & N. Chen (Eds.), The new development of technology enhanced learning: Concept, research and best practices (pp. 165-184). Berlin: Springer-Verlag.

Castronova, E. (2005). *Synthetic worlds: The business and culture of online games*. University of Chicago Press.

Cerniamo, K. S., Ross, J. D., & Ertmer, P. A. (2010). *Technology integration for meaningful classroom use: A standards-based approach*. Belmont, CA: Wadsworth, Cengage Learning.

Chafer, J., & Childs, M. (2008, November 20 21). The impact of the characteristics of a virtual environment on performance: Concepts, constraints and complications. *Proceedings of the ReLIVE 08 conference*, Open University (pp. 94-105).

Chang, L. (2015, June 29). Go shopping from the comfort of your own home with your virtual reality headset. *Digital Trends.* Retrieved from http://www.digitaltrends.com/cool/retail/

Chapman, D. D., & Stone, S. (2010). Measurement of outcomes in virtual environments. *Advances in Developing Human Resources, 12*(6), 665–680. doi:10.1177/1523422310394792

Cheal, C. (2009). Student perceptions of a course taught in Second Life. *Innovate: Journal of online. Education, 5*(5), 2.

Chen, X., Siau, K., & Nah, F. F.-H. (2009). 3-D virtual worlds: Education and learning. *SIGHCI 2009 Proceedings* (p. 13).

Chen, C. J. (2006). The design, development and evaluation of a virtual reality based learning environment. *Australasian Journal of Educational Technology, 22*(1), 39–63.

Chen, C. J. (2010). *Virtual reality (VR)-based learning environment: Design, develop, evaluate.* Saarbrücken, Germany: Lambert Academic.

Chen, C. J., & Teh, C. S. (2000). Design issues of desktop virtual reality educational applications. In H. M. Khalid (Ed.), *Virtual reality: select issues and applications* (pp. 63–78). London: Asean Academic.

Chen, C. J., Toh, S. C., & Ismail, W. M. F. W. (2005). Are learning styles relevant to virtual reality? *Journal of Research on Technology in Education, 38*(2), 123–141. doi:10.1080/15391523.2005.10782453

Chen, C.-M., & Tsai, Y.-N. (2012). Interactive augmented reality system for enhancing library instruction in elementary schools. *Computers & Education, 59*(2), 638–652. doi:10.1016/j.compedu.2012.03.001

Cheng, K.-H., & Tsai, C.-C. (2013). Affordances of augmented reality in science learning: Suggestions for future research. *Journal of Science Education and Technology, 22*(4), 449–462. doi:10.1007/s10956-012-9405-9

Cheng, Y., & Wang, S.-H. (2011). Applying a 3D virtual learning environment to facilitate student's application ability–The case of marketing. *Computers in Human Behavior, 27*(1), 576–584. doi:10.1016/j.chb.2010.10.008

Cheong, D. (2010). The effects of practice teaching sessions in Second Life on the change in pre-service teachers' teaching efficacy. *Computers & Education, 55*(2), 868–880. doi:10.1016/j.compedu.2010.03.018

Childs, M. (2007). Real Learning in Virtual Worlds. *Warwick International Journal, 30*(2).

Childs, M. (2010). *Learners' experience of presence in Virtual Worlds* [Doctoral dissertation]. Institute of Education. Retrieved from https://files.warwick.ac.uk/mchilds1/files/childs+thesis+final.pdf

Choi, S., & Clark, R. E. (2006). Cognitive and affective benefits of an animated pedagogical agent for learning English as a second language. *Journal of Educational Computing Research, 34*(4), 441–466. doi:10.2190/A064-U776-4208-N145

Cho, K., Lee, J., Soh, J., Lee, J., & Yang, H. S. (2007). A realisitc e-learning system based on mixed reality.*Proc 13th Intl Conference on Virtual System and Multimedia* (pp. 57- 64). VSMM.

Chouhan, R., & Sharma, G. K. (2015). Virtual Reality: In gaming. *International Journal of Multidisciplinary Consortium, 2*(2), 36.

Chung, I. C., Huang, C. Y., Yeh, S. C., Chiang, W. C., & Tseng, M. H. (2014). Developing Kinect games integrated with virtual reality on activities of daily living for children with developmental delay. In Advanced technologies, embedded and multimedia for human-centric computing (pp. 1091-1097). Netherlands: Springer. doi:10.1007/978-94-007-7262-5_124

Cifuentes, L., Maxwell, G., & Bulu, S. (2011). Technology integration through professional learning community. *Journal of Educational Computing Research, 44*(1), 59–82. doi:10.2190/EC.44.1.d

Cihak, D. F., & Foust, J. L. (2008). Comparing number lines and touch points to teach addition facts to students with autism. *Focus on Autism and Other Developmental Disabilities*, *23*(3), 131–137. doi:10.1177/1088357608318950

Clarebout, G., Elen, J., Johnson, W. L., & Shaw, E. (2002). Animated pedagogical agents: An opportunity to be grasped? *Journal of Educational Multimedia and Hypermedia*, *11*(3), 267–286.

Clark, R. E., & Choi, S. (2005). Five design principles for experiments on the effects of animated pedagogical agents. *Journal of Educational Computing Research*, *32*(3), 209–225. doi:10.2190/7LRM-3BR2-44GW-9QQY

Clark, R. E., & Choi, S. (2007). The questionable benefits of pedagogical agents: Response to Veletsianos. *Journal of Educational Computing Research*, *36*(4), 379–381. doi:10.2190/2781-3471-67MG-5033

Clark, S., & Maher, M. L. (2001). *The role of place in designing a learner centred virtual learning environment Computer Aided Architectural Design Futures 2001* (pp. 187–200). Springer. doi:10.1007/978-94-010-0868-6_15

Cognition & Technology Group at Vanderbilt. (1993). Anchored instruction and situated cognition revisited. *Educational Technology*, *33*(3), 52–70.

Cohen, A., & Brawer, F. (2003). *The American community college* (4th ed.). San Francisco: Jossey-Bass Publishing.

Colaric, S., & Taymans, J. (2004). Introducing Faculty to Online Learning: An Online Course as Professional Development. In G. Richards (Ed.), *Proceedings of World Conference on E-Learning in Corporate, Government, Healthcare, and Higher Education* 2004 (pp. 549-554). Chesapeake, VA: AACE.

Coleman, K. G. (2010). Computing and Moral Responsibility. Retrieved from http://plato.stanford.edu/archives/win2010/entries/computing-responsibility/

Coleman, K. G. (2007). Casuistry and Computer Ethics. *Metaphilosophy*, *38*(4), 471–488. doi:10.1111/j.1467-9973.2007.00494.x

Colpaert, J. (2006). Pedagogy-driven design for online language teaching and learning. *CALICO Journal*, *23*(3), 477–497.

Common Core State Standards. (2010). Common Core State Standards for Mathematics. Washington, DC: National Governors Association Center for Best Practices and the Council of Chief State School Officers. Retrieved from http://www.corestandards.org/other-resources/key-shifts-in-mathematics/

Community College Research Center. (2014). What we know about developmental education outcomes. Retrieved from http://ccrc.tc.columbia.edu/media/k2/attachments/what-we- know-about-developmental-education-outcomes.pdf

Connolly, P. E. (2008). Virtual reality & immersive technology in education. In C. Van Slyke (Ed.), *Information communication technologies: concepts, methodologies, tools, and applications* (pp. 2168–2172). Hershey, PA: Information Science Reference; doi:10.4018/978-1-59904-949-6.ch158

Consalvo, M. (2003). It's No Videogame: News Commentary and the Second Gulf War. *Proceedings Level Up Conference*. Retrieved from http://citeseerx.ist.psu.edu/viewdoc/summary?doi=10.1.1.77.44

Cooke-Plagwitz, J. (2009). A new language for the Net generation: Why Second Life works for the net generation. In R. Oxford & J. Oxford (Eds.), *Second language teaching and learning in the Net generation* (pp. 173–180). Manoa, HI: National Foreign Language Resource Center, University of Hawaii.

Cooperstock, J. R. (2001). The classroom of the future: Enhancing education through augmented reality.*Proceedings of HCI International* (pp. 688-692). New Orleans: Lawrence Erlbaum Associates, Inc.

Coppola, N. W., Hiltz, S., & Rotter, N. G. (2002). Becoming a virtual professor: Pedagogical roles and asynchronous learning networks. *Journal of Management Information Systems*, *18*(4), 169–189.

Coyle, H., Traynor, V., & Solowij, N. (2015). Computerized and virtual reality cognitive training for individuals at high risk of cognitive decline: Systematic review of the literature. *The American Journal of Geriatric Psychiatry*, *23*(4), 335–359. doi:10.1016/j.jagp.2014.04.009 PMID:24998488

Craig, S. D., Gholson, B., & Driscoll, D. M. (2002). Animated pedagogical agents in multimedia educational environments: Effects of agent properties, picture features, and redundancy. *Journal of Educational Psychology*, *94*(2), 428–434. doi:10.1037/0022-0663.94.2.428

Creative Guerrilla Marketing. (2014). 10 examples of augmented reality in retail. Retrieved from http://bit.ly/OxuyHI

Csikszentmihalyi, M. (1990). *Flow: The psychology of optimal experience*. Harper Perennial Modern Classics.

Cuban, L., Kirkpatrick, H., & Peck, C. (2001). High access and low use of technologies in high school classrooms: Explaining an apparent paradox. *American Educational Research Journal*, *38*(4), 813834. doi:10.3102/00028312038004813

Cummings, J. J., & Bailenson, J. N. (2015). How immersive is enough? A meta-analysis of the effect of immersive technology on user presence. *Media Psychology*, 1–38. doi:10.1080/15213269.2015.1015740

D'Mello, S. K., & Graesser, A. (2010). Multimodal semi-automated affect detection from conversational cues, gross body language, and facial features. *User Modeling and User-Adapted Interaction*, *20*(2), 147–187. doi:10.1007/s11257-010-9074-4

Dafoulas, G., Saleeb, N., & Loomes, M. (2012). The impact of 3D virtual environments on communication patterns. *Paper presented at the Information Technology Based Higher Education and Training (ITHET) 2012 International Conference*. doi:10.1109/ITHET.2012.6246065

Dailey-Hebert, A., Donnelli-Sallee, E., & DiPadova-Stocks, L. (2008). Service-eLearning as integrated pedagogy: An introduction. In A. Dailey-Hebert, E. Donnelli-Sallee, L. & DiPadova-Stocks (Eds.), Service-eLearning: Educating for citizenship (pp.1-5). Charlotte, NC: Information Age Publishing.

Daim, T. U., Letts, M., Krampits, M., Khamis, R., Dash, P., & Monalisa, M. (2012). IT infrastructure refresh planning for enterprises: A business process perspective. *Business Process Management Journal*, *17*(3), 1–16.

Dalgarno, B., Gregory, S., Carlson, L., Lee, M. J. W., & Tynan, B. (2013). *A systematic review and environmental analysis of the use of 3D immersive virtual worlds in Australian and New Zealand higher education institutions* (Final Report) (pp. 1–226). Armidale, Australia: DEHub: Innovation in Distance Education, University of New England. Retrieved from http://www.dehub.edu.au/downloads/VWSSP_Report_V2_TD_200613_dehub.pdf

Damer, B. (1997). *Avatars! Exploring and building virtual worlds on the Internet*. Retrieved from http://www.digitalspace.com/avatars/book/chtu/chtu1.htm

D'Atri, A., Missikoff, O., & Pauselli, E. (2002). FairsNet: A virtual environment to support business education.*Proceedings IASTED International Symposium on Web-based Education (WBE 2002)*, Cancun, Mexico (pp. 394-398).

Davis, J., II, Goel, M., Hylands, C., Kienhuis, B., Lee, E. A., Liu, J., . . . Reekie, J. (1999). *Overview of the Ptolemy project* (ERL Technical Report). UCB/ERL.

Dawley, L. (2007). *Persistent social learning: An emergent ID model for virtual world design* [Video file]. Retrieved from https://admin.acrobat.com/_a768376479/p17101188/

Dawley, L., & Dede, C. (2014). Situated learning in virtual worlds and immersive simulations. In J. M. Spector, M. D. Merrill, J. Elen, & M. J. Bishop (Eds.), *The handbook of research for educational communications and technology* (4th ed., pp. 723–734). New York: Springer. doi:10.1007/978-1-4614-3185-5_58

De Bono, E. (1985). *De Bono's Thinking Course*. New York, NY: Facts On File Publications.

De Freitas, S. (2008). *Serious virtual worlds. A scoping guide: Prepared for the JISC e-Learning Programme, The Joint Information Systems Committee*. UK: JISC.

De Lucia, A., Francese, R., Passero, I., & Tortora, G. (2009). Development and evaluation of a virtual campus on Second Life: The case of SecondDMI. *Computers & Education*, *52*(1), 220–233. doi:10.1016/j.compedu.2008.08.001

Dede, C. (2009). Immersive interfaces for engagement and learning. *Science 2*, 323(5910), 66-69. DOI:.10.1126/science.1167311

Dede, C. (2005). Planning for neomillennial learning styles. *EDUCAUSE Quarterly*, *28*(1), 1–10.

Dehaene, S. (2011). *The number sense: How the mind creates mathematics*. Oxford University Press.

Dehn, D. M., & van Mulken, S. (2000). The impact of animated interface agents: A review of empirical literature. *International Journal of Human-Computer Studies*, *52*(1), 1–22. doi:10.1006/ijhc.1999.0325

Deighton, J. A., & Kornfeld, L. (2007). *Digital interactivity: unanticipated consequences for markets, marketing and consumers*. Boston: Harvard Business School.

Delgarno, B., & Lee, M. (2010). What are the learning affordances of 3-D virtual environments? *British Journal of Educational Technology*, *41*(1), 10–32. doi:10.1111/j.1467-8535.2009.01038.x

Deluna, K. (2014). *10 rockstar examples of augmented reality for 2014*. Retrieved from http://bit.ly/1mIaCib

Deutschmann, M., & Panichi, L. (2009). Talking into Empty Space? Signaling Involvement in a Virtual Language Classroom in Second Life. *Language Awareness*, *18*(3–4), 310–328. doi:10.1080/09658410903197306

Deutschmann, M., Panichi, L., & Molka-Danielsson, J. (2009). Designing oral participation in Second Life—A comparative study of two language proficiency courses. *ReCALL*, *21*(02), 206–226. doi:10.1017/S0958344009000196

Dhir, A. (2004). *The digital consumer technology handbook*. Oxford: Elsevier.

Di Blas, N., & Poggi, C. (2007). European virtual classrooms: Building effective "virtual" educational experiences. *Virtual Reality (Waltham Cross)*, *11*(2-3), 129–143. doi:10.1007/s10055-006-0060-4

Dibbell, J. (1993). A Rape in Cyberspace. *The Village Voice*.

Dibbell, J. (1994). A Rape in Cyberspace: How an Evil Clown, a Haitian Trickster Spirit, Two Wizards, and a Cast of Dozens Turned a Database into a Society. *Annual Survey of American Law*, 1994, 471–481.

Dickey, M. D. (2005). Engaging by design: How engagement strategies in popular computer and video games can inform instructional design. *Educational Technology Research and Development*, *53*(2), 67–83. doi:10.1007/BF02504866

Dickey, M. D. (2005). Three-dimensional virtual worlds and distance learning: Two case studies of Active Worlds as a medium for distance education. *British Journal of Educational Technology*, *36*(3), 439–451. doi:10.1111/j.1467-8535.2005.00477.x

Dickey, M. D. (2005a). Brave new (interactive) worlds: A review of the design affordances and constraints of two 3D virtual worlds as interactive learning environments. *Interactive Learning Environments*, *13*(1–2), 121–137. doi:10.1080/10494820500173714

Dickey, M. D. (2011). The pragmatics of virtual worlds for K-12 educators: Investigating the affordances and constraints of Active Worlds and Second Life with K-12 in-service teachers. *Educational Technology Research and Development*, *59*(1), 1–20. doi:10.1007/s11423-010-9163-4

Diener, S., Windsor, J., & Bodily, D. (2009). Design and development of clinical simulations in SecondLife.*Proceedings of the EDUCAUSE Australasia Conference* (pp. 1–13).

Dieterle, E., & Dede, C. (2006). Building university faculty and student capacity to use wireless handheld devices for learning. In M. van't Hooft (Ed.), *Ubiquitous computing: invisible technology, visible impact* (pp. 303–328). Mahweh, NJ: Erlbaum.

Digitalmeetsculture. (2015). Augmented reality: enriching culture. Retrieved from http://bit.ly/1E46st6

Dionisio, J. D. N., Iii, W. G. B., & Gilbert, R. (2013). 3D Virtual worlds and the metaverse. *ACM Computing Surveys*, *45*(3), 1–38. doi:10.1145/2480741.2480751

Djorgovski, S. G., Hut, P., McMillan, S., Vesperini, E., Knop, R., Farr, W., & Graham, M. J. (2010). Exploring the use of virtual worlds as a scientific research platform: The meta-institute for computational astrophysics (MICA). In *Facets of virtual worlds* (pp. 29–43). Retrieved from http://link.springer.com/chapter/10.1007/978-3-642-11743-5_3

Domagk, S. (2010). Do pedagogical agents facilitate learner motivation and learning outcomes? The role of the appeal of agent's appearance and voice. *Journal of Media Psychology*, *22*(2), 84–97. doi:10.1027/1864-1105/a000011

Domínguez, A., Saenz-de-Navarrete, J., de-Marcos, L., Fernández-Sanz, L., Pagés, C., & Martínez-Herráiz, J.-J. (2013). Pagés, & C. Martínez-Herráiz, J. (2013). Gamifying learning experiences: Practical Implications and Outcomes. *Computers & Education*, *63*, 380–392. doi:10.1016/j.compedu.2012.12.020

Dong, P., Ma, B., & Wang, F. (2010). Development and Evaluation of an Experiential Learning Service in 3D Virtual World. *Paper presented at the Service Sciences (ICSS) 2010 International Conference*. doi:10.1109/ICSS.2010.37

Dorf, Y. J., Belcher, J., Bessetta, M., Danziger, M., McKinney, A., & Hult, E. (2010). Technology for active learning. *Materials Today*, *6*(12), 44–49.

dos Santos, F. R., Guetl, C., Bailey, P. H., & Harward, V. J. (2010). Dynamic virtual environment for multiple physics experiments in higher education. *Paper presented at theEducation Engineering (EDUCON)*. doi:10.1109/EDUCON.2010.5492507

Dreher, C., Reiners, T., Dreher, N., & Dreher, H. (2009). 3D virtual worlds as collaborative communities enriching human endeavours: Innovative applications in e-Learning. *Paper presented at the 3rd IEEE International Conference on Digital Ecosystems and Technologies DEST'09.*

Duncan, I., Miller, A., & Jiang, S. (2012). A taxonomy of virtual world usage in education. *British Journal of Educational Technology*, *43*(6). DOI: 10:1111/j.1467-8535.2011.01263.x

Duncan, I., Miller, A., & Jiang, S. (2012). A taxonomy of virtual worlds usage in education. *British Journal of Educational Technology*, *43*(6), 949–964. http://ishbel.host.cs.standrews.ac.uk/Research/SL_Taxonomy.pdfdoi:10.1111/j.1467-8535.2011.01263.x

Dunleavy, M., Dede, C., & Mitchell, R. (2009). Affordances and limitations of immersive participatory augmented reality simulations for teaching and learning. *Journal of Science Education and Technology*, *18*(1), 7–22. doi:10.1007/s10956-008-9119-1

Dunleavy, M., Dede, C., & Mitchell, R. (2009). Affordances and limitations of immersive participatory augmented reality simulations for teaching and learning. *Journal of Science Education*, *18*, 7–22.

Dunsworth, Q., & Atkinson, R. K. (2007). Fostering multimedia learning of science: Exploring the role of an animated agent's image. *Computers & Education*, *49*(3), 677–690. doi:10.1016/j.compedu.2005.11.010

Duran, J., & Villagrasa, S. (2013). Teaching 3D arts using game engines for engineering and architecture.*Proceedings of the 5th International Conference on Virtual, Augmented and Mixed Reality (VAMR 2013) held as part of HCI International (HCII 2013)* (pp. 113–121). Springer. doi:10.1007/978-3-642-39420-1_13

Dutra, J.P. (2015). *ARgos – augmented reality in Volos – Greece*. Retrieved from http://bit.ly/1BgTVTw

Earnshaw, E., Chilton, N., & Palmer, I. (1997). Visualization and virtual reality on the Internet. In R. Earnshaw & J. Vince (Eds.), *The Internet in 3D information, images and interaction* (pp. 203–222). San Diego, CA: Academic Press.

Eccles, R. G. (1991). The performance measurement manifesto. *Harvard Business Review*, *69*(1), 131–137. PMID:10109469

Edirisingha, P., Nie, M., Pluciennik, M., & Young, R. (2009). Socialisation for learning at a distance in a 3-D multi-user virtual environment. *British Journal of Educational Technology*, *40*(3), 458–479. doi:10.1111/j.1467-8535.2009.00962.x

Education Commission of the States. (1995). *Making quality count in undergraduate education*. Denver, CO: Education Commission of the States.

Edwards, J. (2011). *Digital frontiers media uses augmented reality to market St. Pete/Clearwater tourism with miles media*. Retrieved from http://www.prweb.com/releases/2011/03/prweb5141134.htm

El Sayed, N. A. M., Zayed, H. H., & Sharawy, M. I. (2011). ARSC: Augmented reality student card – an augmented reality solution for the education field. *Computers & Education*, *56*(4), 1045–1061. doi:10.1016/j.compedu.2010.10.019

Ellis, M., Anderson, P. J., & Kibbe, S. (2014). Second Life: Simplifying and enhancing the processes of teaching and learning. In V. C. X. Wang (Ed.), *Handbook of research on education and technology in a changing society* (pp. 483–503). Hershey, PA: IGI Global. doi:10.4018/978-1-4666-6046-5.ch036

eMINTS National Center. (2014). Instructional model. Retrieved from http://www.emints.org/professional-development/instructional-model/

Encyclopædia Britannica. (2015). *Virtual Reality (VR)*. Encyclopædia Britannica Online.

Enyedy, N., Danish, J. A., Delacruz, G., & Kumar, M. (2012). Learning physics through play in an augmented reality environment. *International Journal of Computer-Supported Collaborative Learning*, *7*(3), 347–378. doi:10.1007/s11412-012-9150-3

Epic Games Inc. (2015). *Unreal engine 4* [computer software]. Retrieved from https://www.unrealengine.com/

Erard, M. (2007). A boon to Second Life language schools. Retrieved from http://www.technologyreview.com/communications/18510/page1/?a=f

Erlandson, B. E., Nelson, B. C., & Wilhelmina, C. S. (2010). Collaboration modality, cognitive load, and science inquiry learning in virtual inquiry environments. *Educational Technology Research and Development*, *58*(6), 693–710. doi:10.1007/s11423-010-9152-7

Ertmer, P. A. (1999). Addressing first and second order barriers to change: Strategies for technology integration. *Educational Technology Research and Development*, *47*(4), 4761. doi:10.1007/BF02299597

Ertmer, P. A., & Ottenbreit-Leftwich, A. (2010). Teacher Technology Change: How Knowledge, Confidence, Beliefs, and Culture Intersect. *Journal of Research on Technology in Education*, *42*(3), 255–284. doi:10.1080/15391523.2010.10782551

Ertmer, P. A., Ottenbreit-Leftwich, A., & York, C. (2006). Exemplary technology-using teachers: Perceptions of factors influencing success. *Journal of Computing in Teacher Education*, *23*(2), 55–61.

Eschenbrenner, B., Nah, F. F.-H., & Siau, K. (2008). 3-D virtual worlds in education: Applications, benefits, issues, and opportunities. *Journal of Database Management*, *19*(4), 91–110. doi:10.4018/jdm.2008100106

Estes, J. S. (2015). A call for teacher preparation programs to model integrating technology into the instructional process. In J. Keengwe (Ed.), *Handbook of research on educational technology integration and active learning* (pp. 62–77). Hershey, PA: IGI. doi:10.4018/978-1-4666-8363-1.ch004

EURO Quick server stats. (2015). Retrieved from http://www.warcraftrealms.com/eu_realmstats.php

Evans, C. (1995). *WWW-VRML benefits?* Retrieved from http://www.thinkofit.com/webconf/icde95/0038.htm

Falconer, L. (2013). Situated learning in virtual simulations: Researching the authentic dimension in virtual worlds. *Journal of Interactive Learning Research*, *24*(3), 285–300.

Falloon, G. (2010). Using avatars and virtual environments in learning: What do they have to offer? *British Journal of Educational Technology*, *41*(1), 108–122. doi:10.1111/j.1467-8535.2009.00991.x

Feng, Z., Duh, H. B.-L., & Billinghurst, M. (2008*)*. Trends in augmented reality tracking, interaction and display: A review of ten years of ISMAR. *Paper presented at the7th IEEE/ACM international symposium on mixed and augmented reality (ISMAR)*, Cambridge, UK. doi:10.1109/ISMAR.2008.4637362

Floridi, L. (1999). Information ethics: On the philosophical foundation of computer ethics. *Ethics and Information Technology*, *1*(1), 33–52. doi:10.1023/A:1010018611096

Floridi, L. (2004). Open Problems in the Philosophy of Information. *Metaphilosophy*, *35*(4), 554–582. doi:10.1111/j.1467-9973.2004.00336.x

Floridi, L. (2005). Information ethics, its nature and scope. *ACM SIGCAS Computers and Society*, *35*(2), 3. doi:10.1145/1111646.1111649

Floridi, L. (Ed.). (2010). *The Cambridge Handbook of Information and Computer Ethics*. Cambridge University Press. doi:10.1017/CBO9780511845239

Floridi, L., & Sanders, J. W. (2001). Artificial evil and the foundation of computer ethics. *Ethics and Information Technology*, *3*(1), 55–66. doi:10.1023/A:1011440125207

Fractal landscape. (2015). *Wikipedia, The Free Encyclopedia*. Retrieved from https://en.wikipedia.org/w/index.php?title=Fractal_landscape&oldid=679001052

Franklin, T. (2011). Mobile learning: At the tipping point. *Turkish Online Journal of Educational Technology*, *10*(4), 261–275.

Freitas, R., & Campos, R. (2008). SMART: A system of augmented reality for teaching 2nd grade students.*Proceedings of the 22nd British computer society conference on human-computer interaction (HCI 2008)* (pp. 27-30). LiverpoolJohn Moores University, UK.

Frey, T. (n. d.). 55 Jobs of the Future. Retrieved from http://www.futuristspeaker.com/2011/11/55-jobs-of-the-future /

Friedman, T. (2005). *The world is flat. Farrar, Straus and Giroux*. New York: MacMillan Publishers.

Fry, H., Ketteridge, S., & Marshall, S. (2003). A handbook for teaching and learning in higher education: Enhancing academic practice (2nd ed.). London; Sterling, VA: Kogan Page.

Fullan, M., & Stiegelbauer, S. (1991). *The new meaning of educational change*. New York: Teachers College Press.

Gabriel, K., & Flake, S. (2008). *Teaching unprepared students: strategies for promoting success and retention in higher education*. Stylus Publishing.

Gagne, R. M. (1980). Is Educational Technology in Phase? *Educational Technology*, 1980, 7–14.

Gallagher, A. G., Ritter, E. M., Champion, H., Higgins, G., Fried, M. P., Moses, G., & Satava, R. M. et al. (2005). Virtual reality simulation for the operating room: Proficiency-based training as a paradigm shift in surgical skills training. *Annals of Surgery*, *241*(2), 364–372. doi:10.1097/01.sla.0000151982.85062.80 PMID:15650649

Gallagher, C. (2014). *Minecraft in the classroom: ideas, inspiration, and student projects for teachers*. Peachpit Press.

Gamage, V., Tretiakov, A., & Crump, B. (2011). Teacher perceptions of learning affordances of multi-user virtual environments. *Computers & Education*, *57*(4), 2406–2413. doi:10.1016/j.compedu.2011.06.015

Gao, F., Noh, J. J., & Koehler, M. J. (2009). Comparing role-playing activities in Second Life and face-to-face environments. *Journal of Interactive Learning Research*, *20*(4), 423–443.

Garb, Y. (Winter 1987). Virtual Reality, *Whole Earth Review* (57): 118ff.

Garcia-Zubia, J., Irurzun, J., Angulo, I., Hernandez, U., Castro, M., Sancristobal, E., . . . Ruiz-de-Garibay, J. (2010). *SecondLab: A remote laboratory under Second Life*. Paper presented at the Education Engineering (EDUCON). doi:10.1109/EDUCON.2010.5492556

Gardner, H. (2011). *Frames of mind: The theory of multiple intelligences*. Basic Books.

Gardner, J. W. (1964). *Self-Renewal*. New York: HarperCollins.

Gartner Incorporated. (2014). *Gartner Technology Research*. Retrieved from: http://Online.gartner.com/technology/home.jsp>

Gass, S., & Selinker, L. (2008). *Second language acquisition: An introductory course* (3rd ed.). New York: Routledge/Taylor Francis.

Gay, R., Charlesworth, A., & Esen, R. (2007). *Online marketing: A customer-led approach*. Oxford: Oxford University Press.

Gee, J. P. (2003). *What videogames have to teach us about learning and literacy*. New York: Palgrave Macmillan.

Gee, J. P. (2007). *What video games have to teach us about learning and literacy*. Palgrave Macmillan.

Gerval, J. P., Popovici, M., Ramdani, M., El Kalai, O., Boskoff, V., & Tisseau, J. (2002). Virtual environments for children. *Proceedings International Conference on Computers and Advanced Technology Education (CATE)*, Cancun, Mexico (pp. 416-420).

Gerval, J. P., Popovici, M., & Tisseau, J. (2003). Virtual stories authoring tools for pedagogical purposes.*Proceedings of IASTED International Conference on Computer and Advanced in Education*. Rhodes, Greece (pp. 642-646).

Ghanbarzadeh, R., Ghapanchi, A. H., & Blumenstein, M. (2015). Characteristics of Research on the Application of Three-Dimensional Immersive Virtual Worlds in Health[Springer.]. *Information Science*, 213–224.

Ghanbarzadeh, R., Ghapanchi, A. H., Blumenstein, M., & Talaei-Khoei, A. (2014). A Decade of Research on the Use of Three-Dimensional Virtual Worlds in Health Care: A Systematic Literature Review. *Journal of Medical Internet Research*, *16*(2), e47. doi:10.2196/jmir.3097 PMID:24550130

Ghapanchi, A. H., & Aurum, A. (2011). Antecedents to IT personnel's intentions to leave: A systematic literature review. *Journal of Systems and Software*, *84*(2), 238–249. doi:10.1016/j.jss.2010.09.022

Ghapanchi, A. H., & Ghanbarzadeh, R. (2014). 3DVWs: Three-dimensional virtual worlds to support teaching and learning activities. *E-Learning Update*, *47*, 14–18.

Giroux, H. A. (2002). Neoliberalism, corporate culture, and the promise of higher education: The university as a democratic public sphere. *Harvard Educational Review*, *72*(4), 425–464. doi:10.17763/haer.72.4.0515nr62324n71p1

GoAnimate. (2015). *Make professional animated videos*. Retrieved from http://goanimate.com/

Gomes, T., Abade, T., Campos, J. C., Harriso, M. D., & Silva, J. L. (2014). A Virtual Environment based Serious Game to Support Health Education. *ICST Transactions on Ambient Systems*, *1*(3), e5. doi:10.4108/amsys.1.3.e5

Gordon, E., & Koo, G. (2008). Placeworlds: Using virtual worlds to foster civic engagement. *Space and Culture*, *11*(3), 204–221. doi:10.1177/1206331208319743

Graesser, A. C. (2011). Learning, thinking, and emoting with discourse technologies. *The American Psychologist*, *66*(8), 746–757. doi:10.1037/a0024974 PMID:22082403

Gregory, S., Scutter, S., Jacka, L., McDonald, M., Farley, H., & Newman, C. (2015). Barriers and Enablers to the Use of Virtual Worlds in Higher Education: An Exploration of Educator Perceptions, Attitudes and Experiences. *Journal of Educational Technology & Society*, *18*(1), 3–12.

Grenfell, J. (2013). Immersive Interfaces for Art Education Teaching and Learning in Virtual and Real World Learning Environments. *Procedia: Social and Behavioral Sciences*, *93*, 1198–1211. doi:10.1016/j.sbspro.2013.10.016

Grimes, G., & Bartolacci, M. (2012). Second Life: a virtual world platform for profiling online behavior for network and information security education? An initial investigation. In M. Bartolacci & S. Powell (Eds.), *Research, practice, and educational advancements in telecommunications and networking* (pp. 285–289). Hershey, PA, USA: IGI Global. doi:10.4018/978-1-4666-0050-8.ch017

Grimes, J. M., Fleischmann, K. R., & Jaeger, P. T. (2009). Virtual guinea pigs: Ethical implications of human subjects research in virtual worlds. *International Journal of Internet Research Ethics*, *2*(1).

Grimes, J. M., Fleischmann, K. R., & Jaeger, P. T. (2010). Research ethics and virtual worlds. In C. Wankel & S. Malleck (Eds.), *Emerging Ethical Issues of Life in Virtual Worlds* (pp. 73–99). Information Age Publishing.

Guérin, E., Tosan, E., & Baskurt, A. (2002). *Modeling and approximation of fractal surfaces with projected IFS attractors. Emergent Nature: Patterns, Growth and Scaling in the Science* (pp. 93–303). New Jersey: World Scientific.

Guimaraes, T. (2012). Industry clockspeed's impact on business innovation success factors. *European Journal of Innovation Management*, *14*(3), 322–344. doi:10.1108/14601061111148825

Gulz, A. (2004). Benefits of virtual characters in computer based learning environments: Claims and evidence. *Educational Research Review*, *6*, 27–54.

Häfner, P., Häfner, V., & Ovtcharova, J. (2013). Teaching Methodology for Virtual Reality Practical Course in Engineering Education. *Procedia Computer Science,* 25, 251-260.

Han, D., Jung, T., & Gibson, A. (2014). Dublin AR: Implementing Augmented Reality (AR) in Tourism. In Z. Xiang & I. Tussyadiah (Eds.), *Information and Communication Technologies in Tourism* (pp. 511–523). Wien, New York: Springer International Publishing.

Harris, S. R., & Gerich, E. (1996). Retiring the NSFNET backbone service: Chronicling the end of an era. *ConneXiona*, *10*(4).

Harshman, E. M., Gilsinan, J. F., Fisher, J. E., & Yeager, F. C. (2005). Professional Ethics in a Virtual World: The Impact of the Internet on Traditional Notions of Professionalism. *Journal of Business Ethics*, *58*(1-3), 227–236. doi:10.1007/s10551-005-1417-4

Hartholt, A., Traum, D., Marsella, S., Shapiro, A., Stratou, G., Leuski, A., . . . Gratch, J. (2013). All together now: Introducing the virtual human toolkit. *Proceedings of the International Conference on Intelligent Virtual Humans*. Retrieved from http://ict.usc.edu/pubs/All%20Together%20Now.pdf

Hase, S. (2013). Learning defined learning. In S. Hase & C. Kenyon (Eds.), *Self-determined learning: Heutagogy in action*. London: Bloomsbury.

Hassan, A. (2013). Perspective analysis and implications of visitor management - experiences from the Whitechapel Gallery, London. *Anatolia: An International Journal of Tourism and Hospitality Research*, 24(3), 410-426. doi:.10.1080/13032917.2013.797916

Hax, A. C. (2010). *Reinventing your business strategy*. New York: Springer.

Hedberg, J., Harper, B., & Dalgarno, B. (2002). The contribution of 3D environments to conceptual understanding. In O. J. McKerrow (Eds.), Winds of Change in the Sea of Learning: Proceedings of *the 19th Annual Conference of the Australasian Society for Computers in Learning in Tertiary Education* (Vol 1, pp. 149-158). Auckland, New Zealand: UNITEC, Institute of Technology.

Hedberg, J., & Alexander, S. (1994). Virtual reality in education: Defining researchable issues. *Educational Media International*, *31*(4), 214–220. doi:10.1080/0952398940310402

Heidig, S., & Clarebout, G. (2011). Do pedagogical agents make a difference to student motivation and learning? *Educational Research Review*, *6*(1), 27–54. doi:10.1016/j.edurev.2010.07.004

Heili, J., & Michel, H. (2011, October). Do students Trained using serious games become better sales representatives? An experiment to study the performance of academic serious games. *Proceedings of theEuropean Conference on Games-Based Learning*.

Hemp, P. (2006). Avatar-based marketing. *Harvard Business Review*, *84*(6), 48–57. PMID:16846188

Henckel, A., & Lopes, C. V. (2010). Stellarsim: A plug-in architecture for scientific visualizations in virtual worlds. In *Facets of Virtual environments* (pp. 106–120). Springer-Verlag Berlin Heidelberg. Retrieved from http://link.springer.com/chapter/10.1007/978-3-642-11743-5_9

Hepburn, A. (2015). *Top 10 augmented reality examples- digital buzz blog*. Retrieved from http://bit.ly/1nXdp6l

Hepplestone, S., Holden, G., Irwin, B., Parkin, H., & Thorpe, L. (2011). Using technology to encourage student engagement with feedback: A literature review. *Research in Learning Technology*, *19*(2), 117–127. doi:10.1080/21567069.2011.586677

Hernández-Ramos, P. (2005). If not here, where? Understanding teachers' use of technology in Silicon Valley schools. *Journal of Research on Technology in Education*, *38*(1), 39–64. doi:10.1080/15391523.2005.10782449

Herrera, D. R., Margitay-Becht, A., & Chagas, J. (2010). Cyber-disaporas: The Effects of Migration to Virtual Worlds. In L. DePretto, G. Macri, & C. Wong (Eds.), *Diasporas: Revisiting and Discovering* (pp. 287–298). Oxford: Inter-Disciplinary Press.

Herrington, J., & Oliver, R. (2000). An instructional design framework for authentic learning environments. *Educational Technology Research and Development*, *48*(3), 23–48. doi:10.1007/BF02319856

Hew, K. F., & Brush, T. (2007). Integrating technology into K-12 teaching and learning: Current knowledge gaps and recommendations for future research. *Educational Technology Research and Development*, *55*(3), 223–252. doi:10.1007/s11423-006-9022-5

Hew, K. F., & Cheung, W. S. (2010). Use of three-dimensional (3-D) immersive virtual worlds in K-12 and higher education settings: A review of the research. *British Journal of Educational Technology*, *41*(1), 33–55. doi:10.1111/j.1467-8535.2008.00900.x

Hew, K. F., & Cheung, W. S. (2013). Use of Web 2.0 technologies in K-12 and higher education: The search for evidence-based practice. *Educational Research Review*, *9*, 47–64. doi:10.1016/j.edurev.2012.08.001

Hiebert, J. (1984). Children's mathematics learning: The struggle to link form and understanding. *The Elementary School Journal*, *84*(5), 496. doi:10.1086/461380

High Fidelity. (2015). High Fidelity Inc. Retrieved from https://highfidelity.com/

Hilbelink, A. J. (2009). A measure of the effectiveness of incorporating 3-D human anatomy into an online undergraduate laboratory. *British Journal of Educational Technology*, *40*(4), 664–672. doi:10.1111/j.1467-8535.2008.00886.x

Himma, K. E. (2007). Foundational issues in information ethics. *Library Hi Tech*, *25*(1), 79–94. doi:10.1108/07378830710735876

Himma, K. E., & Tavani, H. T. (Eds.). (2008). *The Handbook of Information and Computer Ethics*. John Wiley & Sons. doi:10.1002/9780470281819

Hislope, K. (2008). Language learning in a virtual world. *The International Journal of Learning*, *15*(11), 51–58.

Hodge, E. M., & Collins, S. (2010). Collaborative efforts: Teaching and learning in virtual worlds.[Retrieved fromhttp://www.educause.edu/ero/article/collaborative-efforts-teaching-and-learning-virtual-worlds]. *EDUCAUSE Review*, *45*(3), 62–63.

Holmberg, B. (2003). Distance education in essence: An overview of theory and practice in the early twenty-first century (2nd ed.). Germany: Oldenburg.

Holmberg, K., & Huvila, I. (2008). Learning together apart: Distance education in a virtual world. *First Monday*, *13*(10). Retrieved from http://firstmonday.org/article/view/2178/2033

Holmes, A., Signer, B., & MacLeod, A. (2011). Professional development at a distance: A mixed-method study exploring inservice teachers' views on presence online. *Journal of Digital Learning in Teacher Education*, *27*(2), 76–85. doi:10.1080/21532974.2010.10784660

Holmes, J. (2007). Designing agents to support learning by explaining. *Computers & Education*, *48*(4), 523–525. doi:10.1016/j.compedu.2005.02.007

Hsieh, M. C., & Lin, H. C. K. (2011). A Conceptual Study for Augmented Reality E-learning System Based on Usability Evaluation. *CISME*, *1*(8), 5–7. doi:10.5963/CISME0108002

Hsu, L. (2012). Web 3D simulation-based application in tourism education: A case study with Second Life. *Journal of Hospitality, Leisure, Sport and Tourism Education*, *11*(2), 113–124. doi:10.1016/j.jhlste.2012.02.013

Huang, H. M., Rauch, U., & Liaw, S. S. (2010). Investigating learners' attitudes toward virtual reality learning environments: Based on a constructivist approach. *Computers & Education*, *55*(3), 1171–1182. doi:10.1016/j.compedu.2010.05.014

Huang, H. W., Wu, C. W., & Chen, N. S. (2012). The effectiveness of using procedural scaffoldings in a paper-plus-smartphone collaborative learning context. *Computers & Education*, *59*(2), 250–259. doi:10.1016/j.compedu.2012.01.015

Huba, M. E., & Freed, J. E. (2000). *Learner-centered assessment on college campuses: Shifting the focus from teaching to learning*. Boston: Allyn & Bacon.

Hughes, J. (2005). The role of teacher knowledge and learning experiences in forming technology-integrated pedagogy. *Journal of Technology and Teacher Education, 13*(2), 277–302.

Hullinger, J. (2015, June 28). *Six innovative uses for virtual reality. The Idea Factory.* Retrieved from http://theweek.com/articles/562851/6

Ibanez, M., Garcia, J., Galan, S., Maroto, D., Morillo, D., & Kloos, C. (2011). Design and Implementation of a 3D Multi-User Virtual World for Language Learning. *Journal of Educational Technology & Society, 14*(4), 2–10.

İbili, E., & Şahin, S. (2013). Software design and development of an interactive 3D geomety book using augmented reality: ARGE3D. *Afyon Kocatepe University Journal of Science and Engineering, 13*(1), 1–8. doi:10.5578/fmbd.6213

Immersion (virtual reality). (2015). In Wikipedia, The Free Encyclopedia. Retrieved from https://en.wikipedia.org/w/index.php?title=Immersion_(virtual_reality)&oldid=690405136

Inman, C., Wright, V. H., & Hartman, J. A. (2010). Use of Second Life in K-12 and higher education: A review of research. *Journal of Interactive Online Learning, 9*(1), 44–63.

International Society for Technology in Education. (2008). *National educational technology standards for teachers* (2nd ed.). Eugene, OR: Author.

International Society for Technology in Education. (2011). Technology, Coaching, and Community: Power partners for improved professional development in elementary and secondary schools. Retrieved from http://www.instructionalcoach.org/images/downloads/ISTE_Whitepaper_June_Final_Edits.pdf

International Society for Technology in Education. (2012). Digital age coaching. Retrieved from http://www.iste.org/standards/nets-for-coaches

International Society for Technology in Education. (2015). Standards for teachers. Retrieved from http://www.iste.org/standards/ISTE-standards/standards-for-teachers

Jabbari, N., Sandoval, S., & Waxman, H. (2015, March). A Meta-Synthesis of Research Using Multiuser Virtual Environments (ie, Second Life) in Teacher Education. *Society for Information Technology & Teacher Education International Conference,* 2015(1), 2375-2381.

Jamlan, M. (2004). Faculty opinions towards introducing e-learning at the University of Bahrain. *International Review of Research in Open and Distance Learning, 5*(2).

Janicki, T., & Steinberg, G. (2003). Evaluation of a computer-supported learning system. *Decision Sciences Journal of Innovative Education, 1*(2), 203–223. doi:10.1111/j.1540-4609.2003.00018.x

Janson, B. (2013). *Faculty Perceptions of Instruction in Collaborative Virtual Immersive Learning Environments in Higher Education* [Dissertation & Theses Collection]. Paper AAI3558390.

Jarmon, L. (2008). Pedagogy and learning in the virtual world of Second Life. In P. Rogers, G. Berg, J. Boettcher, C. Howard, L. Justice, & K. Schenck (Eds.), *Encyclopedia of distance learning* (2nd ed., pp. 1610–1619). Hershey, PA: IGI Global.

Jarmon, L., & Sanchez, J. (2009). The educator's coop: A model for collaboration and LSI communication research in the virtual world. *The Electronic Journal of Communication, 19*(1), 1–29.

Jarmon, L., Traphagan, T., Mayrath, M., & Trivedi, A. (2008). *Exploration of learning in Second Life in an interdisciplinary communication course. Paper presentation at American Educational Research Association*. New York: AERA.

Jarmon, L., Traphagan, T., Mayrath, M., & Trivedi, A. (2009). Virtual world teaching, experiential learning, and assessment: An interdisciplinary communication course in Second Life. *Computers & Education*, *53*(1), 169–182. doi:10.1016/j.compedu.2009.01.010

Jauregi, K., de Graaff, R., & Canto, S. (2012). Integrating Cross-Cultural Interaction through Video-Communication and Virtual Worlds in Foreign Language Teaching Programs: Burden or Added Value? *Paper presented at theEuropean Association for Computer-Assisted Language Learning (EuroCALL) Annual Conference*.

Jayatilaka, D., Wolff, S. K., Grimwood, D. J., McKinnon, J. J., & Spackman, M. A. (2006). Crystal Explorer: A tool for displaying Hirshfeld surfaces and visualising intermolecular interactions in molecular crystals. *Acta Crystallographica. Section A, Foundations of Crystallography*, *62*(a1), s90. doi:10.1107/S0108767306098199

Jestice, R. J., & Kahai, S. (2010). The effectiveness of virtual worlds for education: an empirical study. *Paper presented at theSixteenth Americas Conference on Information Systems (AMCIS)*, Lima, Peru.

Johnson, L., Levine, A., & Smith, R. (2008). 2008 Horizon report Australia-New Zealand edition. In *2008 Horizon Report Australia-New Zealand Edition*. Austin, Texas: The New Media Consortium. Retrieved from http://wp.nmc.org/horizon-anz-2008/

Johnson, A. (2008). A nursing faculty's transition to teaching online. *Nursing Education Perspectives*, *29*(1), 17–22. PMID:18330417

Johnson, A. M., Ozogul, G., Moreno, R., & Reisslein, M. (2013). Pedagogical agent signaling of multiple visual engineering representations: The case of the young female agent. *The Journal of Engineering Education*, *102*(2), 319–337. doi:10.1002/jee.20009

Johnson, A. M., Ozogul, G., & Reisslein, M. (2014). Supporting multimedia learning with visual signaling and animated pedagogical agent: Moderating effects of prior knowledge. *Journal of Computer Assisted Learning*. doi:10.111/jcal.12078

Johnson, D. G. (1997). Ethics online. *Communications of the ACM*, *40*(1), 60–65. http://dl.acm.org/citation.cfm?id=242857.242875 doi:10.1145/242857.242875

Johnson, D. G. (2005). Computer Ethics. In R. G. Frey & C. Heath Wellman (Eds.), *A Companion to Applied Ethics*. Oxford, UK: Blackwell Publishing; doi:10.1002/9780470996621.ch45

Johnson, D. G. (2009). *Computer Ethics* (4th ed.). Pearson.

Johnson-Glenberg, M. C., Birchfield, D. A., Tolentino, L., & Koziupa, T. (2014). Collaborative embodied learning in mixed reality motion-capture environments: Two science studies. *Journal of Educational Psychology*, *106*(1), 86–104. doi:10.1037/a0034008

Johnson, L., Levine, A., Smith, R., & Stone, S. (2010). *The 2010 Horizon Report*. Austin, Texas: The New Media Consortium.

Jonassen, D. H. (1991). Objectivism versus Constructivism: Do we need a new philosophical paradigm? *Educational Technology Research and Development*, *39*(3), 5–14. doi:10.1007/BF02296434

Jonassen, D. H., Peck, K. L., & Wilson, B. G. (1999). *Learning with technology: A constructivist perspective*. Upper Saddle River, NJ: Prentice Hall, Inc.

Jones, C. M., & Youngs, B. L. (2006). Teacher Preparation for Online Language Instruction. In P. Hubbard & M. Levy (Eds.), *Teacher Education in CALL* (pp. 267–280). Amsterdam: John Benjamins. doi:10.1075/lllt.14.22jon

Jung, T., & Han, D. (2014). Augmented reality (AR) in urban heritage tourism. *e-Review of Tourism Research.*

Jung, T., Chung, N., & Leue, M. (2015). The Determinants of Recommendations to Use Augmented Reality Technologies - The Case of a Korean Theme Park. *Tourism Management*, *49*, 75–86. doi:10.1016/j.tourman.2015.02.013

Kalyuga, S., & Sweller, J. (2014). The redundancy principle in multimedia learning. In R. E. Mayer (Ed.), *The Cambridge handbook of multimedia learning* (2nd ed., pp. 247–262).

Kamel Boulos, M. N., Hetherington, L., & Wheeler, S. (2007). Second Life: An overview of the potential of 3-D virtual worlds in medical and health education. *Health Information and Libraries Journal*, *24*(4), 233–245. doi:10.1111/j.1471-1842.2007.00733.x PMID:18005298

Kanuka, H., & Anderson, T. (1999). Using constructivism in technology-mediated learning: Constructing order out of the chaos in the literature. *Radical Pedagogy*, *1*, 1–12. Retrieved from http://www.radicalpedagogy.org/radicalpedagogy/Using_Constructivism_in_Technology-Mediated_Learning__Constructing_Order_out_of_the_Chaos_in_the_Literature.html

Kapp, K., & O'Driscoll, T. (2010). *Learning in 3D: adding a new dimension to enterprise learning and collaboration.* Pfeiffer.

Kapp, K., & O'Driscoll, T. (2010). *Learning in 3D*. San Francisco, CA: Pfeiffer.Lai, K-W. (2008). ICT supporting the learning process: The premise, reality, and promise. In J. Voogt & G. Knezek (Eds.), *International Handbook of Information Technology in Primary and Secondary Education* (pp. 215–230). New York: Springer.

Kastoudi, D. (2011). *Using a Quest in a 3D Virtual Environment for Student Interaction and Vocabulary Acquisition in Foreign Language Learning. European Association for Computer-Assisted Language Learning*. EUROCALL.

Kaufman, I., & Horton, C. (2015). *Digital marketing: Integrating strategy and tactics with values: A guidebook for executives, managers & students*. New York: Routledge.

Kaufmann, H., & Dünser, A. (2007). Summary of usability evaluations of an educational augmented reality application. Virtual Reality,*LNCS* (Vol. *4563*, pp. 660–669). doi:10.1007/978-3-540-73335-5_71

Kaufmann, H., Steinbugl, K., Dunser, A., & Gluck, J. (2005). General training of spatial abilities by geometry education in augmented reality. *Cyberpsychology & Behavior*, *8*(4), 330.

Keller, J. M. (2010). *Motivational design for learning and performance. The ARCS model approach*. New York, NY: Springer. doi:10.1007/978-1-4419-1250-3

Kelton, A. J. (2008). Virtual worlds? Outlook good. *EDUCAUSE Review*, *43*(5). Retrieved from http://www.educause.edu/EDUCAUSE+Review/EDUCAUSE ReviewMagazineVolume43 /VirtualWorldsOutlookGood/163161

Kerawalla, L., Luckin, R., Seljeflot, S., & Woolard, A. (2006). Making it real: Exploring the potential of augmented reality for teaching primary school science. *Virtual Reality (Waltham Cross)*, *10*(3-4), 163–174. doi:10.1007/s10055-006-0036-4

Kerbs, R. W. (2005). Social and ethical considerations in virtual worlds. *The Electronic Library*, *23*(5), 539–546. doi:10.1108/02640470510631254

Kim, J. H., Park, S. T., Lee, H., Yuk, K. C., & Lee, H. (2001). Virtual reality simulations in physics education. Retrieved from http://imej.wfu.edu/articles/2001/2/02/index.asp

Kim, Y. (in press). Pedagogical agents. In M. Spector, et al. (Eds.), *Encyclopedia of Educational Technology.* Thousand Oaks, CA: Sage Publications. Retrieved from http://works.bepress.com/cgi/viewcontent.cgi?article=1056&context=yanghee_kim

Kim, D., & Blankenship, R. J. (2013). Using "Second Life" as a Virtual Collaborative Tool for Preservice Teachers Seeking English for Speakers of Other Languages Endorsement. *Journal of Educational Computing Research, 48*(1), 19–43. doi:10.2190/EC.48.1.b

Kim, M., & Ryu, J. (2003). Meta-analysis of the effectiveness of pedagogical agent. In D. Lassner, & C. McNaught (Eds.), *Proceedings of World Conference on Educational Multimedia, Hypermedia and Telecommunications 2003* (pp. 479-486). Chesapeake, VA: AACE.

Kim, S. H., Lee, J., & Thomas, M. K. (2012). Between purpose and method: A review of educational research on 3D virtual worlds. *Journal of Virtual Worlds Research, 5*(1), 1–18.

Kipper, G., & Rampolla, J. (2014). *Augmented reality: An emerging technologies guide to AR.* London: Elsevier.

Kirkpatrick, D. (1979). Techniques for evaluating training programs. *Training and Development Journal, 33*(6), 78–92.

Kitchenham, B. (2004). Procedures for performing systematic reviews. Keele University, 33.

Klopfer, E. (2008). *Augmented learning: Research and design of mobile educational games.* Cambridge, MA: MIT Press. doi:10.7551/mitpress/9780262113151.001.0001

Knutzen, B., & Kennedy, D. (2012). The Global Classroom Project: Learning a Second Language in a Virtual Environment. *Electronic Journal of E-Learning, 10*(1), 90–106.

Kolb, A.Y., & Kolb, D. A. (2005). *The Kolb Learning Style Inventory – Version 3.1: 2005 Technical Specifications.* Haygroup: Experience Based Learning Systems Inc.

Kolb, D. A. (1984). *Experiential learning: Experience as the source of learning and development.* New Jersey: Prentice-Hall Inc.

Konstantinidis, A., & Tsiatsos, T. (2008). Selecting a networked virtual environment platform and the design of a collaborative e-learning environment. *Paper presented at the 22nd International Conference on Advanced Information Networking and Applications-Workshops AINAW.*

Kopp, G., & Burkle, M. (2010). Using Second Life for just-in-time training: Building teaching frameworks in virtual worlds.[iJAC]. *International Journal of Advanced Corporate Learning, 3*(3), 19–25. Retrieved from http://www.editlib.org/p/45604/article_45604.pdf

Korthagen, F. A. J. (2010). Situated learning theory and the pedagogy of teacher education: Towards an integrative view of teacher behavior and teacher learning. *Teaching and Teacher Education: An International Journal of Research and Studies, 26*(1), 98–106. doi:10.1016/j.tate.2009.05.001

Kotranza, A., Lind, D. S., Pugh, C. M., & Lok, B. (2009, October). Real-time in-situ visual feedback of task performance in mixed environments for learning joint psychomotorcognitive tasks. *Paper presented at the8th IEEE international symposium on mixed and augmented reality (ISMAR)*, Orlando, FL.

Kotsilieris, T., & Dimopoulou, N. (2013). The evolution of e-learning in the context of 3-D virtual worlds. *The Electronic Journal of e-Learning. 11*(2), 147-167.

Kramer, A. D. I., Guillory, J. E., & Hancock, J. T. (2014). Experimental evidence of massive-scale emotional contagion through social networks. *Proceedings of the National Academy of Sciences of the United States of America, 111*(24), 8788–8790. doi:10.1073/pnas.1320040111 PMID:24889601

Kramsch, C. (1995). The cultural component of language teaching. *Language, Culture and Curriculum, 8*(2), 83–93. doi:10.1080/07908319509525192

Krashen, S. D. (1987). *Principles and practice in second language acquisition.* London: Prentice-Hall International.

Krueger, M. W. (1991). *Artificial reality* (2nd ed.). Reading, MA: Addison-Wesley.

Kuhs, T. M., Johnson, R. L., Agruso, S. A., & Monrad, D. M. (2001). *Put to the test – tools and techniques for classroom assessment.* Portsmouth, NH: Heinemann.

Kumar, V., Venkatesan, R., & Reinartz, W. J. (2006). Knowing what to sell when to whom. *Harvard Business Review*, May, 131–145. PMID:16515161

Kurzweil, D., & Marcellas, B. (2008). The faculty - instructional designer dyad. *Proceedings ofWorld Conference on Educational Multimedia, Hypermedia and Telecommunications* (pp. 3445-3446). Chesapeake, VA: AACE.

KZero. (2013). Kzero Worldswide. Retrieved from http://www.kzero.co.uk/blog/category/education-and-academia

KZero. (2014). KZero Reports – Universe Charts. Retrieved from http://kzero.co.uk/

Lai, K.-W. (2008). ICT supporting the learning process: The premise, reality, and promise. In J. Voogt & G. Knezek (Eds.), *International Handbook of Information Technology in Primary and Secondary Education* (pp. 215–230). New York: Springer. doi:10.1007/978-0-387-73315-9_13

Lane, H. C., Cahill, C., Foutz, S., Auerbach, D., Noren, D., Lussenhop, C., & Swartout, W. (2013). The effects of a pedagogical agent for informal science education on learner behaviors and self-efficacy. In *Artificial Intelligence in Education* (pp. 309–318). Springer Berlin Heidelberg. doi:10.1007/978-3-642-39112-5_32

Larsen-Freeman, D. (2007). *Techniques and principles in language teaching* (2nd ed.). Oxford: Oxford University Press.

Laurillard, D. (2002). *Rethinking university teaching: a framework for the effective use of learning technologies* (2nd ed.). London, New York: Routledge/Falmer. doi:10.4324/9780203304846

Lave, G., & Wenger, E. (1991). *Situated learning: Legitimate peripheral participation.* Cambridge: University of Cambridge Press. doi:10.1017/CBO9780511815355

Lawless, K. A., & Pellegrino, J. W. (2007). Professional development in integrating technology into teaching and learning: Knowns, unknowns, and ways to pursue better questions and answers. *Review of Educational Research, 77*(4), 575–614. doi:10.3102/0034654307309921

Lee, H., Chung, N., & Jung, T. (2015). Examining the cultural differences in acceptance of mobile augmented reality: comparison of South Korea and Ireland. In I. Tussyadiah & A. Inversini (Eds.), *Information and Communication Technologies in Tourism* (pp. 477–491). Wien: Springer International Publishing New York. doi:10.1007/978-3-319-14343-9_35

Lee, K. (2012). Augmented reality in education and training. *TechTrends, 56*(2), 13–22. doi:10.1007/s11528-012-0559-3

Lenhart, A., Purcell, K., Smith, A., & Zickuhr, K. (2010). Social media & mobile internet use among teens and young adults. Pew Research Center. Retrieved from http://67.192.40.213/~/media/Files/Reports/2010/PIP_Social_Media_and_Young_Adults_Report_Final_with_toplines.pdf

Lenhart, A., & Madden, M. (2007). *Social networking websites and teens: an overview*. Washington, DC: Pew Internet & American Life Project.

Le, Q. T., Pedro, A., & Park, C. S. (2014). A social virtual reality based construction safety education system for experiential learning. *Journal of Intelligent & Robotic Systems*, 1–20.

Lester, J. (2014). Augmented mind- The evolution of learning tools from language to immersive reality. *Keynote speech presented at the 1st International Conference on e-Learning e-Education and Online Training*. Bethesda, Maryland, United States.

Lester, J. C., Voerman, J. L., Towns, S. G., & Callaway, C. B. (1999). Deictic believability: Coordinated gesture, locomotion, and speech in lifelike pedagogical agents. *Applied Artificial Intelligence*, *13*(4-5), 383–414. doi:10.1080/088395199117324

Leue, M. C., Jung, T., & Tom-Dieck, D. (2015). Google Glass Augmented Reality: Generic Learning Outcomes for Art Galleries. In I. Tussyadiah & A. Inversini (Eds.), Information and Communication Technologies in Tourism (pp. 463-476). Wien: Springer International Publishing.

Levien, R. E. (1972). *The Emerging Technology: Instructional Uses of the Computer in Higher Education*. New York, NY: McGraw-Hill Book Company.

Lewis, C. C., & Abdul- Hamid, H. (2006). Implementing effective online teaching practices: Voices of exemplary faculty. *Innovative Higher Education, 31(*2), 83-98.

Lewis, L. A., Koston, Z., Quartley, M., & Adsit, J. (2011). Virtual communities of practice: Bridging research and practice using Web 2.0. *Journal of Educational Technology Systems*, *39*(2), 155–161. doi:10.2190/ET.39.2.e

Lewis, W., Agarwal, R., & Sambamurthy, V. (2003). Sources of influence on beliefs about information technology use: An empirical study of knowledge workers. *Management Information Systems Quarterly*, *27*(4), 657–678.

Liarokapis, F., Mourkoussis, N., White, M., Darcy, J., Sifniotis, M., & Petridis, P. (2004). Web 3D and augmented reality to support engineering education. *World Transactions on Engineering and Technology Education*, *3*(1), 11–14.

Liarokapis, F., Petridis, P., Lister, P., & White, M. (2002). Multimedia Augmented Reality Interface for E-learning (MARIE). *World Transactions on Engineering and Technology Education*, *1*(2), 173–176.

Ligorio, M., Cesareni, D., & Schwartz, N. (2008). Collaborative virtual environments as means to increase the level of intersubjectivity in a distributed cognition system. *Journal of Research on Technology in Education*, *40*(3), 339–357. doi:10.1080/15391523.2008.10782511

Lim, K. Y. T. (2009). The six learnings of Second Life: A framework for designing curricular interventions in-world.

Linden Lab. (2013). Infographic - 10 Years of Second Life. Retrieved from http://lindenlab.com/releases/infographic-10-years-of-second-life

Linden Lab. (2013). Infographic: 10 years of Second Life. Retrieved from http://www.lindenlab.com/releases/infographic

Linden Lab. (2013). SL10B Infographic: Ten Years of Second Life. Retrieved from http://www.lindenlab.com/releases/infographic-10-years-of-second-life

Linden Lab. (2015). Mainland Pricing and Fees. Retrieved from https://secondlife.com/land/pricing.php

Linden Research. (2011). Second Life education: The virtual learning advantage. Retrieved from http://lecs-static-secondlife-com.s3.amazonaws.com/work/SL-Edu-Brochure-010411.pdf

Lissitz, R. W., & Schafer, W. D. (2002). *Assessment in educational reform: Both means and ends*. Boston: Allyn & Bacon.

Liu, D., Jenkins, S. A., Sanderson, P. M., Fabian, P., & Russell, W. J. (2010). Monitoring with head-mounted displays in general anesthesia: A clinical evaluation in the operating room. *Society for Technology in Anesthesia*, *110*(4), 1032–1038. PMID:20357147

Liu, T.-Y. (2009). A context-aware ubiquitous learning environment for language listening and speaking. *Journal of Computer Assisted Learning*, *25*(6), 515–527. doi:10.1111/j.1365-2729.2009.00329.x

Long, M. H. (1991). Focus on form: a design feature in language teaching methodology. In K. de Bot, R. Ginsberg, & C. Kramsch (Eds.), *Foreign Language Research in Cross-cultural Perspective* (pp. 39–52). Amsterdam: John Benjamins. doi:10.1075/sibil.2.07lon

Long, M. H. (1997). The role of the linguistic environment in second language acquisition. In W. Ritchie & T. Bhatia (Eds.), *Handbook of Second Language Acquisition* (pp. 413–468). San Diego, CA: Academic Press.

Lopes, C. V. (2009). The massification and webification of systems' modeling and simulation with virtual worlds. Proceedings of the 7th joint meeting of the European software engineering conference and the ACM SIGSOFT symposium on The foundations of software engineering (pp. 63–70). ACM; Retrieved from http://dl.acm.org/citation.cfm?id=1595708

Loureiro, A., & Bettencourt, T. (2011). The Extended Classroom: Meeting students' needs using a virtual environment. *Procedia: Social and Behavioral Sciences*, *15*, 2667–2672. doi:10.1016/j.sbspro.2011.04.167

Louvre -DNP Museum Lab. (2015). *Past presentation*. Retrieved from http://www.museumlab.jp/english/tech/04tech.html

Lowendahl, J. M. (2013, July 25). Hype Cycle for Education, 2013. *Gartner*. Retrieved from http://www.gartner.com/DisplayDocument?doc_cd=251104

Low, R., & Sweller, J. (2014). The modality principle in multimedia learning. In R. Mayer (Ed.), *The Cambridge handbook of multimedia learning* (2nd ed., pp. 227–246). New York, NY: Cambridge University Press.

Luciano, C., Banerjee, P., & DeFanti, T. (2009). Haptics-based virtual reality periodontal training simulator. *Virtual Reality (Waltham Cross)*, *13*(2), 69–85. doi:10.1007/s10055-009-0112-7

Ludwig, C., & Reimann, C. (2005). Augmented reality: Information at focus. *Cooperative Computing & Communication Laboratory*, 4(1). Universitat Paderborn.

Lum, R. (2012). *10 mind-blowing augmented reality campaigns*. Retrieved fromhttp://bit.ly/1kMP8AD

Lusk, M. M., & Atkinson, R. K. (2007). Animated pedagogical agents: Does their degree of embodiment impact learning from static or animated worked examples? *Applied Cognitive Psychology*, *21*(6), 747–764. doi:10.1002/acp.1347

Macedo, A., & Morgado, L. (2009). Learning to teach in Second Life.*Proceedings of EDEN seventh open classroom conference* (pp. 120-126).

Macías-Díaz, A. (2008). *Survey of e-business module* (MN5553). St. Andrews University: St. Andrews, Scotland.

Magnenat-Thalmann, N., & Thalmann, D. (1999). Virtual reality software and technology. Encyclopedia of Computer Science and Technology, Marcel Dekker, 41.

Marcelino, R., Silva, J., Gruber, V., & Bilessimo, M. (2012). 3D virtual worlds using open source platform and integrated remote experimentation. *Paper presented at the 2012 9th International Conference on Remote Engineering and Virtual Instrumentation (REV).*

Margitay-Becht, A., & Herrera, D. R. (2008). Fun is Learning: A Case Study of Gaming as Education in Virtual Worlds. In C. Nygaard & C. Holtham (Eds.), *Understanding Learning-centred Higher Education*. Copenhagen: Copenhagen Business School Press.

Margitay-Becht, A., & Herrera, D. R. (2013). Teaching Social Skills in Virtual Worlds: A primer for extending existing social science education to business management. In S. D'Agustino (Ed.), *Immersive Environments, Augmented Realities and Virtual Worlds: Assessing Future Trends in Education.* IGI Global. doi:10.4018/978-1-4666-2670-6.ch011

Marino, P. (2004). *The art of machinima: 3D game-based filmmaking*. Scottsdale: Paraglyph Press.

MarketingWeek. (2015). *Online retail will drive innovation in interactive marketing*. Retrieved from http://bit.ly/1nbpjdM

Martens, R., Bastiaens, T., & Kirschner, P. A. (2007). New learning design in distance education: The impact on student perception and motivation. *Distance Education, 28*(1), 81–93. doi:10.1080/01587910701305327

Martin-Gutierrez, J., Saorin, J. L., Contero, M., Alcaniz, M., Perez-Lopez, D. C., & Ortega, M. (2010). Design and validation of an augmented book for spatial abilities development in engineering students. *Computers & Graphics, 34*(1), 77–91. doi:10.1016/j.cag.2009.11.003

Matsuda, T., Nakayama, H., & Tamada, K. (2015). Using 3D virtual reality technology in cyber ethics education: How can we really evaluate and change students' attitudes? In Human rights and ethics: concepts, methodologies, tools, and applications (pp. 1621-1636). Hershey, PA: IGI Global. doi:10.4018/978-1-4666-6433-3.ch089

Ma, W., Adesope, O. O., Nesbit, J. C., & Liu, Q. (2014). Intelligent tutoring systems and learning outcomes: A meta-analysis. *Journal of Educational Psychology, 106*(4), 901–918. doi:10.1037/a0037123

Maxwell, D., Griffith, T., & Finkelstein, N. M. (2014). Use of Virtual Worlds in the Military Services as Part of a Blended Learning Strategy. In K. S. Hale & K. M. Stanney (Eds.), *Handbook of Virtual Environments: Design, Implementation and Applications* (2nd ed., pp. 959–1000). CRC Press. doi:10.1201/b17360-45

Mayer, R. E. (2005). Principles of multimedia learning based on social cues: personalization, voice, and image principles. In R. Mayer (Ed.), *The Cambridge handbook of multimedia learning* (pp. 201–212). New York, NY: Cambridge University Press. doi:10.1017/CBO9780511816819.014

Mayer, R. E. (2014a). Cognitive theory of multimedia learning. In R. Mayer (Ed.), *The Cambridge handbook of multimedia learning* (2nd ed., pp. 43–71). New York, NY: Cambridge University Press.

Mayer, R. E. (2014b). Principles based on social cues in multimedia learning: Personalization, voice, image, and embodiment principles. In R. Mayer (Ed.), *The Cambridge handbook of multimedia learning* (2nd ed., pp. 345–370). New York, NY: Cambridge University Press. doi:10.1017/CBO9781139547369.017

Mayer, R. E., & DaPra, C. S. (2012). An embodiment effect in computer-based learning with animated pedagogical agents. *Journal of Experimental Psychology. Applied, 18*(3), 239–252. doi:10.1037/a0028616 PMID:22642688

Mayer, R. E., & Moreno, R. (2003). Nine ways to reduce cognitive load in multimedia learning. *Educational Psychologist, 38*(1), 43–52. doi:10.1207/S15326985EP3801_6

Mayer, R. E., & Pilegard, C. (2014). Principles for managing essential processing in multimedia learning: Segmenting, pre-training, and modality principles. In R. Mayer (Ed.), *The Cambridge handbook of multimedia learning* (2nd ed., pp. 316–344). New York, NY: Cambridge University Press. doi:10.1017/CBO9781139547369.016

Mayer, R. E., Sobko, K., & Mautone, P. D. (2003). Social cues in multimedia learning: Role of speaker's voice. *Journal of Educational Psychology, 95*(2), 419–425. doi:10.1037/0022-0663.95.2.419

Mayes, R., Ku, H., Akarasriworn, C., Luebeck, J., & Korkmaz, O. (2011). Themes and strategies for transformative online instruction: A review of literature and practice. *Quarterly Review of Distance Education, 12*(3), 151–166.

Mazuryk, T., & Gervautz, M. (1996). Virtual reality, history, applications, technology and future, 1-72. Institute of Computer Graphics, Vienna University of Technology, Austria. Retrieved August 29, 2015 from https://www.cg.tuwien.ac.at/research/publications/1996/mazuryk-1996-VRH/TR-186-2-96-06Paper.pdf

McArthur, V., Teather, R., & Stuerzlinger, W. (2010). Comparing 3D content creation interfaces in two virtual worlds: World of Warcraft and second life. *Journal of Gaming & Virtual Worlds*, *2*(3), 239–258. doi:10.1386/jgvw.2.3.239_1

McElheran, K. S. (2012). *Do market leaders lead in business process innovation? The case(s) of e-business adoption*. Boston: Harvard Business School.

McInnes, E., & Wimpenny, P. (2008). Using Qualitative Assessment and Review Instrument software to synthesize studies on older people's views and experiences of falls prevention. *International Journal of Evidence-Based Healthcare*, *6*, 337–344. PMID:21631830

McKee, H. A., & Porter, J. E. (2009). Playing a Good Game : Ethical Issues in Researching MMOGs and Virtual Worlds. *International Journal of Internet Research Ethics*, *2*(1).

McKeown, L. (2007). Taking action learning online in the 3D virtual worlds of Second Life. *International Review of Research in Open and Distance Learning*, *8*(3).

McLellan, H. (1996). Virtual realities. In D. H. Jonassen (Ed.), Handbook of research for educational communications and technology (pp. 457-487). New York, NY, USA: Macmillan Library Reference.

McLellan, H. (2003). Virtual realities. In D. H. Jonassen & P. Harris (Eds.), *Handbook of research for educational communications and technology* (2nd ed., pp. 461–498). Mahwah, NJ: Lawrence Erlbaum.

Means, B., & Haertel, G. D. (2004). *Using technology evaluation to enhance student learning*. New York: Teachers College Press.

Medawar, P. (1969). *Induction and Intuition*. Philadelphia: American Philosophical Society.

Mendonça, R. F., Carreira, S. M., & Sampaio, P. N. (2011). *VirtualLabs@ UMa: A customizable 3D learning platform for experimental activities. Paper presented at the 2011 International Conference on Multimedia Computing and Systems (ICMCS).*

Merchant, Z., Goetz, E. T., Cifuentes, L., Keeney-Kennicutt, W., & Davis, T. J. (2014). Effectiveness of virtual reality-based instruction on students' learning outcomes in K-12 and higher education: A meta-analysis. *Computers & Education*, *70*, 29–40. doi:10.1016/j.compedu.2013.07.033

Mergel, B. (1998). Instructional design & learning theory. Retrieved from http://www.usask.ca/education/coursework/802papers/mergel/brenda.htm

Meskill, C. (1999). Computers as Tool for Sociocollaborative Language Learning. In K. Cameron (Ed.), *Computer assisted language learning (CALL): media, design and applications* (pp. 141–162). Lisse: Swets & Zeitlinger.

Meskó, B. (2008). Unique medical simulation in second life! Science Roll Blog. Retrieved from http://scienceroll.com/2008/08/17/unique-medical-simulation-in-second-life/

Messer, S., Evans, S., Cownie, M., & Dawe, C. (2012). Greenbank – A model for situated learning in Second Life. In T. Amiel & B. Wilson (Eds.), *Proceedings of World Conference on Educational Media and Technology 2012* (pp. 844-849). Waynesville, NC: Association for the Advancement of Computing in Education (AACE).

Meyers, C., & Jones, T. B. (1993). *Promoting active learning: Strategies for the college classroom*. San Francisco: Jossey-Bass.

Michel, H. (2013, January). From Haute-Couture to Ready-to-Wear: Typology of Serious Games Implementation Strategies in Higher Education. *Proceedings of theEuropean Conference on Games Based Learning* (p. 386). Academic Conferences International Limited.

Milgram, P., & Kishino, F. (1994). A taxonomy of mixed reality visual displays. *IEICE Trans. Information and Systems. E (Norwalk, Conn.)*, *77-D*(12), 1321–1329.

Milgram, P., Takemura, H., Utsumi, A., & Kishino, F. (1994). Augmented reality: A class of displays on the reality-virtuality continuum, *SPIE. Telemanipulator and Telepresence Technologies*, *2351*, 282–291. doi:10.1117/12.197321

Millar, R. (1991). Why is science hard to learn? *Journal of Computer Assisted Learning*, *7*(7), 66–74. doi:10.1111/j.1365-2729.1991.tb00229.x

Miller, K. F., Kelly, M., & Zhou, X. (2005). Learning mathematics in China and the United States. Handbook of mathematical cognition, 163-178.

Miller, G. A. (1956). The magic number seven, plus or minus two: Some limits on our capacity for processing information. *Psychological Review*, *63*(2), 81–97. doi:10.1037/h0043158 PMID:13310704

Miller, K. F., Smith, C. M., Zhu, J., & Zhang, H. (1995). Preschool origins of cross-national differences in mathematical competence: The role of number-naming systems. *Psychological Science*, *6*(1), 56–60. doi:10.1111/j.1467-9280.1995.tb00305.x

Miller, K. F., & Stigler, J. W. (1987). Counting in Chinese: Cultural variation on a basic cognitive skill. *Cognitive Development*, *2*(3), 279–305. doi:10.1016/S0885-2014(87)90091-8

Miller, R. (2014). The application of virtual reality in higher education distance learning. *Journal of Applied Learning Technology*, *4*(4), 15–18.

Minocha, S., & Roberts, D. (2008). Laying the groundwork for socialisation and knowledge construction within 3-D virtual worlds. *ALT-J. Research in Learning Technology*, *16*(3), 181–196. doi:10.1080/09687760802526699

Mishra, S. (2009). Virtual worlds. In S. Mishra (Ed.), *E-Learning* (pp. 110-113). New Delhi: IndiraGandhi National Open University. Retrieve from http://webserver.ignou.ac.in/institute/STRIDE_Hb8_webCD/STRIDE_Hb8_Full.pdf

Mladenovic, S., Kuvac, H., & Štula, M. (2012). Virtual learning environment. In *Virtual learning environments: concepts, methodologies, tools and applications* (pp. 1–16). Hershey, PA: Information Science Reference; doi:10.4018/978-1-4666-0011-9.ch101

MMOs.com. (2015). Retrieved from http://mmos.com/editorials/most-popular-mmorpgs-world

Mobile Marketer. (2015). *Mobile augmented reality to drive $1.5B in revenue by 2015*. Retrieved from http://bit.ly/1nbq32r

Mohapatra, S. (2009). *Business process automation*. New Delhi: PHI Private Limited.

Molka-Danielsen, J., Richardson, D., Deutschmann, M., & Carter, B. (2007). Teaching and Learning Affectively within a Virtual Campus. *International Journal of Networking and Virtual Organization (Special Issue: Toward Virtual Universities)*, 6(5), 476-498.

Molnar, A. R. (1975). Viable Goals for New Educational Technology Efforts: Science Education and the New Technological Revolution. *Educational Technology*, *15*(9).

Molnar, A. R. (1990). Computers in education: A historical perspective of the unfinished task. *T.H.E. Journal*, *18*(4), 80–83.

Monday, C. (2015). *5 augmented reality examples worth looking at - ignite social media.* Retrieved from http://bit.ly/1mN1qZD

Moore, A. H., Moore, J. F., & Fowler, S. B. (2005). Faculty development for the net generation. In D. G. Oblinger, & J. L. Oblinger (Eds.), *Educating the Net Generation*: Educause. Retrieved from http://www.educause.edu/educatingthenetgen/

Moore, M. G. (1999). Monitoring and evaluation[Editorial]. *American Journal of Distance Education, 13*(2), 1–5. doi:10.1080/08923649909527019

Moravec, J. W. (2008). *Knowmads in society 3.0.* Education Futures.

Moreno-Ger, P., Torrente, J., Hsieh, Y. G., & Lester, W. T. (2012). Usability testing for serious games: Making informed design decisions with user data. *Advances in Human-Computer Interaction, 2012*, 1–13. doi:10.1155/2012/369637

Moreno, R. (2005). Multimedia learning with animated pedagogical agents. In R. Mayer (Ed.), *The Cambridge handbook of multimedia learning* (pp. 507–524). New York, NY: Cambridge University Press. doi:10.1017/CBO9780511816819.032

Moreno, R., Mayer, R. E., Spires, H. A., & Lester, J. C. (2001). The case for social agency in computer-based teaching: Do students learn more deeply when they interact with animated pedagogical agents? *Cognition and Instruction, 19*(2), 177–213. doi:10.1207/S1532690XCI1902_02

Morin, J. E., & Franks, D. J. (2009). Why do some children have difficulty learning mathematics? Looking at language for answers. *Preventing School Failure: Alternative Education for Children and Youth, 54*(2), 111–118. doi:10.1080/10459880903217861

Mueller, J., Wood, E., Willoughby, T., Ross, C., & Specht, J. (2008). Identifying discriminating variables between teachers who fully integrate computers and teachers with limited integration. *Computers & Education, 51*(4), 1523–1537. doi:10.1016/j.compedu.2008.02.003

Muller, D., Chilliischi, A., & Langer, S. (2012). *Integrating immersive 3D worlds and real lab equipment for teaching mechatronics.Paper presented at the 2012 9th International Conference on Remote Engineering and Virtual Instrumentation (REV).* doi:10.1109/REV.2012.6293117

Munezawa, T., Kaneita, Y., Osaki, Y., Kanda, H., Minowa, M., Suzuki, K., & Ohida, T. et al. (2011). The association between use of mobile phones after lights out and sleep disturbances among Japanese adolescents: A nationwide cross-sectional survey. *Sleep, 34*(8), 1013–1020. doi:10.5665/sleep.1152 PMID:21804663

Murray, M., & Tenenbaum, G. (2010). Computerized pedagogical agents as an educational means for developing physical self-efficacy and encouraging activity in youth. *Journal of Educational Computing Research, 42*(3), 267–283. doi:10.2190/EC.42.3.b

Najaftorkaman, M., Ghapanchi, A. H., Talaei-Khoei, A., & Ray, P. (2014). A taxonomy of antecedents to user adoption of health information systems: A synthesis of thirty years of research. *Journal of the Association for Information Science and Technology.*

Najaftorkaman, M., Ghapanchi, A. H., Talaei-Khoei, A., & Ray, P. (2013). Recent research areas and grand challenges in electronic medical record: A literature survey approach. *The International Technology Management Review, 3*(1), 12–21. doi:10.2991/itmr.2013.3.1.2

National Survey of Student Engagement. (NSSE) (2014). Center for Postsecondary Research, Indiana University School of Education, Bloomington, IND. Retrieved from http://nsse.iub.edu/NSSE_2014_Results/pdf/NSSE_2014_Annual_Results.pdf#page=8

Nelson, G. (2001). Do no harm: A first measure of effectiveness in small distance education programs.*Proceedings of ED-MEDIA 2001: World Conference on Educational Multimedia, Hypermedia, and Telecommunications*. Tampere, Finland.

Nettles, K., Dziuban, C., Cioffe, D., Moskal, P., & Moskal, P. (2000). Technology and Learning: The 'no significant difference' phenomenon: A structural analysis of research on technology enhanced instruction. In C. D. Dziuban & P. D. Moskal (Eds.), *Distributed Learning Impact Evaluation*. Orlando: University of Central Florida.

Neuhofer, B., Buhalis, D., & Ladkin, A. (2013). A typology of technology-enhanced tourism experiences. *International Journal of Tourism Research*. doi:10.1002/jtr.1958

New Media Consortium. (2011). The Horizon Report 2011 Edition. Retrieved from http://www.nmc.org/pdf/2011-Horizon-Report.pdf

Nicholls, J., & Philip, R. (2012). Solo life to Second Life: The design of physical and virtual learning spaces inspired by the drama classroom. *Research in Drama Education*, *17*(4), 583–602. doi:10.1080/13569783.2012.727628

Nikolaou, A., & Tsolakidis, C. (2012). The role of three dimensional virtual environments in the development of Personal Learning Networks. *Paper presented at the 2012 15th International Conference on Interactive Collaborative Learning (ICL)*. doi:10.1109/ICL.2012.6402114

Nishide, R., & Ueshima, S. (2004). Digital campus project: a" dream university" over the Internet Web. *Paper presented at the Second International Conference on Creating, Connecting and Collaborating through Computing*.

Nishide, R. (2011). Prospects for digital campus with extensive applications of virtual collaborative space. *Journal of Interactive Learning Research*, *22*(3), 421–443.

Noorman, M. (2014). Computing and Moral Responsibility. Retrieved from http://plato.stanford.edu/archives/sum2014/entries/computing-responsibility/

Nordin, S. (2003). *Tourism clustering and innovation- paths to economic growth and development. Ostersund*. European Tourism Research Institute.

Noteborn, G., Dailey-Hebert, A., Bohle-Carbonell, K., & Gijselears, W. (2013), Essential knowledge for academic performance: Educating in the virtual world to promote active learning. *Teacher and Teacher Education*, 37(January), 217-234. http://authors.elsevier.com/sd/article/S0742051X1300156X

Novak-Marcincin, J., Janak, M., Barna, J., & Novakova-Marcincinova, L. (2014). Application of Virtual and Augmented Reality Technology in Education of Manufacturing Engineers. *New perspectives in information systems and technologies, 2*, 439-446.

O'Connor, E. A., & Sakshaug, L. E. (2009). Preparing for Second Life: Two teacher educators reflect on their initial foray into virtual teaching and learning. *Journal of Educational Technology Systems*, *37*(3), 259–271. doi:10.2190/ET.37.3.c

Oddcast Inc. (2015). *SitePal*. Retrieved from http://www.sitepal.com/

Office of Science and Technology Policy (OSTP). (1992). *Grand Challenges: High Performance Computing and Communications*. Washington, DC. Retrieved from http://www.hpcc.gov

Office of Social and Economic Data Analysis (OSEDA). (2001). *Final results from the e-MINTS teacher survey*. Columbia, MO: Author.

Office of Technology Assessment (OTA). (1995). *Teachers and technology: Making the connection*. Washington, D.C.: U.S. Government Printing Office.

Office of Technology Assessment. (1982). Informational technology and its impact on American education, 128-133. U.S. Congress, Washington, DC.

Okimoto, H., & Heck, R. (2014). Examining the Impact of Redesigned Developmental Math Courses in Community Colleges. *Community College Journal of Research and Practice*, (ahead-of-print), 1-14.

Okita, S. Y., Turkay, S., Mihwa, K., & Murai, Y. (2013). Learning by teaching with virtual peers and the effects of technological design choices on learning. *Computers & Education, 63*, 176–196. doi:10.1016/j.compedu.2012.12.005

Olds, B. M., & Miller, R. L. (1998). An assessment matrix for evaluating engineering programs. *The Journal of Engineering Education, 87*(2), 173–178. doi:10.1002/j.2168-9830.1998.tb00338.x

Oliver, M., & Carr, D. (2009). Learning in virtual worlds: Using communities of practice to explain how people learn from play. *British Journal of Educational Technology, 40*(3), 14. doi:10.1111/j.1467-8535.2009.00948.x

Olson, T., Procci, K., & Bowers, C. (2011). Serious games usability testing: How to ensure proper usability, playability, and effectiveness. In *Design, user experience, and usability: Theory, methods, tools, and practice* (pp. 625–634). Berlin, Heidelberg: Springer. doi:10.1007/978-3-642-21708-1_70

Olsson, T., & Väänänen-Vainio-Mattila, K. (2013). Expected User Experience of Mobile Augmented Reality Services. *Personal and Ubiquitous Computing, 17*(2), 287–304. doi:10.1007/s00779-011-0494-x

Ong, S. K., & Nee, A. Y. C. (2013). *Virtual and augmented reality applications in manufacturing*. Springer Science & Business Media.

Oravec, J. A. (2003). Some influences of online distance learning on US higher education. *Journal of Further and Higher Education, 27*(1), 89–103. doi:10.1080/03098770305628

Ota, D., Loftin, B., Saito, T., Lea, R., & Keller, J. (1995). Virtual reality in surgical education. *Computers in Biology and Medicine, 25*(2), 127–137. doi:10.1016/0010-4825(94)00009-F PMID:7554831

Paas, F., & Sweller, J. (2014). Implications of cognitive load theory for multimedia learning. In R. Mayer (Ed.), Cambridge handbook of multimedia learning (2nd ed., pp. 27-42).

Paas, F. G. W. C. (1992). Training strategies for attaining transfer of problem-solving skill in statistics: A cognitive-load approach. *Journal of Educational Psychology, 84*(4), 429–434. doi:10.1037/0022-0663.84.4.429

Paas, F., & Sweller, J. (2012). An evolutionary upgrade of cognitive load theory: Using the human motor system and collaboration to support the learning of complex cognitive tasks. *Educational Psychology Review, 24*(1), 27–45. doi:10.1007/s10648-011-9179-2

Panda, S., & Mishra, S. (2007). E-learning in a mega open university: Faculty attitude, barriers and motivators. *Educational Media International, 44*(4), 323–338. doi:10.1080/09523980701680854

Pantelidis, V. S. (1997). *Virtual Reality (VR) as an instructional aid: a model for determining when to use VR*. Retrieved from http://www.coe.ecu.edu/vr/vredmod.html

Pantelidis, V. S., & Auld, L. (2002). Teaching virtual reality courses online. *CCAI: The Journal for the Integrated Study of Artificial Intelligence, Cognitive Science and Applied Epistemology.*

Pantelidis, V.S. (2010). Reasons to use virtual reality in education and training courses and a model to determine when to use virtual reality, *Themes in Science and Technology Education (Special Issue),* 59-70.

Pantelidis, V. (2009). Reasons to use virtual reality in education and training courses and a model to determine when to use virtual reality. *Themes in Science and Technology Education, 2*(1), 58–70.

Pantelidis, V. S. (1993). Virtual reality in the classroom. *Educational Technology, 33*(4), 23–27.

Partnership for 21st Century Learning. (2007). *Framework for 21st century learning.* Retrieved from http://www.21stcenturyskills.org

Pasfield-Neofitou, S. (2011). Online domains of language use: Second language learners' experiences of virtual community and foreignness. *Language Learning & Technology, 15*(2), 92–108.

Patrignani, N., & Whitehouse, D. (2014, July 30 – August 1). Slow Tech: The Bridge between Computer Ethics and Business Ethics. In K. Kimppa, D. Whitehouse, T. Kuusela, & J. Phahlamohlaka (Eds.), *Proceedings of 11th IFIP TC 9 International Conference on Human Choice and Computers (HCC11 2014), Turku, Finland* (Vol. 431, pp. 92–106). Berlin, Heidelberg: Springer. doi:10.1007/978-3-662-44208-1

Patterson, D. C., Reiniger, R. L., & Robertson, A. M. (2012). Cross-Reality Math Visualization: The subQuan System Dream Realizations. *Immersive Environments, Augmented Realities, and Virtual Worlds: Assessing Future Trends in Education: Assessing Future Trends in Education*, 57.

Pegrum, M., Oakley, G., & Faulkner, R. (2013). Schools going mobile: A study of the adoption of mobile handheld technologies in western Australian independent schools. *Australasian Journal of Educational Technology, 29*(1), 66–81. doi:10.1234/ajet.v29i1.64

Penner-Wilger, M., Fast, L., LeFevre, J., Smith-Chant, B. L., Skwarchuk, S., Kamawar, D., & Bisanz, J. (2007). The foundations of numeracy: Subitizing, finger gnosia, and fine-motor ability. In *Proceedings of the 29th Annual Cognitive Science Society* (pp. 1385-1390). Austin, TX: Cognitive Science Society.

Pereira, O. R. E., & Rodrigues, J. J. P. C. (2013). Survey and Analysis of Current Mobile Learning Applications and Technologies. *ACM Computing Surveys, 46*(2), 27:1–27:35. doi:10.1145/2543581.2543594

Petersen, C., & Toop, A. (1994). *Sales Promotion in Postmodern Marketing.* Aldershot: Gower Publishing Ltd.

Peterson, B. (2012). It Looks Great but How do I Know If It Fits?: an Introduction to Meta-synthesis Research. In K. Hannes, & C. Lockwood (Ed.), Synthesizing Qualitative Research: Choosing the Right Approach. John Wiley & Sons, LTD: Hoboken, NJ.

Peterson, M. (2011). Towards a Research Agenda for the Use of Three-Dimensional Virtual Worlds in Language Learning. *CALICO Journal, 29*(1), 67–80. doi:10.11139/cj.29.1.67-80

Petrakou, A. (2010). Interacting through avatars: Virtual worlds as a context for online education. *Computers & Education, 54*(4), 1020–1027. doi:10.1016/j.compedu.2009.10.007

Petrina, S. (2007). *Advanced teaching methods for the classroom.* Hershey, PA: Information Science Publishing. doi:10.4018/978-1-59904-337-1

Pew Internet. (2009). Internet, broadband, and cell phone statistics. Retrieved from http://www.distributedworkplace.com/DW/Research/Internet%20broadband%20and%20cell%20phone%20statistics%20-%20Pew%20Internet%20Report%20Jan%202010.pdf

Phan, V. T., & Choo, S. (2010). Interior design in augmented reality in environment. *International Journal of Computers and Applications, 5*(5), 16–21. doi:10.5120/912-1290

Phillips, J. J. (1996). How much is the training worth? *Training & Development, 50*(4), 20–24.

Phillips, J., & Berge, Z. (2009). Second Life for dental education. *Journal of Dental Education, 73*(11), 1260–1264. PMID:19910474

Pierce, D. (2015, March 6). The Future of Virtual Reality is inside your smartphone, Wired, Retrieved from http://www.wired.com/2015/03/future-virtual-reality-inside-smartphone/

Pink, D. H. (2006). *A whole new mind: Why right-brainers will rule the future*. Penguin.

Plant, E. A., Baylor, A. L., Doeer, C. E., & Rosenberg-Kima, R. (2009). Changing middle-school students' attitudes and performance regarding engineering with computer-based social models. *Computers & Education*, *53*(2), 209–215. doi:10.1016/j.compedu.2009.01.013

Popovici, D. M., Gerval, J. P., Hamza-Lup, F., Querrec, R., Polceanu, M., Popovici, N., & Zăgan, R. (2009). 3D virtual spaces supporting engineering learning activities. *International Journal of Computers, Communications & Control*, *IV*(4), 401–414.

Powers, T. M. (2003). Real Wrongs in Virtual Communities. *Ethics and Information Technology*, *5*(4), 191–198. doi:10.1023/B:ETIN.0000017737.56971.20

Prasolova-Forland, E. (2004). Supporting social awareness among university students in 3D CVEs: Benefits and limitations. *Paper presented at the 2004 International Conference on Cyberworlds*. doi:10.1109/CW.2004.59

Prasolova-Førland, E. (2008). Analyzing place metaphors in 3D educational collaborative virtual environments. *Computers in Human Behavior*, *24*(2), 185–204. doi:10.1016/j.chb.2007.01.009

Preexamples. (2015). *Paddy Power augmented reality campaign brings the Queen's face on £10 note to life*. Retrieved from http://bit.ly/1CRur13

Prensky, M. (2001). Digital Natives, Digital Immigrants. *On the Horizon*, *9*(5), 1–6. doi:10.1108/10748120110424816

Prieto-Arranz, J. I., Juan-Garau, M., & Jacob, K. L. (2013). Re-imagining cultural identity: Transcultural and translingual communication in virtual third-space environments. *Language, Culture and Curriculum*, *26*(1), 19–35. doi:10.1080/07908318.2012.759585

Prus, J., & Johnson, R. (1994). A critical review of student assessment options. In T. H. Bers & M. L. Mittler (Eds.), *Assessment & Testing, Myths & Realities. New Directions for Community Colleges, 88* (pp. 69–83). San Francisco: Jossey-Bass Publishers. doi:10.1002/cc.36819948811

Pulse Simulation Technology. (2008). Retrieved from https://www.youtube.com/watch?v=Q11aWO6dg2Q

Putnam, R. T., & Borko, H. (2000). What do new views of knowledge and thinking have to say about research on teacher learning? *Educational Researcher*, *29*(1), 4–15. doi:10.3102/0013189X029001004

Rachel, S., Cobcroft, R., Towers, S., Smith, J., & Bruns, A. (2006). Mobile Learning in Review: Opportunities and Challenges for Learners, Teachers, and Institutions. *Proceedings of the Online Learning and Teaching (OLT) Conference 2006*. doi:10.1016/S0190-9622(06)01179-0

Rawls, J. (1955). Two concepts of rules. *The Philosophical Review*, *64*(1), 3–32. doi:10.2307/2182230

Rayport, J. F., & Jaworski, B. J. (2004). Best face forward. *Harvard Business Review*, *82*(12), 1–12. PMID:15605565

Reigeluth, C. M. (1999). What is instructional-design theory and how is it changing? In C. M. Reigeluth (Ed.), *Instructional-design theories and models - a new paradigm of instructional theory* (pp. 5–29). New Jersey: Lawrence Erlbaum.

Reinick, L. B. (1983). Mathematics and Science and Learning: A New Conception. *Science*, *220*(4596), 477–478. doi:10.1126/science.220.4596.477 PMID:17816206

Reinsmith-Jones, K., Kibbe, S., Crayton, T., & Campbell, E. (2015). Use of Second Life in social work education: Virtual world experiences and their effect on students. *Journal of Social Work Education, 51*(1), 90–108.

Repenning, A., Webb, D., & Ioannidou, A. (2012). Scalable game design and the development of a checklist for getting computational thinking into public schools. Association for Computer Machinery (ACM). Retrieved from http://www.cs.colorado.edu/~ralex/papers/PDF/SIGCSE10-repenning.pdf

Reynolds, R. (2012). Ethics and practice in virtual worlds. In J. R. Sageng, H. Fossheim, & T. M. Larsen (Eds.), *The Philosophy of Computer Games* (Vol. 7, pp. 143–158). Springer; doi:10.1007/978-94-007-4249-9_10

Rheingold, H. (1991). *Virtual reality: The revolutionary technology of computer generated artificial worlds*. New York: Simon & Schuster Publishing.

Richardson, V. (1997). Constructivist teaching and teacher education: Theory and practice. In V. Richardson (Ed.), *Constructivist teacher education: Building a world of new understandings* (pp. 3–14). Florence, KY: Psychology Press.

Rikoon, S., Liebtag, T., Olivera-Aguilar, M., Robbins, S., & Jackson, T. (2014). A Pilot Study of Holistic Assessment and Course Placement in Community College: Findings and Recommendations.

Riva, G. (2006). *Virtual reality, Encyclopaedia of Biomedical Engineering*. London: John Wiley & Sons.

Robinson, D., & Garratt, C. (2000). *Introducing Ethics*. Totem Books.

Roblyer, M. D. (2003). *Integrating educational technology into teaching* (3rd ed.). NJ: Pearson Education.

Rock, D., & Schwartz, J. (2006). *The neuroscience of leadership*. Retrieved from http://www.strategy-business.com/article/06207?gko=6da0a

Roehl, A., Reddy, S., & Shannon, G. (2013). The flipped classroom: An opportunity to engage millennial students through active learning strategies. *Journal of Family and Consumer Sciences, 105*(2), 44–49. doi:10.14307/JFCS105.2.12

Rogers, E. M. (2003). *Diffusion of innovations*. New York, NY: Free Press.

Rokeach, M. (1960). *The open and closed mind*. New York: Basic Books.

Roman, D. (2011, February 11). Online Game's Banker Battles Inflation. *The Wall Street Journal*. Retrieved from http://www.wsj.com/articles/SB10001424052748704132204576135931023983542

Romero-Hall, E., Watson, G. S., Papelis, Y., & Garcia, H. (2014). Nursing pain assessment and management: A 3D interactive simulation. *International Journal of Designs for Learning, 5*(1), 43–56.

Rosemblum, L. J., & Cross, R. A. (1997). The challenge of virtual reality. In W. R. Earnshaw, J. Vince, & H. Jones (Eds.), *Visualization & Modeling* (pp. 325–399). San Diego, CA: Academic Press.

Rosenbaum, E., Klopfer, E., & Perry, J. (2007). On location learning: Authentic applied science with networked augmented realities. *Journal of Science Education and Technology, 16*(1), 31–45. doi:10.1007/s10956-006-9036-0

Rosenberg, A. (2010). Virtual world research ethics and the private/public distinction. *International Journal of Internet Research Ethics, 3*, 23–36.

Rovai, A. P. (2002). A preliminary look at the structural differences of higher education classroom communities in traditional and ALN courses. *Journal of Asynchronous Learning Networks, 6*(1), 41–56.

Rudestam, K. E., & Schoenholtz-Read, J. (2010). The flourishing of adult online education: An overview. In K. E. Rudestam & J. Schoenholtz-Read (Eds.), *Handbook of online learning* (pp. 1–18). Los Angeles, CA: Sage.

Rungtusanatham, M., Ellram, L. M., Siferd, S. P., & Salik, S. (2004). Toward a typology of business education in the Internet age. *Decision Sciences Journal of Innovative Education*, *2*(2), 101–120. doi:10.1111/j.1540-4609.2004.00040.x

Rust, R. T., Katherine, N. L., & Valarie, A. Z. (2004). Return on marketing: Using customer equity to focus marketing strategy. *Journal of Marketing*, *68*(1), 109–127. doi:10.1509/jmkg.68.1.109.24030

Sabourin, J. L., & Lester, J. C. (2014). Affect and engagement in game-based learning environments. *IEEE Transactions on Affective Computing*, *5*(1), 45–56. doi:10.1109/T-AFFC.2013.27

Sadler, R., & Nurmukhamedov, U. (2008, March). Second Life and task-based learning. *Paper presented atCALICO annual conference*, San Francisco, CA.

Sala, N. (2002a). Virtual reality in the educational environments. *ProceedingsIEEE International Conference on Advanced Learning Technologies ICALT 2002*, Kazan, Russia(pp. 417-419).

Sala, N. (2002b). From Virtual Reality to the Virtual Cities. *ProceedingsInternational Conference on New Educational Environment*, Lugano, Switzerland (pp. 21-24).

Sala, N., Metzeltin, S., & Sala, M. (2002). Applications of mathematics in the real world: territory and landscape. *ProceedingsInternational Conference: The Humanistic Renaissance in Mathematics Education*, Città del Mare, Sicilia, Italy(pp. 326-333).

Sala, N. (2009a). Fractal Geometry in Artificial Worlds and in Second Life. *Chaos and Complexity Letters*, *4*(1), 23–34.

Sala, N. (2009b). Fractal Geometry and Computer Science. In J. Gutierrez (Ed.), *Selected Readings on Telecommunications andNetworking* (pp. 385–404). Hershey, PA: Information Science Reference; doi:10.4018/978-1-60566-094-3.ch028

Sala, N. (2012). Virtual reality in architecture, in engineering and beyond. In E. Abu-Taieh, A. El Sheikh, & M. Jafari (Eds.), *Technology Engineering and Management in Aviation: Advancements and Discoveries* (pp. 336–345). Hershey, PA: Information Science Reference; doi:10.4018/978-1-60960-887-3.ch020

Sala, N. (2013a). Applications of Virtual Reality Technologies in Architecture and in Engineering. *International Journal of Space Technology Management and Innovation*, *3*(2), 78–88. doi:10.4018/ijstmi.2013070104

Sala, N. (2013b). Fractals, computer science and beyond. In F. Orsucci & N. Sala (Eds.), *Complexity science, living systems, and reflexing interfaces: new models and perspectives* (pp. 268–291). Hershey, PA: Information Science Reference; doi:10.4018/978-1-4666-2077-3.ch014

Sala, N., & Sala, M. (2005). Virtual reality in education. In D. Carbonara (Ed.), *Technology literacy applications in learning environments* (pp. 358–367). Hershey, PA: Idea Group Inc. doi:10.4018/978-1-59140-479-8.ch025

Saleeb, N., & Dafoulas, G. (2010). Pedagogical immigration to 3D virtual worlds: A critical review of underlying themes and their concepts. *Paper presented at the 2010 International Conference on Information Society* (i-Society).

Salmon, G. (2009). The future for (second) life and learning. *British Journal of Educational Technology*, *40*(3), 13. doi:10.1111/j.1467-8535.2009.00967.x

Salmon, G., Nie, M., & Edirisingha, P. (2010). Developing a five-stage model of learning in Second Life. *Educational Research*, *52*(2), 169–182. doi:10.1080/00131881.2010.482744

Salomon, G., & Perkins, D. (1998). Individual and social aspects of learning. *Review of Research in Education*, *23*, 1–24.

Saposnik, G., & Levin, M. (2011). Virtual reality in stroke rehabilitation a meta-analysis and implications for clinicians. *Stroke*, *42*(5), 1380–1386. doi:10.1161/STROKEAHA.110.605451 PMID:21474804

Satava, R. M. (1995a). Virtual reality, telesurgery, and the new world order of medicine. *Computer Aided Surgery*, *1*(1), 12–16. doi:10.3109/10929089509106821 PMID:9079422

Satava, R. M. (1995b). Medical applications of virtual reality. *Journal of Medical Systems*, *19*(3), 275–280. doi:10.1007/BF02257178 PMID:7643023

Satava, R. M., & Jones, S. B. (1996). Virtual reality and telemedicine: Exploring advanced concepts. *Telemedicine Journal*, *2*(3), 195–200. doi:10.1089/tmj.1.1996.2.195 PMID:10165542

Scacchi, W., Brown, C., & Nies, K. (2012). Exploring the Potential of Virtual Worlds for Decentralized Command and Control Point of Contact. *Proceedings of the 17th International Command and Control Research and Technology Symposium (ICCRTS 2012)*. DTIC Document.

Scardamalia, M., & Bereiter, C. (2006). Knowledge building: Theory, pedagogy, and technology. In K. Sawyer (Ed.), *Cambridge Handbook of the Learning Sciences* (pp. 97–118). New York: Cambridge University Press.

Schiller, S. Z., Goodrich, K., & Gupka, P. B. (2013). Let them play! Active learning in a virtual world. *Information Systems Management*, *30*(1), 50–62. doi:10.1080/10580530.2013.739891

Schroeder, N. L., & Adesope, O. O. (2013). How does a contextually-relevant peer pedagogical agent in a learner-attenuated system-paced learning environment affect cognitive and affective outcomes? *Journal of Teaching and Learning with Technology*, *2*(2), 114–133.

Schroeder, N. L., Adesope, O. O., & Gilbert, R.B. (2013). How effective are pedagogical agents for learning? A meta-analytic review. *Journal of Educational Computing Research*, *49*(1), 1–39. doi:10.2190/EC.49.1.a

Schroeder, R. (2008). Defining virtual worlds and virtual environments. *Journal of Virtual Worlds Research*, *1*(1).

Schroeder, R. (2008). Defining Virtual Worlds and Virtual Environments. *Journal of Virtual Worlds Research*, *1*(1). Retrieved from http://journals.tdl.org/jvwr/article/view/294

Schuemie, M. J., Van Der Straaten, P., Krijn, M., & Van Der Mast, C. A. P. G. (2001). Research on presence in virtual reality: A survey. *Cyberpsychology & Behavior*, *4*(2), 183–201. doi:10.1089/109493101300117884 PMID:11710246

Second Life. (n. d.). Retrieved from the Second Life Wiki: http://en.wikipedia.org/wiki/Second_Life

Seo, B.-K., Kim, K., & Park, J. (2011). Augmented reality-based on-site tour guide: A study in Gyeongbokgung. *Lecture Notes in Computer Science*, *6469*, 276–285. doi:10.1007/978-3-642-22819-3_28

September 21, 2015 from http://www.crito.uci.edu/tlc/FINDINGS/special3/

Sharples, M., Taylor, J., & Vavoula, G. (2005). Towards a Theory of Mobile Learning. *Proceedings of mLearn, 1*, 1–9.

Shelton, B. E., & Hedley, N. R. (2002). Using augmented reality for teaching earth-sun relationship to undergraduate geography students. *Proceedings ofthe First IEEE International Augmented Reality Toolkit Workshop* (pp. 1-8). Darmstadt, Germany: IEEE. doi:10.1109/ART.2002.1106948

Shen, Y., Ong, S. K., & Nee, A. Y. C. (2011). Vision-based hand interaction in augmented reality environment. *International Journal of Human-Computer Interaction*, *27*(6), 523–544. doi:10.1080/10447318.2011.555297

Sherman, W. R., & Craig, A. B. (2003). *Understanding virtual reality. Interface, application and design*. Boston, MA: Morgan-Kaufmann Publishers.

Shieh, R., Gummer, E., & Niess, M. (2008). The quality of a web-based course: Perspectives of the instructor and the students. *TechTrends: Linking Research & Practice to Improve Learning*, *52*(6), 61–68. doi:10.1007/s11528-008-0220-3

Shih, Y., & Yang, M. (2008). A Collaborative Virtual Environment for Situated Language Learning Using VEC3D. *Journal of Educational Technology & Society*, *11*(1), 56–68.

Showcase. (2015). *Shaq augmented reality*. Retrieved from http://bit.ly/1BgTZ5F

Sielhorst, T., Feuerstein, M., & Navab, N. (2008). Advanced medical displays: A literature review of augment reality. *Journal of Display Display Technology*, *4*(4), 451–467. doi:10.1109/JDT.2008.2001575

Skipper, B. (2015, January 27). Greece's new finance minister Yanis Varoufakis is Valve's former Steam Market economist. *International Business Times*. Retrieved from http://www.ibtimes.co.uk/greeces-new-finance-minister-yanis-varoufakis-valves-former-steam-market-economist-1485336

Slater, M., & Steed, A. (2000). A virtual presence counter. *Presence (Cambridge, Mass.)*, *9*(5), 413–434. doi:10.1162/105474600566925

Slater, M., & Wilbur, S. (1997). A framework for immersive virtual environments (FIVE): Speculations on the role of presence in virtual environments. *Presence (Cambridge, Mass.)*, *6*, 603–616.

Sletten Sommerseth, K. (2014). *Facilitating collaborative learning in 3-D virtual worlds. A Qualitative meta study* [Unpublished thesis]. Reprosentralen, University of Oslo.

Sloan Consortium. (2006). Faculty satisfaction. Needham, MA: SloanCWiki. Retrieved from http://www.sloan-c-wiki.org/wiki/index.php?title= Faculty_Satisfaction.

Smart, J., Cascio, J., & Paffendof, J. (2007). *Metaverse roadmap: pathways to the 3D web*. Retrieved from http://www.metaverseroadmap.org/overview

Smith-Robbins, J. (2011, December). Are virtual worlds (still) relevant in education? *elearn Magazine: Education and Technology Perspective*. Retrieved from http://elearnmag.acm.org/archive.cfm?aid=207847

Soares Calado, A. V., Márcio Soares, M., Campos, F., & Correia, W. (2013). Virtual reality applied to the study of the interaction between the user and the built space: A literature review. *Lecture Notes in Computer Science*, *8014*, 345–351. doi:10.1007/978-3-642-39238-2_38

Somekh, B. (2008). Factors affecting teachers' pedagogical adoption of ICT. In J. Voogt & G. Knezek (Eds.), *International Handbook of Information Technology in Primary and Secondary Education* (pp. 449–460). New York: Springer. doi:10.1007/978-0-387-73315-9_27

Song, H., Liu, J., & Chen, G. (2012). Tourism value chain governance- review and prospects. *Journal of Travel Research*, *52*(1), 15–28. doi:10.1177/0047287512457264

Sotiriou, S., & Bogner, F. X. (2008). Visualizing the invisible: Augmented reality as an innovative science education scheme. *Advanced Science Letters*, *1*(1), 114–122. doi:10.1166/asl.2008.012

Soto, V. (2013). Which instructional design models are educators using to design virtual world instruction? *Merlot Journal of Online Learning and Teaching*, *9*(3). Retrieved from http://jolt.merlot.org/vol9no3/soto_0913.htm

Southern, M. (2001). The cultural study of games: More than just games. Retrieved from http://www-bcf.usc.edu/~anthonyb/itp101/articles/cultural.doc

Spencer, A. J., Buhalis, D., & Moital, M. (2012). A hierarchical model of technology adoption for small owner-managed travel firms: An organizational decision making and leadership perspective. *Tourism Management*, *33*(5), 1195–1208. doi:10.1016/j.tourman.2011.11.011

Stamford, C. (2007, April 24). Gartner says 80 percent of active Internet users will have a "Second Life" in the virtual world by the end of 2011. *Gartner Newsroom*. Retrieved from http://www.gartner.com/it/page.jsp?id=503861

Stangel, C., & Pantelidis, V. S. (1997). South Greenville Elementary School virtual reality project. *VR in the Schools, 2*(4). Retrieved from http://www.coe.ecu.edu/vr/vrits/2-4so-gr.htm

Steenbergen-Hu, S., & Cooper, H. (2014). A meta-analysis of the effectiveness of intelligent tutoring systems on college students' academic learning. *Journal of Educational Psychology, 106*(2), 331–347. doi:10.1037/a0034752

Steinberg, A. D., Bashook, P. G., Drummond, J., Ashrafi, S., & Zefran, M. (2007). Assessment of faculty perception of content validity of PerioSim©, a haptic-3-D virtual reality dental training simulator. *Journal of Dental Education, 71*(12), 1574–1582. PMID:18096883

Steinkuehler, C. A. (2004). Learning in massively multiplayer online games. In Y. B. Kafai, W. A. Sandoval, N. Enyedy, A. S. Nixon, & F. Herrera (Eds)., Embracing diversity in the learning sciences: Proceedings of *the Sixth International Conference of the Learning Sciences (ICLS'04)* (pp. 521–528). Mahwah, NJ: Lawrence Erlbaum.

Steinkuehler, C. (2006). Massively multiplayer online videogaming as participation in a Discourse. *Mind, Culture, and Activity, 12*(1), 38–52. doi:10.1207/s15327884mca1301_4

Stephenson, N. (1992). *Snow Crash.* Random House Publishing Group.

Stiubiener, I., Barbosa, W., Kamienski, C. A., & Schweitzer, C. M. (2011). Using Virtual Worlds in distance learning environments. *Paper presented at theFrontiers in Education Conference (FIE).* doi:10.1109/FIE.2011.6142822

Stoutfoot, T. (2007) *How big is Azeroth?* (Pseudonym) Retrieved from http://tobolds.blogspot.com/2007/01/how-big-is-azeroth.html

Stricker, D., Pagani, A., & Zoellner, M. (2009). *In-situ visualization for cultural heritage sites using novel augmented reality technologies*. Retrieved from http://bit.ly/192Vg5N

Subramaniam, K. (2007). Teachers' mindsets and the integration of computer technology. *British Journal of Educational Technology, 38*(6), 1056–1071. doi:10.1111/j.1467-8535.2006.00693.x

Suebnukarn, S., Haddawy, P., Rhienmora, P., & Gajananan, K. (2010). Haptic Virtual Reality for Skill Acquisition in Endodontics. *Journal of Endodontics, 36*(1), 53–55. doi:10.1016/j.joen.2009.09.020 PMID:20003935

Sugar, W., & Slagter van Tryon, P. J. (2014). Development of a virtual technology coach to support technology integration for K-12 educators. *TechTrends, 58*(3), 54–62. doi:10.1007/s11528-014-0752-7

Suh, Y., Shin, C., Woo, W., Dow, S., & MacIntyre, B. (2011). Enhancing and evaluating users' social experience with a mobile phone guide applied to cultural heritage. *Personal and Ubiquitous Computing, 15*(6), 649–665. doi:10.1007/s00779-010-0344-2

Suslov, N. (2012). Krestianstvo SDK towards end-user mobile 3D virtual learning environment. *Proceedings of the 10th International Conference on Creating, Connecting and Collaborating through Computing, C5 2012* (pp. 9–14). doi:10.1109/C5.2012.8

Suter, W. N. (2012). *Introduction to educational research: A critical thinking approach* (2nd ed.). Thousand Oaks, CA: Sage Publications.

Sweller, J. (2005). Implications of cognitive load theory for multimedia learning. In R. Mayer (Ed.), The Cambridge handbook of multimedia learning (pp. 19-30). New York, NY: Cambridge University Press.

Sweller, J. (2010). Element interactivity and intrinsic, extraneous, and germane cognitive load. *Educational Psychology Review*, *22*(2), 123–138. doi:10.1007/s10648-010-9128-5

Sweller, J., Ayres, P., & Kalyuga, S. (2011). The split-attention effect. In *Cognitive Load Theory* (pp. 111–128). Springer New York. doi:10.1007/978-1-4419-8126-4_9

Sweller, J., & Chandler, P. (1994). Why some material is difficult to learn. *Cognition and Instruction*, *12*(3), 185–233. doi:10.1207/s1532690xci1203_1

Sydell, L. (2005). 'Virtual' Virus Sheds Light on Real-World Behavior. *NPR*, Retrieved from http://www.npr.org/templates/story/story.php?storyId=4946772

Tegos, S., Demetriadis, S., & Tsiatsos, T. (2014). A configurable conversational agent to trigger students' productive dialogue: A pilot study in the CALL domain. *International Journal of Artificial Intelligence in Education*, *24*(1), 62–91. doi:10.1007/s40593-013-0007-3

Teoh, J. (2012). Pre-service teachers in second life: Potential of simulations. *Journal of Educational Technology Systems*, *40*(4), 415–441. doi:10.2190/ET.40.4.g

The Associated Press. (2014, March 25). Facebook to buy Oculus virtual reality firm for $2B. Retrieved from http://www.cbc.ca/news/technology/facebook-to-buy-oculus-virtual-reality-firm-for-zb-1,2586318

The New Media Consortium. (2007). *The Horizon Report*. Austin, Texas: New Media Consortium.

The Schome Community. (2007). The schome-NAGTY teen second life pilot final report: a summary of key findings and lessons learnt. Retrieved from http://kn.open.ac.uk/public/getfile.cfm?documentfileid-11344

The World Factbook. (2015). Retrieved from https://www.cia.gov/library/publications/the-world-factbook/rankorder/2119rank.html

The, F. A. Cup. (2015). *About the FA*. Retrieved from http://bit.ly/1GLcZYu

Theodoridou, K. D. (2009). *Learning with Laura. Investigating the effects of a pedagogical agent on Spanish lexical acquisition* (Doctoral dissertation). University of Texas at Austin, Austin, TX.

Thompson, C. W. (2011). Next-Generation Virtual Worlds. *IEEE Internet Computing*, *15*(1), 60–65. doi:10.1109/MIC.2011.15

Thorne, S. L., Black, R. W., & Sykes, J. M. (2009). Second Language Use, Socialization, and Learning in Internet Interest Communities and Online Gaming. *Modern Language Journal*, *93*, 802–821. doi:10.1111/j.1540-4781.2009.00974.x

Thorpe, M., Holm, J., & van den Boer, G. (2014). *Discovering the decisions within your business processes using IBM blueworks live*. New York: International Business Machines Corporation.

Thorsteinsson, G., & Page, T. (2008). Innovative technology education using a virtual reality learning environment, 90, 26-35. Pedagogy Studies/Pedigogika: Vilnius Pedagogical University.

Tokel, S. T., & Karitas, E. C. (2014). *Mersin University Journal of the Faculty of Education*, *10*(1), 1–12.

Toon activity by level. (2015). Retrieved from http://www.wow-stats.info/pact01.html

Trahan, M. P., Adams, N. B., & Dupre, S. (2012). Virtual learning environments: Second Life MUVEs to leverage student ownership. In Virtual Learning Environments: Concepts, Methodologies, Tools and Applications (pp. 200-213). Hershey, PA: IGI Global. doi:10.4018/978-1-4666-0011-9.ch113

Traphagan, T. W., Chiang, Y.-V., Chang, H. M., Wattanawaha, B., Lee, H., Mayrath, M. C., & Resta, P. E. et al. (2010). Cognitive, social and teaching presence in a virtual world and a text chat. *Computers & Education, 55*(3), 923–936. doi:10.1016/j.compedu.2010.04.003

Traub, D. C. (1991). Simulated world as classroom: The potential for designed learning within virtual environments. In S. K. Helsel & J. P. Roth (Eds.), *Virtual reality: Theory, practice, and promise* (pp. 111–121). Westport, CT: Meckler Publishing.

Turban, E., McLean, E. R., & Wetherbe, J. C. (2008). *Information technology for management.* New Jersey: John Wiley & sons, Inc.

Umbach, P. D., & Wawrzynsli, M. R. (2005). Faculty do matter: The role of college faculty in student learning and engagement. *Research in Higher Education, 46*(2), 153–185. doi:10.1007/s11162-004-1598-1

Unity Technologies. (2015). *Unity3D* [computer software]. Retrieved from http://unity3d.com/unity/download

Vaill, P. (1996). *Learning as a way of being.* San Francisco: Jossey-Bass Publishers.

van der Meij, H. (2013). Motivating agents in software tutorials. *Computers in Human Behavior, 29*(3), 845–857. doi:10.1016/j.chb.2012.10.018

van Gog, T. (2014). The signaling (or cueing) principle in multimedia learning. In R. Mayer (Ed.), *The Cambridge handbook of multimedia learning* (2nd ed., pp. 263–278). New York, NY: Cambridge University Press. doi:10.1017/CBO9781139547369.014

van Krevelen, D. W. F., & Poelman, R. (2010). A survey of augmented reality technologies, applications and limitations. *The International Journal of Virtual Reality, 9*(2), 1–20.

van Mulken, S., André, E., & Müller, J. (1998). The persona effect: How substantial is it? In *People and computers XIII* (pp. 53–66). Springer London. doi:10.1007/978-1-4471-3605-7_4

VanLehn, K. (2011). The relative effectiveness of human tutoring, intelligent tutoring systems, and other tutoring systems. *Educational Psychologist, 46*(4), 197–221. doi:10.1080/00461520.2011.611369

VanLehn, K., Graesser, A. C., Jackson, G. T., Jordan, P., Olney, A., & Rose, C. P. (2007). When are tutorial dialogues more effective than reading? *Cognitive Science, 31*(1), 3–62. doi:10.1080/03640210709336984 PMID:21635287

Veletsianos, G., & Russell, G. (2014). Pedagogical agents. In M. Spector, D. Merrill, J. Elen, & M.J. Bishop (Eds.), *Handbook of Research on Educational Communications and Technology* (4th ed., pp. 759-769). Springer Academic. Retrieved from http://www.veletsianos.com/wp-content/uploads/2013/08/pedagogical_agents_synthesis_veletsianos_handbook.pdf

Veletsianos, G. (2007). Cognitive and affective benefits of an animated pedagogical agent: Considering contextual relevance and aesthetics. *Journal of Educational Computing Research, 36*(4), 373–377. doi:10.2190/T543-742X-033L-9877

Veletsianos, G. (2010). Contextually relevant pedagogical agents: Visual appearance, stereotypes, and first impressions and their impact on learning. *Computers & Education, 55*(2), 576–585. doi:10.1016/j.compedu.2010.02.019

Vickerstaff, K. (2015). *Implementation of technology enhanced learning pedagogy and impact on employability and learning within engineering education frameworks* [Unpublished doctoral dissertation]. Plymouth University. Plymouth, UK.

Vincenti, G., & Braman, J. (2010). *Teaching through multi-user virtual environments: applying dynamic elements to the modern classroom.* Hershey, PA: Information Science Reference. doi:10.4018/978-1-61692-822-3

Vincenti, G., & Braman, J. (2011). *Multi-User virtual environments for the classroom: practical approaches to teaching in virtual worlds.* Hershey, PA: IGI Global; doi:10.4018/978-1-60960-545-2

Virtual reality (VR). (2015). In *Encyclopædia Britannica*. Retrieved from http://www.britannica.com/technology/virtual-reality

Virtual reality. (n. d.). Retrieved from http://www.merriamwebster.com/dictionary/virtualreality

Virtual reality. (n. d.). Retrieved from https://en.wikipedia.org/wiki/Virtual_reality

Vlahakis, V., Ioannidis, N., Karigiannis, J., Tsotros, M., Gounaris, M., Stricker, D., Gleue, T., Daehne, P., & Almeida, L. (2002). Archeoguide: An Augmented Reality Guide for Archaeological Sites. *Computer Graphics in Art History and Archaeology, September/October*, 52- 60.

Vong, K. (2015). *How brands are using augmented reality in marketing to engage customers*. Retrieved from http://bit.ly/SrBNTq

Vygotsky, L. S. (1978). *Mind in society*. Cambridge, MA: Harvard University Press.

Wagner, M. (2008). Second life's popularity rests on breadth of activities. *Information Week*. Retrieved from http://www.informationweek.com/news/personal_tech/virtualworlds/showArticle.jhtml?articleID=210602197

Wang, T., & Zhu, Q. (2009). A software engineering education game in a 3-D online virtual environment. *Paper presented at the First International Workshop on Education Technology and Computer Science ETCS'09.*

Wang, Y., & Braman, J. (2009). Extending the classroom through second life. *Journal of Information Systems. Special Issue: Impacts of Web 2.0 and Virtual World Technologies on IS Education, 20*(2), 235-247.

Wang, Y., Dudley, A., Braman, J., & Vincenti, G. (2009). Simulating ethical dilemmas: teaching ethics through immersive virtual environments. *Proceedings of the 12th IASTED International Conference on Computers and Advanced Technology in Education*. St. Thomas, US Virgin Islands.

Wan, G., Yeh, E., & Cheng, H. (in press). Digital Media Use by Chinese Youth and Its Impact. In C. K. Cheung (Ed.), *Media Education in China*. Hong Kong, China: Springer.

Wang, C. X., Song, H., Xia, F., & Yan, Q. (2009). Integrating Second Life into an EFL program: Students' perspectives. *Journal of Educational Technology Development and Exchange*, *2*(1), 1–16.

Wang, C., Calandra, B., Hibbard, S., & McDowell Lefaiver, M. (2012). Learning effects of an experimental EFL program in Second Life. *Educational Technology Research and Development*, *60*(5), 943–961. doi:10.1007/s11423-012-9259-0

Wang, F., & Burton, J. K. (2013). Second Life in education: A review of publications from its launch to 2011. *British Journal of Educational Technology*, *44*(3), 357–371. doi:10.1111/j.1467-8535.2012.01334.x

Wang, F., & Shao, E. (2012). Using Second Life to Assist EFL Teaching: We Do Not Have to Sign in to the Program. *Techtrends: Linking Research and Practice to Improve Learning*, *56*(4), 15–18. doi:10.1007/s11528-012-0582-4

Wang, G. G. (2002). Definition and Review of Virtual Prototyping. *ASME Journal of Computing and Information Science in Engineering*, *2*(3), 232–236. doi:10.1115/1.1526508

Wang, L., Wang, C., & Fournier, C. (2000). Envisioning Yuan Ming Yuan (Garden of Perfect Brightness). *IEEE Computer Graphics and Applications*, *20*(1), 10–14. doi:10.1109/38.814532

Wang, S.-K., & Hsu, H.-Y. (2010). Using the ADDIE model to design Second Life activities for online learners. *TechTrends*, *53*(6), 76–81.

Wankel, C., & Malleck, S. (Eds.), (2009). *Emerging Ethical Issues of Life in Virtual Worlds*. Charlotte, NC, USA: Information Age Publishing.

Warner, T. (2012). E-coaching systems: Convenient, anytime, anywhere, and nonhuman. *Performance Improvement, 51*(9), 22–28. doi:10.1002/pfi.21305

Warren, S., Jones, G., & Lin, L. (2011). Usability and play testing: The often missed assessment. In L. Annetta & S. Bronack (Eds.), *Serious educational game assessment: Practical methods and models for educational games, simulations and virtual worlds* (pp. 131–147). Netherlands: Sense Publishers. doi:10.1007/978-94-6091-329-7_8

Warren, S., & Lin, L. (2012). Ethical considerations for learning game, simulation, and virtual world design and development. In H. H. Yang & S. C.-Y. Yuen (Eds.), *Handbook of Research on Practices and Outcomes in Virtual Worlds and Environments* (Vol. 1). Hershey, PA, USA: IGI Global. doi:10.4018/978-1-60960-762-3.ch001

Wasilik, O., & Bolliger, D. U. (2009). Faculty satisfaction in the online environment: An institutional study. *The Internet and Higher Education, 12*(3-4), 173–178. doi:10.1016/j.iheduc.2009.05.001

Waters, J. (2014, October 9). Could the Oculus Rift redeem virtual reality in higher ed? *Campus Technology*. Retrieved from http://campustechnology.com/articles/2014/10/09/could-the-oculus-rift-redeem-virtual-reality-in-higher-ed.aspx

Waters, J. K. (2009). A 'Second Life' for educators. *The Journal, 36*(1), 29–34.

Webb, D., Repenninga, A., & Koh, K. (2012, February 29-March 3). Toward an emergent theory of broadening participation in computer science education. *Proceeding of the Association for Computer Machinery (ACM) Special Interest Group on Computer Science Conference (SIGCSE)* (pp. 173-178). Raleigh, NC. ACM. doi:10.1145/2157136.2157191

Wegner, S. B., Holloway, K. C., & Garton, E. M. (1999). The effects of internet-based instruction on student learning. *Journal of Asynchronous Learning Networks, 3*(2).

Weimer, M. (2010). *Inspired college teaching: A career-long resource for professional growth*. Hoboken, NJ: John Wiley & Sons.

Whitlock, L. A., McLaughlin, A. C., & Allaire, J. C. (2012). Individual differences in response to cognitive training: Using a multi-modal, attentionally demanding game-based intervention for older adults. *Computers in Human Behavior, 28*(4), 1091–1096. doi:10.1016/j.chb.2012.01.012

Whitton, N., & Hollins, P. (2008). Collaborative virtual gaming worlds in higher education. *ALT-J Research in Learning Technology, 16*(3), 221–229. doi:10.1080/09687760802526756

Wickens, C. D. (1992). Virtual reality and education. *Proceedings of the 1992 IEEE International Conference on Systems, Man and Cybernetics*. doi:10.1109/ICSMC.1992.271688

Wiecha, J., Heyden, R., Sternthal, E., & Merialdi, M. (2010). Learning in a virtual world: Experience with using second life for medical education. *Journal of Medical Internet Research, 12*(1), e1. doi:10.2196/jmir.1337 PMID:20097652

Wiggins, G. (1998). *Educative assessments: Designing assessments to inform and improve student performance*. San Francisco: Jossey-Bass Publishers.

Wigham, C. R., & Chanier, T. (2013). A study of verbal and nonverbal communication in Second Life–the ARCHI21 experience. *ReCALL, 25*(01), 63–84. doi:10.1017/S0958344012000250

Wikipedia: "Fractal terrain texture" by Stevo-88 - self-made, used Adobe Photoshop for Perlin noise creation and Terragen for rendering. Licensed under Public Domain via Wikimedia Commons. (n. d.). Retrieved from http://commons.wikimedia.org/wiki/File:Fractal_terrain_texture.jpg#mediaviewer/File:Fractal_terrain_texture.jpghttp://thejournal.com/articles/2009/01/01/a-second-life-for-educators.aspx

Wind, J., & Mahajan, V. (2001). *Digital Marketing: Global Strategies from the World's Leading Experts*. Chichester: John Wiley & Sons.

Windschitl, M., & Sahl, K. (2002, Spring). Tracing teachers' use of technology in a laptop computer school: The interplay of teacher beliefs, social dynamics, and institutional culture. *American Educational Research Journal*, *39*(1), 165–205. doi:10.3102/00028312039001165

Winn, W. (1993). A conceptual basis for educational applications of virtual reality (Technical Report TR-93-9). Seattle, Washington: Human Interface Technology Laboratory, University of Washington. Retrieved from http://www.hitl.washington.edu/publications/r-93-9/

Wojciechowski, R., & Cellary, W. (2013). Evaluation of learners' attitude toward learning in ARIES augmented reality environments. *Computers & Education*, *68*, 570–585. doi:10.1016/j.compedu.2013.02.014

Wong, J. N. (2010). Searching for good practice in teaching: A comparison of two subject-based professional learning communities in a secondary school in Shanghai. *Compare: A Journal of Comparative and International Education*, *40*(5), 623-639.

Woods, D. (2009). Experiential learning through real space placements undertaken in 'virtual world' spaces. *Proceedings from Ascilite Auckland 2009*.

World of Warcraft Research Assistant. (2015). Retrieved from http://www.hcii.cmu.edu/careers/2011/world-warcraft-research-assistant

World Tourism Organization (UNWTO). (2015). *Understanding tourism: basic glossary*. Retrieved from http://bit.ly/1ki2UGS

Wozney, L., Venkatesh, V., & Abrami, P. C. (2006). Implementing computer technologies: Teachers' perceptions and practices. *Journal of Technology and Teacher Education*, *14*(1), 173–207.

Wu, F., Liu, Z., Wang, J., & Zhao, Y. (2015, March). Establishment virtual maintenance environment based on VIRTOOLS to effectively enhance the sense of immersion of teaching equipment. *Proceedings of the2015 International Conference on Education Technology, Management and Humanities Science (ETMHS 2015)*. Atlantis Press. doi:10.2991/etmhs-15.2015.93

Wu, H.-K., Lee, S. W.-Y., Chang, H.-Y., & Liang, J.-C. (2013). Current status, opportunities and challenges of augmented reality in education. *Computers & Education*, *62*, 41–49. doi:10.1016/j.compedu.2012.10.024

Yalcinalp, S., Sen, N., Kocer, G., & Koroglu, F. (2012). Higher Education Student's Behaviors as Avatars in a Web based Course in Second Life. *Procedia: Social and Behavioral Sciences*, *46*, 4534–4538. doi:10.1016/j.sbspro.2012.06.291

Yang, C. C. (2004). Exploring factors affecting the adoption of mobile commerce in Singapore. *Telematics and Informatics*, *22*(3), 257–277. doi:10.1016/j.tele.2004.11.003

Yang, H. H., & Yuen, C.-Y. S. (Eds.). (2012). Handbook of Research on Practices and Outcomes in Virtual Worlds and Environments (Vol. 2). Hershey, PA, USA: IGI Global.

Ye, E., Liu, C., & Polack-Wahl, J. A. (2007). *Enhancing software engineering education using teaching aids in 3-D online virtual worlds. Frontiers in Education*. FIE.

Yee, N. (2006). Motivations for play in online games. *Cyberpsychology & Behavior*, *9*(6), 772–775. doi:10.1089/cpb.2006.9.772 PMID:17201605

Yee, N. (2006). The demographics, motivations, and derived experiences of users of massively multi-user online graphical environments. *Presence (Cambridge, Mass.)*, *15*(3), 309–329. doi:10.1162/pres.15.3.309

Yeh, E. (2014). Teaching culture and language through the Multiple Intelligences Film Teaching Model in the ESL/EFL classroom. *Journal of Effective Teaching, 14*(1), 63–79.

Yeh, E., & Kessler, G. (2015). Enhancing Linguistic and Intercultural Competencies Through the Use of Social Network Sites and Google Earth. In J. Keengwe (Ed.), *Promoting Global Literacy Skills through Technology-Infused Teaching and Learning*. Hershey, PA, USA: IGI Global. doi:10.4018/978-1-4666-6347-3.ch001

Yılmaz, R. M., Topu, F. B., Goktas, Y., & Coban, M. (2013). Social presence and motivation in a three-dimensional virtual world: An explanatory study. *Australasian Journal of Educational Technology, 29*(6), 823–839.

Yilmaz, R., Topu, F., Goktas, Y., & Coban, M. (2013). Social presence and motivation in a three dimensional virtual world An explanatory study. *Australasian Journal of Educational Technology, 29*(6), 823–839.

Youngblut, C. (1998). *Educational uses of virtual reality technology* (IDA Document D-2128). Retrieved from http://www.sustainable-design.ie/sustain/VE_Education-D2128.pdf

Yovcheva, Z., Buhalis, D., & Gatzidis, C. (2012). Smartphone Augmented Reality Applications for Tourism. *e-Review of Tourism Research (eRTR), 10*(2), 63-66.

Yuen, S., Yaoyuneyong, G., & Johnson, E. (2011). Augmented reality: An overview and five directions for AR in education. *Journal of Educational Technology Development and Exchange, 4*(1), 119–140.

Zech, L. K., Gause-Vega, C. L., Bray, M. H., Secules, T., & Goldman, S. R. (2000). Content-based collaborative inquiry: A professional development model for sustaining educational reform. *Educational Psychologist, 35*(3), 207–217. doi:10.1207/S15326985EP3503_6

Zhang, H. (2013). Pedagogical Challenges of Spoken English Learning in the Second Life Virtual World: A Case Study. *British Journal of Educational Technology, 44*(2), 243–254. doi:10.1111/j.1467-8535.2012.01312.x

Zhao, H., Sun, B., Wu, H., & Hu, X. (2010). Study on building a 3D interactive virtual learning environment based on OpenSim platform. *Paper presented at the2010 International Conference on Audio, Language and Image Processing*. doi:10.1109/ICALIP.2010.5684986

Zhao, Y., Pugh, K., Sheldon, S., & Byers, J. L. (2002). Conditions for classroom technology innovations. *Teachers College Record, 104*(3), 482–515. doi:10.1111/1467-9620.00170

Zheng, D., Li, N., & Zhao, Y. (2008, March). Learning Chinese in Second Life Chinese language school. *Paper presented atCALICO Annual Conference*, San Francisco, CA.

Zheng, B., Warschauer, M., Hwang, J. K., & Collins, P. (2014). Laptop use, interactive science software, and science learning among at-Risk students. *Journal of Science Education and Technology, 1*(5).

Zheng, D., Young, F. M., Brewer, A. R., & Wagner, M. (2009). Attitude and self-efficacy change: English language learning in virtual worlds. *CALICO Journal, 27*(1), 205–231. doi:10.11139/cj.27.1.205-231

Zhong, Y., & Liu, C. (2012). User evaluation of a domain-oriented end-user design environment for building 3D virtual chemistry experiments. *Paper presented at theUser Evaluation for Software Engineering Researchers (USER)*. doi:10.1109/USER.2012.6226585

Zhou, F., Duh, H. L., & Billinghurst, M. (2008). Trends in augmented reality traching, iteraction nd display: A review of ten years in ISMAR. *Proceedings of the Mixed and Augmented Reality, ISMAR 7th IEE/ACM International Symposium* (pp. 193-202). Cambridge: IEEE.

Zhou, Z., Jin, X. L., Vogel, D. R., Fang, Y., & Chen, X. (2011). Individual motivations and demographic differences in social virtual world uses: An exploratory investigation in Second Life. *International Journal of Information Management, 31*(3), 261–271. doi:10.1016/j.ijinfomgt.2010.07.007

Zhu, W., Owen, C., Li, H., & Lee, J.-H. (2004). Personalized in-store e-commerce with PromoPad: An augmented reality shopping assistant. *Electronic Journal for E-commerce Tools and Applications, 1*(3), 1–19.

Ziegler, R., Mueller, W., Fischer, G., & Göbel, M. (1995, January). A virtual reality medical training system. In *Computer vision, virtual reality and robotics in medicine* (pp. 282–286). Springer Berlin Heidelberg. doi:10.1007/978-3-540-49197-2_36

Zoller, U. (1990). Students' misunderstandings and misconceptions in college freshman chemistry (general and organic). *Journal of Research in Science Teaching, 27*(10), 1053–1065. doi:10.1002/tea.3660271011

About the Contributors

Dong Hwa Choi is a teacher, scholar, and researcher who believes that education is a life-long process which requires commitment, self-discipline, and serving others. She has worked in the United States and South Korea focused on teacher preparation, online education, technology integration, and grant-funded projects that serve K-12 teacher candidates. Dr. Choi came to the United States in 1994 from Seoul, South Korea, with a Bachelor of Science in Elementary School Education and a Master of Arts in Educational Psychology, both from Ewha Womans University. A Ph.D. in Early Childhood was earned in 2000 from the University of Missouri-Kanas City. During the following five years, Dr. Choi was an assistant professor at Indiana State University in Terre Haute, Indiana. Dr. Choi has taught at Park University since 2006. Dr. Choi has integrated her international background and experiences into her professional activities including program development and field-based pedagogical practices, and continuously serves professional communities on a national and international level.

Amber Dailey-Hebert Grounded in the belief that education has the power to transform our lives and our society, Amber Dailey- Hebert is an internationally recognized leader in promoting innovation in higher education. Her work directly impacts adult learners as a Full Professor at Park University, and has extended to academic leadership roles as a Department Chair, Program Coordinator, Associate Dean, and as the Founding & Executive Director for the *Center for Excellence in Teaching and Learning*, which serves over 1600 full and part-time faculty around the world. In addition, Dr. Dailey-Hebert is a prolific researcher and collaborator, publishing multiple textbooks, peer reviewed journal articles, serving as editor of peer reviewed journals, and winning awards for her scholarship and pioneering efforts in problem-based learning and service learning in the online, hybrid & face-to-face environments.

Judi Simmons Estes is an Associate Professor and Associate Dean in the School for Education at Park University. Dr. Estes has a research interest in modeling the integration of technology with instruction within teacher preparation coursework, thus educating teacher candidates how to integrate technology to enhance instruction in K-12 classrooms. Dr. Estes is a certified instructional specialist for e-MINTS (Enhancing Missouri's Instructional Network Teaching Strategies).

***

András Margitay-Becht is a developmental economist and systems engineer. His research interests include inequality, growth, ACE, virtual realities and education technologies.

James Braman is an Assistant Professor for the School of Applied and Information Technology at The Community College of Baltimore County (CCBC). He earned a Masters and Bachelor degree in Computer Science from Towson University and is pursuing a Doctorate in Information Technology. He is currently serving as the joint editor-in-chief for the Institute for Computer Sciences, Social Informatics and Telecommunications Engineering (ICST) Transactions on E-Education and E-Learning. James has published several edited books, which include topics related to: teaching through virtual environments, cyber-ethics and technology & art. His research interests include virtual worlds, augmented reality, affective computing, and thanatechnology.

Anita Cassard completed her undergraduate coursework at the Economic Research Institute and Institute of Advanced Studies in Vienna/Austria. She received her MPS from The New School University (Milano-The New School for Management and Urban Policy) NYC, in Hospital and Health Care Administration and her doctoral degree from Walden University in Minneapolis (Applied Management and Decision Sciences) specializing in Leadership and Organizational Change. She collaboratively wrote papers published in peer reviewed scientific journals such as JSBHS- the Journal of Social, Behavioral, and Health Sciences. Her book The Sherpa Leadership Model: A Model of Disempowerment; was published in Europe and the United States by VDM-Publishing in Germany.

Neal M Finkelstein was born in Brooklyn, New York on 5 September 1962. He is a 1980 graduate of Florida Atlantic University with a degree in Electrical Engineering. Dr. Finkelstein also holds a Master of Science degree in Industrial Engineering from Texas A&M University and a Doctorate in Industrial Engineering from the University of Central Florida. Dr. Finkelstein is a graduate of the Army School of Engineering and Logistics. He also holds three Level III Certifications in the Acquisition Corp for Science and Technology Management, Program Management and Engineering and is a past Graduate of the Leadership and Education Development Course, and Graduate of the Manager's Development Course. As the Branch Chief for the Army Research Laboratory located in Orlando, Florida, Dr. Finkelstein serves as a principle senior technical advisor on technical, programmatic and organizational issues that cut across the organization. He is responsible for providing evaluation and recommendations on a wide range of diverse day to day issues arising from research and development of simulations, training and instrumentation solutions. Dr. Finkelstein has contributed to 70 technical publications, been involved in over $2B in acquisition projects and sat on 43 Source Selection Evaluation Boards throughout his career.

Reza Ghanbarzadeh is a doctoral student in the school of Information and Communication Technology at Griffith University, Queensland, Australia. His research area is mainly focused on Information Systems and he is particularly interested in three dimensional immersive virtual worlds and the application of this technology in education and healthcare. He received both his BSc and Msc in computer software engineering. Reza has published several papers in journals like 'Journal of medical Internet Research' and 'Journal of Information Security Research', and for conferences like the IEEE.

Amir Hossein Ghapanchi is a tenured faculty member at the School of Information and Communication Technology, Griffith University, Australia. Prior to that he has worked at University of Technology Sydney and the University of New South Wales (UNSW). He obtained his PhD in Information Systems from the University of New South Wales (UNSW), Australia. Amir has also been an active member of the Institute for Integrated Intelligent Systems (IIIS) and Asia-Pacific ubiquitous Healthcare Research Centre (APuHC). Dr Ghapanchi has been involved in an ongoing Randomised Controlled Trial of robots for aged care in 53 sites in six countries including Australia, as part of the €2.36 Million EU project Victoryahome led by the Norwegian Centre for Integrated Care and Telemedicine (NST). Dr Ghapanchi is a section editor for Australasian Journal of Information System, and an associate editor for International Journal of Enterprise Information Systems, and International Journal of Strategic Decision Sciences. Amir has published over 50 referred publications including 40 journal articles in prestigious information systems and management journals, such as Information and Organization, Communications of Association for Information Systems, Journal of Organizational Computing and Electronic Commerce, Journal of the Association for Information Science and Technology (JASIST), Electronic Markets, Journal of Medical Internet Research, Journal of Computer and System Sciences, International Journal of Project Management, Journal of Systems and Software, and International Journal of Information Management.

Amit Goel has more than two decades of experience in Research and Development. His research interests are parallel and high performance computing, big data, predictive analytics, machine learning, intelligent agents, virtual worlds, and algorithmic game theory. Amit has published internationally in journals, conferences and book chapters. Amit has worked with large, medium and startup scale companies in different countries. He has been responsible for teams of 5-100 people and for budgets from 1-50 million USD. He has worked across multiple domains such as travel, education, finance, stock exchanges, banking, human resource, entertainment, medical informatics, infrastructure and energy with core focus on providing advanced solution with scientific problem solving methods.

Melissa D. Hartley is a Teaching Assistant Professor at West Virginia University in the Department of Special Education. She earned a Ph.D. from Claremont Graduate University and San Diego State University, and an M.S. and a B.S. from Florida State University. Dr. Hartley was previously a special education teacher and worked with students with mild to moderate disabilities in high needs schools. While working as a special education teacher, she served as department chair, and has worked in an administrative capacity as a Site-Based Diagnostic Resource Teacher. Her research interests include virtual reality simulations in preparing special education teachers. Particularly her interests include using virtual reality simulations for skill acquisition, maintenance, and refinement.

Azizul Hassan is a PhD candidate at the Cardiff Metropolitan University, UK and a member of the Tourism Consultants Network of the Tourism Society. His main areas of research interest are technology supported marketing in tourism, innovative marketing dynamics, destination branding in tourism, cultural heritage tourism, heritage interpretation and sustainable management/marketing alternatives for cultural heritage industries.

Timothy Jung is the Director of Creative Augmented Realities Hub (www.creativear.org), Department of Food and Tourism Management at Manchester Metropolitan University, UK. He has been involved in funded research projects at national and international level in the area of ICTs in the tourism and hospitality industry. His current research focuses on the application of mobile and wearable Augmented Reality (AR), Virtual Reality (VR), multi-sensory visitor experience in the context of cultural heritage tourism. Other research interests include social media, mobile marketing and Cittaslow & Slow Food Movement.

Waldemar Karwowski received the M.Sc. degree in production engineering and management from the University of Technology of Wroclaw, Poland in 1978, the Ph.D. degree in industrial engineering from Texas Tech University, USA, in 1982, and the D.Sc. degree in management science from ORGMASZ, Poland in 2004. He is currently Professor and Chairman of the Department of Industrial Engineering and Management Systems, and Executive Director of the Institute for Advanced Systems Engineering, University of Central Florida, Orlando, USA. His research interests include human systems integration, human factors, safety, neuroergonomics, and applications soft computing and nonlinear dynamics to modeling of human-machine systems. Dr. Karwowski is a Fellow of Institute of Industrial Engineers (IIE), Human Factors and Ergonomics Society (HFES), The Institute of Human Factors and Ergonomics (United Kingdom), and International Ergonomics Association (IEA). He serves as Co-Editor of the Human Factors and Ergonomics in Manufacturing and Service Industry journal (Wiley & Sons), and Co-Editor-in-Chief of Theoretical Issues in Ergonomics Science journal (Taylor and Francis, Ltd). He is past President of the Human Factors and Ergonomics Society (2007), and the International Ergonomics Association (2000-2003).

Peter J. Kincaid is founding and current director of the Modeling and Simulation Graduate Program at the University of Central Florida and is affiliated with UCF's Institute for Simulation and Training. During his career, he has worked as a scientist for the US Air Force (AF Human Resources Lab), Army (Army Research Institute), and Navy (Training Analysis and Evaluation Group and NAVAIR Training Systems Division) and as an engineer for a large defense contractor (now Lockheed-Martin). He has held academic positions at two universities and is currently a research professor at UCF. He has published widely in a variety of disciplines, including journal articles in simulation, human factors, engineering, instructional technology and medicine. He developed the widely used Flesch-Kincaid Reading Grade Level formula, which is a feature of MS Word's Style and Grammar Check. Dr. Kincaid's PhD is in human factors from the Ohio State University.

Barbara L. Ludlow, Ed.D. is a Professor and Chair in the Department of Special Education at West Virginia University, where she has been a member of the faculty for over 35 years. She earned an E.D. from WVU, an M.Ed. from the University of Delaware, an M.A. from Cornell University, and a B.A. from St, John's University. Previously, she was a special education teacher in the public school systems of Wilmington, Delaware and Buckhannon, West Virginia. She has authored numerous articles on teacher education in special education and is a leading authority on rural special education and on technology-based delivery of personnel preparation programs. She has authored three professional reference books on distance education, online instruction, and virtual reality. Dr. Ludlow has served as the executive editor of two major professional journals and currently serves on editorial boards of 10 major journals in the disciplines of special education and disability services.

Michele M Montgomery is a 1984 graduate of The Pennsylvania State University with a B.S. degree in Mechanical/Nuclear Engineering, a 1997 graduate of The University of Alabama with an M.S. degree in Physics, and a 2004 graduate of the Florida Institute of Technology with a Ph.D. degree in Physics. Since 2004, Dr. Montgomery has been part of the physics faculty at The University of Central Florida (UCF), where she teaches astronomy, astrophysics, astrobiology, galaxies and cosmology courses to large and small audiences, both face-to-face and online. In addition, she researches fluid flow effects in astrophysical systems via numerical simulations. Besides teaching at UCF, she adjuncts at Valencia College East, where she began the astronomy program in 2006. With Mike Seeds and Dana Backman, she has coauthored several astronomy textbooks including 'Horizons Hybrid: Exploring the Universe' 13e and 'Universe Hybrid: Solar System, Stars, and Galaxies' 7e, all published by Cengage and textbooks that are used world-wide at colleges, universities, and at some high schools.

D. Cooper Patterson received her BSEE and MSEE from the University of Missouri with 40+ post graduate hours in education and virtual world technologies from Texas State University, Avila University, University of Washington, and Boise State University. She solved complex computer problems for Motorola, Intel, IBM, HP, Cisco Systems, Amdahl, Apple Computer, Dreamworks, Disney, Warner Bros., Siemens, U-Haul International, and many more. Cooper has been working for the last fifteen years researching and developing new mathematical curriculum substantiated by the neurological findings on subitizing. She is currently the Cognitive Engineer and Curriculum/Instruction Developer for Dream Realizations and Director of Research and Development at CERLabs.

Rebecca Lynne Patterson graduated from Purdue University with a Math and German BA in 1990. She studied abroad at the University of Hamburg, Germany and after college she taught high school Math and German in Indiana and Oregon. In 2000, her interest shifted to the development of math and language skills in elementary school. She provided math remediation and enrichment at every grade. Her experience expanded to include literature, Junior Great Books, tutoring, and supplementing math curriculum for both TAG and Title I students. Graduate school brought her into contact with others who had the same zest for education, mathematics in particular, and children. Rebecca received her Masters in Secondary Math Education at George Fox University in the summer of 2011. She co-taught math remediation at the college level and instructs virtually in Second Life. She is currently CEO and Educational Coordinator for Dream Realizations, Research Specialist for ItOnlyTakes1, and Development Specialist for CERLabs.

Yvonne Pigatt, Retired Software Engineer- Verizon Communications, is currently a full-time Instructor at The Community College of Baltimore County (CCBC) for School of Applied and Information Technology. She teaches a variety of technology classes ranging from Diversity in a Technological Society to Comprehensive Database Design. Vicky holds a BS in Management Information Systems from the Columbia Union College and a MS in Management Information Systems from American University. She is currently co-Chair of the Teaching and Learning Round-table at CCBC.

William Rivera is CEO and principal research scientist for Cognita Solutions LLC. His research interests include predictive modeling, machine learning, software architecture and engineering and data mining with emphasis on implementing artificial intelligence into software applications.

Anna-Marie Robertson holds a Masters of Educational Technology and a Bachelor's of Science in Secondary Education with emphasis in Mathematics and Business Education. Currently she is the Instructional Designer for Dream Realizations. She also teaches online for a local high school and a local university, both in the Mathematics Department. Prior to becoming a teacher in 1996, she worked for approximately 20 years as a paraprofessional in various accounting firms and businesses. In Second Life, she is known as Alexsis Kamala.

Sami Şahin is a faculty member of Education Faculty of Gazi University in Turkey. His main interest is utilizing emerging technologies into teaching and learning. Dr. Şahin has B.S. in Physics; M.S. in Instructional Design, Development and Evaluation; and PhD. in Curriculum and Instruction with specialization in instructional technology. Dr. Şahin has published several articles, books and book chapters in the field of instructional technology. His recent publications has been on preservice teachers technology use. Dr. Şahin is currently serving as assistant director of distance education and research center at Gazi University.

Nicoletta Melida Sala received the degree in Physics ("Laurea"), applied cybernetics, at the University of Milan (Italy). Ph.D. in Communication Science at Università della Svizzera italiana of Lugano (USI, Lugano, Switzerland). Postgraduate (two years for each) in "Didactics of the communication and multimedia technologies" and "Journalism and mass media". She was professor in Information Technology and in Electronics and she taught at University of Lugano (Mendrisio, Switzerland). She is founder and editor of Chaos and Complexity Letters International Journal of Dynamical System Research (Nova Science, New York). Her research interests concern various scientific topics from an interdisciplinary point of view and comprise the following areas: Fractal Geometry and Complexity; Mathematics in Arts, Architecture and Industrial Design; New media and IT in the learning environments; Virtual Reality in education. She has authored 20 mathematics and information technology books, and edited 10 others. She has written more than 300 scientific papers.

Noah L. Schroeder is an Assistant Professor of Educational Technology and Instructional Design at Wright State University in Dayton, Ohio. His research interests include pedagogical agents, educational video games, meta-analysis, and STEM education.

Brian W Sloboda is currently an economist at the U.S. Department of Labor, Assistant Secretary for Policy. He also teaches courses in economics and statistics at the University of Phoenix and Park University. Brian has published articles in the Journal of Economics, Current Politics and Economics in Africa, Advances in Econometrics, Annals of Regional Science, Advances and Applications in Statistics, Tourism Economics, Journal of Transportation and Statistics, Pennsylvania Economic Review, International Journal of Transport Economics, Journal of Business and Economic Perspectives, and the Virginia Economic Journal. He also edited, Transportation Statistics (2009) by J Ross and also co-edited Econometric and Forecasting Models (2013) with Chandrasekhar Putcha and Kalamogo Coulibaly by Mellen Press.

Çelebi Uluyol Instructor doctor at the Computer Education and Instructional Technology at Gazi University.

Guofang Wan, Ph.D. is director of Office of Graduate Studies and professor of teacher Education at School of Education, Virginia Commonwealth University.

Ellen Yeh holds a Ph.D. in Curriculum and Instruction with a specialization in Second Language Acquisition in Ohio University. She currently serves as a director and lecturer of English as an Additional Language Program at English Department in Columbia College Chicago. Her research interests include media literacy education, Computer Assisted Language Learning (CALL) instruction design, intercultural studies, and the education of diverse populations. She has taught in ESL/EFL (English as a second/ foreign language) institutes in Taiwan and the United States. She was a coordinator in the Helen M. Robison Center for Reading, and is responsible for designing tutor-training sessions, and assisting the coordination of the center. She wrote a book chapter titled "Enhancing linguistic and intercultural competencies through the use of social network sites and Google Earth" and have a publication research article that is entitled "Teaching culture and language through the multiple intelligences film teaching model in the ESL/EFL classroom."

Index

F

G

H

I

J

L

M

N

O

P

R

S

T

V

W

www.ingramcontent.com/pod-product-compliance
Lightning Source LLC
LaVergne TN
LVHW062142200926
848484LV00007B/1845